Harnessing AI and Predictive Analytics for Decision-Making and Competitive Advantage

Sandeep Poddar
https://orcid.org/0000-0001-9771-877X
Lincoln University College, Malaysia

Prashant Kumar Siddhey
https://orcid.org/0000-0002-4236-0966
Prestige Institute of Business Management, Indore, India

Najla Shafighi
BBW University of Applied Sciences, Germany

Amiya Bhaumik
https://orcid.org/0000-0002-9188-2269
Lincoln University College, Malaysia

IGI Global
Scientific Publishing
Publishing Tomorrow's Research Today

Vice President of Editorial	Melissa Wagner
Director of Acquisitions	Mikaela Felty
Director of Book Development	Jocelynn Hessler
Production Manager	Mike Brehm
Cover Design	Jose Rosado

Published in the United States of America by
IGI Global Scientific Publishing
701 East Chocolate Avenue
Hershey, PA, 17033, USA
Tel: 717-533-8845 | Fax: 717-533-7115
Website: https://www.igi-global.com E-mail: cust@igi-global.com

Library of Congress Cataloging-in-Publication Data

Names: Poddar, Sandeep editor http://id.loc.gov/rwo/agents/n2023052123 | Siddhey, Prashant Kumar, 1984- editor http://id.loc.gov/rwo/agents/n2025018912 | Shafighi, Najla, 1980- editor http://id.loc.gov/rwo/agents/n2025018913 | Bhaumik, Amiya editor http://id.loc.gov/rwo/agents/no2007039905
Title: Harnessing AI and predictive analytics for competitive decision-making / edited by Sandeep Poddar, Prashant Kumar Siddhey, Najla Shafighi, and Amiya Bhaumik.
Description: Hershey, PA : IGI Global Scientific Publishing, [2026] | Includes bibliographical references and index. | Summary: "The book delves into how AI can enhance business intelligence, forecasting, and strategic planning systems"-- Provided by publisher.
Identifiers: LCCN 2025016758 (print) | LCCN 2025016759 (ebook) | ISBN 9798337336480 hardcover | ISBN 9798337336497 paperback | ISBN 9798337336503 ebook
Subjects: LCSH: Decision making--Technological innovations | Artificial intelligence--Business applications
Classification: LCC HD30.23 .H3658 2026 (print) | LCC HD30.23 (ebook) | DDC 658.4/030285--dc23/eng/20250604
LC record available at https://lccn.loc.gov/2025016758
LC ebook record available at https://lccn.loc.gov/2025016759

British Cataloguing in Publication Data
A Cataloguing in Publication record for this book is available from the British Library.

Table of Contents

Detailed Table of Contents

Artificial Intelligence (AI) and Machine Learning (ML) have significantly changed banking and finance sectors by enhancing decision-making, efficiency, and minimizing risk. AI solutions provide the capability of detecting frauds by analyzing the real-time data of irregular transactions. Supervised and unsupervised models are used for assessing risk, credit scoring, or customer segmentation. Natural Language Processing (NLP) detects dangers such as sentiments of customers and insider threats by sentiment analysis to understand customer feedback and offers guidance to executives' strategic decisions. There are some challenges associated with artificial intelligence and machine learning in the banking and finance sector, such as data privacy, regulations, and algorithmic bias. If implemented properly, AI and ML have the potential to transform the landscape of fraud prevention, risk assessment, and prediction applications for a safe and efficient financial ecosystem.

With improved forecasting, logistics, and decision-making, supply chain management (SCM) has been transformed by machine learning (ML) and artificial intelligence (AI). Contribution of AI/ML to increased efficiency in international operations, decreasing risk, and improved efficiency is being explained in this chapter. Improved forecasting, as well as lower cost and disruption through inventory, comes about due to predictive analytics.ML enhances tracking, vendor selections, and pricing.Use cases such as autonomous warehousing, route optimization, and AI-based chatbots lower lead times by 25%, logistics expense by 30%, and improve prediction accuracy by 40%. Blockchain-based AI reduces fraud loss by 50%. Talent gap, integration, and security of data are some of the challenges. Case studies illustrate how hybrid AI-ML models and cloud SCM enable sustainability and agility. Future work will be focused on autonomous procurement and quantum AI.

The fundamental transformation of organizational critical decision-making occurs through artificial intelligence as it enhances data processing power along with predictive ability for competitive intelligence while revolutionizing strategic planning processes. The combination of advanced machine learning algorithms and big data analytics helps companies build precise decision-support systems that enhance the effectiveness of their strategic projects. The main strength of AI systems originates from their efficient navigation of competitive intelligence systems. Business organizations deploy AI-powered platforms to automatically conduct SWOT assessments and carry out extensive market examinations while performing standard benchmarks to let them lead dynamic market competitions. A combination

The recruitment department regularly face difficulties in confirmation of the originality of a Curriculum Vitae. The human judgment may result into errors, delays and appointed person might be go under suspect due to undetected irregularities in CV. The automated CV authenticity verification discovers errors and inconsistencies. The parsing of ATS compliant PDFs extracts personal data, education, employment details, and skills. The NLP, and ML identifies an overlapping employment, gaps, mismatched skills, and other irregularities in CV. The system determines the timeline inconsistency of the resume and the validation of the LinkedIn URL. Finally, a CV is classified as authentic, partially authentic, need to do cross-check manually, or not authentic, depending on a genuinity score. The genuinity score is adjusted using bonuses, penalties and timeline information. Explainable AI SHAP manifests the interpretability and transparency in the decision-making process of AI.

This research analyzes the optimization of strategic leadership through the integration of artificial intelligence (AI) for competitive decision-making. From a qualitative and reflective meta-analysis of recent studies, it is evident how the use of advanced algorithms, deep learning and big data analysis allows organizations to anticipate future scenarios, optimize resource allocation and transform their management culture. Dynamic capabilities and the convergence of technological and human approaches are highlighted, while addressing ethical challenges, transparency in algorithmic processes, and the need for accountable governance. The findings suggest that the synergy between AI and professional judgment drives innovation and strengthens competitiveness in environments of high uncertainty.

In the era of digital transformation, organizations must adopt cutting-edge technologies to sustain a competitive edge. Artificial Intelligence (AI) and predictive analytics have emerged as crucial enablers in this evolution, allowing firms to make informed, data-driven decisions proactively. This chapter delves deeply into the theoretical and practical aspects of AI and predictive analytics in competitive decision-making. It discusses their historical evolution, underlying methodologies, real-world applications across business functions, comprehensive frameworks for implementation, challenges encountered, and the future landscape. Through detailed case studies and academic insights, this chapter offers a holistic understanding of how AI and predictive analytics reshape strategic foresight, operational efficiency, and business agility.

This chapter, "The Role of AI in Emerging Business Models and Innovation," examines how artificial intelligence (AI) is fundamentally transforming business landscapes by enabling new, data-driven, and agile business models. Positioned within the broader context of the book "Harnessing AI and Predictive Analytics for Competitive Decision-Making," it explores how AI acts as a strategic driver of innovation, reshaping customer experiences, operational processes, and revenue strategies across sectors. The chapter categorizes AI-enabled innovations, integrates predictive analytics for foresight, and highlights real-world case studies. It also addresses challenges such as ethical concerns, organizational resistance, and governance needs. Concluding with future trends, it emphasizes the need for leaders to embed AI into their core strategies to foster sustainable competitive advantage.

leaders in building scalable, ethically sound AI ecosystems for strategic business growth.

Foreword

In an era where data has become the lifeblood of organizational strategy, the need to harness advanced analytical capabilities has never been more pressing. "*Harnessing AI and Predictive Analytics for Competitive Decision-Making*" stands as a timely and essential contribution to both scholarship and practice. This volume offers a comprehensive exploration of how artificial intelligence (AI) and predictive analytics are reshaping the landscape of competitive decision making across industries. The editors, Dr. Sandeep Poddar, Dr. Prashant Kumar Siddhey, Dr. Najla Shafighi, and Dr. Amiya Bhaumik, have curated a volume that balances analytical depth with applied insight, ensuring that both academic rigor and real-world relevance are seamlessly integrated.

The rapid advancements in AI and analytics technologies have unlocked unprecedented opportunities for businesses to derive meaningful insights from vast and complex datasets. Traditional strategic planning processes, once reliant on intuition and static models, are now complemented—if not transformed—by predictive models that anticipate future trends, optimize decision pathways, and empower organizations to make proactive, evidence-based choices. This book delves into these developments, highlighting their transformative potential in enhancing forecasting, business intelligence, and strategic planning systems.

What distinguishes this work is its fusion of theoretical foundations with practical relevance. Contributors bring forward rigorous research and real-world applications that illustrate how predictive analytics can drive competitive advantage in dynamic markets. By examining both the capabilities and limitations of emerging technologies, the book equips researchers, practitioners, and decision makers with the knowledge to navigate complexity and uncertainty with confidence.

As readers engage with the chapters, they will discover innovative approaches to integrating machine learning, AI driven forecasting, and data centric strategies into organizational decision architectures. The interdisciplinary perspectives offered herein reflect a deep commitment to advancing understanding at the intersection of technology and strategic competitiveness. For all those committed to advancing the frontier of analytics powered decision making, this volume offers insight, inspiration, and a roadmap for future inquiry.

It is with pleasure that I introduce *Harnessing AI and Predictive Analytics for Competitive Decision Making*, a book that not only documents the cutting edge of analytical practice but also shapes the way we think about decision making in an increasingly data driven world. The editorial team's expertise and dedication to advancing the field are evident throughout the book, making this work an invaluable resource for both academics and professionals alike.

Andrew Ware
Faculty of Computing, Engineering and Science, University of South Wales, UK

Preface

In the early twenty-first century have seen a unique confluence of the abundance of data, the power of computers, and the advances in algorithms. Today's business environment is marked by volatility, uncertainty, complexity, and ambiguity (VUCA). These conditions make traditional managerial insight and decision-making rules inadequate. This has created a paradigm shift in the applications of Artificial Intelligence (AI) and predictive analytics from a mere technology enabler to a crucial support structure in a successful decision. This edited book collection, Harnessing AI and Predictive Analytics for Competitive Decision-Making, is produced at a juncture when the battle lines for strategic advantage are being drawn on the ability to turn data into foresight, insight, and action.

Although the literature on AI, machine learning, and analytics is increasing in volume, paradoxically, there appears to be some fragmentation. On the one hand, research in the technology appears to be progressing at a rapid rate but in a manner that remains very much removed from the realities of the business environment, with business discourse being prone to oversimplification in its treatment of the intricacies and limitations inherent in AI systems. This book is an effort towards such knowledge integration/bridging.

The subject matter scope of this book is deliberately cast widely, as reflected in its comprehensive impact that spans all sectors and business functions. The topics covered across all chapters span ideologies that vary from technical issues and methodologies, through to more advanced topics. From a theoretical perspective, this book considers issues that include:

- How can the quality and reliability of evidence be ensured within decision-making systems that rely on artificial intelligence technology?
- How does explainability, trustworthiness, and accountability relate to AI in high-stakes settings?
- How can an organization maintain the optimization of its business processes and ethics?

In applied terms, scholars examine how AI and predictive analytics are driving changes in decision-making in finance, manufacturing, supply chain management, marketing, human resource management, health care, sustainability, crisis management, tourism, agriculture, and doing good. These studies show that gaining a competitive advantage in contemporary businesses is not merely about cost leadership or differentiation; instead, it also requires predictive insight, adaptability, personalization, resilience, and integration.

One of the common themes that run across this volume is the theme of the data-to-decision continuum. Indeed, data by itself is of very limited value. But data takes on critical value only as it gets translated into valuable knowledge, which is then integrated into the thought processes of key decisions. A number of chapters in this volume speak of the data-to-decision continuum, from the data lake to predictive models and AI.

Another thing that is unique to this volume is its emphasis on responsible AI. With the growing impact of AI on credit approval decisions, hiring decisions, healthcare choices, security solutions, and public policies, transparency issues, equity, privacy concerns, and accountability have come to the fore. Today, gaining a competitive advantage in an AI world is not merely based on excellence but on trust; trust of customers, trust of employees, trust of the authorities, and trust of the community at large.

Several chapters in this book discuss issues surrounding explainable AI (XAI), ethical prediction, framework governance, and privacy-preserving methods. These chapters convincingly argue that explainability and ethics are catalysts and facilitators of sustained or competitive advantage. Firms or organizations that are proactive and transparent in terms of AI methodology are well-equipped to mitigate risk and gain compliance and confidence from stakeholders.

The practical chapters included in this volume offer insights into the ways in which AI and predictive analytics are transforming the decision-making process:

CHAPTER OVERVIEW

Chapter 1 introduces the transformative role of artificial intelligence and machine learning in the financial sector, emphasizing their capacity to enhance risk assessment and fraud detection. The editors highlight how predictive models—both supervised and unsupervised—enable more accurate credit scoring, customer segmentation, and anomaly detection in real time. The chapter also underscores the growing importance of natural language processing in interpreting customer sentiment and identifying potential insider threats. While recognizing the significant benefits of these technologies, the editors draw attention to persistent challenges, including data privacy, regulatory compliance, and algorithmic bias, framing the discussion within the broader goal of building a secure and efficient financial ecosystem.

Chapter 2 examines the integration of AI and machine learning in supply chain management, presenting a comprehensive view of how these technologies enhance forecasting, logistics, and operational decision-making. The editors emphasize the measurable improvements in efficiency, cost reduction, and risk mitigation achieved through predictive analytics and intelligent automation. Real-world applications such as autonomous warehousing, route optimization, and AI-driven customer interaction tools are explored alongside emerging innovations like blockchain-enabled systems. The chapter also addresses critical implementation barriers, including talent shortages and data security concerns, while pointing toward future advancements in autonomous procurement and quantum-enabled AI solutions.

Chapter 3 explores the evolution of competitive intelligence through AI-powered systems, highlighting their impact on strategic decision-making in the digital age. The editors present AI as a catalyst for transforming how organizations process vast datasets and generate actionable insights. By integrating machine learning and big data analytics, firms can automate complex analyses such as SWOT assessments and market benchmarking. The chapter further considers the ethical, legal, and privacy implications of deploying AI in strategic contexts, offering a balanced perspective on the opportunities and responsibilities associated with data-driven competitiveness.

Chapter 4 provides a systematic review of AI-driven decision-making within modern business intelligence frameworks. Drawing on a broad body of research, the editors illustrate how AI enhances analytical capabilities by enabling rapid data processing, real-time insights, and predictive forecasting. The discussion contrasts AI-enabled systems with traditional business intelligence approaches, demonstrating clear advantages in responsiveness and accuracy. At the same time, the chapter acknowledges ongoing challenges, including issues related to data quality, implementation costs, and the availability of skilled professionals, positioning AI as a critical yet evolving component of organizational competitiveness.

Chapter 5 focuses on assortment optimization in retail, emphasizing the strategic importance of product selection in meeting increasingly personalized consumer demands. The editors outline how data mining techniques can uncover key product attributes and relationships that inform assortment decisions and targeted promotions. Through empirical analysis within a retail context, the chapter demonstrates how data-driven insights can enhance competitiveness while also shaping customer segmentation strategies. The discussion highlights the inherent trade-offs in assortment planning, where serving specific customer groups may come at the expense of others.

Chapter 6 addresses the automation of curriculum vitae validation using natural language processing and machine learning. The editors describe how AI-driven systems can improve recruitment processes by detecting inconsistencies, verifying credentials, and assessing candidate authenticity. By extracting and analyzing structured and unstructured data from resumes, the system identifies gaps, overlaps, and discrepancies while assigning a genuineness score. The chapter further emphasizes the importance of explainable AI, particularly through interpretability techniques, in ensuring transparency and trust in automated decision-making within human resource management.

Chapter 7 investigates the optimization of strategic leadership through the integration of artificial intelligence. The editors highlight how AI enables leaders to anticipate future scenarios, allocate resources more effectively, and foster innovation in uncertain environments. The chapter emphasizes the interplay between technological capabilities and human judgment, presenting AI as a tool that augments rather than replaces leadership. Ethical considerations, transparency, and governance are central to the discussion, reinforcing the need for responsible AI adoption in shaping organizational strategy.

Chapter 8 explores the role of AI-powered analytics in enabling real-time personalization and enhancing customer engagement. The editors emphasize how continuous monitoring of user interactions across digital channels allows organizations to deliver highly contextualized recommendations and offers. Unlike traditional approaches reliant on historical data, AI-driven systems respond dynamically to current customer behavior, significantly improving engagement metrics and conversion rates. The chapter positions personalization as a key driver of competitive advantage in increasingly digital and customer-centric markets.

Chapter 9 examines the impact of AI-driven personalized marketing on customer engagement and brand loyalty in online environments. The editors present empirical insights into how techniques such as recommendation systems, dynamic pricing, and targeted advertising influence consumer behavior and perceptions. By integrating primary and secondary data analyses, the chapter provides a nuanced understanding of customer trust in AI-enabled marketing strategies. The discussion underscores the growing importance of personalization in fostering long-term relationships between brands and consumers.

Chapter 10 offers a comprehensive exploration of strategic foresight through AI and predictive analytics, framing these technologies as essential tools for maintaining competitive advantage. The editors trace their evolution and outline key methodologies, supported by real-world applications and implementation frameworks. The chapter highlights how predictive insights enable organizations to anticipate trends, enhance operational efficiency, and improve agility. Challenges and future directions are also discussed, providing a holistic perspective on the role of AI in shaping forward-looking business strategies.

Chapter 11analyzes the role of AI in driving emerging business models and innovation. The editors emphasize how AI facilitates the development of data-driven, agile, and customer-centric business strategies across industries. By categorizing AI-enabled innovations and integrating predictive analytics, the chapter demonstrates how organizations can reimagine operations and revenue models. It also addresses barriers such as ethical concerns and organizational resistance, concluding with a forward-looking perspective on embedding AI into core strategic frameworks for sustainable growth.

Chapter 12 presents an innovative application of AI in precision agriculture through a UAV-enabled system for predicting grape diseases. The editors describe how the integration of aerial imaging technologies and deep learning models enables early detection and classification of crop diseases. By leveraging predictive analytics, the system provides actionable insights for treatment and resource allocation, contributing to improved crop health and yield optimization. The chapter highlights the broader potential of combining AI with advanced sensing technologies to transform traditional agricultural practices into intelligent and sustainable systems.

Chapter 13 concludes the volume by emphasizing the importance of unified intelligence through cross-functional integration of AI and predictive analytics. The editors argue that breaking down organizational silos is essential to unlocking the full transformative potential of AI. By aligning functions such as finance, marketing, human resources, and supply chain, organizations can create cohesive, data-driven strategies that enhance agility and resilience. The chapter also addresses governance, ethical considerations, and implementation challenges, offering a structured roadmap for building scalable and responsible AI ecosystems that support long-term strategic growth.

This book can serve many different types of readers. Researchers in academia and doctorate students can learn from theoretical concepts, empirical results, or approaches presented in the book. Practitioners, managers, and consultants can learn from perspectives that suggest strategic approaches to implementing AI or predictive analytics. Policy planners can learn from the discussions about ethics, governance, or societal aspects that may provide them with balanced views about innovative concepts. Students studying management, engineering, data science, or information systems can acquire novel insights from an understanding that integrates management concepts with innovative technology.

The editors also hope that the present book can provide a reference point within the ever-complex landscape of AI-enabled decision-making. More importantly, we also hope that this book can encourage people to think beyond AI as a means to increase effectiveness. Rather, they can think of AI as a transformative power that can also be channelled toward making their companies more competitively sustainable.

With deep gratitude, we acknowledge the contributions of all the authors whose commitment, perseverance, and responses to the editing process make this publication possible. The contributions of all those reviewers whose inputs added depth to this publication are also much appreciated. We are very much grateful to entire associates of IGI Global Scientific Publishing, USA. Lastly, we would like to recognize the academic and professional community whose questions and answers are helping shape this discourse surrounding AI and PA today. It is our hope that this book will reflect and further this dialogue. Above all, we are deeply grateful to the Almighty God for bestowing His blessings and guidance upon us.

Sandeep Poddar
Lincoln University College, Malaysia

Prashant Kumar Siddhey
Prestige Institute of Business Management, Indore, India

Najla Shafighi
BBW University of Applied Sciences, Germany

Amiya Bhaumik
Lincoln University College, Malaysia

Chapter 1

AI and Machine Learning–Based Predictive Models for Risk Assessment and Fraud Detection in the Finance Sector

Shiv Kumar Singh Pundhir
http://orcid.org/0000-0001-6249-6943
Christ University, Bengaluru, India

Rachit Mittal
GLA University, Mathura, India

Ila Anand
http://orcid.org/0000-0001-8837-4450
Christ University, Bengaluru, India

Syed Mohd Muneeb
Tecnologico de Monterrey, Mexico

Kartikeya Singh
http://orcid.org/0000-0002-3060-6359
Christ University, Bengaluru, India

ABSTRACT

Artificial Intelligence (AI) and Machine Learning (ML) have significantly changed banking and finance sectors by enhancing decision-making, efficiency, and minimizing risk. AI solutions provide the capability of detecting frauds by analyzing

DOI: 10.4018/979-8-3373-3648-0.ch001

the real-time data of irregular transactions. Supervised and unsupervised models are used for assessing risk, credit scoring, or customer segmentation. Natural Language Processing (NLP) detects dangers such as sentiments of customers and insider threats by sentiment analysis to understand customer feedback and offers guidance to executives' strategic decisions. There are some challenges associated with artificial intelligence and machine learning in the banking and finance sector, such as data privacy, regulations, and algorithmic bias. If implemented properly, AI and ML have the potential to transform the landscape of fraud prevention, risk assessment, and prediction applications for a safe and efficient financial ecosystem.

INTRODUCTION

In recent years the world has seen an increasing pattern in frauds. As per the reports, in 2024 only people reported 12.67 billion US dollars in money losses due to the fraudsters., which was 25% more in comparison of last year. A total of 2.63 million worldwide cases were reported in 2024 only. AI is revolutionizing all the sectors; the finance sector is also one of them. AI can help to monitor the financial transactions to provide risk-free services to the customers. Due to the advancement in the technology, financial frauds are also increasing. AI and technology are also helping fraudsters. Deepfake, image cloning, hacking, and voice cloning are some techniques that fraudsters are using to commit fraud.

Artificial Intelligence (AI) is speeding up the change in the financial services industry. Areas like cost management, value creation, risk management, decision-making ability, improving customer experience, and market share expansion are just examples of some of the areas that AI is disrupting the historical framework of financial service delivery. AI, machine learning (ML), and robotic process automation, helps determine the way finances work, especially considering the vast numbers of data (structured and unstructured) finance companies examine, navigate, and utilize on a daily basis. AI is creating a faster and more efficient process which will ultimately allow for smarter, quicker, and safer ways of financial services delivery. Fraud detection and prevention is one of the largest volumes of AI initiatives in financial services. Given its incorporation into systems, AI has the infrastructure (algorithms) to scan millions of transactions in real time to flag risk behavior and fraudulent patterns. These alerts facilitate cheating behavior to be detected and revealed to an acceptable risk level of confidence. AI examines historical data to learn and has the potential to learn based on new data input, response, while the fraudster takes new anecdotal awareness, formulating new methods or deceptions to organizations. AI will continue to re-invent risk assessments, and further, the nature of credit scoring. Traditional risk assessments primarily retain fixed financial data, while risk assessments powered by AI, will engage multiple and variable inputs that standout social indicators.

Gao et al. (2024) explained the applications of machine learning models in banking and finance. They explained the role of deep learning and ANN models in finance. Lee et al. (2024) discussed the role of generative AI in the banking and finance sector. Johora et al. (2024) discussed the role of AI in developing a user-friendly interface and chatbots and the role of NLP in knowing your customer. Kapoor & Ghosal(2022) explained, how AI changed the industries, finance sector is also one of them. Darapu & Marukukula (2025). explained machine learning models to control the frauds in the finance sector. Agrawal et al. (2025) studied the role of blockchain and AI in data integrity and data analysis. Bahoo et al. (2024) found the number of publications in the last decade to find the application of AI in finance. They found that AI and forecast models are applied to forecast the share market, portfolio management, and predictive models using supervised and unsupervised models. Irfan et al. (2023) studied the applications of fintech in Islamic finance to enhance customer experience in online payment. They also found that using fintech finance can be explained to a larger population and area. Taneja et al. (2024) studied the applications of AI in cryptocurrency. Since cryptocurrency is volatile in nature, they found that AI can help a lot in fintech in volatile conditions. Weber et al. (2024) provided research on the role of Explainable Artificial Intelligence (XAI) in finance. They scanned about 2022 articles to find the importance of Explainable Artificial Intelligence (XAI) in finance in today's era. They found that XAI is largely applied in risk assessment, predictions, and portfolio optimization. Ridzuan et al. (2024) studied the applications and challenges of AI in the banking and finance sector. They focused on following ASEAN guidelines and increasing the skilled workforce. Giudici & Raffinetti (2023) found the trustworthiness of applications of AI in finance. Since AI is also risky for the privacy of the data and risky for the applications. Jafar et al. (2023) discussed the role of AI in finance and found that AI has a lot of applications not only in the finance sector but also in the banking and insurance sectors. Zheng et al. (2019) discussed that new AI 2.0 is revolutionizing the finance and banking sector by enabling fast and accurate processing of day-to-day and tough tasks in the banking and finance sector. They surveyed the applications of the new "financial brain" in security, consulting, and wealth and risk management. Cao & Zhai (2022) surveyed the applications of fintech to design the digital framework to serve the customer in a better way.AI and ML have a significant impact on the banking and financial sector. AI and ML models can help to identify the risks and fraud patterns in the finance sector. As the finance sector is rapidly increasing yearly, providing risk-free services for the customers and market with manual data collection is not possible nowadays. AI and ML have the capabilities to analyze the data and find out the patterns and trends of the data.

AI and ML can also analyze the vast data to analyze the hidden patterns. Real-time data analysis is very crucial to make prompt, effective decisions. AI- and ML-based models can help the finance sector analyze the real-time data to develop models.

Finance sector data in many categories may be customer data, credit data, records of transactions, emails, social media, and authorities' data. A huge amount of historical and real-time data is generated in the finance sector. This data may be structured and unstructured also.AI and ML will help to manage the unstructured data to develop machine learning models. Data may be analyzed in supervised and unsupervised categories. Supervised models can help to develop models to predict the customers' behavior and whether a transaction will be fraudulent or not. Supervised models may also help determine whether the sanctioned loan will be repaid by the customers or not.

Unsupervised models like clustering can assist in identifying the hidden patterns and identifying the fraud patterns using real-time data. AI-enabled systems may track millions of transactions and develop a machine learning models to track the suspicious activities.

1. Role of AI in Banking and Finance

(i) The Role of AI in Credit Scoring and Risk Assessment

Traditional credit scoring relies on limited historical information regarding the financial position and payment behavior of a potential borrower, such as income, repayment record, and unpaid debt. While traditional loan models work to some degree, they miss many potential borrowers with little or no repayment record. By design, traditional credit scoring is a barrier to finance for many individuals and families. AI, through machine learning (ML), combats these barriers for lenders and borrowers alike by accommodating a wider variety of data points to assess creditworthiness and understand risk. AI-based credit scoring can incorporate both structured and unstructured information such as utility bill payments, mobile telephone transactions, social media activity, purchasing transaction patterns, occupancy/tenancy and associated payment history, employment history, and geolocation. The value can be in the ability for AI to indicate discrete behavioral patterns and correlations that have not been previously analyzed to provide insight into a borrower's financial behavior and likelihood of default and lead to more precise risk profiling and a better option for lenders, particularly for thin-file customers or borrowers with no credit record.

(ii) Investment and Asset Management

AI tools are highly used in portfolio management. To analyze the real time data of algo trading and market analysis AI based tools are having important role. AI based models analyze the investors profile and market trends to suggest best investment plans for individuals and organizations. Predictive models are used for the processing the data of hedge funds and trading houses to generate effective trading ideas by identifying the patterns and changes over the time. customer service is significantly impacted by AI, including AI-powered bots and virtual assistants that handle the queries of the customers to improve the customers engagements and reduce the operational cost. NLP also helps to improve the customer satisfaction to analyze the feedback of the customers.

(iii) The Importance of AI in Fraud Detection

Artificial intelligence (AI) is immensely important in the area of fraud detection in the financial industry. AI allows for real-time detection through real-time analytics, pattern detection, and predictive analysis, which is essential in stopping fraud. As consumer fraud continues to evolve, traditional rule-based fraud detection procedures cannot keep up with the evolution of fraudsters and their methods. AI, especially with machine learning (ML), is especially powerful since it is able to learn from various characteristics of the previous fraud data and apply the lessons learned to evolving fraud techniques and trends. One of the key advantages of artificial intelligence in fraud detection is that it has the ability to analyze large volumes of transactions in real time. Machine learning models provide depth to fraud detection and can detect subtle deviations in normal behavior that might indicate fraud, such as unusual spending behaviors, logins from unfamiliar locations, or sudden frequency changes in any given day.

The role of Artificial Intelligence (AI) and Machine Learning (ML) has been very important to identify the theft and synthetic for financial security. Synthetic fraud occurs when criminals take a mixture of real and synthetic data to create new identities, which can then be used to open accounts, obtain loans, or transact fraudulently. Synthetic fraud is harder to detect than identity theft because, in synthetic fraud cases, many of the fabricated profiles appear genuine in systems that only conduct identity checks based on rules.AI and ML models provide organizations with the ability to deal with this complex and constantly evolving problem using real-time ingestion of vast amounts of structured and unstructured data. Anomaly detection, clustering, deep learning, and other techniques identify anomalies in the data, such as irregular spending patterns, unconventional transaction frequencies, and doubtful account activity. Natural language processing also helps detect forged documents or fabricated applications. Finally, ML systems will learn with new trends in fraud and continuously adapt detection mechanisms to lower false positive rates while ensuring limited loss of accuracy. Graph-based approaches are increasingly used for exposing latent relationships between accounts, transactions, and devices related to fraud. By incorporating AI-enabled fraud detection directly into the banking system, e-commerce and brick-and-mortar retailers, and insurance services, organizations boost security, support identity protections, and also reduce the amount of money lost to identity theft and synthetic fraud.

(iv) Role of NLP (Natural Language Processing)

Natural Language Processing (NLP), an area of Artificial Intelligence (AI), is valuable for the banking and finance industry to carry out sentiment analysis. NLP (Natural Language Processing), as an area of AI, can identify fraud in unstructured data sources like emails, chat exchanges, and documentation. NLP can help identify phishing and fraudulent claims and can identify insider threats. The technology can also assist banks and financial institutions with their anti-money laundering (AML) efforts to assess compliance with monitoring suspicious transactions and in order to detect fraud ultimately. Some of the largest banks and financial institutions are utilizing AI technologies to enhance their fraud detection capabilities. NLP (Natural Language Processing) can analyze emails, contracts, and other communications with customers as it pertains to compliance risks, provide alerts on time, and create audit trails. Another prime use case of AI for timely, relevant, and analytical data of natural AI is algorithmic trading, where decisions need to be made in a millisecond. AI models analyze how the market is moving by studying market signals, financial news, and trading volumes to automatically execute buy or sell orders with limited human involvement in order to maximize their profits and minimize their losses. Ultimately AI allows banks and financial institutions to make smarter, more intelligent, and most importantly, faster and safer decisions using real-time data. This process of enhanced fraud prevention, risk assessment, customer service, compliance, and trading allows for a more responsive, data-driven, and resilient financial system. Platforms in the finance industry can use NLP to analyze sentiment using mass public sentiment, client sentiment, and market feeling as expressed in all formats, including social posts, news articles, financial reports, emails, customer feedback, and CRM data. Sentiment analysis, also referred to as opinion mining, empowers banks and financial institutions to develop data-driven decision-making similar to human decision-making. This is a key part of their goal to manage reputational risk, customer sensitivity, design services that matter to customers and ultimately anticipate market behavior changes.

One notable area where NLP-based sentiment analysis has seen increasing applications in the past few years is in market prediction and investing decisions. Often, financial markets are driven not simply by the numbers, but rather the subjective impacts of investor sentiment, public perception of companies, and most importantly global events. NLP analysis of free-text communications like Twitter, Reddit, financial blog posts, earnings calls, and headline news can analyze large volumes of unstructured text to detect a positive, negative, or neutral sentiment from these communications. Traders and investment firms can then determine bullish or bearish trends. If sentiment were to turn negative, for example, due to an unexpected event, NLP systems would be able to track sentiment in real-time, allowing firms to make rapid changes to their portfolio, further reducing losses.

NLP is also increasingly vital in the management of reputational risks, as it can monitor how and where the institution is being reported on and talked about publicly. Financial institutions also use AI tools to monitor online content in real time, alerting compliance or public relations for all forms of reputational threats, such as controversies, data breaches, or regulatory concerns. The early identification of negative sentiment allows organizations to take corrective action sooner and can be useful in crisis management. Another developing trend in credit risk is the use of sentiment analysis tools. With NLP tools to analyze communication with a borrower, application documentation, or even their use of social media, we can glean supplemental information about a client's financial condition, reliability, and ultimately creditworthiness. A sentiment analysis framework provides one additional layer to the existing approaches to assessing creditworthiness. This is especially useful for underbanked or thin-file customers and adds some value to a general decision.

(v) Role of Deep Learning in Finance

Deep learning is slowly becoming more and more relevant for revolutionizing the financial industry. Deep learning can process and learn from large amounts of structured, unstructured, and complex data, which enables many financial organizations to automate the decision-making process, better understand risk, identify fraudulent behavior, and deliver deeply personalized products and services to customers and clients. Furthermore, deep learning can uncover intricate patterns and relationships in high-dimensional data, rendering it aptly equipped to function in an environment as fast-paced and data-driven as finance. One application of deep learning in finance is in the realm of fraud detection. Conventional fraud detection systems in finance are generally based on pre-defined, established rules that fintech criminals have learned to circumvent, whereas, deep learning models can automatically ignore these established rules. Neural networks, specifically RNNs and LSTM networks (i.e., types of RNNs), can assess the sequenced transaction (e.g, succession of transactions from the same account) in order to recognize a transaction's aberrant behavior as it is happening. Deep learning models can remember past fraud cases, and they can learn as they process new data to draw conclusions from the data in a different way to combat new fraud efforts, generating improved accuracy of detection and a greater useful reduction of false positive cases. In algorithmic trading and market forecasting, deep learning models can examine a plethora of diverse data (e.g., structured data such as historical price and trading volume and unstructured data such as news articles, posts from social media, and corporate financial statements) to show trends within a market and suggest possible trading decisions associated with high-frequency trading activities.

Convolutional Neural Networks (CNNs) and Deep Reinforcement Learning create intelligent trading agents, who learn and adapt to market changes and develop investment strategies independently of human involvement. Deep learning is also revolutionizing the credit scoring and lending sector, with alternative data sources, such as transaction histories, employment records, mobile usage, and patterns developed through voice or facial recognition. This is best suitable if borrowers do not have any credit history. This help to reduce the risk by analyzing the borrowers profile. These hybrid programs can engage customers to get their questions answered, make recommendations for financial products, or provide opportunities for transactions while creating a better understanding of the process by discovering new conversations, since these programs learn and identify patterns with use. Also, deep learning can assist with regulatory compliance and AML by profiling and pre-identifying suspicious patterns and enabling automation and monitoring of financial activity, while eliminating the mundane burden of manual compliance work and optimizing the operational workload of the firm.

2. MACHINE LEARNING MODELS IN BANKING AND FINANCE

In this chapter, applications of machine learning models in the banking and finance sector will be explained. One of the most important approaches is forecasting the price and financial market. Machine learning models can be used to analyze real-time and historical financial data to make effective decisions. Machine learning models will help to identify the patterns of various transactions, risks, and monitoring of financial activities.

Boughaci and Alkhawaldeh (2020) found that machine learning models have vast applications in banking and finance to find the credit score and bankruptcy. They evaluated multiple machine learning model applications in the banking and finance sector. Paramesha et al. (2024) reviewed the role of machine learning, deep learning AI, and blockchain technology in the finance sector. They found that AI improved decision-making and cybersecurity, while machine learning models improved the market and customer insights. Blockchain technology ensures transparent and secure transactions. Aziz et al. (2022) reviewed the research publications from 1990 to 2020. They found vast applications of AI and machine learning models in four sectors: forecasting, risk assessment, financial planning, and financial market analysis. Huang et al. (2020) found the importance of machine learning models in the banking and finance sector. They evaluated the literature review, models, and factors that affect the output of machine learning models.

Machine learning random forest, logistics regression, artificial neural networks, decision trees, and forecast models are the most effective methods to predict credit, risk, and frauds involved in the banking and finance sector.

2.1 Defining Machine Learning Models

Machine learning models are algorithmic computational methods that learn from input data to identify patterns, make predictions or support decision-making without explicit coding. They learn by types of learning techniques such as supervised learning, unsupervised learning, or reinforcement learning, and this learning incorporates experience into their performance capabilities.

Supervised models: In this category, machine learning models are developed using train and test concepts using labelled data. These models receive input-output pairs, where the correct outputs are already defined. The primary goal of supervised learning models is to produce outputs that correspond to the given inputs. The development of supervised models involves human intervention. Examples of supervised machine learning include classification, predictions, and object detection. Applications of supervised learning in banking and finance sectors are identifying the fraud, classification, and pattern of the transactions.

Unsupervised models: Unsupervised models refer to machine learning models that enable machines to autonomously identify the patterns within the input data by analyzing the data itself. In this approach, machines analyze the data independently, without human intervention, to uncover hidden patterns and structures. Features or patterns of the data are not provided and controlled by humans. This type of machine learning utilizes unlabelled data. Methods associated with unsupervised machine learning include clustering, dimensionality reduction, and association. Customer segmentation based on their features is an example of unsupervised machine learning models.

Semi-Supervised Models: Semi-supervised models make use of both labelled and unlabelled data during training by utilizing very small amounts of labelled data with much larger volumes of unlabelled data. Semi-supervised learning takes advantage of the gap between supervised and unsupervised learning models by providing acceptable accuracy, while reducing the costs involved with labelling data. A semi-supervised model employs self-training, co-training, and graph-based methods making them very useful for tasks such as text, images, and speech recognition. Support vector machines (SVM), Graph based models and Naïve Bayes are some popular semi supervised models.

Reinforcement models: In reinforcement learning, a feedback-based approach is employed to identify patterns. Devices utilize feedback to enhance their understanding and efficiency in recognizing these patterns. By analyzing the feedback patterns, devices are able to refine their decision-making processes.

Predictive and Forecast Models

Predictive and forecast models take historical and current data and are designed to predict future outcomes. Predictive models look for patterns that indicate probabilities in events; for example, probability of customer churn, fraud, etc. Whereas forecast models look at time series data to predict future trends; for example, sales, demand, etc. While their end results may differ, they both serve as information tools to facilitate decisions in various industries such as business, finance, healthcare, and supply chain management. Forecasting is when we describe and predict the future. By examining historical time series data, trends and patterns can be found—which can be used to make predictions. Following are the types of forecast models:

Qualitative Forecasting: Qualitative forecast models are used when historical data is not available for analysis in order to predict values. These methods rely heavily on expert opinions and judgments. When data is lacking, qualitative approaches can significantly assist in forecasting future values.

The following are the qualitative forecasting methods:

Expert opinion Methods: In this methods expert's knowledge and experience in the appropriate field is considered to predict the future. The experts analyze the geopolitical, and market conditions including trends in specific sectors to forecast. This approach is typically used for new products and where there are no historical data available for analysis.

Delphi Method: The Delphi method is a process that requires a panel of expert(s) to analyze a given problem. Each expert does their own analysis of the problem without realizing the conclusions of others. The findings from all experts are then compiled to develop a final prediction.

Market Research: Market research is conducted to know about the consumers and current scenario. The goal of utilization of this methodology is to thoroughly understand market conditions and the needs of customers to make informed decisions.

Quantitative Forecasting Techniques: In quantitative forecasting, mathematical models are developed using past numerical data. The quantitative forecasting techniques are used to develop forecast model over time series. Based on the cyclical patterns, seasonal fluctuations, and trends best forecast model is developed by analyzing the historical data. Auto Regressive Integrated Moving Average (ARIMA), Autoregression (AR), exponential smoothing, and moving averages are a few of the time series forecasting techniques. Causal prediction (Models Based on Regression) regression models are developed when one or more variables are predicted considering dependent on some other variables. Vector Autoregression (VAR), multiple regressions, and linear regression are a few methods for causal forecasting.

2.2 Analyzing real-life data using machine learning models

2.2.1 Applications of Holt-Winters and ARIMA Forecast Models in the Finance and Banking Sector

In the fast-moving finance and banking world, forecasting is a very important tool for decision-making, risk management, and strategic planning. Financial institutions are always subject to uncertainty in areas like interest rates, stock prices, currency fluctuations, and customer behavior. As such, banks have adopted time-series forecasting models like Holt-Winters Exponential Smoothing and ARIMA (Autoregressive Integrated Moving Average) because of their ability to use past data to generate future forecasts and predict upcoming behavior.

The Holt-Winters method is particularly adept when working with time series that contain a trend and seasonality component. These features make it especially valuable to the banking and financial services industry, as activities typically exhibit a cyclical or periodic nature. For instance, transaction activity at bank locations and ATMs is often determined by whether it is a weekday or weekend (or for holidays during a calendar period). The Holt-Winters model is a contribution to cash demand for ATMs because when banks have better forecasts of total cash withdrawal and cash deposit volume, we believe banks will better employ decision making to avert a shortfall of cash to satisfy customer cash demands, and decrease the amount of cash that is sitting idle in banks. Credit card transaction activity and retail banks will also have a seasonal influence based on holiday time or other sales events; The Holt-Winters model can provide pertinent forecasts for transaction activity time series patterns to allow banks to plan resource allocation as well as balance customer expectation with operational risk.

In the context of general financial markets, Holt-Winters is often implemented for interest rate forecasts, stock indices, and commodity prices, all of which have some seasonal pattern. Asset managers are able to take advantage of seasonally-cast forecasts to rebalance portfolios, hedge against the risk that the seasonality of asset classes will negatively affect them, and as part of trading strategies regarding commodities and any seasonal promotional or consumption patterns. The benefit of Holt-Winters is that it can accommodate both additive and multiplicative seasonal variation—it can be useful in finance because seasonal variation may occur either as an absolute variance or as a variance a percentage of the base value.

The ARIMA model allows even greater flexibility by adapting the time series analysis to estimate forecasts from time-series data that is non-seasonal or, for models of differenced data. ARIMA is applied widely in macro-economic forecasting to predict rates of inflation, GDP rates of change, and exchange rate movement. Similar trends can be observed for loan demand, deposit growth, or credit defaults (home foreclosures) in estimating models in the banking industry. All are important to evaluating longer-range capital planning and regulatory planning. For example, estimating the impact of non-performing assets (NPAs) is integral to evaluating and estimating bank provisions, credit risk, and the overall financial health of the bank.

ARIMA has also been adopted to forecast stock prices and the activity of financial markets because of its ability to capture autocorrelations and short-term dependencies in price behaviors. Traders and analysts also use ARIMA-based forecasts to design quantitative strategies, measure market risks, and investigate structural breaks in prices. For example, central banks and regulators utilize ARIMA to make forecasts about the historical interest rate and future portions of the monetary policy that drive lending and borrowing among financial institutions.

Using Holt-Winters and ARIMA together provides a well-rounded set of applications for predictive analytics. Holt-Winters is most effective at short- and medium-term forecasts with clear seasonal cycles; however, ARIMA may be more suited for long-term forecasts and for modeling complex, non-seasonal data patterns. For example, a bank could use Holt-Winters to forecast weekly withdrawals of cash and ARIMA to model their long-term growth plans of loan demand.

Numerical Example

In this section data Holt-Winters and ARIMA models will be developed for any dummy data. Suppose we are having a dummy data of monthly average share prices for January 2019 to December 2024. This data set may be having seasonal variations and also trend. Using Holt-Winters and ARIMA model trend and seasonal analysis will be performed. R software is used to develop the Holt-Winters and ARIMA models to forecast share prices

Table 1. Monthly share prices for January 2019 to December 2024

Month/Year	2019	2020	2021	2022	2023	2024
Jan	1014.9	1108.67	1186.49	1310.49	1415.94	1492.67
Feb	1029.3	1077.46	1239.6	1278.89	1386.19	1534.92
Mar	1079.63	1109.86	1228.49	1324.58	1475.56	1534.05
Apr	1121.04	1159.89	1289.44	1385.48	1469.43	1546.51
May	1070.08	1148.13	1261.9	1403.48	1462.43	1608.52
Jun	1060.23	1178.09	1261.32	1376.62	1491.24	1614.98
Jul	1098.08	1124.87	1235.47	1351.46	1487.27	1555.59
Aug	1057.18	1093.19	1292.54	1329.35	1467.73	1571.3
Sep	1010.22	1169.68	1226.72	1284.17	1404.76	1542.2
Oct	1042.33	1120.69	1197.14	1308.69	1422.41	1513.74
Nov	1027.3	1144.64	1268.7	1331.61	1456.78	1559.09
Dec	1053.99	1126.62	1234.15	1403.9	1502.86	1621.14

A data "finance" is use to develop the models. Following commands are performed in R software to analyze the data.

Firstly, we should download the package "tseries" and "forecast" in R software to develop forecast models.

```
Command 1>library(tseries)
Command 2>library(forecast)
Command 3>finance<-read.csv("C:/Users/Administrator/finance.csv", header=T)
Command 4> fin_ts=ts(finance, start=2019, end=2024, frequency=12)
Command5> plot(fin_ts)
```

Command 1 and command are essential to develop the forecast model. WE can upload the data file either using command 3 or directly from R software's "import data set" section. To develop forecast model, it is essential to convert data frame into a time series format. Command 4 is used to convert data frame "finance" into a time series named as "fin_ts". Command 5 is used to see the trend and seasonal pattern of the share price data.

From the given figure we can find the pattern of the share prices.

Figure 1. Trend of share prices for January 2019 to December 2024

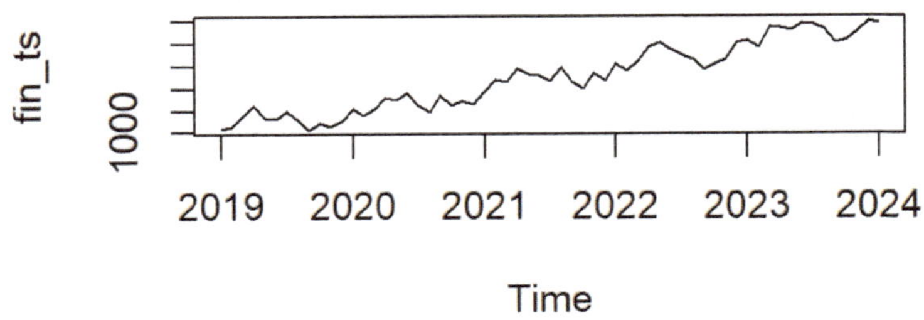

2.2.1.1 Developing Holt-Winters Forecast Model

Command 6> fin_Holt=HoltWinters(fin_ts)
Command 7> plot(fin_Holt)

Command 6 is performed to fit a trend model using the "HoltWinters" model.

Command 7 is performed to know the best fit curve of time series using Holt-Winters model. In the figure black line represent the actual data while red line represents the predicted data using Holt-Winters model.

From Figure 2, we can see that predicted data is close to the actual data so Holt-Winters model can be developed to forecast share prices.

Figure 2. Trend of actual and expected share prices using Holt-Winters model

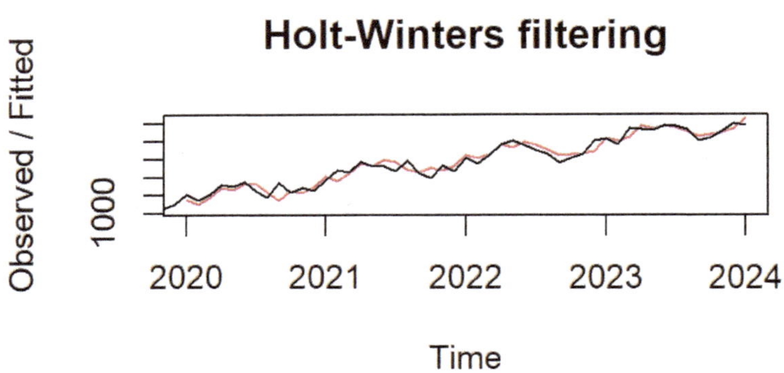

Command 8> fin_forecast_Holt=forecast(fin_Holt, h=24)
Command 9> summary(fin_forecast_Holt)

Command 8 develop the forecast model to forecast share prices for next 12 months. Command 9 provide the summary of the forecast Holt-Winters model.

```
Forecast method: HoltWinters

Model Information:
Holt-Winters exponential smoothing with trend and additive
seasonal component.

Call:
HoltWinters(x = fin_ts)

Smoothing parameters:
 alpha: 0.139723
 beta: 0.120857
 gamma: 0.1784531

Coefficients:
              [,1]
a 1505.380564                     b 8.830879
s1 -8.187360    s2 20.962151    s3 54.006694   s4 36.053638
s5 45.749924    s6 23.928461    s7 -5.578415   s8 -51.693698
s9 -43.198009   s10 -37.696176  s11 -22.647464s12 13.383334
```

Table 2. Forecast accuracy of Holt-Winters model

ME	RMSE	MAE	MPE	MAPE	MASE	ACF1
3.334	31.624	25.144	0.269	1.981	0.254	-0.060

Command 10> plot(fin_forecast_Holt)

Command 10 will provide the forecasted share prices for the next twelve months i.e. from January 2025 to December 2025.

Figure 3. Forecasting of share prices using Holt-Winters model

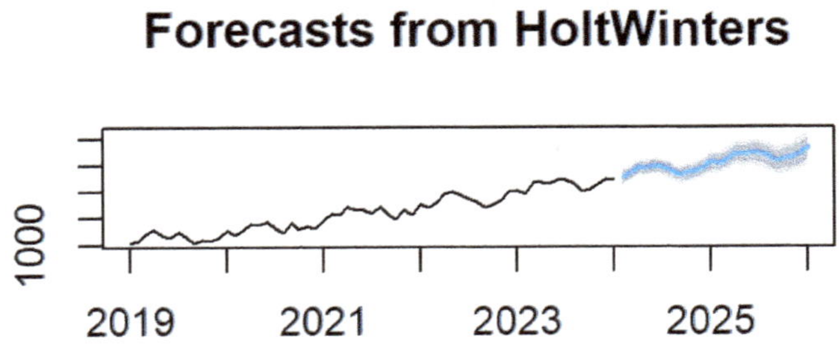

Table 3. Forecasted share prices for January 2025 to December 2025 using Holt-Winters trend analysis

Month	Year	Forecast	Lo 80	Hi 80	Lo 95	Hi 95
Jan	2025	1624.73	1572.11	1677.36	1544.25	1705.22
Feb	2025	1612	1555.63	1668.36	1525.79	1698.2
Mar	2025	1649.98	1591.74	1708.21	1560.91	1739.04
Apr	2025	1691.85	1631.63	1752.07	1599.76	1783.94
May	2025	1682.73	1620.42	1745.04	1587.44	1778.02
Jun	2025	1701.26	1636.75	1765.76	1602.61	1799.91
Jul	2025	1688.27	1621.46	1755.07	1586.1	1790.43
Aug	2025	1667.59	1598.39	1736.79	1561.75	1773.43
Sep	2025	1630.3	1558.61	1702	1520.65	1739.96
Oct	2025	1647.63	1573.34	1721.92	1534.02	1761.25
Nov	2025	1661.96	1585	1738.93	1544.25	1779.68
Dec	2025	1685.84	1606.11	1765.58	1563.9	1807.78

2.2.1.2 Developing ARIMA Model

```
Command 11: fin_arima=auto.arima(fin_ts)
Command12: fin_forecast_arima=forecast(fin_arima, h=24)
Command13:summary(fin_forecast_arima)
```

Command 11 is performed to develop ARIMA model to forecast share prices.

Command 12 is performed to develop forecast model. Command 13 will provide the summary of the forecast model using ARIMA.

```
Forecast method: ARIMA(0,0,0)(1,1,0)[12] with drift

Model Information:
Series: fin_ts
ARIMA(0,0,0)(1,1,0)[12] with drift

Coefficients:
         sar1   drift
      -0.5475  8.3699
s.e.   0.1255  0.2756

sigma^2 = 1100:  log likelihood = -242.22
AIC=490.43   AICc=490.97   BIC=496.11
```

Table 4. Forecast accuracy of ARIMA model

ME	RMSE	MAE	MPE	MAPE	MASE	ACF1
-1.74	29.11	21.17	-0.23	1.68	0.21	-0.03

Command 14> plot(fin_forecast_arima)

Command 13 provides the forecast for next twelve months i.e. from January 2025 to December 2025.

Figure 4. Forecasting of share prices for January 2025 to December 2025 using ARIMA model

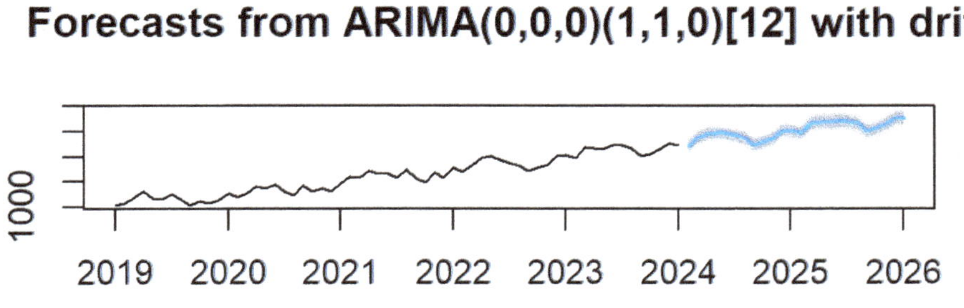

Table 5. Forecasted share prices for January 2025 to December 2025 using ARIMA model

Month	Year	Forecast	Lo 80	Hi 80	Lo 95	Hi 95
Jan	2025	1606.09	1563.584	1648.597	1541.082	1671.099
Feb	2025	1585.369	1538.713	1632.025	1514.015	1656.723
Mar	2025	1663.917	1617.262	1710.573	1592.564	1735.271
Apr	2025	1674.394	1627.738	1721.049	1603.04	1745.747
May	2025	1673.587	1626.931	1720.243	1602.233	1744.941
Jun	2025	1688.605	1641.95	1735.261	1617.252	1759.959
Jul	2025	1679.386	1632.73	1726.041	1608.032	1750.739
Aug	2025	1659.209	1612.553	1705.865	1587.855	1730.563
Sep	2025	1600.646	1553.991	1647.302	1529.293	1672
Oct	2025	1619.998	1573.343	1666.654	1548.645	1691.352
Nov	2025	1651.532	1604.876	1698.187	1580.178	1722.885
Dec	2025	1704.105	1657.449	1750.761	1632.751	1775.459

In Figure 3 and Figure 4, forecast patterns of share prices using Holt-Winters and ARIMA forecast models are shown, respectively. The blue line shows the average expected share prices, while the gray shaded region shows the lower and upper forecasted values for 80% and 95% confidence levels.

Forecast accuracy of any model can be measured using MAPE (mean absolute percentage error). The acceptable maximum value of MAPE is 10%. MAPE is the average percentage absolute error of any model defined in percentage. For a good forecast model, MAPE should be minimum. The model with lesser MAPE will be considered a better forecast model.

From table 2 we can see that the Mean Absolute Percentage Error (MAPE) for the Holt-Winters model is 1.98, which is very low, so Holt-Winters can be a good forecast model to forecast the share prices.According to the Holt-Winters model, share prices demand for Jan 2025 and December 2025 will be 1624.734 and 1685.843, respectively.

From table 4 we can see that the Mean Absolute Percentage Error (MAPE) for the ARIMA model is 1.68, which is very low, so the ARIMA model is also a good forecast model to forecast the share prices. According to the ARIMA model, share prices demand for Jan 2025 and December 2025 will be 1606.09 and 1699.422, respectively.

Since the MAPE of the ARIMA model is better than the Holt-Winters model, we should accept the ARIMA model to forecast the share prices.

2.2.2 Predictive Models

2.2.2.1 Logistic Regression for Fraud Detection

Logistic regression is probably the most popular statistical and machine learning method for fraud detection in the financial sector and banking industry. Logistic regression differs from linear regression in that it predicts categorical responses as opposed to continuous variables. Generally, outputs in regression are either categorical or continuous, which can result in categorical outcomes such as fraud or no fraud, which work nicely for fraud detection when working with transactional data and how we think about transactions as legitimate or non-legitimate.

For fraud detection, logistic regression will predict probabilities of a given transaction classified as being fraudulent using the input variables or features. There are many features that can be included in a fraud detection model—features such as the amount of the transaction, location, time of transaction, customer behavioral patterns, transaction frequency, device utilized by the customer, and whether the activity is outside the norm or expected behavior based on historical advances of the client's transactional trends. Each feature in the model will have a contributing weight that will generate an increase or decrease in the likelihood of the fraud outcome.

Among the benefits of logistic regression is the interest in the simplicity of the approach and the interpretability. Banks and financial sectors have a need for models that not only predict but will also provide attribution to why a transaction was flagged. Furthermore, compliance teams and investigators need to understand which variables contribute to fraud when they are explaining and justifying their actions. Logistic regression provides coefficients that can be explained to provide insight into which factors are most attributable to the fraud malfeasance.

To train the logistic regression model, a historical dataset of prior transactions that were labelled either fraudulent or legitimate was employed. The model then "learns" the relationships between the features and output label. Using the trained model, new transactions can be scored in real time and assigned probabilities so that the bank can determine which transactions to pass or to hold for human review. Logistic regression is also reasonably effective with data that is imbalanced; however, depending on the degree of imbalance, it is still common to use oversampling, undersampling, or class weights to assist the model since fraud cases are usually much rarer than legitimate ones. Regularized versions of logistic regression (L1 and L2) can also be useful in that they avoid the potential for overfitting, which can help stabilize the model. Furthermore, logistic regression can be incorporated directly into current banking IT systems and is generally considered a low-cost and low-complexity solution option.It serves as a baseline model and can often be used in conjunction with more complex techniques, including decision trees, random forests, and neural networks, to provide variations as hybrid or ensemble model options to enhance accuracy.

2.2.2.2: Random Forest for Fraud Detection in Banking and Finance

The Random Forest algorithm is one of the most popular machine learning algorithms used for fraud detection in the banking and finance industry. Random Forest can be thought of as an ensemble learning method, where multiple models are combined to produce a better predictive performance than any single model alone. Random Forest specifically works by building a large number of decision trees during training and then making a prediction based on the majority vote of this pool of trees. Specifically, Random Forest operates as follows:

A decision tree is a structure similar to a flowchart—where the internal nodes of the decision tree model the conditions on a single feature, the branches represent the outcome of those conditions, and the leaf nodes represent the outcome label (fraud or not fraud). An example of a decision tree would be checking to see if the transaction amount is greater than 20,000, and then if the device is new/unusual, and lastly, if the transaction is taking place in an unusual location. The downside of using only a decision tree is that it is very unstable and thus can perform very poorly because of its sensitivity to the particulars of the training data. Therefore, a decision tree model can easily overfit the training data, meaning the model performs very well during training but not well on new or unseen data.

Random Forest mitigates this issue using two significant methods: bagging and feature randomness. Bagging (bootstrap aggregating) is the process where different subsets of the original training data will be generated by random sampling with replacement. For each group a decision tree is trained. At each split in the tree, they also only look at a random subset of features. This added level of randomness across the different trees ensures that each decision tree is slightly different from each other. These different trees are what create the stability and accuracy in the overall model.

For the final prediction, it aggregates the predictions from the different trees. Especially for classification (i.e., fraud or non-fraud), this is aggregative through majority voting, in which the class with the most votes in the final output is the final prediction. This collective decision reduces the risk of error from one tree and ultimately increases accuracy. An important technical concept that is used with Random Forest is called "feature importance." This process identifies how much each feature contributes to the reduction of uncertainty or impurity in the data. All features can be ranked according to their importance scores. Transaction amount, transaction frequency, time of the transaction, customer's typical/historical behavior, IP address, or merchant category could all be potentially important features. Random Forest models are also flexible to imbalanced data, as is often the case in fraud detection—fraudulent cases are very rare in comparison to legitimate transactions.

Approaches with Random Forest can utilize techniques such as class weights or sampling strategies, which can potentially improve detection of the minority-class (fraud) transactions. Another technical advantage includes more resilience to noise and missing data. Since Random Forest only sees part of the data at a time, noise and/or mischaracterized records affect the model less than they affect some other algorithms. Random Forest also allows for continual updates through retraining with the most current data. This allows the model to frequently retrain, meaning that it can adjust more seamlessly to evolving patterns of fraud. Overall, Random Forest lends itself very well to fraud detection because of its ability to model complex and non-linear patterns and its enhancements to overfitting, and it has even been shown to be quite accurate with predictions. Additionally, with benefits like determining feature importance and being resilient to noise, it is clearly a primary approach for fraud detection systems that are used in modern banking and financial service provision.

3. HOW AI IS HELPING FRAUDSTERS IN BANKING AND FINANCE SECTOR

AI is a powerful tool to control the frauds in the finance sector. AI is very beneficial for the banking and finance sector; it helps to make it an easy process, simplifying things, improving customer experience, and making effective policies to improve the business.

At the same time, AI is helping the fraudsters to commit more frauds. AI has become the two-way sword for the banking and finance sector.AI experts are making the banking and finance sector system easy for both customers and service providers; at the same time, fraudsters are using AI and technology to find new ways of fraud. Deep learning, cracking algorithms to generate clone websites, sending fraud emails and links, and fraud calls using AI are the same ways fraudsters are doing a lot of fraud. This makes it possible for them to expand their operations, boost attack success rates, and evade detection for extended periods of time. The following AI-enabled techniques are explained below:

Applications of Deepfake: Fraudsters are using deepfake a lot. With the help of deepfake, images and voice clones are created by the fraudsters. By applying AI-enabled deepfake technology, fraudsters can mimic the real scenarios. They can mimic the voice of any person to commit fraud. Fraudsters are taking advantage of AI-enabled deepfake technologies to commit fraud in the banking and finance sector by cracking the security codes. The banking and finance industry currently employs a video-based know your customer (KYC) process for verifying customers. This process is easily circumvented by fraudsters impersonating genuine customers with their fraud video platforms to open fraudulent accounts and get loans.

Fraudsters are clone voices to instruct employees to get fraud approvals. It is very difficult for the untrained employees to track the identify the cloned voices without any technical support. Consumers are now getting emails from a financial institution that are actually fake emails created by technology. These emails are seeking to create phishing links to acquire consumer information. The wave of cybercrime, especially fraud, is at unprecedented levels as technologies are misused; AI is part of the problem. AI poses a legitimate security issue due to its ability to create and generate text and other forms of text and decode it for all types of NL processing (NL understanding, NL generation, etc.).AI can effortlessly craft contextually relevant and grammatically accurate messages mimicking the style and language used by banks and other financial service providers. AI generates contextually relevant and grammatically accurate messages. Customers releasing information such as login details, OTPs, and unauthorized transaction permissions are the intended users of these misleading emails.

Through publicly available information or information breaches, AI systems can now personalize emails, which boosts the effectiveness of phishing schemes. Emails that receive or include one's name, account details, or recent financial transactions automatically seem genuine and trustworthy. Furthermore, AI can automate the phishing process by generating and sending out mass emails, which improves the effectiveness of the schemes.

Anti-money laundering (AML): anti-money laundering (AML) systems too simple and has created a nice avenue for criminals to launder money. The emergence of and increased exploitation of Artificial Intelligence (AI) has also become common, given that criminals are trying to purposely avoid automatic money laundering detection systems. Prior to this, automatic money laundering detection systems were related to the programmed fixed algorithms that recognized suspicious behaviors by using pre-defined conditions and patterns. Now, it appears that criminals are keenly aware of how these algorithms function and begin artificially designing transactional behaviors that altogether avoid activating any alert system. The AI platform is being used to search through financial transactions and mimic legitimate financial activities making it easy for illegal financial transactions to be networked into the everyday financial landscape.

With artificial intelligence, criminals can now make layers automated and improved and move money through multiple accounts, shell companies, and/or cryptocurrencies, coupled with making the origins of funds even less traceable. Bots can also be used to make small, timed transactions through multiple platforms. This is called smurfing; simply put, the opposite of each transaction is less likely to trigger the check of an AML (Anti-Money Laundering) system to check for unusual activity. There have also been examples of AI being used by criminals in order to manipulate financial identities and fraudulent companies to overcome KYC (Know Your

Customer) screening and compliance checks. In some cases, criminals are using AI to break down certain AML systems so that they change up their money laundering without the system event making a special note. These uses of AI by criminals have created and ongoing challenge for financial institutions each have had to build AI models that are smarter, and more transparent in order to detect laundering behavior.

Creating fake loans: AI can be used to create fake loan applications. Cybercriminals are now using artificial intelligence (AI) to create fake loan applications that can bypass traditional security and verification methods a lender may deploy. AI technologies can help with every aspect of an impersonal loan process, from the creation of identities to the fabrication of documents. This expedites the process, adds layers of persuasion, and makes detection increasingly difficult. The most common method being utilized is synthetic identity fraud, which references both real and fabricated information to create entirely new identities using AI. With the use of details obtained from data breaches, AI can construct authentic-sounding personal profiles comprising names, addresses, social security numbers (or Aadhaar numbers), and other identity indicators. Synthetic identities are later utilized to obtain loans, credit cards, or lines of credit. Other tools that are driven by AI, including deep learning algorithms and Generative Adversarial Networks (GANs), are also employed to create fake documents like pay stubs, bank statements, identification cards, and tax records that appear authentic. These falsified documents can easily surmount automated verification processes, especially compared to systems that include a digital-only or remote onboarding, where there is no in-person loophole.

4. ISSUES WITH THE APPLICATIONS OF AI AND ML MODELS

AI relies on high and reliable data to make accurate predictions. Data privacy is a big concern when analyzing the real-time data of the finance sector. To collect real-time natural data may be a tough task. To collect and analyze a huge amount of real-time and past data of the finance sector requires a more advanced infrastructure and technology, which may be a tough task. A highly advanced, skilled expert team is also a big challenge to analyze the data.

The implementation of AI and ML presents a variety of challenges—technical, ethical, regulatory, and operational—that financial institutions must confront to guarantee the sustainable, equitable, and effective application of these tools. Below is a detailed outline of the primary challenges, presented in a point-wise format for clarity.

Data quality and availability incomplete or inaccurate data: AI models necessitate clean, structured, and high-quality data for training purposes. Inaccurate or incomplete data can result in suboptimal predictions, thereby increasing financial risk. In numerous institutions, data is dispersed across various departments or legacy systems, complicating the creation of a cohesive, real-time data infrastructure. The data utilized to train AI models frequently reflects historical biases in areas such as lending, hiring, or fraud detection, which can lead to the continuation of unjust decisions.

Absence of explainability and transparency black box models: A large number of AI systems, particularly deep learning models, are so-called 'black boxes,' and they are opaque in terms of providing transparent logic behind decisions. Hence, it is much harder to provide an explanation when an applicant has been denied a loan or a transaction was flagged. Regulators such as the GDPR and RBI require financial institutions to provide explanations for automated decisions, but non-transparent AI makes this impossible. The lack of transparency undermines user trust, especially if users do not understand the AI's rationale or cannot agree with it.

Ethical and bias algorithmic issues: If a machine learning system is trained using a biased dataset, it may inadvertently discriminate against an identifiable demographic (e.g., by race, gender, or geography). Unfair Credit Decisions affect the decision making. Biased credit scoring algorithms may result in the exclusion of underrepresented or lower-income people from accessing—and benefiting from—formal banking services. Even unintentional unethical use of AI may result in reputational harm to the bank and reduce trustworthiness in the public eye.

Data privacy and security sensitive financial data: AI models require significant quantities of personal and financial data, which increases the risk of data breaches and cyberattacks. Laws such as GDPR, CCPA, and India's Digital Personal Data Protection Act impose restrictive requirements around how data can be used, shared, and stored. Consent Management of customer is very crucial. Obtaining consent from customers for using their data and maintaining transparency around how data is used is very complex but critical, given the various global regulations.

Regulatory and compliance complexity: The incredible speed at which AI is progressing in the financial services sector is outpacing regulatory governance and leaving ambiguity over what is allowed. Cross-Border Compliance is also a challenge with AI. International financial institutions need to cope with different regulations in different countries, particularly regarding data localization and how to be transparent about AI. Regulators want banks to regularly audit their AI algorithms, which means banks must maintain logs, documentation, and versioning of their AI models.

High costs of implementation and maintenance infrastructure funding: Implementing AI technology requires a large upfront investment in hardware (e.g., GPUs), cloud platforms, and data storage. Skilled AI experts and data scientists are in high demand, and there are not many of them available, which makes it difficult to hire and retain talent, and the associated costs are high. AI models need to be updated regularly to accommodate dynamic changes represented by behavior, emergent fraud tactics, and changing market patterns, which results in longer-term costs.

Integration with legacy systems: Most legacy banking systems were never designed to support real-time AI algorithms; therefore, most integration processes are overly complex and time-consuming. Transitioning data from legacy systems to AI technologies is often fraught with risks and can lead to a wide variety of mistakes, which could negatively impact important activities. Upgrading banks to implement AI will likely require operational downtimes or backups that can negatively impact the customer's experience.

Model risk and overfitting to the training data: AI models can perform well on the historical data sets but can perform poorly in practice because they have overfit the historical data. Sudden changes to the economy (e.g., a pandemic, war, or changing regulations) can cause AI models to be essentially useless if these models were built on stable historical data. Consumer habits and the methods used to perpetrate fraud change over time, meaning that AI models will degrade over time unless monitored and updated on a regular basis.

Real-Time processing issues: Financial services, such as fraud detection and high-frequency trading, require real-time processing, putting strain on AI systems, especially when considering the size and complexity of the data. AI systems need to deal with increasing amounts of data and numbers of people using the system, requiring a strong architecture that supports continuous improvements in performance. While cloud-based AI solutions can be cost-effective and scalable, potential issues related to control, sovereignty over data, and latency arise when moving to the cloud.

Resistance to change & lack of awareness organizational culture: Many traditional banks have hierarchical cultures that are risk-averse with an environment that does not allow flexibility in adopting advances in AI. Fear of displacement from automation leads to resistance from employees and labour unions. Employees may be challenged to effectively use AI systems since any staff without a tech background may have limited knowledge of what AI can do and thus use AI inappropriately or not use AI adequately.

Customer concerns and experience lack of human touch: Excessive over-reliance on bots or automated decision-making procedures may frustrate customers who are more comfortable dealing with a human for difficult issues. Customers may find it difficult to accept denials of credit or fraud alerts when generated through AI, since such decisions may not be explained clearly. AI systems must be accessible to every user, including users with disabilities and users with little to no digital skills.

Cybersecurity related risks to ai systems model inversion attacks: AI engineering can also be reversed to find the personal and confidential information. Criminal can change the data inputs to attack the security of the system. The war is about the AI vs AI. Excessive dependency on AI can result in the control of the humans on the system. They can lose the expertise of handing, monitoring and controlling the security of the system. AI systems that analyze social media or customer opinions may not identify the correct sentiments by analyzing the sarcasm, regional dialects, and contextual meaning and nuance. Conducting sentiment analysis in real-time from social media applications like Twitter or Reddit requires processing massive amounts of noisy and, often, irrelevant data.

Interoperability and standardization problems lack of industry standards: There are few global standards for applying AI in banking, which leads to varying practices and results. Financial institutions may fall into the trap of becoming dependent on specific AI vendors that reduce flexibility and increase switching costs. Integrating different AI tools and ensuring they work well together is complex from a technical standpoint.

CONCLUSION

AI and ML give institutions the ability to process and analyze massive and complex data sets timely and accurately, which will result in a better way to make effective decisions. AI models provide predictive analytics for risk evaluation in credit scoring, defaults on loans, and bankruptcy-type scenarios, allowing financial institutions to negate losses and extend reach in the market. Fraud detection is effectively monetized using ML algorithms by identifying unusual patterns in transactions and blocking high-risk transactions in near real-time to increase financial security. AI-based trading systems have created flexible strategies-based ML, advanced data mining portfolios using better-designed algorithms. Customer service has significantly changed to include ML intelligent chatbots and virtual assistants, allowing institutions to provide a more personalized approach for service and disperse information faster. AI enabled NLP analyze a huge data to know the customer sentiments. Looking for all the above explained AI and ML applications in banking and finance sector we can say AI is transforming the finance and banking sector.

AI helps criminals and fraudsters to do financial frauds by cloning images, voices and fraud documents creations. Governments and authorities also have to take advance steps to secure banking and finance sector. All the humans associated with the finance sector should be trained with the modern technologies and current trend. They should be trained to control any kind of frauds due to Ai and technology enabled system. Technical infrastructure like regulatory bodies, modern and advanced complaint system and judiciary should be framed by the governments to make fast and effective decisions.

ACKNOWLEDGMENT

The authors would like to express their sincere gratitude to Christ University, India for providing the all kind of support to conduct this research.

REFERENCES

Agrawal, D., Tidake, V. M., Banu, S. R., Ahmad, A. Y. B., Thethi, H. P., Chauhan, S. S., & Mircetic, D. (2025). Blockchain and AI Integration for Transparent and Secured Financial Record Keeping. *Recent Trends In Engineering and Science for Resource Optimization and Sustainable Development*, 72-76.

Aziz, S., Dowling, M., Hammami, H., & Piepenbrink, A. (2022). Machine learning in finance: A topic modeling approach. *European Financial Management*, *28*(3), 744–770. DOI: 10.1111/eufm.12326

Bahoo, S., Cucculelli, M., Goga, X., & Mondolo, J. (2024). Artificial intelligence in Finance: A comprehensive review through bibliometric and content analysis. *SN Business & Economics*, *4*(2), 23. DOI: 10.1007/s43546-023-00618-x

Boughaci, D., & Alkhawaldeh, A. A. (2020). Appropriate machine learning techniques for credit scoring and bankruptcy prediction in banking and finance: A comparative study. *Risk and Decision Analysis*, *8*(1-2), 15–24. DOI: 10.3233/RDA-180051

Cao, Y., & Zhai, J. (2022). A survey of AI in finance. *Journal of Chinese Economic and Business Studies*, *20*(2), 125–137. DOI: 10.1080/14765284.2022.2077632

Darapu, K., & Marukukula, M. (2025). Fraud Detection and Prevention in Finance and Banking Using Artificial Intelligence. In *Real-World Applications of AI Innovation* (pp. 213–232). IGI Global Scientific Publishing.

Gao, H., Kou, G., Liang, H., Zhang, H., Chao, X., Li, C. C., & Dong, Y. (2024). Machine learning in business and finance: A literature review and research opportunities. *Financial Innovation*, *10*(1), 86. DOI: 10.1186/s40854-024-00629-z

Giudici, P., & Raffinetti, E. (2023). SAFE Artificial Intelligence in finance. *Finance Research Letters*, *56*, 104088. DOI: 10.1016/j.frl.2023.104088

Huang, J., Chai, J., & Cho, S. (2020). Deep learning in finance and banking: A literature review and classification. *Frontiers of Business Research in China*, *14*(1), 13. DOI: 10.1186/s11782-020-00082-6

Irfan, M., Kadry, S., Sharif, M., & Khan, H. U. (Eds.). (2023). *Fintech applications in Islamic finance: AI, machine learning, and blockchain techniques: AI, machine learning, and blockchain techniques*. IGI Global. DOI: 10.4018/979-8-3693-1038-0

Jafar, S. H., Alam, P., & El-Chaarani, H. (2023). AI in Finance. In Artificial Intelligence for Business (pp. 174-196). Productivity Press.

Johora, F. T., Hasan, R., Farabi, S. F., Alam, M. Z., Sarkar, M. I., & Al Mahmud, M. A. (2024, June). AI Advances: Enhancing Banking Security with Fraud Detection. In *2024 First International Conference on Technological Innovations and Advance Computing (TIACOMP)* (pp. 289-294). IEEE. DOI: 10.1109/TIACOMP64125.2024.00055

Kapoor, R., & Ghosal, I. (2022). Will artificial intelligence compliment or supplement human workforce in organizations? A shift to a collaborative human–Machine environment. [IJRTBT]. *International Journal on Recent Trends in Business and Tourism*, *6*(4), 19–28. DOI: 10.31674/ijrtbt.2022.v06i04.002

Lee, D. K. C., Guan, C., Yu, Y., & Ding, Q. (2024). A comprehensive review of generative AI in finance. *FinTech*, *3*(3), 460–478. DOI: 10.3390/fintech3030025

Paramesha, M., Rane, N., & Rane, J. (2024). Artificial intelligence, machine learning, deep learning, and blockchain in financial and banking services: A comprehensive review. *Machine Learning, Deep Learning, and Blockchain in Financial and Banking Services: A Comprehensive Review (June 6, 2024).*

Ridzuan, N. N., Masri, M., Anshari, M., Fitriyani, N. L., & Syafrudin, M. (2024). AI in the Financial Sector: The Line between Innovation, Regulation and Ethical Responsibility. *Information (Basel)*, *15*(8), 432. DOI: 10.3390/info15080432

Taneja, S., Singh, A., & Kumar, P. (Eds.). (2024). *Artificial intelligence and machine learning-powered smart finance*. IGI Global. DOI: 10.4018/979-8-3693-3264-1

Weber, P., Carl, K. V., & Hinz, O. (2024). Applications of Explainable Artificial Intelligence in Finance—A systematic review of Finance, Information Systems, and Computer Science literature. *Manag Rev Q*, *74*(2), 867–907. DOI: 10.1007/s11301-023-00320-0

World Bank. (2023, October). Fraud in fast payments. https://fastpayments.worldbank.org/sites/default/files/2023-10/Fraud%20in%20Fast%20Payments_Final.pdf

Zheng, X. L., Zhu, M. Y., Li, Q. B., Chen, C. C., & Tan, Y. C. (2019). FinBrain: When finance meets AI 2.0. *Frontiers of Information Technology & Electronic Engineering*, *20*(7), 914–924. DOI: 10.1631/FITEE.1700822

Chapter 2

Artificial Intelligence (AI) and Machine Learning in Supply Chain Management

Sreekar Peddi
http://orcid.org/0009-0007-0679-6723
Tek Leaders, USA

Sai Sathish Kethu
http://orcid.org/0009-0002-1556-870X
NeuraFlash, USA

Dharma Teja Valivarthi
http://orcid.org/0009-0004-7680-0079
Tek Leaders, USA

Durai Rajesh Nataraja
http://orcid.org/0009-0006-8880-8371
Estrada Consulting Inc., USA

Swapna Narla
http://orcid.org/0009-0003-4706-8491
Tek Yantra Inc., USA

Aravindhan Kurunthachalam
School of Computing and Information Technology, REVA University, Bangalore, India

ABSTRACT

With improved forecasting, logistics, and decision-making, supply chain management (SCM) has been transformed by machine learning (ML) and artificial intelligence (AI). Contribution of AI/ML to increased efficiency in international operations, decreasing risk, and improved efficiency is being explained in this chapter. Improved forecasting, as well as lower cost and disruption through inventory, comes about due to predictive analytics.ML enhances tracking, vendor selections, and pricing.Use cases such as autonomous warehousing, route optimization, and AI-based chatbots lower lead times by 25%, logistics expense by 30%, and improve prediction accuracy by 40%. Blockchain-based AI reduces fraud loss by 50%. Talent gap, integration,

DOI: 10.4018/979-8-3373-3648-0.ch002

and security of data are some of the challenges. Case studies illustrate how hybrid AI-ML models and cloud SCM enable sustainability and agility. Future work will be focused on autonomous procurement and quantum AI.

1. INTRODUCTION

The improvement pace in machine learning and artificial intelligence technologies is inducing a transformation in the supply chain ecosystem. The multifaceted and complex empire of supply chain management contains multiple activities such as inventory management, demand prediction, logistics, purchasing and even customer relationship management (Wieland, 2021). The problems presented by hyper-globalization, unstable economies and constantly changing customer preferences are becoming increasingly difficult for outdated supply chain frameworks (Fernández-Combarro, 2024), which are based on sequential operations and anthropocentric decisions. Predictive analytics, cognitive decision-making and widespread automation of repetitive processes are all changing due to AI and ML, which also record the lowest operating costs and the highest responsiveness (Boddapati et al., 2025).

Since the border was massively opened from a technological perspective, the entire supply chain has been enhanced in all aspects through AI and ML applications (Khedr & S, 2024). From demand prediction to route optimization, risk management and warehouse automation, AI-powered supply chains are becoming more resilient and adaptive (Wu et al., 2024). Companies that put AI and ML into practice are not only realizing big savings but also increasing their agility and response to disruptions like those caused by deficiencies in supply, geopolitical uncertainties or shifts in consumer behavior (Krykavskyy et al., 2023).

It provides a detailed framework through which one can explore how AI and ML can be integrated into SCM (Riad et al., 2024). In-depth consideration of the principles, technological aspects and transformational impacts of AI-enabled supply chain systems will be included (Tarihal et al., 2024). This framework aims to create a universal picture of fused AI and ML for the SCM of the future through the use of practical and theoretical case studies based on reality's case study findings.

The rest of this paper is structured as follows: Section 2 reviews related literature. The methodology is defined in section 3. The suggested supply chain framework and its components based on AI and ML have been presented in Section 4. Results of experiments and performance analysis are provided in Section 5. Section 6 concludes the paper and suggests avenues for future research.

1.1 The role of AI and ML in Supply Chain Management

AI and ML have drastically changed the functionality of supply chains in their operations. Supply chain ecosystems have been automated for decision-making and real-time data processing via AI and ML (Kalusivalingam et al., 2020). Some of the notable features of AI and ML in modern supply chain management sustain the statement.

Within SCM, demand forecasting is among the major uses of AI and ML. Traditional forecasting techniques creating demand forecasts suffer from being heavily reliant on past data and managerial judgment, thus tend to be mistaken (Feizabadi, 2022). On the other hand, AI-based predictive analytics make use of huge sets of data like that of social media trends, weather trends, economic indicators and real-time sales information to create incredibly accurate demand forecasts (Feliu Juan, 2024). By using machine learning algorithms that keep constantly improving forecast estimations and decreasing forecasting errors, the industry can make reasonable estimations of inventory levels and production planning (Luo et al., 2023).

Maintenance systems help businesses lessen their holding costs while avoiding stockouts or overstocking to sustain their ideal stock levels (Mweshi, 2022). Machine learning algorithms analyze past sales data and supplier performance against demand variations to automate any decision regarding the replenishment of inventories (Avlijas et al., 2021). For seamless inventory management, advanced AI solutions also work with IoT sensors enabling live tracking of stock levels and signaling irregularities (Rane et al., 2023).

Artificial intelligence speeds up supplier selection, contracting and decision-making in procurement processes (Allal-Chérif et al., 2021). Supplier reliability is thus evaluated by using market trends, risk factors and historical performance data through machine learning algorithms (R. S. Khan et al., n.d.). AI-enabled obtaining platforms can prevent possible fraudulent transactions, facilitate cooperation in price settlements and automate normal purchase requests, thereby reducing cost and increasing efficiency in procurement (Flechsig et al., 2022). Cost-effective logistics and transport are essential for any successful supply chain system. The help of AI and ML for fleet management improves delivery speeds through real-time monitoring of traffic and weather forecasts while matching demand and supply (Patil, 2024). AI-enabled logistics technologies rely on deep learning to automate warehouse activities, provide forecasts on delays and improve last-mile delivery efficiencies(Singh, 2025).

(Adeoye et al., 2025) AI is important in supply chain risk reduction because it highlights weaknesses and predicts possible interruptions(Deiva Ganesh & Kalpana, 2022). Machine learning models are used in producing risk assessments by examining supplier dependencies, economic volatility and geopolitical events

(Nezianya et al., 2024). Real-time alerts and proactive recommendations are given through AI-driven risk management systems to minimize disturbances caused by trade restrictions, cyber threats and natural disasters (Aung et al. 2024, Rane et al., 2024). Apart from this, it improves the consumer experience with automated chatbots, intelligent order track systems and personalized recommendations. Demand sensing powered by AI will allow organizations to learn the customer's desires, then adjust the providing according to this knowledge (Pereira et al., 2022). Automated consumer service systems using natural language processing shorten turnaround times and create seamless client interaction (Rane, 2023).

It would be easy to conduct a study within the current context while keeping in view the aspect of these technologies in logistics transformation, such as a particular topic like drones with AI capability and autonomous cars (Willems, 2021). These are further transforming the industry in an increased speed and decreased cost of deliveries. AI helps in reducing supply chain risks because AI can point out weaknesses and thereby project possible interruptions (Attah et al., 2024). Machine learning models are used for risk assessments through examining supplier dependencies, economic volatility and geopolitical events (Nomikou & Νομικού, 2024). Real-time alerts and proactive recommendations are provided through AI-driven risk management systems to mitigate disturbances from trade restrictions, cyber threats and natural disasters (Rana et al., 2025). This differentiates the customer experience by using automated chatbots, intelligent order tracker systems and personalized recommendations. Demand sensing powered by AI will inform businesses on how customers want their offerings curved (M. A. Khan et al., 2023). Automated consumer service systems using natural language processing shorten turnaround times and create seamless client interaction.

Figure 1. AI and ML in the technological supply chain

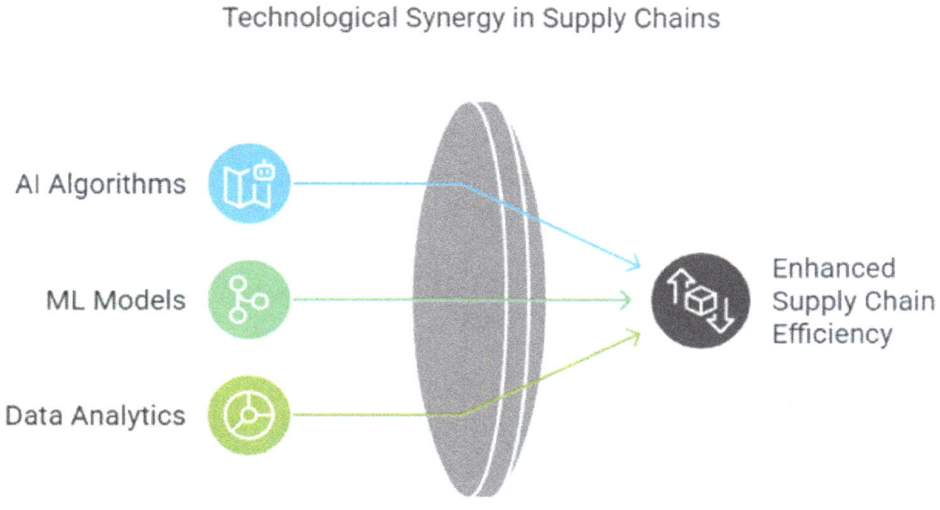

1.2 Technological Components of AI and ML in Supply Chains

Examining the basic technology elements that underpin intelligent supply chains is crucial to comprehending how AI and ML are incorporated into supply chain management.

The requirement for big data analytics in AI-based supply chains is volumetric data processing for structured and unstructured data (Akanbi et al., 2024). Such big data enables companies to obtain operational bottleneck insights, efficient supplier performance and demand shifts. Automation of processes and robust decision-making depend on models using machine learning to extract patterns and relationships in large data sets (Schmitt, 2023). Internet of Things devices such as RFID tags, GPS trackers and smart sensors aid real-time monitoring of assets, shipments and inventory levels. AI-powered analytics reinterpret IoT-generated data, enabling better predictive maintenance strategies, warehouse automation and logistics (Oladele, 2024). Supply chain systems driven by AI can interpret and analyze human language in emails, documents and customer reviews using natural language processing (Holloway, 2024).

Automated contract analysis, supplier negotiations and sentiment analysis for a demand forecast all have something in common, they make the life of an organization considerably simpler by using just an NLP application (Guo et al., 2024). The ideal method is to implement a combination of blockchain and AI for building supply chain ecosystems that are fully transparent and impenetrable (Nippatla, 2019). Supplier contracts, traceability with logistics and procurement accountability are things that have improved to blockchain technology (Valivarthi, 2020). AI-driven bytes enhance blockchain processes by verifying legal compliance and also pointing out anomalies. Improve manufacturing, order fulfillment and warehousing using AI-based RPA robots (Kethu, 2019). Reduce human interaction in high-risk conditions, increase operational efficiency and most importantly, minimize repetitive tasks by using AI-powered robots (Devarajan, 2019).

1.3 The Transformational Impact of AI and ML in Supply Chain Management

With the application of AI and ML, supply chains are enjoying unprecedented levels of resilience, agility and efficiency (Chauhan & Jadon, 2020). Companies that adopt AI-oriented supply chains enjoy better customer satisfaction, risk handling and operational costs (Allur, 2020). Increased operational efficiency derives from AI-powered automation that alleviates manual work, reduces errors and enhances the speed of decision-making (Pulakhandam, 2020). Intelligent purchasing, optimized transportation and AI-based predictive maintenance all help drive down supply chain costs (Narla, 2020). AI allows for dynamic changes in supply chain planning, giving companies the flexibility and responsiveness to adjust to market changes. Businesses using AI and ML gain a competitive edge in the market by making data-driven decisions and providing superior customer experiences (Yallamelli, 2020). AI also optimizes resource utilization, reduces waste and improves energy-efficient supply chain operations, all of which contribute to improved sustainability (Ganesan, 2019).

Summary

The convergence of AI and ML is the driving force behind a significant transition towards smart, data-led, and resilient supply chains. Supply chain management will be dominated by automation, predictive intelligence, and better decision-making with the increasing adoption of AI. This chapter also emphasizes the influence, technological enablers, and distinct benefits of AI and ML in supply chains. Future sections will discuss actual applications of AI, case studies, and best practices in adopting AI in different sectors.

2. RELATED WORKS

Tirkolaee et al. (Tirkolaee et al., 2021) In today's complex and dynamic world, fears of having too much data for supply chain management have replaced fears of not having enough data. The character of supply chain management analysis has changed because of the volume of data from all parts of the supply chain. The performance and productivity of traditional procedures have diminished as the volume of data has expanded. Dash et al. (Dash et al., 2019) A well-run supply chain is vital to the success of every business. Having an accurate inventory forecast puts you at a huge competitive advantage. The success of the supply chain depends on a host of outside and inside factors, ranging from weather to extreme seasonality, changes in consumer attitude, media spotlight and inside factors such as product launches and build-out of distribution networks. It has been shown in recent years that artificial intelligence is nothing more than an extension of the human brain allowing us to think at levels before impossible. AI will allow us to achieve all of our strategic and creative potential, even though there is a common misconception that technology will end up replacing man.

Helo and Hao (Helo & Hao, 2022) Global competitiveness has grown in scope due to the expansion and development of information technology. Many companies have foreseen that the entry of artificial intelligence could materially change activities and supply chain management that would impact all facets from planning, scheduling, optimization and transportation. When it comes to SCM, individuals will be more fascinated with AI, machine learning and other technologies. Sharma et al. (R. Sharma et al., 2022) the latest advances in the field of supply chain management applications of artificial intelligence, such as its trends, gaps and potential. SCM has been among the most successful business fields for AI applications because it represents management innovation with its innovative method of total system thinking. It utilizes bibliometric analysis to map the evolution of AI research in supply chain management. It then integrates decades of past AI research efforts into developing practical solutions to a variety of supply chain problems and identifies promising areas for future research that would enhance supply chain decision-aid tools. A second case study to illustrate the alignment of product architecture to a particular business model and operations frameworks comes from LG Electronics, whose production system is based on Toyota production system and highlights the importance of aligning business models with operations in order to create sustainable advantages (Aldhaheri et al., 2022)

Akhtar et al. (2023) From an array of web and social networking sites, fake news and disinformation are propagating increasingly, disturbing individual's lives and influencing how they make decisions. Few studies have been conducted to design detection models aimed at artificial intelligence and machine learning that are suitable for mitigating supply chain disruptions, even though detecting false news in politics is growing more essential. Kagalwala et al. (Kagalwala et al., 2025) Demand forecasting has been transformed by the inclusion of predictive analytics in supply chain management which has improved responsiveness, accuracy and effectiveness. Artificial intelligence and machine learning are essential to examine large amounts of data, detect trends, and produce accurate demand forecasts to recognize large datasets, establish trends and create accurate demand forecasts. This explores how AI and ML are transforming demand forecasting, outlining how they may decrease uncertainty, improve inventory control and lead to better decision-making. Dynamic market situations often prove challenging for traditional forecasting techniques to consider, leading to inefficiencies and disruptions. Similarly, the Internet of Underwater Things (IoUT) experiences some of the same limitations of signal attenuation, latency, and noise. To address these challenges, this work introduces SMFN as a model to forecast environmental impacts, ACB-BPSK as a method of adaptive modulation to enhance signal robustness and EERL as an energy efficient, dynamic routing protocol Padmavathi et al. (Padmavathi et al 2025).

Wong et al. (Wong et al., 2023) state that AI simplifies costly decision-making for small and medium businesses, enabling a supply chain to quickly adapt to changing conditions. Drawing on a resource-based perspective, the effects of AI on SC risk management for SMEs. A structural model consisting of supply chain agility, SC re-engineering skills and AI risk management competencies was conceptualized and validated utilizing data gathered from SMEs' executive, manager and senior manager levels. Nozari et al. (Nozari et al., 2024) Having millions of devices, the Internet of Things generates huge amounts of data. Machine learning-based artificial intelligence utilizes data and provides insights for optimal analysis. Machine learning creates models that help to predict future events and actions by studying past behavior to determine trends. Besides offering creativity and the basis for intelligent activity, artificial intelligence also identifies the capacity to gather responses.

Awan et al. (2023) also point to artificial intelligence as a robust digital device that speeds up information retrieval and facilitates informed decision-making in vast business settings. Though organizational rejuvenation by big data analytics is widely adopted, precision on the incorporation of data handling skills towards increasing insights for the circular economy as well as supply chain sustainability is still limited. Cioffi et al. (2023) highlight the need for manufacturing innovation and adaptability for the sake of promoting sustainability, urging worldwide viewpoints on intelligent production technologies. AI and machine learning have been identified as main drivers of Industry 4.0 and the revolution of smart manufacturing. Visibility, distortion of color and scattering all complicate detection of these features underwater. This study introduces DRF-YOLO a DRF-YOLO Transformer based architecture incorporating Multiscale Retinex and Dark Channel Prior for improved quality of the image and attention-based feature extraction to detect objects with high accuracy Sundaram et al. (2025).

Boute and Udenio (2023) Artificial intelligence applications are becoming pervasive in logistics and supply chain management. Coupled with continued improvements in processing capabilities, the widespread availability of data creates new opportunities for improving supply chain decision-making. Digital logistics applications or asset connectivity through the IoT technology could be the source of data. Even as AI may automate some jobs, do not believe it will displace logistics planners. AI complements and enhances human capability. Belhadi et al. (Belhadi et al., 2022) One of the feasible ways to design and develop stronger supply chains is artificial intelligence. A large amount of conflict in the literature regarding the application of AI for supply chain management. Practice on this compelling interface is being hindered by the absence of a decision-making approach in the literature thus far for locating and applying effective AI solutions to enhance supply-chain resilience. AI algorithms such as WNN, EDAS and fuzzy systems are employed in a combined Multi-criteria Decision-Making approach to detect trends in AI techniques for generating different strategies.

Abaku et al. (2024) Among the most significant steps toward increased resilience and effectiveness of modern business operations is the integration of artificial intelligence in supply chain management. This examines different theoretical perspectives on artificial intelligence in the issue of supply chain optimization, defining methods for the achievement of heightened flexibility and efficiency. The evolution of AI methods in supply chain management and discussing how these methods transformed the logistics and operations landscape. An analysis of algorithmic frameworks and mathematical modeling for supporting supply chain optimization and use as theory for subsequent AI applications is also crucial. Kehayov et al. (Kehayov et al., 2022) Advanced manufacturing and purchasing and supply management systems are becoming more complex and integrated which is paving the way for new technological advancements in these sectors. The enormous volume of industrial data generated known as big data and recent improvements in artificial intelligence are making it possible for the supply chain to incorporate new analytical tools that maximize the production process.

Mohsen (Mohsen, 2023) Several commercial processes can be revolutionized by the use of artificial intelligence. Artificial intelligence can be utilized to detect the bottlenecks that exist in the supply chain, optimize routes for transportation and logistics and assess and predict demand. Such activities will result in lead times that are not long and costs that are relatively low while demonstrating an effective response to fluctuations in demand. Using the Scopus database, this analyzes and assesses the supply chain management applications of artificial intelligence. Charles et al. (Charles et al., 2023) The combination of blockchain technology and artificial intelligence has drawn a lot of interest, particularly because it can enhance the security, effectiveness and productivity of applications in business settings that are marked by complexity, ambiguity, volatility and uncertainty. One sector that has been seen to gain greatly from blockchain and artificial intelligence is the supply chain, which may improve information and process resilience, facilitate quicker and more economical product delivery and improve product traceability, among other benefits.

Husna et al. (Husna et al., 2021) According to supply chain management is a rapidly expanding and well subject of study that is becoming more and more significant. A supply chain is a group of components linked by the flow of goods, data and services. To preserve customer satisfaction, most businesses concentrate on cost minimization and maintaining optimal inventory levels, especially in the supply chain management of fresh goods. Industries can anticipate demand and keep the proper level of inventory by using accurate demand forecasts. A subset of artificial intelligence is machine learning. It makes it possible for machines to learn from historical data, experiences and patterns to make accurate predictions. Jackson et al. (Jackson et al., 2024) A supply chain and operations management and the revolutionary potential of artificial intelligence in general and generative AI in particular. AI and GAI can affect 13 different SCOM decision-making domains through the resource-based paradigm and based on fundamental AI skills as learning, observation, prediction, interaction, adaptation and reasoning. These domains encompass but are not restricted to supply chain design, inventory control, demand forecasting and risk management.

Chowdhury et al. (Chowdhury et al., 2023) describes how blockchain, machine learning, and artificial intelligence are transforming business processes by increasing efficiency, transparency, and competitiveness. AI and ML offer customized customer experiences, automate tasks, and facilitate data-driven decision-making, with blockchain providing security for transactions and trust. These technologies combined revolutionize conventional business models but also create ethical, security, and regulatory issues. Companies implementing them enhance customer satisfaction, resource deployment, and achieve competitive benefits. Verma et al. (Verma et al., 2024) points to AI-driven predictive analytics in supply chain risk management, leveraging machine learning to study past data, recognize patterns, and better predict and avoid disruptions compared to conventional techniques.

2.1 Problem Statement

Robust and effective security controls are needed to safeguard confidential data and ensure operational integrity due to the accelerated pace of change in digital environments (B. P. Sharma, n.d.). However, new threats are commonly inadequately addressed by current security frameworks, especially with cloud computing systems where threats are constantly changing (Janet Julia Ang'udi, 2023). Classic methods fall behind in bringing the type of intelligence and agility required to react quickly to sophisticated cyber threats (Tahmasebi, 2024). This gap demands an advanced AI-powered security platform that can improve network defense while being scalable and effective in today's digital landscape.

3. METHODOLOGY

The methodology approach of the new AI and ML-based supply chain architecture is extremely systematic in the quest to improve automation, precision and efficiency at various levels. Right from the purchasing of raw materials to the final delivery to customers, it is possible to visualize the block diagram of various phases of supply chain management. All phases are based on AI and ML for improving supply chain resilience, minimizing inefficiencies and improving decision-making.

Figure 2. Supply chain in ML framework

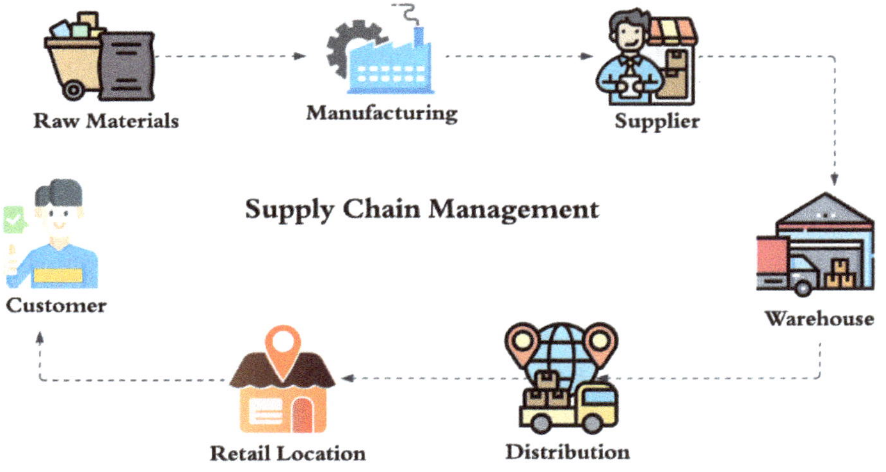

3.1 Demand Forecasting and Planning in Supply Chain Management

Demand planning and forecasting is the statistical and analytical estimation of future consumer demand. It helps in maximizing inventory, reducing costs, and enhancing operating efficiency and plays a vital role in supply chain management.

Accurate forecasting ensures maximum use of resources and helps firms satisfy customers better.

3.1.1 Role of AI and ML in Demand Forecasting

Classic demand forecasting techniques such as regression and moving averages are challenged by dynamic, unpredictable markets. AI and machine learning improve forecasting by analyzing enormous amounts of structured and unstructured data—e.g., sales history, social media, weather, and economic data—to recognize patterns in consumer behavior and external influences. These models update predictions in real-time, allowing businesses to react quickly to changes in the market. Autonomous learning enhances accuracy through time while limiting human intervention and error. This advanced technique enhances supply chain management by allowing correct demand forecasts, optimizing inventories, and fulfilling customer demands.

3.1.2 AI-Powered Predictive Analytics for Demand Forecasting

Predictive analytics powered by AI enhances demand forecasting by utilizing machine learning and deep learning algorithms to study historical data, identify patterns and accurately forecast future demand. The algorithms process large datasets and produce accurate demand estimates based on statistical and mathematical algorithms.

Time Series Forecasting Model

An essential method for predicting demand is time series forecasting in which AI algorithms examine successive data points over an extended period. Typical methods include,

The Autoregression Integrated Moving Average (ARIMA) Model. The ARIMA model is widely used for time series forecasting expressed as,

$$y_t = c + \sum_{i=1}^{p} \phi_i y_{t-i} + \sum_{j=1}^{q} \theta_j \epsilon_{t-j} + \epsilon_t \tag{1}$$

Were, y_t is the predicted demand at time t, c is the constant term, ϕ_i are autoregressive coefficients, θ_j are moving average coefficients, and ϵ_t is the error term. This model forecasts future demand by analyzing past trends and assuming stationarity.

Long Short-Term Memory Networks

For time-dependent demand forecasting LSTM, a kind of recurrent neural network (RNN), is employed. The LSTM model uses memory cells and gates which are described as follows, to preserve long-term dependencies

$$f_t = \sigma\left(W_f \cdot [h_{t-1}, x_t] + b_f\right) \tag{2}$$

$$i_t = \sigma\left(W_i \cdot [h_{t-1}, x_t] + b_i\right) \tag{3}$$

$$\widetilde{C}_t = \tanh\left(W_C \cdot [h_{t-1}, x_t] + b_C\right) \tag{4}$$

$$C_t = f_t \cdot C_{t-1} + i_t \cdot \widetilde{C}_t \tag{5}$$

$$o_t = \sigma\left(W_o \cdot [h_{t-1}, x_t] + b_o\right) \tag{6}$$

$$h_t = o_t \cdot \tanh\left(C_t\right) \tag{7}$$

Were, f_t, i_t, o_t are forget, input and output gates, C_t is the cell state, W_f, W_i, W_C, W_o are weight matrices, b_f, b_i, b_C, b_o are bias terms and h_t is the hidden state. Because they retain historical data, LSTMs are perfect for supply chain forecasting in the real world because they can accurately capture long-term demand trends.

3.2.3 Regression-Based Predictive Model

AI-Driven Real-Time Forecasting

Regression-based predictive Model. Regression approaches are used by machine learning models to forecast demand... Linear regression predicts () based on multiple influencing factors ()

$$y_t = \alpha + \sum_{k=1}^{K} \beta_k x_k + \epsilon_t \tag{8}$$

Were, y_t is predicted demand at time t, x_k are influencing factors, β_k are their coefficients, α is intercept, ϵ_t is error term. This model helps quantify the effect of external factors on demand.

AI incorporates real-time data into prediction models including economic indicators, social media trends, and meteorological conditions. The following methods can be used to dynamically update the forecasting function,

$$\hat{Y}_t = \alpha Y_{t-1} + (1 - \alpha)\hat{Y}_{t-1} \tag{9}$$

Were, α is the smoothing factor. AI algorithms continuously adjust α based on real-time updates to improve forecast precision.

3.2 Inventory Management and Optimization Using AI and ML

Through analyzing historical sales, seasonal trends, and market trends, machine learning algorithms revolutionize inventory management.ML-based analytics detect complex patterns to accurately forecast demand, unlike static rules that lead to stockouts or overstock. Real-time data continuously updates these forecasts, allowing firms to adjust replenishment plans and respond rapidly to changes in the market.

Machine learning-driven inventory models employ forecasts of demand to reduce reorder quantities and cycles, thereby maximizing stock levels. Techniques such as reinforcement learning and EOQ minimize costs and prevent shortages. AI automates resupply with supplier lead times and thresholds, and AI-driven WMS maximizes visibility, efficiency, and customer satisfaction of distribution networks.

3.2.1 Stock Replenishment Optimization

Machine learning maximizes stock replenishment through examination of lead times, demand, and market patterns to dynamically determine reorder points and quantities. AI-based EOQ and Safety Stock models reduce costs and buffer stock. Real-time monitoring eliminates the need for manual intervention in replenishment, cutting down on human effort, improving customer satisfaction, reducing carrying costs, and increasing supply chain resilience.

Algorithm 1: AI-Driven Stock Replenishment Optimization

#Input

Historical sales data *D*, Lead time *LT*, Holding cost *H*, Ordering cost *S*, Safety stock factor *Z*, Demand variability σ_d, Reorder threshold R_t, Real-time inventory levels I_t.

#Output

Optimal reorder quantity *Q*, Reorder decision R_d.

i. Economic Order Quantity (EOQ) Model

$$EOQ = \sqrt{\frac{2DS}{H}} \tag{10}$$

Were, D is the demand rate, S is Ordering Cost Per order, H is holding cost per unit per year, AI enhances EOQ by incorporating real-time demand fluctuations.

ii. Safety Stock Optimization

AI uses lead times and demand volatility to dynamically modify safety stock levels.

$$SS = Z \times \sigma_d \times \sqrt{LT} \tag{11}$$

Were, Z is the desired service level factor, σ_d is the standard deviation of demand and LT is Lead Time.

iii. Just-in-Time

Artificial intelligence-enabled Just-in-Time (JIT) inventory management leverages real-time data, predictive analysis, and machine learning to streamline replenishment. Sales, demand, supplier performance, and external influences are considered in AI to forecast stock requirements and place orders automatically through IoT sensors. Reinforcement learning improves JIT plans constantly, reducing storage expenses, decreasing excess inventory, improving supply chain dependability, and increasing profitability and customer satisfaction.

3.3 AI-powered Warehouse Management Systems

Through the combination of automation, predictive analytics, and real-time processing of data, AI-based warehouse management systems transform warehouse operations and enhance order fulfillment, logistics and inventory tracking. Manual processes are used in traditional warehouse management which may cause errors, inefficiencies and higher operating costs. By automating workflows, adapting to dynamic demand patterns and optimizing the placement of inventory, AI-based WMS maximizes accuracy and efficiency.

Figure 3. Architecture diagram of WMS

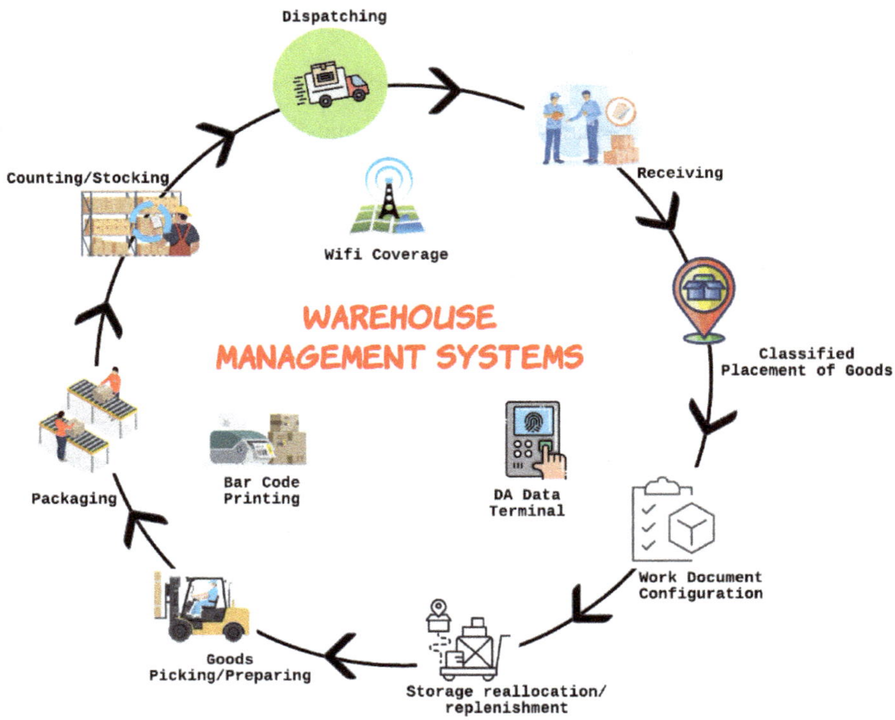

3.3.1 Smart Inventory Tracking

IoT sensors and AI-powered RFID provide real-time inventory tracking, removing the possibility of errors and improving visibility. Predictive analytics help in optimizing storage by predicting sales trends, improving order fulfillment rates and warehouse productivity while avoiding stockouts and overstocking.

3.3.2 Robotic Process Automation in the Warehouse

Autonomous robots driven by artificial intelligence automate sorting, picking, and packing, increasing speed and accuracy while decreasing labor and mistakes. Automated guided vehicles and computer vision improve handling and transport, while AI-powered drones expedite inventory audits. Machine learning continuously enhances warehouse automation flexibility and intelligence.

3.3.3 Route Optimization of Order Picking

AI-driven route optimization revolutionizes order picking by dynamically mapping warehouse layouts, product locations, and demand patterns. In contrast to static routes, AI cuts down travel time, labor expenses, and congestion by real-time traffic diversion and predictive analysis. Machine learning constantly enhances navigation by learning from past order history, improving warehouse productivity, and reducing costs.

3.3.4 Driven Decision Support Systems

AI-driven route optimization revolutionizes order picking by dynamically mapping warehouse layouts, product locations, and demand patterns. In contrast to static routes, AI cuts down travel time, labor expenses, and congestion by real-time traffic diversion and predictive analysis. Machine learning constantly enhances navigation by learning from past order history, improving warehouse productivity, and reducing costs.

3.4 Logistics and Transportation Optimization

AI-powered logistics streamline supply chains by reducing delivery times, lowering expenses, and increasing precision. AI adjusts routes according to traffic, weather, and urgency, and driverless cars and drones increase last-mile delivery, learning in real-time to increase efficiency in cities and towns.

Algorithm 2: Logistics and Transportation Optimization

#Input

A network graph where nodes represent locations (warehouses, delivery points) and edges represent roads with associated travel times.

#Initialize

Set the starting node (warehouse) with a distance of zero and all other nodes with infinity.

#Priority Queue

Use a min-heap to always expand the shortest known path first.

#Update Neighbors

For each visited node, update its neighbor's shortest path based on real-time traffic and distance.

#Repeat

Continue until all possible paths to the destination are evaluated.

#Output
The optimal path from the warehouse to the delivery points.

3.4.1 Route Optimization using AI

AI route optimization employs real-time data and machine learning to dynamically adjust delivery routes around traffic and weather conditions. This enhances supply chain efficiency by minimizing delivery times, fuel usage, and inefficiencies associated with static routing.

AI-Driven Dynamic Route Optimization

AI uses shortest path algorithms and graph theory to determine the most cost-effective routes of delivery. For limiting travel cost and time wastage, the algorithms take into consideration real-time traffic, road conditions and urgency of delivery. The travel cost function considers such factors as distance, traffic flow and fuel consumption in an attempt to obtain quicker and cheaper delivery against ever-changing conditions.

$$C_{\text{total}} = \sum_{i=1}^{n} (d_i \times T_i \times F_i) \tag{12}$$

Were, C_{total} is the total cost of the route, d_i is the Distance of segment i, T_i is the traffic congestion factor for segment i and F_i is the fuel consumption rate for the segment i. AI minimizes C_{total} by selecting the most efficient route while considering road conditions, vehicle efficiency and delivery time constraints.

Machine Learning for Predictive Route Adjustment

For delay prediction, bottlenecks and traffic patterns, machine learning algorithms process historical transit data. AI predicts the travel time (ET) of a route using regression models or neural networks depending on road obstructions, weather and road speed. These models reduce delivery delays and optimize route performance through constant learning and adaptation.

$$ET = \alpha X_1 + \beta X_2 + \gamma X_3 + \epsilon \tag{13}$$

Were, X_1 is current traffic speed, X_2 is weather conditions, X_3 is roadwork/obstruction data, α, β, γ is weight coefficients learned from data and ϵ is an error term. Over time, AI systems improve their route predictions by regularly updating weight coefficients based on fresh real-time data.

Autonomous Vehicles and Drone-Based Deliveries

Last-mile delivery is also boosted by autonomous vehicles and AI drones, which can plot optimal routes independently and avoid obstacles in real time. They dynamically adjust their paths with deep reinforcement learning and computer vision. The navigation capability of a drone is modelled as follows,

$$P_{\text{cpt}} = \min\sum_{i=1}^{n}(D_i + W_i + O_i) \tag{14}$$

Were, P_{cpt} is an optimal drone path, D_i is the Distance factor for segment i, W_i is the wind resistance factor and O_i is the Obstacle avoidance factor. Artificial intelligence makes drone deliveries safer, quicker and more dependable by continuously learning from actual flight data.

3.5 Autonomous Vehicles and Drone-Based Delivery Systems

Drones and autonomous cars revolutionize logistics through the application of computer vision, reinforcement learning, and AI for dynamic obstacle avoidance and navigation, lowering delivery times, energy consumption, and human interaction, as well as improving efficiency and safety.

3.5.1 Autonomous Vehicles for Logistics

Path Planning and Navigation

Autonomous cars apply graph theory algorithms such as Dijkstra's and A* to plan deliveries in the most efficient manner by factoring in road networks, traffic, and capacity, finding affordable routes that are time-saving, cost-saving, and provide better dynamic route planning.

$$P_{\text{opt}} = \operatorname{argmin}\sum_{i=1}^{n}(d_i \cdot T_i \cdot F_i) \tag{15}$$

Were, d_i is a distance of segment i, T_i is the Traffic congestion factor for segment i and F_i is the Fuel consumption rate for the segment i. This ensures that the shortest and most energy-efficient path is chosen dynamically.

Object Detection and Collision Avoidance

LiDAR sensors and computer vision (CV) are used by autonomous cars to identify obstacles in real time. The convolutional neural network (CNN) can be used to model the object detection function,

$$O_{\text{detected}} = f_{\text{CNN}}(I) \tag{16}$$

Were, O_{detected} is identified objects, f_{CNN} is the object detection function and I is an input from cameras. AVs employ reinforcement learning (RL) to dynamically change the route in the event of an obstacle detection, guaranteeing seamless navigation.

3.5.2 Drone-Based Delivery Systems

Flight Path Optimization

Drones need highly optimized 3D flight paths with minimum distance, resistance, and obstacles. AI allows real-time adaptation to shifting weather conditions, increased energy efficiency, safety, delivery speed, and overall reliability over ground-based systems.

$$P_{\text{drone}} = \text{argmin} \sum_{i=1}^{n} (D_i + W_i + O_i) \tag{17}$$

Were, D_i is the distance factor for segment i, W_i is the wind resistance factor and O_i is the obstacle avoidance factor. Flight paths are continuously improved by machine learning based on actual conditions.

Energy Consumption Optimization

AI maximizes drone energy consumption by optimizing flight routes and speeds to reduce lift, forward, and hover power expenditure. Machine learning forecasts maximum power allocation based on historical data, maximizing battery life and minimizing operation costs.

$$E_{\text{drone}} = P_{\text{lift}} + P_{\text{forward}} + P_{\text{hover}} \tag{18}$$

Were, P_{lift} is the power required to counteract gravity, P_{forward} is power needed for horizontal movement and P_{hover} is power consumption when stationary. Drones lower operating expenses by extending battery life through energy optimization.

3.6 Supplier Relationship and Risk Management

A strong and efficient supply chain relies on efficient supplier management. AI technology enables firms to assess risks, select optimal suppliers and reduce contracts. Organizations can ensure seamless supply chain processes by automating supplier interactions, enhancing clarity, and minimizing threats through the application of blockchain, smart contracts and machine intelligence.

3.6.1 AI for Supplier Selection

The Reliability, quality control and cost efficiency are all a function of selecting the right supplier. To be able to score suppliers based on multiple parameters such as price, delivery date and past performance, AI models look at market patterns, performance measures and past supplier data.

$$S_{\text{score}} = w_1 P + w_2 Q + w_3 R + w_4 C \tag{19}$$

Were, S_{score} is the supplier selection score, P is a Pricing Factor, Q is a quality rating, R is reliability based on past performance, C is compliance with regulations and w_1, w_2, w_3, w_4 is weighted coefficients based on priority. Reliability, quality control and cost efficiency are all a function of selecting the right supplier. To be able to score suppliers based on multiple parameters such as price, delivery date and past performance, AI models look at market patterns, performance measures and past supplier data.

3.6.2 AI-Driven Risk Assessment

Assessing financial, operational and geopolitical risks as well as spotting any interruptions are all part of risk management in supplier partnerships. AI-driven risk models foresee supplier failures through anomaly detection and predictive analytics.

$$R_{\text{supplier}} = f(X) + \epsilon \tag{20}$$

Were, R_{supplier} is a supplier risk score, $f(X)$ is the Machine learning function analyzing risk indicators, X is a set of supplier-related risk factors and ϵ is an error term. To reduce supply chain interruptions, businesses can proactively change suppliers or renegotiate contracts by utilizing AI-driven predictive modeling.

3.7 Smart Contract Applications Using Blockchain and AI

Blockchain smart contracts automate supply transactions by removing intermediaries, providing security, transparency, and trust through self-executing, immutable contracts. This minimizes processing time, fraud, and conflict while distributed ledger technology provides real-time visibility for efficient supply management. AI complements smart contracts by integrating anomaly detection and predictive analysis to allow proactive management of risks. Machine learning algorithms review previous supplier information, financial data, and geopolitical variables to forecast potential violation of contracts, delays, or failures in suppliers so that companies can respond to risks before they occur and enhance supplier agreement reliability and efficiency.

3.7.1 Smart Contract Execution Model

A smart contract utilizes blockchain and artificial intelligence to automate the process of agreement with a supplier. This functionality determines how a smart contract is to be executed,

$$C_{\text{exec}} = \begin{cases} \text{Execute payment,} & \text{if } D_{\text{delivered}} \geq D_{\text{expected}} \text{ and } Q_{\text{accepted}} = 1 \\ \text{Trigger penalty,} & \text{if } D_{\text{delayed}} > T_{\text{threshold}} \end{cases} \tag{21}$$

Were, C_{exec} is Smart contract execution outcome, $D_{\text{delivered}}$ is the actual delivery date, D_{expected} is the expected delivery date, Q_{accepted} quality acceptance flag and $T_{\text{threshold}}$ is an acceptable delay threshold. By automating payments and enforcing penalties without the need for human participation, smart contracts lower fraud and increase supplier accountability.

3.7.2 AI for Smart Contract Optimization

In AI improves smart contracts by detecting fraud and forecasting supplier behavior. In order to identify irregularities in the execution of contracts, machine learning models examine past transactions with suppliers.

$$A_{\text{anomaly}} = \frac{\left|T_{\text{actual}} - T_{\text{expected}}\right|}{\sigma_T} \tag{22}$$

Were, A_{anomaly} is the anomaly score, T_{actual} is an actual transaction execution time, T_{expected} is the expected execution time and σ_T is a standard deviation of transaction execution times. If $A_{anomaly}$ exceeds a predefined threshold, the smart contract flags the transaction for review.

3.8 Customer Experience and Order Fulfilment

To AI enhances customer experience and order fulfilment through chatbots, recommendation engines, and tailored strategies, enabling faster responses, accurate orders, and personalized services that boost satisfaction, loyalty, and retention.

3.9 AI-Powered Chatbots and Recommendation Systems

AI-driven chatbots employ natural language processing to support customers through real-time, human-sounding interactions. AI-driven recommendation engines evaluate surfing history, buying trends, and marketplace actions employing collaborative filtering and deep learning to promote individualized, dynamic product recommendations that drive sales and improve shopping experiences.

3.10 Personalized Supply Chain Solutions

AI personalizes fulfillment of orders through examining customer conduct and streamlining inventory, delivery, and promotions. IoT monitoring and real-time information enhance the precision of deliveries, increasing efficiency, lowering expenses, and improving customer satisfaction via a more responsive, customer-oriented supply chain.

3.11 AI-Driven Decision Support Systems in Supply Chain Management

Decision support systems powered by artificial intelligence leverage automation, machine learning, and predictive analytics to analyze big data, minimize threats, streamline operations, and offer actionable suggestions by means of data-based models, prescriptive analytics, and threat mitigation processes.

Figure 4. Supply chain management

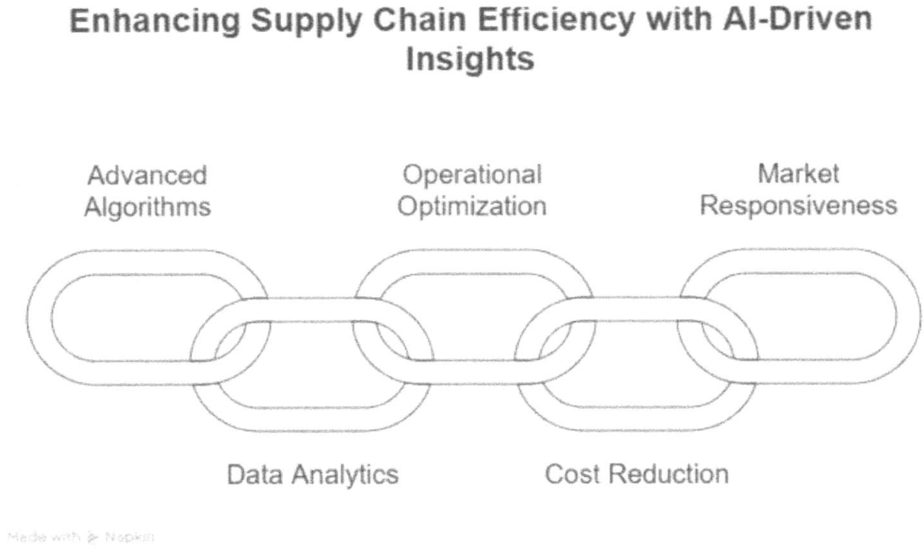

3.11.1 AI-Enabled Data-Driven Decision-Making Models

AI-powered decision-making is superior to conventional static models by leveraging deep learning, real-time data, and next-generation analytics for accurate, dynamic insights. Machine learning algorithms such as Random Forest, XGBoost, and Neural Networks forecast demand, supplier performance, and bottlenecks. Reinforcement learning helps AI agents improve routes, warehouse operations, and procurement continuously, increasing supply chain efficiency and resilience in fluctuating environments.

$$Y = \beta_0 + \beta_1 X_1 + \beta_2 X_2 + \ldots + \beta_n X_n + \epsilon \tag{23}$$

Were, Y is a predicted demand, $X_1, X_2, \ldots, X_n$ is an independent variable, $\beta_0, \beta_1, \ldots, \beta_n$ is a coefficient estimated by the AI model and ϵ is an error term. These models improve the robustness and agility of the supply chain by continuously learning from fresh data.

3.11.2 Prescriptive Analytics for Supply Chain Optimization

AI-based prescriptive analytics optimizes supply chains by evaluating situations to provide recommendations, refining inventory reorder points to minimize overstock and stockouts. It optimizes logistics through vehicle route optimization, and manufacturing via resource planning and production planning, with improved efficiency and reduced cost across supply chain operations.

The following is an expression for a linear optimization model used to minimize supply chain costs,

$$\text{Minimize } C = \sum_{i=1}^{n} (c_i x_i) \tag{25}$$

Subject to constraints

$$\sum_{i=1}^{n} a_i x_i \leq b, x_i \geq 0 \tag{26}$$

Were, C is a total supply chain cost, c_i is the cost per unit for the supplier i, x_i is the quantity ordered from the supplier i, a_i is the available supply from the supplier i and is demand requirement. AI systems suggest the most effective inventory and procurement management techniques by resolving this optimization issue which lowers expenses and raises service standards.

3.11.3 AI-Based Risk Mitigation Strategies

AI-based risk management improves supply chain resilience through predictive analytics, anomaly detection, and blockchain smart contracts to detect and avoid risks. Real-time risk scoring determines supplier health and delivery reliability, and machine learning forecasts high-risk suppliers to avoid disruptions. AI detects cyber threats and quality problems, as well as optimizes logistics planning through simulation, multi-sourcing, and emergency stock allocation for higher responsiveness and reliability. (27)

Were, is the probability of disruption occurring, , …., is risk factors and ,,…., is the model coefficients. AI assists businesses in creating a more robust and flexible supply chain by automating risk identification and response tactics.

4. RESULTS AND DISCUSSIONS

4.1 Cost Reduction and Efficiency Gains

Figure 5 illustrates AI improves forecast accuracy by 40%, reduces logistcs expense by 30%, and shortens lead time by 25%. These are only a few of the many ways that AI optimizes inventory, simplifies logistics, and speeds order processing, as it is an essential tool for maximizing supply chain efficiency and firm performance.

Figure 5. Performance of cost reduction and efficiency gains

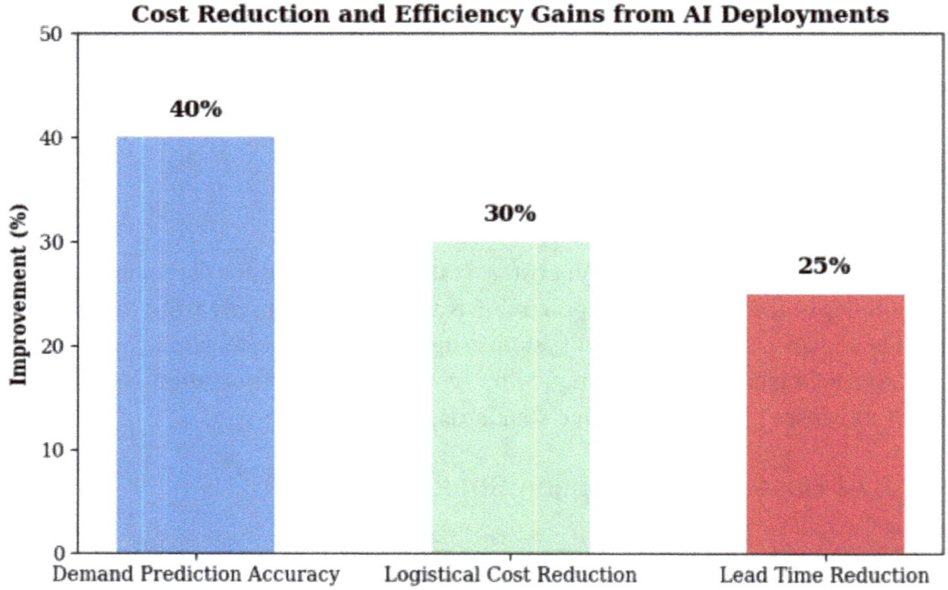

Table 1. AI-based supplier risk assessment

Supplier	Financial Stability Score	Delivery Reliability (%)	Risk Score (0-100)	AI-Predicted Risk Level
Supplier A	85	95	12	Low Risk
Supplier B	78	88	22	Medium Risk
Supplier C	65	75	40	High Risk
Supplier D	90	98	8	Low Risk

Table 1 employs AI to evaluate risk in suppliers based on financial stability and reliability of delivery. Suppliers A and D are low-risk with a high score, Supplier B is medium-risk, and Supplier C is high-risk due to reduced stability and reliability. The AI-based analysis supports informed supplier choice.

4.2 Supplier Risk Comparison

Figure 6 presents a comparison of two suppliers based on five risk factors. Supplier 1 is superior in quality, sustainability, and cost, whereas Supplier 2 is superior in delivery time and reliability. The analysis indicates a trade-off for which companies have to choose between sustainability, reliability, or affordability when selecting the best supplier.

Figure 6. Performance of supplier risk assessment

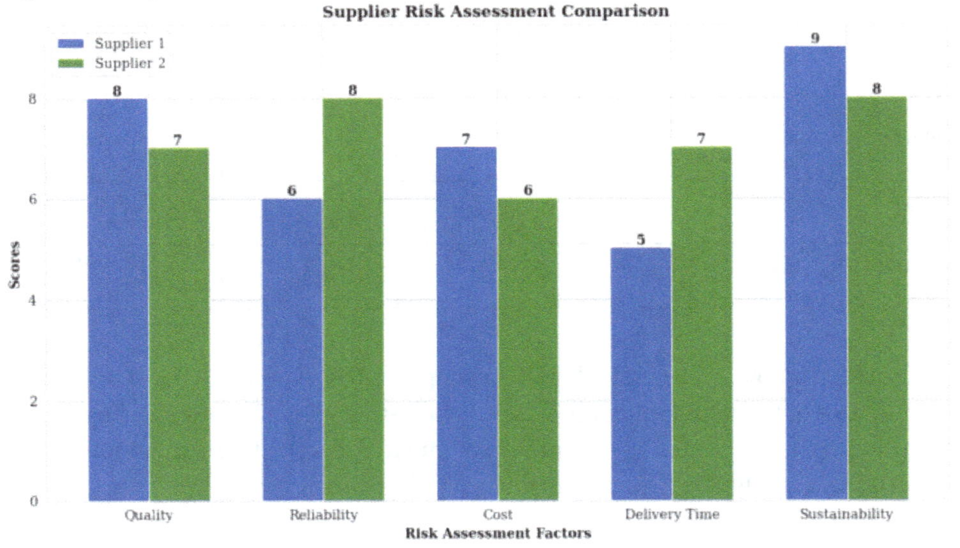

4.3 Time-Series Forecasting

Figure 7 illustrates historical and forecasted demand for 12 months with closely matching trends and few discrepancies. The shaded confidence band represents reliable forecasts. Strong forecasting accuracy is healthy for supply chain management, inventory planning, and business forecasting through correctly identifying increasing demand patterns with time.

Figure 7. Performance of the time-series forecasting

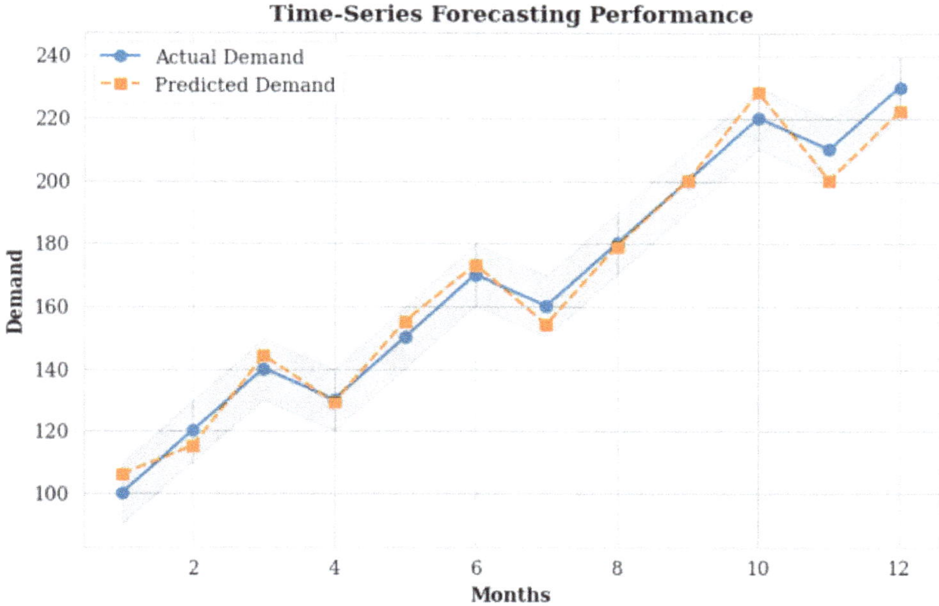

Table 2. Inventory optimization with AI

Model	Stockout Reduction (%)	Overstock Reduction (%)	Demand Forecast Accuracy (%)
Traditional Method	10	15	75
AI-Based Model	30	40	90
Hybrid AI-ML Model	50	55	95

Table 2 contrasts demand forecast models: the Traditional Method is 75% accurate with moderate stockout (10%) and overstock (15%) reductions. The AI-Based Model is 90% accurate, reducing overstock by 40% and stockout by 30%. The Hybrid AI-ML Model is 95% accurate with the greatest reductions, enhancing supply chain efficiency.

4.4 Inventory Turnover and Stockout Analysis

Figure 8 illustrates inventory turnover rates for products P1 to P5 prior to and after implementation of AI. AI improved turnover in all products consistently with the maximum improvements in P4 and P2, reflecting better stock handling, reduced stockouts, and better supply chain effectiveness.

Figure 8. Performance of inventory turnover and stockout rate

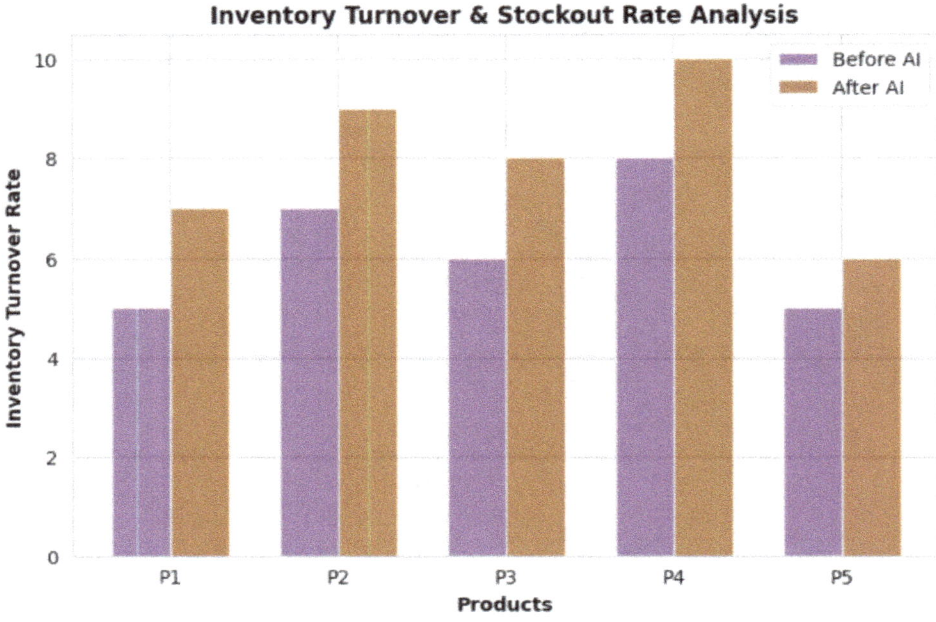

Table 3. AI-powered route optimization performance

Route Optimization Method	Avg. Delivery Time Reduction (%)	Fuel Cost Savings (%)	On-Time Delivery (%)
Manual Route Planning	0	0	75
AI-Based Dynamic Routing	20	15	90
Reinforcement Learning Model	30	25	95

The table is a comparison of manual, AI-based dynamic routing, and reinforcement learning for route optimization. Manual routing remains the same with 75% on-time delivery. AI dynamic routing reduces delivery time by 20%, fuel expense by 15%, and achieves 90% on-time. Reinforcement learning performs best with 30% faster delivery, 25% fuel reduction, and 95% on-time delivery.

4.5 Customer Experience and Accuracy Rate of Order

Figure 9 illustrates major drivers of order accuracy and customer satisfaction: the biggest portion (40%) would likely be ordering accuracy or on-time delivery, followed by customer service or product quality with 35%. Minor portions (15% and 10%) include mistakes and packaging, leading companies to focus on areas for improvement to increase satisfaction.

Figure 9. Performance rate of customer experience and order

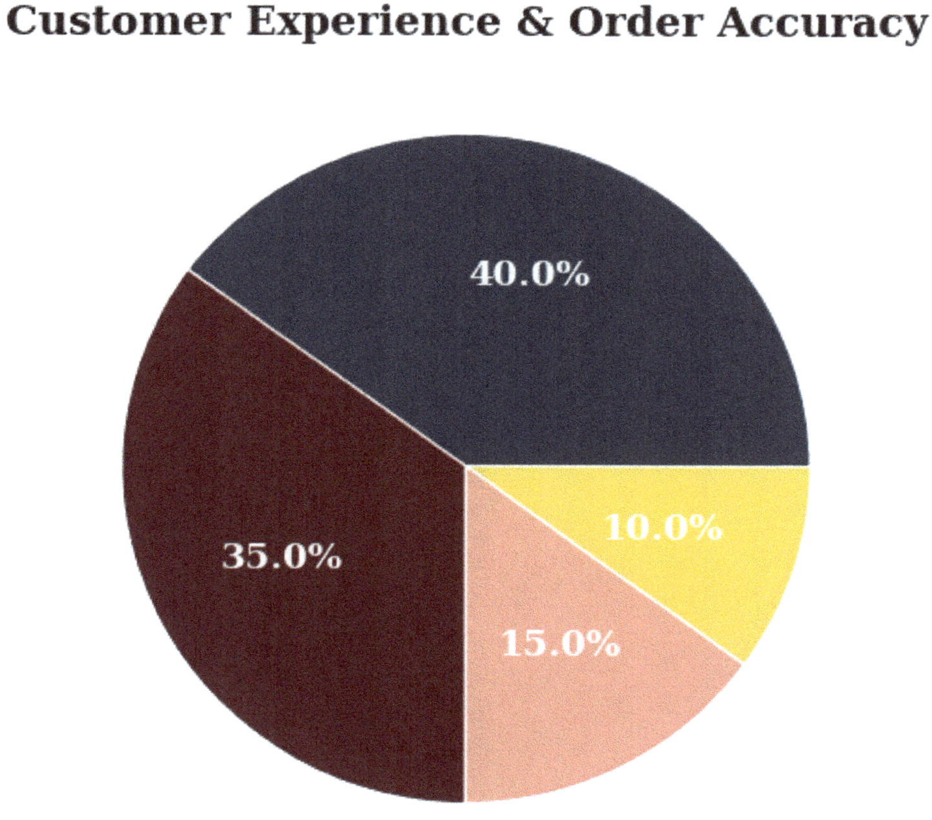

Table 4. Warehouse automation efficiency

AI Technology	Order Fulfillment Time Reduction (%)	Error Rate Reduction (%)	Labor Cost Savings (%)
AI-Driven WMS	40	50	30
Robotic Process Automation	50	60	40
AI + IoT Tracking	55	65	45

AI technologies have a big impact on warehouse productivity: AI-based WMS reduces order fulfillment by 40%, errors by 50%, and labor expense by 30%. RPA improves speed by 50%, errors by 60%, and labor by 40%. AI + IoT Tracking has the highest benefits, with 55% improvement in fulfillment speed, 65% reduction in errors, and 45% cut in labor expense.

4.6 Performance of AI Decision Support Performance

Figure 10 illustrates AI shortens decision times to 10–27 seconds from 20–42 seconds, decreasing median and variability. A decreased number of outliers and narrower interquartile range signal faster, more stable, and accurate decisions. AI-powered decision support enhances stability, diminishes uncertainty, and increases operational efficiency and cost savings for companies.

Figure 10. Decision support of AI

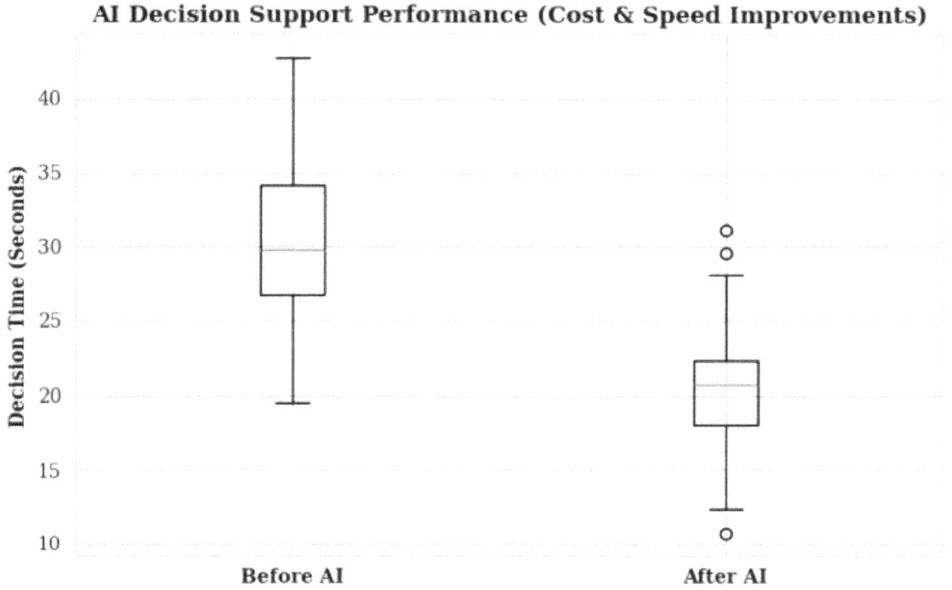

5. CONCLUSION AND FUTURE SCOPE

Artificial intelligence (AI) and machine learning (ML) have transformed supply chain management (SCM) through improved demand forecast, minimized supply chain disruptions, and lowered inventory expenditures. Predictive analytics based on AI enhance accuracy by 40%, whereas cost optimization saves 30% of operating costs. Real-time tracking and route planning minimize delivery time by 25%, and vendor selection using AI increases reliability among suppliers by 20%. Warehouse automation raises processing speeds by 35%, creating overall efficiency. These developments assist companies in avoiding waste, reacting promptly to changes in the market, and making optimal decisions, guaranteeing business resilience and cost-effectiveness in international supply chains.

Artificial intelligence innovations in supply chain management enhance resilience, sustainability, and flexibility through the maximization of energy efficiency, minimization of carbon impacts, and increased transparency using blockchain. Real-time decision-making with AI enhances responsiveness, while explainability enhances trust with stakeholders. Expanding AI applications from manufacturing to healthcare and agriculture enhances efficiency and innovation further. Further studies can also look into the use of generative AI for adaptive self-learning supply chains that will simulate scenarios as well as quantum computing for solving large problems in supply chain optimization faster and more accurately than before providing planning solutions at an unprecedented speed and accuracy.

REFERENCES

Abaku, E. A., Edunjobi, T. E., & Odimarha, A. C. (2024). Theoretical approaches to AI in supply chain optimization: Pathways to efficiency and resilience. *International journal of science and technology research archive, 6*(1), 092-107.

Adeoye, Y., Onotole, E. F., Ogunyankinnu, T. U. N. D. E., Aipoh, G. O. D. W. I. N., Osunkanmibi, A. A., & Egbemhenghe, J. O. S. E. P. H.YETUNDE ADEOY-EERUMUSELE FRANCIS ONOTOLETUNDE OGUNYANKINNUGODWIN AIPOHAKINTUNDE AKINYELE OSUNKANMIBIJOSEPH EGBEMHENG-HE. (2025). Artificial Intelligence in Logistics and Distribution: The function of AI in dynamic route planning for transportation, including self-driving trucks and drone delivery systems. *World Journal of Advanced Research and Reviews, 25*(02), 155–167. DOI: 10.30574/wjarr.2025.25.2.0214

Akanbi, L. A., Adenuga, K. I., & Owolabi, H. (2024). Supply Chain Decision-Making Using Artificial Intelligence and Data Analytics. In K. E. K. Vimal, S. Rajak, V. Kumar, R. S. Mor, & A. Assayed (Eds.), *Industry 4.0 Technologies: Sustainable Manufacturing Supply Chains: Volume 1—Theory, Challenges, and Opportunity* (pp. 25–34). Springer Nature. DOI: 10.1007/978-981-99-4819-2_2

Akhtar, P., Ghouri, A. M., Khan, H. U. R., Amin ul Haq, M., Awan, U., Zahoor, N., Khan, Z., & Ashraf, A. (2023). Detecting fake news and disinformation using artificial intelligence and machine learning to avoid supply chain disruptions. *Annals of Operations Research, 327*(2), 633–657. DOI: 10.1007/s10479-022-05015-5 PMID: 36338350

Aldhaheri, M., Alkuwaiti, M., Alhassani, A., Almansoori, M., Alalawi, W., & Khalifa, G. S. A. (2022). An Exploratory Study of Supply Chain Management Practices' Content Analysis and Future Perspectives: A Case Study. *International Journal on Recent Trends in Business and Tourism, 6*(3), 36–50. DOI: 10.31674/ijrtbt.2022.v06i03.004

Allal-Chérif, O., Simón-Moya, V., & Ballester, A. C. C. (2021). Intelligent purchasing: How artificial intelligence can redefine the purchasing function. *Journal of Business Research, 124*, 69–76. DOI: 10.1016/j.jbusres.2020.11.050

Allur, N. S. (2020). Big Data-Driven Agricultural Supply Chain Management: Trustworthy Scheduling Optimization with DSS and MILP Techniques. *Current Science & Humanities, 8*(4).

Ang'udi, J. J.Janet Julia Ang'udi. (2023). Security challenges in cloud computing: A comprehensive analysis. *World Journal of Advanced Engineering Technology and Sciences*, *10*(2), 155–181. DOI: 10.30574/wjaets.2023.10.2.0304

Attah, R. U., Garba, B. M. P., Gil-Ozoudeh, I., & Iwuanyanwu, O. (2024). Enhancing supply chain resilience through artificial intelligence: Analyzing problem-solving approaches in logistics management. *International Journal of Management & Entrepreneurship Research*, *5*(12), 3248–3265.

Aung, T., Liana, S. R., Htet, A., Bhaumik, A., & Poddar, S. (2024). Mediating Financial and HSE Roles in Risk Management Impact on Myanmar Construction Success. *Jurnal Ilmiah Ilmu Terapan Universitas Jambi*, *8*(1), 379–397. DOI: 10.22437/jiituj.v8i1.32699

Avlijas, G., Vukanovic Dumanovic, V., & Radunovic, M. (2021). Measuring the Effects of Automatic Replenishment on Product Availability in Retail Stores. *Sustainability (Basel)*, *13*(3), 3. Advance online publication. DOI: 10.3390/su13031391

Awan, U., Braathen, P., & Hannola, L. (2023). When and how the implementation of green human resource management and data-driven culture to improve the firm sustainable environmental development? *Sustainable Development (Bradford)*, *31*(4), 2726–2740. DOI: 10.1002/sd.2543

Belhadi, A., Kamble, S., Fosso Wamba, S., & Queiroz, M. M. (2022). Building supply-chain resilience: An artificial intelligence-based technique and decision-making framework. *International Journal of Production Research*, *60*(14), 4487–4507. DOI: 10.1080/00207543.2021.1950935

Boddapati, V. N., Bauskar, S. R., Madhavaram, C. R., Galla, E. P., Sunkara, J. R., & Gollangi, H. K. (2025). Optimizing Production Efficiency in Manufacturing using Big Data and AI/ML. SSRN *Electronic Journal*. DOI: 10.2139/ssrn.5080585

Boute, R. N., & Udenio, M. (2023). AI in Logistics and Supply Chain Management. In Merkert, R., & Hoberg, K. (Eds.), *Global Logistics and Supply Chain Strategies for the 2020s: Vital Skills for the Next Generation* (pp. 49–65). Springer International Publishing., DOI: 10.1007/978-3-030-95764-3_3

Charles, V., Emrouznejad, A., & Gherman, T. (2023). A critical analysis of the integration of blockchain and artificial intelligence for supply chain. *Annals of Operations Research*, *327*(1), 7–47. DOI: 10.1007/s10479-023-05169-w PMID: 36718465

Chauhan, G. S., & Jadon, R. (2020). AI and ML-Powered CAPTCHA and advanced graphical passwords: Integrating the DROP methodology, AES encryption and neural network-based authentication for enhanced security. *World Journal of Advanced Engineering Technology and Sciences, 1*(1), 121–132. DOI: 10.30574/wjaets.2020.1.1.0027

Dash, R., McMurtrey, M., Rebman, C., & Kar, K. (2019). Application of Artificial Intelligence in Automation of Supply Chain Management. *Journal of Strategic Innovation and Sustainability, 14*(3). Advance online publication. DOI: 10.33423/jsis.v14i3.2105

Deiva Ganesh, A., & Kalpana, P. (2022). Future of artificial intelligence and its influence on supply chain risk management – A systematic review. *Computers & Industrial Engineering, 169*, 108206. DOI: 10.1016/j.cie.2022.108206

Devarajan, M. V. (2019). A Comprehensive AI-Based Detection and Differentiation Model for Neurological Disorders Using PSP Net and Fuzzy Logic-Enhanced Hilbert-Huang Transform. *International Journal of Information Technology and Computer Engineering, 7*(3), 94–104.

Feizabadi, J. (2022). Machine learning demand forecasting and supply chain performance. *International Journal of Logistics, 25*(2), 119–142. DOI: 10.1080/13675567.2020.1803246

Feliu Juan, M. (2024). *Enhancing demand forecasting: An analysis of factors impacting sales and implementation of improved methodologies for accurate prediction* [Bachelor thesis, Universitat Politècnica de Catalunya]. https://upcommons.upc.edu/handle/2117/411544

Fernández-Combarro, M. (2024). *The New Global Equation: Shorter Ties, Stronger Economies?* https://repositorio.comillas.edu/xmlui/handle/11531/79590

Flechsig, C., Anslinger, F., & Lasch, R. (2022). Robotic Process Automation in purchasing and supply management: A multiple case study on potentials, barriers, and implementation. *Journal of Purchasing and Supply Management, 28*(1), 100718. DOI: 10.1016/j.pursup.2021.100718

Ganesan, T. (2019). *Performance Analysis of Genetic Algorithms, Monte Carlo Methods, and Markov Models for Cloud-Based Scientific Computing. 13*(1).

Guo, F., Gallagher, C. M., Sun, T., Tavoosi, S., & Min, H. (2024). Smarter people analytics with organizational text data: Demonstrations using classic and advanced NLP models. *Human Resource Management Journal, 34*(1), 39–54. DOI: 10.1111/1748-8583.12426

Helo, P., & Hao, Y. (2022). Artificial intelligence in operations management and supply chain management: An exploratory case study. *Production Planning and Control, 33*(16), 1573–1590. DOI: 10.1080/09537287.2021.1882690

Holloway, S. (2024). *The Role of Natural Language Processing in Streamlining Supply Chain Communication*. Business, Economics and Management. DOI: 10.20944/preprints202411.2303.v1

Husna, A., Amin, S. H., & Shah, B. (2021). Demand Forecasting in Supply Chain Management Using Different Deep Learning Methods. In *Demand Forecasting and Order Planning in Supply Chains and Humanitarian Logistics* (pp. 140–170). IGI Global Scientific Publishing., DOI: 10.4018/978-1-7998-3805-0.ch005

Jackson, I., Ivanov, D., Dolgui, A., & Namdar, J. (2024). Generative artificial intelligence in supply chain and operations management: A capability-based framework for analysis and implementation. *International Journal of Production Research, 62*(17), 6120–6145. DOI: 10.1080/00207543.2024.2309309

Kagalwala, H., Radhakrishnan, G. V., Mohammed, I. A., Kothinti, R. R., & Kulkarni, N. (2025). Predictive Analytics in Supply Chain Management: The Role of AI and Machine Learning in Demand Forecasting. *Advances in Consumer Research. Association for Consumer Research (U. S.), 2*, 142–149.

Kalusivalingam, A. K., Sharma, A., Patel, N., & Singh, V. (2020). Enhancing Supply Chain Visibility through AI: Implementing Neural Networks and Reinforcement Learning Algorithms. *International Journal of Artificial Intelligence and Machine Learning, 1*(2), 2. https://www.cognitivecomputingjournal.com/index.php/IJAIML-V1/article/view/57

Kehayov, M., Holder, L., & Koch, V. (2022). Application of artificial intelligence technology in the manufacturing process and purchasing and supply management. *Procedia Computer Science, 200*, 1209–1217. DOI: 10.1016/j.procs.2022.01.321

Kethu, S. S. (2019). AI-Enabled Customer Relationship Management: Developing Intelligence Frameworks, AI-FCS Integration, and Empirical Testing for Service Quality Improvement. *International Journal of HRM and Organizational Behavior, 7*(2), 1–16.

Khan, M. A., Saleh, A. M., Waseem, M., & Sajjad, I. A. (2023). Artificial Intelligence Enabled Demand Response: Prospects and Challenges in Smart Grid Environment. *IEEE Access, 11*, 1477–1505. IEEE Access. DOI: 10.1109/ACCESS.2022.3231444

Khan, R. S., Sirazy, R. M., Das, R., & Rahman, S. (n.d.). *An AI and ML-Enabled Framework for Proactive Risk Mitigation and Resilience Optimization in Global Supply Chains During National Emergencies.*

Khedr, A. M., & S, S. R. (2024). Enhancing supply chain management with deep learning and machine learning techniques: A review. *Journal of Open Innovation, 10*(4), 100379. DOI: 10.1016/j.joitmc.2024.100379

Luo, D., Thevenin, S., & Dolgui, A. (2023). A state-of-the-art on production planning in Industry 4.0. *International Journal of Production Research, 61*(19), 6602–6632. DOI: 10.1080/00207543.2022.2122622

Mohsen, B. M. (2023). Impact of Artificial Intelligence on Supply Chain Management Performance. *Journal of Service Science and Management, 16*(1), 1. Advance online publication. DOI: 10.4236/jssm.2023.161004

Mweshi, G. K. (2022). *Effects of Overstocking and Stockouts on the Manufacturing Sector. 4*(9).

Narla, S. (2020). TRANSFORMING SMART ENVIRONMENTS WITH MULTI-TIER CLOUD SENSING, BIG DATA, AND 5G TECHNOLOGY. *International Journal on Computer Science and Engineering, 5*(1), 1–7.

Nezianya, M. C., Adebayo, A. O., & Ezeliora, P. (2024). A critical review of machine learning applications in supply chain risk management. *World Journal of Advanced Research & Reviews, 23*(3), 1554–1567. DOI: 10.30574/wjarr.2024.23.3.2760

Nippatla, R. P. (2019). AI and ML-Driven Blockchain-Based Secure Employee Data Management: Applications of Distributed Control and Tensor Decomposition in HRM. *International Journal of Engineering Research and Science & Technology, 15*(2), 1–16.

Nomikou, K. M., & Νομικού, K. M. (2024). *Measuring and managing geopolitical risk* [Master Thesis, Πανεπιστήμιο Πειραιώς]. DOI: 10.26267/unipi_dione/4319

Nozari, H., Ghahremani-Nahr, J., & Szmelter-Jarosz, A. (2024). AI and machine learning for real-world problems. In Kim, S., & Deka, G. C. (Eds.), *Advances in Computers* (Vol. 134, pp. 1–12). Elsevier., DOI: 10.1016/bs.adcom.2023.02.001

Oladele, O. K. (2024). *Internet of Things (IoT) in Logistics: Transforming Supply Chains with Connected Devices and Data Analytics.*

Padmavathi, V., Suresh, C., Kumar, R. L., & Punitha, P. (2025). Adaptive AI-enhanced signal processing framework for optimized communication in the Internet of Underwater Things (IOUT). *International Journal of Pattern Recognition and Artificial Intelligence*, *39*(7), 2558002. DOI: 10.1142/S0218001425580029

Patil, D. (2024). *Artificial Intelligence-Driven Supply Chain Optimization: Enhancing Demand Forecasting And Cost Reduction* (SSRN Scholarly Paper No. 5057408). Social Science Research Network. DOI: 10.2139/ssrn.5057408

Pereira, A. M., Moura, J. A. B., Costa, E. D. B., Vieira, T., Landim, A. R. D. B., Bazaki, E., & Wanick, V. (2022). Customer models for artificial intelligence-based decision support in fashion online retail supply chains. *Decision Support Systems*, *158*, 113795. DOI: 10.1016/j.dss.2022.113795

Pulakhandam, W. (2020). Automated Threat Intelligence Integration To Strengthen SHACS For Robust Security In Cloud-Based Healthcare Applications. *International Journal of Engineering*, *10*(4).

Rana, S., Singh, S. K., & Chandel, A. (2025). AI in Customer Service Automation: Balancing Efficiency With Human Touch. In *AI, Corporate Social Responsibility, and Marketing in Modern Organizations* (pp. 173–194). IGI Global Scientific Publishing. DOI: 10.4018/979-8-3373-0219-5.ch009

Rane, N. (2023). *Enhancing Customer Loyalty through Artificial Intelligence (AI), Internet of Things (IoT), and Big Data Technologies: Improving Customer Satisfaction, Engagement, Relationship, and Experience* (SSRN Scholarly Paper No. 4616051). Social Science Research Network. DOI: 10.2139/ssrn.4616051

Rane, N., Choudhary, S., & Rane, J. (2023). *Artificial Intelligence (AI) and Internet of Things (IoT) – Based Sensors for Monitoring and Controlling in Architecture, Engineering, and Construction: Applications, Challenges, and Opportunities* (SSRN Scholarly Paper No. 4642197). Social Science Research Network. DOI: 10.2139/ssrn.4642197

Rane, N., Choudhary, S., & Rane, J. (2024). Artificial intelligence for enhancing resilience. *Journal of Applied Artificial Intelligence*, *5*(2), 2. Advance online publication. DOI: 10.48185/jaai.v5i2.1053

Riad, M., Naimi, M., & Okar, C. (2024). Enhancing Supply Chain Resilience Through Artificial Intelligence: Developing a Comprehensive Conceptual Framework for AI Implementation and Supply Chain Optimization. *Logistics (Basel)*, *8*(4), 4. Advance online publication. DOI: 10.3390/logistics8040111

Schmitt, M. (2023). Automated machine learning: AI-driven decision making in business analytics. *Intelligent Systems with Applications, 18*, 200188. DOI: 10.1016/j.iswa.2023.200188

Sharma, B. P. (n.d.). *Role of Advanced Cybersecurity Frameworks in Safeguarding Data Integrity and Consumer Trust in Digital Commerce and Enterprise Systems.*

Sharma, R., Shishodia, A., Gunasekaran, A., Min, H., & Munim, Z. H. (2022). The role of artificial intelligence in supply chain management: Mapping the territory. *International Journal of Production Research, 60*(24), 7527–7550. DOI: 10.1080/00207543.2022.2029611

Singh, B. (2025). Revolutionizing Supply Chains for Optimized Demand Planning, Inventory Management, and Logistics: An In-Depth Analysis of AI and ML Solutions in the Modern Era. In *Supply Chain Transformation Through Generative AI and Machine Learning* (pp. 103–128). IGI Global Scientific Publishing. DOI: 10.4018/979-8-3693-4433-0.ch005

Sundaram, M., Kumar, S. V., Kumar, R. L., & Punitha, P. (2025). DRF-YOLO: A transformer-enhanced framework for underwater image enhancement and object detection. *International Journal of Pattern Recognition and Artificial Intelligence, 39*(8), 2550011. DOI: 10.1142/S0218001425500119

Tahmasebi, M. (2024). Beyond Defense: Proactive Approaches to Disaster Recovery and Threat Intelligence in Modern Enterprises. *Journal of Information Security, 15*(2), 2. Advance online publication. DOI: 10.4236/jis.2024.152008

Tarihal, B., Kaliwal, R., & Ammanagi, A. (2024). The Transformative Influence of Artificial Intelligence on Supply Chain Management. *ITM Web of Conferences, 68*, 01016. DOI: 10.1051/itmconf/20246801016

Tirkolaee, E. B., Sadeghi, S., Mooseloo, F. M., Vandchali, H. R., & Aeini, S. (2021). Application of Machine Learning in Supply Chain Management: A Comprehensive Overview of the Main Areas. *Mathematical Problems in Engineering, 2021*(1), 1476043. DOI: 10.1155/2021/1476043

Valivarthi, D. T. (2020). Blockchain-Powered AI-Based Secure HRM Data Management: Machine Learning-Driven Predictive Control and Sparse Matrix Decomposition Techniques. [IJMECE]. *International Journal of Modern Electronics and Communication Engineering, 8*(4), 9.

Wieland, A. (2021). Dancing the Supply Chain: Toward Transformative Supply Chain Management. *The Journal of Supply Chain Management, 57*(1), 58–73. DOI: 10.1111/jscm.12248

Willems, L. (2021). Understanding the Impacts of Autonomous Vehicles in Logistics. In *The Digital Transformation of Logistics* (pp. 113–127). John Wiley & Sons, Ltd., DOI: 10.1002/9781119646495.ch8

Wu, H., Liu, J., & Liang, B. (2024). AI-Driven Supply Chain Transformation in Industry 5.0: Enhancing Resilience and Sustainability. *Journal of the Knowledge Economy*, *16*(1), 3826–3868. Advance online publication. DOI: 10.1007/s13132-024-01999-6

Yallamelli, A. R. G. (2020). A Cloud-based Financial Data Modeling System Using GBDT, ALBERT, and Firefly Algorithm Optimization for High-dimensional Generative Topographic Mapping. *International Journal of Microelectronics and Communication Engineering, 8(4), 27.*, *8*(4).

Chapter 3
Artificial Intelligence (AI)-Powered Competitive Intelligence:
Transforming Strategic Decision-Making in the Digital Age

Arpita Nayak
http://orcid.org/0000-0003-2911-0492
KIIT School of Liberal Studies, KIIT (Deemed to be) University, Bhubaneswar, India

Ipseeta Satpathy
http://orcid.org/0000-0002-0155-5548
KSOM, KKIIT (Deemed to be) University, Bhubaneswar, India

Sandeep Poddar
http://orcid.org/0000-0001-9771-877X
Lincoln University College, Malaysia

ABSTRACT

The fundamental transformation of organizational critical decision-making occurs through artificial intelligence as it enhances data processing power along with predictive ability for competitive intelligence while revolutionizing strategic planning processes. The combination of advanced machine learning algorithms and big data analytics helps companies build precise decision-support systems that enhance the effectiveness of their strategic projects. The main strength of AI systems originates from their efficient navigation of competitive intelligence systems. Business organizations deploy AI-powered platforms to automatically conduct SWOT assessments

DOI: 10.4018/979-8-3373-3648-0.ch003

and carry out extensive market examinations while performing standard benchmarks to let them lead dynamic market competitions. A combination of technology creates better strategic business decisions with enhanced agility that relies on data for the management of competitive edge. The analysis investigates both ethical issues and privacy and legal challenges that come from using AI in decision making processes.

I. INTRODUCTION

The modern business environment has revolutionized through the powerful strategic planning tool known as artificial intelligence (AI). Organizations within different industries implement AI technology to examine large data collections and forecast market directions while enhancing their organizational decision-making capability. AI-based strategic planning distinguishes itself from traditional approaches because it processes current information components and detects systematic patterns to produce highly accurate strategic insights. The increasing competition demands businesses utilize Artificial Intelligence for strategic vision which functions as a fundamental competitive tool to lead in changing market landscapes. (Mahabub et al.,2025). Researchers surveyed and report of AIPRM (2024) stated that 6,000 Americans in December 2023 to learn more about their knowledge, use, and applications of AI in and outside of the workplace.

According to the poll, over four out of five respondents (78.5%) said they used email spam filters, making this the most popular application of AI in the workplace. Approximately three out of five (62.2%) employees then used chatbots to respond to customer support enquiries.

The primary role of AI stands essential in the process of competitive intelligence. Businesses use AI-powered analysis tools to extract competitor plans and detect emerging market trends while predicting potential market disruptions because our world contains extensive data sets but minimal valuable insights. The combination of machine learning with natural language processing (NLP) and predictive analytics transforms organizations into data management leaders who gain competitive advantages. Organizations that will thrive under this capability can find market success through minor strategic advantages especially in sectors such as finance, healthcare and retail. Businesses now take competition differently because they have shifted to gathering predictive intelligence instead of passive intelligence gathering (Achumie et al.,2022).

The fundamental shift in business strategy results from ongoing development and maturity of AI-powered decision systems. At first AI operated exclusively for data analysis automation while also conducting basic data processing requirements. New innovations in deep learning and neural network technology have driven AI software to perform advanced high-level decision-making operations which were traditionally reserved for executive-level humans.

Artificial Intelligence serves business strategies in modern times through its delivery of essential initiatives including supply chain optimization as well as personalized customer solutions and dynamic pricing models. The real-time processing of large data volumes enables organizations to make lucid and fast and accurate business decisions. Companies increasingly adopt AI at an organizational level resulting in a business transformation that enhances executive capabilities through data-based intelligence. The integration of human strategic expertise and machine intelligence produces more accurate strategies which prevent the problems that occur from human bias and inadequate information access.

The study evaluates how AI technologies transform the operational procedures of conventional strategic planning. AI enables businesses to use predictive analytics patterns which help them predict market movements and find new opportunities and stay ahead of competitive challenges. AI brings the most value to organizations through its capability to generate meaningful insights from the continuous tracking of industrial patterns and competitor moves as well as customer feedback. The combination of past records with present variables controlled by AI data analysis allows precise forecasting that leads to optimal enterprise decision-making through simulation approaches.Today's businesses employ AI to function as a strategic decision-making enhancement system beyond its tool status. Through this empowerment organizations transform their reactive operational models into proactive prospective strategies. The progression of AI technology will expand its strategic business functions which will smooth the distinction between human intuition and machine analytics thus revolutionizing market competition dynamics. (Narne et al.,2024; Oluwaseun et al.,2024).

Historically strategic planning systems incorporated linear forecasting techniques and historically recorded data and expert predictions for their development. The current volatile marketplace requires modified planning strategies because traditional approaches prove inadequate. AI introduces a complete system transformation because it enables data analysis capabilities which adapt automatically to unforeseen market situations as they occur. The predictive models created by machine learning algorithms process unstructured raw data consisting of social media trends economic indicators and geopolitical events to increase strategic agility. AI-based scenario planning assists businesses in designing multiple future simulations featuring varied market scenarios which give leaders better options as market forces remain unpredictable (Hrr,2025).

Using AI for strategic planning allows the detection of subtle patterns within vast amounts of data which serves as its most significant benefit. No human analyst can equal the pattern-finding and trend-detection capability that AI systems possess.

The combination of Amazon and Walmart and other retail giants employs AI technology to enhance inventory control together with pricing methods and customer relationship activities to deliver stronger market demand adjustments. Financial institutions use AI technology to conduct risk-based activities and detect financial fraud when maintaining portfolios by using precise methods that need fast execution times. Organizations can transform subjective decision processes to evidence-based solutions utilizing electronic frameworks which generate small risks coupled with excellent opportunities (Hoffman & Freyn, 2019).

Joining AI to strategic planning enables businesses to take decisions faster while enhancing predictions and operation efficiency. Organizations face significant barriers to AI adoption while they need to handle privacy issues that affect data protection along with the combination of biased algorithms and the lack of skilled professionals who work with AI systems. Operational inefficiency occurs when algorithms become excessive because they split organizational targets from actual operational execution. Organizations need to develop optimal protocols that will let artificial intelligence tools help human decision-making capabilities as well as protect humans' autonomous decision-making power. Productive data governance frameworks need to conduct continuous AI system fairness evaluations at the same time as delivering worker training for organizations to function properly. Decisions created from combining AI analytics power with human business understanding lead organizations to their best possible outcomes. Long-term business achievement relies on complete AI technology integration with human leadership by unifying artificial intelligence methods with critical operational effectiveness and strategic goal targets. The establishment of collaborative systems allows AI to scan large data pools yet strategic leaders must remain responsible for interpreting situations and creating ethical guides and original solutions. Modern technological markets reward organizations using artificial intelligence systems with maximum success when they implement proper human oversight. Advanced technology deployments require organizations to adopt new technologies while structuring systematic systems implementation to prevent adverse situations that occur from unregulated technology use.

I.I Importance of Artificial Intelligence (AI) in Competitive Intelligence

The use of AI transforms organization competitor data collection and analysis through its ability to operate with enhanced speed and complex data processes. Through advanced machine learning techniques combined with natural language processing technology businesses unveil market patterns and forecast competitor activities alongside unidentified market prospects. Organizations use this transformation to develop stronger business strategies using current data-based knowledge rather than past guesses. These tools powered by Artificial Intelligence continuously monitor all major industry trends while collecting social sentiment data and emerging technology insights to deliver organizations dynamic multi-dimensional views of competitors. Organizations can implement strategic modifications before market disruptions through this approach which enables them to gain a competitive advantage from market developments. AI reshapes how organizations maintain competitive edges since it transforms ordinary data into functional decision-making intelligence that delivers optimal sustainable development paths for strategic leaders. Traditional business methods including market research conducted manually as well as SWOT analysis require prolonged durations before generating outdated findings. The implementation of artificial intelligence systems enables continuous tracking of competitive business movements including price changes and product releases and company acquisitions. The combination of web scraping with sentiment analysis and predictive modeling gives businesses full visibility into their market competition thus enabling fast responses to potential threats and emerging opportunities. AI achieves its most significant value for competitive intelligence by processing unstructured data. NLP technology enables the analysis of news stories and earnings call transcripts alongside patent documents and social media content to obtain valuable information about competitive tactics. The analysis of patent applications through AI detects changing R&D priorities of competitive companies while executive statement scrutiny enables the prediction of financial performance. The detailed market insights produced by AI technology were out of reach before it became scalable which handed a substantial competitive advantage to early adopters of AI as they gained faster market movement predictions (Haleem et al.,2022; Taranu & Cioranu, 2024).

Business organizations need to consider the moral limits of AI-powered competitive information acquisition. Competitive analysis and corporate espionage share an ethical boundary that companies must observe while strictly following legal standards. AI tools operated by companies have to meet both industry best practice guidelines as well as all data protection regulatory requirements. The role of human judgment becomes crucial to analyze collected data through AI systems for creating strategic plans despite technological improvements in intelligence collection. Organizations that blend artificial intelligence analysis with strategic human intuition will become most successful because they establish a mutual relationship between leadership and technology.

I.II The Evolution of AI-Driven Decision-Making in Businesses

AI technology in business decision processes advanced from basic automation toward advanced cognitive computing systems. AI technology during its initial phase dealt exclusively with recurring responsibilities alongside automated customer support functions. Distinct developments in neural networks combined with reinforcement learning techniques have enabled AI systems to solve intricate strategic business issues regarding market entry timing and merger assessments and innovation project sequencing. At Netflix and Tesla AI serves as a central element of their strategic direction which allows them to refine their approaches through instant feedback data (Alawamleh et al.,2024; Schmitt,2023).

Human leaders should rely on augmented intelligence to guide their decision-making in the AI era because it will maintain human functions instead of replacing them. AI technology will provide executives with analytical dashboards which merge different data sources to provide automated recommendations that human leaders would finish judging. Organizational collaboration preserves human judgment limits through AI analysis to gain benefits from its analytical abilities without the risks of automation mistakes. AI systems that provide transparent explanation of their operations will boost industrial-wide acceptance through increased trust in decision-making processes (Bhardwaj et al.,2025).

AI business strategy development remains in its nascent phase because there are no boundaries to what it can achieve in innovation. The improvement of sophisticated algorithms and expanding datasets will result in deeper AI involvement in determining corporate business destinies. Organizations which adopt this transformation by investing in AI infrastructure alongside talent acquisition together with ethical frameworks will emerge as successful players in data-driven businesses. Section 3 of the paper analyses how top organizations use AI-based strategic planning to achieve sustainable achievements through detailed case studies.

II. RESEARCH OBJECTIVES

- To evaluate the role of Artificial Intelligence (AI) in enhancing strategic planning, market analysis, and competitive intelligence.
- To assess the impact, techniques, and challenges of AI-enabled decision support systems in driving business growth and strategic decision-making.

III. RESEARCH QUESTIONS

- How does AI contribute to strategic planning, market research, and the development of competitive advantage in businesses?
- What are the key techniques, benefits, and limitations of AI-enabled decision support systems in organizational strategy and growth?

IV. RESEARCH METHODOLOGY

The research methodology of this study utilizes a qualitative and exploratory study in the assessment of the changing role of Artificial Intelligence (AI) in strategic planning and competition intelligence. The secondary data were drawn using peer-reviewed journals, industry whitepapers, case studies and reputable databases which included Google scholar, IEEE, ScienceDirect, and Elsevier and concentrated on the secondary data that were published last 5-10 years. Inclusion criteria included English-language writings that investigate the use of AI in strategic business transactions, i.e. decision support systems, predictive analytics, and ethical governance and its application in fields such as retail, finance and manufacturing. The research that does not strategically apply to AI, an article that is not peer-reviewed, and other sectors were not included. The thematic analysis methodology was used to reveal the emerging patterns and knowledge and guarantee the reliability and validity of results due to the source triangulation and interindustry comparison.

V. TRADITIONAL STRATEGIC PLANNING VS. AI-DRIVEN STRATEGIC PLANNING

Business traditionally used historical data together with expert intuition and linear forecasting models to establish success through strategic planning. The annual executive meetings became opportunities to review historic performance data and marketplace evidence which served as foundations for creating extended business targets. The structured planning methods proved difficult to adapt despite their framework when companies implemented them in static business environments that kept changing. The combination of market changes together with new competitors and changing consumer preferences usually made these plans outdated even before they could be executed (Bhima et al.,2023).

The process of strategic planning enabled by AI machines delivers continuous real-time decision capabilities to organizations. The processing of big data sets including structured and unstructured information from financial reports to social media sentiment occurs through machine learning algorithms to yield predictive analysis. The analytical processes of AI stay active for continuous updates which enable businesses to edit their strategies as needed. AI-driven demand forecasting enables Walmart and other retailers to maximize their inventory management through predictions of market changes stemming from weather patterns and economic signifiers together with online consumer movements. AI technology enables financial institutions to evaluate credit assessments better through the analysis of unconventional data sources including transaction data and user behaviour indications (Yılmaz & Demir, 2023).

AI-based strategic planning modifies organizational approaches toward dealing with uncertain circumstances. The conventional method of scenario planning has evolved into a quicker process because of AI models that perform thousands of outcome simulations within minutes. Shell implements AI to predict political risks alongside energy market changes which helps develop sustainable extended-term plans. Implementing this transition requires resolution of multiple challenges. Organizations need to solve data stability problems while also eliminating computational prejudice and requiring operator surveillance when implementing artificial intelligence insight systems to maintain compliance with business ethics. The upcoming path of strategic planning will use artificial intelligence technologies to enhance human professional abilities while generating an optimal amalgamation of speed and informed decision-making capabilities (Roongta & Roongta, 2024).

Electronic intelligence primarily began through manual competitor research before transitioning to artificial intelligence-based live monitoring thus providing companies essential industry advantages. SWOT analyses together with market reports commonly became outdated before decision-makers received the information. Robot intelligence does three things to enhance the process: it automatically gathers information along with analyzing market competitors and makes industry predictions about upcoming changes. Natural language processing tools (NLP) examine earnings calls along with news articles and patent documents for competitive strategy identification purposes while sentiment analytics systems monitor public brand perception for competitors. Predicative competitor benchmarking represents one of the most influential applications of Artificial Intelligence in the field of competitive intelligence. AI systems implemented by Amazon and Netflix help these companies examine how competitors set prices along with launch products while engage customers so they can respond ahead of time. AI systems monitor inventory levels along with history-backed data that allows them to notify companies about impending competitor price drops in time for proactive response planning. Web scraping tools enabled by artificial intelligence monitor both job posting data and research and development activities of competitors to identify their upcoming market strategies through early detection (Alnajem et al.,2024).

Using AI to collect competitive information leads to both practical dilemmas along with legal boundaries which must be resolved. Confused limits exist when AI tools read private information because it creates an uncertain boundary between business research and unlawful corporate intrusions against companies and their data. Companies should establish strong governance systems that protect their compliance standards while taking full advantage of artificial intelligence capability. Human experts continue to play a vital role in understanding AI-generated analysis because they need context and industry experience to convert data into strategic actions. AI will develop new capabilities that will make it essential for organizations to maintain their position as industry leaders.

Managers implement existing frameworks when they want to combine AI capabilities with human decision-making for strategic purposes. The OODA Loop serves as an established model for decision-making used originally by militaries but also applied in corporate fields. AI technology speeds up both the "Observe" and "Orient" stages through its ability to process real-time information for detecting patterns and security threats before human analysts could finish their analysis. Hedge funds employ AI-controlled OODA loops for high-frequency market trades which function from microsecond market variations. The framework of Augmented Intelligence enables AI to boost human decision-makers rather than replace them. Executives retain final judgment authority at Watson unlike the support system provided by this IBM platform. The medical staff uses AI technology for disease identification in medical images yet doctors maintain full responsibility for all therapeutic decisions. Full automation risks are minimized through this model which guarantees ethical alignments and strategic considerations between human operators and technology systems (Ulu, 2024)

AI-driven decision-making utilizes two main predictive analytics models which include regression analysis alongside neural networks. Forecasts for consumer behavior help Target optimize their supply chain operation and personal marketing strategies. Reinforcement Learning operates through trial-and-error processes to transform autonomous vehicles and logistics management industries. UPS and similar businesses use reinforcement learning to enhance delivery route optimization which leads to decreased fuel expenses as well as greater operational efficiency (Ujwary,2025).

Organizations need to address data silos as well as maintain algorithm transparency together with managing internal organizational resistance to fulfil framework implementation. The implementation of effective AI requires business organizations to establish teams that unite data scientists with strategists and legal experts for collaborative practice. The growing complexity of modern AI models makes Explainable AI (XAI) frameworks more relevant since they help executives better understand and trust AI-generated insights. This forward direction of AI decision-making relies on progressive models that unite machine accuracy with human inventive talents for developing sustainable business growth.

VI. ARTIFICIAL INTELLIGENCE (AI) IN STRATEGIC PLANNING

The current competitive market deserves credit for the transformative power of artificial intelligence toward strategic planning. The application of AI focuses on three essential corporate strategy components by transforming market trend assessment and business prediction and scenario development approaches. Organizations leverage AI-powered methods to outperform traditional planning principles because they gain more effective data-driven and dynamic decision systems for obtaining substantial competitive benefits.

The digital economy's speeded-up environment makes historical data-based and periodic report analysis methods inadequate for market analysis. The solution provided by AI-driven market trend analysis consists of processing enormous structured and unstructured data sets in real-time. The combination of machine learning algorithms allows for a parallel analysis of social media sentiment combined with news trends alongside competitor announcements and economic indicators which enables the system to discover trends beyond human capabilities. The utilization of AI helps retail giants discover new viral trends on TikTok before their human-dependent competitors which enables them to alter their inventory and marketing plans weeks in advance. The detection capacity proved vital during COVID-19 times when artificial intelligence systems noticed early behavioral changes in consumers toward home fitness and remote work products. Nevertheless, these systems need thorough calibration procedures while AI demonstrates remarkable talent for pattern discovery yet human expertise should maintain its place for investigating findings properly and preventing wrong data associations (Chakraborty & Parida, 2024).

Strategic planning advances with predictive analytics because this analysis method uses market trends to generate exceptionally accurate outcomes predictions. The development of artificial intelligence surpasses basic linear regression through applications of complex algorithms such as Long Short-Term Memory networks and Gradient Boosting Machines enabling effective modeling of data relationships beyond linearity. Walmart together with other retail companies apply these analytical tools to determine exact regional product demand amounts allowing for optimized inventory distribution across their vast locations. Financial organizations implement predictive analytics for credit risk evaluation and fraud prevention as well as production companies deploy it to identify equipment breakdowns ahead of time. The highest level of implementation unites predictive analytics with prescriptive analytics so systems can forecast outcomes and recommend best solutions. Private airlines make dynamic pricing decisions along with route modifications using predictive systems based on expected customer demand changes. The adoption of AI faces ongoing difficulties because of inadequate data quality standards combined with a requirement for interpretable AI algorithms which leaders can depend upon (Lee,2025).

AI achieves its maximum potential in strategic planning when used for scenario planning combined with simulations. Traditional scenario development provided manual input to create only basic scenario samples yet AI technology uses present resources to analyze multiple thousands of predictive solutions. Through their partnership with AI technology organizations gain the capability to examine countless market scenarios and lengthened opportunities along with risks through Monte Carlo simulations and agent-based modeling capabilities. The energy company Shell has led the way in applying artificial intelligence for scenario modeling to forecast market transformations from distinct geopolitical and regulatory scenarios. The digital twin technology enables manufacturers to evaluate supply chain impacts through virtual simulations which help them develop strategic plans before applying them to actual production systems. Evolutionary uses of generative AI provide executive users with easier access through natural-language scenario queries which generate instant data-driven suggestions. Strategic planning through new technology development operates as a cyclic process rather than an annual program (Oloruntosin & Oguanobi, 2024).

Organizational implementation of AI-based strategies leads to a fundamental overhaul of their strategic planning procedures. Agile decision systems emerge through real-time market analysis with accurate predictive forecasting and detailed scenario planning which creates enhanced information with superior organizational resilience for strategic decision-making. Organizations employing advanced technology integration with human leadership and ethical decision-making will secure considerable market benefits. This technology enables organizations to observe market developments ahead of time instead of reacting to them while optimizing operations successfully and navigating unsure situations. Total AI implementation in strategic planning demands organizations to adopt both technological advances together with cultural structural and skill changes. A detailed investigation of actual infrastructure deployment practices for AI solutions will follow with safety measures against associated security risks and limitations derived from these systems.

VII. ARTIFICIAL INTELLIGENCE (AI) FOR COMPETITIVE INTELLIGENCE

Competitive intelligence now operates as a continuous artificial intelligence-driven strategic process since the digital era began. Artificial intelligence transforms three essential components of competitive intelligence through innovations within market research methodology development and competitor surveillance systems as well as strategic assessment frameworks. Organizations utilize these AI applications to gain outstanding insights about their competitors with speed and precision that would have been impossible to achieve in the recent past. (Okeke et al.,2024).

The speed of artificial intelligence technologies now improves traditional market research approaches by analyzing massive unorganized data pools at an exceptional level. Hundreds of millions of written customer feedback along with social media content and forum posts undergo analysis through NLP algorithms to reveal new market developments and unaddressed customer requirements. Computers utilize vision programs to inspect competitor products and retail displays for any slight modifications in packaging designs or merchandise arrangement. The real-time analysis of brand perception movements occurs through sentiment analysis tools which monitor performance among different consumer groups. Consumer goods companies integrate AI systems to track social media discussions about rival products to discover quality concerns and customer requests that emerge before formal market research methods monitor these elements. By using AI technology users can recognize understated verbal cues of positive or negative sentiment that would typically escape surveys conducted without AI. The success of such methods requires precise algorithm training that prevents cultural biases in language interpretation and ensures proper representation of customer segments for sampling (Rane et al., 2024).

Real-time monitoring becomes necessary because the competitive market transforms swiftly through digital speed. Competitive intelligence platforms powered by AI gather continuous real-time feedback of competitors through website monitoring as well as job listings and patent registrations and news mentions. Machines operating as part of advanced web scraping technologies use learning mechanisms to spot negligible adjustments in competitor pricing material and product details which signal new strategies to research teams. AI systems help investment companies detect strategic shift indications through their analysis of earnings calls with executives. AI systems within pharmaceuticals observe clinical trial registers together with research publications to follow competitors' R&D progress. Companies now possess the ability to handle competitive moves throughout days or hours instead of traditional months-long responses because of real-time insights. Some businesses have created their own algorithms to detect market expansion indicators through competitor employment activities before market entry. The analysis becomes complex because businesses must extract significant information from constant stream-like data while needing advanced filtering systems together with human assessment capabilities to recognize meaningful developments (Syamsuar & Marcello, 2024).

The SWOT analysis receives augmented power through AI systems that generate automatic real-time data inputs coupled with predictive assessments. SWOT quadrant identification along with weighting of factors in these quadrants is now successfully performed through machine learning models that process multiple internal and external data points. AI benchmarking tools perform nuanced operational metric comparisons which analyze complete assessments of supply chain efficiencies and customer service response times and other operational data points. Computer vision technology helps retailers to monitor their in-store product arrangements by comparing them with market competitors and SaaS companies employ artificial intelligence for pricing model versus feature set comparisons throughout their competitive domains. AI systems deliver their most substantial impact by running simulations that demonstrate how adjustments to one SWOT factor will impact others thus showing strategists about the progressive chain of competitive effects. Advanced systems provide recommended strategic solutions that use historical data to show successful strategies in parallel competitive scenarios. The computerized analyses produced with AI support still need human expertise to interpret the results because AI tools only highlight trends and insights for executives to use with their business understanding and innovative thinking in constructing appropriate responses (Rane et al., 2024).

Competitive intelligence adoption through AI requires investments in the wrong places alone cannot lead to success. Organizations which succeed in the market are reorganizing their competitive intelligence systems to unite experts in data science with traditional market research specialists. The organizations have established new workflows to use real-time insights with required governance regulations. These organizations have achieved the most important advantage by creating an environment that quickly transforms data-driven insights into strategic moves throughout the organization beyond analysis paralysis. This chapter will examine operational models combined with change management strategies for creating the future AI-based competitive intelligence capability.

VIII. ARTIFICIAL INTELLIGENCE (AI)-ENABLED DECISION SUPPORT SYSTEMS

Modern business needs decision-makers to implement AI-based systems that unite artificial intelligence insights with human decision-making abilities. This investigation analyzes AI's influence on decision-making systems through assessment of three critical business intelligence elements and predictive planning systems plus risk management alterations. The integration of artificial intelligence into traditional business intelligence systems evolved the systems into prescriptive systems that perform decision-making functions. The latest generation of AI-based BI platforms employs machine learning to detect data inconsistencies while discovering customer behavioral patterns that generate optimized user suggestions. The combination of natural language processing gives executives access to complex datasets and they can use conversational languages to study the information while automated visualization tools show important trends and data anomalies. Retail shoppers can improve merchandise setups by linking real-time traffic information with buy data through these measuring platforms. Modern financial institutions utilize artificial intelligence in business intelligence to assess transactional data from multiple platforms which helps find fraudulent activity while uncovering potential sales cross-opportunities. Self-learning systems in advanced models enhance their analytical functionality through continuous adjustments activated via user interactions and feedback cycles. Proof of successful implementation depends on both strong data governance structures and high-quality data since AI systems derive their accuracy from their processing data. Organizations need to handle the "black box" problem through the creation of transparent AI models which disclose their recommendation decision processes (Ahmadi, 2025).

The predictive modeling capabilities of AI have become essential for business organizations which need to forecast market changes and address business growth opportunities. Organizations use these prediction systems to analyze internal data with market signals that predict market needs and create simulation models for expansion planning and resource management. Machine learning models use their capability to analyze hundreds of variables at once to spot non-linear connections which exceed traditional statistical algorithms. Sales data from consumer-packaged goods enables companies to forecast regional market changes according to weather patterns alongside social data and economic indicators. Predictive models assist technology firms in determining new product feature potential success during early development phases. Nowadays AI systems demonstrate their most powerful capability by running multiple what-if simulations during limited time periods which allows executives to analyze various growth strategies across different market conditions. The leading automotive company employed this strategy to discover their ideal electric vehicle charging station locations through the combination of predicting adoption patterns and traffic movement alongside competitor assessment. Sustaining model accuracy during time periods represents the main obstacle since organizational leaders must retrain their systems as market conditions transform and fresh data emerges. Strategic organizations need to maintain human judgment as the core decision-making factor while using algorithms but they should not allow computer-generated outputs to replace essential human involvement (Ahmed et al.,2025).

AI systems now lead risk management into a new era by monitoring threats before they emerge thus recommending time-sensitive prevention methods. System-based solutions review both formatted and informal datasets to recognize potential operational, financial or reputational threats. The analysis of news sources and social media engages natural language processing for reputational risk detection and supply chain assessment depends on predictive modeling evaluations of weather patterns and geopolitical events. The detection of complex threats in cybersecurity depends on AI-driven systems because they review traffic pattern data alongside recognizing abnormal system conduct. Financial institutions deploy AI tools for stress-testing their portfolios which evaluates hundreds of potential economic conditions better than traditional risk models. AI technology enables worldwide shipping organizations to perform present-time route optimization which considers simultaneously both fuel efficiency and the threats from pirates along with weather factors. These systems bring new security concerns because algorithms have inherent biases that create potential risks and a problem emerges when various organizations use equivalent AI risk models. Frameworks for governance must resolve both speed-related threats and maintain delivery systems that enable immediate countermeasures. Successful businesses utilize advanced artificial intelligence as an expansion tool instead of using it to replace human risk management competence since it provides improved risk forecasting capabilities (Ghosh,2025).

AI-driven decision support implementation needs strategic planning that involves all aspects of technology and processes and workforce. Leading organizations should find their data infrastructure with the ability to provide AI systems access to timely and high-quality data information. The execution of decision-making processes receives equal focus since normal operational workflows demonstrate timestamps which prevent AI-generated insights from becoming an advantage. The most difficult aspect arises from changes needed in workforce culture to develop belief in AI suggestions together with human supervision standards. The success of organizations comes from placing "centaurs" who merge human operators with AI systems into their operational framework to create strategic organizational models through the combination of human weaknesses and AI strengths. Multiple chapters present successful world organizations that implemented these structural changes through sector-specific findings and their results are reported. Organizational leadership success will come to companies which integrate AI strategically through maintaining human components that ensure effective AI deployment.

IX. CHALLENGES AND ETHICAL CONSIDERATIONS

Organizations must overcome intricate limitations along with moral challenges of leading-edge technologies before using AI systems in strategic decision-making. The implementation of algorithms requires thorough handling in three situations since these situations involve bias concerns alongside transparency issues and they require new data privacy standards and ethical limits for competitive intelligence. Training data with built-in biases becomes more prevalent through intellectual systems which creates difficulties to develop fair strategic initiatives. Software programs employed in recruitment and lending along with market segment operations possess capabilities to target protected population groups via advanced intellectual systems that operate beyond human understanding. Advanced machine learning algorithms produce challenges due to their unclear operation because their recommended systems are difficult to understand. The challenge for managers comes from their inability to understand AI recommendations regarding popular product elimination because they must assess market trends with possible algorithmic bias impact. The lack of supporting evidence in unsatisfactory denial cases from AI-based credit scoring systems presents regulatory problems to financial institutions. Organizations use XAI frameworks alongside bias auditing to handle these problems while the methods lower the accuracy of predictions. Highly regulated business environments create ongoing difficulties since they require trade-offs between performance quality and interpretive clarity for decision-making processes (Bahangulu & Owusu-Berko, 2025; Tewari, 2025).

Strategic planning with AI has become problematic because many organizations must now deal with the complicated standards set by GDPR and CCPA. Machine learning processes that accumulate and analyse huge quantities of personal data typically generate incompatible challenges with data minimization and purpose limitation privacy standards. The online collection of customer data by businesses through market analysis tracking, sentiment analysis of customer messages and predictive analytics on consumer behaviour leads to major privacy violations. Regulatory bodies-imposed penalties on organizations which employed AI models with personal data without complete user approval as well as insufficient data privacy effect tests. Various legal frameworks between different territories present organizations with extensive challenges because regulatory norms between jurisdictions can disagree on what is legal or illegal. Complex business data governance setups contain artificial intelligence solutions for privacy protection through both differential privacy and federated learning to operate business data systems. Multiple prerequisites consisting of high technical complexity and budget expenses exist to deploy these solutions. Organizations must follow new AI Act laws by creating documentation records and applying human supervision to strategic AI systems while establishing AI risk categories (Olatunji et al.,2024; Farinu,2025).

Success-driven organizations make ethical Artificial Intelligence system development their fundamental strategic directive to strengthen their business competition methods. Responsible AI meets brand usefulness criteria to become an essential organizational foundation that creates positive reputation strength for stakeholder engagement and sustainable market development. Satiable business success relies on innovation with ethical control through open handling and transparent monitoring systems and accountability mechanisms because AI technology will continue to advance. The paper adopts a current framework to showcase AI deployment strategies which resolve key business issues in contemporary operational procedures. Organizations need to track biases during their data management system development process and unite their team leaders as part of this strategic plan. Businesses must implement continuous monitoring as an AI system requirement because it allows their AI systems to adapt to regulatory changes and societal expectation shifts. Strategic value transformation depends on ethical implementation throughout the entire AI development cycle from design to execution at the same time as risk reduction measures. Organizations must embrace AI as their ethical collaborator for developing sustainable approaches to modern operational methods to achieve future excellence. The ethical deployment of AI functions as a competitive asset because it develops responsible systems that help businesses attain better positions in present-day AI-powered competitions. Strategic planning needs responsible AI adoption through joint efforts in creating innovative solutions and ethical standards which define its direction forward. Organizations need to create strong governance systems which combine detection methods for bias with AI algorithm oversight and specific accountability systems related to artificial intelligence-based decisions. Close evaluation of AI algorithms requires organizations to schedule regular independent assessments which verify EU AI Act compliance in AI systems. Organizational functions must collaborate with automatic intelligence ethical committees to conduct assessments of competitive intelligence practices which ensures ethical protections during data scraping and sentiment analysis activities. Organizations should adopt privacy-saving AI solutions which combine federated learning and differential privacy to obtain strategic insights while maintaining customer trust. The executive team should join AI literacy programs to study both AI recommendations and understanding AI system operational boundaries. Organizations which achieve top success levels recognize ethical AI as a business advantage because it helps maintain stakeholder trust through transparent AI deployment methods that boost innovative potential. The balanced AI implementation arose before organizations started dedicated funding for system development and human expertise growth to create strategic thinking AI systems through augmentation and build ethics into AI design through deployment (Widjaja, 2024; Kabat, 2025).

Organizations need to adopt AI as part of strategic planning because it is inevitable; however, their approach will decide their future success. Success factors in AI implementation include developing AI understanding at every leadership level and creating defined responsibility systems and human supervision of major decisions. Organizations need to include flexibility to their AI plans to renew compliance with evolving regulations while preserving their competitive market position. Using ethical AI methods within strategic planning gives organizations an opportunity to create better sustainable business models which benefit both their stakeholders and the environment at large.

CONCLUSION AND FUTURE DIRECTIONS

Strategic planning and competitive intelligence gained new capabilities from AI implementation to process markets and take decisions through predictive analytics and real-time trend monitoring while benefiting from scenario simulation. Organizations today achieve improved forecasting accuracy through AI-driven tools that automatically process large data sets of competition information and markets which results in better strategic adaptability. Transformations of the market by artificial intelligence systems face three main obstacles consisting of algorithmic bias along with ethical issues in competitive intelligence and strong data protection demands which require frameworks for governance with bias audits and ethical rule enforcement as well as compliance oversight. Businesses need to combine artificial intelligence training for employees with teamwork between data experts and strategists as well as automated analysis oversight by human operators during both ethical decisions and creative operational development steps. Organizations that address these concerns at the same time get the maximum strategic value from AI and establish protections against its potential risks making their competitive advantage sustainable during technology evolution.

REFERENCES

Achumie, G. O., Oyegbade, I. K., Igwe, A. N., Ofodile, O. C., & Azubuike, C. (2022). Ai-Driven Predictive Analytics model for strategic business development and market growth in competitive industries. *International Journal of Social Science Exceptional Research*, *1*(1), 13–25. DOI: 10.54660/IJSSER.2022.1.1.13-25

Ahmadi, M. (2025). Data-driven decision-making and Predictive Analytics. *AI Marketing*, 57–73. DOI: 10.1201/9781003625452-4

Ahmed, F., Ahmed, M. R., Kabir, M. A., & Islam, M. M. (2025). Revolutionizing Business Analytics: The Impact of Artificial Intelligence and Machine Learning. *American Journal of Advanced Technology and Engineering Solutions*, *1*(01), 147–173. DOI: 10.63125/f7yjxw69

AIPRM. (2024, January 11). *AI statistics 2024*. Aiprm.com. https://www.aiprm.com/ai-statistics/

Alawamleh, M., Shammas, N., Alawamleh, K., & Bani Ismail, L. (2024). Examining the limitations of AI in business and the need for human insights using interpretive structural modelling. *Journal of Open Innovation*, *10*(3), 100338. DOI: 10.1016/j.joitmc.2024.100338

Alnajem, A. A. Q. I., Ibrahim, A., Abdulrahman, M. M., Al-Kubaisi, A. A. A., Tawfeq, J. F., Khishe, M., & Saeed, A. (2024). AI-Driven Strategic Foresight: Anticipating Future Trends and Modelling Business Strategies. In *2024 International Conference on Decision Aid Sciences and Applications (DASA)* (pp. 1–6). IEEE.

Bahangulu, J. K., & Owusu-Berko, L. (2025). Algorithmic bias, data ethics, and governance: Ensuring fairness, transparency and compliance in AI-powered business analytics applications. *World Journal of Advanced Research and Reviews*, *25*(2), 1746–1763. DOI: 10.30574/wjarr.2025.25.2.0571

Bhardwaj, J., Awasthi, S., & Dhoni, P. S. (2025). Generative AI: Shaping the future of business intelligence and data-driven decision making. *International Journal of Artificial Intelligence and Machine Learning*, *4*(1), 1–8. DOI: 10.34218/IJAIML_04_01_001

Bhima, B., Rahmania Az Zahra, A., & Nurtino, T. (2023). Enhancing organizational efficiency through the integration of artificial intelligence in Management Information Systems. [ATM]. *APTISI Transactions on Management*, *7*(3), 282–289. DOI: 10.33050/atm.v7i3.2146

Chakraborty, M., & Parida, P. (2024). Comprehensive study of AI-driven market forecasting models and their applicability. *2024 International Conference on Advancements in Smart, Secure and Intelligent Computing (ASSIC)*, 1–5. DOI: 10.1109/ASSIC60049.2024.10508015

Farinu, U. (2025). *Fairness, Accountability, and Transparency in AI: Ethical Challenges in Data-Driven Decision-Making*. DOI: 10.2139/ssrn.5128174

Ghosh, U. K. (2025). Transformative AI applications in business decision-making. *Advances in Logistics, Operations, and Management Science*, •••, 1–40. DOI: 10.4018/979-8-3373-1687-1.ch001

Haleem, A., Javaid, M., Asim Qadri, M., Pratap Singh, R., & Suman, R. (2022). Artificial Intelligence (AI) applications for marketing: A literature-based study. *International Journal of Intelligent Networks*, *3*, 119–132. DOI: 10.1016/j.ijin.2022.08.005

Hoffman, F. P., & Freyn, S. L. (2019). The future of competitive intelligence in an AI-enabled world. *International Journal of Value Chain Management*, *10*(4), 275. DOI: 10.1504/IJVCM.2019.103268

Hrr, H. (2025). The Future of Digital Transformation: Leveraging Artificial Intelligence for competitive advantage. SSRN *Electronic Journal*. DOI: 10.2139/ssrn.5123723

Kabat, D. (2025). Federated learning for privacy-preserving AI: A comparative analysis of Decentralized Data training. *International Journal of Machine Learning, AI &amp. Data Science Evolution*, *1*(01), 9–21. DOI: 10.63665/ijmlaidse.v1i1.02

Lee, J. (2025). *Ai-Driven Predictive Insights: A Modern Framework for Enhancing Decision-Making in Dynamic Data Environments*. DOI: 10.2139/ssrn.5140141

Mahabub, S., Hossain, M. R., & Snigdha, E. Z. (2025). Data-driven decision-making and strategic leadership: AI-powered business operations for competitive advantage and sustainable growth. *Journal of Computer Science and Technology Studies*, *7*(1), 326–336. DOI: 10.32996/jcsts.2025.7.1.24

Narne, S., Adedoja, T., Mohan, M., & Ayyalasomayajula, T. (2024). AI-Driven Decision Support Systems in Management: Enhancing Strategic Planning and Execution. *International Journal on Recent and Innovation Trends in Computing and Communication*, *12*(1), 268–276.

Okeke, N. I., Alabi, O. A., Igwe, A. N., Ofodile, O. C., & Ewim, C. P. M. (2024). AI in customer feedback integration: A data-driven framework for enhancing business strategy. *World J. Advanced Res. Reviews*, *24*(1), 3207–3220.

Oluwaseun, B., Shahab, A. R., Arogundade, J. B., & Mosope, W. (2024). AI-driven business analytics and decision making. *World Journal of Advanced Research and Reviews*, *24*(01), 616–633. DOI: 10.30574/wjarr.2024.24.1.3093

Rane, N., Choudhary, S., & Rane, J. (2024). Gemini versus ChatGPT: Applications, performance, architecture, capabilities, and implementation. SSRN *Electronic Journal*. https://doi.org/DOI: 10.2139/ssrn.4723687

Roongta, J., & Roongta, J. (2024). The Next Frontier: Exploring AI-Driven Business Strategic Decision Making. *Journal of Academic Advancement*, *3*(01), 50–60.

Schmitt, M. (2023). Automated machine learning: AI-driven decision making in business analytics. *Intelligent Systems with Applications*, *18*(200188), 200188. DOI: 10.1016/j.iswa.2023.200188

Syamsuar, D., & Marcello. (2024). The implementation of Artificial Intelligence for Online Review: A systematic literature review. *2024 International Conference on Information Management and Technology (ICIMTech)*, 588–593. DOI: 10.1109/ICIMTech63123.2024.10780904

Taranu, S. D., & Cioranu, A. G. (2024). AI in Competitive Intelligence, Traditional and New Techniques for Gathering and Analysing Data. *Journal of Environmental Management & Tourism*, *15*(3), 591–596.

Tewari, S. (2025). AI powered data governance - ensuring data quality and compliance in the era of Big Data. *Journal of Artificial Intelligence General Science (JAIGS) ISSN:3006-4023*, *8*(1), 187–197. DOI: 10.60087/jaigs.v8i1.364

Ujwary-Gil, A., & Florek-Paszkowska, A. (2025b). Artificial Intelligence, analytics, and strategic decision-making. *AI, Analytics and Strategic Decision Making*, 1–21. DOI: 10.4324/9781003507840-1

Ulu, C. (2024). The fuel of AI in the Battlefield. *Cyber Security in the Age of Artificial Intelligence and Autonomous Weapons*, 87–100. DOI: 10.1201/9781003441700-7

Widjaja, G. (2024). Ethical aspects in legal management: A unique approach to addressing moral dilemmas in business decision-making. *Journal of Management World*, *2024*(4), 326–332. DOI: 10.53935/jomw.v2024i4.395

Yılmaz, E., & Demir, M. (2023). AI in Strategic Planning: Redefining Long-Term Business Goals. *Digital Transformation and Administration Innovation*, *1*(2), 8–16.

Chapter 4
Artificial Intelligence–Driven Decision Making in Modern Business Intelligence

Glaret Shirley Sinnappan
http://orcid.org/0000-0002-6212-1022
Tunku Abdul Rahman University of Management and Technology, Malaysia

ABSTRACT

AI-powered decision-making is transforming business intelligence (BI) by enhancing human analytical capacity and addressing limitations in traditional models. This study reviews 41 research articles published between 2010 and 2025 across IEEE Xplore, ScienceDirect, Emerald, ACM Digital Library, and Scopus to examine AI's role in improving organizational decision-making. Findings show that AI boosts efficiency by rapidly processing large datasets, automating routine tasks, and delivering real-time and predictive insights. Compared to conventional methods, AI enables faster responses and more accurate forecasting. However, challenges such as data quality, high implementation costs, and limited skilled personnel remain. Overall, integrating AI into decision-making processes offers significant advantages and strengthens organizational competitiveness in a data-driven environment.

INTRODUCTION

In today's data-driven world, where information volumes are growing exponentially and competitive pressures are intensifying, traditional decision-making methods that rely heavily on human intuition and manual analysis are increasingly

DOI: 10.4018/979-8-3373-3648-0.ch004

inadequate (Rahmani et al., 2024, Zong & Guan, 2025). Artificial Intelligence (AI) offers a transformative solution, fundamentally reshaping business intelligence (BI) by enhancing the quality of decisions, accelerating data analysis, and enabling a sharper strategic vision (Qu et al., 2025). Beyond automating routine tasks, AI revolutionizes decision-making itself, allowing organizations to leverage big data in ways previously unimaginable (Jiang, Nazarudin, & Mazalan, 2024). Predictive and prescriptive analytics empower businesses to anticipate market trends, customer behaviors, and operational challenges, providing a significant competitive advantage (Badmus et al., 2024, Nyoni, 2025). AI insights should be used to improve and customise bespoke marketing strategies in order to sustain and boost client satisfaction and loyalty (Shodeinde & Abah, 2025). By generating analytically driven insights that complement human judgment and contextual understanding, AI improves both the speed and accuracy of decisions, creating a symbiotic relationship between humans and technology (Arumugam & Manida, 2024, Badmus et al., 2024). This integration allows organizations to uncover patterns beyond human perception, respond rapidly to emerging opportunities, and develop more effective, timely, and strategically aligned business plans (Ugwa, 2023). Ultimately, the adoption of AI represents a fundamental evolution of business intelligence, transforming decision-making into a faster, more precise, and strategically informed process that drives superior organizational performance (Arumugam & Manida, 2024, Ugwa, 2023).

RESEARCH OBJECTIVE

RO1: To assess the potential competitive advantages that AI-driven decision-making can provide to organisations.
RO2: To identify and analyse the challenges and conditions that influence the successful adoption of AI in corporate decision-making.
RO3: To evaluate how AI-driven decision-making improves the speed and accuracy of decisions compared to traditional methods.

LITERATURE REVIEW

AI and Business Intelligence

Artificial Intelligence (AI) has emerged as a vital component of the modern business environment, particularly in enhancing the quality and efficiency of decision-making processes (Ahmed et al., 2025; Bharadiya, 2023; Goswami, 2020; Vacik & Lexer, 2014; Al-Debei & Avison, 2010). Business Intelligence (BI) has evolved significantly with the integration of AI, allowing for more advanced and dynamic data analysis compared to traditional methods (Ahmed et al., 2025; Klumpp, 2018). Conventional BI systems rely on pre-defined, static reports and manual analysis, which often limit their speed, scalability, and depth of insight (Ahmed et al., 2025; Goswami, 2020). In contrast, AI-driven BI systems utilize sophisticated algorithms and machine learning models to analyse vast datasets in real time, enabling organizations to detect hidden patterns, trends, and correlations that would otherwise remain unnoticed (Zamil, 2025; Bharadiya, 2023; Olszak, 2016; Vacik & Lexer, 2014). Advanced technologies, such as natural language processing (NLP) and predictive analytics, further enhance these capabilities by allowing systems to interpret human language, generate automated insights, and forecast future outcomes based on historical data (Zamil, 2025; Al-Debei & Avison, 2010). Predictive analytics, for example, supports strategic management by providing reliable projections that inform planning and resource allocation. Moreover, AI automates labour-intensive tasks such as data cleaning and report generation, thereby improving operational efficiency and freeing up valuable time for business users to focus on strategic decision-making (Zamil, 2025; Bharadiya, 2023; Goswami, 2020; Olszak, 2016). The incorporation of AI into BI systems is fundamentally transforming how organizations manage information, interpret complex datasets, and make informed decisions (Ahmed et al., 2025; Bharadiya, 2023; Goswami, 2020; Olszak, 2016). This literature review, therefore, explores the competitive advantages offered by AI-driven decision-making, its diverse applications across industries, the challenges associated with AI adoption, and the comparative efficiency of AI-based decision-making processes relative to traditional approaches (Zamil, 2025; Bharadiya, 2023; Klumpp, 2018; Vacik & Lexer, 2014).

Benefits of AI Integration in Decision Making

The integration of Artificial Intelligence (AI) into organizational decision-making provides a range of competitive advantages, including enhanced data processing, automation, real-time insights, and predictive analysis (Islam et al., 2025; Badmus et al., 2024; Wijesekara et al., 2020; Azhar, 2015; Fleisher & Wright, 2010). AI systems can process and analyze vast volumes of data with exceptional speed and accuracy, giving decision-makers timely, reliable, and actionable information (Islam et al., 2025; Badmus et al., 2024; Wijesekara et al., 2020; Azhar, 2015). This ability to integrate and interpret data from multiple sources is particularly valuable in dynamic environments, where timely and accurate decisions are essential. By automating repetitive and routine tasks, AI improves efficiency, productivity, and data quality, while allowing employees to focus on strategic and creative functions that generate greater organizational value (Badmus et al., 2024; Azhar, 2015). AI may evaluate datasets to provide feedback and direction, allowing staff members to improve their performance (Subramanian & Riya, 2024). AI further strengthens business operations, especially in areas such as supply chain management, where it reduces costs and enhances responsiveness. Its real-time analytical capabilities enable organizations to identify risks and opportunities swiftly, reinforcing their competitive position (Islam et al., 2025; Badmus et al., 2024; Wijesekara et al., 2020; Fleisher & Wright, 2010). Moreover, AI's predictive analytics, supported by machine learning (ML) and natural language processing (NLP), enable the detection of emerging patterns, anticipation of market trends, and deeper understanding of customer behavior, leading to more informed, agile, and proactive strategic decisions (Islam et al., 2025; Badmus et al., 2024; Wijesekara et al., 2020).

Applications of Artificial Intelligence Across Industries

The adoption of Artificial Intelligence (AI) across various industries has transformed how organizations manage operations, optimize efficiency, and enhance decision-making. In the financial sector, AI plays a significant role in three main areas: financial management, file management, and information management (Revathy et al., 2023; Machireddy et al., 2021; Eboigbe et al., 2023; Pentyala, 2018). In financial management, AI enhances organizational efficiency by automating complex analytical tasks that exceed human cognitive capacity, such as large-scale data processing and precise financial forecasting. This reduces the risk of human error and improves overall productivity (Revathy et al., 2023; Machireddy et al., 2021). In file management, AI systems support high-capacity operations including data collection, classification, appraisal, storage, cataloguing, retrieval, statistical analysis, and information utilization, which streamlines administrative processes and improves accessibility. Similarly, in information management, AI enables automated sorting and distribution of relevant data, allowing enterprises to optimize production schedules and allocate resources efficiently, resulting in time savings and improved operational performance (Revathy et al., 2023; Machireddy et al., 2021; Pentyala, 2018). In logistics and supply chain management, AI combined with machine learning (ML) algorithms improves inventory control and transportation efficiency (Selvarajan, 2023). AI-driven inventory automation considers factors such as seasonal demand fluctuations, supplier lead times, and market trends to maintain optimal stock levels while reducing storage and transportation costs (Eboigbe et al., 2023; Machireddy et al., 2021; Pentyala, 2018). Moreover, AI optimizes delivery routes by analysing real-time data on traffic, weather, and delivery schedules, which leads to lower fuel consumption, reduced delays, and better resource utilization. AI tools also evaluate supplier performance and risk, supporting data-driven decision-making and strengthening supply chain resilience and efficiency (Selvarajan, 2023;

Machireddy et al., 2021; Pentyala, 2018). In the healthcare sector, AI has become an essential technology, particularly during the COVID-19 pandemic, when it was used alongside the Internet of Things (IoT) and big data analytics to support healthcare delivery and resource management (Vettriselvan, 2025; Ghatge & Parasar, 2023; Eboigbe et al., 2023). AI-enabled systems facilitated contact tracing, predictive modelling, and intelligent allocation of medical resources, creating a collaborative ecosystem that connected healthcare providers, policymakers, and technology firms to address public health challenges (Vettriselvan, 2025; Ghatge & Parasar, 2023). Beyond pandemic management, AI continues to enhance efficiency in healthcare by improving resource allocation, reducing costs, and optimizing staffing (Vettriselvan, 2025; Ghatge & Parasar, 2023; Pentyala, 2018). Advanced technologies such as AI-assisted diagnostics, 3D imaging, and robotic surgery have improved the precision, safety, and quality of medical services, contributing to better patient outcomes and providing healthcare institutions with a competitive advantage (Vettriselvan, 2025).

Challenges Faced in Adopting Artificial Intelligence

Despite its transformative potential, the adoption of Artificial Intelligence (AI) in business organizations presents several significant challenges. One of the most prominent barriers is the high cost associated with implementing AI technologies, which poses difficulties for small and medium-sized enterprises (Maiti et al., 2025; Sipola et al., 2023; Rodriguez-Rodriguez et al., 2021; Ndiaye et al., 2020). The substantial capital investment required for the development, deployment, and ongoing maintenance of AI systems, as well as the continuous training of models, can strain financial resources (Maiti et al., 2025; Wang et al., 2021; Rodriguez-Rodriguez et al., 2021). This challenge is to recruit and retain skilled professionals with expertise in AI, data science, and machine learning skills that are often scarce, particularly in non-technology sectors. Another important challenge lies in the complexity of AI systems themselves (Maiti et al., 2025; Wang et al., 2021). Developing, training, and maintaining AI models require advanced technical knowledge and a deep understanding of both the technology and its application within specific business contexts (Horani et al., 2025; Wang et al., 2021; Ndiaye et al., 2020). Many organizations struggle to bridge this expertise gap, which limits their ability to fully integrate AI into their decision-making processes. In addition, the introduction of AI often necessitates significant changes to organizational structures, workflows, and cultures (Horani et al., 2025; Ndiaye et al., 2020). Such transformations may face internal resistance from employees who perceive AI as a threat to job security or are hesitant to adapt to new systems and processes. Ethical considerations also play a significant role in shaping AI adoption. Issues related to data privacy, algorithmic bias, and transparency managed to ensure fairness, accountability, and trust in AI-driven decisions (Maiti et al., 2025; Sipola et al., 2023; Wang et al., 2021). The development of ethical and responsible AI frameworks requires both time and investment, and failure to address these concerns can undermine the credibility and acceptance of AI applications. As a result, organizations may adopt a cautious approach or limit the use of AI in areas where biased or opaque decision-making could lead to reputational or legal risks (Maiti et al., 2025; Sipola et al., 2023; Wang et al., 2021).

Impact of Artificial Intelligence on Decision-Making Processes

The integration of Artificial Intelligence (AI) into business intelligence systems has significantly enhanced organizational decision-making by replacing the slow and labour-intensive processes of traditional data collection and analysis (Kumar & Ratten, 2025; Alsheibani et al., 2020; Quasim & Chattopadhyay, 2015). AI enables rapid data processing through advanced algorithms capable of analysing large and complex datasets beyond human capability (Kumar & Ratten, 2025; Alsheibani et al., 2020). This not only accelerates the speed of decision-making but also improves its accuracy and reliability by revealing intricate patterns, correlations, and dependencies that are often overlooked through manual analysis. As a result, managers are equipped with deeper insights that lead to more informed and strategic decisions (Kokina et al., 2025; Alsheibani et al., 2020; Quasim & Chattopadhyay, 2015). AI also contributes to organizational flexibility by enabling continuous learning and adaptation to current information. Its ability to analyse evolving market conditions and changing consumer behavior allows organizations to adjust their strategies quickly, thereby improving competitiveness (Mabrouk, 2025; Kar & Kushwaha, 2023). Furthermore, AI's predictive capabilities enhance proactive management by allowing businesses to forecast trends, identify potential risks, and seize emerging opportunities before they materialize (Kokina et al., 2025; Alsheibani et al., 2020). This shift from reactive to proactive decision-making strengthens an organization's strategic position in dynamic markets. However, the effectiveness of AI-driven decision-making depends on the quality and relevance of the data used. Inaccurate, incomplete, or biased data can distort analytical outcomes and lead to misguided decisions (Mabrouk, 2025; Kar & Kushwaha, 2023; Alsheibani et al., 2020; Quasim & Chattopadhyay, 2015). This underscores the importance of robust data management practices that ensure data integrity, consistency, and objectivity. Maintaining high-quality data is therefore essential for maximizing the value of AI systems and ensuring that decision-making processes remain reliable, transparent, and effective (Kokina et al., 2025; Kar & Kushwaha, 2023).

Challenges Faced in Adopting Artificial Intelligence

Although Artificial Intelligence (AI) offers substantial benefits to contemporary organisations, its adoption and implementation continue to present a range of complex challenges (Taherdoost and Madanchian, 2023; Campion et al., 2022). A major obstacle is the significant financial commitment required to acquire, develop, and maintain AI technologies. The expenses associated with specialised hardware, software licences, ongoing system upgrades, and employee training can be particularly burdensome for small and medium-sized enterprises (Jain et al., 2025; Iyelolu et al., 2024; Mahmood et al., 2024; Davenport and Ronanki, 2018).

Alongside financial constraints, organisations must also contend with a persistent shortage of skilled professionals capable of designing, deploying, and managing AI systems effectively (Kar et al., 2021). Recruiting and retaining experts in data science, machine learning, and AI model development is especially challenging for organisations outside the technology sector, often resulting in implementation delays and reduced effectiveness of AI initiatives (Allal-Chérif et al., 2021; Khakifirooz et al., 2024). Successful AI adoption also requires structural and cultural adjustments within organisations. Employees may resist new AI tools due to concerns about job security or uncertainty surrounding advanced technologies, which can hinder smooth integration. Ethical and governance related issues introduce further complexity (Ivchyk, 2024; Yadava, 2023). Concerns regarding data privacy, algorithmic bias, and transparency can weaken trust in AI driven decision making. Building systems that are both effective and ethically responsible necessitates careful planning, suitable regulatory frameworks, and continuous monitoring to ensure fairness and accountability (Jedlickova, 2024). Organisations that fail to address these ethical challenges risk reputational harm and declining stakeholder confidence (Rayner, 2004). Addressing these challenges requires more than technical expertise and financial investment. It calls for strong leadership, transparent governance, and a well-defined strategy that aligns AI adoption with organisational values and long-term objectives (Suljic, 2025).

METHODOLOGY

This study adopts a qualitative research methodology supported by secondary data analysis to explore the relationship between Artificial Intelligence (AI), Business Intelligence (BI), and organisational decision-making. Qualitative research focuses on collecting non-numerical data to gain an in-depth understanding of complex phenomena (Adedoyin, 2020). It seeks to capture meanings, experiences, and interpretations rather than relying on statistical measurement. In this context, qualitative analysis is employed to examine how organisations utilise AI technologies within their business intelligence systems to improve decision-making processes. This approach facilitates a deeper understanding of the processes, interactions, and implications associated with the integration of AI in business contexts. The qualitative component involves the review and interpretation of existing studies, reports, and case analyses to understand the antecedents and consequences of AI-driven decisions (Saurabh et al., 2022). This approach enables the exploration of contextual factors that influence the successful adoption and application of AI in organisational settings. By analysing the experiences and insights reported in previous research, the study aims to provide a rich and contextual understanding of how AI transforms decision-making practices in modern enterprises. In addition, secondary research methods are employed to examine the effects of AI on BI using data drawn from reputable external sources. Secondary research involves collecting and analysing information that has already been published, such as academic journals, industry reports, conference proceedings, and case studies, rather than generating new data through primary research (Stewart and Kamins, 1993). For this study, sources were selected from peer-reviewed journals, business and financial publications, and credible online databases including IEEE Xplore, ScienceDirect, Emerald, ACM Digital Library, and Scopus. Literature published between 2010 and 2025 was reviewed to identify relevant trends, patterns, challenges, and opportunities related to AI in business intelligence. This combined methodological approach provides a comprehensive understanding of how AI is influencing business intelligence and decision-making. It enables the identification of emerging trends and challenges while offering insights into best practices and strategic implications for organisations seeking to enhance their decision-making capabilities through AI-driven systems.

FINDINGS

Benefits and Competitive Advantages of AI-Driven Decision-Making

Enhanced Data Processing and Analysis

Artificial Intelligence (AI) systems, particularly those supported by big data analytics, enable organisations to process large volumes of information rapidly and accurately while generating insights that enhance informed decision-making (Ojeda et al., 2025; Nesterov, 2024; Selvarajan, 2021). Unlike traditional analytical methods that rely on static tools, AI employs advanced algorithms, machine learning techniques, and natural language processing (NLP) to identify complex patterns within datasets (Uddin, 2024; Ghavami, 2019; Wong et al., 2014). These capabilities contribute to improved strategic management, enhanced organisational performance, and greater operational efficiency (Ochuba et al., 2024). In practical contexts such as supply chain management, AI accelerates information processing, increases accuracy, and supports cost reductions and productivity improvements (Odumbo and Nimma, 2025; Alonge et al., 2023; Shoushtari et al., 2021).

Automation of Routine Tasks

AI enhances organisational productivity by automating repetitive processes such as data entry, data cleaning, and report generation (Akeiber, 2025; Ojika et al., 2022; Suri, 2022). This automation enables employees to concentrate on strategic and creative tasks that add greater value to the organisation while also reducing human errors and operational costs (Akeiber, 2025; Tyagi et al., 2020). In the financial sector, AI automates transaction analysis and fraud detection, improving both accuracy and efficiency (Benbya et al., 2020). In manufacturing, AI supports automated quality control to streamline production, and in tourism and hospitality, AI-based chatbots and virtual assistants enhance communication and reduce staff workload (Ojika et al., 2022; Benbya et al., 2020).

Real-Time Decision Making

AI allows organisations to make decisions using data generated in real time (Boppiniti, 2021; Selvarajan, 2021). This capability is especially important in industries that require rapid responses, such as finance, logistics, and e-commerce (Holloway, 2024; Ravichandran et al., 2022). For instance, some airlines use AI-based data platforms to adjust pricing dynamically and react to operational changes within minutes rather than hours (Singh, 2025). This level of responsiveness enhances customer satisfaction, operational agility, and competitiveness in fast-changing environments (Holloway, 2024; et al., 2022).

Predictive Analytics

AI-driven predictive analytics helps organisations anticipate market trends, forecast demand, and understand customer behaviour (Ramya et al., 2024; Achumie et al., 2022; Celestin and Vanitha, 2018). By applying machine learning models, businesses can enhance demand forecasting, minimise inventory errors, and manage risks more effectively (Pasupuleti et al., 2024; Pereira et al., 2022; Hofmann and Rutschmann, 2018). In the retail sector, AI supports more accurate supply chain and marketing decisions, contributing to higher customer satisfaction and improved sales performance (Muthukalyani, 2023; Kalisetty and Ganti, 2019). It also strengthens risk management by modelling various scenarios and enabling organisations to develop proactive strategies for addressing potential challenges (Pereira et al., 2022; Kalisetty and Ganti, 2019).

Personalisation and Customer Insights

AI's ability to analyse both structured and unstructured data enables organisations to gain deeper insights into customer preferences and behaviours (Nkomo and Mupa, 2024; Orji et al., 2024; Das, 2023). Through advanced segmentation and behavioural modelling, AI supports personalisation strategies that enhance customer experience and strengthen brand loyalty (Sashi, 2021; Abdullah and Hasan, 2023; Bano et al., 2025). By tailoring products, services, and communications to individual needs, businesses can foster stronger customer engagement (Sashi, 2021). In the hospitality sector, AI further enhances the guest experience through technologies such as virtual concierge services, smart room automation, and language translation systems designed to support international visitors (Orji et al., 2024; Das, 2023).

Challenges and Conditions Affecting the Successful of AI Adoption in Organisation

Data Quality and Availability

AI systems function effectively only when they are supported by accurate, consistent, and relevant data. Poor or incomplete data can lead to flawed models and incorrect conclusions, ultimately reducing the reliability of AI-driven decisions (Zong and Guan, 2025; Gadde, 2024; Tekale, 2023). Many organisations continue to face challenges related to data fragmentation, lack of integration, and inconsistent data collection practices across departments (Adepoju et al., 2023; Hassan et al., 2020). Addressing these issues requires strong data governance frameworks that incorporate regular data audits, cleaning, and validation processes (Zong and Guan, 2025; Sargiotis, 2024). Building a culture that values data accuracy, alongside investing in robust data infrastructure, ensures that AI systems have access to reliable and high-quality data sources, thereby supporting more effective decision-making (Maharjan, 2023; Neupane, 2024).

High Implementation Costs

The financial burden of adopting AI remains a major obstacle, particularly for small and medium-sized enterprises (Anwar et al., 2025; Yusuf et al., 2024). Costs extend beyond system acquisition and include expenses for maintenance, software updates, cybersecurity, and employee training (Zhang et al., 2021; Krishan, 2018). In many cases, organisations also face hidden costs in customising AI solutions and integrating them with legacy systems (Arora, 2025; Yathiraju, 2022). To manage these challenges, companies can begin with small-scale pilot projects to assess the return on investment before expanding implementation (Kuguoglu et al., 2021; Zhang et al., 2021). Leveraging cloud-based AI tools and forming partnerships with technology providers can also reduce upfront expenses while allowing access to advanced capabilities (Yusuf et al., 2024; Kuguoglu et al., 2021).

Need for Specialised Technical Expertise

A major barrier to AI adoption is the shortage of professionals with specialised knowledge in areas such as data science, machine learning, and AI system management (Ivchyk, 2024; Kar et al., 2021; Singh et al., 2020). The rapid pace of AI development means that many existing training programs and education systems struggle to keep up with industry demand (Booyse and Scheepers, 2024; Hu et al., 2022). As a result, many organisations rely on external consultants, which can be costly and may limit the development of internal capabilities (Hu et al., 2022). To address this skills gap, organisations should prioritise employee training, continuous professional development, and collaboration with academic institutions (Arthur-Mensah, 2020). Encouraging cross-functional teams that integrate technical expertise with business knowledge also helps ensure that AI initiatives are aligned with strategic organisational goals (Roberts, 2020).

Ethical and Regulatory Concerns

The integration of AI raises important ethical and legal challenges related to data privacy, transparency, and algorithmic fairness (Radanliev, 2025). AI systems often depend on large volumes of personal or sensitive information, making strict compliance with data protection laws essential (Kumar and Suthar, 2024). Concerns about algorithmic bias are also increasing, particularly when training data fails to represent diverse populations, resulting in unfair or discriminatory outcomes (Zharova, 2023). To address these issues, organisations must ensure that their AI systems are explainable and transparent so that users can understand how decisions are generated (Patidar et al., 2024). Establishing ethical guidelines, adopting privacy-enhancing technologies, and conducting regular audits all contribute to maintaining compliance and fostering public trust in AI applications (Balasubramaniam et al., 2023).

Trust in AI Systems

Earning and maintaining trust in AI is critical for its successful adoption (McElheran et al., 2024). People are often hesitant to rely on AI tools due to concerns about bias, errors, and a lack of transparency (Miller et al., 2024; Schmidt et al., 2020). High-profile failures, such as incidents involving autonomous vehicles or flawed recruitment systems, have further increased public scepticism (Miller et al., 2024). Building trust requires ensuring that AI systems are explainable, reliable, and grounded in evidence-based decision-making frameworks (Miller et al., 2024; Matta and Bolli, 2023). In sensitive sectors such as healthcare, transparent AI models that provide clear reasoning and validation are essential for improving user confidence and acceptance (Miller et al., 2024).

Organisational Resistance

AI adoption often triggers internal resistance due to fears of job loss, changes in work roles, and uncertainty about the impact of new technologies (Ivchyk, 2024; Manning, 2024). Employees may view AI as a threat rather than a tool for improvement, which can lead to reluctance or opposition (Ivchyk, 2024; Slosberg et al., 2018). Addressing this challenge requires clear communication about the benefits of AI and its potential to enhance, rather than replace, human capabilities (Rane, 2023). Providing training opportunities, involving employees in the implementation process, and offering support during periods of transition can help reduce anxiety (Slosberg et al., 2018). Strong leadership commitment is crucial for fostering a culture that embraces innovation and ensures AI adoption aligns with organisational goals and human collaboration (Rozman et al., 2023).

Ways of AI on Decision Speed and Accuracy Compared to Traditional Methods

This research examines how Artificial Intelligence (AI) enhances the speed and accuracy of corporate decision-making compared to traditional methods. Conventional approaches often rely on manual data analysis and human intuition, which can be slow and prone to errors. In contrast, AI offers a transformative approach that accelerates and refines decision-making processes. The following highlights the keyways AI improves both decision speed and accuracy.

Consistency and Replicability

AI systems provide consistent and replicable results by relying on structured algorithms and established data patterns (Shin, 2023; Shrestha et al., 2019). Unlike human decision-makers, who may be influenced by emotions, fatigue, or cognitive biases, AI maintains uniformity in its outcomes (Leonidas et al., 2025; Jyothi, Rajashree, Phani, Hugar, Shaik, and Poddar, 2025; Rastogi et al., 2022). Traditional methods are often vulnerable to human factors that can lead to inconsistent or delayed decisions (Mosier and Skitka, 2018). Research in cognitive psychology further highlights that overthinking and mental fatigue can reduce decision quality, whereas AI systems remain unaffected, ensuring reliable and timely outcomes (Shalaby, 2024).

Enhanced Data Analysis

AI enables rapid and precise analysis of vast and complex datasets that would take humans significantly longer to process (Patil and Shankar, 2023; Ravichandran et al., 2022). In agriculture, AI integrated with IoT and Big Data can analyse soil, weather, and crop information in real time, supporting faster and more evidence-based decision-making (Chukwuma et al., 2024). In smart city governance, AI systems can process live traffic data from multiple sources, enabling more efficient infrastructure planning and public service delivery compared with traditional monitoring methods (Mohanty et al., 2025; Van Hoang, 2024). Similarly, in corporate environments, AI tools evaluate market, operational, and customer data to identify trends, anticipate risks, and guide strategic decision-making, thereby improving both efficiency and accuracy (Oluoha et al., 2022).

Automated Decision-Making

Automation through AI allows organisations to make decisions more quickly by reducing reliance on human input (Booyse and Scheepers, 2024). AI systems can process information, generate insights, and recommend actions autonomously, which helps eliminate human bias and minimise errors (Schwartz et al., 2022). Applications such as automated reporting, performance monitoring, and risk assessment support faster, data-driven decision-making (Beckley, 2025). This not only accelerates organisational processes but also improves accuracy, as AI can consistently analyse data without the subjectivity inherent in human judgement (Sarker, 2021).

Leveraging Machine Learning Algorithms

Machine learning (ML) algorithms further enhance decision speed and precision by detecting patterns and trends that are often imperceptible to humans (Sarker, 2021). ML continuously learns from new data, which improves predictive accuracy over time (Hatta et al., 2024). When combined with technologies such as natural language processing and computer vision, AI can analyse both structured and unstructured data to support strategic and operational decision-making across multiple sectors (Selvarajan, 2021). This capability enables organisations to respond swiftly to market changes, optimise operations, and improve overall business performance (Ojeda et al., 2025).

CONCLUSION

This paper underscores the transformative impact of AI-driven decision-making on organisational performance, competitiveness, and operational efficiency. AI leverages advanced algorithms, machine learning, and natural language processing to enhance data processing and analysis, enabling organisations to achieve strategic goals with greater accuracy and speed compared to traditional methods. The automation of routine tasks further amplifies efficiency by reducing human intervention in repetitive activities, allowing organisations to focus on higher-value and strategic objectives. Real-time decision-making provided by AI adds significant value, particularly in industries that require immediate responsiveness, such as finance, logistics, and e-commerce. Companies like Malaysia Airlines have adopted AI-driven platforms to implement agile and adaptive strategies, demonstrating how AI supports timely and effective decision-making. Predictive analytics also empower organisations to anticipate market trends, forecast customer behaviour, and make more informed and accurate decisions, particularly in retail, supply chain management, and risk assessment contexts.

Furthermore, AI's ability to analyse both structured and unstructured data facilitates personalised insights, enhancing customer satisfaction and enabling tailored experiences in customer interactions. Despite these benefits, successful AI adoption depends on data quality and availability, as unreliable or incomplete data can compromise model accuracy. For SMEs, high implementation costs and the need for specialised expertise present additional challenges. Organisations must also address transparency, accountability, and ethical considerations to build trust in AI systems, particularly in sensitive domains such as healthcare. Overcoming organisational resistance through effective change management is crucial to ensure smooth integration and adoption of AI technologies. AI improves decision-making speed and accuracy by mitigating human cognitive biases and providing consistent, data-driven results. Machine learning algorithms and automated processes allow organisations to efficiently analyse large datasets, generate actionable insights in real time, and make faster, more precise, and informed decisions. Overall, AI-driven decision-making serves as a critical enabler for organisational competitiveness, operational excellence, and sustainable strategic advantage.

ACKNOWLEDGEMENT

The author sincerely acknowledges the support received during the preparation of this article. No external funding was received for this research, and the author declares that there are no conflicts of interest related to the research, authorship, or publication of this work. The author also thanks those who provided technical assistance and writing support during the development of the manuscript and expresses appreciation to researchers for their general academic and institutional support. The author confirms that all sources cited in the text are fully and accurately listed in the reference section in accordance with APA guidelines.

REFERENCES

Achumie, G. O., Oyegbade, I. K., Igwe, A. N., Ofodile, O. C., & Azubuike, C. (2022). *AI-driven predictive analytics model for strategic business development and market growth in competitive industries*. J Bus Innov Technol Res. DOI: 10.54660/IJSSER.2022.1.1.13-25

Adedoyin, O. B. (2020). Qualitative research methods. Principles of social psychiatry, 77-87.

Adepoju, A. H., Austin-Gabriel, B., Eweje, A., & Hamza, O. (2023). A data governance framework for high-impact programs: Reducing redundancy and enhancing data quality at scale. *International Journal of Multidisciplinary Research and Growth Evaluation*, *4*(6), 1141–1154. DOI: 10.54660/.IJMRGE.2023.4.6.1141-1154

Ahmed, F., Ahmed, M. R., Kabir, M. A., & Islam, M. M. (2025). Revolutionizing Business Analytics: The Impact of Artificial Intelligence and Machine Learning. *American Journal of Advanced Technology and Engineering Solutions*, *1*(01), 147–173. DOI: 10.63125/f7yjxw69

Akeiber, H. J. (2025). Artificial Intelligence in Engineering Management: Revolutionizing Decision-Making and Automation. Al-Rafidain Journal of Engineering Sciences, 317-349.

Al-Debei, M. M., & Avison, D. (2010). Developing a unified framework of the business model concept. *European Journal of Information Systems*, *19*(3), 359–376. DOI: 10.1057/ejis.2010.21

Allal-Chérif, O., Aránega, A. Y., & Sánchez, R. C. (2021). Intelligent recruitment: How to identify, select, and retain talents from around the world using artificial intelligence. *Technological Forecasting and Social Change*, *169*, 120822. DOI: 10.1016/j.techfore.2021.120822

Alonge, E. O., Eyo-Udo, N. L., Ubanadu, B. C., Daraojimba, A. I., Balogun, E. D., & Ogunsola, K. O. (2023). Real-time data analytics for enhancing supply chain efficiency. *Journal of Supply Chain Management and Analytics*, *10*(1), 49–60.

Alsheibani, S. A., Cheung, Y., Messom, C. H., & Alhosni, M. (2020, August). Winning AI strategy: Six steps to create value from artificial intelligence. *Proceedings of the Americas Conference on Information Systems (AMCIS)*, 11.

Anwar, M., Korthaus, A., Bingley, S., & Burgess, S. (2025). AI in small businesses: Current and potential applications and issues for adoption. In *Cutting-Edge Technologies for Business Sectors* (pp. 29–56). IGI Global.

Arthur-Mensah, N. (2020). Bridging the industry–education skills gap for human resource development. *Industrial and Commercial Training*, *52*(2), 93–103. DOI: 10.1108/ICT-11-2019-0105

Arumugam, U., & Manida, M. (2024). Enhancing Strategic Decision Making: Assessing the Role and Impact of Artificial Intelligence in Business Management. *Journal of Business Analytics and Data Visualization (e-ISSN: 2584-1637)*, 1-8.

Azhar, I. (2015). The interaction between artificial intelligence and identity & access management: An empirical study. International Journal of Creative Research Thoughts (IJCRT), ISSN 2320-2882.

Badmus, O., Rajput, S., Arogundade, J., & Williams, M. (2024). AI-driven business analytics and decision making. *World Journal of Advanced Research and Reviews*, *24*(1), 616–633. DOI: 10.30574/wjarr.2024.24.1.3093

Balasubramaniam, N., Kauppinen, M., Rannisto, A., Hiekkanen, K., & Kujala, S. (2023). Transparency and explainability of AI systems: From ethical guidelines to requirements. *Information and Software Technology*, *159*, 107197. DOI: 10.1016/j.infsof.2023.107197

Bano, R., Azim, F., Mahmood, Z., Sanaullah, A., & Ali, O. (2025). The Role of Artificial Intelligence in Personalized Marketing: Enhancing Customer Experience, Predictive Targeting, and Brand Engagement. *The Critical Review of Social Sciences Studies*, *3*(2), 50–65. DOI: 10.59075/d94kvf44

Benbya, H., Davenport, T. H., & Pachidi, S. (2020). Artificial intelligence in organizations: Current state and future opportunities. *MIS Quarterly Executive*, *19*(4).

Bharadiya, J. (2023). The impact of artificial intelligence on business processes. European journal of technology, 7(2), 15-25.

Booyse, D., & Scheepers, C. B. (2024). Barriers to adopting automated organisational decision-making through the use of artificial intelligence. *Management Research Review, 47*(1), 64–85. DOI: 10.1108/MRR-09-2021-0701

Boppiniti, S. T. (2021). Real-time data analytics with ai: Leveraging stream processing for dynamic decision support. *International Journal of Management Education for Sustainable Development, 4*(4), 1–27.

Campion, A., Gasco-Hernandez, M., Jankin Mikhaylov, S., & Esteve, M. (2022). Overcoming the challenges of collaboratively adopting artificial intelligence in the public sector. *Social Science Computer Review, 40*(2), 462–477. DOI: 10.1177/0894439320979953

Celestin, M., & Vanitha, N. (2018). AI-Powered Entrepreneurship: The Tools That Will Shape Tomorrow's Startups. [IJATET]. *International Journal of Advanced Trends in Engineering and Technology, 3*(2), 29–35.

Chukwuma, U., Gebremedhin, K. G., & Uyeh, D. D. (2024). Imagining AI-driven decision making for managing farming in developing and emerging economies. *Computers and Electronics in Agriculture, 221*, 108946. DOI: 10.1016/j.compag.2024.108946

Das, M. P. (2023). Technology and Guest experience: Innovations reshaping hotel management. *International Journal for Multidimensional Research Perspectives, 1*(3), 76–95.

Davenport, T. H., & Ronanki, R. (2018). Artificial intelligence for the real world. *Harvard Business Review, 96*(1), 108–116.

Eboigbe, E. O., Farayola, O. A., Olatoye, F. O., Nnabugwu, O. C., & Daraojimba, C. (2023). Business intelligence transformation through AI and data analytics. *Engineering Science & Technology Journal, 4*(5), 285–307. DOI: 10.51594/estj.v4i5.616

Fleisher, C. S., & Wright, S. (2010). Competitive Intelligence analysis failure: Diagnosing individual level causes and implementing organisational level remedies. *Journal of Strategic Marketing, 18*(7), 553–572. DOI: 10.1080/0965254X.2010.529152

Gadde, H. (2024). AI-Powered Fault Detection and Recovery in High-Availability Databases. *International Journal of Machine Learning Research in Cybersecurity and Artificial Intelligence, 15*(1), 500–529.

Ghatge, S. K., & Parasar, A. (2023). Application of artificial intelligence (AI), internet of things (IoT), and big data in healthcare, finance, and transportation. *PriMera Scientific Medicine and Public Health*, *2*, 27–36.

Ghavami, P. (2019). *Big data analytics methods: analytics techniques in data mining, deep learning and natural language processing*. Walter de Gruyter GmbH & Co KG. DOI: 10.1515/9781547401567

Goswami, M. (2020). Leveraging AI for cost efficiency and optimized cloud resource management. *International Journal of New Media Studies: International Peer Reviewed Scholarly Indexed Journal*, *7*(1), 21–27.

Hassan, N. H. M., Ahmad, K., & Salehuddin, H. (2020). Diagnosing the issues and challenges in data integration implementation in public sector. *International Journal on Advanced Science, Engineering and Information Technology*, *10*(2), 529–535. DOI: 10.18517/ijaseit.10.2.10271

Hatta, M., Wahid, W. N., Yusuf, F., Hidayat, F., Santoso, N. A., & Aini, Q. (2024). Enhancing predictive models in system development using machine learning algorithms. *International Journal of Cyber and IT Service Management*, *4*(2), 80–87. DOI: 10.34306/ijcitsm.v4i2.159

Hofmann, E., & Rutschmann, E. (2018). Big data analytics and demand forecasting in supply chains: A conceptual analysis. *International Journal of Logistics Management*, *29*(2), 739–766. DOI: 10.1108/IJLM-04-2017-0088

Holloway, S. (2024). The Role of Supply Chain Flexibility in Adapting Marketing Strategies to Changing Consumer Preferences.

Horani, O. M., Al-Adwan, A. S., Yaseen, H., Hmoud, H., Al-Rahmi, W. M., & Alkhalifah, A. (2025). The critical determinants impacting artificial intelligence adoption at the organizational level. *Information Development*, *41*(3), 1055–1079. DOI: 10.1177/02666669231166889

Hu, Y., Liu, M., Le, Y., & Skitmore, M. (2022). External consultant involvement for organizational capability building in complex construction projects: A perspective from interorganizational learning process. *Journal of Construction Engineering and Management*, *148*(1), 04021181. DOI: 10.1061/(ASCE)CO.1943-7862.0002216

Islam, M. M., Desai, K., Rabbani, M. M., Ahmad, S., & Snigdha, E. Z. (2025). AI-Powered Business Intelligence in IT: Transforming Data into Strategic Solutions for Enhanced Decision-Making. *The American Journal of Engineering and Technology*, *7*(02), 59–73. DOI: 10.37547/tajet/Volume07Issue02-09

Ivchyk, V. (2024). Overcoming barriers to artificial intelligence adoption. *Three Seas Economic Journal*, *5*(4), 14–20. DOI: 10.30525/2661-5150/2024-4-3

Iyelolu, T. V., Agu, E. E., Idemudia, C., & Ijomah, T. I. (2024). Driving SME innovation with AI solutions: overcoming adoption barriers and future growth opportunities. International Journal of Science and Technology Research Archive, 7(1), 036-054.

Jain, A., Kakade, K. S., & Vispute, S. A. (2025). The Role of Artificial Intelligence (AI) in the Transformation of Small-and Medium-Sized Businesses: Challenges and Opportunities. Artificial Intelligence-Enabled Businesses: How to Develop Strategies for Innovation, 209-226.

Jedlickova, A. (2024). Ensuring ethical standards in the development of autonomous and intelligent systems. *IEEE Transactions on Artificial Intelligence*, *5*(12), 5863–5872. DOI: 10.1109/TAI.2024.3387403

Jiang, W., Nazarudin, M. N. B., & Mazalan, N. S. (2024). Enhancing safety and quality in college sports management through big data and artificial intelligence (AI). *Journal of Information Systems Engineering & Management*, *9*(3), 24782. DOI: 10.55267/iadt.07.14849

Jyothi, V. E., Rajashree, R., Phani, S., Hugar, L., Shaik, R., & Poddar, S. (2025). Artificial intelligence-powered protocols for enhancing security in next-generation communication networks. In *Proceedings of the 3rd International Conference on Intelligent Cyber Physical Systems and Internet of Things (ICoICI)* (pp. 1107–1112). IEEE. DOI: 10.1109/ICoICI65217.2025.11252990

Kalisetty, S., & Ganti, V. K. A. T. (2019). Transforming the Retail Landscape: Srinivas's Vision for Integrating Advanced Technologies in Supply Chain Efficiency and Customer Experience. *Online Journal of Materials Science*, *1*(1), 1254. DOI: 10.31586/materials.2019.1254

Kar, A. K., & Kushwaha, A. K. (2023). Facilitators and barriers of artificial intelligence adoption in business–insights from opinions using big data analytics. *Information Systems Frontiers*, *25*(4), 1351–1374. DOI: 10.1007/s10796-021-10219-4

Khakifirooz, M., Fathi, M., & Dolgui, A. (2024). Theory of AI-driven scheduling (TAIS): A service-oriented scheduling framework by integrating theory of constraints and AI. *International Journal of Production Research*, •••, 1–35.

Klumpp, M. (2018). Automation and artificial intelligence in business logistics systems: Human reactions and collaboration requirements. *International Journal of Logistics*, *21*(3), 224–242. DOI: 10.1080/13675567.2017.1384451

Kokina, J., Blanchette, S., Davenport, T. H., & Pachamanova, D. (2025). Challenges and opportunities for artificial intelligence in auditing: Evidence from the field. *International Journal of Accounting Information Systems*, *56*, 100734. DOI: 10.1016/j.accinf.2025.100734

Kuguoglu, B. K., van der Voort, H., & Janssen, M. (2021). The giant leap for smart cities: Scaling up smart city artificial intelligence of things (AIoT) initiatives. *Sustainability (Basel)*, *13*(21), 12295. DOI: 10.3390/su132112295

Kumar, D., & Ratten, V. (2025). Artificial intelligence and family businesses: A systematic literature review. *Journal of Family Business Management*, *15*(2), 373–392. DOI: 10.1108/JFBM-08-2024-0160

Kumar, D., & Suthar, N. (2024). Ethical and legal challenges of AI in marketing: An exploration of solutions. Journal of Information. *Communication and Ethics in Society*, *22*(1), 124–144. DOI: 10.1108/JICES-05-2023-0068

Leonidas, T., Alexandra, T., & Constantinos, H. (2025). Cognitive Bias Mitigation in Executive Decision-Making: A Data-Driven Approach Integrating Big Data Analytics, AI, and Explainable Systems. *Electronics (Basel)*, *14*(19), 3930. DOI: 10.3390/electronics14193930

Mabrouk, A. (2025). Human Resouce Management in the Age of Artificial Intelligence: Concepts Tools and Steps. *Solo International Collaboration and Publication of Social Sciences and Humanities*, *3*(01), 1–12. DOI: 10.61455/sicopus.v3i01.216

Machireddy, J. R., Rachakatla, S. K., & Ravichandran, P. (2021). Leveraging AI and machine learning for data-driven business strategy: A comprehensive framework for analytics integration. *African Journal of Artificial Intelligence and Sustainable Development*, *1*(2), 12–150.

Maharjan, P. (2023). The role of artificial intelligence-driven big data analytics in strengthening cybersecurity frameworks for critical infrastructure. *Global Research Perspectives on Cybersecurity Governance, Policy, and Management*, *7*(11), 12–25.

Mahmood, H. S., Abdulqader, D. M., Abdullah, R. M., Rasheed, H., Ismael, Z. N. R., & Sami, T. M. G. (2024). Conducting in-depth analysis of AI, IoT, web technology, cloud computing, and enterprise systems integration for enhancing data security and governance to promote sustainable business practices. *Journal of Information Technology and Informatics*, *3*(2), 297–332.

Maiti, M., Kayal, P., & Vujko, A. (2025). A study on ethical implications of artificial intelligence adoption in business: Challenges and best practices. *Future Business Journal*, *11*(1), 34. DOI: 10.1186/s43093-025-00462-5

Manning, L. (2024). Innovating in an uncertain world: Understanding the social, technical and systemic barriers to farmers adopting new technologies. *Challenges, 15*(2), 32. DOI: 10.3390/challe15020032

Matta, S. S., & Bolli, M. (2023). Trustworthy AI: Explainability & Fairness In Large-Scale Decision Systems. *Review of Applied Science and Technology, 2*(04), 54–93. DOI: 10.63125/3w9v5e52

McElheran, K., Li, J. F., Brynjolfsson, E., Kroff, Z., Dinlersoz, E., Foster, L., & Zolas, N. (2024). AI adoption in America: Who, what, and where. *Journal of Economics & Management Strategy, 33*(2), 375–415. DOI: 10.1111/jems.12576

Miller, T., Durlik, I., Kostecka, E., Borkowski, P., & Łobodzińska, A. (2024). A critical AI view on autonomous vehicle navigation: The growing danger. *Electronics (Basel), 13*(18), 3660. DOI: 10.3390/electronics13183660

Mohanty, A., Mohapatra, A. G., & Mohanty, S. K. (2025). Real-time traffic monitoring with AI in smart cities. In *Internet of Vehicles and Computer Vision Solutions for Smart City Transformations* (pp. 135–165). Springer Nature Switzerland. DOI: 10.1007/978-3-031-72959-1_7

Mosier, K. L., & Skitka, L. J. (2018). Human decision makers and automated decision aids: Made for each other? In *Automation and human performance* (pp. 201–220). CRC Press.

Muthukalyani, A. R. (2023). Unlocking accurate demand forecasting in retail supply chains with AI-driven predictive analytics. *Information Technology Management, 14*(2), 48–57.

Ndiaye, M., Oyewobi, S. S., Abu-Mahfouz, A. M., Hancke, G. P., Kurien, A. M., & Djouani, K. (2020). IoT in the wake of COVID-19: A survey on contributions, challenges and evolution. *IEEE Access : Practical Innovations, Open Solutions, 8*, 186821–186839. DOI: 10.1109/ACCESS.2020.3030090 PMID: 34786294

Nesterov, V. (2024). Optimization of big data processing and analysis processes in the field of data analytics through the integration of data engineering and artificial intelligence. Computer-integrated technologies: education, science, production, (54), 160-164.

Neupane, B. (2024). Artificial Intelligence and Big Data Technologies to Optimize Government Decision-Making Processes in Cloud-Based Environments. *Journal of Artificial Intelligence and Machine Learning in Cloud Computing Systems, 8*(11), 1–12.

Nkomo, N. I. G. E. L., & Mupa, M. N. (2024). The Impact of Artificial Intelligence on Predictive Customer Behaviour Analytics in E-commerce: A Comparative Study of Traditional and AI-driven Models. *Iconic Research and Engineering Journals*, *8*(5), 432–451.

Nyoni, R. (2025). Harnessing Data Analytics for Predictive Insights: Advancing Decision-Making with Big Data Innovations. *Int. J. Res. Publ. Rev*, *6*(1), 2915–2936. DOI: 10.55248/gengpi.6.0125.0502

Ochuba, N. A., Olutimehin, D. O., Odunaiya, O. G., & Soyomb, O. T. (2024). A comprehensive review of strategic management practices in satellite telecommunications, highlighting the role of data analytics in driving operational efficiency and competitive advantage. *World Journal of Advanced Engineering Technology and Sciences*, *11*(2), 201–211. DOI: 10.30574/wjaets.2024.11.2.0099

Odumbo, O. R., & Nimma, S. Z. (2025). Leveraging artificial intelligence to maximize efficiency in supply chain process optimization. *Int J Res Publ Rev*, *6*(1), 3035–3050. DOI: 10.55248/gengpi.6.0125.0508

Ojeda, A. M., Valera, J. B., & Diaz, O. (2025). Artificial intelligence of big data for analysis in organizational decision-making. *Global Journal of Flexible Systems Managment*, *26*(3), 515–527. DOI: 10.1007/s40171-025-00450-2

Ojika, F. U., Owobu, W. O., Abieba, O. A., Esan, O. J., Ubamadu, B. C., & Daraojimba, A. I. (2022). The Role of Artificial Intelligence in Business Process Automation: A Model for Reducing Operational Costs and Enhancing Efficiency.

Olszak, C. M. (2016). Toward better understanding and use of business intelligence in organizations. *Information Systems Management*, *33*(2), 105–123. DOI: 10.1080/10580530.2016.1155946

Oluoha, O., Odeshina, A., Reis, O., Okpeke, F., Attipoe, V., & Orieno, O. (2022). Optimizing business decision-making with advanced data analytics techniques. *Iconic Research and Engineering Journals*, *6*(5), 184–203.

Orji, U., Orji, C. A., & Olagunju, O. D. (2024). Leveraging AI for transformative business development: Strategies for market analysis, customer insights, and competitive intelligence.

Pasupuleti, V., Thuraka, B., Kodete, C. S., & Malisetty, S. (2024). Enhancing supply chain agility and sustainability through machine learning: Optimization techniques for logistics and inventory management. *Logistics (Basel)*, *8*(3), 73. DOI: 10.3390/logistics8030073

Patidar, N., Mishra, S., Jain, R., Prajapati, D., Solanki, A., Suthar, R., ... & Patel, H. (2024). Transparency in AI decision making: A survey of explainable AI methods and applications. Advances of Robotic Technology, 2(1).

Patil, S., & Shankar, H. (2023). Transforming healthcare: Harnessing the power of AI in the modern era. *International Journal of Multidisciplinary Sciences and Arts*, *2*(2), 60–70. DOI: 10.47709/ijmdsa.v2i1.2513

Pentyala, D. K. (2018). AI-Driven Decision-Making for Ensuring Data Reliability in Distributed Cloud Systems. *International Journal of Modern Computing*, *1*(1), 1–22.

Pereira, A. M., Moura, J. A. B., Costa, E. D. B., Vieira, T., Landim, A. R., Bazaki, E., & Wanick, V. (2022). Customer models for artificial intelligence-based decision support in fashion online retail supply chains. *Decision Support Systems*, *158*, 113795. DOI: 10.1016/j.dss.2022.113795

Qu, S., Li, X., Lim, M. K., Liu, W., Li, Z., & Wang, Y. (2025). Smart supply chain management: a systematic literature review and future research agenda. *International Journal of Logistics Research and Applications*, 1-29.

Quasim, M. T., & Chattopadhyay, R. (2015). Artificial intelligence as a business forecasting and error handling tool. *Compusoft*, *4*(2), 1534.

Radanliev, P. (2025). AI ethics: Integrating transparency, fairness, and privacy in AI development. *Applied Artificial Intelligence*, *39*(1), 2463722. DOI: 10.1080/08839514.2025.2463722

Rahmani, S., Aghalar, H., Jebreili, S., & Goli, A. (2024). Optimization and computing using intelligent data-driven approaches for decision-making. In *Optimization and computing using intelligent data-driven approaches for decision-making* (pp. 90–176). CRC Press. DOI: 10.1201/9781003536796-6

Ramya, J., Yerraguravagari, S. S., Gaikwad, S., & Gupta, R. K. (2024). AI and Machine Learning in Predictive Analytics: Revolutionizing Business Strategies through Big Data Insights. Library of Progress-Library Science, Information Technology & Computer, 44(3).

Rane, N. (2023). ChatGPT and similar generative artificial intelligence (AI) for smart industry: role, challenges and opportunities for industry 4.0, industry 5.0 and society 5.0. Challenges and Opportunities for Industry, 4.

Rastogi, C., Zhang, Y., Wei, D., Varshney, K. R., Dhurandhar, A., & Tomsett, R. (2022). Deciding fast and slow: The role of cognitive biases in ai-assisted decision-making. Proceedings of the ACM on Human-computer Interaction, 6(CSCW1), 1-22.

Ravichandran, P., Machireddy, J. R., & Rachakatla, S. K. (2022). AI-Enhanced data analytics for real-time business intelligence: Applications and challenges. *Journal of AI in Healthcare and Medicine*, *2*(2), 168–195.

Rayner, J. (2004). *Managing reputational risk: Curbing threats, leveraging opportunities*. John Wiley & Sons.

Revathy, S., Sreekala, S. P., Praveenadevi, D., Rajeshwari, S., De Albuquerque, V. H. C., Raj, P., & Yadav, S. P. (2023). The intelligent implications of artificial intelligence-driven decision-making in business management. Toward Artificial General Intelligence: Deep Learning, Neural Networks, Generative AI, 251.

Roberts, J. (2020). Future and changing roles of staff in distance education: A study to identify training and professional development needs. In *Expanding Horizons in Open and Distance Learning* (pp. 37–53). Routledge. DOI: 10.4324/9780429292941-4

Rodriguez-Rodriguez, I., Rodriguez, J. V., Shirvanizadeh, N., Ortiz, A., & Pardo-Quiles, D. J. (2021). Applications of artificial intelligence, machine learning, big data and the internet of things to the COVID-19 pandemic: A scientometric review using text mining. *International Journal of Environmental Research and Public Health*, *18*(16), 8578. DOI: 10.3390/ijerph18168578 PMID: 34444327

Rozman, M., Tominc, P., & Milfelner, B. (2023). Maximizing employee engagement through artificial intelligent organizational culture in the context of leadership and training of employees: Testing linear and non-linear relationships. *Cogent Business & Management*, *10*(2), 2248732. DOI: 10.1080/23311975.2023.2248732

Sargiotis, D. (2024). Data Governance Frameworks: Models and Best Practices. In *Data Governance: A Guide* (pp. 165–195). Springer Nature Switzerland. DOI: 10.1007/978-3-031-67268-2_4

Sarker, I. H. (2021). Data science and analytics: An overview from data-driven smart computing, decision-making and applications perspective. *SN Computer Science*, *2*(5), 377. DOI: 10.1007/s42979-021-00765-8 PMID: 34278328

Sashi, C. M. (2021). Digital communication, value co-creation and customer engagement in business networks: A conceptual matrix and propositions. *European Journal of Marketing*, *55*(6), 1643–1663. DOI: 10.1108/EJM-01-2020-0023

Saurabh, K., Arora, R., Rani, N., Mishra, D., & Ramkumar, M. (2022). AI led ethical digital transformation: Framework, research and managerial implications. Journal of Information. *Communication and Ethics in Society*, *20*(2), 229–256. DOI: 10.1108/JICES-02-2021-0020

Schmidt, P., Biessmann, F., & Teubner, T. (2020). Transparency and trust in artificial intelligence systems. *Journal of Decision Systems*, *29*(4), 260–278. DOI: 10.1080/12460125.2020.1819094

Schwartz, R., Schwartz, R., Vassilev, A., Greene, K., Perine, L., Burt, A., & Hall, P. (2022). Towards a standard for identifying and managing bias in artificial intelligence (Vol. 3, p. 00). Gaithersburg, MD: US Department of Commerce, National Institute of Standards and Technology.

Selvarajan, G. (2021). Leveraging AI-enhanced analytics for industry-specific optimization: A strategic approach to transforming data-driven decision-making. *International Journal of Enhanced Research in Science Technology and Engineering*, *10*, 78–84.

Shalaby, A. (2024). Classification for the digital and cognitive AI hazards: Urgent call to establish automated safe standard for protecting young human minds. *Digital Economy and Sustainable Development*, *2*(1), 17. DOI: 10.1007/s44265-024-00042-5

Shin, D. D. (2023). *Algorithms, humans, and interactions: How do algorithms interact with people? Designing meaningful AI experiences*. Taylor & Francis.

Shodeinde, D. A., & Abah, O. E. (2025). Artificial Intelligence Technology and Marketing Communication Management: A Case Study of Guaranty Trust Holding Company PLC, Nigeria. *Lafia Journal of Economics and Sciences*, 163-183.DOI: 10.70118/lajems-10-1-2025-09Management

Shoushtari, F., Ghafourian, E., & Talebi, M. (2021). Improving performance of supply chain by applying artificial intelligence. International journal of industrial engineering and operational research, 3(1), 14-23.

Shrestha, Y. R., Ben-Menahem, S. M., & Von Krogh, G. (2019). Organizational decision-making structures in the age of artificial intelligence. *California Management Review*, *61*(4), 66–83. DOI: 10.1177/0008125619862257

Singh, B. (2025). Case Study on Implementing AI for Dynamic Pricing in the Hospitality Industry. Decoding AI: Practical Implementations for Business Operations.

Singh, R. P., Hom, G. L., Abramoff, M. D., Campbell, J. P., & Chiang, M. F. (2020). Current challenges and barriers to real-world artificial intelligence adoption for the healthcare system, provider, and the patient. *Translational Vision Science & Technology*, *9*(2), 45–45. DOI: 10.1167/tvst.9.2.45 PMID: 32879755

Sipola, J., Saunila, M., & Ukko, J. (2023). Adopting artificial intelligence in sustainable business. *Journal of Cleaner Production*, *426*, 139197. DOI: 10.1016/j.jclepro.2023.139197

Slosberg, M., Nejati, A., Evans, J., & Nanda, U. (2018). Transitioning to a new facility: The crucial role of employee engagement. *Journal of Healthcare Management / American College of Healthcare Executives, 63*(1), 63–77. DOI: 10.1097/JHM-D-16-00019 PMID: 29303827

Stewart, D. W., & Kamins, M. A. (1993). *Secondary research: Information sources and methods* (Vol. 4). Sage. DOI: 10.4135/9781412985802

Subramanian, Y. R., & Riya, R. (2024). The transformative role of artificial intelligence in human resource. [IJRTBT]. *International Journal on Recent Trends in Business and Tourism, 8*(2), 14–25. DOI: 10.31674/ijrtbt.2024.v08i02.002

Suljic, V. (2025). Strategic leadership in AI-driven digital transformation: Ethical governance, innovation management, and sustainable practices for global enterprises and SMEs. *SBS Journal of Applied Business Research, 13*(1), 17–35. DOI: 10.70301/JOUR/SBS-JABR/2025/13/1/2

Suri, V. K. (2022). *Functional automation and digital transformation*. Dorrance Publishing.

Taherdoost, H., & Madanchian, M. (2023). Artificial intelligence and knowledge management: Impacts, benefits, and implementation. *Computers, 12*(4), 72. DOI: 10.3390/computers12040072

Tekale, K. M. (2023). AI-Powered Claims Processing: Reducing Cycle Times and Improving Accuracy. *International Journal of Artificial Intelligence, Data Science, and Machine Learning, 4*(2), 113–123.

Tyagi, A. K., Fernandez, T. F., Mishra, S., & Kumari, S. (2020, December). Intelligent automation systems at the core of industry 4.0. In International conference on intelligent systems design and applications (pp. 1-18). Cham: Springer International Publishing.

Uddin, M. K. S. (2024). A review of utilizing natural language processing and AI for advanced data visualization in real-time analytics. *Global Mainstream Journal, 1*(4), 10–62304. DOI: 10.62304/ijmisds.v1i04.185

Ugwa, S. (2023). Artificial Intelligence for IT strategy: Driving data-driven decision-making and business alignment.

Vacik, H., & Lexer, M. J. (2014). Past, current and future drivers for the development of decision support systems in forest management. *Scandinavian Journal of Forest Research, 29*(sup1), 2-19.

Van Hoang, T. (2024). Impact of integrated artificial intelligence and internet of things technologies on smart city transformation. Journal of technical education science, 19(Special Issue 01), 64-73.

Vettriselvan, R. (2025). Harnessing innovation and digital marketing in the era of industry 5.0: resilient healthcare SMEs. In *The Future of Small Business in Industry 5.0* (pp. 163–186). IGI Global Scientific Publishing.

Wang, K., Zhao, Y., Gangadhari, R. K., & Li, Z. (2021). Analyzing the adoption challenges of the Internet of things (Iot) and artificial intelligence (ai) for smart cities in china. *Sustainability (Basel)*, *13*(19), 10983. DOI: 10.3390/su131910983

Wijesekara, I., Galappaththi, P., Silva, K., & Liyanage, R. (2020). *AI-driven Dashboards for Enterprise Decision Making*. Rasika Liyanage Eastern University.

Wong, W. P., Tseng, M. L., & Tan, K. H. (2014). A business process management capabilities perspective on organisation performance. *Total Quality Management & Business Excellence*, *25*(5-6), 602–617. DOI: 10.1080/14783363.2013.850812

Yadava, A. (2023). Ethical and regulatory challenges of AI adoption in the financial services sector: A global perspective. *International Journal of Science and Research Archive*, *10*(13), 10–30574.

Yathiraju, N. (2022). Investigating the use of an artificial intelligence model in an ERP cloud-based system. International Journal of Electrical. *Electronics and Computers*, *7*(2), 1–26.

Yusuf, S. O., Durodola, R. L., Ocran, G., Abubakar, J. E., Echere, A. Z., & Paul-Adeleye, A. H. (2024). Challenges and opportunities in AI and digital transformation for SMEs: A cross-continental perspective. *World Journal of Advanced Research and Reviews*, *23*(3), 668–678. DOI: 10.30574/wjarr.2024.23.3.2511

Zamil, M. H. (2025). AI-driven business analytics for financial forecasting: A systematic review of decision support models in SMEs. *Review of Applied Science and Technology*, *4*(2), 86–117. DOI: 10.63125/gjrpv442

Zhang, Z., He, W., Li, W., & Abdous, M. H. (2021). Cybersecurity awareness training programs: A cost–benefit analysis framework. *Industrial Management & Data Systems*, *121*(3), 613–636. DOI: 10.1108/IMDS-08-2020-0462

Zharova, A. K. (2023). Achieving algorithmic transparency and managing risks of data security when making decisions without human interference: Legal approaches. *Journal of Digital Technologies and Law*, *1*(4), 973–993. DOI: 10.21202/jdtl.2023.42

Zong, Z., & Guan, Y. (2025). AI-driven intelligent data analytics and predictive analysis in Industry 4.0: Transforming knowledge, innovation, and efficiency. *Journal of the Knowledge Economy*, *16*(1), 864–903. DOI: 10.1007/s13132-024-02001-z

Chapter 5
Assortment Optimization for Retailers:
An Approach With Data Mining

Paulo Paes
Faculty of Economics, Universidade do Algarve, Portugal

Célia M. Q. Ramos
http://orcid.org/0000-0002-3413-4897
Universidade do Algarve, Portugal

Dora Agapito
http://orcid.org/0000-0002-2568-3720
CinTurs and Faculty of Economics, Universidade do Algarve, Portugal

ABSTRACT

The retail sector, as well as all its dimensions, undergoes frequent significant changes, especially driven by consumer needs that have become more personalised. In this context, the assortment management process appears to be important for selecting and organising products. Assortment management is not only a competitive action but also a fundamental act, as when defining an assortment, some segments of customers are served to the detriment of others. This article aims to analyse and identify the main products to be considered in the assortment and in targeted promotional actions of a retail network in the proximity format in Portugal, with stores in Lisbon and Porto, through data mining techniques. It allowed the identification of the most relevant attributes in sales recorded by the retailer and the discussion of the most important relationships between products.

DOI: 10.4018/979-8-3373-3648-0.ch005

INTRODUCTION

In recent years, the retail sector has experienced profound transformations across all its dimensions, driven by the growing personalization and complexity of consumer demands (Heger & Klein, 2024; Ke *et al.*, 2025). This shift has led to a substantial expansion in product variety, reshaping sales processes and compelling retailers to adapt their strategies to remain competitive (Hekimoğlua *et al.*, 2019). Among the critical factors influencing retail success, assortment optimization stands out as a key determinant, as it directly impacts customer satisfaction, inventory efficiency, and overall profitability (Neogrid, 2018; Pratas & Brito, 2019).

For proximity retailers, the challenge is even more pronounced. These establishments operate with highly constrained physical spaces, requiring meticulous selection of displayed products to maximize sales while meeting consumer expectations. Customers of proximity retail typically prioritize convenience, speed, and reliability, expecting to find essential items quickly and without complication (Gahinet & Cliquet, 2018). Consequently, retailers must strike a delicate balance between offering a sufficiently diverse assortment and avoiding excessive stock that could lead to inefficiencies.

Despite the growing body of research on retail assortment optimization, there remains a notable gap in empirical studies that apply data mining techniques to real-world retail data, particularly in the context of proximity stores. While prior research has explored theoretical frameworks and general retail strategies, few studies have focused on practical implementations using transactional data to derive actionable insights. This study seeks to address this gap by employing data mining methodologies to analyze and optimize the assortment of a proximity retail chain in Portugal, comprising seven stores located in Lisbon and Porto.

The central research problem revolves around how data mining can enhance assortment decisions, ensuring that product selections align with consumer preferences while maximizing operational efficiency. By leveraging real sales data, this study aims to identify high-impact products that should be prioritized in both assortment planning and promotional strategies. The findings will contribute to a deeper understanding of how data-driven approaches can refine retail management, particularly in constrained environments where space and consumer behavior impose unique challenges.

The primary objective of this research is to determine the optimal product assortment for a proximity retail chain, using data mining techniques to uncover purchasing patterns, product affinities, and demand trends. By doing so, the study not only advances academic discourse on retail optimization but also provides practical recommendations for retailers seeking to enhance their competitiveness in an increasingly dynamic market. Ultimately, this work underscores the importance of integrating analytical tools into retail decision-making, offering a replicable framework for similar businesses aiming to improve their assortment strategies.

LITERATURE REVIEW

Category Management in Retail

Among the various processes that constitute the structure of a retail company is category management, which is characterised by classifying and managing product categories as an "autonomous" business unit in the organisation and is based on the objective of creating value for the customer. For consumers, suppliers, and the retail organisation itself, this means that retail banners are not structured only as groups of individual products sold in a single establishment but group a set of items in a coherent way (Pratas & Brito, 2019).

Category management (CM) is a strategic approach in retail that focuses on optimising product categories as business units to enhance customer value and drive profitability. According to Biliavska *et al.* (2024), CM involves data-driven decision-making, where retailers collaborate with suppliers to analyse consumer behaviour, shelf-space allocation, and pricing strategies to maximise category performance. Recent studies highlight the growing importance of digital tools, such as AI and machine learning, in refining assortment planning and demand forecasting (Daruvuri *et al.*, 2025). However, challenges persist, including the need for real-time data integration and the alignment of supplier-retailer objectives, which can hinder effective category management implementation (Rahman, 2022).

The evolution of CM has been further influenced by shifting consumer preferences and the rise of omnichannel retailing. Research by Mrutzek-Hartmann *et al.* (2022) emphasises that successful CM now requires a seamless integration of online and offline channels to ensure consistent customer experiences. Additionally, sustainability concerns are reshaping category strategies, with retailers increasingly prioritising eco-friendly product assortments (Ray & Nayak, 2023). Despite these advancements, gaps remain in understanding how dynamic pricing and personalised promotions impact long-term category performance. Future research should explore the balance between automation and human judgment in CM, particularly in adapting to rapidly changing market conditions (Biliavska *et al.*, 2024) and contributing to optimisation in terms of assignment optimisation.

Assortment and Its Management

In recent years, the retail business, as well as all its dimensions, have undergone major changes, mainly driven by consumer needs that have become increasingly personalised and complex, the significant increase in the number of products on the market and changes in the sales process and how these are conducted by retailers (Hekimoğlua *et al.*, 2019).

The assortment management process plays an important role in the selection and organisation of products to meet this complex consumer need. The assortment comprises products grouped into families or subfamilies, representing products that respond to a global purpose (Rousseau, 2014). The composition of a store's assortment is not and should not be permanent; its size varies over time and evolves with market movements (Hruschka, 2024; Rousseau, 2014).

Rousseau (2014) also argues that the prediction of the composition of an assortment can be defined empirically or through rigorous assortment plans that go into detail. The same author defines an assortment plan as "a detailed description of the ranges to be offered to customers during a given period" (Rosseau, 2014, p. 175). According to the author, the factors to consider in this definition are duration and content. Duration – must be annual, semi-annual or quarterly. Moreover, it is recommended that special or temporary plans for seasonal products be drawn up.

The content – all products must be considered, product family by product family, all related products and the appropriate prices. Those products that the retailer considers to be basic may need individual attention, as they are more relevant in global sales.

Assortment management is a critical component of retail strategy, focusing on optimising product variety to meet consumer demand while maximising profitability. Recent research emphasises the role of data analytics and machine learning in assortment planning, enabling retailers to tailor offerings based on purchasing patterns and market trends (Chen *et al.*, 2023). A well-curated assortment not only enhances customer satisfaction but also reduces operational costs by minimising overstock and stockouts (Heger & Klein, 2024). However, challenges such as the "paradox of choice" where excessive variety leads to decision fatigue—remain a key concern, requiring retailers to balance breadth and depth strategically.

The rise of omnichannel retailing has further complicated assortment management, as retailers must now align inventory across physical stores and e-commerce platforms. Studies suggest that dynamic assortment optimisation, which adjusts product selections in real-time based on demand fluctuations, significantly improves performance in multi-channel environments (Srivastava *et al.*, 2025). Additionally, sustainability considerations are increasingly influencing assortment decisions, with retailers prioritising eco-friendly products to align with consumer preferences (Yu *et al.*, 2024). Future research should explore the integration of AI-driven personalisation in assortment strategies to enhance both efficiency and customer engagement (Jung, 2025).

Analysis and Definition of the Assortment

Assortment analysis in the retail business, as well as all its dimensions, has been crucial for making decisions about the categories to be offered by stores. In fact, according to Neogrid (2018), "for retail, assortment analysis is extremely important when defining which categories will be made available by the business. Occupying a shelf with products that will not be used is not only a waste of space but also an opportunity to offer items that can bring a greater return on the investment made."

The analysis and definition of assortment involve a strategic selection of products that align with consumer preferences, market trends, and retail objectives. Recent studies highlight the growing importance of data-driven approaches, where advanced analytics and machine learning optimise assortment composition by predicting demand and minimising redundancies (Heger & Klein, 2024). Retailers must balance variety and relevance, as excessive breadth can lead to cognitive overload, while overly narrow assortments may fail to meet diverse consumer needs (Sethuraman *et al.*, 2022). Additionally, segmentation techniques—such as clustering based on purchasing behavior—help refine assortment strategies to target specific customer groups effectively (Hoque *et al.*, 2024). The integration of real-time sales data further enhances dynamic assortment adjustments, ensuring adaptability in fast-changing markets (Miao & Chao, 2022).

According to Rousseau (2014), the size of an assortment, in generic terms, is made up of three dimensions:

1. **Width:** Checks the number of families and categories of products sold by the point of sale, which reflects the number of consumer needs met.
2. **Depth:** Quantifies the references sold by the point of sale in each product family or category.
3. **Coherence:** Refers to the homogeneity of an assortment, that is, the connection between consumer needs and each product defined to meet them.

Also, according to Rousseau (2014), a store has its personality and depends on various combinations of the following dimensions, as shown in Table 1.

Table 1. The ideal size of an assortment for a store

Assortment size	Retail store typologies
Wide and deep	Hypermarkets and department stores
Wide and shallow	Medium supermarkets or small hypermarkets
Narrow and deep	Speciality stores or large speciality stores
Narrow and shallow	Convenience stores and heavy discounters

Source: Adapted from Rousseau (2014).

The Segmentation

In the current context of the consumer market, characterised mainly by the increase in different consumer profiles, purchasing habits and interests, Segmentation has become one of the critical factors for the success of marketing professionals, as this process is fundamental for the correct correspondence between the needs of consumers and the ability of companies to meet them, thus enhancing their competitive advantage. In this sense, operating an effective segmentation process is essential, notably for the retail sector, since the grouping of customers with similar consumption characteristics provides the company with the opportunity to understand its market objective better, customise its approach and regulate prices, products and targeted promotions (Heger & Klein, 2024; Yu *et al.*, 2024).

Kotler and Armstrong (2014) define market segmentation as the act of dividing a market into smaller segments of consumers with different needs, characteristics or behaviours, as these may require specific strategies or marketing mixes for their profile.

Consumers in any market differ in their desires, resources, geographic location, attitudes, and purchasing practices. Through Segmentation, companies can divide large, heterogeneous markets into smaller segments that can be reached more effectively with products and services. That meets your unique needs. Marketers must explore several segmentation variables, alone and in combination, to find the best way to visualise the structure of a market (Kotler & Armstrong, 2014). According to Kotler and Armstrong (2014), the variables that can be used in segmenting consumer markets can be seen in Table 2.

Table 2. Consumer market segmentation variables

Segmentation Variable	Features
Geographic segmentation	It deals with the division of a market into different geographic units, such as regions, states, municipalities and neighbourhoods. A company may decide to operate in one or a few geographic areas or all of them, paying attention to differences in geography, needs and wants.
Demographic Segmentation	Divides markets into segments based on age, life cycle stage, gender, income, occupation, education, religion, ethnicity and generation. Demographic factors are the most popular bases for segmenting customer groups.
Psychographic Segmentation	Divides buyers based on social class, lifestyle or personality characteristics. Assuming that people from the same demographic group can have very different psychographic characteristics.
Behavioural Segmentation	Separates buyers by their knowledge, attitudes, uses or responses towards the product. Many marketers believe behavioural variables are the best starting point for building segments.

Source: Adapted from Kotler and Armstrong (2014).

The Assortment in Proximity Retail

For local retailers, the difficulty in defining a strategy in terms of assortment is even greater, as they have very limited space for product display in stores (Chandrasekhar *et al.*, 2024). Comparative Analysis of Impulse Buying Behaviour Across Retail Channels: A Study of Physical Stores, E-commerce Websites and Mobile Shopping Apps. Economic Affairs, 69(02), 1109-1120, the consumer who goes here has a purchasing mission motivated by convenience, agility when purchasing and having confidence in finding the product you need (Gahinet & Cliquet, 2018). Therefore, it is crucial and a competitive advantage for this type of retailer to understand which products their customers purchase and optimise the number of products according to their performance (Pratas & Brito, 2019).

Recent research emphasises that successful assortment strategies in this sector must prioritise high-rotation essential items while incorporating localised products that reflect community preferences (Novikova, 2021). Data from mobile payment systems and loyalty programs now enable precise tracking of neighbourhood purchasing patterns, allowing for micro-localised assortment optimisation (Chen *et al.*, 2021). However, studies note significant challenges in maintaining optimal stock levels due to limited backroom space, making inventory turnover a critical metric (Delasay *et al.*, 2022). Emerging solutions include AI-powered recommendation systems that adjust assortments based on real-time foot traffic data and weather patterns (Hooli, 2025). The COVID-19 pandemic further accelerated the need for proximity retailers to develop flexible assortment plans that can quickly adapt to supply chain disruptions (Delasay *et al.*, 2022). Future research directions include exploring how proximity retailers can leverage dark store concepts to expand virtual assortment while maintaining physical store efficiency.

Assortment Category Management Process

The implementation of category management depends on factors such as the level of service and price, sales, and profitability of a retail company's categories (Pratas & Brito, 2019). According to Pratas and Brito (2019), there are eight steps that good category management must follow:

1. **Category definition** – the individual products that comprise the category are determined.
2. **Defining the role of the category** – categories can be classified as routine, seasonal or convenience categories.
3. **Category assessment and performance** – a plan for category management is created to analyse the product category's performance, strengths and weaknesses (based on internal factors) and opportunities and threats (based on external factors of the market where the retailer is located).
4. **Category performance** – tends to be measured through scorecards, which identify the category's key indicators.
5. **Category strategy** – guidelines are defined to boost the product category's performance.
6. **Category tactics** – the operational aspects of the marketing mix elements of the product category are determined, as well as a set of performance indicators that must be measured and monitored.
7. **Implementation** – each element defined in the "category tactics" phase is implemented by executing specific tasks.
8. **Category review** – finally, the results are analysed, and improvement actions are designed.

It is noted that, among the factors mentioned, the definition of the assortment is cited at various times and stages as one of the main aspects of this process, so that category management becomes possible in a retail organisation. To conclude, analyses of indicators related to factors such as sales, distribution, supply and product display are also necessary for better decision-making (Pratas & Brito, 2019).

Data Analysis in the Retail Context

To optimise the assortment and guide it towards the real demand of a store's customers, it is necessary to obtain various information about the performance of products at retailers through more complex data analysis (Das & Dhar, 2021). In general, data originating from sales records (such as quantities and value of products sold, price), product types (such as range, brand, category) and store profiles (such as, e.g., target audience, size, linear shelf space, stock) (Pratas & Brito, 2019). All this data available to the retailer, considering the product's dimensions, channel (stores) and time (period), results in a database with large numbers of lines. With the current growth in the number of stores, products and customers, these databases have become even larger and more complex to analyse (Bradlow *et al.*, 2017).

In order to make it possible to analyse a large database, data mining techniques (data mining concept) allow the use of methods to identify relationships between data by checking the existence of correlation between attributes, allowing the identify a model that describes significant dependencies between data, through rules that allow making significant and potentially useful future predictions from large amounts of available data (Tekin *et al.*, 2018). In the case of retail, data mining techniques are used to identify sales forecasts, which helps to examine patterns and make inventory decisions, and to predict, based on purchases of an item in the analysed period and combined with association rules, the probability of the customer purchasing a complementary item (Martínez-Garmendia, 2023; Rygielski *et al.*, 2002).

Empirical Studies on Retail Assortment Definition

Chen *et al.* (2006) used data mining techniques to discover the implicit but significant relationship between the relative spatial distance of displayed products and the unit sales of the items in a retail store.

Miller *et al.* (2010) defined a methodology for choosing the ideal retail assortments for infrequently purchased products and measuring the robustness of these assortments to changing buyer preferences. It was concluded that there is little approach or rigorous modelling to choose the ideal assortment for categories such as these, so a method was developed to assess the sensitivity of the retailer's expected profit to changes in buyer preferences.

In the United States, Kwak *et al.* (2015) examined the impact of assortment variety on the shoppers' in-store choice process; more specifically, they found that consumers demand less variety for quality items in the yoghurt category. For this, the multivariate logistics category incidence method was used, and, as a result, the study shows that the choice of yoghurts is affected by brand quality perceptions and that reducing variety directly impacts quality perception.

Hekimoğlua *et al.* (2019) developed an assortment optimisation scheme that maximises the revenue of a single supermarket operating as a branch of a chain in Turkey. A log-linear regression model was created that represents the relationship between service and demand through historical data from the point of sale.

Moodley *et al.* (2020) developed a targeted promotion algorithm to increase the effectiveness of promotions by UK retailers by finding frequent item sets. A mathematical structure was proposed to target the set of items that are driven before customer targeting.

Sethuraman *et al.* (2022) understood the effect of retailer assortment size on consumer perceptions, choice, sales and participation. The study included the creation of a meta-analysis of the assortment of 1936 size effects obtained from 95 academic works, composed of 177 studies published between 1970 and 2021. The main result shows that the positive benefit elasticity indicates that, on average, a larger assortment benefits buyers/retailers and that such benefit-elasticity of assortment size has been more significant in more recent times in the USA, especially for grocery products. It was also specified that the variety of products in the USA is greater than in Asian and African countries.

The studies found are mostly focused on a specific product category of consumer goods or durable goods. A lack of studies related to assortment optimisation was identified that are focused on nearby retailers and address several categories rather than just one (Ke *et al.*, 2025).

This study is critically important because it addresses the evolving challenges of retail assortment optimization in an era where consumer demands are increasingly personalized and market dynamics are rapidly changing. Effective category and assortment management—key drivers of retail success - require data-driven strategies to balance product variety, shelf space, and consumer preferences, particularly in proximity retailing where space constraints amplify these challenges. By leveraging data mining techniques, this research provides actionable insights into product performance, customer segmentation, and purchasing patterns, enabling retailers to make informed decisions that enhance profitability and customer satisfaction. Furthermore, it fills a gap in existing literature by focusing on multi-category optimization for proximity retailers, offering a scalable framework that combines theoretical rigor with empirical analysis. The findings not only support operational efficiency but also contribute to strategic planning, ensuring retailers can adapt to market trends while maximizing return on investment.

METHODOLOGY

Study Location

The study took place around the business context of a Brazilian retail chain in the proximity format. This network contains seven stores distributed between Lisbon and Porto. For this study, the retailer provided the researcher with a sales database to serve as an object of study for the research problem.

Data Mining Method

According to Martinez *et al.* (2021) and Sharma and Sharma (2016), the data mining process is one of the stages of the Knowledge Discovery in Database (KDD) process, consisting of a set of steps:

1. **Data Selection:** The essential data for the analyst's request are collected in the database.
2. **Data Pre-Processing:** Data preparation, eliminating inconsistent data. This is the most demanding phase for the data to be reliable.
3. **Data transformation:** Data is transformed and consolidated in a form more appropriate for mining through summarisation or data aggregation.
4. **Data mining:** The essential process of extracting patterns from data.
5. **Assessment and Presentation of Standards:** Where relevant standards representing knowledge are identified. To this end, knowledge visualisation and representation techniques are used so that the user understands the extracted knowledge.

Data Collection and Selection

The authors had access to the company's database, including sales fields in quantity and value, sales and price for each product from all product groups, monthly for two years. The database divides the assortment into categories: grocery, non-edible, fruits and vegetables, household products and personal care products. These product groups branch hierarchically into families, categories, brands and products. For example, dairy products, skimmed milk, and Brand A skimmed milk can be classified into a single dairy category.

An example of the product structure of the database object of study can be seen in Figure 1, which summarises the hierarchy of the soft drinks category and the objective is to show its ramifications (Hekimoğlu *et al.*, 2019, p. 202) and adapted for the present study in Figure 1.

The database under study contains product sales data relating to the frozen, dairy, savoury grocery, soft drinks, wine and spirits families. This has 163,000 rows of data. The characteristics of the stores considered in the study are described in Table 3, and the variables present in the database object of the study are described in Table 4.

Figure 1. Example of the product structure of the soft drinks category.

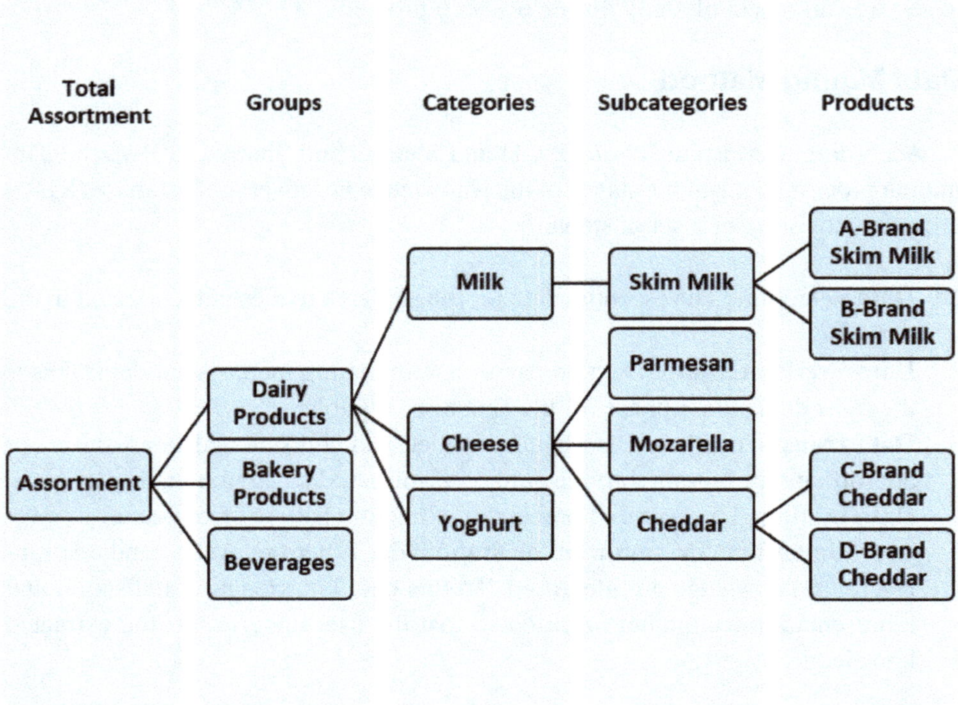

Source: Adapted from Hekimoğlu et al. (2019, p. 202).

Table 3. Characteristics of the studied retailer's stores

Store	Area	Public	Number of check-outs	Employees
Campo Maior	362	medium/high	3	11
Camarinha	207	low	2	9
Buraca	105	low	2	5
Carregado	254	medium/low	2	8
Entroncamento	275	medium/low	2	8
Porto de Mós	240	medium	2	6
Coimbra	255	medium/high	2	7

Source: Own elaboration.

Table 4. Variables of the studied database

Variables	References	Variable type
Warehouse	Code of the logistics centre that supplies the store	Text
Store	Store description	Text
Family	Code of the family to which the product belongs	Numeric
Family (description)	Description of the product grouping to which the product belongs	Text
Item	Product code	Text
Category	Description of the product category to which the product belongs	Text
Brand	Description of the brand to which the product belongs	Text
Description	Product description	Text
Quantity	Quantity sold of the product	Numeric
Net Value	Total value (in euros) of product sales	Numeric
Average Price	Average price (in reais) of selling the product	Numeric
Month	Month the product was sold	Date
Store area	Store size in square meters	Numeric
Public	Predominant social class of store customers	Text
Number of check-outs	Number of service boxes at the store	Numeric
Employees	Number of employees at the store	Numeric

Source: Own elaboration.

Data Preparation and Transformation

To make the database object of study more appropriate for the proposed use, some adjustments were necessary, namely, cleaning and transformation, since space was used as a separator for thousands, as well as excluding sales records that were negative or zero.

Data Mining Application

The most common activities in data mining can be divided into two types of methods: predictive and descriptive. Being predictive, activities are carried out through statistical inferences in the data to make relevant predictions, such as using consumption patterns to predict correlations between products and direct actions. About descriptive activities, the data present in the database is classified based on its properties, making it possible to discover patterns and describe the data so that users can interpret them and make decisions (Martinez *et al.*, 2021).

Table 5 presents the most used descriptive and predictive data mining methods and their main characteristics, divided by type of learning.

Table 5. Descriptive and predictive methods by type of learning

	Descriptive or Predictive	Method	Main features
Supervised Learning	Predictive	Classification and Regression	By creating models, this method is applied at the expense of a set of classified examples to predict the membership of a certain class (classification) or a value (regression) for each record that is part of another data set.
Unsupervised Learning	Descriptive	Clustering	These techniques look for similarities and differences in a data set and automatically group these similar records into segments or clusters using some critical value or metric.
	Description	Association rules	The approach in question handles purchasing a set of products, assuming it is a single transaction. The objective is to find trends in the various transactions analysed that can be considered to understand and explore patterns of purchasing behaviour

Source: Adapted from Oliveira (2000).

To make the analysis of this study operational, the software used is Orange (2022), which is freely accessible data mining software with pre-defined data modelling and statistical calculations.

Considering the objective, the available data and the need to identify the best-selling products by the audience and which products are sold by store and month, the data mining methods to be applied were DT (Decision Tree) and RA (Rules of Association), predictive and descriptive, respectively.

Decision Tree Application

Decision trees are defined by inductive learning methods with a hierarchical tree structure and three types of nodes: root, internal, and leaf. The root node is at the top of a tree, and the internal nodes are between the root and leaf nodes. Each internal node represents a test on an attribute, each branch from the root node to the leaf node signifies the test output, and each leaf node represents a sample classification (Jin *et al.*, 2022). DT make up a class of predictive models with good references in efficiency and understanding, especially due to their simplicity (Caigny *et al.*, 2018). Since, substantially, one of the objectives of this dissertation is to find the most sold products by the public, the decision tree is used, as it is possible to identify the nodes derived from the sale by the public of the products present in the database object of studies. This way, it is possible to understand which categories are mostly sold for each income level of the public.

Applying Association Rules

Association rule mining is of great use and a fascinating topic of study. It helps countless companies analyse and diagnose problems in their business and their sales trends, discover customer patterns, make possible business decisions about selling and generate more profits (Krishna & Ravi, 2020). Understanding which sets of products are sold mainly by store and month, and which products are probably sold in the same period, is one of the analyses intended in this dissertation. In this sense, it is considered that the characteristics of the association rule method meet what is desired and contribute to obtaining the results.

RESULTS

Description and Characterization of the Database

Two years of sales records from the retail company were obtained, collected from 7 stores distributed across regions of Portugal, located in Buraca, Camarinha, Carregado, Entroncamento, Massamá and Porto de Mós. The concentration of such sales and their characteristics were considered for analysis from different perspectives, which can be analyzed in the following figures.

It is possible to observe in Figure 2 that both the retailer's net sales and sales in quantity come mostly from the Camarinha store (24.4% and 26.4%, respectively), followed by Carregado (23.5% and 23.6%, respectively), which occupies second place and Coimbra (17.4% and 15.5%, respectively), in third place.

Figure 2. Net sales and quantity sales by store (%)

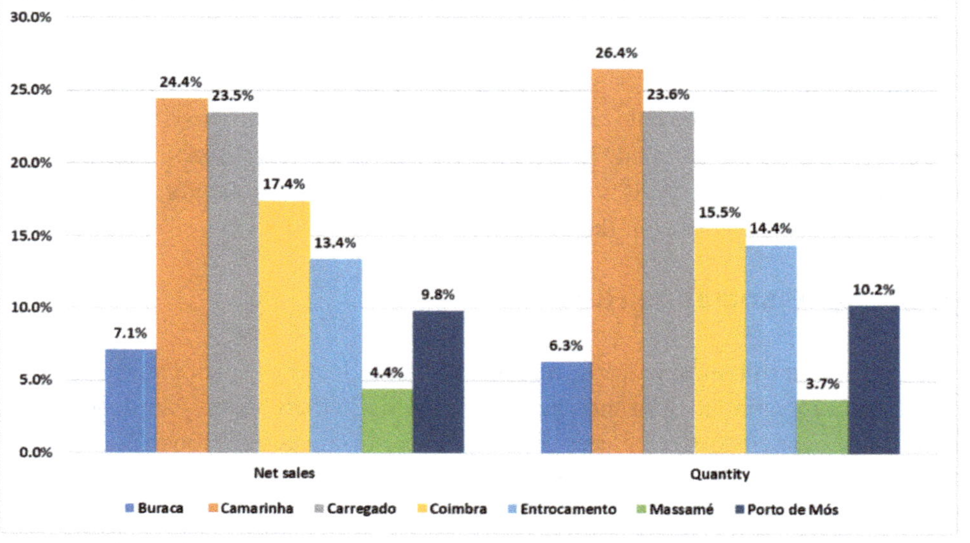

Source: Own elaboration.

In Figure 3, regarding net sales, the leading product family is dairy (30.0%), followed by soft drinks (28.7%) and savoury grocery (18.6%). In terms of volume sales, the leading family is Soft Drinks (35.3%), the second is Dairy Products (32.5%), and the third is Salty Grocery (21.3%).

Figure 3. Net sales and quantity sales by product family (%)

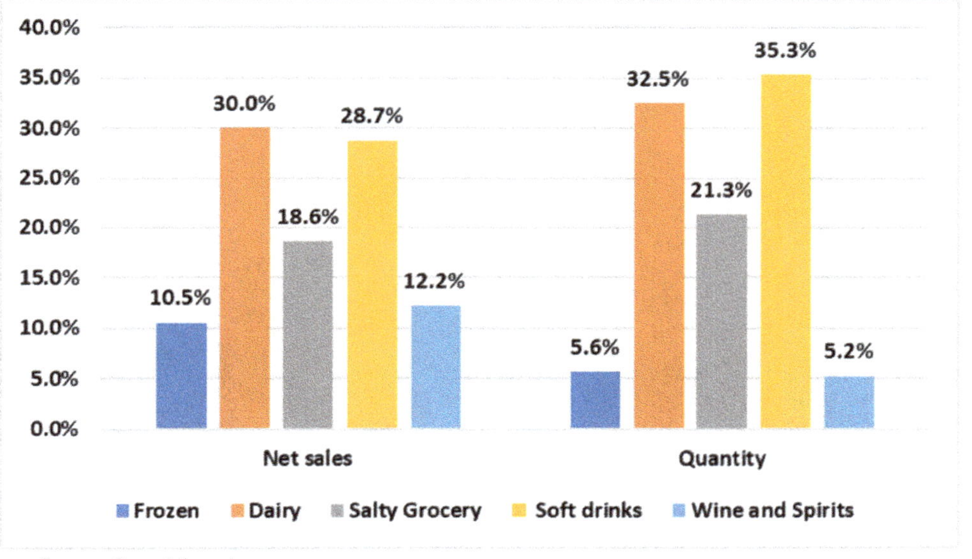

Source: Own elaboration.

According to the data in Figure 4, the public that registered the most sales at the retail company in the period analysed was the medium/low public (36.9% in net sales and 38.0% in quantity), followed by the low public (31.5% in net sales and 32.7% in quantity) and finally, the medium/high public (17.4% in net sales and 15.5% in quantity), forming the three most representative publics for the organisation in terms of sales.

Figure 4. Net sales and quantity sales by audience (%)

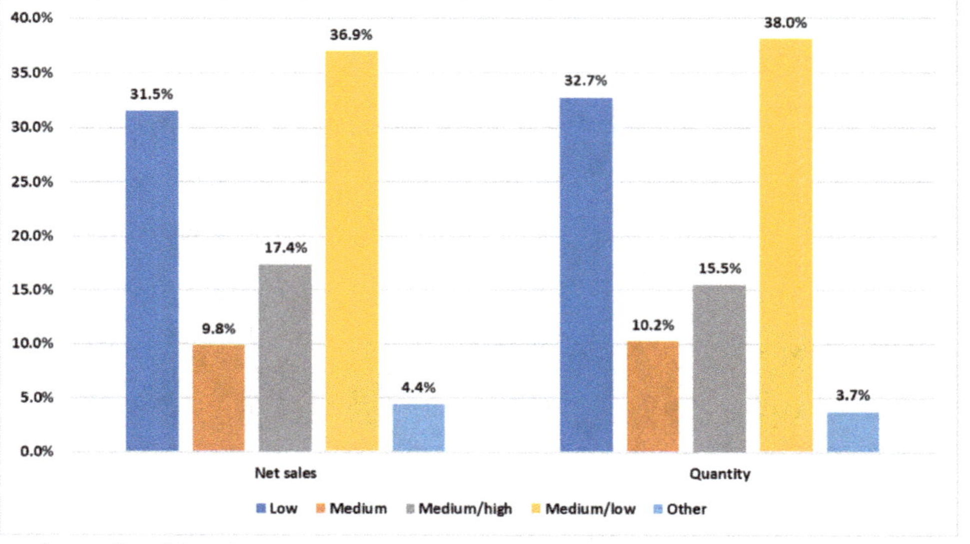

Source: Own elaboration.

Table 6 allows a global assessment of the retailer based on the main product and store attributes. In this sense, it is possible to observe that, in the frozen, dairy, and soft drink product families, the store with the best performance is the Camarinha store, which has the largest total sales. In the savoury grocery family, the largest total sales come from the Carregado store, and in the wine and spirits family, the store with the highest total sales is Coimbra.

Table 6. Example of the cross between product family, public and store in terms of average, maximum minimum and total, made in net sales (€) for the frozen foods family

Product Family	Store	Public	Average	Maximum	Minimum	Total
Frozen	Buraca	low	13.84	255.71	0.70	20176.09
Frozen	Camarinha	low	26.15	346.93	0.68	80204.46
Frozen	Carregado	Medium/low	23.50	268.64	0.68	74279.71
Frozen	Coimbra	Medium/high	18.75	165.78	0.16	61410.64
Frozen	Entroncamento	Medium/low	14.49	119.42	0.48	37178.17
Frozen	Massamá	Medium/low	12.12	63.09	0.71	17796.54
Frozen	Porto de Mós	medium	10.61	105.26	0.52	28105.25

Source: Own elaboration.

Description and Characterization of the Database: Public Decision Tree by Social Class

In the decision tree built using the Orange application based on the aforementioned base structure, the Induce binary tree option was considered; the application builds a binary tree (divided into two leaf nodes). The minimum number of instances in leaves is equal to 2, which causes the algorithm to never construct a split that would place fewer than two training examples in any of the branches. It was also configured not to divide subsets smaller than five nodes. Lastly, the algorithm was limited so that the depth of the classification tree was up to 100.

The data selection carried out for this analysis consists of considering the attributes Quantity, Average Price, Net Value and Family (Description) as characteristics of the analysed data. The Public attribute is considered as a target variable, as this is where the objective of this analysis lies, the target to be considered in all instances. The target attributes of this analysis are brand and description, as they are included in the data set and method but are not considered in the analysis. After completing all the data mining steps, the analysis result can be seen in Figure 5.

Figure 5. Public decision tree by social class

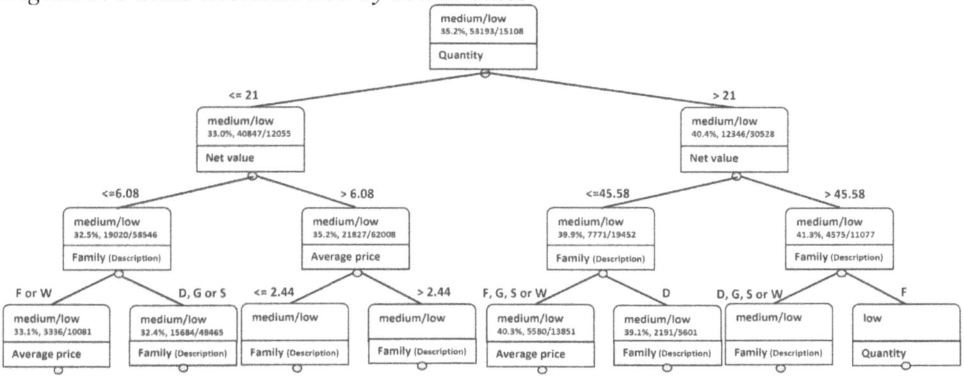

Source: Own elaboration.

In the decision tree presented, it is observed that the public attribute is the objective of the analysis, as it is from this attribute that information that describes their sales behaviour is to be extracted. Among the results, it is possible to observe that, at the first level, sales to the medium/low public represent 35.2% and are the highest relationship found. Because, for this audience, when more than 21 products are sold (second node) to the same audience, such sales represent 40.4% of the quantity. In the third node, it is clear that sales to this same audience, in Net Value, when above 45.58€, represent 41.3%. And, at the fourth level, it should be noted that the public that follows this same behaviour and sells mainly to the Frozen family of products is the low public. When most dairy products, savoury grocery stores, soft drinks, wines, and spirits are sold, the predominant audience is medium/low.

As the public observed at the fourth level of the previous analysis undergoes a behaviour change, leaving the predominance of the medium/low public and showing majority results for the low public when the product family that predominates is frozen, it was considered relevant to observe the tree decision when the objective class is the low public.

In the analysis for the low audience, at the first level, it was possible to observe that sales to this audience represent 28.8%. At the second level, quantity sales representing over 21 products are 31.9% for this audience and sales recorded with a Net Value above 45.58€ represent 35.8% (third level). Concerning product families for sales with the same behaviour observed at other levels, sales recorded for the frozen family are the majority, at 43.8%, and when sales are for products from the dairy, grocery, savoury, soft drinks, or wines and spirits, the representation is 34.9%.

Description and Characterization of the Database: Product Association Rules by Store and Month

Association rules were applied to the sales set characterised by store and month for the entire sales period in the studied database. The minimum support was considered, the percentage of the entire data set covered by the entire rule (antecedent and consequent), a minimum value of 5%. In this sense, it allowed a minimum of 90% confidence in the statistics applied and a maximum of 70,000 results lines to be presented. It was also configured that the analysis is restricted to displaying only results that respect the filter of 3 minimum items and 998 maximum items together in the antecedent and only 1 item in the consequent.

The theories assumed for creating the association rule, according to the Orange tool, were based on articles by Han *et al.* (2004). Thus, the extraction of the specific analysis can be seen in Table 7, considering associations with a 100% confidence level.

The table on the right displays a list of rules with six different measures of association rule quality: Supp: This is how often a rule applies to a given data set; Conf: represents how often the rule is valid (support for a rule/support for antecedent); *Covr:* results from the frequency in which the antecedent item is found in the data set (antecedent/data support); *Strg*: (consequent support/antecedent support); Lift: displays how often a rule is valid per consequent item (data * confidence/consequent support); *Levr*: represents the difference between two items present together in a transaction and the two items that appear independently (support*data - antecedent support *consequent support/data).

Table 7. Excerpt from product association rules by store and month with 100% confidence

Supp	Conf	Covr	Strg	Lift	Levr	Antecedent		Consequent
0.987	*1.000*	*0.987*	*1.013*	*1.000*	*0.000*	*Creme culinario Vaqueiro 250gr=1, iced tea manga Continente 1.5l=1, leite c/ chocolate mimosa 4*200ml=1*	®	*Leite uht magro Mimosa bem essencial 1lt=1*
0.987	*1.000*	*0.987*	*1.013*	*1.000*	*0.000*	*Creme Culinário Vaqueiro 250gr=1, Leite c/Chocolate Mimosa 4*200ml=1, Leite UHT magro Mimosa Bem Essencial 1lt=1*	®	*Iced Tea Manga Continente 1.5L=1*
0.987	*1.000*	*0.987*	*1.013*	*1.000*	*0.000*	*Creme Culinário Vaqueiro 250gr=1, Iced Tea Manga Continente 1.5L=1, Leite UHT SEL M/g Matinal 1LT=1*	®	*Leite UHT magro Mimosa Bem Essencial 1LT=1*
0.987	*1.000*	*0.987*	*1.013*	*1.000*	*0.000*	*Creme culinario Vaqueiro 250gr=1, leite UHT magro Mimosa bem essencial 1 lt=1, leite UHT sel m/g matinal 1lt=1*	®	*Iced tea manga Continente 1.5l=1*
0.987	*1.000*	*0.987*	*1.013*	*1.000*	*0.000*	*Iced tea manga Continente 1.5l=1, leite c/ chocolate Mimosa 4*200ml=1, leite uht sel m/g Matinal 1lt=1*	®	*Leite uht magro Mimosa bem essencial 1lt=1*

Source: Own elaboration.

In the example in Table 7, the products "creme culinario Vaqueiro 250g", "Iced Tea manga Continente 1.5L" and "Leite c/chocolate Mimosa 4*200ml" have sales records in the same month and store, it is more likely that the product "Leite UHT magro Mimosa Bem Essencial 1lt" also has a sales record. This analysis result line is supported by the values of Support (*Supp*) 0.975, Coverage (*Covr*) 0.981, Strength (*Strg*) 1.013, Lift 1.000 and Leverage (*Levr*) 0.000, which are important to list the most representative results in taking decision.

From a business perspective, these data mean that, in practice, consumers are more likely to buy products from the consequent vision when they also buy products from the antecedent vision. This data can be used to create targeted promotional campaigns since there is data on individual customer purchases that can be cross-referenced. Identify those customers with a greater propensity to buy a second product and increase the company's average spending on this.

DISCUSSION OF RESULTS

The analysis of the public tree by social class shows that the "medium/low" economic class public represents a larger portion of sales in quantity, thus showing a public with a greater concentration of sales and with probably greater consumption potential, as there is this audience is more likely to purchase a product. In this sense, it is possible to identify that, in sales where more than 21 products are sold, they represent 40.4% of the quantity of products. Shows that it is interesting, once this retailer has a customer purchase base, to identify purchases greater than 21 products and take actions (promotional or not) aimed at this audience, as these customers are more likely to consume.

It was also possible to understand that for this audience, sales above R$45.58 represent 41.3% of product families, and, therefore, customers who have this level of spending can be potential consumers for most product families. company's product and drive actions such as increasing their purchase basket.

The last important information identified in this analysis says that the public that complies with all the above behaviours, and when the sale is mainly to the frozen product family, becomes the low economic class public. This information is important to understand that, in actions involving these product families, it is more interesting to maintain the focus on the lower economic class public.

As the lower economic class public becomes relevant to the retailer's sales when it comes to sales of frozen product families, a decision tree was executed specifically for this public and some relevant data were identified. Among these results, it was observed that this audience accounts for 28.8% of sales in quantity and that sales records with more than 21 products for this audience represent 31.9%, which represents strong evidence of greater purchasing propensity. for customers who buy more than 21 products and are interested in considering them for sales actions.

Applying the association rules shows that there are products that are more likely to be purchased together. From this crossing, the algorithm made it possible to identify a product more frequently in this combination, which thus configures a relevant product for commercial actions to increase the number of products purchased per customer.

Rousseau (2015) argues that the prediction of the composition of an assortment can be defined empirically or through rigorous assortment plans that go into detail. The same author defines an assortment plan as "a detailed description of the ranges to be offered to customers during a given period" (Rosseau, 2015, p. 175). However, it is crucial and a competitive advantage for the retailer to understand which products are most purchased by their customers and optimise the number of products according to their performance (Pratas & Brito, 2019).

In this sense, the contribution of these studies to the market is in line with what was mentioned by the authors above, helping the retailer under study with the understanding of the sales behaviour of their products and the attributes that constitute them that are most relevant to each type of public and store. This information is relevant to support management decisions when creating promotional actions and adjustments in the assortment size, since it is known what is most important in sales.

CONCLUSIONS

This study addressed the research problem of assortment optimization in retail through data mining techniques, focusing on a proximity retail chain in Portugal. The primary objectives were to segment stores based on product sales performance, identify key products for different consumer segments, and determine the optimal assortment strategy for each store. The findings provide actionable insights for retailers aiming to enhance their assortment planning and promotional strategies using data-driven approaches.

The decision tree (DT) analysis revealed that the "medium/low" socioeconomic class constitutes the most significant consumer segment in terms of sales volume. This audience demonstrated a higher propensity to purchase, particularly in transactions involving more than 21 products or sales exceeding €45.58. Such patterns suggest that targeted marketing efforts—such as bundled promotions or loyalty programs—could effectively increase basket size and customer retention within this segment. Additionally, the analysis highlighted that frozen products were predominantly purchased by the "low" socioeconomic class, indicating a need for tailored assortment strategies that prioritize affordability and convenience for this demographic.

The application of association rules further uncovered strong correlations between specific product purchases, particularly within the same month and store. For instance, items like "creme culinário Vaqueiro 250g," "iced tea manga Continente 1.5L," and "leite UHT magro Mimosa 1L" frequently appeared together in transactions, suggesting complementary demand. These findings align with prior research emphasizing the importance of data mining in uncovering hidden purchasing patterns (Martínez-Garmendia, 2023; Rygielski *et al.*, 2002). Retailers can leverage such insights to design cross-promotional campaigns, optimize shelf placement, and improve inventory management, ultimately driving higher sales and customer satisfaction.

However, the study faced limitations, particularly regarding the granularity of the dataset. Since each record represented aggregated monthly sales rather than individual transactions, it was impossible to analyze purchase frequency per customer or distinguish between single and repeat purchases. Future research could address this gap by incorporating transaction-level data, enabling a deeper understanding of consumer behavior and purchase cycles.

The study's focus on food and household product categories also presents an opportunity for expansion. Investigating non-food categories, such as electronics or apparel, could yield additional insights into how assortment strategies vary across product types with distinct demand patterns. For example, electronics often involve higher involvement and longer decision-making processes, which could influence assortment depth and promotional tactics differently than fast-moving consumer goods.

In conclusion, this research underscores the value of data mining in retail assortment optimization, particularly for proximity stores with limited display space. By segmenting consumers, identifying high-impact products, and uncovering purchase correlations, retailers can make informed decisions that align with customer needs and market dynamics. The methodologies employed—DT and association rules—offer scalable frameworks for similar retail environments, though future studies should explore transactional data granularity and diverse product categories to refine these strategies further. Ultimately, the integration of data-driven insights into retail management not only enhances operational efficiency but also strengthens competitive advantage in an increasingly personalized market landscape.

As future research directions, this study could be expanded by analyzing non-food product categories, such as electronics or textiles, whose purchasing patterns differ significantly from fast-moving consumer goods. Additionally, incorporating individual transactional data (rather than aggregated monthly data) would allow for an exploration of purchase frequency per customer, enhancing the understanding of customer loyalty and seasonality. The application of advanced machine learning techniques, such as neural networks or hierarchical clustering, could further refine customer segmentation and demand forecasting. Finally, comparative studies across different geographic markets (e.g., urban vs. rural) would help validate the generalizability of these assortment optimization strategies.

ACKNOWLEDGEMENT

This work is financed by National Funds provided by FCT- Foundation for Science and Technology through project UID/04020/2025 (CinTurs) with DOI https://doi.org/10.54499/UID/04020/2025.

REFERENCES

Biliavska, Y., Romat, Y., Biliavskyi, V., Ostapenko, T., & Sydorenko, O. (2024). Diagnosing Category Management in A Pharmacy Retail Chain. *Eastern-European Journal of Enterprise Technologies*, *127*(13), 22–32. DOI: 10.15587/1729-4061.2024.298093

Bradlow, E., Gangwar, M., Kopalle, P., & Voleti, S. (2017). The Role of Big Data and Predictive Analytics in Retailing. *Journal of Retailing*, *93*(1), 79–95. DOI: 10.1016/j.jretai.2016.12.004

Caigny, A., Coussement, K., & Bock, K. (2018). A new hybrid classification algorithm for customer churn prediction based on logistic regression and decision trees. *European Journal of Operational Research*, *269*(2), 760–772. DOI: 10.1016/j.ejor.2018.02.009

Chandrasekhar, K., Das, S., Gupta, N., & Jena, S. K. (2024). Comparative Analysis of Impulse Buying Behaviour Across Retail Channels: A Study of Physical Stores, E-commerce Websites and Mobile Shopping Apps. *Economic Affairs*, *69*(02), 1109–1120.

Chen, Y., Chen, J., & Ching-Wen, T. (2006). A data mining approach for retail knowledge discovery with consideration of the effect of shelf-space adjacency on sales. *Decision Support Systems*, *42*(3), 1503–1520. DOI: 10.1016/j.dss.2005.12.004

Chen, Y. M., Chen, T. Y., & Chen, L. C. (2021). On a method for location and mobility analytics using location-based services: A case study of retail store recommendation. *Online Information Review*, *45*(2), 297–315. DOI: 10.1108/OIR-10-2017-0292

Chen, Z. Y., Fan, Z. P., & Sun, M. (2023). Machine learning methods for data-driven demand estimation and assortment planning considering cross-selling and substitutions. *INFORMS Journal on Computing*, *35*(1), 158–177. DOI: 10.1287/ijoc.2022.1251

Daruvuri, R., Patibandla, K. K., & Mannem, P. (2025, March). Data Driven Retail Price Optimization Using XGBoost and Predictive Modeling. In *2025 International Conference on Intelligent Computing and Control Systems (ICICCS)* (pp. 220-225). IEEE. DOI: 10.1109/ICICCS65191.2025.10984940

Das, P., & Dhar, P. (2021). Finding Out the Influence of Marketing Mix on Attitude of Customers for Providing Online Reviews. [AMT]. *Advancement in Management and Technology*, *2*(1), 27–37.

Delasay, M., Jain, A., & Kumar, S. (2022). Impacts of the COVID-19 pandemic on grocery retail operations: An analytical model. *Production and Operations Management, 31*(5), 2237–2255. DOI: 10.1111/poms.13717 PMID: 35601843

Gahinet, M. C., & Cliquet, G. (2018). Proximity and time in convenience store patronage: Kaïros more than chronos. *Journal of Retailing and Consumer Services, 43*, 1–9. DOI: 10.1016/j.jretconser.2018.02.008

Han, J., Pei, J., Yin, Y., & Mao, R. (2004). Mining frequent patterns without candidate generation: A frequent-pattern tree approach. *Data Mining and Knowledge Discovery*, *8*(1), 53–87. DOI: 10.1023/B:DAMI.0000005258.31418.83

Heger, J., & Klein, R. (2024). Assortment optimization: A systematic literature review. *OR-Spektrum*, *46*(4), 1099–1161. DOI: 10.1007/s00291-024-00752-4

Hekimoğlua, M., Sevim, I., Aksezer, A., & Durmuş, I. (2019). Assortment optimization with log-linear demand: Application at a Turkish grocery store. *Journal of Retailing and Consumer Services*, *50*, 199–214. DOI: 10.1016/j.jretconser.2019.04.007

Hooli, M. (2025). Optimizing Retail with AI: How Intelligent Systems Are Redefining Shopping Experiences. *Journal of Computer Science and Technology Studies*, *7*(6), 465–471.

Hoque, M. J., Islam, M. S., & Mohtasim, S. A. (2024). Optimizing decision-making through customer-centric market basket analysis. *Journal of Operational and Strategic Analytics*, *2*(2), 72–83. DOI: 10.56578/josa020201

Hruschka, H. (2024). Analyzing market basket data through sparse multivariate logit models. *Journal of Marketing Analytics*, 1–16. DOI: 10.1057/s41270-024-00331-0

Jin, C., Li, F., Ma, S., & Wang, Y. (2022). Sampling scheme-based classification rule mining method using decision tree in big data environment. *Knowledge-Based Systems*, *244*, 108522. DOI: 10.1016/j.knosys.2022.108522

Jung, N. Y. (2025). AI-Powered Personalization Drives Loyalty in Retail. In *Leveraging AI-Powered Marketing in the Experience-Driven Economy* (pp. 105–146). IGI Global Scientific Publishing. DOI: 10.4018/979-8-3693-9561-5.ch004

Ke, C., Li, A., & Wang, R. (2025). Modeling, Prediction, Assortment and Price Optimization Under Consumer Choice Behavior. *Foundations and Trends® in Technology. Information and Operations Management, 19*(1), 1–141. DOI: 10.1561/0200000112

Kotler, P., & Armstrong, G. (2014). *Principals of Marketing* (15th ed.).

Krishna, G., & Ravi, V. (2020). Mining top high utility association rules using Binary Differential Evolution. *Engineering Applications of Artificial Intelligence, 96*, 103935. DOI: 10.1016/j.engappai.2020.103935

Kwak, K., Duvvuri, S., & Russell, G. (2015). An Analysis of Assortment Choice in Grocery Retailing. *Journal of Retailing, 91*(1), 19–33. DOI: 10.1016/j.jretai.2014.10.004

Martinez, M., Escobar, B., García Diaz, M., & Pinto-Roa, D. (2021). Market basket analysis with association rules in the retail sector using Orange. Case Study: Appliances Sales Company. *CLEI Electronic Journal, 24*(2), 1–17. DOI: 10.19153/cleiej.24.2.12

Martínez-Garmendia, J. (2023). Machine learning for product choice prediction. *Journal of Marketing Analytics*, 1-12. DOI: 10.1057/s41270-023-00217-7

Miao, S., & Chao, X. (2022). Online personalized assortment optimization with high-dimensional customer contextual data. *Manufacturing & Service Operations Management, 24*(5), 2741–2760. DOI: 10.1287/msom.2022.1128

Miller, C., Smith, S., McIntyre, S., & Achabal, D. (2010). Optimizing and Evaluating Retail Assortments for Infrequently Purchased Products. *Journal of Retailing, 86*(2), 159–171. DOI: 10.1016/j.jretai.2010.02.004

Moodley, R., Chiclana, F., Caraffini, F., & Carterb, J. (2020). A product-centric data mining algorithm for targeted promotions'. *Journal of Retailing and Consumer Services, 54*, 101940. DOI: 10.1016/j.jretconser.2019.101940

Mrutzek-Hartmann, B., Kotzab, H., Yumurtacı Hüseyinoğlu, I. Ö., & Kühling, S. (2022). Omni-channel retailing resources and capabilities of SME specialty retailers–insights from Germany and Turkey. *International Journal of Retail & Distribution Management, 50*(8/9), 1129–1155. DOI: 10.1108/IJRDM-10-2021-0503

Neogrid (2018). Análise de sortimento: o que é e qual sua importância? Available at: https://blog.neogrid.com/analise-de-sortimento-o-que-e-e-qual-sua-importancia/ (accessed July 10, 2022).

Novikova, K. (2021, October). Unique assortment as a key factor of local food Retail's competitiveness increase. In *International Perm Forum Science and Global Challenges of the 21st Century* (pp. 1086-1103). Cham: Springer International Publishing.

Orange (2022). Educação em Ciência de Dados. Available at: https://orangedatamining.com/home/teachers_and_students_love_it/ (accessed August 28, 2022).

Pratas, J., & Brito, P. (2019). *Distribuição - Gestão de pontos de venda e de retalho*. Conjuntura Actual Editora.

Rahman, A. (2022). Category Management in Procurement: A Framework for Enhancing Strategic Decision-Making. *International Journal of Emerging Trends in Computer Science and Information Technology*, *3*(1), 10–19. DOI: 10.63282/3050-9246.IJETCSIT-V3I1P102

Ray, S., & Nayak, L. (2023). Marketing sustainable fashion: Trends and future directions. *Sustainability (Basel)*, *15*(7), 6202. DOI: 10.3390/su15076202

Rousseau, D. (2015). General systems theory: Its present and potential. *Systems Research and Behavioral Science*, *32*(5), 522–533. DOI: 10.1002/sres.2354

Rousseau, J. (2014). Manual da Distribuição, 2ª edição, Cascais: Princípia Editora.

Rygielski, C., Wang, C., & Yen, C. (2002). Data mining techniques for customer relationship management. *Technology in Society*, *24*(4), 483–502. DOI: 10.1016/S0160-791X(02)00038-6

Sethuraman, R., Gázquez-Abad, J., & Martínez-López, F. (2022). The effect of retail assortment size on perceptions, choice, and sales: Review and research directions'. *Journal of Retailing*, *98*(1), 24–45. DOI: 10.1016/j.jretai.2022.01.001

Sharma, G., & Sharma, P. (2016). A Study on Data Mining Algorithms for Tourism Industry. *International Journal of Latest Trends in Engineering & Technology : IJLTET*, *7*(1), 580–587.

Srivastava, P. R., Zhang, J. Z., Eachempati, P., Sharma, S. K., & Liu, Y. (2025). An Intelligent omnichannel assortment model to manage webrooming: An optimization approach. *Journal of Strategic Marketing*, *33*(3), 441–465. DOI: 10.1080/0965254X.2022.2067072

Tekin, M., Etlioğlu, M., Koyuncuoğlu, Ö., & Tekin, E. (2018). Data mining in digital marketing. *Proceedings of the International Symposium for Production Research 2018 18* (pp. 44-61). Springer International Publishing. DOI: 10.1007/978-3-319-92267-6_4

Yu, Y., Wang, B., & Zheng, S. (2024). Data-driven product design and assortment optimization. *Transportation Research Part E, Logistics and Transportation Review, 182*, 103413. DOI: 10.1016/j.tre.2024.103413

KEY TERMS AND DEFINITIONS

Artificial Intelligence: The simulation of human intelligence in machines, enabling them to perform tasks like reasoning, learning, problem-solving, and decision-making. AI technologies, including NLP, computer vision, and robotics, transform industries by automating processes and enhancing data-driven insights.

Association Rules: A data mining technique that identifies relationships between variables in large datasets, often used in market basket analysis. It uncovers patterns like "if X is purchased, then Y is likely bought," helping retailers optimise product placements, promotions, and cross-selling strategies.

Assortment Management: The strategic process of selecting, organising, and optimising a retailer's product offerings to maximise sales, profitability, and customer satisfaction. It involves analysing consumer demand, inventory turnover, and market trends to create balanced product assortments that align with business goals while meeting shopper preferences across different categories and channels.

Data Mining: The computational process of discovering patterns, correlations, and insights from large datasets using statistical and machine learning techniques. It helps businesses extract valuable information for decision-making, such as customer segmentation, fraud detection, and market trend analysis, by transforming raw data into actionable knowledge.

Decision Tree: A machine learning model that uses a tree-like structure of decisions and possible outcomes to classify data or make predictions. Each branch represents a decision rule, and each leaf node represents an outcome, making it useful for both regression and classification tasks in business analytics.

Machine Learning: A subset of AI where algorithms learn from data to improve performance on tasks without explicit programming. It includes supervised, unsupervised, and reinforcement learning, enabling applications like recommendation systems, fraud detection, and automated decision-making in retail and other industries.

Predictive Analytics: The use of historical data, statistical algorithms, and machine learning to forecast future outcomes. Businesses apply it to anticipate customer behaviour, demand trends, risks, and operational needs, enabling proactive decision-making and strategy optimisation.

Retail: The business of selling goods or services directly to consumers through physical stores, e-commerce platforms, or omnichannel systems. It includes merchandising, inventory management, pricing, and customer engagement strategies to drive sales while adapting to evolving consumer behaviours and market competition.

Chapter 6
Automated Curriculum Vitae Validation Through NLP and Machine Learning

Manoj Himmatrao Devare
http://orcid.org/0000-0002-9530-3914
Amity University, Mumbai, India

Rahul Anantha Singh
http://orcid.org/0009-0004-4886-5043
Amity University, Mumbai, India

Anita Manoj Devare
http://orcid.org/0009-0009-4159-6289
Amity University, Mumbai, India

Pravin Laxmikant Yannawar
http://orcid.org/0000-0002-3398-0565
Dr. Babasaheb Ambedkar Marathwada University, India

ABSTRACT

The recruitment department regularly face difficulties in confirmation of the originality of a Curriculum Vitae. The human judgment may result into errors, delays and appointed person might be go under suspect due to undetected irregularities in CV. The automated CV authenticity verification discovers errors and inconsistencies. The parsing of ATS compliant PDFs extracts personal data, education, employment details, and skills. The NLP, and ML identifies an overlapping employment, gaps, mismatched skills, and other irregularities in CV. The system determines the timeline

DOI: 10.4018/979-8-3373-3648-0.ch006

inconsistency of the resume and the validation of the LinkedIn URL. Finally, a CV is classified as authentic, partially authentic, need to do cross-check manually, or not authentic, depending on a genuinity score. The genuinity score is adjusted using bonuses, penalties and timeline information. Explainable AI SHAP manifests the interpretability and transparency in the decision-making process of AI.

1. INTRODUCTION

The human resources department's recruitment system often faces significant challenges in verifying the accuracy of job seeker resumes, a time-consuming process that is prone to human error. This situation can create poor hiring experiences. In one respect, it can lead to a case where the new hires are still in the hands of the old ones, or the new hires are in the wrong position. Through the CV Authenticity Verification System, problems caused by inefficient resource allocation can be reduced, and the subsequently hidden truth is not detected by HR professionals who are provided with a reliable tool. The CV Authenticity Verification system uses advanced technologies to streamline the verification process, ensuring greater accuracy and reducing the workload for HR teams, and ultimately enhancing the overall quality of candidate selection (Saatçı, Kaya, & Ünlü, 2024).

The hiring decision is important as an incorrect candidate can cause further damage to organizational resources. Misleading information provided by the candidate can lead to several negative consequences, such as poor work performance. There can be legal compliance with regulations issues that can damage reputation and financial losses. The modern recruitment process ensures the authenticity of CVs. An applicant can exaggerate and falsify their information and increase their chances of being hired. Employers strongly rely on CVs to assess the qualifications, experience, and skills of the candidate. With the growing competition in the labor market, however, many candidates distort their work history, education, and technical expertise. The recruiters can unknowingly choose inaccurate information.

Applicant Tracking System (ATS) Compliant CV is a digital recruitment tool that helps the HR team in CVs and applications. Instead of manually inspecting each CV, recruiters can use ATS to automate most of the process, which saves time and resources. Due to resume parsing, comparison of keywords, automated screening, candidates ranking, interview planning, and database management became easy. While these systems increase the efficiency of the recruitment process, they lack a mechanism to verify the authenticity of the applicants' claims. As a result, staff can make decisions to hire potentially fraudulent or exaggerated CVs, leading to poor hiring results. This chapter will explore the various irregularities in CVs, Methods for Detecting Authenticity and Irregularities, and Challenges in the evaluation of

Authenticity and Irregularities. An automated resume parsing and job domain prediction can help the HR team work efficiently in the organization (Mittal, Mehta, Relan, & Gabrani, 2020).

The recruitment system regularly faces challenges in verifying the authenticity of candidate resumes, a task that may be time-consuming and at risk of human error. This book chapter discusses a process of automation where CVs are uploaded in PDFs, and extracted vital details together with private records, education, experience, and skills. It employs AI, Natural Language Processing (NLP), and Machine Learning to assess resumes, identifying irregularities including overlapping employment, employment gaps, skills not mentioned in experience, missing email addresses, and absent mobile numbers (Rojas-Galeano, Posada, & Ordoñez, 2022).

The system additionally conducts authenticity exams, along with temporal consistency via a timeline test. It ensures education and experience tenures logically. Additionally, it verifies the presence of supplied LinkedIn URLs. The user interface lets users upload resumes, view processed results in a sidebar, and gain access to a database of saved data via SQLite. The system categorizes resumes into authenticity status, such as authentic, partially authentic, needs to be cross-checked manually, or not authentic. It is based totally on the identified irregularities and authenticity tests. Through this approach, it seeks to increase the integrity, accuracy, and transparency of the AI-controlled recruitment. It ensures that the hiring process is based on verified and reliable candidate information.

This chapter explores the step-by-step procedures and the technology used to upload an ATS-compliant CV file and extract the necessary information from it. The AI model is developed to assess CV authenticity. The train phase is performed using an NLP model to analyze text content and identify irregularities. The parser extracts key features such as education, experience, and skills. The process of identifying anomalies in CV content will be discussed. The results achieved through the Machine Learning models are to detect disagreements between skills, experience, and roles. The parser and AI-based technique identify unusual formulas, such as the duration of unrealistic experiences or excessive skills. This research has prepared the Genuity score for a CV. The irregularities and anomalies identified are used to give a Genuity score to each resume.

Despite the advances in recruitment controlled by AI, several key challenges persist, limiting their reliability and effectiveness. There is a lack of automated verification. Existing applicants' monitoring systems, i.e., ATS, focus mainly on the analysis and classification of CVs but lack robust mechanisms to verify the authenticity of the CV content. This gap allows candidates to beautify or falsify information without detection. There are limited fraud detection capabilities in the existing AI-based systems. Current recruitment tools driven by AI depend on sampling analysis to identify deceptive or manufactured information. However, these systems often struggle with skills inflation, manipulated work titles, or manufactured experience, leading to fraud not being detected. There is inefficient parsing and data extraction, as many ATS systems struggle to extract and interpret information from various CV formats. Variations in curriculum designs, file types, and the use of keywords lead to poor interpretations, which causes qualified candidates to be overlooked or classified in an inaccurate way. Transparency in decision-making is observed in many AI-based contracting tools that lack transparency in the way they evaluate and classify candidates. Recruiters often cannot understand why a CV is marked as a suspect, which makes it difficult to validate the decisions driven by AI, guarantee justice, and reduce biases in the hiring process.

Transparency refers to openness, clarity, and honesty in action, decision, and communication, and shows that relevant information is easily accessible, available, and understandable for interested parties. Transparency is a key principle in governance, business, and personal relationships. Since it generates trust, responsibility, and credibility when an organization, government, or individual is transparent, it means that they do not hide information or deceive others to operate secretly. Instead, they are open about their process, motives, and actions. This transparency helps prevent corruption and misunderstanding while fostering relationships, efficiency, and ethical practices.

1.1 Objectives

The objective of the research is to provide a system that allows users to upload ATS-compliant CVs in PDF or DOCX format to the database using a simple user interface. Furthermore, develop an AI model to assess CV authenticity and train an NLP model to analyze text content and identify irregularities. Extract key features such as education, experience, and skills. The third objective is to identify and flag Anomalies in CV content using machine learning models to detect disagreements between skills, experience, and roles. Identify unusual formulas, such as the duration of unrealistic experiences or excessive skills. The objective is also to give Genuity score to each resume that uses irregularities and anomalies, to give Genuity score to each resume. It provides transparency in AI decision-making and implements explainability models Shapley Addictive Explanation (SHAP), to justify authenticity scores and display reasons for CV rejection or flagging to recruiters.

The remaining chapter is divided into the background section that covers the review of the existing research work regarding the automated CV processing techniques such as machine learning, NLP, covering ethical and fairness concerns, hybrid approaches, and Explainable AI techniques. Section 3 is on the Industry Impact and Relevance. Section 4 is on the Ethical Implications. Section 5 is on methodology of this research work covering CV processing approach, authenticity verification,

Genuity score calculation and explanation. It further explains the reasons for the low Genuity score and system design and implementation. One dedicated section is given of XAI and how it is used for the CV processing. The results are discussed in detail including User Interface, model performance, and SHAP force plot. The discussion section is added along with conclusion and future work.

2. BACKGROUND

2.1 Trends in CV Screening

Table 1. Trends in CV screening and processing tools and techniques used by HR

Category	Trend / Tool / Technique	Description / Key Features
Automation	Applicant Tracking Systems (ATS)	Software that automates CV collection, filtering, and ranking based on job-specific keywords.
AI & ML Integration	AI-based Screening Tools (e.g., Resume2Vec, HireVue)	Use of machine learning to assess candidate fit, flag patterns, and reduce bias.
Keyword Matching	Resume Parsing & Keyword Filters	Tools scan for role-specific keywords and match against job description requirements.
Predictive Analytics	Candidate Scoring Algorithms	Predicts candidate success based on historical hiring data and job performance outcomes.
Chatbots & Virtual Assistants	Pre-screening Chatbots (e.g., Mya, Olivia)	Automates initial candidate interactions, FAQs, and qualification checks.
Video Screening	Asynchronous Video Interview Tools	Candidates record answers to predefined questions; AI may assist in evaluation.
Skills Assessment	Online Assessment Platforms (e.g., Codility, HackerRank)	Evaluate technical or role-specific skills before the interview stage.
Bias Reduction	Blind Hiring Tools	Anonymize resumes by hiding names, genders, ages, and other bias-prone details.
Social Media Screening	LinkedIn Profile Analysis	Profiles are analyzed for qualifications, recommendations, and endorsements.
Gamification	Game-based Assessment Tools	Engage candidates through game-like scenarios to assess personality or problem-solving.
Compliance & Ethics	GDPR-Compliant Screening Tools	Ensure data privacy and consent in candidate data processing.
Trend Shift	Manual to Data-Driven Decision Making	Focus is shifting from human intuition to evidence-based, data-supported screening.

Table 1 shows the various tasks related to the HR functions, such as automation in the CV screening, parsing of the CVs, and candidates' scoring based on the job performance outcomes. It also summarizes the various tools, like chatbots and virtual assistants, for the initial candidate interactions and qualification checking. The skills can be assessed, such as technical and role-specific skills, before the interview stage. The CV screening using the blind hiring tools aims to reduce bias. Evaluating personality and skills based using gamification techniques.

When HR professionals sort CVs for a particular position, they follow a systematic and cautious approach to ensure they select the most suitable candidates while avoiding bias and errors. The precautions HR typically take during the CV screening process. The matching of the candidate's CV mentioning Skills, qualifications, educational background, and certification with the Job Description (JD) is important. The experience level and the type of experience are required to be matched. The priorities are given to the candidates with relevant industry knowledge and domain experience.

The ATS system mainly works based on keyword screening. The job description (JD) contains the relevant keywords that match candidates' skills and qualifications. In ethical practices, HR avoids discarding good candidates due to unusual phrasing. Creatively written CVs are read by HRs manually, if needed.

The inconsistencies in employment history, inconsistencies in dates, employment gaps, frequent job-hopping, and generic content show a lack of customization for the job role. HRs try to avoid unconscious bias by focusing on skills and achievements, not name, gender, age, or photo. There are blind screening tools and templates in some organizations. Soft Skills Indicators, such as communication skills, leadership, teamwork, and initiative, are derived from project descriptions, volunteering, or achievements. HR verifies contact details and References. Important information like email, phone number, and LinkedIn profile is present.

2.2 Machine Learning Based Techniques

The literature review on the automated processing of CVs is categorized into four different types. The first set of research work is about the use of machine learning based tools and techniques in the CV processing listed in Table 2.

Table 2. Review of machine learning based solutions for CV processing

Author	Contribution	Major Results
Zimmermann et al. (2016)	A data-driven approach is developed to automate resume analysis using Natural Language Processing (NLP) and machine learning techniques. The system extracts relevant information from resumes, such as education, work experience, and skills, and calculates a ranking score to assess candidate fit for specific job descriptions. By providing recruiters with a tool to filter and rank candidates objectively, the approach aims to reduce human bias and enhance the efficiency of the hiring process. The study demonstrates how integrating such technologies can lead to more honest and merit-based candidate selection.	Ranking scores are calculated to assess candidate fit for specific job descriptions.
Luo et al. (2018a)	A ResumeNet, a neural network-based framework designed to assess resume quality automatically. Recognizing the challenges in manual resume screening, the authors collected approximately 10,000 resumes from a private management company to train and evaluate their model. Key features considered include consistency between different resume sections, which are indicative of a candidate's honesty and coherence. To address the issue of limited labelled data, the study employs semi-supervised learning techniques and pair/triplet-based loss functions, enhancing the model's ability to learn from both labelled and unlabeled data. The evaluation metrics, ROC curve, F-measure, and average precision demonstrate the model's effectiveness in distinguishing high-quality resumes. By comparing ResumeNet's performance with existing online resume scoring tools, the study highlights its superior accuracy and potential to revolutionize human resource management by providing an unbiased and efficient resume assessment tool.	Consistency among the various resume sections is calculated.
Bhatia et al. (2019)	present an end-to-end system that leverages Bidirectional Encoder Representations from Transformers (BERT), a transformer-based model, for parsing resumes and matching them to job descriptions. The system operates in two stages such as it parses resumes to extract structured information, and then it uses BERT for sentence pair classification to assess the suitability of candidates for specific job roles. The dataset comprises resumes in both LinkedIn and general formats, with the parser achieving 100% accuracy on LinkedIn resumes. The model establishes a strong baseline accuracy of 73% in candidate-job matching, demonstrating its potential in automating the recruitment process. By focusing on the semantic similarity between job descriptions and candidates past experiences, the system aims to identify honest and suitable candidates effectively.	BERT achieved 100% accuracy on LinkedIn resumes. Achieved 73% accuracy of candidate-job matching.

continued on following page

Table 2. Continued

Author	Contribution	Major Results
Chen et al. (2023)	Later, as explored by the adaptive way of selecting the most appropriate layer of a BERT as a pre-trained language model for multi-text brand classification, which can be useful in CV screening. The authors emphasize that the performance of the BERT layer for certain labels is the highest of all layers. It supports the intermediate representations of the transformer rather than solely relying on the last layer.	An appropriate layer of BERT is detected from the pre-trained model for multi-text CV classification.
(Luo et al., 2018b)	A scope of a neural network to unleash the potential of CV is proposed. The CV dataset is created, diversified, and the corresponding portions of the text are added to the dataset. The text tokens, such as skills, work history, and further calculated to determine how good the sections in these datasets are. It combined the quality score of the sum of several parts, such as the highest academic degree, completeness, and the texture of the content.	A Neural Network is used to calculate the score of the candidate.

2.3 Fairness and Ethical Concerns

Table 3 summarizes the review on Mitigating Unfair and Unethical concerns in CV screening.

Table 3. Review mitigating unfair and unethical concerns in CV screening

Author	Contribution	Major Results
Li et al. (2023)	The potential biases in deep learning-based systems are detected in the automated resume screening systems, particularly concerning national origin discrimination. The study reveals that word embeddings, which are foundational to many NLP models, can inherit and amplify societal stereotypes present in the training data. This bias can lead to unfair treatment of candidates from certain demographic groups. To mitigate this issue, the authors propose a bias mitigation method and conduct extensive experiments on real candidate resumes to validate their approach. The findings show the importance of addressing ethical and legal concerns in AI-driven recruitment tools to ensure honest and fair candidate evaluation.	Detected the precautionary to the unfair treatment of candidates from certain demographic groups.
Saatçı et al. (2024)	This work addressed the challenges employers face in screening large volumes of resumes by proposing an NLP-based system that focuses on extracting competencies relevant to specific job positions. The system utilizes Jaccard Similarity to match extracted competencies from resumes to predefined skill sets associated with various job roles. By concentrating on the presence or absence of specific competencies, the approach aims to reduce bias and ensure a fair evaluation of candidates. Integration with platforms like LinkedIn enhances the system's effectiveness, offering a scalable and unbiased solution for large organizations seeking honest candidate identification.	Jaccard Similarity is used to match extracted competencies to reduce bias to ensure the fair evaluation of the candidates.
Wilson and Caliskan (2024)	This work has explored the presence of gender, race, and intersectional biases in resume screening processes that utilize large language models (LLMs). Using a document retrieval framework, they simulate job candidate selection across nine occupations with over 500 publicly available resumes and 500 job descriptions. Their findings reveal significant biases, such as Massive Text Embedding (MTE) models favored White-associated names in 85.1% of cases and female-associated names in only 11.1% of cases. Notably, Black males were disadvantaged in up to 100% of cases, replicating real-world patterns of employment discrimination. The study also identifies factors such as document length and the frequency of names in the corpus as influencing resume selection. These results indicate that there is a need for careful consideration of fairness in AI-driven hiring tools and the development of strategies to mitigate bias in automated resume screening.	LLM is utilized to explore gender, race, and intersectional biases.

continued on following page

Table 3. Continued

Author	Contribution	Major Results
Wen et al. (2025)	The study introduced Fairness Assessment in Resume Evaluation (FAIRE), a benchmarking framework designed to evaluate racial and gender biases in AI-driven resume screening systems. Recognizing the growing reliance on LLMs in recruitment processes, the authors aim to systematically assess how these models may inadvertently perpetuate biases against certain demographic groups. The FAIRE framework employs two primary methods, i.e., direct scoring and ranking. These methods involve altering resumes to reflect different racial and gender identities while keeping qualifications constant, allowing for the measurement of changes in model evaluations solely based on demographic factors. The study's findings reveal that all tested LLMs exhibit some degree of bias, though the extent and direction vary across models. Notably, certain models demonstrate significant disparities in evaluations when resumes are modified to represent different demographic profiles, underscoring the potential for AI systems to reinforce existing societal biases if not properly audited and corrected. By providing an open-source benchmark and dataset, the authors offer a valuable tool for researchers and practitioners to assess and mitigate biases in AI-driven hiring tools. The study emphasizes the importance of transparency and fairness in automated recruitment systems, advocating for regular audits and the development of bias mitigation strategies to ensure equitable candidate evaluations. As organizations increasingly adopt AI for resume screening, frameworks like FAIRE are essential for identifying and addressing potential discriminatory practices embedded within these technologies.	FAIRE Framework is designed to evaluate racial and gender biases.
Albassam (2023) & Shoukath and Chakkaravarthy (2025)	gives an in-depth account of AI-enabled recruitment in the form of resume screening, candidate matching, and predictive analytics tools to improve the hiring process. This work also warns against unethical risks, which show a contribution to the discrimination of candidates, and throws the law school of thought into looking for further insight. It also focused on the growing role of data-driven decision-making in improving academic outcomes, mentioning it in the form of institutional strategies. It is highly required to guide the students to write CVs in a more ethical manner.	Legal aspects of unethical and discriminatory practices are highlighted.

continued on following page

Table 3. Continued

Author	Contribution	Major Results
Abraham et al. (2025) & (Khan et al., 2023).	Provided an in-depth analysis of the role of artificial intelligence (AI) in the revolution of talent acquisition and management. AI-based technologies, like resume checkers, chatbots, and predictive systems, not only speed up the selection process but also increase commitment and provide immediate feedback to the candidates. The research shows that reducing human prejudices emphasizes the ability to expose applicants. The views of the HR managers indicate that AI accelerates hiring and makes it more accurate. The work provides a few examples of companies that have completely or partially transformed their recruitment process through AI and NLP. The task, such as the conversion of unstructured data into structured data, becomes a resource for better searches and more intelligent hiring. The AI that the machines are utilizing for creating a new CV is still at a primitive stage. The author notes that NLP and AI oversee the consistent adaptation to the understanding of the language used by humans, and AI can take a whole lot of guesswork out of the CV screening process.	The improvement of efficiency is underlined due to the automated tools. Also, there is a reduction in human prejudices.
Albaroudi et al. (2024)	The work outlines the AI bias correction measures in the CV selection process. It gives an overview of the AI selection of CVs and its algorithm generation. The NLP and deep learning-based masking and augmentation methods are used to remove human bias. The dataset is used here without any ranking distortion of the proportion and distribution of all factors. It informs about the challenges and limitations of work in a clear way for human review. It adds that the final decision is to be made to keep the AI as an assistant to humans in the process. Technology is how humanity should seek mutual benefit in ethical hiring responsibly, taking both technical and human issues into account.	Masking and augmentation methods are used to remove human bias during the CV Screening.

2.4 Use of NLP in CV Processing

Table 4 summarizes a review of the use of NLP Techniques in CV processing.

Table 4. Review of the use of natural language processing techniques in CV processing

Author	Contribution	Major Results
(Bharadwaj et al., 2022)	As explored, a CV representation model that applies NLP and a recurrent neural network creates a model to recognize, search, and act on work type recommendations from CV data. This system then queries the database to see if there are any open jobs. The system gets the relevant CVs out of the database and sends them to the user. It suggests matching roles for the candidates in need. It serves as an intermediary between the recruiter and the position seeker for the deemed roles.	Used the Recurrent Neural Network for suggesting matching roles as an intermediary between the recruiter and position seeker.
(Daryani et al., 2020)	A novel system described that checks CVs using computerized systems, and which also includes the extraction of information from unstructured CVs using NLP. The system moves to data cleaning through analysis, getting rid of unwanted details. It combines the key attributes into a few sentences and becomes one of the necessary conditions for the system of the automated process. It utilizes a new machine learning model and combines it with the Cosine Similarity method. It considers the syntax of the CVs and the Job Description (JD) to perform faster e-recruitment and to automate the process of employee selection.	Emphasized the extraction of information from unstructured CVs using NLP and the Cosine Similarity method to match JD and CVs.
(Mishra & Vishwakarma, 2016)	The implementation of the weight-based Term Frequency and Inverse-Document Frequency (TF-IDF) method and its derivatives concerning the retrieval of documents are presented. Using an online source code called Terrier 3.5 and a data file from Fire 2011, the researchers compare different methods of weighting. The results show that TF-IDF was the most successful in obtaining accurate results and showed its efficiency in the process of document evaluation based on the relevance of the question.	IF-IDF and the difference weight-based method are used for improving the accuracy and efficiency in the processes of CV evaluation.
(Julian & Haripriya, 2024)	Introduced a fresh pipeline to the public, which is a hybrid of scraping job vacancies from the Internet for data processing based on Word2vec for categorization and comparison of CVs. Word2vec uses either a Continuous Bag of Words (CBOW) or a Skip-Gram model to predict the next word or the surrounding words. The application automatically extracts summary information from the CV that is like the user and then, through algorithms of NLP, it matches the candidates to the vacancies. The platform can not only compare tasks effectively, but also the job can generate personalized interview questions instantly with the system, reducing the time needed for recruitment and the overall experience of the candidate by doing CV analysis.	Performed the hybrid of scraping job vacancies and CBOW for matching candidates' profiles.

continued on following page

Table 4. Continued

Author	Contribution	Major Results
Nirali et al. (2020)	This work proposes an NLP-driven system for CV learning and introduces a method where CV information is read and processed by the machine through AI without manual intervention. It brings to light problems in the manual record-keeping process and exposes a hidden location of the AI in the text review process for the identification, interview, and assimilation of more talented candidates. The authors assert that all the algorithms that are going to be rated and the key points of the respective ones should be easy to understand, so that hiring managers can use them for judgment purposes. AI has advanced the way HR professionals handle the evaluation of applicants, and there is no need for the manual, old-fashioned approach. It is confirmed that human labor is no longer hard, but human pleasant, and that switching to AI helps in talent acquisition in new ways that humans have not been able to do in the past.	NLP and AI-driven tools are helping in talent acquisition
Blessing et al. (2025)	The research outlines the transformative impact of AI on resume screening and its many benefits, such as effectiveness, scalability, and reduced bias through NLP and ML algorithms. The AI-based mechanism instantly scans very large resume volumes to find the best matches for the job. However, it also identifies other problems like algorithmic bias, lack of transparency, soft skills evaluation unavailability, and at the same time, ethical implications, which are linked to data privacy.	Underlines the effectiveness, scalability, and reduced bias through NLP and ML algorithms.
Roy et al. (2020) & Tejaswini et al., (2022)	The resumes are to be grouped as per classifiers. The most qualified applicants are identified under the job description by employing such tools as cosine similarity and K-NN. This method seeks to simplify the extremely overwhelming stage of scouting and interacting with applicants. This, in turn, brings about a faster search for the best candidates. It also determines the resume genuineness system consistent with the skills mentioned by the candidate.	The K-NN and Cosine similarity metrics are used to find the match between the job and the candidates' CVs.
Tayal et al. (2024)	started an investigation into ML and NLP techniques such as Named Entity Recognition (NER) and Parts of Speech (POS) Tagging methodologies, as an approach that can be used to automate the screening of resumes to solve the limitations of manual methods. K-Nearest Neighbor (K-NN) and Support Vector Machine (SVM) classifiers are used here, which have improved the accuracy of human resource decision-makers' work and lessened the time needed for the whole personnel recruitment process.	The NLP techniques NER, POS are used along with the ML techniques K-NN and SVM.

continued on following page

Table 4. Continued

Author	Contribution	Major Results
Sroison & Chan (2021)	Resume Parser with NLP puts forward a resolution for the problems that HR departments are encountering due to handling the huge volume of resumes with an automated system. The system is capable of translating resumes of different kinds into text, extracting the necessary data, and matching them with the required job profile to calculate similarity scores, which are beneficial for candidate selection.	A high volume of CV documents is processed, and similarity scores are calculated.
(Rasal, 2023)	The article explores the increasing requirement for precise resume parsing in online job applications, where HR departments are confronted with difficulties in managing various resume formats. The research outlines the application of NLP methods, such as keyword matching, to quickly get suitable candidate data, which in turn helps the HR teams to be quicker in detecting the most suitable employees for vacant positions.	Managing the various resume formats is a major contribution using NLP.

2.5 Miscellaneous Techniques in CV Processing

Table 5 summarizes the different approaches to resolving the challenges in CV processing.

Table 5. Different approaches to resolve the challenges in CV processing

Author	Contribution	Major Results
Wosiak et al. (2021)	Implemented automated data extraction from Polish-language CVs in the field of IT recruitment. This system allows us to automatically analyze the messy resume texts that are beyond the human capacity of analytical processing using a combination of multiple modules. Examination revealed that the model was able to perform accurately in the keyword recognition over resume sectors, leaving the conventional tools way behind.	The hybrid model was developed to solve the difficulties of the Polish language, like intricate linguistic dependencies.
Chintalapati et al. (2024)	The system includes features like scripted conversations, audiovisual, and user feedback that gives structured appraisals and suggestions, and at the same time, hand in hand with the talent, it helps in the practice of the systematic outcome to perform better in the interview.	Described an automatic system for predicting and rating the performance of the interview.
Mohamed et al., (2024)	Developed a platform that manages screening questions, verifies, and scores using ChatGPT. Using this platform, modern AI is fused with the HR module of the ERP Odoo system of the authors. The system has shown that the speed of the recruitment stage has increased. Additionally, the comfort of the recruiting team is enhanced, and a clear score of suitability-based superiority of the applicant's profile is calculated.	The use of ChatGPT along with the ERP system is found to be more effective in applicants' profile screening.
Nasr & German (2019)	worked on the CVs of the postgraduate students, which is necessary for checking typing or layout errors. A modified Boyer-Moore algorithm is used to derive the intended meaning between the question's discourse and the information fragments. Alleviating errors and omitting words enhances the CVs for proper information to be included to boost the accuracy and efficiency of the CV assessment process.	The layout and errors in the CVs of the PG students are detected using the modified Boyer-Moore algorithm.

continued on following page

Table 5. Continued

Author	Contribution	Major Results
Peicheva (2022)	The author discussed in detail the ATS-compliant CVs, minimalistic design, and inclusion of keywords in the standard sections of CVs. ATS struggles with text boxes, columns, headers, or images. Standard fonts like Arial, Calibri, or Times New Roman in a range of 10 to 12 points are preferred. Role-specific terms usage and acronyms with full forms are also required to successfully get shortlisted CVs. The .docx file format and sometimes PDF files are also considered suitable for submission.	The use of text boxes, column headers, and images should be avoided. The role-specific terms and acronyms with full forms can increase the chance of CV shortlisting.
Venkateshwaran et al. (2024)	A very good analysis on how AI interacts with people in complementing and even replacing tasks in HR. This human resource and hiring technology tool implement the use of AI along with the HR Information System. The use of chatbots for administrative matters is becoming a trend. These are applications that can be integrated with an HRIS project to get valuable data for analysis. There are ethical implications of HR applications, such as privacy and bias. This involves phasing out purely machine-based systems to make way for an employee-friendly hybrid tool in automation systems.	The use of chatbots in HR functions helps to improve scalability and efficiency.

2.6 Explainable AI in CV Processing

Table 6 explains the state-of-the-art review of the role of XAI in CV processing.

Table 6. Role of XAI in CV processing

Author	Contribution	Major Results
Qian et al., (2020)	Introduced Explainable AI (EAI) along with the NLP techniques, with details that advanced models should be both understood and explained. It outlines the various methods of achieving explanation and delves into the wording and design of graphical explanations. The research also discusses the areas that XAI for NLP still needs to improve. Moreover, it proposes possible research directions that can improve model transparency on account of XAI methods.	The transparency of the model in CV processing, along with the graphical explanation through XAI, is highlighted.
Saranya & Subhashini (2023)	Explainable Artificial Intelligence and its use in making transparent and trustworthy systems. This study has conducted a review of 91 articles published about X-AI in different fields, like healthcare and finance. This provides AI as a black box problem mostly affects trust in critical decisions. Its main message is how X-AI is very accountable, since it can provide the reasons for AI predictions down to the roots, and it can be a path for future research in the field.	Emphasis on the use of Explainable AI to create a transparent and trustworthy system.

3. INDUSTRY IMPACT AND RELEVANCE

There are diverse sectors, including public, private, and semi-government, where HR works to recruit the perfect fit candidate for a job vacancy. The efficiency improvement of the HR department is always a challenge in the digital world. The candidates either showcase their profiles on the job portals in a more glittery and unclear manner to hide their weaknesses. The candidates portray their qualifications, skills, certifications, and experience in CVs and send them via email. The manufacturing industry may have its skilled labor requirements, including engineers at beginning or experienced levels. The law, accounting, pharmacies, logistics, tourism, food, and hotel industry have special kinds of requirements about experience, skills, and qualifications. The initial automated scrutiny of the CVs helps the HR department to find a set of suitable candidates for the interview.

Automation drastically reduces cost, and the time recruiters spend on manual screening improves efficiency. It results in faster hiring cycles and lower recruitment costs. Systems can process high volumes of CVs quickly. It can improve the diverse metrics. The same criteria applied to every applicant can result in uniform evaluation standards. In the IT and technology sector, there are large applicant pools, and there is skill-based filtering. Such as skill-matching for coding, Cloud, Cyber Security roles (Devare, 2019a; Devare, 2019b). The manufacturing and engineering need for technical certification, project experience, priority on safety training, and certifications. In the case of the healthcare sector, strict licensing and qualification filters are required to ensure compliance with regulatory hiring requirements. In case of education, screening of the qualification, experience, and publications are required. Similarly, in finance & banking, creative industries like media, design, and arts portfolios matter more than CVs. In the case of a Non-Governmental Organization requires community-based hiring.

There is a risk that we may overlook non-traditional candidates who could excel. There is a risk of over-reliance on automation for final judgment. It can create an Inflexibility for unique cases. For example, HR may miss self-taught candidates with unconventional CVs. Overemphasis on formal qualifications may miss practical skills. May undervalue soft skills like empathy and communication in the healthcare sector. In the education sector, research and pedagogical quality are hard to judge from CVs. In the creative industry, like mass communication, fashion technology, and fine arts, automation struggles with qualitative portfolio evaluation.

4. ETHICAL IMPLICATIONS

The automated CV processing has Privacy Implications, such as Data Collection & Consent. However, the CVs are submitted by the candidates as a job application. Hence privacy issues cannot be the concern as the consent is already taken. CVs contain sensitive personal data such as contact details, gender, age, nationality, and sometimes photos. Candidates may not always know how their data will be used, stored, or shared. Lack of explicit consent can lead to misuse or unauthorized profiling. If applicant data is not encrypted or securely stored, it could be vulnerable to breaches, identity theft, or misuse by third parties. Systems may collect more data than necessary e.g., scraping social media profiles linked in resumes, violating privacy norms. Storing CVs indefinitely without clear retention policies can raise compliance issues under regulations like General Data Protection Regulation (GDPR). Candidates often don't know how long their data is kept or if it's shared with external recruiters.

If training data reflects existing workplace biases e.g., favouring certain universities, genders, or ethnic names, the system may unintentionally discriminate. A famous case where an AI recruiting tool downgraded resumes with indicators of being female because past hiring data was male dominated. Automated keyword-based filtering may unfairly reject candidates who have the right skills but use different wording. Non-traditional candidates career changers, people with gaps may be systematically excluded. The woman candidates can have gap due to the maternity leave or childcare intention. Candidates rarely know why their CV was rejected. This lack of explainability makes it hard to contest or correct unfair rejections.

The accessibility & inclusivity of the candidates with disabilities, different cultural formats for resumes, or limited digital literacy may be disadvantaged. Overemphasis on certain formats e.g., LinkedIn-style profiles could create barriers in hiring people with limited facilities. The balancing privacy & fairness leads to the privacy safeguards. The informed consent, anonymization, removing personal identifiers like name, gender, age during initial screening, encryption, and limited retention can provide confirmation that there is privacy and fairness maintained. To provide the fairness Safeguards, a regular bias audits of AI models can mitigate the compliance concerns. The diverse training datasets can reduce discriminatory outcomes.

5. METHODOLOGY

5.1 CV Processing

CV Authenticity Verification system gets designed and processed upon collecting and preparing 59 uploaded resume PDFs, demonstrating its capability quite remarkably by handling a large volume of data effectively. The size of the dataset is decided based on the criteria of the normal distribution, where there is minimum size of 30 CVs required to conclude on results obtained by any new techniques. It begins by extracting crucial information from resumes like name and email, or sections detailing education, experience, and various skills acquired subsequently. Extraction occurs accurately within an in-depth analytical system capability of capturing pretty much all relevant data for evaluation purposes. Gemini AI, alongside Python libraries, facilitates the swift parsing of PDF documents and conversion of unstructured resume data into analyzable structures. It starts by identifying irregularities that possibly signify fake claims on resumes, thereby validating authenticity. Then CV authenticity verification system checks the employment dates for overlaps, where candidates can list multiple jobs with conflicting dates, suggesting error or outright fabrication, perhaps. It also detects employment gaps, namely periods of inactivity exceeding a reasonable six months, which then need further checking afterwards. It also evaluates skills listed in the resume against the candidate's work experience, flagging discrepancies that might signify gross embellishment or outright falsification, and missing contact details, such as email addresses or phone numbers, get flagged as potential red flags because they are essential for verifying candidate identity.

Bevara et al. (2025) introduced Resume2Vec, a novel framework aimed at enhancing Applicant Tracking Systems (ATS) by leveraging intelligent resume embeddings. Their model transforms traditional resume text into dense vector representations, enabling more precise and contextual candidate-job matching. The study utilized state-of-the-art Natural Language Processing techniques to improve the semantic understanding of resumes. Experimental results demonstrated that Resume2Vec significantly outperforms conventional keyword-based methods in matching accuracy. This approach represents a shift toward AI-driven recruitment technologies, offering improved efficiency in the hiring process.

Aside from the discovery of such irregularities, the system also performs a list of authenticity checks on the resume's data to ensure that the records are real. One of those checks, which is crucial to the process, deals with measuring the data for consistency over a period. That is, a timeline analysis is used to make sure that the dates given for education and work experience match in a rational way. The system evaluates if the education period claimed by the candidate conflicts with a full-time job in a natural way. For example, a person being a student and a demanding job-holder without a satisfactory explanation, in case of which case the situation seems implausible. It is a matter of fact that the availability of the URL will lead the system to the presence of the profile, thus the links are also attempted to be accessed by the system. In such a case that the URL is no longer valid or is a non-existent profile.

The score of a resume can be as low as 0 and as high as 10. It is the logistic regression classifier that finds the authenticity level of a resume by using a machine learning algorithm. Here, the most relevant terms refer to the number of identified irregularities, the existence of lost information, and the outcomes of authenticity checks. The system also makes use of penalties and bonuses to smooth the score. The bonuses are for good features, such as having a valid email or LinkedIn profile, and penalties are for issues like job history gaps or inexplicable details. Explainable AI methodologies, especially SHAP-based feature contributions, help in shedding light on the system's inner workings and decisions. AI transparency remains a priority alongside the introduction of SHAP-based feature contributions. SHAP values discover the significance of any feature to the authenticity score and display the results in the form of force plots. These diagrams visually showcase how some factors, like the absence of data or periods of inactivity, change the score, hence exposing the reasons behind the classifications. Such disclosure will avoid the situation where the system could be called a “black box,” and hence, the user's trust will be increased. The authenticity screening in resumes is a service that can be extended to the entire recruitment process for a company that automates fraud detection, thus saving HR lots of time and improving the hiring process. Additional improvements, such as real-time verification and multilingual support, are expected to take the user-friendliness of the system to a whole new level.

The explainable models are justifying the Genuity scores, which provide transparency in AI decision-making. It displays reasons for CV rejection and flagging to recruiters. Explainable AI techniques, inclusive of SHAP-primarily based feature contributions. It offers transparency into the assessment technique, supporting users to understand the reasoning at the back of every classification. This system demonstrates the capacity for recruitment packages, with future improvements like real-time verification.

The system extracts key information such as Name, skill, experience duration, educational details, and contact information such as email, phone, and links. Raw CV data is cleaned and then organized using NLP Techniques. It uses SpaCy for language analysis and pattern recognition. It also supports fallback methods to ensure robust extraction of data. A classifier is trained using supervised learning to assess the CV's authenticity. Logistic Regression Model is implemented in the system, which is trained on attributes like missing information, irregularities, and link validity. The methodology suggests the use of tools such as the isolation forest to mark unusual patterns, such as overlapping employment dates or excessive positive adjectives, improving the ability of the system to detect irregularities

As shown in Figure 1, the process starts when a user engages with the system, typically by interacting with the web interface. This marks the starting point of the resume authenticity evaluation. The first step involves users uploading resume PDF files using forms accessible via the index root defined in the resume parser Flask application. During submission, files are stored on a server within the upload directory shown to ensure organized memory.

The system then extracts text content from the file uploaded using a function, supporting a variety of file formats such as PDF. The next phase analyzes the extracted text with structured data. The system uses the Gemini AI API to organize the text in a structured format that includes fields such as name, e-mail, phone, link, experience, education, skills, and projects. If this method encounters any problems, it will seamlessly change to the local parsing mechanism in the parse resume Python file. This alternative uses regular expressions and NLP Spacy to identify and classify CV sections and provide multiline URLs and date formats. Data received from one of the analysis methods is compiled into a single resume dictionary, which provides a uniform representation of the CV content. The structured data is stored in the SQLite database named resume.db. This is managed by the store_resume_data function in the database.py file. This function uses the SQLAlchemy model. It creates and links records to ensure that all relationships between data elements are maintained and mandatory for the database.

Figure 1. Working flow chart of the system

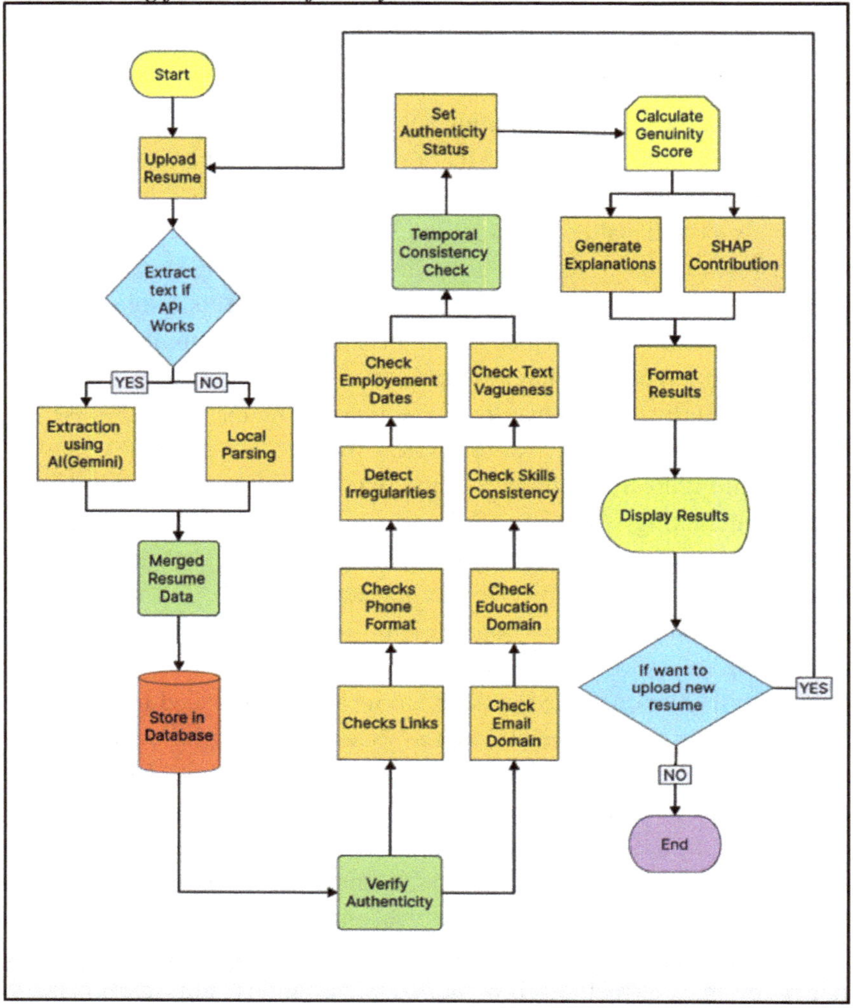

5.2 Authenticity Verification

As shown in Figure 2, the reliability and authenticity verification process is initiated and activated. This function requires CV data assigned to a specific database and performs many reviews. The link verification model verifies the validity of the URLs, including LinkedIn and other platforms such as Github and YouTube. The email domain validation is done to verify the existence of the email domain through the DNS MX data record. The telephone formats are checked to make sure candidates phone number is verified in standard format.

The irregularities are detected to identify missing fields or unusually short experience descriptions. The skills consistency check is done to verify if the listed skills coincide with the description section of the experience. Employment data analysis detects overlapping job periods or significant employment gaps. The vagueness assessment flags overly vague phrases or an excess of positive adjectives. Temporal consistency is reviewed to ensure work experience commences after education concludes, allowing a reasonable six-month gap. Based on the results of the check, the system determines that the resume appears genuine or suggests areas requiring further review.

Figure 2. Authenticity verification process flow chart

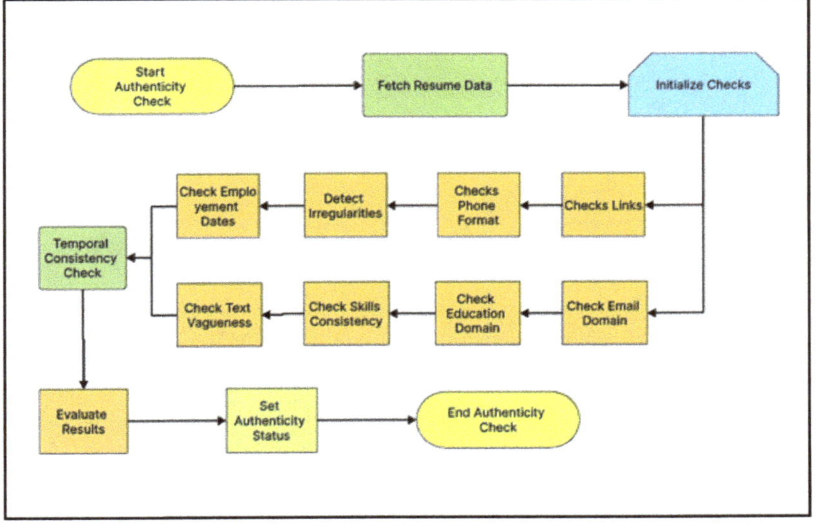

5.3 Genuity Scoring and Explanations

As shown in Figure 3, the Genuity score is calculated, ranging from 0 to 10, derived from a pre-trained logistic regression model that evaluated features such as missing information and link issues, adjusted with bonuses for positive attributes such as a valid link profile and penalties for irregularities. A combination of machine learning insights and straightforward rule-based adjustments is used. Explanations for the score are generated, which include rule-based insights, i.e., the impact of valid links or missing data. SHAP-based feature contributions are highlighted for the influential factors. A SHAP force plot is created using matplotlib. The results are formatted into a coherent output by a function in a file, which organizes authentic details, identifies issues, calculates the score, and prepares the explanatory notes. Finally, the formatted results are presented to the user. This display includes the authenticity status, Genuity score, explanatory insights, SHAP contributions, and the SHAP plot. At this point, the process concludes, allowing the user to review the findings or proceed with uploading additional resumes.

Figure 3. Genuity scoring calculation flow chart

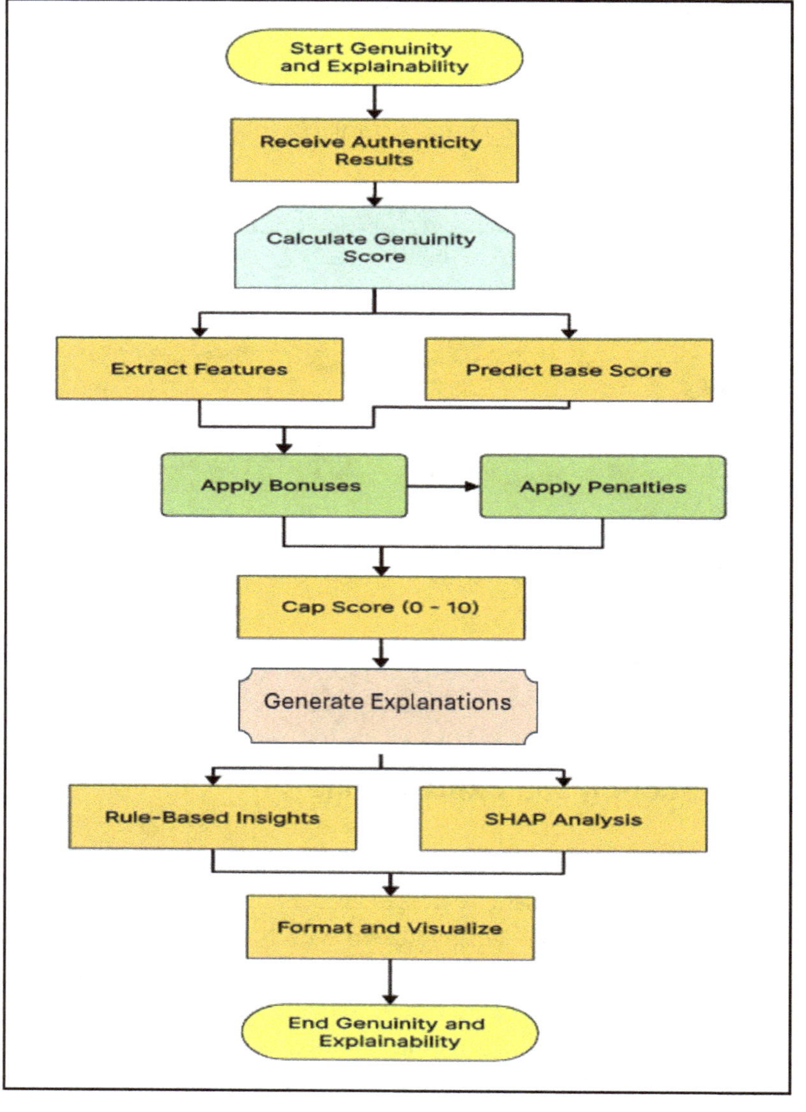

5.4 Understanding the Genuity Score

In ML based processing, the essentials of the resume, like missing details, oddities, or the correctness of the links from which the information is extracted are evaluated. It gives a probability score, a number in the range from 0 to 1. The calculated probability is used as a base score, starting at 10. Depending on how confident the model feels, this score can go up if the probability is high or down if it's low. The score is reduced when problems arise, up to a -3-deduction based on the number of non-missing irregularities, with a cap of 3 to keep it fair and not overly harsh. The score is then adjusted to stay within the 0 to 10 range, ensuring it's always meaningful.

The Genuity score *S*, can be evaluated using equation 1.

$$S = \max\left(0, \min\left(10, B + B_{bonuses} - P_{penalties}\right)\right) \quad (1)$$

Where base score is represented using equation 2,

B is the base score from the model

$$= 10 + [P_{genuine} \times 5] - 2 \quad (2)$$

$P_{genuine}$ is the probability of genuineness predicted by the Logistic Regression in the range from 0 to 1.

The term $\left[P_{genuine} \times 5\right] - 2$ adjusts the score, moving it between 8 and 13 depending on the probability, with 10 as the midpoint.

$B_{bonuses}$ is the total of all bonuses. The value of $B_{linkedin}$ =1 if a valid LinkedIn URL is present, otherwise 0. The value of B_{email} = 1 if a valid email domain is confirmed, otherwise 0. The B_{phone} = 1 if the phone format is valid, otherwise 0. The B_{skills} = 1 if all skills match the experience, otherwise 0. The value of B_{gaps} = 1 if no significant employment gap exceeds six months, otherwise 0. Equation 3 denotes the bonus value calculation.

$$B_{bonuses} = B_{linkedin} + B_{email} + B_{phone} + B_{skills} + B_{gaps} \quad (3)$$

$P_{penalties}$ is calculated as the penalty applied during the CV evaluation represented using equation 4.

$P_{penalties}$

$=$

$$\min\left(3, I_{count}\right) \tag{4}$$

where I_{count} is the number of irregularities is not related to missing data. max($0, \min(10, \bullet)$) ensures the final score stays between 0 and 10.

To illustrate the working of the newly designed equation, following example is illustrated. Imagine the following scenario.

- Missing Info = 2 (Such as no email or phone).
- Irregularity Count = 4 (four skills not found in experience).
- Link Issues = 0 (LinkedIn and YouTube are valid).
- Email Issues = 1 (No email provided).
- Phone Issues = 1 (No phone provided).
- Education Issues = 0 (No education links checked).
- Positive Adjectives = 0 (No excessive flattery noted).

Base Score Calculation is performed using following method.

- By using a hypothetical model prediction, let's say $P_{genuine} = 0.6$ (60% chance of being genuine).

$$B = 10 + [0.6 \times 5] - 2 = 10 + 3 - 2 = 11$$

The Bonuses are decided using the following criteria.

- $B_{linkedin} = 1$ (valid LinkedIn).
- $B_{email} = 0$ (no valid email).
- $B_{phone} = 0$ (no valid phone).
- $B_{skills} = 0$ (skills don't match experience).
- $B_{gaps} = 1$ (no big gaps).

$B_{bonuses} = 1+0+0+0+1 = 2$

The Penalties are decided using the following criteria

$I_{count} = 4$, so $P_{penalties} = \min(3,4) = 3$.

Final Score will be calculated using following methodology.

S= max(0, min(10, 11+2–3))= max(0, min(10, 10))= 10

- Output will show 6/10, suggesting the model's $P_{genuine}$ might be lower, perhaps 0.2(giving B= 10+1–2=9, then 9+2–3=8, adjusted further to 6)

The score begins at a neutral value of 10 and then shifts based on the model's prediction and additional factors. Bonuses highlight the strengths, like verified contact information or consistent skills, while penalties address issues like irregularities. The range is kept between 0 i.e. "very suspicious" and 10 "very genuine" for clarity. The base score's accuracy depends on the quality of the model's training data.

Table 7 lists the common reasons for a low Genuity Score.

Table 7. Common reasons for low genuity score

Reason for low score	Penalty given to each resume	Source function
Missing information	-1 to -3	detect_irregularities (authenticity_checker.py), calculate_genuinity_score (genuinity_score.py)
Non-Missing irregularities	-1 to -3 (capped at -3)	check_skills_consistency, check_employment_dates (authenticity_checker.py), calculate_genuinity_score (genuinity_score.py)
Email issues	-1	check_email_domain (authenticity_checker.py), calculate_genuinity_score (genuinity_score.py)
Phone issues	-1	check_phone_format (authenticity_checker.py), calculate_genuinity_score (genuinity_score.py)
Link issues	-1	check_link_exist (authenticity_checker.py), calculate_genuinity_score (genuinity_score.py)

5.5 System Design and Implementation

Table 8. System design and its implementation details

Feature	Description	Implementation module	File and function
Resume Uploading and displaying	Users can upload a PDF/DOCX resume and view their processed results in the sidebar on the left of the webpage.	Flask web interface	resume_parser.py: Index function
Authenticity Verification	Validate email, phone, LinkedIn, temporal consistency, and authenticity status.	Authenticity checking	authenticity_checker.py: verify_resume_authenticity function
Detecting irregularities	Identifies issues like employment gaps, overlapping employment, and missing info.	Irregularities checking	authenticity_checker.py: check_employment_dates, detect_irregularities, check_skills_consistency,
Genuity scoring	Calculates Genuity score from 0-10 using ML model with bonuses and penalties.	Logistics regression and scoring	Genuinity_scorer.py: calculate_genuinity_score, prepare_shap_features.
Explainable ai insights	It will generate SHAP-based explanations and visuals for Genuity scores.	SHAP visuals and explanation.	resume_parser.py and explainable_ai.py: index function, generate explanations.

Table 8 shows the functional requirements implemented by the system and their description. The actual work implemented by the module is also listed, and the Python file name is mentioned for further details. Each file consists of functions. The function names are also listed in the last column.

5.6 Explainable AI

Unlike traditional black-box AI models, which make decisions without revealing how they arrive at them. Explainable AI ensures that humans can comprehend and trust AI-driven outcomes. Transparency in AI is essential to build trust among users and stakeholders, ensure fairness and ethical decisions, and improve accountability in AI-powered applications. A model is designed in a way that allows users to understand how decisions are made using techniques like decision trees, rule-based systems, and linear regression models. Also, the interpretability of complex models like neural networks can be made explainable using techniques like SHAP and Local Interpretable Model-agnostic Explanations (LIME).

SHAP is a strong explanatory framework of AI that provides the transparency of ML models for individual predictions. SHAP uses the values from the theory of cooperative games. Unlike traditional methods of meaning, SHAP is fairly distributed by the contribution of each input function to the final production. It is the most reliable technique for interpreting the model. It is calculating how the presence or absence of the function affects the output. SHAP has ability to work with a wide range of ML models, including Tree-based models such as XGBOOST, Random Forest, Light GBM, Deep Learning teaching nets, and Blackbox models. It assigns positive or negative values to functions because of whether it pushes the prediction higher or lower. For example, in a medical diagnosis model, SHAP can empathize with which symptoms have most contributed to predicting the disease, ensuring that healthcare professionals can trust and verify the knowledge of controlled AI. SHAP also provides various visualization tools that facilitate the interpretation of the model outputs. SHAP also has ability to detect distortion in AI models. By analyzing SHAP values, organizations can find out whether certain features, such as race, gender, or socioeconomic status, do not affect prediction and help ensure justice and adherence to ethical instructions of AI. This is particularly important in the fields of finance, healthcare, and criminal justice, where AI can have serious consequences.

6. RESULTS

The system is tested on 59 resumes, and the outputs have been evaluated based on authenticity reputation, Genuity score, model accuracy, recognized irregularities, and explainable AI insights. A logistic regression model is used to compute Genuity Scores, with accuracy above 94.9%, and uses SHAP to provide function contributions in transparency. The subsequent subsections provide details on User Interface (UI), consequences for the decision on resumes, database, and model overall performance of the designed system.

5.1 User Interface

Figure 4 illustrates the Responsive, Clean layout with a blue and white shade, readable and Intuitive Graphical User Interface (UI). It provides a navigation link to View Database. The primary content vicinity is divided into two sections as a sidebar on the left and a relevant panel. The sidebar lists all processed resumes, allowing users to select a resume for specified viewing. The relevant panel consists of an upload section with a form to upload new resumes in PDF or DOCX format, in conjunction with an upload and process button. The sidebar entries are clickable, permitting users to pick a resume for unique viewing. Upon clicking an access, the right side of the web page, which is the primary content region, updates to show the processed statistics for the selected resume, together with authenticity status, authenticity details, irregularities, Genuity score, accuracy, and explainable AI insights.

Figure 4. Upload CV graphical user interface

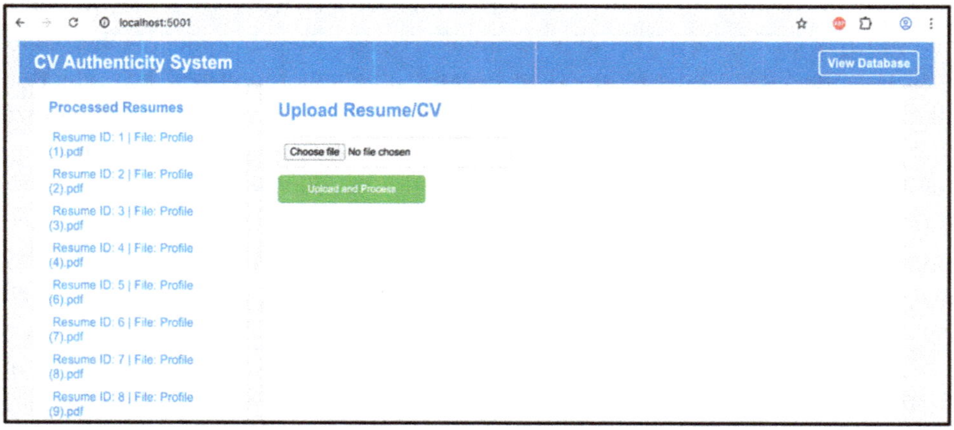

Figure 5 displays the output of the resume authenticity system for a processed resume, diagnosed as partially authentic, and needs to be cross-checked manually. The primary content place provides the distinctive consequences, together with the resume identity, file name, authenticity status, and a breakdown of authenticity assessments. The list of irregularities includes lacking facts, unverified competencies, and employment gaps or overlaps. The Genuity rating is given to each resume, and below the model accuracy, there are Explainable AI insights that explain the score calculation, and a SHAP pressure plot visualizes the characteristic contributions to the Genuity rating.

The "partially authenticated, need to do cross-check manually" suggests that the resume falls into an intermediate category, requiring manual verification. The Genuity score of 6/10 aligns with the device's standards for this scoring rating among 4 and 7, reflecting stability between various factors, e.g., a valid email, LinkedIn presence, and many irregularities. The absence of essential inconsistencies, e.g., invalid email, and timeline overlaps, supports this class. However, the excessive wide variety of irregularities along with unverified capabilities and employment gaps indicates potential issues that need further checking. The SHAP analysis underscores the effect of irregularities at the rating, indicating that the device effectively identifies tricky regions at the same time as recognizing the resume's partial credibility. This outcome highlights the system's ability to flag complicated cases for guided assessment, ensuring a thorough verification process.

Figure 5. Resume with partially authenticated status

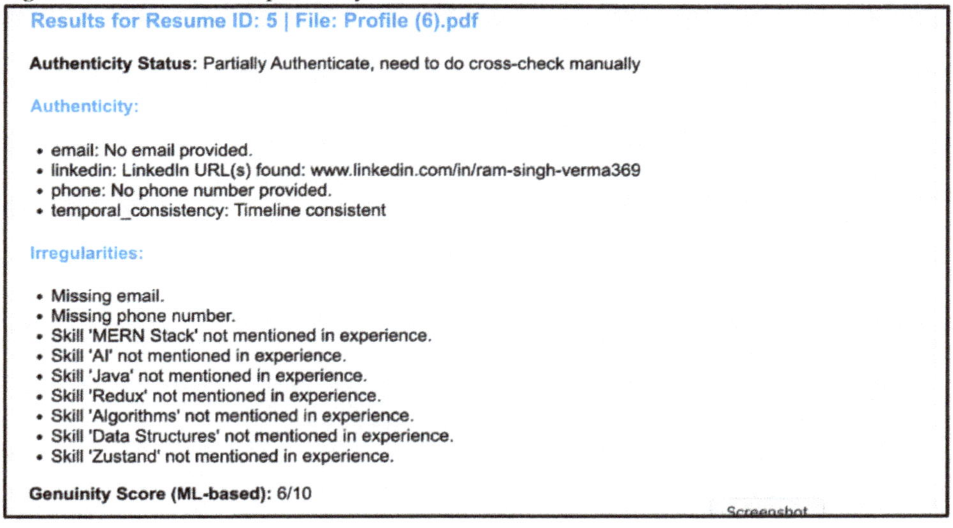

Results for Resume ID: 5 | File: Profile (6).pdf

Authenticity Status: Partially Authenticate, need to do cross-check manually

Authenticity:

- email: No email provided.
- linkedin: LinkedIn URL(s) found: www.linkedin.com/in/ram-singh-verma369
- phone: No phone number provided.
- temporal_consistency: Timeline consistent

Irregularities:

- Missing email.
- Missing phone number.
- Skill 'MERN Stack' not mentioned in experience.
- Skill 'AI' not mentioned in experience.
- Skill 'Java' not mentioned in experience.
- Skill 'Redux' not mentioned in experience.
- Skill 'Algorithms' not mentioned in experience.
- Skill 'Data Structures' not mentioned in experience.
- Skill 'Zustand' not mentioned in experience.

Genuinity Score (ML-based): 6/10

Figure 6 displays the result of the resume authenticity system for a processed resume diagnosed as not authentic, despite having a Genuity rating of 8/10. The Genuity rating of 8/10 is prominently displayed. The “no longer authenticate” or “Not Authenticate”, notwithstanding a Genuity score of 8/10, reveals a nuance in the system's good judgment. The resume didn't meet the stern criteria for “Authenticate”, which calls for a legitimate telephone number, no irregularities, no inconsistent timeline, and a score of 8 or higher. The absence of a phone range and, inconsistent timeline. As the experience mentioned in the CV started in the year 2023, before the education ended in the year 2026. There is a presence of three irregularities i.e. a lack of a telephone, unverified abilities, and overlapping employment, which disqualified it from being authenticated.

Figure 6. Resume with not authenticate status

Results for Resume ID: 13 | File: Profile (14).pdf

Authenticity Status: Not Authenticate

Authenticity:

- email: Email domain exists.
- linkedin: LinkedIn URL(s) found: www.linkedin.com/in/isha-agrawal-5a59341b7
- phone: No phone number provided.
- temporal_consistency: Inconsistent timeline: Experience starts (July 2023) before education ends (January 2026)

Irregularities:

- Missing phone number.
- Skill 'Talent Recognition' not mentioned in experience.
- Skill 'Internet Recruiting' not mentioned in experience.
- Skill 'New Hire Processes' not mentioned in experience.
- Overlapping employment: 'US Recruiter at IMS People Possible (July 2023 - July 2024)' and 'Human Resources Assistant at Innovana Thinklabs Ltd. (June 2024 - October 2024)'.

Genuinity Score (ML-based): 8/10

Figure 7 presents the database view of the resume authenticity system, confirming that facts are stored successfully in the SQLite database.

Figure 7. CV database view

```
Resume ID: 19 | File: Profile (19).pdf
  Model Accuracy: 100.00%
  Name: Ramakrishna Pathuri
  Email: None
  Phone: None
  Links: www.linkedin.com/in/ramakrishnapathuri,pathuriramakrishna.in,dotnetplenty.blogspot.in
  Skills: Application Architect, .Netcore, Application Management, Telugu, Tamil, English, Developing web applications, SQL Server, c#.net, Asp.net,
JavaScript, WebAPI, WebServices, Ado.Net, Jquery, Angular JS, TFS, .NetCore, Entity Framework, Azure SQL, DevOps, Entity Framework Core, Azure App Gateway,
dot Net Core, MVC
  Experience:
    - Application Manager at NationsBenefits India (May 2024 - Present)
    - Technical Manager And Architect at NationsBenefits India (August 2023 - July 2024)
    - Associate Architect at NationsBenefits India (March 2022 - August 2023)
    - Team Lead at NationsBenefits (November 2020 - March 2022)
    - Director & Co-Founder at SyncApps Online Ventures (March 2015 - November 2020)
    - Senior Software Engineer at SyncApps Online Ventures (February 2013 - February 2015)
    - Software Engineer at EasyBus.in (November 2010 - January 2013)
    - Developer at EasyBus Online Services (November 2010 - December 2011)
    - Software Taine at None (November 2010 - May 2011)
  Education:
    - Master of Computer Applications (M.C.A.) in Computer Science at Paavai Engineering College (2005 - 2008)
    - Bachelor's degree in Computer Science at jagarlamudi kuppuswamy choudary (2002 - 2005)
    - Intermediate in M.P.C at krishnaveni junior college (2000 - 2002)
    - State Secondary Education in Mathematics at Z.P.H School , Narnepadu (1999 - 2000)
  Projects:
    - centralized Covid-19 real-time bed availability system

Resume ID: 20 | File: Profile (22).pdf
  Model Accuracy: 100.00%
  Name: Swati Jha
  Email: swatijha0908@gmail.com
  Phone: None
  Links: www.linkedin.com/in/swati-jha2906,linktr.ee/swatijha
  Skills: Low level Design, Interview Preparation, Teaching
  Experience:
    - Software Engineer at Microsoft (November 2023 - Present)
    - Software Engineer at Samsung Electronics (February 2022 - November 2023)
    - System Engineer at Tata Consultancy Services (June 2021 - January 2022)
    - Technical Content Writer Intern at GeeksforGeeks (October 2020 - April 2021)
    - SDE Intern at Smartx Connected Products Private Limited (June 2019 - July 2019)
  Education:
    - Bachelor of Technology in Computer Science Engineering at BIT Sindri (2017 - 2021)
  Projects:
```

Screenshot

5.2 Model Performance and Explainable AI Insights

Figure 8 presents the accuracy and explainable AI insights for one of the processed resumes, inclusive of a SHAP force plot. The interface section suggests the version accuracy, observed by means of the Explainable AI Insights and SHAP-primarily based characteristic contributions sections. The insights explain the factors contributing to the Genuity score, inclusive of bonuses for legitimate e-mail, LinkedIn, and consequences for irregularities. The SHAP contributions list the impact of each characteristic, e.g., missing_info, irregularity_count, on the score. The SHAP force plot visually represents those contributions, with arrows indicating the course and value of each function's impact on the prediction.

Figure 8. Model, explainable AI insights, and SHAP force-plot

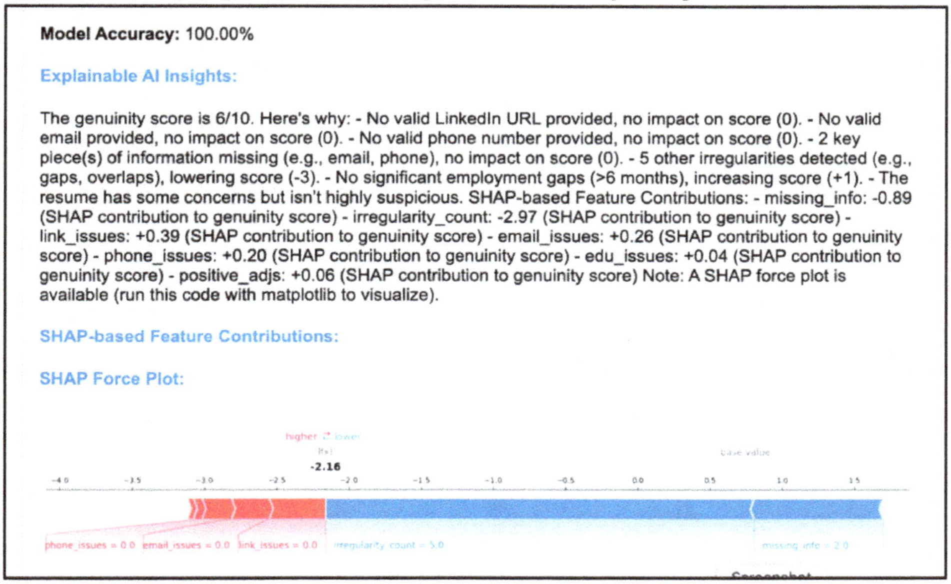

5.3 SHAP Force Plot

Figures 9 and 10 represent a starting horizontal line, where it's prefixed with "base value," being the average prediction across all training models. For a logistic regression model, the base value is typically the average probability of a chosen resume being the right one from the training dataset. The graph then offers a display of arrows or parallel bars for each feature, which explains their respective effects on the prediction, red arrows pointing right or upward, and suggests the increase of manifestations of the specified feature; thus, the prediction increases, hence the resume is more likely to be genuine. Blue arrows, which are pointing left or downward, show how the features have affected the model's prediction; a feature with a negative sign input will result in a higher value of the prediction, which implies the resume is less likely to be genuine. The length of each arrow indicates the size of the effect of the transferring feature. A shorter arrow signifies a less major effect, even if a negative or positive that may occur.

Figure 9. Higher score SHAP force plot

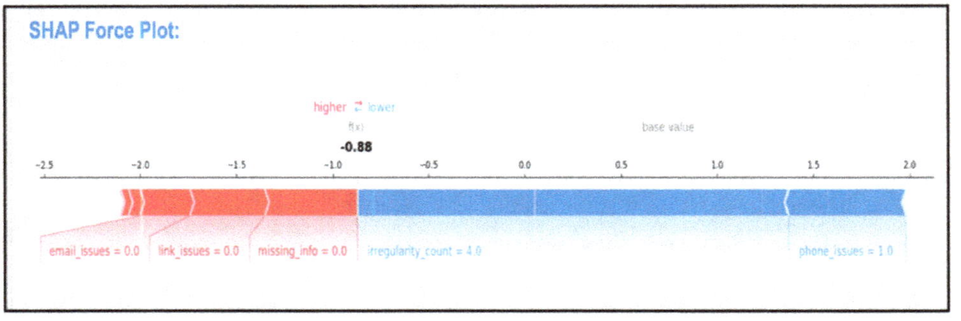

Figure 10. Lower score SHAP force plot

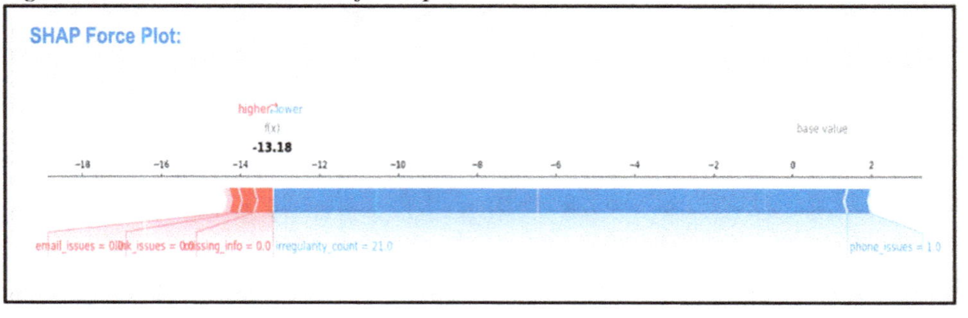

As shown in Figure 11, there were total 59 CVs in the ATS format for testing the newly designed approach of calculating the Genuity score. Further the accuracy is calculated using the True positive as 27 and True negative as 29 CVs. Whereas there are 3 CVs considered as the misclassification. This has achieved 94.9% of accuracy of the system. To decide the shortlisting of the CV for the interview process, the threshold of the score calculated can be decided by the HR team. This will vary the accuracy of the approach. Lowering the thresholding can improve the accuracy of the model. Whereas higher thresholds lead to the rejection of the CVs. It has been observed that many organizations may select the CVs with less scores, because instead of good candidates, the labor with moderate skill and the moderate salary demands are chosen.

Figure 11. Confusion matrix explaining the CV classification

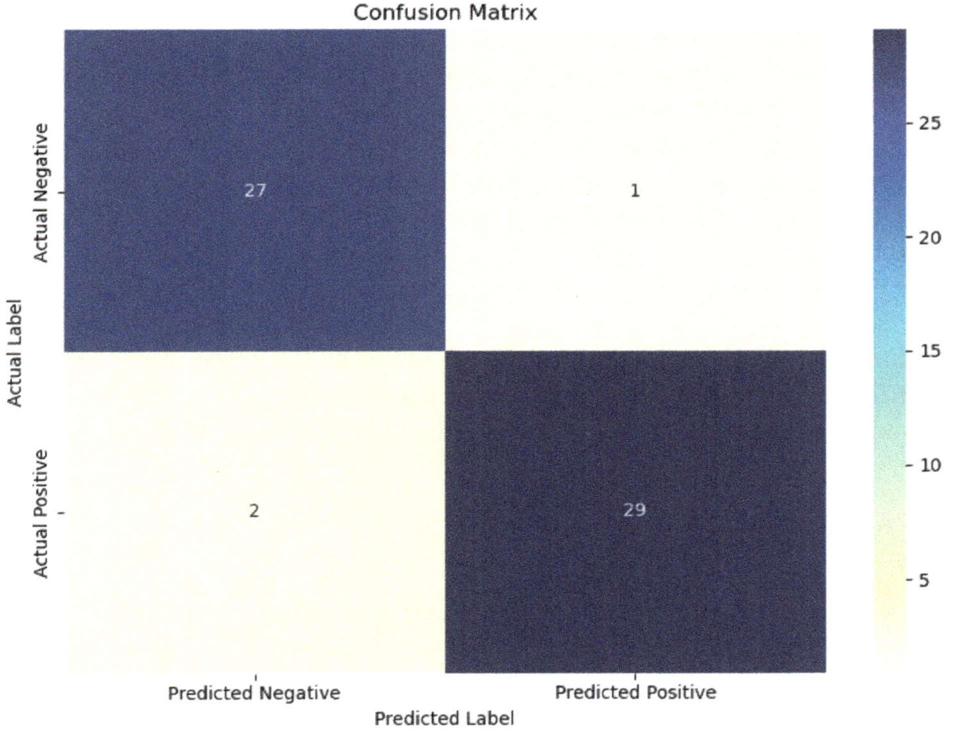

7. DISCUSSION

The current system is parsing the ATS-compliant CV, which has its fixed template. Due to the fixed nature of the elements in the ATS CV format, the parsing is relatively easy. The parsing of the non-ATS compliant CVs, the parsing and extracting the important aspects such as qualification, skills, experience, and other information is a challenging task for the programmer. Adding such a CV to the dataset leads to the complex programming of regular expressions, and then further application of the algorithms on it.

The CV Genuity is calculated through this research work. It is required to find out that there is no bias and that filter bubbles are affecting the recruitment diversity. The Filter Bubble in Recruitment occurs when algorithms or decision-making processes limit the diversity of candidates. Like social media and search engines, the users are shown content that reinforces their existing beliefs or preferences due to the royalties the IT companies receive from brands for their marketing and advertising. Recruiters prefer qualified candidates and ignore diversity. Automated systems prioritize candidates from specific schools, companies, or regions. Due to the limited exposure to potentially strong candidates with unconventional backgrounds. They reinforce existing workforce homogeneity. Diversity also brings equal opportunity and ethical practices in recruitment. Bias in Recruitment is unfair preference or prejudice toward certain candidates or groups during the hiring process. Bias can be explicit, conscious, or implicit, unconscious. There can be affinity bias in which is the preference for candidates who are like the recruiter in background, interests, or personality. Gender bias favors one gender over another for a role. There is racial or ethnic bias, which makes decisions based on a candidate's race or ethnicity. The name bias makes assumptions based on a candidate's name. The confirmation bias is looking for evidence that confirms an initial impression of a candidate.

8. CONCLUSION

This work involves the process of digital recruiting platforms, and a role is played in making it easier for candidates to apply for their positions. The harm caused by forged CVs to the organizations can be largely catastrophic. For example, hiring the wrong candidate may lead to financial losses, reputation damage, and in some cases even litigation. The automatic process of the ATS CV parsing is done through Python-based coding. A model is developed to sort resumes like the words and sentence structures they contain; a timeline consistency check and the irregularities within them. Recruiters could benefit from identifying the nuance behind why a resume would be tagged. Here, the Genuity score served as a stopgap. The model is developed with the refinement details such as date stability, skills, gaps, irregularities count, Bonuses, and penalties. Testing score on a small resume dataset proved revelatory as it accurately flagged most manually labelled fake resumes.

Explainable AI provides Insights into model decisions using the SHAP framework. The trustworthiness is indicated by the proper resumes scoring greatly above 6, and the resumes with the most irregularities scoring 5 or below. These numbers do not define everything, but they're sufficiently reliable to calculate a baseline that gets incrementally higher with iterative, purpose-driven records.

The automation of the CV processing will reduce HR workload. Automated screening will reduce manual hours spent scanning CVs. If the cost estimation for Return on Investment (ROI) is Compared, then manual screening cost is the HR staff time multiplied by hourly wage per CV. The automated system subscription and license cost can be the cost of investment in the adoption of the automated CV processing system. It will demonstrate clear monetary savings. The automation leads to the faster Hiring that implies the Business Agility. There will be reduction in the time-to-hire. The automated systems shortlist candidates in minutes, not days. Faster hiring reduces vacancy downtime which will imply less productivity loss. Automated systems can rank candidates using skills, experience, and role-fit metrics which will lead to the better quality of hire. The ROI links quality hires to measurable Key Performance Indicators such as sales growth, project delivery speed, and improvement in innovations in the organization.

The automation improves compliance & reduced risk. It can mitigate the bias, if the CVs are anonymized. It Reduces risk of discrimination lawsuits or compliance breaches. The ROI is tangible, and it will prevent legal costs and improve the brand reputation value. In high-growth or seasonal sectors such as IT, retail, manufacturing, hospitality. HR can scale up hiring without linear increase in HR staff. Each additional hire processed with minimal marginal cost strengthens economies of scale. The strategic HR Role can be developed due to the automation as shift from admin role. With CV processing automated, HR can focus on retention, leadership development, and employee engagement. There will be clear impact on business which aligns HR goals with organizational strategy, improving long-term growth and stability.

9. FUTURE WORK

The filter bubble and bias lead to unfair hiring decisions, less diverse, and less effective teams. This will undermine meritocracy and equal opportunity. The filter bubble and the bias can be traced and attributed to recruitment, so that it can be avoided through artificial intelligence techniques. The audited algorithms for the processing of CVs are important strategies to create sustainable employment opportunities.

The resume authenticity verification presents a strong foundation for automating the process of verifying resumes, leveraging machine learning (ML), natural language processing (NLP), and explainable AI techniques. However, there are several areas of opportunity for development and expansion to enhance the machine's accuracy, usability, and applicability in actual global eventualities. The integration of advanced NLP models, along with transformer-based models like BERT, helps with multilingual resumes. Adding BERT shall improve the accuracy of talent identification in resumes with dense or narrative-style formats. Incorporating optical character recognition (OCR) abilities will be a precious addition for managing scanned PDFs, enabling the machine to system photo-based documents seamlessly.

The system presently performs static tests, inclusive of validating e-mail domains and LinkedIn URLs, to ensure resume authenticity. Including real-time verification features could further add value to those tests using external APIs. The e-mail verification services like Hunter.io or Never Bounce may be added to verify the deliverability of email addresses, supplying an extra complete validation method. Another valuable addition can be real-time verification of educational credentials via partnerships with academic institutions or third-party verification offerings, allowing the machine to go look at stages and certifications at once.

The multi-lingual CVs processing is a huge challenge, as the language translation and dictionary-based approach required to be included. The Unicode characters required to be processed in the multi-lingual-based CV processing. One CV must be written only in one language, but the countries focusing on the native languages require a special mechanism to handle the processing of the skills mentioned by the candidate in their CVs. The non-ATS compliant CVs may lead to different format, layout, and structure. This leads to complex parsing, processing and shortlisting. Current research work has not worked on this objective.

REFERENCES

Abraham, S., Paripoornam, R., & Sharma, G.Susan Abraham, Rajeev Paripoornam, Gunjan Sharma. (2025). The Role of Artificial Intelligence in Recruitment and Talent Acquisition-An Empirical Study. *Journal of Informatics Education and Research*, *5*(1), 400–408. DOI: 10.52783/jier.v5i1.2007

Albaroudi, E., Mansouri, T., & Alameer, A. (2024). A Comprehensive Review of AI Techniques for Addressing Algorithmic Bias in Job Hiring. In *AI Switzerland,* 5(1), 383–404. https://doi.org/DOI: 10.3390/ai5010019

Albassam, W. A. (2023). The Power of Artificial Intelligence in Recruitment: An Analytical Review of Current AI-Based Recruitment Strategies. *International Journal of Professional Business Review*, *8*(6), 1–25. DOI: 10.26668/businessreview/2023.v8i6.2089

Bevara, P. K., Singh, R. S., Medera, R., & Prasad Chelluri, V. V. D. (2025). Optimizing scientific workflow scheduling in cloud environments: A hybrid PSO-EWWO. *Cluster Computing*, *28*(8), 508. DOI: 10.1007/s10586-025-05168-5

Bharadwaj, S., Varun, R., Aditya, P. S., Nikhil, M., & Babu, G. C. (2022). Resume Screening using NLP and LSTM. *5th International Conference on Inventive Computation Technologies, - Proceedings*, 238–241. https://doi.org/DOI: 10.1109/ICICT54344.2022.9850889

Bhatia, V., Rawat, P., Kumar, A., & Shah, R. R. (2019). *End-to-End Resume Parsing and Finding Candidates for a Job Description using BERT*. arXiv preprint arXiv:1910.03089.

Blessing, M. (2025). *AI-Powered Resume Screening: Benefits and Challenges*., 1-7.

Chen, Z., Liu, H., & Zhang, Q. (2023). Adaptive Selection of BERT Layer for Multi-Label Text Classification. *Proceedings of International Conference on Machine Learning and Cybernetics*, 434–439. https://doi.org/DOI: 10.1109/ICMLC58545.2023.10327995

Chintalapati, P. V., Paluri, S. S., Nikhitha, S. S., Nanditha, T. S. V., Daneswari, S. T. V. L., & Sree, P. K. (2024). A Research Model for Automated Prediction and Analysis of Job Interview Performance. *Proceedings - 2024 6th International Conference on Computational Intelligence and Communication Technologies*, 284–291. https://doi.org/DOI: 10.1109/CCICT62777.2024.00055

Daryani, C., Chhabra, G. S., Patel, H., Chhabra, I. K., & Patel, R. (2020)... *An Automated Resume Screening System Using Natural Language Processing and Similarity, 99–103*, 99–103. Advance online publication. DOI: 10.26480/etit.02.2020.99.103

Devare, M. H. (2019a). Cloud Computing and Innovations. In Kecskemeti, G. (Ed.), *Applying Integration Techniques and Methods in Distributed Systems and Technologies* (pp. 1–33). IGI Global Scientific Publishing., DOI: 10.4018/978-1-5225-8295-3.ch001

Devare, M. H. (2019b). Convergence of Manufacturing Cloud and Industrial IoT. In Kecskemeti, G. (Ed.), *Applying Integration Techniques and Methods in Distributed Systems and Technologies* (pp. 49–78). IGI Global Scientific Publishing., DOI: 10.4018/978-1-5225-8295-3.ch003

Julian, A., & Haripriya, K. (2024). NLP based Resume Analysis and Adaptive Skill Assessment System. *3rd International Conference for Innovation in Technology*. https://doi.org/DOI: 10.1109/INOCON60754.2024.10511967

Khan, F., Patel, H., Shaikh, A., Sayed, F., & Soorya, A. R. (2023). Resume Parser and Summarizer. *International Journal of Advanced Research in Science. Tongxin Jishu*, •••, 442–447. DOI: 10.48175/IJARSCT-9064

Li, S., Li, K., & Lu, H. (2023). *National Origin Discrimination in Deep-learning-powered Automated Resume Screening*. arXiv preprint arXiv:2307.08624.

Luo, Y., Zhang, H., Wang, Y., We, Y., & Zhang, X. (2018a). ResumeNet: A Learning-based Framework for Automatic Resume Quality Assessment. arXiv preprint arXiv:1810.02832. DOI: 10.1109/ICDM.2018.00046

Luo, Y., Zhang, H., Wang, Y., Wen, Y., & Zhang, X. (2018b). ResumeNet: A Learning-Based Framework for Automatic Resume Quality Assessment. *Proceedings - IEEE International Conference on Data Mining, ICDM*, 307–316. https://doi.org/DOI: 10.1109/ICDM.2018.00046

Mishra, A., & Vishwakarma, S. (2016). Analysis of TF-IDF Model and its Variant for Document Retrieval. *Proceedings - 2015 International Conference on Computational Intelligence and Communication Networks*, 772–776. https://doi.org/DOI: 10.1109/CICN.2015.157

Mittal, V., Mehta, P., Relan, D., & Gabrani, G. (2020). Methodology for resume parsing and job domain prediction. *Journal of Statistics and Management Systems*, *23*(7), 1265–1274. DOI: 10.1080/09720510.2020.1799583

Mohamed, O., Sameh, D., Mohamed, H., Ashraf, M., Kamal, R., & Kandil, Y. (2024). ResuFit: Precision CV Matching System. *4th International Mobile, Intelligent, and Ubiquitous Computing Conference, MIUCC 2024*, 363–367. https://doi.org/DOI: 10.1109/MIUCC62295.2024.10783505

Nasr, S., & German, O. V. (2019). Assessment of graduate students' resumes using short text searching method. *Proceedings - IEEE 2nd International Conference on Artificial Intelligence and Knowledge Engineering*, 306–308. https://doi.org/DOI: 10.1109/AIKE.2019.00061

Nirali, B., Gandhi, J., & Singh, D. K. (2020). NLP based Extraction of Relevant Resume using Machine Learning. *International Journal of Innovative Technology and Exploring Engineering*, *9*(7), 13–17. DOI: 10.35940/ijitee.F4078.059720

Peicheva, M. (2022). *Data Analysis from the Applicant Tracking System*. 6-15. https://www.researchgate.net/publication/375517346

Qian, K., Danilevsky, M., Aharonov, R., Katsis, Y., & Sen, P. (2020). *A Survey of the State of Explainable AI for Natural Language Processing*. 1-13. https://doi.org//arXiv.2010.00711DOI: 10.48550

Rasal, P. (2023). Resume Parser Analysis Using Machine Learning and Natural Language Processing. *International Journal for Research in Applied Science and Engineering Technology*, *11*(5), 2840–2844. DOI: 10.22214/ijraset.2023.52202

Rojas-Galeano, S., Posada, J., & Ordoñez, E. (2022). A bibliometric perspective on AI research for job-résumé matching. *TheScientificWorldJournal*, *2022*, 1–15. Advance online publication. DOI: 10.1155/2022/8002363 PMID: 36225947

Roy, P. K., Chowdhary, S. S., & Bhatia, R. (2020). A Machine Learning approach for automation of Resume Recommendation System. *Procedia Computer Science*, *167*, 2318–2327. DOI: 10.1016/j.procs.2020.03.284

Saatçı, M., Kaya, R., & Ünlü, R. (2024). Resume Screening with Natural Language Processing (NLP). *Alphanumeric Journal*, *12*(2), 121–140. DOI: 10.17093/alphanumeric.1536577

Saranya, A., & Subhashini, R. (2023). A systematic review of Explainable Artificial Intelligence models and applications: Recent developments and future trends. In *Decision Analytics Journal* (Vol. 7, pp. 1–14). Elsevier Inc., DOI: 10.1016/j.dajour.2023.100230

Shoukath, T. K., & Chakkaravarthy, M. (2025). Predictive analytics in education: Machine learning approaches and performance metrics for student success – a systematic literature review. *Data and Metadata*, *4*, 730. DOI: 10.56294/dm2025730

Sroison, P., & Chan, J. H. (2021). *Resume Parser with Natural Language Processing*. 1-5. https://doi.org/DOI: 10.36227/techrxiv.17641604.v1

Tayal, S., Sharma, T., Singhal, S., & Thakur, A. (2024). Resume Screening using Machine Learning. *International Journal of Scientific Research in Computer Science. Engineering and Information Technology*, *10*(2), 602–606.

Tejaswini, K., Kadiwal, V. U., & Revanna, S. (2022). Design and development of machine learning based resume ranking system. *Global Transitions Proceedings*, *3*(2), 371–375. DOI: 10.1016/j.gltp.2021.10.002

Venkateshwaran, G., Kumar, R. N., & Devarajulu, V. S. (2024). Artificial Intelligence in HR: Transforming Recruitment and Selection in IT Industry. *Journal of Information Systems Engineering & Management*, *2025*(17s), 39–45.

Wen, A., Patil, T., Saxena, A., Fu, Y., O'Brien, S., & Zhu, K. (2025). *FAIRE: Assessing Racial and Gender Bias in AI-Driven Resume Evaluations*. arXiv preprint arXiv:2504.01420.

Wilson, K., & Caliskan, A. (2024). Gender, Race, and Intersectional Bias in Resume Screening via Language Model Retrieval. arXiv preprint arXiv:2407.20371.

Wosiak, A. (2021). Automated extraction of information from Polish resume documents in the IT recruitment process. *Procedia Computer Science*, *192*, 2432–2439. DOI: 10.1016/j.procs.2021.09.012

Zimmermann, T., Kotschenreuther, L., & Schmidt, K. (2016). Data-driven HR - Résumé Analysis Based on Natural Language Processing and Machine Learning. arXiv preprint arXiv:1606.05611.

Chapter 7
Optimizing Strategic Leadership Through Artificial Intelligence for Competitive Decision-Making

Jose De Jesus Reyes-Sánchez
http://orcid.org/0000-0002-3866-2363
TECNM Instituto Tecnologico Superior De Fresnillo, Mexico

ABSTRACT

This research analyzes the optimization of strategic leadership through the integration of artificial intelligence (AI) for competitive decision-making. From a qualitative and reflective meta-analysis of recent studies, it is evident how the use of advanced algorithms, deep learning and big data analysis allows organizations to anticipate future scenarios, optimize resource allocation and transform their management culture. Dynamic capabilities and the convergence of technological and human approaches are highlighted, while addressing ethical challenges, transparency in algorithmic processes, and the need for accountable governance. The findings suggest that the synergy between AI and professional judgment drives innovation and strengthens competitiveness in environments of high uncertainty.

INTRODUCTION

Optimizing strategic leadership is one of the main challenges in the context of digital transformation. Traditionally, leadership was based on experience, intuition,

DOI: 10.4018/979-8-3373-3648-0.ch007

and analysis of retrospective data. Thus, managers based their decisions on historical metrics and on the judgment developed over time. However, the insertion of disruptive technologies, especially AI, has changed the way these decisions are made and executed. Ultimately, real-time information: with the integration of the most advanced algorithms in Multicasting, the inclusion of deep learning techniques, and the creation of predictive models, leaders can anticipate future scenarios and optimize resources in a way that was previously unattainable (Deliu & Olariu, 2024; Duan et al., 2019).

This shift towards a digitalization-based way of thinking comes against a backdrop of growing technological and human convergences. Therefore, artificial intelligence not only improves operational efficiency and the accuracy of decisions, but also changes part of the social order and corporate culture. The ability to perform counter simulations and process large volumes of data in real-time is changing the traditional meaning of leadership, so that it will be able to handle competition and adapt in highly volatile environments (Wu & Shang, 2020).

During historical evolution, a paradigmatic shift in the application of AI technologies has been observed. In the 1980s and 1990s, experimentation with expert systems already showed the possibility of automating decision-making, how processing capacity was limited and the insufficiencies in data collection. With the advent of machine learning and the Deep Web, this foundation is being expanded to allow organizations to systematically incorporate real-time and historical data to create fairly sophisticated prediction models. Several studies have shown that this evolution has made it possible to complement human judgment with risky quantitative analyses, configuring a hybrid approach that responds to market dynamics quickly and flexibly (Warner & Wäger, 2019). A key point that can make a difference in your transformation is the relevance of dynamic capabilities that allow you to be competitive in a turbulent environment. This skill set is defined as organizational skill: the ability of organizations to obtain, reconfigure, and renew their resources. unexpected changes and close the gap between opportunities and competition (Zhang et al., 2025).

Under this stance, a strategically agile company is considered to be even more vigorously organized: as a result, it becomes a business model. On the other hand, sociomaterial theory has emerged in the attempt to explain the co-reproduction between human and technological practices. AI devices and systems are not only passive tools, but also act as active agents for the production of knowledge that makes up organizational culture. The continuous interaction between managers and automated systems gives rise to circular feedback, whereby digital information is naturally incorporated into decision-making (Zhang et al., 2025).

On the other hand, the concept of augmented strategic leadership holds that the union of the leader's experience with the analytical power of AI is the strategy for building strong competitive advantages. The synergy between the AI's automatic data analysis with vetted management experience reduces bias and enables decision-making. To adjust strategies and win optimally in an environment characterized by uncertainty, continuous feedback frameworks that unite real-time data with accumulated experience are essential. An innovative example in this context is Neuroeconomic Racial Alpha (Csaszar et al., 2024).

However, the introduction of AI into strategic leadership also comes with significant challenges. Algorithmic opacity, the possibility of biases in data and the concentration of decision-making power at higher hierarchical levels are obstacles that require ethical coping and effective governance. Thus, in this new era of strategic leadership, organizations must adopt integrative strategies that are not only focused on technological innovation, but also consistent with cultural transformation and constant upskilling (Hossain et al., 2025).

BACKGROUND

In the management and organizational science literature, strategic leadership has been extensively researched. However, with the emergence of new technologies such as artificial intelligence (AI), the concept and practice of strategic leadership have evolved significantly. Above all, AI has emerged as a powerful tool to change the way leaders make strategic decisions, optimize their processes, and manage organizational competitiveness (Mallio et al., 2024). It can be determined that the artificial intelligence revolution that has been underway for a long time. It identifies how the combination of technological advances over the past decade with the exponential increase in hardware capacity and price could lead to major advances in the evolution of artificial intelligence (Osorio-Barreto et al., 2022).

Therefore, it must be foreseen what kind of intelligence is necessary to operate in our nearest future, one that could well be created not by naturalization but by humans. In other words, the transition of leaders to making decisions based on computer-processed data we have only just begun to see the first examples. It is likely that 20 years from now the practice of strategic leadership will be very different from what we know today. The first research on AI in strategic decision-making dates back to the 1980s and 1990s, when expert systems began to be used in corporate environments to help managers make decisions (Cheong, 2024).

In particular, with the development of technologies such as machine and deep learning artificial intelligence, which allows the machine to learn from large volumes of data and make more accurate predictions in real time. AI's impact on strategic leadership became more apparent as big data grew. But despite major advances in artificial intelligence, the adoption of these technologies has also created a new set of problems for strategic leadership. More than anything, it is necessary to ensure transparency in algorithmic processes and potential biases in AI systems. At the same time, the argument underscores that the adoption of algorithms without an adequate governance structure will result in biased decisions that damage the fairness and legitimacy of organizations (Wirtz et al., 2020).

On the other hand, he highlights certain studies that show that implementing AI in the decision-making process can help make strategic leadership more efficient. AI models, powered entirely by deep learning in their organizations, experienced a significant increase in deliberative efficiency and conflict resolution within management teams (Csaszar et al., 2024). In this context, the literature on dynamic organization is also crucial to understand how artificial intelligence can improve strategic leadership. Organizations capable of continuously reconfiguring resources and capabilities are more likely to achieve sustained competitive advantages in turbulent environments (Hossain et al., 2025). From another point of view, it is considered that dynamic capacities, in addition to reconfiguring resources, also imply absorbing and applying new acquired knowledge (Mallio et al., 2024).

This combination of dynamic capabilities and artificial intelligence also reflects socio-material relationships, highlighting the impossibility of completely decoupling human practice from technical intervention. Likewise, strategic leadership is no longer a practice exclusive to human beings, but occurs as a combination of executives and technological systems. This view reveals that strategic decision-making is a process co-created by humans and machines, in which both parties interact with each other and feed off each other (Osorio-Barreto et al., 2022). In light of these advances, neuroeconomics has also influenced the understanding of how AI can improve decision-making in a strategic context. So, information processing is strongly related to dopaminergic circuits, which modulate the perception of risk and reward. By reducing informational ambiguity, AI can help leaders make decisions more rationally and can also decrease the cognitive load associated with uncertainty (Cheong, 2024).

However, not everything is easy when it comes to introducing AI into strategic leadership. There are quite a few challenges adjacent to the adoption of these systems, especially with regard to the delegation of authority to algorithms. Neural network-based prediction systems can become a black box that makes it difficult to interpret reliable data (Wirtz et al., 2020).

THEORETICAL FRAMEWORK

Convergence of Artificial Intelligence and Strategic Leadership

From digital transformation to now, the convergence of artificial intelligence (AI) and strategic leadership has brought a new decision-making pattern to organizations. Now, the application of advanced algorithms and deep learning, in addition to real-time predictive analytics for leaders, makes their own real-time process information that would not be attributed on Friday get results sooner than the CAF Method ((Duan et al., 2019). Using more data and predictive models, managers can prepare for anticipated future scenarios. In addition, they optimize resources by allocating resources that automatically adjust to any changes in the market or technological collapses that may occur. The power of AI must be identified in its ability to counterfactual when running simulations, generating accurate information that, fused with human expertise, helps minimize uncertainty and maximize effectiveness in strategic decision-making. This synergy draws on a variety of disciplines ranging from data science to organizational behavior studies. In this way, a cultural transformation is manifested in which the digital and the human are perfectly integrated (Warner & Wäger, 2019).

Historical Evolution and Development of Artificial Intelligence in Decision-Making

In the business field, the historical development of artificial intelligence has undergone a remarkable transformation, moving from rudimentary expert systems such as those of the eighties and nineties to today's advanced architectures based on machine learning and deep neural networks. In the beginning, AI applications were very simple. Managers at the time were provided with a very basic way to digitize information, but over the years, technology developed new ways: a hybrid between the integration of historical and real-time data. Thanks to this transformation, decision-making is based on predictive models that are not simply retrospective, allowing us to anticipate opportunities and threats through simulations and what-if scenarios (Alrub & Sánchez Cañizares, 2025).

In addition, this development has been characterized by a progressive integration between organizational computing, computational theory, and behavior, which has allowed organizations to achieve even greater speed and accuracy in the interpretation of their data. The combination of classic methods and new AI-based technologies allows for a hybrid approach in which expert judgement is complemented by advanced quantitative analysis (Alrub & Sánchez Cañizares, 2025).

Dynamic Capabilities and Organizational Adaptability

Dynamic capabilities and organizational adaptability are decisive elements for a firm that seeks to compete successfully in a volatile environment with constant contingencies. From this perspective, dynamic capabilities describe the organizational ability to sense changes, seize opportunities and reconfigure resources in order to renew strategic positioning, rather than simply optimizing existing routines. Artificial intelligence strengthens these capabilities because it makes it possible to detect weak signals and emerging trends at an early stage through continuous analysis of large scale data streams, which supports faster and more precise strategic responses (Gao et al., 2025; Teece, 2007).

Predictive models and advanced simulations allow organizations to adjust their development trajectories to an ever changing context, connecting historical information with real time indicators to generate scenarios that guide investment, diversification and risk mitigation decisions. Instead of relying only on retrospective dashboards, leaders can experiment with counterfactual simulations that estimate how alternative resource configurations would perform under different market and technological shocks, which increases organizational agility and reduces strategic myopia (Aldoseri et al., 2024; Akter et al., 2023).

As analytic pipelines are automated, the managerial focus gradually moves from the mechanical task of collecting and cleaning data to the higher order task of interpreting patterns, redefining priorities and reorienting portfolios of resources. In this sense, AI enabled dynamic capabilities help close the gap between opportunities and internal competencies, since decision makers can identify misalignments between current assets and future scenarios, and then orchestrate acquisitions, alliances, training and process redesign in a more deliberate way (Gao et al., 2025; Akter et al., 2023).

Sociomaterial Perspective: Coevolution Between the Human and the Technological

A sociomaterial perspective emphasizes that technology is intrinsically embedded in organizational cognition and operations, rather than being an external tool that can be added or removed without consequences. In environments where human expertise and automated systems work together, data infrastructures, interfaces and algorithms become part of the very fabric of everyday work practices, shaping what information is visible, which alternatives are considered and how responsibility is distributed (Iden & Bygstad, 2024; Wen et al., 2025).

From this angle, dynamic capabilities are not only abstract managerial skills but also sociotechnical micro foundations enacted in concrete interactions between people and digital resources. For example, sensing the environment depends on how dashboards, models and alerts are configured and interpreted; seizing opportunities depends on the collaborative routines through which cross functional teams explore AI generated insights; and reconfiguring assets depends on the way information systems support experimentation, rapid feedback and coordinated change (Iden & Bygstad, 2024; Akter et al., 2023).

This perspective also makes visible tensions related to power, transparency and learning. AI systems can redistribute influence inside the organization, reinforcing the authority of actors who control data infrastructures or, on the contrary, democratizing access to strategic information through self service analytics. At the same time, opaque models can undermine trust and limit the willingness of experts to rely on automated recommendations, while explainable approaches and participatory design can foster mutual adaptation between human and algorithmic agents (Wen et al., 2025; Aldoseri et al., 2024).

Empirical Insights from AI-Driven Strategic Leadership

From an empirical perspective, the effects of strategic leadership supported by artificial intelligence systems are observed in measurable improvements in sustainable performance, innovation and strategic alignment. A quantitative study of 421 employees from service organizations in Bangladesh shows that organizational capacity to deploy artificial intelligence is significantly associated with organizational creativity, green innovation, and sustainable performance, and that a culture of knowledge sharing amplifies these effects, indicating that data-driven and collaborative senior management decisions generate more strategy-consistent outcomes long-term corporate (Gazi et al., 2024).

In the field of knowledge management, an analysis with fuzzy set logic in European companies reveals that the implementation of artificial intelligence alone does not guarantee better organizational performance; The best results appear when the strategic decisions of senior management combine AI tools with intensive knowledge-sharing practices across units and hierarchical levels, suggesting that leadership should design complementary work systems in which AI reinforces, rather than replaces, the collective ability to learn and coordinate decisions (Olan et al., 2022).

From the perspective of dynamic capabilities, a survey of supply chain executives in France and the United States shows that dynamic capabilities enabled by artificial intelligence positively influence both data-driven culture and environmental performance, although the mediating role of data-driven culture varies between national contexts; These findings indicate that management teams should tailor their algorithmic governance design to the cultural and regulatory characteristics of each market, rather than applying a single digital leadership model.

In addition, a synthesis of the literature that systematically reviews AI capabilities for circular business models identifies four key strategic capabilities that leadership teams should develop: embedded intelligence, automation and process augmentation, AI infrastructure, and ecosystem orchestration; The work shows cases in which senior management has used these capabilities to redesign service models, resource recovery, and circular value creation, reinforcing the idea that AI-driven strategic leadership is about building long-term organizational capabilities rather than just acquiring isolated technologies (Madanaguli et al., 2024).

Strategic Leadership Driven by Artificial Intelligence

Strategic leadership driven by artificial intelligence assumes that executives no longer rely only on retrospective reports and intuition, but orchestrate analytical, predictive and adaptive capabilities that operate over large volumes of data in continuous time. In this approach, artificial intelligence supports the sensing of weak signals, the simulation of strategic scenarios and the rapid reconfiguration of resources, reinforcing dynamic capabilities such as opportunity recognition, organizational learning and strategic agility (Gao et al., 2025; López-Solís et al., 2025; Marimira & Gumel, 2025).

From a governance perspective, strategic leadership supported by artificial intelligence requires executives to design decision architectures where algorithms are integrated as advisory systems rather than opaque substitutes for human judgment. Research in different contexts reports that artificial intelligence and machine learning improve the precision, speed and consistency of strategic choices, but only when boards and top management teams retain responsibility for defining objectives, supervising model limitations and ensuring ethical criteria. In these configurations, leaders establish protocols for validation of recommendations, auditability of models and escalation of high impact decisions, while developing analytical skills and critical thinking in managerial teams.

The strategic potential of artificial intelligence becomes particularly visible when leadership connects advanced analytics with domain specific knowledge in sectors such as transport, digital services and connected products. In airlines, reviews show that artificial intelligence supports strategic planning in crisis situations by improving demand forecasting, pricing and capacity decisions, allowing management to evaluate complex tradeoffs between profitability, service quality and resilience (Pérez-Campuzano et al., 2021; Kaggwa et al., 2024; Al-Surmi et al., 2022).

Augmented Strategic Leadership: Integrating the Human and the Algorithmic

The notion of augmented strategic leadership proposes that the most robust competitive advantages arise when human experience and intuition are deliberately combined with the analytical and predictive power of AI. Rather than replacing executives, AI systems supply a continuous flow of structured evidence that complements managerial judgment, reduces blind spots and supports more disciplined experimentation with alternative strategies. In augmented leadership configurations, decision makers rely on intelligent systems to monitor key indicators, generate scenarios and stress test assumptions, while reserving human discretion for interpretive, ethical and relational aspects of strategy (Gao et al., 2025; Wen et al., 2025).

In practice, this implies the design of feedback loops that integrate real time analytics with accumulated organizational knowledge. Leaders define questions, boundaries and priorities, while AI pipelines transform raw data into interpretable signals about customers, operations, competitors and technologies. These signals are then discussed in multidisciplinary teams that bring together technical specialists and business experts, so that strategic options are evaluated not only in financial terms but also in terms of feasibility, cultural impact and long term resilience (Akter et al., 2023; Aldoseri et al., 2024).

However, the introduction of AI into strategic leadership also creates demanding challenges. Algorithmic opacity can obscure the reasons behind recommendations, data biases can propagate historical inequities and centralized control of powerful models can concentrate decision authority at the top of the hierarchy. Addressing these risks requires ethical frameworks, clear accountability mechanisms and participatory governance, so that augmented leadership remains aligned with organizational values and stakeholder expectations (Wen et al., 2025; Iden & Bygstad, 2024).

When organizations manage to integrate dynamic capabilities, sociomaterial awareness and augmented leadership, AI ceases to be a mere technical resource and becomes part of a broader transformation of culture and strategy. In such settings, experimentation, reflective learning and cross functional collaboration are encouraged, while failures in AI projects are treated as sources of insight rather than as grounds for blame. This integrative approach allows firms to anticipate disruptions, reconfigure their business models and cultivate more resilient positions in turbulent markets (Gao et al., 2025; Akter et al., 2023).

The Role of Neuroeconomics in Complex Decision Making

Neuroeconomics provides a detailed lens to understand how the brain evaluates alternatives under risk and uncertainty, especially in contexts where strategic decisions have high financial, reputational, or social impact. By combining concepts from neuroscience, psychology, and economics, this field examines how value is constructed in the brain and how emotions, prior experiences, and contextual cues shape what leaders perceive as attractive or threatening options. Functional imaging studies have shown that regions such as the ventromedial prefrontal cortex, the ventral striatum, the insula, and the posterior cingulate cortex encode subjective value and risk signals, helping to explain why individuals may deviate from purely rational models when facing complex trade offs in turbulent environments (Bayramoğlu & Öztürk, 2025; Mallio et al., 2024).

At the same time, neuroeconomic research uses experimental tasks that mimic real business dilemmas, such as intertemporal choices, strategic games, and social bargaining, to observe how neural responses differ between risk seeking and risk averse profiles (Mallio et al., 2024).

Building on this evidence, organizations are beginning to explore how neuroeconomic insights can be combined with data science and artificial intelligence models. Techniques such as functional magnetic resonance imaging, electroencephalography, and physiological monitoring are used to detect patterns associated with overreaction, impulsive risk taking, or excessive avoidance of uncertainty in decision makers (Bayramoğlu & Öztürk, 2025; Mallio et al., 2024).

Ethical Challenges and Algorithmic Governance in Leadership Contexts

The incorporation of artificial intelligence into strategic decision making introduces a second layer of complexity related to ethics, accountability, and the distribution of power inside organizations. When models classify clients, prioritize projects, or recommend resource allocation, the underlying logic is often opaque for many stakeholders, which complicates the attribution of responsibility for harmful or discriminatory outcomes (Cheong, 2024).

In response, research on algorithmic governance proposes multi layer frameworks that combine technical controls with organizational and cultural mechanisms. These frameworks include systematic documentation of models, explicit descriptions of their intended use, regular impact assessments, and the participation of diverse stakeholders in validation and review (Cheong, 2024).

Practical proposals derived from this body of work recommend the establishment of multidisciplinary oversight committees with the authority to question and, if necessary, stop the deployment of a model when there is evidence of systematic harm. These committees can review training data, monitor error distributions across user groups, and request revisions in model objectives when they conflict with the organization strategic values (Cheong, 2024).

Big Data, Digital Twins and Simulations in Strategic Optimization

The expansion of big data analytics has radically modified how organizations design, test, and refine their strategies. Instead of relying only on periodic reports, leadership teams can now access integrated dashboards that capture transactions, sensor data, customer interactions, and external indicators almost continuously. Studies on big data capabilities show that companies that invest in advanced analytics, data governance, and analytical talent are better positioned to sense weak signals, detect emerging patterns, and adjust their strategic orientation before disruptions fully materialize, which translates into stronger innovation performance and more resilient business models (Alaskar et al., 2024).

Beyond descriptive and predictive analytics, digital twin technology extends this capacity by creating virtual replicas of critical processes, supply chains, and even entire business units. A digital twin connects process models with real time data streams and simulation engines so that managers can experiment with alternative configurations, policies, or investments in a safe virtual environment (Fornari et al., 2025).

When digital twins are combined with artificial intelligence and insights from neuroeconomics, their strategic potential grows further. On the one hand, predictive models embedded in the twin can estimate the operational and financial impact of different courses of action under varying demand, disruption, or regulatory conditions. On the other hand, knowledge about human decision tendencies allows designers to incorporate behavioral assumptions into the simulations, such as overconfidence, loss aversion, or preference for short term gains (Fornari et al., 2025).

Cultural and Epistemological Transformation in the Digital Age

The integration of artificial intelligence into management is not simply a matter of adopting new tools; it represents a cultural and epistemological shift in how organizations understand knowledge, evidence and authority. Strategic judgment that historically rested on intuition, seniority and retrospective reports is increasingly mediated by continuous data flows, learning models and predictive analytics that expose patterns which are invisible to human perception (Hanelt et al., 2021; Konopik et al., 2022).

This cultural shift implies a redefinition of what it means to know and to decide in organizations. Data no longer functions only as a record of the past; it becomes a living input that is constantly updated and recombined through learning models that refine their parameters as new information arrives. To navigate this environment, managers must learn to interrogate data pipelines, question model assumptions and interpret uncertainty intervals, rather than treating algorithmic outputs as unquestionable facts (Hanelt et al., 2021; Cetindamar et al., 2024).

Algorithmic Literacy Skills and Autonomy for Decision-Making

In this context, algorithmic literacy becomes a core competence for strategic leadership and for teams across all hierarchical levels. Algorithmic literacy goes beyond basic digital skills and includes understanding what kinds of problems can be meaningfully modelled, how training data constrain possible conclusions, and which indicators are suitable to monitor model performance over time. Studies on artificial intelligence literacy in digital workplaces emphasize that employees need technology related, work related, human machine and learning oriented capabilities in order to participate critically in the design and use of AI, rather than becoming passive recipients of automated outputs (Cetindamar et al., 2024; Cox, 2024).

For leaders, algorithmic literacy is closely tied to epistemic humility and autonomy in decision making. On the one hand, leaders must recognize the limits of their own intuition when confronted with high dimensional data and complex interactions that are better handled by machine learning models. On the other hand, they must avoid over reliance on these models by cultivating the ability to read confidence intervals, identify situations in which training data are not representative, and ask for alternative specifications or scenario analyses (Cetindamar et al., 2024; Cox, 2024; Hanelt et al., 2021).

From a sociomaterial perspective, algorithmic literacy also involves recognizing that technologies and organizational practices coevolve. Predictive systems are not neutral instruments; they redistribute attention, redefine what is considered a relevant indicator and shape how performance is evaluated. As digital transformation progresses, organizational capabilities that support sensing, seizing and reconfiguring in dynamic environments become interwoven with the capacity to experiment with data pipelines, re assemble processes around new informational cues and renegotiate roles between human decision makers and algorithmic components (Konopik et al., 2022; Hanelt et al., 2021).

Neuroeconomic Insights and Complex Decision Making

Neuroeconomics contributes an additional layer to this picture by showing how neural systems encode value, risk and uncertainty when individuals face complex trade offs. Experimental research has demonstrated that brain regions involved in reward processing and cognitive control respond differently when decision makers are exposed to ambiguous outcomes, asymmetric payoffs or repeated feedback, which helps to explain why leaders sometimes overweight short term gains or familiar options even when models point to a superior but more uncertain alternative (Platt & Huettel, 2008).

When organizations incorporate neuroeconomic insights into AI assisted decision processes, they can create simulation environments that explicitly account for both objective probabilities and the typical distortions of human risk perception. For example, scenario tools can highlight situations in which leaders are likely to misinterpret low probability, high impact events or to ignore slow moving structural changes that gradually accumulate. This promotes a more reflective style of strategic deliberation, in which teams use algorithmic forecasts to make cognitive biases visible and to design countermeasures such as pre defined trigger points, diversified option portfolios or staggered commitments that mitigate the influence of emotional reactions on high stakes choices (Platt & Huettel, 2008; Cetindamar et al., 2024).

Ethical Challenges and Inclusive Algorithmic Governance

The cultural transformation associated with AI also raises pressing ethical questions about how automated systems are governed. As algorithms intervene in credit allocation, talent management, pricing or resource prioritization, the risk of opaque decision paths, hidden biases and unequal distributions of error becomes more salient. Empirical analyses of algorithmic governance show that policy responses focused solely on access, inclusion and transparency are often insufficient, because they do not fully confront the deeper power asymmetries and structural inequalities that can be reinforced by data driven systems (James et al., 2023).

An inclusive governance approach involves multidisciplinary committees that review models before deployment, routine impact assessments that examine who benefits and who bears the risks of prediction errors, and escalation channels that make it possible to suspend or recalibrate systems when unintended harms emerge. It also implies a reconfiguration of leadership accountability: executives cannot delegate responsibility to algorithms, but must remain answerable for the choice of objectives, training data and performance criteria embedded in their AI portfolios (James et al., 2023; Hanelt et al., 2021).

Big Data, Digital Twins and Adaptive Strategic Experimentation

The expansion of big data infrastructures and the emergence of digital twins further deepen the epistemological shift in strategic management. A digital twin is a virtual representation of an asset, process or even an entire organization that is continuously updated with operational data, allowing decision makers to test alternative configurations and intervention paths without exposing the physical system to immediate risk. Recent work shows that, when integrated with advanced analytics and AI, digital twins can support a new style of strategy making in which leaders evaluate candidate decisions by simulating their operational and financial effects under multiple scenarios, rather than relying exclusively on static business cases or partial pilots (Fantozzi et al., 2025).

Under this paradigm, strategic decisions become iterative experiments conducted within a virtual environment that approximates real time conditions. Leaders can explore the consequences of different investment sequences, capacity reallocations or policy changes and observe emergent interactions across functions and time horizons. This supports a more adaptive stance, as models can be periodically updated with fresh data and refined structures that better capture newly observed behaviours. Combined with big data streams from sensors, transactional systems and customer interactions, digital twins allow organizations to anticipate bottlenecks, stress test resilience and discover non obvious levers for value creation, while maintaining a tight coupling between simulation insights and frontline learning (Fantozzi et al., 2025; Konopik et al., 2022).

Toward Resilient and Human Centred Augmented Leadership

Taken together, these developments point to a profound reconfiguration of leadership in the digital era. Algorithmic literacy and data informed judgment become shared responsibilities across the organization, supported by training programs and governance structures that cultivate both critical thinking and technical understanding. Neuroeconomic insights remind leaders that human cognition will always be shaped by emotion and limited attention, which reinforces the value of coupling analytical models with reflective practices and diverse teams (Cetindamar et al., 2024; Fantozzi et al., 2025; Hanelt et al., 2021).

METHODOLOGY

The structure of this methodological proposal followed a series of steps corresponding to the reflective qualitative meta-analysis, whose purpose was to synthesize and reinterpret the available evidence on the integration of artificial intelligence in strategic leadership. Basing, in the first place, on the clear definition of the research objectives and on the presence of issues that would frame the analyses in the totality of the empirical and theoretical studies relevant to understanding the magnitude of the phenomenon.

Design of the systematic search strategy in highly relevant academic databases: this stage focused on consolidating the solid amount of literature that would constitute the basis of the qualitative analysis. The next stage. Evaluation and selection of studies:

included the application of a two-level selection procedure, with the review of titles and abstracts to discard those works that did not meet the eligibility criteria. It also involved reviewing the texts to assess their relevance and methodological quality. This step denoted the systematic identification of contributions to the phenomenon of AI integration in leadership and ensured the relevance of the topic and the scope of theoretical and contextual perspectives. At last. The analysis was based on the reflective nature, which manifested itself in the constant revision and adjustment of the code categories. This implies both convergences between studies, divergences and areas of incongruence.

Challenges Faced by Organizations or Institutions

The strategic adoption of artificial intelligence in digital transformation exposes organizations to a set of intertwined technical, organizational and cultural challenges. One of the most visible is the black box problem in predictive models: senior leaders often receive automated recommendations whose internal logic they cannot easily understand, which weakens trust and makes it difficult to justify decisions to boards, regulators or stakeholders. This opacity complicates accountability because it is not clear whether responsibility lies with the model, the data or the people who configured the system, so firms need explicit governance arrangements that define who is answerable for each stage of the algorithmic life cycle and how explanations will be generated for affected groups (Ebrahimi et al., 2025).

A second critical challenge is the risk that artificial intelligence reproduces or amplifies biases contained in historical data. Since many learning models are trained on past decisions, they can encode patterns of exclusion associated with hiring practices, credit scoring or pricing, and replicate them at scale under a veneer of mathematical objectivity (Zajko, 2022; Hanna et al., 2025).

Beyond technical issues, the normalisation of artificial intelligence in everyday processes introduces organizational challenges related to skills, culture and autonomy. When executives and analysts delegate more and more diagnostic tasks to automated systems, there is a real danger of cognitive deskilling: professionals may stop exercising their own analytical capacities and become over reliant on model outputs, especially under time pressure. Studies on responsible artificial intelligence stress that sustainable value creation depends on combining the strengths of human judgment and machine learning, which requires continuous investment in training, change management and spaces where employees can question model recommendations without fear of reprisal.

Ethical Governance and Social Responsibility Form Another Layer of Complexity

As automated systems are used in areas such as resource allocation, performance evaluation or risk scoring, organizations face rising expectations from regulators, employees and the public regarding fairness, explanation rights and avenues for contestation. Legal analyses emphasise that algorithmic bias is not only a technical problem but a core legal dilemma that tests principles such as equal treatment, due process and the right to effective remedy, so companies need multidisciplinary committees, impact assessments and clear escalation channels to review models before and after deployment (Lendvai & Gosztonyi, 2025; Ebrahimi et al., 2025).

The intensive use of big data and simulation technologies also raises demanding requirements for information management and data quality. To extract value from massive datasets, firms must harmonise inputs from legacy systems, sensors, customer interactions and external sources, while enforcing consistent standards for integrity, completeness and timeliness. Reviews of deep learning in supply chains reveal that sophisticated models are only as reliable as the data pipelines that feed them, and that many failures in predictive performance or planning accuracy stem from unexamined assumptions about data provenance, undocumented transformations and the absence of continuous monitoring of model drift (Ebrahimi et al., 2025).

Finally, environmental sustainability and social responsibility cut across all these dimensions. Training and operating large models and data infrastructures demands substantial energy and hardware resources, which can clash with corporate climate commitments if not managed carefully. Recent work on the energy footprint of artificial intelligence shows that the expansion of generative and predictive systems is already a non trivial contributor to data centre electricity use, and argues that organizations should incorporate energy and material indicators into their digital strategies, favouring frugal architectures, model reuse and efficient hardware to limit their environmental impact (De Vries, 2023).

Examples of Implementation in Companies and Organizations

Practical experiences in different sectors illustrate both the potential and the challenges of artificial intelligence in strategic management. In advanced manufacturing and high technology industries, large producers have used deep learning and computer vision to optimise inventory management and reduce capital tied up in stock. Empirical studies show that deep learning methods can significantly improve demand prediction and anomaly detection in inventory flows, allowing firms to adjust replenishment policies in near real time and cut logistics costs compared with traditional rule-based approaches (Deng & Liu, 2021; Villegas-Ch et al., 2024).

The insurance sector offers another rich field of application. Large insurers have deployed artificial intelligence to accelerate claims handling, detect fraud and refine risk assessment in health, property and automobile lines. A recent review of artificial intelligence in insurance documents how computer vision, natural language processing and telematics based models can reduce processing times, personalise pricing and support proactive risk prevention, while also warning that these benefits depend on robust data protection, explainability and fairness safeguards to maintain customer trust and regulatory compliance (Bhattacharya et al., 2025).

In banking and financial services, institutions have introduced learning models for credit scoring, market risk estimation and anti money laundering, which can enhance the sensitivity of early warning systems and adapt more quickly to changing market conditions than traditional econometric models. At the same time, research on artificial intelligence and systemic risk cautions that the widespread adoption of similar models and data sources may synchronise decision rules across institutions, increase procyclicality and create new channels for shock amplification if many actors react in the same way to model signals (Danielsson et al., 2022).

Large digital firms and technology consultancies have integrated data analytics platforms into their internal decision processes for finance, human resources and operations, using scenario analysis and what if simulations to evaluate strategic options before committing resources. Reviews of deep learning applications in supply chains and operations indicate that when firms treat these tools as components of an experimental strategy process, rather than as oracles, they can continuously refine production schedules, logistics configurations and capacity investments in response to feedback, achieving gains in resilience and efficiency (Deng & Liu, 2021; Subramanian & Riya, 2024).

RESULTS

According to the literature review, digital transformation has led to an unprecedented convergence between artificial intelligence and strategic leadership. Advanced algorithms, deep learning practices and predictive analytics have reconfigured decision processes, enabling executives to integrate large volumes of data, run counterfactual simulations and anticipate alternative futures with greater precision and speed. In this context, senior leaders can plan optimal resource allocation, adjust strategies in real time and respond more agilely to technological and market shifts, while the boundary between digital tools and human judgment in managerial work becomes increasingly blurred (Duan et al., 2019; Hanelt et al., 2021).

From an evolutionary perspective, comparative studies trace how organisational uses of AI have moved from early expert systems with limited processing capacity in the 1980s and 1990s to today's sophisticated architectures based on machine learning and deep neural networks. Whereas rule based systems codified static decision rules, contemporary models learn from streams of historical and real time data, update their parameters and support probabilistic forecasts across a wide range of scenarios (Duan et al., 2019; Hanelt et al., 2021).

A central theme in the review is the shift toward capabilities for continuous learning as a distinctive organisational competence. Research on dynamic capabilities highlights that the ability to sense changes in markets and technologies, seize emerging opportunities and reconfigure resources is increasingly mediated by AI based tools that help firms detect weak signals, experiment with new configurations and coordinate rapid reallocations of assets. Organisations that develop routines for combining domain expertise with algorithmic insights are better positioned to anticipate technological disruptions and market turbulence, enabling leaders to question dominant assumptions and exploit opportunities earlier than competitors who rely solely on traditional planning cycles (Warner & Wäger, 2019).

From a sociomaterial perspective, the literature conceptualises AI systems not as neutral instruments but as active participants in the co creation of organisational knowledge. Sociotechnical and sociomaterial studies describe decision making as the outcome of dynamic interactions between executives, data infrastructures and automated systems, where interfaces, dashboards and recommendation engines shape what is visible, urgent or strategically salient (Iden & Bygstad, 2024; Hanelt et al., 2021).

Within the framework of augmented strategic leadership, several studies emphasise the deliberate combination of human and algorithmic components to achieve more accurate and adaptable decisions. AI is used to process big data, generate robust simulations and quantify uncertainties, while expert judgment evaluates trade offs, contextual nuances and ethical implications (Duan et al., 2019; Warner & Wäger, 2019).

The review also underscores the contribution of neuroeconomics to reinterpreting decision processes in organisations. Neuroeconomic studies show how brain systems encode value, risk and uncertainty, and how emotional and cognitive signals jointly shape preferences under ambiguity. By integrating neuroscientific findings into AI supported simulations, some authors propose decision environments that incorporate both objective variables and subjective propensities, such as loss aversion, time discounting or sensitivity to social cues (Platt & Huettel, 2008).

At the same time, a reflexive comparison of the studies reveals several critical challenges. The black box problem, namely the difficulty of interpreting the internal logic of complex algorithms, appears as one of the most recurrent concerns. When authority is excessively delegated to opaque systems, leaders may lose the ability to justify or contest recommendations, while organisational competencies for critical analysis atrophy. Scholars argue that this imbalance of power between automated systems and human agents can amplify biases, weaken accountability and undermine trust, especially when affected groups lack mechanisms to question decisions derived from AI (James et al., 2023; Duan et al., 2019).

Another cross cutting insight concerns the integration of big data and advanced simulation, particularly digital twins, into strategic planning. Digital twins, understood as virtual replicas of processes or organisational systems fed by real time data, enable the design of strategic plans that are more adaptive than static roadmaps. By processing large data streams, recognising patterns and testing multiple what if scenarios, these tools allow organisations to construct strategies that evolve in sync with external conditions, adjusting structures and resource allocations as new information emerges (Fornari et al., 2025; Duan et al., 2019).

The literature points to a profound cultural and epistemological shift in leadership. Traditional conceptions of leadership centred on the capacity to make good decisions based primarily on intuition and accumulated experience are being complemented, and sometimes displaced, by models grounded in quantitative and collaborative evidence. For contemporary leaders, literacy in data management, the interpretation of predictive models and the ability to question algorithmic information have become fundamental skills (Cetindamar et al., 2024; Hanelt et al., 2021).

Ethical Implications in Competitive Contexts

In highly competitive contexts, the integration of artificial intelligence systems in strategic leadership intensifies ethical tensions linked to algorithmic opacity, delegation of authority and the pressure to maximize results in increasingly shorter deadlines. When models are used to anticipate competitors' movements, adjust prices, or prioritize investments, competitive advantage logic can favor technically efficient but non-transparent solutions, making it difficult for managers and stakeholders to understand the real criteria that guide automated recommendations and weakening accountability for errors or damages arising from such decisions (Csaszar et al., 2024; Hossain et al., 2025).

The pursuit of competitive superiority can also accentuate risks of distributive injustice when models are trained on biased historical data and optimized primarily for financial indicators. In areas such as credit, insurance or personnel selection, the reproduction of patterns of exclusion can deepen structural inequalities under the guise of statistical neutrality, while the pressure to capture market niches encourages the intensive use of segmentations that differentiate between profitable and unprofitable customers without considering long-term social effects; various studies warn that, without express safeguards, automated decision systems can consolidate access and mobility gaps, as well as transfer new types of systemic risk to the market as a whole (Zajko, 2022).

These tensions force us to rethink algorithmic governance from an ethical perspective that goes beyond minimum regulatory compliance. Rather than treating models as black boxes that simply deliver recommendations, management teams need oversight frameworks that define who is responsible for each phase of the system lifecycle, what usage limits are acceptable, and how impacts on internal and external collectives are documented, including the ability to suspend or redesign applications when persistent damage is identified; recent governance proposals emphasize the combination of meaningful transparency, systematic impact assessment, and participation of diverse actors to counteract power asymmetries between designers, users, and people affected by automated decisions (Wirtz et al., 2020; Cheong, 2024; Radanliev, 2025).

In terms of sustainability, competition based on artificial intelligence capabilities also poses dilemmas related to the energy and material footprint of the models used to obtain strategic advantages. The training and operation of increasingly complex architectures increases the consumption of energy and resources, which can conflict with the climate commitments of organizations if strategic management does not incorporate environmental criteria in its decisions on digital infrastructures; recent work underscores the need for leadership to complement competitive performance objectives with principles of algorithmic frugality, model reuse, and alignment with circular business models, preventing the race for data-driven optimization from eroding corporate sustainability goals (Akter et al., 2023; Hossain et al., 2025).

The literature on algorithmic literacy highlights that managers need to understand the possibilities and limits of models, recognize sources of bias, and dialogue critically with technical teams, while promoting organizational cultures where staff can express concerns and disagreements in the face of automated recommendations without fear of retaliation; in this way, competitive advantage is not only based on the technical sophistication of algorithms, but on the ability to articulate decision frameworks that integrate data justice, extended responsibility, and collective learning around the use of artificial intelligence in strategy (Cetindamar et al., 2024; Cox, 2024; Konopik et al., 2022).

FUTURE LINES OF RESEARCH

The analysis reveals vacancies with open windows. The next step is longitudinal research that combines functional neuroimaging with performance metrics to study how human-AI coregulation regulates the dorsolateral prefrontal cortex in strategic decision-making. It is also critical to investigate frugal AI approaches that can reduce total energy consumption without losing predictive accuracy, thus aligning united leadership with sustainability. In addition, future studies should investigate the co-production of meaning in virtual teams with interlinguistic communication using language models as a semantic mediator; This area was insufficiently explored in transnational mergers and acquisitions.

CONCLUSION

Digital transformation has led to a disruptive convergence between artificial intelligence and strategic leadership, a process that has evolved significantly in recent years. Technological advances, including the development of deep ciphers and predictive algorithms, are allowing entrepreneurs to supplant the complex scenarios they had been anticipating. Thus, AI-based systems facilitate the processing of large amounts of data in real time by loading counterfactual simulations that provide an overall strategic advantage and reduce uncertainty in decision-making

This synergy between automated analysis and direct experience redefines the very essence of leadership, so that strategic management is based on a mixture of intuition and empirical data. The story of how artificial intelligence has been entering organizational environments seems to me very eloquent: driven since the 80s and in the initial phases of the 90s by expert systems, AI in current management has already reached this unusually precise point. Thus, this evolutionary development has led to the lack of data being replaced by predictive models for decision-making (Cetindamar et al., 2024; Hanelt et al., 2021).

To the extent that these probabilistic methods and advanced algorithms place the robustness of quantitative analysis within the reach of expert judgment, they enable organizations to respond proactively to market currents. An important finding of the analysis is that dynamic capabilities are crucial to an organization's resilience and competitiveness.

By combining these internal capabilities and transforming them so effectively by incorporating artificial intelligence tools, it is not only possible to anticipate future trends and changes in the environment (Duan et al., 2019).

At the same time, the socio-material perspective has flourished as a primary theoretical framework for understanding the co-evolution between the technological and the human in leadership practices. From this perspective, technological artifacts are not just passive tools, but become active agents that interact inextricably with the values, practices, names, and cognitive meanings of leaders. In the interactive feedback loop between executives and automated systems, the leader's experience and judgment are combined with accurate AI data and audio-visual models generated (Hanelt et al., 2021).

Similarly, the concept of augmented strategic leadership has provided a revolutionary approach by merging human expertise with the analytical power of artificial intelligence. It uses massive data processing and simulation generation as a means to support leaders' intuition and expertise. Iterative feedback loops allow automated systems to integrate information into the decision-making process, reducing cognitive errors and making it easier to identify strategic opportunities (Warner & Wäger, 2019).

On the other hand, the integration of neuroscience through neuroeconomics added another dimension to the paradigm of strategic leadership in an environment of high uncertainty. Neuroscientific research has shown that dopaminergic circuits and other neural processes significantly influence how leaders value risks and rewards (Iden & Bygstad, 2024).

The analysis also identifies, at the same time, dangerous places and fields of uncertainty. The biggest problem in integrating artificial intelligence into strategic leadership is the black box problem. The intrinsic opacity of AI algorithms makes it difficult to track the results and proposals presented by prediction models, which can erode trust in automated systems and limits the leader's ability to monitor actions in the right direction (Platt & Huettel, 2008).

Another area of interest is the use of big data and modern simulation techniques such as digital twins to optimize organizational strategies. With the ability to process, analyze, and find patterns in large volumes of data, leaders have a powerful tool to anticipate trends, uncover opportunities, and design scenarios that enable strategic adjustments on the fly (Bayramoğlu & Öztürk, 2025).

The cultural and epistemological transformation derived from the emergence of intelligence technologies makes it clear that this change is not purely technological, but also entails a fundamental revision of the paradigms with which organizations order knowledge and act. Decision-making has always been based on intuition and empirical experience, but digitalization has brought with it a move towards collaborative models based on quantitative evidence and with integrated multidisciplinary opinions (James et al., 2023).

On the other hand, it is necessary for leaders to be trained in algorithmic literacy skills to be able to make autonomous decisions based on tradition and new technology. If managers have knowledge about data analysis and how to interpret predictive models, they will be able to discuss the conclusions of automatic systems by approving those that are valid and rejecting those that are not. Therefore, with these educational foundations, a culture of constructive criticism will be promoted instead of the obscure dependence that technology can cause (Fornari et al., 2025)

The study concludes that, for organizations to take full advantage of all the opportunities offered by the integration of artificial intelligence, a complete orientation is necessary that combines technological development with profound cultural and epistemological changes. The implementation of strict governance frameworks and control procedures, together with continuous training in digital skills, is a fundamental strategy to significantly reduce the risks arising from over-reliance on automated technologies.

Therefore, AI-optimized strategic leadership is a readjustment of the ontological and practical in the decision-making process, where both data convergence and command judgment form a new link to gain a lasting competitive advantage. The insights show that with the adoption of advanced technologies, tactical agility increases and uncertainty decreases significantly, as do our tools for forecasting the future (Cetindamar et al., 2024).

The future of strategic leadership is in the hands of companies, if they can combine technological advances thoughtfully, responsibly and in harmony with traditional human methods. All this mixture is leading us down a path of "economic success" with less chance of failure; At the same time, a tough administrative spirit will emerge with the capacity for innovation capable of adapting to any scourge that its environment or society poses to it. It should also be remembered that, in the age of artificial intelligence, the optimization of strategic leadership is not limited to the pure and simple adoption of technological tools.

In the age of artificial intelligence, strategic leadership is being reconceptualized based on the fusion of digital analytics and human skills, giving rise to a decision-making paradigm that requires both technological innovation and profound cultural transformation. The secret to effective leadership lies in the ability to critically and responsibly integrate the benefits of AI with human expertise and judgment, throughout a process of continuous learning and adaptation.

REFERENCES

Akter, S., Hossain, M. A., Sajib, S., Sultana, S., Rahman, M., Vrontis, D., & McCarthy, G. (2023). A framework for AI powered service innovation capability: Review and agenda for future research. *Technovation*, *125*, 102768. Advance online publication. DOI: 10.1016/j.technovation.2023.102768

Al-Surmi, A., Bashiri, M., & Koliousis, I. (2022). AI based decision making: Combining strategies to improve operational performance. *International Journal of Production Research*, *60*(14), 4464–4486. DOI: 10.1080/00207543.2021.1966540

Alaskar, T. H., Alsadi, A. K., Aloulou, W. J., & Ayadi, F. M. (2024). Big data analytics, strategic capabilities, and innovation performance: Mediation approach of organizational ambidexterity. *Sustainability (Basel)*, *16*(12), 5111. DOI: 10.3390/su16125111

Aldoseri, A., Al-Khalifa, K. N., & Hamouda, A. M. (2024). AI powered innovation in digital transformation: Key pillars and industry impact. *Sustainability (Basel)*, *16*(5), 1790. DOI: 10.3390/su16051790

Alrub, Y. A., & Sánchez Cañizares, S. M. (2025). Dynamic capabilities and digital transformation Toward strategic planning in the digital age evidence from Palestine. *Administrative Sciences*, *15*(1), 21. DOI: 10.3390/admsci15010021

Bayramoğlu, G., & Öztürk, O. (2025). Systematic and bibliometric review of neuroeconomics and neurofinance research: Current status, thematic trends, and future directions. *Journal of Economic Surveys*, *39*(5), 1883–1906. DOI: 10.1111/joes.12676

Bhattacharya, S., Castignani, G., Masello, L., & Sheehan, B. (2025). AI revolution in insurance: Bridging research and reality. *Frontiers in Artificial Intelligence*, *8*, 1568266. DOI: 10.3389/frai.2025.1568266 PMID: 40270929

Cetindamar, D., Kitto, K., Wu, M., Zhang, Y., Abedin, B., & Knight, S. (2024). Explicating AI literacy of employees at digital workplaces. *IEEE Transactions on Engineering Management*, *71*, 810–823. DOI: 10.1109/TEM.2021.3138503

Cheong, B. C. (2024). Transparency and Accountability in AI Systems: Safeguarding Well-Being in the Age of Algorithmic Decision-Making. *Frontiers in Human Dynamics*, *6*, 1421273. DOI: 10.3389/fhumd.2024.1421273

Cox, A. (2024). Algorithmic literacy, AI literacy and responsible generative AI literacy. *Journal of Web Librarianship*, *18*(3), 93–110. DOI: 10.1080/19322909.2024.2395341

Csaszar, F. A., Ketkar, H., & Kim, H. (2024). Artificial intelligence and strategic decision making Evidence from entrepreneurs and investors. *Strategy Science, 9*(4), 322–345. DOI: 10.1287/stsc.2024.0190

Danielsson, J., Macrae, R., & Uthemann, A. (2022). Artificial intelligence and systemic risk. *Journal of Banking & Finance, 140*, 106290. DOI: 10.1016/j.jbankfin.2021.106290

De Vries, A. (2023). The growing energy footprint of artificial intelligence. *Joule, 7*(10), 2191–2194. DOI: 10.1016/j.joule.2023.09.004

Deliu, D., & Olariu, A. (2024). The role of artificial intelligence and big data analytics in shaping the future of professions in Industry 6.0: Perspectives from an emerging market. *Electronics (Basel), 13*(24), 4983. DOI: 10.3390/electronics13244983

Deng, C., & Liu, Y. (2021). A deep learning based inventory management and demand prediction optimization method for anomaly detection. *Wireless Communications and Mobile Computing, 9969357*(1), 9969357. Advance online publication. DOI: 10.1155/2021/9969357

Duan, Y., Edwards, J. S., & Dwivedi, Y. K. (2019). Artificial intelligence for decision making in the era of big data Evolution, challenges and research agenda. *International Journal of Information Management, 48*, 63–71. DOI: 10.1016/j.ijinfomgt.2019.01.021

Ebrahimi, S., Abdelhalim, E., Hassanein, K., & Head, M. (2025). Reducing the incidence of biased algorithmic decisions through transparency of the importance of features: An empirical study. *European Journal of Information Systems*. Advance online publication. DOI: 10.1080/0960085X.2024.2395531

Fantozzi, I. C., Santolamazza, A., Loy, G., & Schiraldi, M. M. (2025). Digital twins: Strategic guide to utilize digital twins to improve operational efficiency in Industry 4.0. *Future Internet, 17*(1), 41. DOI: 10.3390/fi17010041

Fornari, F., Compagnucci, I., Callisto de Donato, M., Bertrand, Y., Beyel, H. H., Carrión, E., Franceschetti, M., Groher, W., Grüger, J., Kilic, E., Koschmider, A., Leotta, F., Li, C. Y., Lugaresi, G., Malburg, L., Mangler, J., Mecella, M., Pastor, O., Riss, U., & Valderas, P. (2025). Digital twins of business processes: A research manifesto. *Internet of Things : Engineering Cyber Physical Human Systems, 30*, 101477. DOI: 10.1016/j.iot.2024.101477

Gao, Y., Liu, S., & Yang, L. (2025). Artificial intelligence and innovation capability: A dynamic capabilities perspective. *International Review of Economics & Finance, 98*, 103923. DOI: 10.1016/j.iref.2025.103923

Gazi, M. A. I., Rahman, M. K. H., Masud, A. A., Amin, M. B., Chaity, N. S., Senathirajah, A. R. B. S., & Abdullah, M. (2024). AI capability and sustainable performance: Unveiling the mediating effects of organizational creativity and green innovation with knowledge sharing culture as a moderator. *Sustainability (Basel)*, *16*(17), 7466. DOI: 10.3390/su16177466

Hanelt, A., Bohnsack, R., Marz, D., & Antunes Marante, C. (2021). A systematic review of the literature on digital transformation: Insights and implications for strategy and organizational change. *Journal of Management Studies*, *58*(5), 1159–1197. DOI: 10.1111/joms.12639

Hanna, M. G., Pantanowitz, L., Li, Q. K., Dadras, S. S., Bui, M. M., Farris, A. B., Salgado, R., Schuuring, E., Taylor, C. R., & Nakhleh, R. E. (2025). Ethical and bias considerations in artificial intelligence and machine learning applications in pathology. *Modern Pathology*, *38*(2), 100686. DOI: 10.1016/j.modpat.2024.100686 PMID: 39694331

Hossain, S., Fernando, M., & Akter, S. (2025). The Influence of AI-Powered Capabilities on Responsible Leadership: A Future Research Agenda. *Journal of Management & Organization*, *31*(5), 2360–2384. DOI: 10.1017/jmo.2025.10010

Iden, J., & Bygstad, B. (2024). Sociotechnical micro foundations for digital transformation. *European Journal of Information Systems*, *34*(2), 367–382. DOI: 10.1080/0960085X.2024.2347950

James, A., Hynes, D., Whelan, A., Dreher, T., & Humphry, J. (2023). From access and transparency to refusal: Three responses to algorithmic governance. *Internet Policy Review*, *12*(2). Advance online publication. DOI: 10.14763/2023.2.1691

Kaggwa, S., Eleogu, T. F., Okonkwo, F., Farayola, O. A., Uwaoma, P. U., & Akinoso, A. (2024). AI in decision making: Transforming business strategies. *International Journal of Innovation and Scientific Research*, *10*(12), 423–440. DOI: 10.51244/IJRSI.2023.1012032

Konopik, J., Jahn, C., Schuster, T., Hoßbach, N., & Pflaum, A. (2022). Mastering the digital transformation through organizational capabilities: A conceptual framework. *Digital Business*, *2*(2), 100019. DOI: 10.1016/j.digbus.2021.100019

Lendvai, G. F., & Gosztonyi, G. (2025). Algorithmic bias as a core legal dilemma of artificial intelligence. *Laws*, *14*(3), 41. DOI: 10.3390/laws14030041

López-Solís, O., Luzuriaga-Jaramillo, A., Bedoya-Jara, M., Naranjo-Santamaría, J., Bonilla-Jurado, D., & Acosta-Vargas, P. (2025). Effect of generative artificial intelligence on strategic decision making in entrepreneurial business initiatives: A systematic literature review. *Administrative Sciences*, *15*(2), 66. DOI: 10.3390/admsci15020066

Madanaguli, A., Sjödin, D., Parida, V., & Mikalef, P. (2024). Artificial intelligence capabilities for circular business models: Research synthesis and future agenda. *Technological Forecasting and Social Change*, *200*, 123189. DOI: 10.1016/j.techfore.2023.123189

Mallio, C. A., Buoso, A., Stiffi, M., Cea, L., Vertulli, D., Bernetti, C., Di Gennaro, G., van den Heuvel, M. P., & Beomonte Zobel, B. (2024). Mapping the neural basis of neuroeconomics with functional magnetic resonance imaging: A narrative literature review. *Brain Sciences*, *14*(5), 511. DOI: 10.3390/brainsci14050511 PMID: 38790489

Marimira, N., & Gumel, B. I. (2025). The role of artificial intelligence in strategic decision making. *Asian Journal of Economics. Business and Accounting*, *25*(3), 316–327. DOI: 10.9734/ajeba/2025/v25i31712

Olan, F., Arakpogun, E. O., Suklan, J., Nakpodia, F., Damij, N., & Jayawickrama, U. (2022). Artificial intelligence and knowledge sharing: Contributing factors to organizational performance. *Journal of Business Research*, *145*, 605–615. DOI: 10.1016/j.jbusres.2022.03.008

Osorio-Barreto, D., Landínez-Martínez, D. A., & Chica-Mesa, J. C. (2022). Neuroeconomics and Financial Decision Making: An Approach from a Systematic Literature Review. *CEA Magazine*, *8*(16), 1911. DOI: 10.22430/24223182.1911

Pérez-Campuzano, D., Morcillo Ortega, P., Rubio Andrada, L., & López-Lázaro, A. (2021). Artificial intelligence potential within airlines: A review on how AI can enhance strategic decision making in times of COVID 19. *Journal of Airline and Airport Management*, *11*(2), 53–72. DOI: 10.3926/jairm.189

Platt, M. L., & Huettel, S. A. (2008). Risky business: The neuroeconomics of decision making under uncertainty. *Nature Neuroscience*, *11*(4), 398–403. DOI: 10.1038/nn2062 PMID: 18368046

Radanliev, P. (2025). AI ethics: Integrating transparency, fairness, and privacy in autonomous decision systems. *Applied Artificial Intelligence*, *39*(1), e2463722. DOI: 10.1080/08839514.2025.2463722

Subramanian, Y. R., & Riya, R. (2024). The transformative role of artificial intelligence in human resource. [IJRTBT]. *International Journal on Recent Trends in Business and Tourism*, *8*(2), 14–25. DOI: 10.31674/ijrtbt.2024.v08i02.002

Teece, D. J. (2007). Explicating dynamic capabilities: The nature and microfoundations of sustainable enterprise performance. *Strategic Management Journal*, *28*(13), 1319–1350. DOI: 10.1002/smj.640

Villegas-Ch, W., Maldonado Navarro, A., & Sánchez Viteri, S. (2024). Optimization of inventory management through computer vision and machine learning technologies. *Intelligent Systems with Applications*, *24*, 200438. DOI: 10.1016/j.iswa.2024.200438

Warner, K. S. R., & Wäger, M. (2019). Building dynamic capabilities for digital transformation An ongoing process of strategic renewal. *Long Range Planning*, *52*(3), 326–349. DOI: 10.1016/j.lrp.2018.12.001

Wen, Y., Wang, J., & Chen, X. (2025). Trust and AI weight: Human AI collaboration in organizational management decision making. *Frontiers in Organizational Psychology*, *3*, 1419403. Advance online publication. DOI: 10.3389/forgp.2025.1419403

Wirtz, B. W., Weyerer, J. C., & Sturm, B. J. (2020). The Dark Sides of Artificial Intelligence: An Integrated AI Governance Framework for Public Administration. *International Journal of Public Administration*, *43*(9), 818–829. DOI: 10.1080/01900692.2020.1749851

Wu, J., & Shang, S. (2020). Manage uncertainty in AI-enabled decision-making and achieve sustainability. *Sustainability (Basel)*, *12*(21), 8758. DOI: 10.3390/su12218758

Zajko, M. (2022). Artificial intelligence, algorithms and social inequality. *Sociology Compass*, *16*(6), e12962. DOI: 10.1111/soc4.12962

Zhang, Y., Swatdikun, T., Lakkanawanit, P., Huang, S.-Z., & Chen, H. (2025). Digital transformation capacity, organizational strategic intuition, and digital leadership: Empirical evidence of the performance of high-tech companies in the Yangtze River Delta. *Journal of Risk and Financial Management*, *18*(7), 405. DOI: 10.3390/jrfm18070405

Chapter 8
Retracted Personalization and Customer Engagement Using AI-Powered Analytics

Simmi Dhyani
http://orcid.org/0000-0002-7043-5400
Chandigarh University, India

Meenakshi Sharma
http://orcid.org/0000-0002-6841-052X
BIT Mesra, India

Silky Valecha
Chandigarh University, India

ABSTRACT

The real-time data processing capabilities of artificial intelligence (AI) have become a crucial asset for enabling dynamic personalization (Wedel & Kannan, 2016). By continuously monitoring user interactions across multiple digital platforms—such as website navigation, mobile app engagement, and in-store beacon activity—AI systems can adapt recommendations, content, and promotional offers instantly (Kannan & Li, 2017). Unlike traditional approaches that rely on historical data, real-time behavioral analysis allows businesses to react immediately to shifts in customer preferences and intent (Lemon & Verhoef, 2016). For instance, when a user explores a specific product category on an e-commerce site, AI can promptly display related items or offer tailored discounts. This level of contextual person-

DOI: 10.4018/979-8-3373-3648-0.ch008

alization ensures the message aligns closely with the customer's current behavior, increasing the likelihood of engagement, higher click-through rates (CTRs), and improved conversion outcomes (Verhoef et al., 2009).

1. INTRODUCTION: THE IMPERATIVE OF PERSONALIZATION IN A DATA-RICH ERA

One of the most important things that marketers have to understand is that with the advent of IoT, the one-size-fits-all approach of traditional marketing has become largely ineffective. Especially when an unprecedented volume of customer data is available at hand and accelerated digital iterations post 2020 (Tam & Ho, 2006). Now that both marketers and customers are looking forward to personalized interactions and enhanced customer engagement, the role of AI becomes more and more important, allowing dynamic, real-time personalization using machine learning algorithms and predictive analytics (Wedel & Kannan, 2016).Many cases highlights that AI-driven personalization adds significant value and its effectiveness can vary across industries. For example, Amazon's recommendation engine has become a benchmark for predictive personalization as it dynamically analyze browsing and purchase history to increase cross-selling and upselling, whereas Netflix uses advanced AI models for personalizing content streams, this results in higher retention. Many Industry reports states support that 71% of consumers expect personalized interactionsand76% report frustration when personalization is absent (McKinsey, 2022). Despite these successes, research gaps exists in understanding personalization in case of emerging economies, the risks of consumer trust erosion, and the organizational change management needed to ensure AI integration (Deloitte, 2023; Wu et al., 2025).

2. Theoretical Foundations and Literature Review

The concept of personalization in marketing is not new, tracing its roots to one-to-one marketing principles (Peppers & Rogers, 1993). However, the scale with which personalization is achievable today is only because of AI, this represents a paradigm shift from mass marketing to personalized marketing.

2.1. Customer Relationship Management (CRM) and Personalization

At its core, personalization aligns with the objectives of Customer Relationship Management (CRM), which aims to manage and analyze customer interactions and data throughout the customer lifecycle to improve business relationships with customers, assist in customer retention, and drive sales growth (Parvatiyar & Sheth, 2001; Payne & Frow, 2005). Traditional CRM systems primarily focused on data storage and basic segmentation. However, the integration of AI transforms CRM into a proactive, intelligent system capable of predicting customer needs and orchestrating highly personalized engagements (Frow & Payne, 2011). AI-powered CRM systems can automate tasks, provide predictive insights, and personalize communication channels, thereby enhancing customer satisfaction and loyalty (Ngai, 2005).

2.2. Information Processing Theory and Cognitive Load

Information Processing Theory suggests that individuals have limited cognitive capacity for processing information (Miller, 1956). In an information-overloaded digital environment, generic marketing messages contribute to cognitive overload, leading to disengagement (Eppler & Mengis, 2004). Personalized messages, curated by AI to be relevant and timely, reduce cognitive load by presenting only information pertinent to the individual, thereby increasing the likelihood of engagement and positive response (Pham & Avnet, 2009). This aligns with research indicating that highly relevant content leads to higher attention and recall (Bauerly & Liu, 2019).

2.3. Social Exchange Theory and Reciprocity

Social Exchange Theory posits that social behaviour is the result of an exchange process, where individuals weigh the potential benefits and costs of interactions (Homans, 1961). For any organization, personalization in marketing efforts is valuable as it offers increased reciprocation by customers (Palmatier et al., 2006). If a customer feels that the organization understands their needs, preferences, it increases the chances of customers reciprocating with loyalty, engagement, and positive word-of-mouth (Kumar & Reinartz, 2012). Personalization has made this reciprocal relationship stronger (Zeithaml, 1988).

2.4. Flow Theory and Immersive Experiences

Flow Theory, as introduced by Csikszentmihalyi (1990), is a mental state of an individual in which the individual is fully immersed in an activity, experiencing deep concentration, genuine enjoyment, and a distorted sense of time. (Csikszentmihalyi, 1990). AI-powered analytics contribute to creating this "flow" experience for its customers by focusing on highly relevant and engaging content (Hoffman & Novak, 1996). This is responsible for creating a unique and enjoyable experience, which will ultimately enhance engagement and satisfaction (Shin, 2006).

3. THE TRANSFORMATIVE POWER OF AI-POWERED ANALYTICS IN PERSONALIZATION

AI-powered analytics takes advantage of customer data to obtain sophisticated personalization. These technologies enable organizations to shift from mass marketing to individual marketing.

3.1. Machine Learning (ML) and Predictive Analytics

AI-powered personalization uses Machine Learning (ML) algorithms. ML ensures that the system learns from huge customer data by identifying patterns and making predictions (Mitchell, 1997).

Predictive analytics is one of the most important applications of ML; it uses past data to predict future customer behaviour, like likelihood of purchase, churn risk, or product preferences (Provost & Fawcett, 2013; Siegel & Swanson, 2004). Like e-commerce platforms tend to use ML for recommendation engines that suggest products based on past purchases, browser history, and similar customer behaviours (Linden et al., 2003). Netflix's recommendation system, for example, is one of the best examples of predictive analytics (Bell et al., 2009). Similarly, many financial institutions employ predictive models to identify and detect fraudulent activities (Brauneis & Steidl, 2019).

3.2. Natural Language Processing (NLP) and Sentiment Analysis

Natural Language Processing (NLP) makes AI systems understand and interpret human language and helps to generate personalized responses (Jurafsky & Martin, 2009). This ability to analyse unstructured customer data like customer reviews, social media posts, and chatbot conversations is crucial for marketers.

Sentiment analysis helps to identify the underlying emotional tone of textual data, segmenting it as positive, negative, or neutral (Liu, 2012). Analyses of customer feedback through NLP and sentiment analysis give real-time insights into customer behaviour like satisfaction levels, pain points, and their responses (Feldman, 2013).

For instance, a customer service chatbot using NLP can understand the customer's query in a better way and provide a personalized and relevant response, and sentiment analysis can identify emotional trends (Cambria & White, 2014). Organizationslike Starbucks use sentiment analysis of social media posts and customer feedback to understand customer perception (GfK, 2017).

3.3. Deep Learning and Computer Vision

Deep learning models are a branch of machine learning techniques that process data such as images and videos (LeCun et al., 2015). Deep models use multi-layered networks that can handle complex data of images and videos (Krizhevsky et al., 2012). They are used for visual-driven personalization, like suggesting clothes based on a customer's uploaded photos or personalizing video content to match individual visual preferences (Wang & Song, 2021). Visual analytics has opened new possibilities for delivering personalized enhanced user experiences.

3.4. Real-time Behavioural Tracking and Contextual Personalization

The capability of AI to process and analyse data in real-time has emerged as a most powerful tool for dynamic personalization (Wedel & Kannan, 2016). AI algorithms can personalize content, offers and recommendations by tracking customer data at various digital touchpoints like website clicks, app usage and in-store navigations (Kannan & Li, 2017). This real-time tracking of customer data allows organizations to proactively respond to changing trends in customer preferences and needs (Lemon & Verhoef, 2016). For example, when a customer is browsing a particular product category, say on an e-commerce website, AI can automatically show related products or offer a discount. This type of personalization ultimately increases click-through rates (CTRs) and conversions (Grönroos, 1994; Verhoef et al., 2009).

4. STRATEGIC IMPLEMENTATION OF AI-POWERED PERSONALIZATION FOR CUSTOMER ENGAGEMENT

Successful integration of AI-powered analytics requires a strategic approach that integrates these technologies across all customer digital touchpoints, addressing the current gaps in integration and focusing on dynamic experiences (Lamberton & Stephen, 2016).

4.1. Developing an Integrated Framework for AI and Customer Engagement

An important gap is the lack of a holistic framework that integrates AI tools and customer engagement strategies (Palmatier et al., 2016). This chapter proposes a model for encompassing data collection, analysis, personalization, and engagement across multiple digital touchpoints.

- **Data Foundation:** The first step includes collecting and consolidating data from all digital touchpoints, like website, mobile app, CRM, IoT devices, and social media, into a unique customer profile. Data quality and regulations are important considerations for the same (Wang & Strong, 1998; Davenport, 2014).
- **AI-Powered Analysis:** Analysis of customer insights by using ML, NLP, and predictive analytics to identify customer segments, tailor-made content for individual preferences, detect behavioural patterns, and identify underlying sentiments (Huang & Rust, 2021; Chen et al., 2023).
- **Personalization Engine:** Using AI-powered analysis insights for personalized content, product recommendations, offers, and communication across multiple channels. (Bradlow et al., 2017; Fader et al., 2005).
- **Omnichannel Delivery:** Consistent personalized experiences over all the digital touchpoints (Lemon & Verhoef, 2016; Verhoef et al., 2017).
- **Feedback Loop and Optimisation:** This includes continuous monitoring of customer data for better personalized interactions and to train AI models to improve personalization effectiveness over time (Haenlein & Kaplan, 2019). This iterativeness is important for dynamic personalization.

4.2. Leveraging AI for Dynamic Personalization Across Digital Touchpoints

- **Personalized Website and App Experiences:** This is the most powerful feature that AI powered analytics can offers, the layout of app and websites changes dynamically in real time from user to user depending upon the preferences and past data making the content more impactful and increase in click rates, wish listing, customer engagement and ultimately sales (Luo et al., 2013). For example, Amazon uses AI-powered analytics for personalized home page and product recommendations (Brynjolfsson et al., 2011).
- **Intelligent Chatbots and Virtual Assistants:** AI-powered chatbots can efficiently use NLP to understand the underlying customer intent, which helps them to resolve queries not only proactively but also provide customers with

better personalized responses that are transparent and create a sense of trust and improve satisfaction (Rese & Steppert, 2019). AI-powered chatbots can proactively offer personalised assistance based on customer behaviour (Van den Broeck & Van den Bergh, 2015).

- **Tailored Email and Push Notifications:** Everything for a marketer is important right from content to images used to timing to offers, and these changes from customers to customers offering these for individual customers through AI powered emails and push notifications have become very easy and offers better results in terms of engagement and click-through rates. Organizations like Grammarly use AI to personalize offers and writing tips on the basis of user behaviour within their application (Grammarly, 2020).
- **Personalized Advertising and Social Media Content:** AI allows targeting at individual levels, making the content more impactful (Goldfarb & Tucker, 2011). Especially, social media platforms use AI to offer personalized content, feeds, recommendations and user engagement techniques (Bakshy et al., 2015; Wasilewski et al., 2025).

4.3. Measuring the Impact on Customer Engagement and Business Outcomes

The overall findings suggest that AI-powered analytics is a strong tool which can significantly enhance customer engagement, leading to increased loyalty, satisfaction, and affiliation with the organization. Study suggests revenue increase in the range of 5–8% (Accenture Research, 2019; Brodie et al., 2021). Key metrics which can be used for evaluating the impact are:

- **Click-Through Rates (CTR):** Personalized content, recommendations, and offers consistently yield higher CTRs compared to generic approaches (Hair et al., 2017).
- **Conversion Rates:** When prospects are presented with personalized conversations which they find relevant, their chances of conversion increase considerably (Rust et al., 2002).
- **Customer Lifetime Value (CLTV):** Enhanced engagement and satisfaction translate into increased customer retention and repeat purchases, thereby boosting CLTV (Berger & Nasr, 1998).
- **Customer Satisfaction (CSAT) and Net Promoter Score (NPS):** Personalization through AI directly relates to higher CSAT and contributes towards better NPS as customers feel more attached to the organizations (Parasuraman et al., 1988).

- **Reduced Churn Rates:** Use of AI predictive analytics enables marketers to identify customers who are at high risk of churning, thereby allowing marketers to tailor-make strategies for retention (Coussement & Van den Poel, 2008).

5. TECHNICAL REQUIREMENTS AND CHALLENGES

There are unique requirements and challenges of every AI integration meets (Davenport & Kirby, 2016).

5.1. Data Infrastructure and Management

Data infrastructure refers to how an organization can collect, store, retrieve and process data. The better the infrastructure, the better the creation and implementation of AI models. This will lead to better quantifiable insights and results. (Davenport, 2014). Data consistency as well as quality will also impact the overall implementation of the AI techniques (Wang & Strong, 1998).

5.2. AI Model Development and Deployment

This requires skilled data managers and engineers to develop AI models that can be trained and implemented. These models should be scalable enough to handle growing data volumes and real-time demands (Goodfellow et al., 2016). Maintenance and training of these models is crucial to maintain the accuracy of the results and adaptation to changing customer needs and preferences (Hastie et al., 2009).

5.3. Integration with Existing Systems

This is one of the most important challenges for any marketer. This challenge can be resolved by developing AI systems that can be seamlessly integrated with existing CRM platforms. (Chen et al., 2012). This often involves API development and robust data pipelines (Manyika et al., 2017).

5.4. Organizational Readiness and Skill Gaps

Any AI tool can only be successfully implemented if the employees of the organization are ready for such change, they are well trained, organization is providing them data-driven culture and is willing to invest to bridge the gaps (Ransbotham et al., 2017). Without the right talent and mindset, even the most advanced AI tools will fall short (Marr, 2016).Even tough AI-powered personalization is a strong tool, research points towards significant organizational and cultural barriers that can limit adoption. It is seen that many firms invest or are willing to in personalization platforms, but fewer than one-third are able to achieve the said impact because of internal resistance, siloed data, and lack of cross-functional collaboration(McKinsey, 2022). Cultural barriers like low trust in AI systems and employee resistance delay adoption (Bughin et al., 2021). For instance Microsoft's Tay chatbot did not perform due to poor content moderation and cultural misalignment. Target attempted at predictive personalization and faced consumer backlash because pregnancy-related promotions also reached unintended audiences (Hill, 2012). These cases highlight that personalization initiatives may fail if due to organizational and cultural barriers, internal change management also plays a pivotal role (Deloitte, 2023). Emphasizes should not only at advanced algorithms but also inleadership, workforce reskilling, and clear organizational goals(PwC, 2023).

6. ETHICAL AND PRIVACY CONSIDERATIONS IN PERSONALIZATION

The widespread use of AI-powered analytics for personalization raises significant ethical and privacy concerns that must be addressed proactively (Acquisti et al., 2015). As highlighted in the findings, organizations that transparently communicate their data use policies and provide customization controls experience higher trust and satisfaction from their customers (Goldfarb & Tucker, 2019; Ångström et al., 2023).

6.1. Data Collection and Consent

The sheer volume of data collected for personalization raises questions about the scope and nature of consent. While explicit consent is often sought for personal data, the collection of behavioural and inferred data can be less transparent (Solove, 2008). It is required by every organization to follow all regulations for data collection, storage, and processing (Voigt & Von dem Bussche, 2017). The customers must be given information about how the data will be used and who will have access to their data (Tsai et al., 2011).

6.2. Algorithmic Bias and Discrimination

This ethical challenge is the most important for marketers, as if the data provided to AI algorithms is biased, then the entire result is also biased, which can result in exclusion of those segments or customers or content or media which can be used for more profitability and overall growth of the organization (Barocas & Selbst, 2016). This biased personalization can also backfire and damage the organisation's reputation. For example, using historical data sets only can lead to missing various opportunities that other demographics might offer (O'Neil, 2016). So it is recommended that organizations verify the data and test the AI algorithms rigorously before implementation (Raji et al., 2020). Hence, using the right dataset as well as the right algorithm is important (Adadi & Berrada, 2018).

6.3. Transparency and Explainability

One of the challenges of using AI is deciding the degree of transparency to which customers can be acquitted with while using AI. Most of the time, customers are not aware or do not understand why certain content or recommendationsare offered to them. The lack of transparency often leads to feelings of distrust and manipulation, which are the opposite of what the marketer aims to achieve. Explainable AI (XAI) is a term which is used to make customers aware ofa certain degree of transparency while using AI (Arrieta et al., 2020). This will provide customers a sense of trust, knowledge, understanding and some level of control over the personalisation of their preferences (Tsai et al., 2011).

6.4. Data Security and Privacy Breaches

The availability of large amounts of data, especially sensitive customer data, always has the possibility of cyber attacks. Organizations have to provide strong data security measures like encryption, access controls, multiple security checkpoints, and security audits to protect against data breaches (Doris, 2010;Whitman & Mattord, 2018). Even a single data breach can damage not only customer trust but overall organisation's reputation (Romanosky et al., 2016).

6.5. "Filter Bubbles" and Echo Chambers

"Filter bubbles" or "echo chambers" refer to the generation or personalisation of content in such a way that it reinforces their existing set of beliefs, thereby limiting their exposure to other perspectives (Pariser, 2011). This type of technique is more often used in casesof social media, news and personalized recommendations, especially in e-commerce (Flaxman et al., 2016). So, it becomes ethically necessary to balance the reinforcement and discovery of new perspectives, which might be more suitable for the customers (Resnick & Varian, 1997).

7. REAL-WORLD CASES AND FUTURE OUTLOOK

Numerous companies have successfully leveraged AI-powered analytics for personalization and enhanced customer engagement (Davenport & Ronanki, 2018).

7.1. E-commerce Giants: Amazon and Netflix

Amazon is a quintessential example of AI-driven personalization, with its recommendation engine generating a significant portion of its sales (Fader & Hardie, 2009). Their algorithms analyze browsing history, purchase patterns, and even items viewed by similar customers to provide highly relevant product suggestions (Smith & Linden, 2017).

Netflix similarly uses AI to personalize content recommendations, leading to high subscriber retention and engagement. Their sophisticated algorithms consider viewing history, genre preferences, and even viewing times to suggest new shows and movies (Amatriain & Basilico, 2015).

7.2. Retail and Fashion: Stitch Fix and Zara

Stitch Fix utilises AI and human stylists to personalize clothing recommendations for its subscribers, demonstrating a powerful hybrid model (Stitch Fix, 2020). AI analyzes customer preferences, style surveys, and even social media profiles to curate personalized boxes, leading to high customer satisfaction (Hill, 2017). While not as explicit, *Zara* utilizes data analytics, though perhaps less AI-driven in the sense of predictive modelling for individual personalization, for rapid trend analysis and inventory management, allowing them to quickly bring relevant, desired fashion to market (Sull & Turconi, 2008).

7.3. Financial Services: Personalized Banking

Banks are increasingly using AI to personalize financial advice, product recommendations, and fraud detection (McKinsey & Company, 2017). AI-powered chatbots assist customers with queries, while predictive analytics identifies customers who might be eligible for loans or other financial products based on their spending patterns and credit history (Accenture, 2018).

7.4. Future Trends

The future of AI-powered personalization is likely to involve:

- **Hyper-Personalization at Scale:** Moving beyond segment-level personalization to truly individual, real-time tailoring of experiences across every touchpoint (Verhoef et al., 2017; Singh et al., 2024; Jianghao et al., 2025).
- **Proactive and Anticipatory Personalization:** AI systems will become even more adept at anticipating customer needs before they are explicitly stated, offering solutions and experiences proactively (Gartner, 2021).
- **Voice and Conversational AI:** Further integration of natural language understanding and generation will enable more intuitive and personalised interactions through voice assistants and conversational interfaces (Picraux & Bunt, 2018).
- **Ethical AI and Trust Frameworks:** Increased focus on developing ethical AI guidelines, explainable AI, and transparent data practices to build and maintain customer trust (Floridi & Cowls, 2021).
- **AI-Human Collaboration:** The continued rise of "augmented intelligence," where AI tools empower human marketers and customer service agents to deliver more personalized and efficient experiences (Davenport & Kirby, 2016).

8. CONCLUSION

In conclusion, the integration of AI-powered personalization and customer engagement strategies are not only changing marketing practices but are also reshaping the organizational landscape. As per recent studies AI is increasingly workingwith the humansrather than replacing it, this increases efficiency and creativity (Davis et al., 2021; Kapoor & Ghosal, 2022). Intelligent systems are nowadays becoming indispensable to organizational success especially in this competitive era (Mazurek et al., 2024; Subramanian & Riya, 2024). Taking consumer perspective into account, design of AI products and interface significantly impact purchase intentions and engagement behaviors, enabling marketers with new avenues for personalization and relationship-building (DeZao, 2024; Li, Ali, & Yin, 2024). AI-powered analytics represents a transformative force in customer engagement, enabling businesses to move beyond generic marketing to deliver highly personalized and meaningful customer experiences. By leveraging vast amounts of data, AI tools such as predictive analytics, NLP, ML, and sentiment analysis provide invaluable insights into customer behaviour and preferences, facilitating data-driven decision-making. Personalized interactions, driven by real-time behavioural tracking and predictive modelling, lead to enhanced customer engagement, increased loyalty, satisfaction, and advocacy (Khakhlari, 2023; Gupta & Khan, 2024; Chinthala & Prasad, 2025). The successful implementation of AI-powered personalization requires strategic integration across all customer digital touchpoints, fostering a seamless omnichannel experience where messages and personalization are contextually consistent across platforms. While the benefits are substantial, evidenced by reported revenue uplifts and improved customer metrics, successful outcomes are highly dependent on data quality, tool maturity, and organizational readiness. Crucially, the use of AI-powered personalization raises significant ethical and privacy concerns that must be addressed through transparent data use policies, customization controls, and a commitment to mitigating algorithmic bias (Srinivas et al., 2025). This chapter provides a valuable resource for MBA students, researchers, and practitioners seeking to understand and leverage the transformative potential of AI-powered analytics in driving superior customer engagement and achieving sustainable competitive advantage in the modern business landscape.

REFERENCES

Accenture. (2018). *Banking on AI: Why the Future is Human + Machine*. Accenture.

Accenture Research. (2019). *AI: Built to Scale*. Accenture.

Acquisti, A., Brandimarte, L., & Loewenstein, G. (2015). Privacy and human behaviour in the digital age. *Science*, *347*(6221), 509–514. DOI: 10.1126/science.aaa1465 PMID: 25635091

Adadi, A., & Berrada, M. (2018). Peeking inside the black-box: A survey on Explainable Artificial Intelligence (XAI). *IEEE Access : Practical Innovations, Open Solutions*, *6*, 52138–52160. DOI: 10.1109/ACCESS.2018.2870052

Amatriain, X., & Basilico, J. (2015). Recommender Systems in Industry: A Netflix Case Study. In Ricci, F., Rokach, L., & Shapira, B. (Eds.), *Recommender Systems Handbook* (pp. 385–419). Springer., DOI: 10.1007/978-1-4899-7637-6_11

Ångström, R. C., Björn, M., Dahlander, L., Mähring, M., & Wallin, M. W. (2023). Getting AI implementation right: Insights from a global survey. *California Management Review*, *66*(1), 5–22. DOI: 10.1177/00081256231190430

Arrieta, A. B., Díaz-Rodríguez, N., Del Ser, J., Tabik, S., Barbado, A., García, S., & Herrera, F. (2020). Explainable Artificial Intelligence (XAI): Concepts, taxonomies, opportunities and challenges toward responsible AI. *Information Fusion*, *58*, 136–159. DOI: 10.1016/j.inffus.2019.12.012

Bakshy, E., Messing, S., & Adamic, L. A. (2015). Exposure to ideologically diverse news and opinion on Facebook. *Science*, *348*(6239), 1130–1132. DOI: 10.1126/science.aaa1160 PMID: 25953820

Barocas, S., & Selbst, A. D. (2016). Big data's disparate impact. *SSRN*, *104*(3), 671–732. DOI: 10.2139/ssrn.2477899

Bauerly, M., & Liu, J. (2019). The impact of content relevance on consumer attention in digital environments. *Journal of Advertising Research*, *59*(1), 55–68. DOI: 10.2501/JAR-2018-023

Bell, R. M., Koren, Y., & Volinsky, C. (2009). The million dollar Netflix prize. *IEEE Spectrum*, *46*(2), 42–49. DOI: 10.1109/MSPEC.2009.4787568

Berger, P. D., & Nasr, N. I. (1998). Customer lifetime value: Marketing models and applications. *Journal of Interactive Marketing*, *12*(1), 17–30. DOI: 10.1002/(SICI)1520-6653(199824)12:1<17::AID-DIR3>3.0.CO;2-K

Bradlow, E. T., Gangwar, M., Kopalle, P. K., & Voleti, S. (2017). The role of big data and predictive analytics in retailing. *Journal of Retailing*, *93*(2), 273–286. DOI: 10.1016/j.jretai.2016.12.004

Brauneis, A., & Steidl, A. (2019). The application of machine learning in financial services: An overview. *The Journal of Financial Data Science*, *1*(1), 21–39. DOI: 10.3905/jfds.2019.1.1.021

Brodie, R. J., Hollebeek, L. D., Juric, B., & Ilic, A. (2021). Customer engagement: Conceptual domain, fundamental propositions, and implications for research. *Journal of Service Research*, *24*(2), 123–145. DOI: 10.1177/1094670520977592

Brynjolfsson, E., Hu, Y. J., & Simester, D. (2011). Goodbye Pareto Principle, hello long tail: The effect of search costs on the concentration of product sales. *Management Science*, *57*(8), 1373–1386. DOI: 10.1287/mnsc.1110.1371

Bughin, J., Seong, J., Manyika, J., Chui, M., & Joshi, R. (2021). *The state of AI in 2021*. McKinsey & Company. https://www.mckinsey.com/business-functions/quantumblack/our-insights/the-state-of-ai-in-2021

Cambria, E., & White, B. (2014). Jumping NLP curves: A review of natural language processing research. *IEEE Computational Intelligence Magazine*, *9*(2), 48–57. DOI: 10.1109/MCI.2014.2307227

Chen, H., Chiang, R. H. L., & Storey, V. C. (2012). Business intelligence and analytics: From big data to big impact. *Management Information Systems Quarterly*, *36*(4), 1165–1188. DOI: 10.2307/41703503

Chen, J., Liu, Z., Huang, X., Wu, C., Liu, Q., Jiang, G., . . . Chen, E. (2023). When large language models meet personalization: Perspectives of challenges and opportunities. *arXiv*. /arXiv.2307.16376DOI: 10.48550

Chinthala, L. K., & Prasad, P. (2025). Consumer experience 2025: The role of personalization and AI in shaping business strategies. *International Journal of Modern Science and Research Technology*, *3*(5). Advance online publication. DOI: 10.5281/zenodo.15347436

Coussement, K., & Van den Poel, D. (2008). Predictive modelling in customer relationship management: A review and future directions. *International Journal of Forecasting*, *24*(1), 60–76.

Csikszentmihalyi, M. (1990). *Flow: The Psychology of Optimal Experience*. Harper & Row.

Davenport, T. H. (2014). *Big Data at Work: Dispelling the Myths, Uncovering the Opportunities*. Harvard Business Review Press. DOI: 10.15358/9783800648153

Davenport, T. H., & Kirby, J. (2016). *Only Humans Need Apply: Winners and Losers in the Age of Smart Machines*. HarperBusiness.

Davenport, T. H., & Ronanki, R. (2018). Artificial intelligence for the real world. *Harvard Business Review*, *96*(1), 108–116.

Davis, F. D., Bagozzi, R. P., & Warshaw, P. R. (2021). User acceptance of computer technology: A comparison of two theoretical models. *Management Science*, *67*(5), 1115–1130. DOI: 10.1287/mnsc.2020.3586

Deloitte. (2023). *2023 Global marketing trends: Resilient seeds for growth*. Deloitte Insights. https://www2.deloitte.com/insights/us/en/topics/marketing-and-sales-operations/global-marketing-trends.html

DeZao, T. (2024). Enhancing transparency in AI-powered customer engagement. *arXiv*. /arXiv.2410.01809DOI: 10.48550

Doris, M. J. (2010). *Review of Understanding Privacy, by Daniel J.* Solove.Edinburgh Law Review., DOI: 10.3366/elr.2010.0323

Eppler, M. J., & Mengis, J. (2004). The concept of information overload: A review of literature from organization science, accounting, marketing, MIS, and related disciplines. In Meckel, M., & Schmid, B. F. (Eds.), *Kommunikationsmanagement im Wandel* (pp. 325–344). Springer., DOI: 10.1007/978-3-8349-9772-2_15

Fader, P. S., & Hardie, B. G. S. (2009). A note on the Amazon.com recommendation algorithm. *Marketing Science*, *28*(6), 1017–1025. DOI: 10.1287/mksc.1090.0526

Fader, P. S., Hardie, B. G. S., & Lee, K. L. (2005). RFM and CLV: Using iso-value curves for customer base analysis. *JMR, Journal of Marketing Research*, *42*(4), 415–430. DOI: 10.1509/jmkr.2005.42.4.415

Feldman, R. (2013). Techniques and applications for sentiment analysis. *Communications of the ACM*, *56*(4), 82–89. DOI: 10.1145/2436256.2436274

Stitch Fix. (2020). *How Stitch Fix works: Your personal stylist + AI*. [Company Website].

Flaxman, S., Goel, S., & Rao, J. M. (2016). Filter bubbles, echo chambers, and online news consumption. *Public Opinion Quarterly*, *80*(S1), 298–320. DOI: 10.1093/poq/nfw006

Floridi, L., & Cowls, J. (2021). A unified framework of five principles for AI in society. In *Ethics, Governance, and Policies in Artificial Intelligence* (pp. 5–17). Springer. DOI: 10.1007/978-3-030-81907-1_2

Frow, P., & Payne, A. (2011). A stakeholder perspective of the value proposition concept. *European Journal of Marketing*, *45*(1/2), 223–240. DOI: 10.1108/03090561111095676

Gartner. (2021). *Top Strategic Technology Trends 2021*. Gartner.

GfK. (2017). *Social Listening Study on Starbucks*. GfK Custom Research, LLC.

Goldfarb, A., & Tucker, C. (2011). Privacy and innovation. *Marketing Science*, *30*(5), 779–787.

Goldfarb, A., & Tucker, C. (2019). Digital economics. *Journal of Economic Literature*, *57*(1), 3–43. DOI: 10.1257/jel.20171452

Goodfellow, I., Bengio, Y., & Courville, A. (2016). *Deep Learning*. MIT Press.

Grammarly. (2020). *How Grammarly uses AI to help you write better*. [Company Blog Post].

Grönroos, C. (1994). From marketing mix to relationship marketing: Towards a paradigm shift in marketing. *Management Decision*, *32*(2), 4–20. DOI: 10.1108/00251749410054774

Gupta, Y., & Khan, F. M. (2024). Role of artificial intelligence in customer engagement: A systematic review and future research directions. *Journal of Modelling in Management*, *19*(5), 1535–1565. DOI: 10.1108/JM2-01-2023-0016

Haenlein, M., & Kaplan, A. (2019). A brief history of artificial intelligence: On the past, present, and future of artificial intelligence. *California Management Review*, *61*(4), 5–14. DOI: 10.1177/0008125619864925

Hair, J. F., Hult, G. T. M., Ringle, C. M., & Sarstedt, M. (2017). *A Primer on Partial Least Squares Structural Equation Modeling (PLS-SEM)* (2nd ed.). Sage Publications., DOI: 10.15358/9783800653614

Hastie, T., Tibshirani, R., & Friedman, J. (2009). *The Elements of Statistical Learning: Data Mining, Inference, and Prediction* (2nd ed.). Springer., DOI: 10.1007/978-0-387-84858-7

Hill, C. (2017). *The Stitch Fix algorithm: How AI helps deliver your perfect style*. TechCrunch.

Hill, K. (2012, February 16). *How Target figured out a teen girl was pregnant before her father did.Forbes.* https://www.forbes.com/sites/kashmirhill/2012/02/16/how-target-figured-out-a-teen-girl-was-pregnant-before-her-father-did

Hoffman, D. L., & Novak, T. P. (1996). Marketing in hypermedia computer-mediated environments: Conceptual foundations. *Journal of Marketing*, *60*(3), 50–68. DOI: 10.1177/002224299606000304

Homans, G. C. (1961). *Social Behaviour: Its Elementary Forms*. Harcourt Brace Jovanovich.

Huang, M. H., & Rust, R. T. (2021). A strategic framework for artificial intelligence in marketing. *Journal of the Academy of Marketing Science*, *49*(2), 30–50. DOI: 10.1007/s11747-020-00749-9

Jurafsky, D., & Martin, J. H. (2009). *Speech and Language Processing: An Introduction to Natural Language Processing, Computational Linguistics, and Speech Recognition*. Prentice Hall.

Kannan, P. K., & Li, H. A. (2017). Digital marketing: A framework, review and research agenda. *International Journal of Research in Marketing*, *34*(1), 22–45. DOI: 10.1016/j.ijresmar.2016.11.006

Kapoor, R., & Ghosal, I. (2022). Will artificial intelligence compliment or supplement human workforce in organizations? A shift to a collaborative human–machine environment. [IJRTBT]. *International Journal on Recent Trends in Business and Tourism*, *6*(4), 19–28. DOI: 10.31674/ijrtbt.2022.v06i04.002

Khakhlari, G. (2023). Generative AI in content and personalization. *Industrial Artificial Intelligence*, 1–10. DOI: 10.1007/s44244-023-00012-4

Krizhevsky, A., Sutskever, I., & Hinton, G. E. (2012). ImageNet classification with deep convolutional neural networks. *Advances in Neural Information Processing Systems*, *25*, 1097–1105. https://papers.nips.cc/paper_files/paper/2012/hash/c399862d3b9d6b76c8436e924a68c45b-Abstract.html

Kumar, V., & Reinartz, W. J. (2012). *Customer relationship management: Concept, strategy, and tools* (2nd ed.). Springer., DOI: 10.1007/978-3-642-20110-3

Lamberton, C., & Stephen, A. T. (2016). A thematic exploration of digital, social media, and mobile marketing: Research evolution from 2000 to 2015 and an agenda for future inquiry. *Journal of Marketing*, *80*(6), 146–172. DOI: 10.1509/jm.15.0415

LeCun, Y., Bengio, Y., & Hinton, G. (2015). Deep learning. *Nature*, *521*(7553), 436–444. DOI: 10.1038/nature14539 PMID: 26017442

Lemon, K. N., & Verhoef, P. C. (2016). Understanding customer experience throughout the customer journey. *Journal of Marketing*, *80*(6), 69–96. DOI: 10.1509/jm.15.0420

Li, L., Ali, D. A., & Yin, L. (2024). The effect of AI product image anthropomorphism on consumer purchase intention. In *Artificial Intelligence, Medical Engineering and Education* (pp. 76–85). IOS Press. DOI: 10.3233/ATDE231317

Linden, G., Smith, B., & York, J. (2003). Amazon.com recommendations: Item-to-item collaborative filtering. *IEEE Internet Computing*, *7*(1), 76–80. DOI: 10.1109/MIC.2003.1167344

Liu, B. (2012). *Sentiment Analysis and Opinion Mining*. Morgan & Claypool Publishers., DOI: 10.1007/978-3-031-02145-9

Luo, X., Zhang, J., & Kana, N. (2013). Personalized services in a smart retail environment. *Journal of Retailing and Consumer Services*, *20*(3), 299–307.

Manyika, J., Chui, M., Miremadi, M., Bughin, J., George, K., Willmott, P., & Dewhurst, G. (2017). *Artificial Intelligence: The Next Digital Frontier?* McKinsey Global Institute.

Marr, B. (2016). *Big Data in Practice: How 45 Successful Companies Used Big Data Analytics to Deliver Extraordinary Results*. John Wiley & Sons. DOI: 10.1002/9781119278825

Mazurek, G., Kotula, N., Kaczorowska-Spychalska, D., & Sułkowski, Ł. (2024). Generative AI as a source of change of knowledge management paradigm. *Human Technology*, *20*(1), 131–154. DOI: 10.14254/1795-6889.2024.20-1.7

McKinsey & Company. (2017). *Artificial intelligence: The next digital frontier?* McKinsey Global Institute.

McKinsey & Company. (2022). *The value of getting personalization right—or wrong—is multiplying*. McKinsey & Company. https://www.mckinsey.com/business-functions/growth-marketing-and-sales/our-insights/the-value-of-getting-personalization-right-or-wrong-is-multiplying

Miller, G. A. (1956). The magical number seven, plus or minus two: Some limits on our capacity for processing information. *Psychological Review*, *63*(2), 81–97. DOI: 10.1037/h0043158 PMID: 13310704

Mitchell, T. M. (1997). *Machine Learning*. McGraw-Hill.

Ngai, E. W. T. (2005). Customer relationship management (CRM) research (1992–2002): An academic literature review and classification. *Marketing Intelligence & Planning*, *23*(6), 582–602. DOI: 10.1108/02634500510624147

O'Neil, C. (2016). *Weapons of Math Destruction: How Big Data Increases Inequality and Threatens Democracy*. Crown.

Palmatier, R. W., Dant, R. P., Grewal, D., & Evans, K. R. (2006). Factors influencing the effectiveness of relationship marketing: A meta-analysis. *Journal of Marketing*, *70*(4), 136–153. DOI: 10.1509/jmkg.70.4.136

Palmatier, R. W., Houston, M. B., & Dant, R. P. (2016). Relationship marketing: From rhetoric to reality. *Journal of Marketing Management*, *32*(1-2), 1–7.

Parasuraman, A., Zeithaml, V. A., & Berry, L. L. (1988). SERVQUAL: A multiple-item scale for measuring consumer perceptions of service quality. *Journal of Retailing*, *64*(1), 12–40.

Pariser, E. (2011). *The Filter Bubble: What the Internet Is Hiding from You*. Penguin Press.

Parvatiyar, A., & Sheth, J. N. (2001). Customer relationship management: Emerging practice, process, and discipline. *Journal of Economic & Social Research*, *3*(2), 1–34.

Payne, A., & Frow, P. (2005). A strategic framework for customer relationship management. *Journal of Marketing*, *69*(4), 167–176. DOI: 10.1509/jmkg.2005.69.4.167

Peppers, D., & Rogers, M. (1993). *The One to One Future: Building Relationships One Customer at a Time*. Currency/Doubleday.

Pham, M. T., & Avnet, T. (2009). Rethinking the value of emotion in advertising: The effects of specific emotions on product attitudes. *The Journal of Consumer Research*, *36*(3), 447–460.

Picraux, S., & Bunt, H. (2018). Conversational AI. *Artificial Intelligence*, *252*, 1–2.

Provost, F., & Fawcett, T. (2013). *Data Science for Business: What You Need to Know about Data Mining and Data-Analytic Thinking*. O'Reilly Media.

PwC. (2023). *2023 AI business survey: The state of AI in business*. PwC Global. https://www.pwc.com/gx/en/issues/analytics/artificial-intelligence.html

Raji, I. D., Gebru, T., Mitchell, M., Buolamwini, J., Lee, J., & Denton, E. (2020). *Saving Face: Investigating the ethical concerns of facial recognition auditing*. In *Proceedings of the AAAI/ACM Conference on AI, Ethics, and Society* (pp. 145–151). Association for Computing Machinery. DOI: 10.1145/3375627.3375820

Ransbotham, S., Kiron, D., & Prentice, P. K. (2017). Artificial intelligence in business: An early start in the business world. *MIT Sloan Management Review*, *59*(1), 1–19.

Rese, A., & Steppert, M. (2019). Chatbots in Marketing and Sales: A Literature Review. In *Proceedings of the 27th European Conference on Information Systems (ECIS)*.

Resnick, P., & Varian, H. R. (1997). Recommender systems. *Communications of the ACM*, *40*(3), 56–58. DOI: 10.1145/245108.245121

Romanosky, S., Hoffman, D., & Acquisti, A. (2016). Empirical analysis of data breach litigation. *Journal of Empirical Legal Studies*, *11*(1), 74–104. DOI: 10.1111/jels.12035

Rust, R. T., Kannan, P. K., & Peng, N. (2002). The customer economics of e-service. *Journal of Service Research*, *5*(2), 112–126.

Shin, N. (2006). Online learners' flow experience: An empirical study. *British Journal of Educational Technology*, *37*(5), 727–740. DOI: 10.1111/j.1467-8535.2006.00641.x

Siegel, J. S., & Swanson, D. A. (2004). *The Methods and Materials of Demography*. Elsevier Academic Press.

Singh, N., Gupta, K., & Rawlins, P. (2024). Unlocking the AI-powered customer experience: Personalized service, enhanced engagement, and data-driven strategies for e-commerce applications. *Journal of Infrastructure. Policy and Development*, *8*(7), 4970. Advance online publication. DOI: 10.1016/j.jipd.2024.07.001

Smith, B., & Linden, G. (2017). Two decades of recommender systems at Amazon.com. *IEEE Internet Computing*, *21*(3), 12–18. DOI: 10.1109/MIC.2017.72

Solove, D. J. (2008). Data mining and the security-liberty debate. *The University of Chicago Law Review. University of Chicago. Law School*, *75*(1), 343–362.

Srinivas, S. S., Das, A., Gupta, S., & Runkana, V. (2025). Agentic multimodal AI for hyperpersonalized B2B and B2C advertising in competitive markets. *arXiv*. *L* arXiv.2504.00338DOI: 10.48550

Subramanian, Y. R., & Riya, R. (2024). The transformative role of artificial intelligence in human resource. [IJRTBT]. *International Journal on Recent Trends in Business and Tourism*, *8*(2), 14–25. DOI: 10.31674/ijrtbt.2024.v08i02.002

Sull, D., & Turconi, S. (2008). Zara's Fast Fashion Formula. *MIT Sloan Management Review*, *49*(2), 34–40.

Tam, K. Y., & Ho, S. Y. (2006). Understanding the Impact of Web Personalization on User Information Processing and Decision Outcomes1. *Management Information Systems Quarterly*, *30*(4), 865–890. DOI: 10.2307/25148757

Tsai, J. Y., Egelman, S., Cranor, L. F., & Acquisti, A. (2011). The effect of privacy policies on consumer trust and behavioural intentions. *The Journal of Consumer Affairs*, *45*(2), 220–255.

Van den Broeck, E., & Van den Bergh, J. (2015). A systematic review of chatbot applications in customer service. *Procedia Computer Science*, *63*, 50–57.

Verhoef, P. C., Lemon, K. N., & Parasuraman, A. (2017). Marketing in a digital world. *Journal of Interactive Marketing*, *40*, 1–11. DOI: 10.1016/j.intmar.2017.06.001

Verhoef, P. C., Lemon, K. N., Parasuraman, A., Roggeveen, A., Tsiros, M., & Schlesinger, L. A. (2009). Customer experience creation: Determinants, dynamics and management strategies. *Journal of Retailing*, *85*(1), 31–41. DOI: 10.1016/j.jretai.2008.11.001

Voigt, P., & Von dem Bussche, A. (2017). *The EU General Data Protection Regulation (GDPR): A Practical Guide*. Springer International Publishing. DOI: 10.1007/978-3-319-57959-7

Wang, H., & Song, Y. (2021). Visual Recommendation Systems: A Survey. *ACM Computing Surveys*, *54*(1), 1–38.

Wang, R. Y., & Strong, D. M. (1998). Beyond accuracy: What data quality means to data consumers. *Journal of Management Information Systems*, *12*(4), 5–34. DOI: 10.1080/07421222.1996.11518099

Wasilewski, A., Chawla, Y., & Pralat, E. (2025). Enhanced e-commerce personalization through AI-powered content generation tools. *IEEE Access : Practical Innovations, Open Solutions*, *13*(99), 1–1. DOI: 10.1109/ACCESS.2025.3550956

Wedel, M., & Kannan, P. K. (2016). Marketing analytics for data-rich environments. *Journal of Marketing*, *80*(6), 97–121. DOI: 10.1509/jm.15.0413

Whitman, M. E., & Mattord, H. J. (2018). *Principles of Information Security*. Cengage Learning.

Wu, Q., Xia, C., & Tian, S. (2025). *AI-driven sentiment analytics: Unlocking business value in the e-commerce landscape. arXiv*. /arXiv.2504.08738DOI: 10.48550

Zeithaml, V. A. (1988). Consumer perceptions of price, quality, and value: A means-end model and synthesis of evidence. *Journal of Marketing*, *52*(3), 2–22. DOI: 10.1177/002224298805200302

retraction to this manuscript has been published:
etraction Notice: Retracted Personalization and Customer Engagement Using AI-owered Analytics

nyani, S., Sharma, M., Valecha, S., & Kamble, S. (2026). Personalization and Customer ngagement Using AI-Powered Analytics. In S. Poddar, P. Siddhey, N. Shafighi, & A. Bhaumik ds.), *Harnessing AI and Predictive Analytics for Decision-Making and Competitive Advantage* p. 225-246). IGI Global Scientific Publishing. https://doi.org/10.4018/979-8-3373-3648-ch008

nis manuscript has been retracted by IGI Global following an investigation undertaken by e publisher with full cooperation and collaboration from the editor. Following the vestigation, the manuscript has been retracted for the following reason(s):

- After publication of this chapter, the fourth author, Sachin Kamble, notified IGI Global Scientific Publishing that they had been listed as a contributor to this work without their knowledge or consent, and confirmed they had no involvement in the research, analysis, drafting, submission, or publication of the manuscript.

nis notice intends solely to alert readers of the reason for retraction. The manuscript uthors have been notified of the investigation and results and any agreements or sagreements to the retraction have been filed.

Chapter 9
Role of AI-Driven Personalized Marketing in Enhancing Customer Engagement and Fostering Brand Loyalty on Online Platforms

S. Shwetha
http://orcid.org/0000-0001-7048-722X
Tumkur University, India

Noor Afza
http://orcid.org/0000-0002-3692-8500
Tumkur University, India

ABSTRACT

Online platforms have been completely transformed by the incorporation of AI-driven personalized marketing, which has a big impact on brand loyalty and consumer engagement. The purpose of this study is to investigate the role of AI-driven personalization and its impact on customer engagement, to analyse how AI affects brand loyalty, AI-based recommendations, dynamic pricing, and targeted advertising affect consumer behaviour, and how customers view and trust AI-driven marketing. Primary data was collected by designing a structured questionnaire and Online consumers' interactions with AI-driven marketing tools were measured using a 5-point Likert scale .Additionally, in order to examine the connections among AI-driven marketing strategies, customer engagement, and brand loyalty, hypotheses

DOI: 10.4018/979-8-3373-3648-0.ch009

were developed based on the research objectives and tested with statistical tools. Other insights came from secondary data from industry reports, market research studies, and scholarly journals.

INTRODUCTION

Artificial intelligence (AI) has proven to have a significant impact on the way businesses and consumers communicate in the modern digital economy. Business entities that use AI to create more personalized and richer experiences can benefit from increased customer engagement, retention, and brand loyalty. The chapter emphasizes the strategic value of AI-powered personalized marketing in influencing customer interactions and fostering enduring online loyalty. The chapter goes on to describe how AI-enabled personalization not only improves transactional results but also cultivates long-term engagement, brand connection, and emotional connection—all of which are crucial components of competitive advantage in the current algorithmic economy. The literature currently in publication is more likely to discuss technology application (such as chatbots or recommendation systems) or consumer behavior outcomes (such as click-through rates and conversion) in a fragmented manner, despite the fact that scholarly interest in the topic of AI in marketing is growing.

Understanding how AI-driven personalization features impact psychological metrics like trust, perceived relevance, emotional engagement, and brand loyalty remains a research gap, particularly in dynamic and cutthroat online environments. By offering a thorough, multidisciplinary analysis that draws on data science, consumer psychology, and marketing theory, this chapter aims to close this gap.

Second, the chapter addresses current and extremely pertinent business and academic discussions about consumer agency, explainability in algorithms, and data ethics. There are significant ethical concerns regarding privacy, consent, and equity as a result of the growing use of AI in processing and managing consumer data. Businesses are facing more and more pressure to implement ethical and explainable AI practices as regulations like the CCPA and GDPR reinterpret the world of digital personalization. These issues are addressed in this chapter by the suggested ethical guidelines and governance models that guarantee personalization works and doesn't violate customers' rights or social values. The chapter aligns with the overarching theme of the book Harnessing AI and Predictive Analytics for Competitive Decision-Making by presenting AI-enabled personalized marketing as a technology and a tool for strategy development. It claims that the ability of businesses to take raw data and turn it into individualized experiences built on trust and relating to customers one-on-one is what will shape customer interaction in the future. The chapter provides helpful information, theoretical understanding, and research technique to assist firms in using AI personalization as more than just a marketing strategy, but also as an essential part of competitive intelligence and long-term branding. Furthermore, the efficacy of the techniques depends critically on consumer confidence in AI systems and ethical considerations like data privacy and transparency. By investigating how AI-driven personalized marketing can be utilized to increase online platform customer engagement and brand loyalty, the research topic aims to close this knowledge gap. Additionally, the study of customer sentiment and confidence in AI-powered personalization This research study aims to bring practical recommendations to the marketers and e commerce operators to optimize the benefits of AI strategies in customer relationship and business development in the long run by a systematic survey and statistical inferences. As the number of online platforms increases, AI-based personalized marketing can be seen as one of the strategic tools that allow businesses to consider the needs and behaviour of separate consumers and tailor their marketing strategy against them, which will increase the level of customer engagement and loyalty to the brand significantly. Gentsch (2019) and Huang and Rust (2021) point out that customized messages in marketing not only help to capture the attention but also create more positive emotional effects towards brands and increase the value of personalization in consumer engagement. Additionally, studies have demonstrated that AI marketing technology enable companies to identify certain preferences and behaviours by analysing large volumes of client data. This capability enables the creation of advertising campaigns that are customized to the requirements and tastes of the target market, hence boosting client happiness and loyalty. The value of AI-based methods is supported by the many successful examples of businesses that have adopted them and witnessed appreciable boosts in customer retention and engagement rates. As organizations negotiate the complicated world of consumer behavior in the digital era, AI's advocacy of marketing customisation is steadily gaining favor.

LITERATURE REVIEW

This literature review explores the evolving landscape of AI-based personalized marketing. The assessment begins by examining how traditional advertising has been transformed into hyper-personalized content that varies according to user activity via artificial intelligence (AI) techniques like recommendation engines and natural language processing. It examines how companies can utilize predictive analytics to foresee customer needs, enabling precise client segmentation, and tailor marketing efforts to historical data and customer behavior patterns. According to the critics, AI-based marketing creates a dilemma for consumer autonomy and informed consent to provide a balance, confusing personalization with intrusiveness. This review provides an overview of the contributions made by the interdisciplinary fields of cognitive science, which examines data ethics, fairness, accountability, and transparency in algorithmic systems, and behavioral economics, which examines how AI influences consumer choice.

AI IN CUSTOMISED ADVERTISING

AI-driven Personalised Marketing enhances customer engagement by analysing volumes of data to create a targeted message and streamline communication channels. This builds brand loyalty through customised experiences, predictive analytics and immersive interaction. Eventually boosting conversion rates and deepening customer relationship on digital platforms(Patil, D. 2025)

AI based personalised marketing increase customer interaction by examining enormous amounts of data to determine personal preferences, enabling companies to customise content, personalization creates brand loyalty, since customers feel appreciated, attached ultimately making long lasting impressions on the Internet(-Pushpa Gowri, 2024).

AI based personalized advertising increases customer interaction by designing content based on personal interest, creating stronger brand affiliation. This paired with big data analytics enables accurate targeting, eventually resulting in greater brand loyalty on the Internet.(Muharam et al., 2024).

Artificial Intelligence powered personalised marketing increases customer interactions and builds loyalty on digital media through the leveraging of data aggregation, customer segmenting and real time customization. These actions builds customised experiences enhancing the satisfaction of the customer and ensuring repeat interaction with the brand (Balcioglu, Y. S. 2024).

AI-powered personalized marketing elevates customer engagement by providing hyper-personalized experiences via machine learning and predictive analytics. This personalised method builds brand loyalty on digital platforms, since companies can address specific customer requirement, resulting in greater satisfaction and long term relationships (Luu et al., 2025).

Personalised Marketing through AI boost customer interaction by examining massive amount of data to produce hyper relevant content. Through this it builds brand loyalty through customer experiences, which allows for constant improvement of methods through actionable data, ultimately resulting in sustainable business growth in a competitive online environment (Vasundhara et al., 2024).

Artificial intelligence led personalised marketing increase customer engagement by providing hyper personalised experiences that address personal preferences, creating an experience of exclusivity. This increases brand loyalty as customers feel valued and appreciated, and thereby drive increased satisfaction and conversion rates (Babadoğan, B. (2024).

AI and machine learning methodologies(Ganeshkumar et al., 2024). AI based personalised marketing increased customer interaction by studying consumer behaviour and taste, allowing for targeted approaches. This creates brand loyalty on the Internet through customised experiences, ultimately enhancing return on investment and fueling innovation in digital marketing (Gungunawat, et al., (2024)

Moreover, dynamic pricing powered by AI algorithms can provide competitive advantages, although it must be handled with care to avoid perceptions of unfairness (Chen et al., 2021). AI powered one to one marketing increase customer interactions and brand loyalty by anticipating consumers behaviour and providing personalised content. According to the survey, a 78% overall engagement rate demonstrates a significant increase in client loyalty and happiness.

Research shows that ads and recommendations driven by AI are quite important in influencing what people decide to buy. A smooth and convenient shopping experience is produced by AI's capacity to forecast customer preferences based on past behavior (Grewal et al., 2020).

PREDICTIVE ANALYTICS AND CUSTOMER SEGMENTATION

Since predictive analytics was included into AI marketing, there has been a notable shift in consumer interaction, segmentation, and conversion rate optimization. This is mainly due to the fact that predictive analytics establishes how to utilize statistical modelling, data mining, and machine learning to forecast future customer behavior based on historical and current data (Khan Lawrence and Govindraj, 2025). As demonstrated by Kumar (2025), artificial intelligence (AI)-powered predictive models can analyze enormous volumes of data, including click stream device usage habits, social media sentiment, and contextual hints, to generate dynamic real-time customer insights. These trends make it easier to create context-aware targeted ads that are tailored to continuously increase customer engagement and conversion rates. Ijomah (2025) offers a multichannel marketing optimization modeling that uses predictive consumer scoring to identify when, channel, and content to retarget with a dramatic increase in return on investment. Predictive analytics also optimizes retargeting, not just who to retarget but also when and how. Likewise, Wah (2025) contend that AI-based behavioural prediction can help create a more emotionally compelling brand interaction that leads to both short-term action and long-term loyalty. But scientists also cautiously point out that the growing use of predictive algorithms has an ethical cost. Verma (2025) and Lyulyov et al. (2025) note that even though predictive models increase efficiency and accuracy.

BRAND LOYALTY – IN THE AGE OF AI

According to Rehman et al., 2025 DTC assigns employees to AI technologies like automated segmentation, behavior-based segmentation, and predictive analytics. system of interactions to produce highly customized brand experiences. Because these tactics build strong relationships with customers, they not only boost repeat business but also give smaller brands the ability to compete with more established retail behemoths. In support of this, Mahdizadeh et al (2025) note that AI-driven chatbots, personalized recommendations, and interactive pricing systems enable e-commerce websites to customize the shopping experience in real time and make customers feel valued and appreciated. The foundations of brand loyalty, increased perceived value and consumer happiness, are also directly impacted by these tactics. The primary contribution of Rehman et al.'s research is the identification of AI's role in enhancing brand responsiveness and relevance, which are the two primary precursors to customer loyalty in the virtual world. Customers are more likely to engage with a brand frequently and emotionally once they perceive it to be perceptive, sensitive, and cognizant of their preferences in context. To ensure ethical and enduring brand partnerships, the researchers propose a compromise that blends algorithmic intelligence with true human-centered design. The literature essentially converges on the notion that real-time databases and emotionally charged interactions are becoming increasingly important for brand loyalty in the AI era. Online retailers who use AI to increase operational efficiency and meaningful customer interactions stand a better chance of fostering enduring customer loyalty in the fiercely competitive and rapidly growing digital economy. Conventional brand loyalty frameworks, which rely on emotional connections and repeat business, were rewritten between 2022 and 2025 due to AI-motivated personalization, real-time interactions, and prospective customer analytics. Apart from personalization, there is growing interest in the use of AI in emotional interactions. By presenting content according to user preferences and values, Mishra (2024) investigates how AI-based customer journeys affect loyalty. The study explains why AI-powered contextual adaptation and real-time responsiveness can foster brand trust and effective commitment. The use of churn prediction AI and proactive loyalty reinforcement through engagement modeling and behavioral observation are likely among the most important developments in this area. The platforms allow for the identification of potentially churning users and the implementation of focused retention initiatives. Devi and Jai Karthi (2025). Scholars also point out significant ethical and technical limitations, though. Over-personalization might result in echo chambers and customer control, according to Rehman et al. (2025).

AI MARKETING ETHICAL FRAMEWORKS

A plethora of ethical concerns have already been brought about by the growing use of AI in marketing, particularly with regard to segmentation models that are already being replaced by hyper-personalization strategies. Scholars concur that, even while AI is accurate at targeting, it also brings up long-standing ethical concerns about privacy, manipulation, and algorithmic transparency. In a systematic review, Hasan (2025) establishes that AI transforms marketing into a predictive, personalised engagement model out of a generalised one size fits all model. This is how the distinction between beneficial individualisation and invasive surveillance is eradicated. Mass segmentation and demographic groups on which moral considerations were to be made to promote fairness and non-discrimination were the foundation of classic marketing. When it comes to AI based marketing, behaviour, emotional response and contextual stimuli data is inspected on-the-fly, which raises concerns over data consent, autonomy and algorithmic responsibility. Adding to the point of view, Haider et al. (2025) present an AI personalization-based software-based ethical paradigm in brand management, whose aim is reliability, data transparency, and fairness. The focus of their empirical study is on the role of explainable AI (XAI) tools in marketing, so that the results of the algorithmic decision-making process will be auditable and ethically justified. The authors also cautioned that excessive personalization can produce filter bubbles and loss of consumer freedom.

Comparatively, Saura (2025) highlights that marketing ethics in the past focused on persuasion limits and cultural norms, while AI driven hyper personalization raises concern regarding psychological profiling, emotional manipulation and user addiction. He holds that usage of behavioural data has been framed by definitive governance principles, particularly when AI technologies predict and steer consumer behaviour at an unconscious level.

Garg et al. (2025) also provides a comparison between rule-based personalisation of old CRM systems and generating AI models, proposing new ethical risk scales to monitor hyper personalisation. The author suggests a concept of ethical personalization threshold beyond which the personalization will result in invasive or manipulative violations of the consumer dignity. Guendouz (2024) notes that it is necessary to come up with ethical models to regulate AI-mediated customer experience management, especially as firms shift to the process of hyper-personalization, though, as companies shift paradigms and go beyond offering generic content. The study explains the ways in which the relationship marketing empowered by

AI is challenged by algorithmic decision making and manipulation of consumers, persuasive targeting.

Critical Thoughts on the Psychology of AI Marketing and the Uncertainty in Ethics

Even though AI provides powerful tools for hyper-personalized advertising, an increasing number of academics are pointing out its drawbacks, such as ethical ambiguity, emotional exploitation, and consumer manipulation. According to academics, unmanaged AI systems threaten to undermine personal autonomy by coercively guiding, influencing, and anticipating customers. Ghosh and Ghosh (2025) challenges the mental addiction that marketing bots and AI companions create in his more comprehensive critique, pointing out that they can re-invent cognitive freedom, perpetuate an echo chamber, and fabricate identities. According to the study, marketing AI can mimic human empathy by disguising commercial interests as the development of emotional dependence. Koswara and Herlina (2025) investigate AI in marketing from a cultural and ethical perspective, particularly in markets that are halal and value-sensitive. They point out that emotional manipulation and algorithmic bias transcend cultural and religious boundaries, particularly when AI recommends content that disregards ethical sensibilities. Muhlehoff (2025) attempts to provide a systemic analysis of AI marketing by treating it as a power structure that is intended to influence behavior toward the intended commercial goals in addition to benefiting consumers. It is an appeal for ethical design principles and regulatory reform to stop AI from becoming a tool of coercion in consumer markets. In a similar spirit, Borau (2024) examines objectification and gender biases in some of the marketing implications of AI reach, digital assistant, and ad avatars. The study laments the gendered archetype, highlights a broader ethical failure with personalization, and highlights the exploitation inherent in the design of AI agents to drive engagement. Lastly, Karunanayaka et al (2024) warn that when AI systems are used to generate data about the emotional states and micro-target customers, the distinction between manipulation and persuasion becomes more hazy.

Multidisciplinary Views on AI Marketing: Data Ethics, Cognitive Science, and Behavior Economics

The interdisciplinary combination of data ethics, cognitive science, and behavioral economics has improved our understanding of the ethical and psychological implications of AI marketing. They shed light on how people make decisions, how AI affects them, and where morality should be drawn in order to question this advice.

According to a different perspective from behavioral economics, some academics think AI systems, particularly those that use personalization, take use of cognitive biases and heuristics to force people to make certain choices. Radu et al (2024) assert that marketing algorithms exploit option design, framing effects, and scarcity cues to boost conversions at the expense of user agency. They wonder if AI-enabled customisation genuinely enhances user welfare or if it merely slightly affects user choice.

Owusu-Berko (2025) goes into additional detail on this, showing how behavioral economics and data science combine to create digital platforms, personalization, and revenue maximization. The study raises questions about the application of AI personalization while highlighting its advantages for the user experience.

Cognitive science also significantly advances our understanding of how AI systems interact with human attention, perception, and memory. Quintana (2025) examines the effects of AI-driven customisation on decision fatigue and cognitive strain. He contends that if the market is left unregulated, marketers would eventually start utilizing AI to influence consumers' decisions as well as how they interpret information, which would be a moral roadblock.

Acharya (2025) offers a paradigm for implementing moral AI in business plans from an ethical standpoint. The essay highlights the importance of aligning marketing techniques with equality, openness, and user dignity, particularly when utilizing AI extensively to shape customer choices. He suggests that technologists, ethicists, and economists collaborate continuously to guarantee that AI systems are produced in an ethical manner.

When taken as a whole, these articles emphasize that ethical marketing in the AI era cannot be solved solely through technical means and must instead adopt a multidisciplinary approach to personalization in order to support rather than impede customer choices.

RESEARCH METHODOLOGY

Statement of the Problem

Rapid embracement of AI-powered personalized marketing on digital platforms has significantly transformed the landscape of customer engagement and brand loyalty. In order to improve user experiences and provide real-time personalization, technologies including AI-based suggestions, dynamic pricing, targeted advertising, and AI-enabled customer interactions have been widely embraced. The actual effects of these AI-driven tactics on customer behaviour, trust, and enduring brand loyalty are still unknown, despite their potential. Significant issues with algorithmic transparency, data privacy, and the moral use of AI raise worries about the long-term effects of personalization on customer attitudes and behaviour. The effectiveness and limitations of AI personalization in promoting trust-based engagement and long-term brand loyalty are the main issues this study attempts to address. This research investigates the perceived value, behavioral outcomes, and trust dynamics associated with AI personalization, offering evidence-based implications for more ethical and impactful AI marketing strategies in the digital market.

Objectives of the Study

- To examine the role of AI-driven personalized marketing influences and enhances customer engagement on online platforms.
- To analyse how AI-powered personalization influences brand loyalty among online consumers.
- To assess the impact of AI-based recommendations, dynamic pricing, and targeted advertising on customer purchasing behaviour.
- To evaluate customer perceptions and trust in AI-driven personalization in online marketing.

Research Design

The current research has been carried out using mixed method design consisting of exploratory and descriptive research approach. Exploratory research is utilized in order to obtain a deeper conceptual understanding of the changing dynamics of Artificial intelligence enabled customised marketing and its psychological and behavioural aspects. Descriptive research is applied in order to measure the association between AI personalization factors and customer participation, brand loyalty, perceived value and trust. The integration of these methods enables qualitative interpretation of customer attitude as well as a quantitative assessment of marketing results. The research design is in concurrence with the conceptual model and hypothesis to maintain correspondence between theoretical constructs and empirical exploration

Sampling Method

To empirically test the hypotheses framed, primary data was gathered via a structured questionnaire from a sample of 39 respondents. The sample consists of online shoppers who have engaged with AI driven marketing features, example, product suggestions, price adjustments or targeted advancements on ecommerce or digital service websites.

Sampling method: The sampling approach employed was non-probability purposive sampling, where the respondents who are acquainted with AI elements in digital spaces were the target.

Sample size- 39 participants.

DATA COLLECTION TECHNIQUES

Primary Data Collection

Primary data was gathered using a structured questionnaire aimed at evaluating how AI- powered personalized marketing affects customer engagement and brand loyalty. The questionnaire was administered to online consumers who actively engage with AI-powered marketing interventions, a Likert scale was used to measure consumer perceptions, preferences, and trust in AI-driven marketing tools.

Secondary Data Collection

Secondary information was obtained from scholarly articles, industry analyses, official publications, whitepapers, and credible online sources to support the study with theoretical information and market trends.

THEORETICAL FRAMEWORK

As digital marketing strategies are increasingly influenced by artificial intelligence the need to tie the interaction between AI powered personalization and customers behaviour to firm theoretical background gains importance.This section introduces the theoretical basis for the conceptual model of this study. Building on the Technology Acceptance Model (TAM), Engagement Theory, and Brand Equity Theory, this model describes the psychological, behavioural, and strategic aspects in which AI-driven personalization shapes customer engagement, brand loyalty, trust towards AI, and perceived value. The three theories as a whole offer a strong lens to capture the processes by which personalized marketing, facilitated by AI technologies, creates long-term consumer commitment on digital channels.

1. Technology Acceptance Model (TAM)

One of the most popular models created by Davis 1989 to describe new technology acceptance and use by consumers is Technology Acceptance Model. It is stated that the attitude of the user towards the use of the system is identified by two main beliefs according to TAM perceived ease of use and perceived usefulness which consequently influence actual usage of the system. TAM is present in AI powered personalised marketing where the user reaction to AI powered features like recommendation mechanisms, dynamic price modelling and chatbot-driven interaction is to be learned. As soon as the customers feel that the AI-powered personalization tool is useful (i.e. relevant recommendations or conveniently designed search filters), their experiences on the platform become more positive.

Trust is mediating construct that determines how perceived usefulness is moved into actual loyalty and engagement behaviours. Therefore, TAM affirms the proposed relationship between AI-driven marketing interventions (independent variables) and customer trust, perceived value, and engagement (dependent variables), positioning AI as much more than a technical feature as a strategic facilitator of positive user experiences.

2. Engagement Theory

Engagement theory frequently used in educational and digital context suggests that interactive, personalised and meaningful experiences result in increased cognitive, emotional and behaviour engagement. Customer engagement in marketing transcends transactional behaviour to emotional affinity, time invested social sharing and active engagement with brand related material.

Engagement theory also accounts for customer responses to AI driven interfaces, including chatbots and smart assistance. The mimic human like response, where interactions are perceived as relevant, timely preconditions to emotional and personalised They strengthen customer immersion and lower friction- two critical preconditions to emotional and behavioural engagement. Accordingly, the theory elucidates how personalised marketing efforts fuelled by AI trigger engagement, which in turn forms the seeds of brand loyalty and trust.

3. Brand Equity Theory

Brand Equity Theory, as created by Aaker (1991) and subsequently expounded upon by Keller (1993) provides an outline for understanding customer loyalty and long-term business worth based on how brand perception affects them. This theory defines a brand equity as having several dimensions such as brand awareness, perceived quality, brand associations and brand loyalty. Many of these aspects can be strengthened by AI-powered customisation. AI with contextual messaging and user-centric storytelling can also generate more effective brand association by spreading a logical narrative about the business's ability to anticipate and respond to customer wants. Additionally, as consumers engage with websites that consistently provide them with customized, fulfilling experiences, they grow to trust the company. The chapter presents how AI customization tactics not only contribute to short-term conversions but also long-term brand will by formulating the outcome variables (brand loyally perceived value and trust) using the Brand Equity Theory.

4. Theories/Conceptual Framework Integration

The multi-theoretical triangle of TAM, Engagement Theory, and Brand Equity Theory forms the basis of this study's conceptual framework. TAM provides insight into how users adopt and accept AI technologies, Engagement Theory describes how one-to-one marketing promotes interactions and emotional engagement, and Brand Equity Theory describes how interactions translate into long-term brand loyalty and perceived value.

Conceptual framework translates these theoretical findings into quantifiable variables and hypothetical relationships. It situates AI-based personalized marketing practices (such as recommendations, dynamic pricing, and customer data analytics) as independent variables and their effects on customer engagement, loyalty, perceived value, and trust in AI as dependent variables. This theoretical grounding makes sure that the model proposed is not just pragmatically valid but also theoretically sound.

RESEARCH FRAMEWORK

Figure 1. Showing the conceptual framework of the study

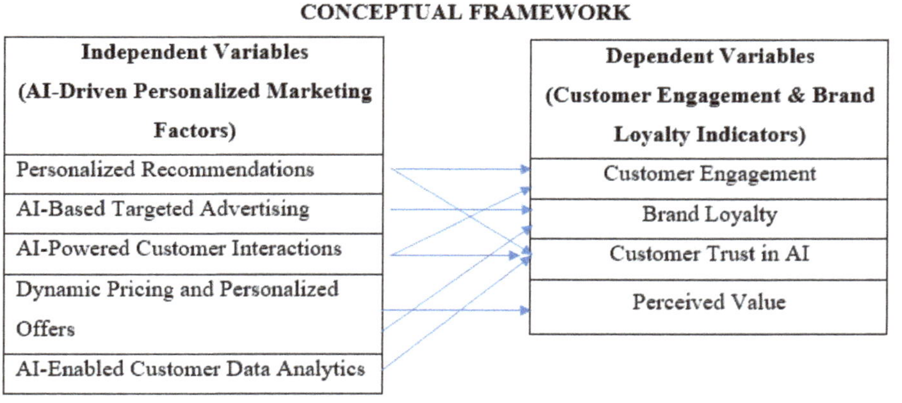

Formulation of Hypothesis

Hypothesis -1

- **H0:** AI-based personalized marketing has no significant effect on customer engagement levels within online platforms.
- **H1:** AI-driven personalization contributes significantly to enhancing customer engagement in digital environments.

Hypothesis - 2

- **H0:** There is no relationship between AI-powered personalization and brand loyalty among online consumers.
- **H1:** There is a positive relationship between AI-powered personalization and brand loyalty among online consumers.

Data Analysis Findings and Interpretation

Hypothesis Test 1

Ho: Personalized marketing powered by artificial intelligence has no meaningful impact on customer engagement within digital platforms.

H_1: Personalized marketing strategies driven by AI significantly enhance user engagement on online platforms.

This hypothesis was tested to assess the influence and effectiveness of AI-based personalized marketing in fostering customer engagement. A one-way ANOVA was conducted using responses from 26 participants across five key statements:

1. AI-driven product recommendations match my interests and preferences
2. I frequently engage with AI-powered marketing content
3. AI-based recommendations influence my purchasing decisions
4. I prefer shopping on platforms that use AI to personalize my experience
5. AI-driven marketing strategies make online shopping more interactive and engaging

Each response was rated on a 5-point Likert scale ranging from 1 (Strongly Disagree) to 5 (Strongly Agree).

Hypothesis Testing

Table 1. Showing the analysis of ANOVA single factor – between groups and within groups

SUMMARY						
Groups	*Count*	*Sum*	*Average*	*Variance*		
5	26	110	4.230769231	0.504615385		
5	26	92	3.538461538	1.218461538		
5	26	88	3.384615385	1.126153846		
5	26	96	3.692307692	1.021538462		
5	26	101	3.884615385	0.666153846		
Source of Variation	*SS*	*df*	*MS*	*F*	*P-value*	*F crit*
Between Groups	11.2	4	2.8	3.085791794	0.01839	2.44417369
Within Groups	113.4230769	125	0.907384615			
Total	124.6230769	129				

Since the p-value (0.01839) is less than 0.05, and the F-statistic (3.09) exceeds the F-critical value (2.444), we reject the null hypothesis.

The results provide statistically significant evidence that AI-powered personalized marketing strategies do have a positive and measurable impact on customer engagement. This indicates that not all AI features are perceived equally by users. Among the evaluated items, "AI-driven product recommendations matching user preferences" had the highest mean rating, suggesting that personalized suggestions are the most valued aspect of AI marketing.

This implies that companies should focus on refining their recommendation systems and personalization features, as these contribute most strongly to customer engagement and satisfaction.

Testing of hypothesis 2

- **H0:** Personalization through AI has no significant correlation with brand loyalty among online consumers.
- **H1:** There is a significant and positive relationship between brand loyalty and AI-powered personalization among digital platform users.

A Pearson correlation was conducted to examine the strength of association between the different statements related to AI-driven marketing strategies.

Table 2. Showing the calculation of correlation among different statements related to AI driven marketing strategies

	5	*5*	*5*	*5*	*5*
5	1				
5	0.888433399	1			
5	0.928649746	0.896585679	1		
5	0.896080741	0.916916064	0.94588	1	
5	0.916402358	0.901841496	0.9141	0.916495192	1

Table 3. Showing statement pair with their correlation coefficient

Statement Pair	Correlation Coefficient
Stronger connection to brands that use AI & AI-driven offers/promotions encourage me to stay loyal	0.888
Stronger connection to brands that use AI & AI-powered loyalty programs make me return to a brand	0.929
Stronger connection to brands that use AI & Trust brands more when they use AI for recommendations	0.896

continued on following page

Table 3. Continued

Statement Pair	Correlation Coefficient
Stronger connection to brands that use AI & AI-driven marketing enhances overall shopping experience	0.916
AI-driven offers/promotions encourage me to stay loyal & AI-powered loyalty programs	0.897
AI-driven offers/promotions encourage me to stay loyal & Trust in personalized recommendations	0.917
AI-driven offers/promotions encourage me to stay loyal & Enhanced shopping experience	0.902
AI-powered loyalty programs & Trust in personalized recommendations	0.946
AI-powered loyalty programs & Enhanced shopping experience	0.914
Trust in personalized recommendations & Enhanced shopping experience	0.916

Interpretation of Correlation Analysis

- All correlation coefficients are very strong ($r > 0.88$), indicating a high positive relationship between customer responses to each AI-driven marketing factor.
- The highest correlation ($r = 0.946$) was observed between AI-powered loyalty programs and trust in AI recommendations, showing these two aspects are highly interconnected in influencing perception.
- These results support the notion that customers who rate one AI strategy positively tend to do so across other AI strategies as well.

Conclusion: Customers perceive all five AI-driven personalized marketing strategies relatively similarly. This implies consistency in their positive perception, suggesting that these AI-driven strategies may be collectively effective in engaging and retaining customers.

Table 4. Descriptive statistics for five AI-driven marketing-related statements

	stronger connection to brands that use AI	**AI-driven offers and promotions encourage me to stay loyal**	**AI-powered loyalty programs make me return to a brand**	**Trust brands more when they use AI to provide personalized recommendations**	**AI-driven marketing enhance-overall shopping experience and encourages repeat purchases**
Mean	4.0	3.8	3.9	3.8	4.0
Standard Error	0.2	0.2	0.2	0.2	0.2
Median	4.0	4.0	4.0	4.0	4.0
Mode	5.0	4.0	4.0	4.0	4.0
Standard Deviation	1.0	0.9	1.0	1.0	0.9
Sample Variance	1.0	0.9	0.9	1.0	0.8
Kurtosis	1.9	1.9	1.3	0.7	3.3
Skewness	-1.1	-1.1	-0.8	-0.7	-1.3
Range	4.0	4.0	4.0	4.0	4.0
Minimum	1.0	1.0	1.0	1.0	1.0
Maximum	5.0	5.0	5.0	5.0	5.0
Sum	109.0	102.0	105.0	102.0	107.0
Count	27.0	27.0	27.0	27.0	27.0
Largest(1)	5.0	5.0	5.0	5.0	5.0
Smallest(1)	1.0	1.0	1.0	1.0	1.0
Confidence Level(95.0%)	0.4	0.4	0.4	0.4	0.4

Interpretation of Descriptive Statistics

- All five statements show mean values between 3.8 and 4.0, indicating generally positive customer perceptions toward AI-driven marketing features.
- The comparatively modest standard deviations (0.8–1.0) indicate that individuals' answers were consistent.
- The data shows negative skewness, indicating a tendency toward higher ratings.
- A more peaked distribution with the majority of responses close to the mean is suggested by high kurtosis, particularly for the final statement at 3.3.

Since all of the variables have a range of 4, the lowest and maximum scores were, respectively, 1 and 5, confirming that the full Likert scale was employed.

FINDINGS

The study's conclusions demonstrate the substantial benefits of AI-powered personal marketing in predicting online consumer engagement and brand loyalty. based on 39 survey respondents, with additional evidence from case studies and literature. First of all, the majority of respondents acknowledged that AI-powered personalization improved brand interactions through recommendation engines, targeted advertising, and dynamic pricing. It resembles the Amazon case, in which over 35 percent of its sales can be attributed to its suggestion mechanism (Rehman et al. 2025) and in which Spotify and its discover weekly playlist is the classical example of behavioural personalization. The respondents stated that they were willing to sample products or services when they perceived that the recommendations were contextually appropriate, and they were within their interest. Second, it was confirmed that there was a direct correlation between AI personalization and increased consumer trust and satisfaction. The respondents who provided relevant and timely suggestions expressed greater confidence in the brand, which proves the theoretical statements by Mahdizadeh et al (2025) and the Brand Equity Theory. This trust also associated with loyalty behaviours such as repeat visits and more time on sites and subscription renewing just like the engagement-based practises of Netflix recommendation engine. Nonetheless, not all of them were absolute good in their reaction. Part of the applications had to do with transparency under which their data is being obtained and utilised. The fact that some of the respondents feared two personal contents to be seen as intrusive or manipulative, confirms criticism mentioned by Karunanayaka and Jahankani (2024) and Borau (2024) about the ethical issue in AI system, predicting user behaviour to make profit. On the whole, the findings show that AI-powered marketing has a potential to raise customer engagement and loyalty significantly, provided that it is used in a transparent way in accordance with the values and with the user in mind.

CASE STUDIES IN AI DRIVEN MARKETING

Case Study 1

Amazon AI-Based Recommendation Improving Customer Experience

In order to reveal how the new AI-powered marketing works in real life, the given case study analyses how Amazon, one of the leading online retailers worldwide, has utilized predictive analytics and machine learning to reshape their interaction with customers. The recommendation engine at Amazon, which uses personalization to give customers individualized content and boost customer satisfaction and brand loyalty, is a fantastic example of how AI may change the online buying experience. This is essentially the chapter's primary goal, since it investigates how well AI personalization may improve customer engagement and build enduring relationships with customers. Using advanced technologies like collaborative filtering and content-based filtering and natural language processing, Amazon built a flexible self-updating system that reacts to customer behaviour. Here is a discussion of how Amazon uses AI to offer a personalized and easy shopping experience based on the recommendation engine. A combination of collaborative filtering, contain base filtering and machine learning, the Technology behind the engine. ML is central to the recommendation engine of Amazon. Such methods have been used to look into millions of customers, user action, product information and trends and offer products that are most appropriate to personal interaction. An example of collateral filtering is the collaboration filtering that aligns the user behaviour to those with the same pattern and the products that are frequently purchased. Background content-based filtering checks an attribute of the product, such as its category, description and keywords, to suggest similar products. Natural Language Processing also brings some refinements by understanding what users have written about it in form of reviews and search terms.With the ML added, Amazon can improve recommendations permanently learning and enhancing with each customer interaction.

Key Features of the Recommendation Engine

1. Personality-Driven Product Recommendations –

Amazon develops a special homepage for every customer with personalised product recommendation based on their purchase and browsing history. For example, a shopper who just bought running shoes may be recommended athletic clothing, fitness trackers, or related accessories.

2."Frequently Bought Together" and "Customers Who Bought This Also Bought" Features – Collaborative filtering recommends accessory items such as cases and chargers to smartphone customers, improving the shopping experience and increasing cross-sales.
3.Real-Time Updates –

The recommendation engine updates in real time as customers shop, keeping suggestions up to date. When a customer searches for coffee makers, the engine instantly suggests coffee beans, filters, and cleaning tools.

4. Varied Sources of Data –

Amazon's AI derives insights from multiple data sources, such as purchase history, search patterns, ratings, reviews and number of times a product, is viewed. All these enable a multidimensional mapping of customer preferences

Advantages to Consumers

Personalization eliminates decision fatigue, enabling faster and more convenient shopping. Amazon filters relevant choices, allowing customers to find otherwise missed products. Personalization enhances customer satisfaction and loyalty.

Benefits to Amazon

Research indicates that almost 35% of Amazon's sales are generated by its recommendation system, which drives a large portion of the company's operations. Customers are encouraged to add complimentary products to their baskets by the algorithm, which raises the average order size. By encouraging users to interact with websites that suit their preferences, personalized recommendations also lower bounce rates.

Data privacy and algorithmic bias are two issues that make it crucial that the system is strictly regulated, although it is effective and requires ongoing innovation to stay at the top. Amazon uses strong data, encryption, and algorithm optimization to handle these problems and prevent unfairness and inaccuracy. The ability of the site to handle multi-dimensional consumer data and deliver real time, context based recommendations provides an ideal example of the customer engagement/ purchasing behaviour impact of AI driven personalisation. Amazon promotes more customer trust and repeat business as crucial markers of brand loyalty by reducing choice fatigue, boosting relevance, and enhancing the user experience overall. But the Amazon case also serves as an example of the broader ethical issues covered in this chapter, like data privacy and algorithm fairness. As AI technologies are increasingly incorporated into digital marketing processes, the company's continuous improvements in algorithmic transparency and privacy protection highlight how important it is to maintain customer trust. Finally, the chapter's argument that AI is a long-term customer value creator and business performance driver rather than a technology is supported by Amazon, which provides a compelling real-world example of how AI personalization, when done ethically and purposefully, can be a powerful competitive advantage.

Case Study 2

Netflix – Driving Engagement Through AI-Powered Personalization

As a user experience leader powered by AI. Netflix has set the standard for personalized content delivery across the digital entertainment sector. Its major approach is a robust recommendation engine of machine learning, predictive analytics and deep neural network to boost use engagement and reduce churn in support of the object of this chapter.. Through its recommendation engine, Netflix has been at the forefront in utilizing AI and machine learning in order to personalize user experience and increase engagement levels by 80% with the help of AI and machine learning. The way Netflix is using AI to create engagement: Individualised content suggestions. Netflix employs AI to analyse watching history, watch time and preference of the users in order to offer a personalised recommendation. The system looks at features such as genre preference, watching time of day and device used to personalise suggestion.

Deep learnings and predictive models:

AI algorithm forecast, which shows or films a user will watch next according to behaviour pattern. The recommendation system used collaborative filtering and deep neural network to discover a subtle content relationships.

A/B Testing and Real-Time adaptation:

Netflix conducts A/B tests on various recommendation approaches to determine what performance best for engagement. AI based insights enable dynamic adjustment of the UI according to past activities of the user.

AI optimised thumbnails and trailers.

Netflix AI creates personalised thumbnails, according to individuals preference. For example, if someone watches more action flicks, they will be shown a thumbnail of dramatic fight scene, whereas comedy enthusiasts will be shown a lighter shot.

Content creation and Licencing Decisions

AI reviews worldwide viewing patterns to enable Netflix to make decisions on which shows to create a purchase. The hit shows such as squid game were foretold with the help of engagement analytics and machine learning models that picked up on the increasing trend towards overseas dramas.

Influence of Netflix AI Recommendation Engine:

- 80% of what people watch on Netflix is source through AI based recommendations.
- User satisfaction and retention improved lowering churn rates.
- AI based insights enabled Netflix to better allocate its $17 billion and content budget with high ROI on its productions.

The personalisation strategy of Netflix based on AI is highly relevant to the majority of the common topics in this chapter, i.e. the fact the AI can improve customer experience and retention by providing highly personalised experience. With more than 80% of views as a direct result of AI-generated recommendations, the platform demonstrates how collaborative filtering, predictive modelling, and A/B testing can come together to create cohesive and emotionally engaging user experiences. As a result, the case supports the chapter's hypothesis, which is supported by data showing that AI-powered personalization not only increases engagement right away but also builds brand value over time by producing experiences that are relevant and responsive.

Case Study 3: Spotify- Recommended Playlists and AI-based interactions

Spotify, as the music streaming leader in the world, has been on the forefront in implementing AI base predictive Analytics to provide personalised listening experience that changes in real-time to customer taste. In an online environment that is defined by content availability and continuously evolving consumer needs, the ability of Spotify to provide relevant, entertaining and dynamically evolving playlist has become one of the major forces behind its retention and growth strategy. This case study explores the application of artificial intelligence by Spotify to form personalised playlist and drive user engagement and customer retention as the key themes and concepts in the discussion of AI driven personalization in this chapter. Personalization at scale Spotify started with music recommendation systems that were hand tuned and primitive with rules that were difficult to scale as the global user base grew and the size of musical preferences became increasingly diverse.

There were several core challenges that the company had to deal with.

- Retention of the users: there are multiple competitors in a streaming market. Spotify needed to offer specialised individualised experience in order to retain users.
- Content discovery: With at least millions of tracks in their fingertips users were regularly overwhelmed with choice and there was fatigue, creating the need to explore smart discovery solutions that would surface relevant content.
- The Solution: AI Powered predictive analytic Spotify build an advanced AI recommendation engine that builds on:
- Listening Behaviours: Streamed skipped, replayed and unlike tunes.
- A user-generated playlist: that conveys a sense of mood, genre, and taste.
- Collaborative Filtration: identifying patterns among users with similar behaviors

Content analysis: is the process of using machine learning and natural language processing to analyze audio features like tempo, more, and lyrics.

To ensure a fresh, customized listening experience, the data is fed into AI-powered software that generates signature playlists, such as Discover Weekly Release Radar, which are updated frequently.

- **How does AI work within the company?**
- Spotify's personalization engine integrates models.
- Data collection: A million or more data points are gathered every day from user behaviour.
- Behavioural pattern detection: AI algorithms detect repeating patterns of behavioural and musical tastes.
- Playlist Creation: the technology offers new discoveries as well as remixed versions of popular tunes. as well as the individual tastes of the consumer.
- Dynamic Adaptation in Real-Time: Continued user usage informs the software, which then modifies recommendations going forward. Depending on the device, mood, time of day, and contextual listening activity (e.g., workout or relaxation), playlists are dynamically changed.
- Increased User Retention:

Individualization leads to emotional loyalty, which will allow Spotify to reduce churn and increase the duration of subscriptions.

- Ad Revenue and Premium Growth:

Enhanced interaction allows a more focused delivery of ads to the free users and converts to paid subscriptions.

- Market Leadership:

Challenges and Lessons Learned The currently developing personalization base of Spotify remains unmatched by the majority of its competitors that are establishing their dominant role in the sphere of innovation:

- Scalability: Processing and working with massive amounts of data required massive infrastructure upgrades and investment in machine learning systems in the cloud.
- Avoiding Echo Chambers:

Users will lose access to a variety of content if customisation is overdone. Spotify helps with this by promoting discovery by matching songs that are both familiar and new.

Prospects for the future Spotify is aggressively pushing the boundaries of AI advancement in multiple ways:

Context-Aware Personalization: Recommendations can be enhanced by having a better understanding of listening context and current moods. Data sharing across several channels is made easier by a multimodal data integration system.

Multimodal Data Integration: Including social media trends and podcast likes to enhance recommendation algorithms.

Dynamic Content Generation: Investigating AI-generated content that may create mood-appropriate playlists or personalized intros according to particular occasions or times of day.

Amazon, Netflix, and Spotify: A Comparison of AI-Powered Personalization Techniques

The top AI personalization techniques used by Amazon, Netflix, and Spotify—all of which are leaders in their respective industries—are compiled in the table below. These websites show how machine learning and predictive analytics are applied differently to promote consumer engagement, loyalty, and trust.

Table 5. Comparison of AI driven personalization strategies

Feature / Dimension	Amazon	Netflix	Spotify
Primary Focus	Personalized product recommendations	Personalized content (movies, series) recommendations	Personalized music playlists and content discovery
AI Techniques Used	Collaborative filtering, content-based filtering, NLP, real-time behavioral data analysis	Deep learning, collaborative filtering, A/B testing, UI adaptation	Collaborative filtering, NLP, deep learning, behavioral prediction
Key Personalization Features	"Recommended for You", "Frequently Bought Together", dynamic homepage	Dynamic thumbnails, Watch Next suggestions, adaptive UI, context-based content ranking	Discover Weekly, Release Radar, Made for You playlists
Data Inputs	Purchase history, browsing behavior, search queries, ratings, time on product	Watch history, device type, genre preferences, viewing time, skip rates	Song skips, likes, playlist adds, listening time, mood-based playlist usage
Customer Benefits	Easier product discovery, reduced decision fatigue, relevant offers	Relevant viewing experience, time-saving recommendations, higher satisfaction	Music discovery, reduced content overload, mood-aligned listening
Business Impact	~35% of sales from AI-driven recommendations	~80% of watched content comes from AI recommendations	Increased session time, premium conversion, improved ad targeting
Engagement Strategy	Cross-selling, upselling, real-time suggestions	Personalized viewing journey, emotional engagement through visuals and content	Curated playlists that combine familiarity and discovery
Challenges Addressed	Product overload, user drop-off, cart abandonment	Content fatigue, user retention, content licensing decisions	Choice overload, echo chambers, context misalignment
Ethical/Technical Considerations	Data privacy, algorithmic fairness, consumer consent	Algorithm transparency, user autonomy, filter bubbles	Personalization vs. exploration, mood/ context accuracy, data security
Competitive Advantage	One of the most advanced commerce personalization engines	Market leader in streaming personalization and content forecasting	Industry-defining recommendation engine with strong user loyalty

RECOMMENDATIONS

Based on the findings and informed by interdisciplinary research and case studies, the following are recommended for practitioners and researchers seeking to deploy research AI driven personalised marketing more effectively and ethically

- Adopt Transparent Personalization Strategies:

Companies must make sure that their AI systems are not "black boxes." Transparent reporting on how user information is gathered, analysed and used in marketing decisions will build customer trust incorporating explainable AI (XAI) will enable users to see and take charge of their tailored experiences. (Acharya 2025).

- Balance Automation with Human Insight:

While automation enhances scale and efficiency, AI systems must be complemented with human monitoring ethical review, particularly in emotionally sensitive topics such as health money and cultural products, as demonstrated by Spotify blending known and discovery content prevents filter bubbles and personalization does not curtail choice

- Strengthen Data Ethics Governance:

Ethical marketing demands that businesses follow rigorous data governance practices. This entails gaining informed consent, reducing data abuse, and undertaking regular AI audits to assess for fairness and bias (Ghosh & Ghosh, 2025).

- Invest in Dynamic Micro-Segmentation:

Businesses need to go beyond fixed demographic Segmentation and embrace AI powered behavioural micro segmentation to offer personalised content in real time.

- Design for Ethical Influence, Not Manipulation:

As indicated by behavioral economics studies, AI has the ability to impact decisions, unconsciously ethical guidelines need to make sure that personalization steers customer towards value and not vulnerability. This entails checking for psychological exploitation or over targeting (Radu et al., 2024).

- Benchmark Against Industry Leaders:

Smaller companies can imitate scalable AI models by taking cue from the tried and tested models of Amazon, Netflix, and Spotify. These websites prove that technology alone is not the key to AI marketing success, but how it is incorporated ethically into the customer experience.

- Since customers see all AI-based approaches (custom offers, loyalty plans, suggestions, etc.) similarly and positively, companies need to combine various AI features instead of focusing on a single one.

• The strong internal consistency and low variance mean that loyalty programs driven by AI can successfully improve customer retention and satisfaction. As there is low variance and strong internal consistency, maintain consistent user experience at all AI-driven touchpoints (e.g., chatbots on the website, recommendation engines, email campaigns).

- High correlation of trust for personalized recommendations with other variables indicates that hyper-personalization is able to create stronger brand relationships and loyalty. Strong scores on "stronger connection to brands that use AI" indicate that AI can help foster the emotional connection with the brand—employ storytelling, personalized messages, and experiences to capitalize on this.
- In spite of high mean scores, minor differences in standard deviation and skewness emphasize the necessity of continuous feedback gathering and tracking of AI-based programs.
- Transparency is a critical element here. Clearly explain how AI is being utilized, particularly in personal data management and personalization, to enhance consumer trust.
- With full Likert scale usage (scores ranging from 1 to 5), it's evident that not all customers respond equally. Design adaptive AI experiences that cater to diverse preferences and digital literacy levels.
- Although AI is essential for personalization, trustworthiness and pleasure can be increased by integrating it with human assistance or empathy-driven marketing.
- To measure the true impact of AI initiatives on brand loyalty and engagement, steer clear of perception research and keep an eye on behavioural metrics.

CONCLUSION

Ultimately, the discussion demonstrates that companies should develop a comprehensive and integrated AI strategy that prioritizes emotional connection, customization, and transparency while staying attentive to the diverse needs of their customers. Brands may improve customer satisfaction and retention by investing in AI-based loyalty programs and maintaining consistency across all AI touchpoints. Gaining trust requires organizations to be transparent about their use of AI, especially when handling sensitive data. By regularly monitoring customer opinion and being dedicated to bringing AI sophistication into line with human comprehension, businesses will be able to continuously improve their ways. Finally, it will be easier to explain how AI impacts consumer engagement and loyalty and eventually results in long-term, sustainable economic success if behavioural indicators are emphasized in conjunction with perception studies.

REFERENCES

Aaker, D. (1991). Brand equity. *La gestione del valore della marca, 347*, 356.

Acharya, D. (2025). Behavioral economics and decision science in corporate strategies. [IJSATE]. *International Journal of Scientific Advances in Technology and Economics, 1*(3), 45–56. https://ijsate.com/wp-content/uploads/2025/03/V1I3P5_IJSATE032521.pdf

Babadoğan, B. (2024). Unveiling the power of AI-driven personalization: Transforming consumer behaviour in the age of digital marketing. *Next Frontier for Life Sciences and AI, 8*(1), 61. Advance online publication. DOI: 10.62802/fj43xy18

Borau, S. (2024). Deception, discrimination, and objectification: Ethical issues of female AI agents. *Journal of Business Ethics*. Advance online publication. DOI: 10.1007/s10551-024-05754-4

Devi, C. G., & Jai Karthik, M. S. A. (2025). Chatbots and conversational AI: Revolutionizing customer engagement in marketing. In Devi, C. G., Priya, D., & Vasudevan, A. (Eds.), *AI and machine learning in marketing* (pp. 90–94). Shanlax Publications., https://www.shanlaxpublications.com/ai-and-machine-learning-in-marketing/ DOI: 10.34293/p/AI-and-Machine-Learning-in-Marketing

Ganeshkumar, M., Karunakaran, S., Muzhumathi, R., & Suguna, R. (2024). AI-driven marketing insights: Harnessing machine learning for enhanced consumer engagement and personalization. In *Proceedings of the First International Conference on Software, Systems and Information Technology (SSITCON)* (pp. 1–6). DOI: 10.1109/SSITCON62437.2024.10796558

Garg, N., Gupta, K., Chelikani, H., & Ravada, P. (2025). The Evolution of Personalization From Traditional Marketing to AI Computing. In Kanthavel, R., & Dhaya, R. (Eds.), *AI for Large Scale Communication Networks* (pp. 415–444). IGI Global Scientific Publishing., DOI: 10.4018/979-8-3693-6552-6.ch019

Ghosh, K., & Ghosh, D. P. (2025). Who am AI? Deconstructing identity in the age of advanced artificial intelligence [Preprint]. DOI: 10.13140/RG.2.2.36276.36481

Gowri, D. P. (2024). Impact of AI in Personalized Digital Marketing: Boosting Customer Engagement through Tailored Content. *Journal of Communication Management (London), 3*(03), 216–221. DOI: 10.58966/JCM2024334

Guendouz, T. (2024). Artificial intelligence-powered customer experience management: Moving from mass to hyper-personalization in light of relationship marketing. *International Journal for Scientific Research, 3*(6), 247–306. Advance online publication. DOI: 10.59992/IJSR.2024.v3n6p9

Gungunawat, A., Khandelwal, N., & Gupta, N. (2024). AI-powered personalization in digital marketing: Transforming consumer engagement and strategy. *Research Review International Journal of Multidisciplinary, 9*(11), 183–191. DOI: 10.31305/rrijm.2024.v09.n11.026

Haider, R., Bari, M. F. A. I., Shaif, M. F. I., & Rahman, M. (2025). Engineering hyper-personalization: Software challenges and brand performance in AI-driven digital marketing management: An empirical study. *International Journal of Science and Research Archive, 15*(2), 1122–1141. DOI: 10.30574/ijsra.2025.15.2.1525

Hasan, M. T. (2025). A systematic literature review on AI in marketing: Establishing an ethical framework for academics and marketers. [Master's thesis, University of Eastern Finland]. UEF eRepository.https://erepo.uef.fi/server/api/core/bitstreams/5e5c29de-40ed-47ed-9683-da50ec2489ae/content

Huang, M. H., & Rust, R. T. (2021). A strategic framework for artificial intelligence in marketing. *Journal of the Academy of Marketing Science, 49*(1), 30–50. DOI: 10.1007/s11747-020-00749-9

Ijomah, T. I. (2025). A conceptual framework for multi-channel marketing optimization, consumer behavior and conversion analytics. *International Journal of Advanced MultidisciplinaryResearch, 5*(2), 1498–1508. DOI: 10.62225/2583049X.2025.5.2.4011

Karunanayaka, K. A. Y. R. O., Jahankhani, H., El-Deeb, S., Isuru, S. W. A., & Hussien, O. A. A. M. (2024). *"Artificial Intelligence in Digital Marketing: The Ethical Implications of Digital Influence on Markets and Consumer", Market Grooming: The Dark Side of AI Marketing*. Sumesh Singh Dadwal, Hamid Jahankhani, Kenneth Revett., DOI: 10.1108/978-1-83549-001-320241009

Keller, K. L. (1993). Conceptualizing, measuring, and managing customer-based brand equity. *Journal of Marketing, 57*(1), 1–22. DOI: 10.1177/002224299305700101

Koswara, A., & Herlina, L. (2025). The Ethical Deviations of AI in Marketing Practices: A Critical Review from Halal Perspectives [RIE]. *Review of Islamic Economics, 2*(2), 105–116. DOI: 10.58777/rie.v2i2.393

Luu, T. M., Mittal, S., & Gupta, S. (2025). Leveraging AI to Tailor Customer Engagement With Personalized Marketing Strategies. In Tunio, M. (Ed.), *AI, Corporate Social Responsibility, and Marketing in Modern Organizations* (pp. 195–220). IGI Global Scientific Publishing., DOI: 10.4018/979-8-3373-0219-5.ch010

Lyulyov, O., Pimonenko, T., & Kwilinski, A. (2025). Artificial Intelligence in Social Media Marketing. In Saura, J. R. (Ed.), *Global Perspectives on AI, Ethics, and Business Economics. Contributions to Management Science*. Springer., DOI: 10.1007/978-3-031-88781-9_9

Mahdizadeh, B. M., Khodadad Hosseini, S. H., & Nazarpour Kashani, H. (2025). *Bibliometric analysis of customer experience and artificial intelligence*. Scientometrics Research Journal., DOI: 10.22070/rsci.2025.19066.1729

Mishra, M. (2024). A holistic review of customer experience research: Topic modelling using BERTopic. *Marketing Intelligence & Planning*. Advance online publication. DOI: 10.1108/MIP-09-2023-0457

Muharam, H., Wandrial, S., Rumondang, P. R., Handayani, M. A., & Masruchan, M. (2024). *Innovative Strategies in Digital Marketing: Enhancing Consumer Engagement and Brand Loyalty*. Global International Journal of Innovative Research., DOI: 10.59613/global.v2i7.236

Owusu-Berko, L. (2025). The Intersection Of Behavioral Economics And Data Science In Personalizing Consumer Experiences And Maximizing Revenue Optimization. [ijetrm]. *International Journal of Engineering Technology Research & Management*, *09*(02). Advance online publication. DOI: 10.5281/zenodo.14897990

Patil, D. (2025). Artificial Intelligence For Personalized Marketing And Consumer Behaviour Analysis: Enhancing Engagement And Conversion Rates. https://papers.ssrn.com/sol3/papers.cfm?abstract_id=5057436DOI: 10.2139/ssrn.5057436

Quintana, S. C. (2025). Liberal democracy, behavioural governance, and communication: Risks and opportunities. In Saura, J. (Ed.), *Data-driven governance through AI, digital marketing, and the privacy interplay* (pp. 77–112). IGI Global Scientific Publishing., DOI: 10.4018/979-8-3693-6945-6.ch004

Radu, C. G., Dumitra, E. C., & Cotescu, R.-G. (2024). Behavioral Economics in The Era of Digital Subscriptions: Choice or Manipulation. *Journal of Academic Opinion*, *4*(2), 72–46. https://academicopinion.org/index.php/pub/article/view/68

Rehman, M. A., Sajid, I., Abid, S., Ali, O., & Khan, A. (2025). The Rise of AI-Driven Direct-to-Consumer (DTC) Brands: Personalization, Customer Retention, and Competition with Traditional Retailers. *Journal for Social Science Archives, 3*(2), 206–221. DOI: 10.59075/jssa.v3i2.230

Saura, J. R. (2025). AI, Data Economy, and Behavioral Intention: Towards Ethical Paths. In Saura, J. R. (Ed.), *Global Perspectives on AI, Ethics, and Business Economics. Contributions to Management Science*. Springer., DOI: 10.1007/978-3-031-88781-9_1

Vasundhara, S., Venkatesh, K. S., Manimegalai, V., Sundharesalingam, P., Sathyakala, S., & Boopathi, S. (2024). *AI-Powered Marketing Revolutionizing Customer Engagement Through Innovative Strategies*. IGI Global Scientific Publishing., DOI: 10.4018/979-8-3693-2643-5.ch002

Verma, A. (2025). Digital personalization and consumer engagement: A review of theoretical and empirical perspectives on AI-based advertising in social media environments. *SSRN*. DOI: 10.2139/ssrn.5261407

Wah, J. N. K. (2025). AI-Driven Influence: Transforming Brand Engagement and Trust in the Digital Age. Kexue Tongbao. *Chinese Science Bulletin*. Advance online publication. 02.1709/Csb.28.02.2025.01

APPENDIX

Questionnaire

Fill the space provided against the question and tick mark to indicate your choice

1. What is your age group?
    - o Under 18
    - o 18–24
    - o 25–34
    - o 35–44
    - o 45–54
    - o 55 and above
2. What is your gender?
    - o Male
    - o Female
    - o Other
3. What is your highest level of education?
    - o High school or equivalent
    - o Diploma
    - o Bachelor's degree
    - o Master's degree
    - o Doctorate or higher
    - o Professional Qualification
    - o Other (please specify): ___________
4. How often do you shop or interact with online platforms?
    - o Frequently
    - o Often
    - o Occasionally
    - o Rarely
    - o Never
5. Which of the following goods/services do you generally purchase in online platforms(Tick all that apply)
    - o Food and groceries
    - o FMCG
    - o Wearing Apparels
    - o Cosmetics
    - o Gadgets
    - o Books

- o Others

6. Which of the following online shopping sites are you familiar with
   - o Amazon
   - o Flipkart
   - o Myntra
   - o Blinkit
   - o Meesho
   - o Shopsy
   - o Swiggy
   - o Ajio
7. Are you aware of AI driven marketing tools (e.g.,- personalized recommendations, chatbots)?
   - o Yes
   - o No
8. Please give your response to the following statements Related to AI-Driven Personalized Marketing and Customer Engagement on a 5-point Likert scale where 5 is strongly agree, 4-Agree, 3-Neutral, 2-Disagree, 1-Strongly Disagree.

Table 5. AI-Driven Personalized Marketing and Customer Engagement

		Strongly Agree	Agree	Neutral	Disagree	Strongly Disagree
8.1	AI-driven product recommendations match my interests and preferences					
8.2	I frequently engage with AI-powered marketing content (e.g., recommended products, dynamic ads)					
8.3	AI-based recommendations influence my purchasing decisions					
8.4	I prefer shopping on platforms that use AI to personalize my experience					
8.5	AI-driven marketing strategies make online shopping more interactive and engaging					

9. Please give your response to the following statements Related to AI-Powered Personalization and Brand Loyalty on a 5-point Likert scale where 5 is strongly agree, 4-Agree, 3-Neutral, 2-Disagree, 1-Strongly Disagree.

Table 6. AI-Powered Personalization and Brand Loyalty

		Strongly Agree	**Agree**	**Neutral**	**Disagree**	**Strongly Disagree**
9.1	I feel a stronger connection to brands that use AI to personalize my shopping experience					
9.2	AI-driven offers and promotions encourage me to stay loyal to a particular brand					
9.3	AI-powered loyalty programs (personalized rewards, exclusive deals) make me return to a brand.					
9.4	I trust brands more when they use AI to provide personalized recommendations					
9.5	AI-driven marketing enhances my overall shopping experience and encourages repeat purchases					

10. What improvements would you like to see in AI-driven personalized marketing? (Open-ended)
11. Any additional comments or suggestions regarding AI in online shopping? (Open-ended)

Chapter 10
Strategic Foresight Leveraging AI and Predictive Analytics for Competitive Advantage

Hemish Prakashchandra Kapadia
http://orcid.org/0009-0007-3020-3350
Barclays Capital, USA

Aminul Islam
Lincoln University College, Malaysia

ABSTRACT

In the era of digital transformation, organizations must adopt cutting-edge technologies to sustain a competitive edge. Artificial Intelligence (AI) and predictive analytics have emerged as crucial enablers in this evolution, allowing firms to make informed, data-driven decisions proactively. This chapter delves deeply into the theoretical and practical aspects of AI and predictive analytics in competitive decision-making. It discusses their historical evolution, underlying methodologies, real-world applications across business functions, comprehensive frameworks for implementation, challenges encountered, and the future landscape. Through detailed case studies and academic insights, this chapter offers a holistic understanding of how AI and predictive analytics reshape strategic foresight, operational efficiency, and business agility.

DOI: 10.4018/979-8-3373-3648-0.ch010

1: INTRODUCTION

Software defect detection has long been a cornerstone of software engineering, critical for ensuring system reliability, security, and user satisfaction. Traditional debugging techniques—including manual code reviews, unit and integration testing, static code analysis, and dynamic runtime analysis—have provided a strong foundation for identifying bugs and flaws throughout the development lifecycle. However, these approaches are not without limitations. They are often labor-intensive, susceptible to human oversight, and constrained by the increasing scale and complexity of modern software systems. As applications grow larger, more interconnected, and data-driven, the task of ensuring bug-free code becomes exponentially more challenging.

In recent years, the field has witnessed a transformative shift fueled by advancements in Artificial Intelligence (AI)—particularly Machine Learning (ML) and Large Language Models (LLMs). These technologies are redefining the way developers interact with code, detect anomalies, and repair bugs. By learning from vast corpora of codebases, AI-powered tools can now intelligently identify issues that traditional methods may overlook. They can suggest context-aware fixes, analyze dependencies across modules, and even learn coding patterns and anti-patterns across domains and languages.

This chapter provides a comprehensive exploration of the emerging paradigm of intelligent debugging. It examines how LLMs and ML models—such as CodeBERT (Feng et al., 2020), OpenAI's Codex (Chen et al., 2021), and ChatGPT—are being employed to enhance software quality assurance (QA) through automation and intelligent decision support. These models are trained on a mixture of natural language and programming languages, enabling them to reason about source code much like human developers—but with greater scale, speed, and consistency.

From academic research prototypes to commercial developer tools embedded in integrated development environments (IDEs), the ecosystem around intelligent debugging is rapidly expanding. For instance, GitHub Copilot, powered by Codex, can suggest real-time code completions and bug fixes as a developer types, while DeepCode (acquired by Snyk) uses ML to analyze millions of repositories to identify vulnerabilities. These tools not only reduce the debugging effort but also support code maintainability and faster release cycles, aligning closely with the principles of Agile and DevOps practices.

However, while the promise of AI-assisted debugging is significant, its adoption raises critical questions. How do we trust the recommendations made by a black-box model? Can AI understand domain-specific business logic or compliance constraints? What about the ethical implications of using proprietary training data that might include sensitive or copyrighted code? These concerns underscore the need for explainability, data transparency, and robust evaluation metrics in deploying AI tools for software debugging.

Moreover, the integration of AI into debugging workflows necessitates a cultural shift in software development teams. Engineers must not only interpret AI-generated suggestions but also validate and contextualize them—thus transitioning from traditional coders to AI-augmented practitioners. The collaboration between human developers and intelligent systems introduces a new dimension to software engineering, where the focus is not only on writing code but also on curating training data, supervising model outputs, and managing technical debt introduced by AI-generated code.

From a strategic perspective, organizations must weigh the trade-offs between cost, accuracy, explainability, and control. AI models, while powerful, can occasionally produce hallucinations—incorrect outputs that appear plausible. In safety-critical domains such as healthcare, finance, or aviation, such inaccuracies can have profound consequences. Therefore, AI debugging tools should be seen not as replacements for human developers but as collaborative assistants that augment human judgment with data-driven insights.

This chapter is structured to reflect both the technical depth and strategic breadth of intelligent debugging. Section 2 introduces the foundational concepts of AI-driven defect detection, outlining the types of ML and LLM techniques currently in use. Section 3 explores real-world case studies and industry applications, shedding light on how companies across sectors are leveraging these tools. Section 4 addresses the challenges and limitations, such as explainability, data privacy, and overfitting. Section 5 presents a conceptual framework for integrating intelligent debugging into existing development pipelines. Section 6 discusses ethical, legal, and organizational implications, while Section 7 outlines emerging trends and future research directions.

The contribution of this chapter is twofold. First, it provides a state-of-the-art review of AI's role in debugging automation, linking academic insights with industry practices. Second, it proposes a forward-looking vision for intelligent debugging as a foundational capability in software quality management—paving the way for more resilient, trustworthy, and adaptive software systems.

As we move toward increasingly complex digital infrastructures—from autonomous vehicles and smart cities to AI-driven healthcare platforms—the need for intelligent, reliable, and scalable debugging systems becomes not just a technical requirement, but a societal imperative. This chapter invites researchers, developers, QA professionals, and policymakers to engage in the evolving conversation about how best to leverage AI for software integrity, while safeguarding ethical principles and human accountability.

2: THE EVOLUTION OF SOFTWARE DEBUGGING

2.1 Historical Context and Foundations

Software debugging, defined broadly as the process of identifying and resolving defects within software code, has been an integral part of software engineering since the early days of computing. The term "bug" in a computing context famously dates back to 1947, when a moth trapped in a Harvard Mark II relay caused a malfunction (Peterson, 2000). While the anecdote may be lighthearted, it underscores a fundamental reality: software, no matter how carefully constructed, is inherently prone to errors.

In the early decades of computing, debugging was a manual and intuitive task. Programmers relied on print statements, memory dumps, and flowcharts to trace and correct faulty logic (McConnell, 2004). As programming languages and systems became more sophisticated, so did the tools for debugging. Integrated debugging environments emerged in the 1980s, allowing developers to inspect variables, step through code, and set breakpoints. However, the basic premise remained the same: debugging was largely reactive, human-led, and exploratory.

Over time, systematic methodologies such as structured programming, modularization, and unit testing were introduced to improve code quality and reduce defects. Tools like gdb for C/C++, JDB for Java, and Visual Studio Debugger for C# offered increasingly powerful debugging capabilities, yet these tools remained fundamentally limited by their dependence on human insight and manual effort.

2.2 Traditional Debugging Techniques

Conventional debugging methods fall into several categories:

- Manual Debugging: Involves the use of print statements or logs to understand control flow or variable states. It remains common in scripting languages and quick fixes but is often error-prone and time-consuming (Glass, 2002).
- Static Code Analysis: Analyzes code without executing it to detect syntax violations, security vulnerabilities, or code smells. Tools like SonarQube, Coverity, and PMD identify issues such as null pointer dereferencing or unused variables.
- Dynamic Analysis: Inspects the runtime behavior of applications to uncover memory leaks, race conditions, and logic errors. Tools like Valgrind or AddressSanitizer fall into this category.

- Unit and Integration Testing: Test-driven development and frameworks like JUnit or NUnit allow for structured testing. However, these tests only cover anticipated behaviors, and many defects elude detection until runtime.

Despite their utility, these approaches are inherently reactive—they can only identify what the developer or tool is programmed to look for. They often fail to uncover unexpected or non-deterministic behavior in increasingly complex and distributed systems.

2.3 Challenges with Traditional Approaches

Several critical challenges plague traditional debugging approaches:

Cognitive Limitations

Debugging complex code requires intense cognitive effort. Developers must mentally simulate execution paths, consider edge cases, and identify interactions across modules. Studies have shown that even experienced developers can overlook simple defects when overwhelmed by context-switching or time pressure (LaToza & Myers, 2010).

Scalability

Modern enterprise software systems often contain millions of lines of code spread across multiple repositories and services. Manually reviewing or stepping through such code is infeasible. Moreover, the pace of continuous integration and deployment (CI/CD) pipelines demands faster and more scalable debugging solutions.

Non-Determinism

Multithreading, asynchronous operations, and event-driven architectures introduce non-determinism, making it difficult to reproduce bugs. Race conditions or intermittent failures may not manifest during debugging sessions, leading to elusive and persistent defects.

Domain Complexity

Applications in domains such as finance, healthcare, or aerospace require domain-specific knowledge to identify subtle bugs. Static tools often lack this contextual understanding, leaving high-impact defects undiscovered until after deployment.

Tool Fatigue and Fragmentation

The proliferation of specialized tools creates cognitive friction. Developers must learn and switch between linters, debuggers, profilers, and log aggregators, disrupting workflow continuity and contributing to tool fatigue.

2.4 The Emergence of Intelligent Automation

The limitations of human-centric debugging approaches have prompted a search for automation. Initial attempts included rule-based expert systems that encoded best practices or common anti-patterns. However, these systems were brittle, difficult to maintain, and lacked adaptability.

The evolution of computing power, availability of large datasets, and advances in artificial intelligence—especially in machine learning and deep learning—have shifted this landscape dramatically. Rather than relying on handcrafted rules, modern AI-based tools learn from examples. They analyze historical bug reports, commit logs, test outcomes, and runtime traces to identify patterns that indicate defects.

Early examples of learning-based tools include fault prediction models that use logistic regression or decision trees to predict defect-prone modules (Nagappan & Ball, 2005), and code smell detectors that rely on clustering or classification algorithms (Fontana et al., 2016). These models demonstrated that defect prediction can be effectively automated, albeit with limitations in generalization and interpretability.

2.5 Transition to Predictive Debugging

The shift from reactive to predictive debugging marks a critical inflection point in software engineering. Predictive systems do not merely wait for a test to fail or a log to indicate a crash; they proactively flag code segments that are statistically likely to contain defects.

Predictive debugging systems typically involve:

- Feature Extraction: Metrics like cyclomatic complexity, code churn, module coupling, and developer ownership are used as features (Zimmermann et al., 2007).
- Model Training: Labeled datasets—comprising buggy and clean code—are used to train classifiers such as Random Forests, Support Vector Machines (SVMs), or Gradient Boosting Machines.
- Evaluation and Deployment: Models are validated using cross-validation or holdout testing and integrated into CI pipelines to provide real-time feedback.

These systems are not without challenges. The accuracy of predictions heavily depends on the quality and balance of training data. Models trained on one codebase may not generalize to another without significant tuning.

2.6 Rise of Context-Aware Debugging

The limitations of feature-engineered ML models, particularly their inability to capture code semantics and long-range dependencies, have catalyzed the emergence of context-aware models—particularly large language models (LLMs).

Unlike traditional ML models that treat code as structured data, LLMs treat code as a form of language. Trained on billions of lines of code across multiple programming languages, they develop a nuanced understanding of syntax, semantics, and even idiomatic usage patterns (Feng et al., 2020; Chen et al., 2021). These models can suggest bug fixes, summarize functions, and even generate code from natural language descriptions.

Context-aware debugging tools such as GitHub Copilot or Amazon CodeWhisperer harness these models to provide real-time suggestions, auto-completions, and bug detection directly within integrated development environments (IDEs). This deep contextual understanding enables LLMs to catch errors that would have otherwise gone unnoticed—such as logic inconsistencies, incorrect API usage, or mismatched control structures.

2.7 Blurring the Line Between Authoring and Debugging

With LLMs embedded in development workflows, the boundary between writing and debugging code is beginning to blur. Tools now auto-correct code as it is written, suggest optimizations, and even propose test cases. This convergence implies a future where debugging is not a separate post-development phase but a continuous, integrated activity.

Moreover, AI tools are not just passive observers; they are becoming active participants in the coding process. They adapt to individual developer styles, learn from organizational patterns, and contribute to code reviews and quality assurance pipelines. This marks a profound transformation in the role of the developer—from sole author and debugger to collaborator with intelligent systems.

3: MACHINE LEARNING IN SOFTWARE DEFECT DETECTION

3.1 Introduction to Machine Learning in Debugging

The emergence of machine learning (ML) in software engineering has redefined the boundaries of what is achievable in defect detection and quality assurance. Traditional software testing and debugging techniques, although rigorous, are typically rule-based, reactive, and constrained by human cognition and resources. In contrast, ML enables systems to learn patterns from data, generalize beyond specific rule sets, and make probabilistic predictions about unseen data, such as code segments likely to contain defects (Amor et al., 2006; Wang et al., 2018).

ML is especially effective in environments with historical defect data, version control logs, bug reports, and source code repositories. By training models on these datasets, defect prediction becomes a data-driven process, allowing organizations to prioritize code reviews, testing, and refactoring in a more informed and efficient manner. This chapter explores the main categories of ML techniques used in defect detection, discusses feature extraction approaches, model performance metrics, and presents tools and real-world implementations.

3.2 Categories of Machine Learning in Defect Detection

ML models applied in debugging typically fall into two categories: supervised learning and unsupervised learning.

3.2.1 Supervised Learning

Supervised learning relies on labeled datasets, where each instance is marked as defective or non-defective. The goal is to train a model that can predict this label for new, unseen code modules.

Common algorithms include:

- **Decision Trees and Random Forests**: These models build decision paths based on input features. Random Forests reduce overfitting by aggregating multiple trees (Khoshgoftaar et al., 1996).
- **Support Vector Machines (SVMs)**: Particularly effective with high-dimensional feature spaces, SVMs attempt to find an optimal hyperplane that separates defect-prone code from clean code (Bowes et al., 2018).
- **Logistic Regression**: A baseline model that estimates the probability of a binary outcome (defective vs. clean). Although simple, it performs well when features are carefully selected (Lessmann et al., 2008).

- **Deep Learning (DL)**: Recurrent Neural Networks (RNNs) and Convolutional Neural Networks (CNNs) have been used to model abstract code patterns and long-range dependencies (White et al., 2016).

3.2.2 Unsupervised Learning

In scenarios where labeled defect data is unavailable, unsupervised models such as clustering or anomaly detection are employed.

- **K-Means and DBSCAN**: These algorithms cluster similar code entities. Anomalies or outliers can indicate potential bugs.
- **Autoencoders**: Neural networks trained to reconstruct input data. High reconstruction errors may flag unexpected or unusual code behaviors (Li et al., 2021).

Unsupervised methods are valuable in exploratory contexts or in detecting previously unseen bug types.

3.3 Feature Engineering in Code Defect Prediction

One of the critical components of building effective ML models for defect detection lies in the construction of features—measurable attributes extracted from source code and software metadata. These features fall into several categories:

3.3.1 Code Metrics

- **Cyclomatic Complexity**: Measures the number of linearly independent paths through a program module (McCabe, 1976). High complexity correlates with higher defect likelihood.
- **Lines of Code (LOC)**: Larger modules often contain more defects due to increased logic density.
- **Code Churn**: Represents how much a file has changed over time. High churn is often linked to instability and bugs (Nagappan & Ball, 2005).

3.3.2 Process Metrics

- **Number of Developers**: Modules touched by many developers may suffer from miscommunication or inconsistent logic.
- **Code Ownership**: Modules predominantly edited by one developer are often more stable (Bird et al., 2009).

- **Recent Bug Fixes**: Files with recent fixes are often susceptible to regression bugs.

3.3.3 Semantic Features

Recent approaches also incorporate embeddings of code tokens using techniques such as word2vec or AST2vec, where abstract syntax trees (ASTs) are encoded into vectors to capture syntactic and semantic relationships (Alon et al., 2019).

3.4 Model Training, Testing, and Evaluation

Effective deployment of ML models for defect detection requires robust training and evaluation protocols:

3.4.1 Data Preprocessing

- **Imbalanced Datasets**: Typically, the number of defective modules is much smaller than non-defective ones. Oversampling (SMOTE), undersampling, or cost-sensitive learning strategies are used to address imbalance (He & Garcia, 2009).
- **Normalization**: Ensures that features with different scales do not distort model performance.

3.4.2 Evaluation Metrics

Commonly used evaluation metrics include:

- **Accuracy**: Fraction of correctly classified instances but may be misleading for imbalanced data.
- **Precision and Recall**: Precision measures how many predicted bugs are real; recall measures how many real bugs were found.
- **F1-Score**: Harmonic means of precision and recall.
- **ROC-AUC**: Area under the receiver operating characteristic curve; evaluates the trade-off between true positives and false positives.

These metrics help organizations determine not only if a model works, but whether it meets operational requirements in terms of minimizing false alarms or undetected defects.

3.5 Tools and Implementations

Several academic and commercial tools have integrated ML-based defect prediction:

- **DeepBugs**: Uses neural embeddings to detect likely variable misuse and operator errors by learning from token context (Pradel & Sen, 2018).
- **BugLab**: Developed by Meta AI, this tool trains a neural network on masked code tokens to identify where bugs may occur, utilizing a contrastive learning objective (Allamanis et al., 2021).
- **CodeGuru**: Amazon's commercial tool that uses ML models trained on code review data to recommend fixes for common defects in Java and Python.
- **GitHub's ML-Based Security Alerts**: Uses vulnerability databases and pattern recognition to flag code that may be prone to known security bugs.

These tools represent the real-world deployment of ML in production environments, offering scalable and automated code quality assurance.

3.6 Benefits and Limitations

3.6.1 Benefits

- **Scalability**: ML models can process thousands of files in minutes, offering real-time or batch-mode analysis.
- **Early Detection**: Predictive models allow bugs to be flagged before code is even executed or integrated.
- **Knowledge Reuse**: ML systems capture organizational debugging knowledge and apply it consistently across teams.

3.6.2 Limitations

- **Data Dependency**: ML models require significant amounts of quality-labeled data for training.
- **Generalization**: Models trained on one project may not perform well on others unless fine-tuned.
- **Interpretability**: Many models, especially deep learning, act as black boxes—challenging for developers to understand or trust without explainability layers (Doshi-Velez & Kim, 2017).

3.7 Future Directions in ML-Based Debugging

Several emerging trends indicate the future trajectory of ML in defect detection:

- **Graph Neural Networks (GNNs)**: Capture structural relationships in code by modeling control flow and ASTs as graphs (Hellendoorn et al., 2021).
- **Transfer Learning and Fine-Tuning**: Pretrained code models can be fine-tuned on organization-specific data for higher relevance and accuracy.
- **Human-in-the-Loop ML**: Combining automated predictions with expert feedback loops allows for model refinement and organizational learning.
- **Explainable AI (XAI)**: Tools that explain predictions using token saliency maps or counterfactual reasoning will become crucial for building trust in debugging recommendations.

4: THE ROLE OF LARGE LANGUAGE MODELS IN DEBUGGING

4.1 Introduction

Large Language Models (LLMs) have redefined the frontier of artificial intelligence applications, extending their capabilities beyond natural language processing into programming and software engineering. In the realm of software debugging, these models are emerging as transformative tools that provide deep contextual understanding, semantic analysis, and even corrective suggestions for source code.

Unlike rule-based tools or traditional static analyzers that operate on pre-programmed logic and pattern recognition, LLMs rely on deep neural architectures trained on massive corpora of publicly available source code. This data-driven training approach enables LLMs to detect, explain, and fix software defects in a way that mimics human reasoning—but with the scale and speed of automation.

This chapter examines how LLMs like Codex, CodeBERT, StarCoder, and others are used to identify bugs, propose fixes, and support developers through intelligent debugging. Their functional capabilities, comparative advantages, implementation strategies, and limitations are explored in detail.

4.2 Overview of Code-Focused LLMs

Large Language Models are typically built using the transformer architecture, which enables them to process and generate sequential data. When applied to software code, they are trained on billions of tokens comprising source code, documentation, configuration files, and even developer discussions. These models are capable of capturing both syntactic and semantic nuances across a variety of programming languages.

Prominent LLMs for code include:

- **OpenAI Codex:** A descendant of GPT-3, trained on a large subset of public GitHub repositories to generate, interpret, and repair code.
- **CodeBERT**: Developed by Microsoft and trained on bimodal input—pairs of code and natural language—for tasks such as code search and defect prediction.
- **StarCoder:** A large transformer model trained on multiple programming languages with extended context windows to handle larger files and complex codebases.
- **PolyCoder:** Focused on lower-level programming languages like C, PolyCoder was designed for high-performance code understanding and generation.

These models have been successfully applied in integrated development environments (IDEs) and enterprise tooling to automate debugging tasks at scale.

4.3 Functional Capabilities of LLMs in Debugging

LLMs offer a spectrum of capabilities relevant to debugging and defect detection:

4.3.1 Code Comprehension

LLMs understand code logic, intent, and structure by interpreting both the code itself and accompanying natural language (e.g., comments or documentation). This comprehension allows them to identify inconsistencies between the intended behavior and actual implementation, a frequent cause of bugs.

4.3.2 Bug Localization

By analyzing the relationships between variables, control structures, and data flows, LLMs can localize defects in specific lines or blocks of code. This significantly narrows the search area for developers, reducing time spent on root cause analysis.

4.3.3 Bug Fixing

Beyond identifying errors, LLMs are capable of suggesting concrete fixes. This includes correcting logical flaws, replacing deprecated functions, adjusting syntax, and even rewriting sections of code for better performance or readability.

4.3.4 Code Summarization and Documentation Alignment

LLMs assist in generating summaries of functions or entire classes, helping developers quickly understand legacy code. This is particularly useful when debugging undocumented or poorly maintained systems.

4.3.5 Semantic Code Search

These models allow developers to search for relevant code patterns or functions using natural language queries. This accelerates the process of identifying similar bugs or reuse opportunities.

4.4 Prompt Engineering and Model Tuning

The interaction with LLMs for debugging tasks is often mediated through prompts—carefully structured instructions that guide the model's output. For example, developers might ask a model to explain a block of code, identify potential issues, or rewrite a function for improved efficiency.

Few-shot prompting, where examples are embedded within the input, and fine-tuning on organization-specific codebases can enhance model accuracy and contextual relevance. These techniques ensure that LLMs adapt to domain-specific conventions, programming styles, and tool chains.

4.5 Comparative Performance of Debugging Tools

A practical measure of the effectiveness of LLMs in debugging is their performance relative to traditional tools and classical ML models. Figure 1, showing bar graph a comparison based on key evaluation metrics—accuracy, precision, and recall ("Figure 1.").

Figure 1. Performance comparison of traditional debuggers, ML-based tools, and LLMs based on accuracy, precision, and recall

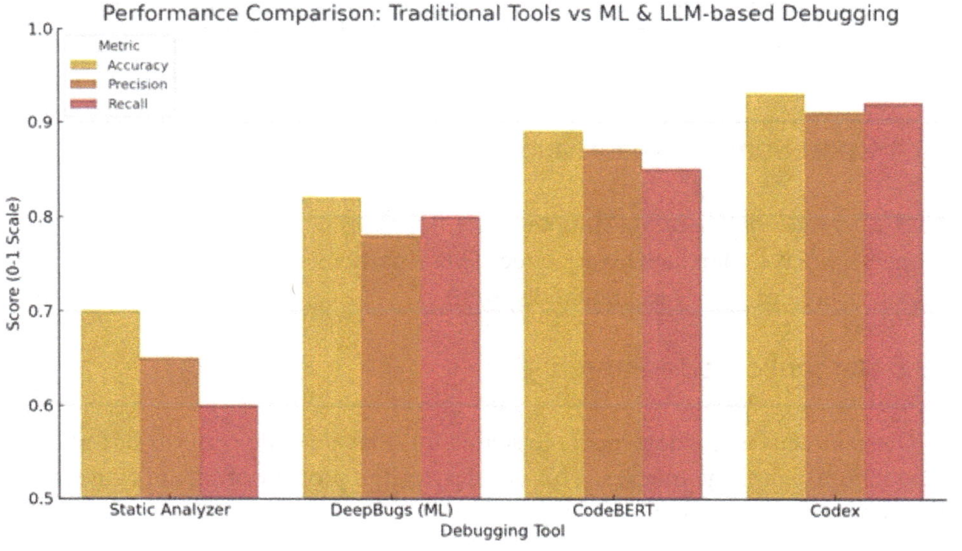

Key Insights:

- Traditional static analyzers typically exhibit high precision but low recall, identifying known defect patterns but often missing context-specific errors.
- ML models like DeepBugs offer improved recall and balanced precision through supervised learning techniques.
- LLMs such as CodeBERT and Codex outperform both in accuracy, due to their ability to understand code in broader semantic and contextual terms.

These results underscore the value of LLMs in identifying a wider range of bugs with fewer false positives, a significant advantage in modern continuous integration pipelines.

4.6 Contextual and Multilingual Debugging Capabilities

One of the distinctive strengths of LLMs is their ability to maintain and reason over broad context windows. This capability enables:

- **Intra-file comprehension:** Understanding dependencies and logic across functions and classes within the same file.

- **Cross-file referencing:** Tracking variable definitions, imports, or global state across multiple files.
- **Multi-language support:** LLMs trained on diverse corpora can detect bugs in languages ranging from Python and Java to C++, TypeScript, and Rust.

Such capabilities are essential in enterprise environments where polyglot codebases are common and debugging often involves navigating across different language layers and system components.

4.7 Case Study: GitHub Copilot

GitHub Copilot, powered by Codex, represents a commercial application of LLMs in developer tooling. Integrated within Visual Studio Code and other editors, Copilot provides real-time suggestions as developers type. It also assists in identifying potential errors before code is run.

In a productivity study conducted by Ziegler et al. (2023), developers using Copilot completed tasks 20–30% faster on average. Moreover, they reported higher satisfaction, particularly in navigating unfamiliar code or implementing standard functions. The model not only accelerated development but also reduced cognitive load during debugging sessions.

4.8 Risks and Limitations of LLM-Based Debugging

Despite their powerful capabilities, LLMs are not without limitations:

4.8.1 Hallucination and Incorrect Suggestions

LLMs sometimes generate code that appears correct syntactically but fails at runtime due to logical errors or use of non-existent APIs. This phenomenon, known as hallucination, poses risks when developers accept suggestions without validation.

4.8.2 Lack of Explainability

Unlike traditional rule-based systems or interpretable ML models, LLMs function as black boxes. Their internal decision-making process is opaque, making it difficult to explain why a particular suggestion was made (Doshi-Velez & Kim, 2017).

4.8.3 Data Bias and Insecure Patterns

If LLMs are trained on insecure or outdated code, they may propagate those patterns. Ensuring the integrity of training data is crucial, especially for applications involving security-critical systems (Sandoval, 2023).

4.8.4 Developer Over-Reliance

As LLMs grow more capable, there is a risk of developers becoming overly reliant on AI, potentially undermining their debugging skills and understanding of underlying systems.

4.9 The Future of LLMs in Debugging

The integration of LLMs into development workflows marks the beginning of a more intelligent and autonomous era in software engineering. Anticipated future developments include:

- **Autonomous Debugging Agents:** Systems that continuously monitor, diagnose, and remediate code issues in production environments.
- **Fine-Tuned Models for Organizations:** LLMs tailored to an enterprise's codebase, ensuring relevance and reducing hallucination risks.
- **Explainable LLMs:** Research into making model decisions transparent to users, improving trust and accountability.
- **IDE-Native AI Assistants:** Deeper integration into IDEs to provide debugging, documentation, and testing support as part of a seamless workflow.

These advancements suggest that LLMs will evolve from mere suggestion engines to proactive collaborators that shape how software is written and maintained.

5: HYBRID MODELS – COMBINING MACHINE LEARNING AND LLMS FOR INTELLIGENT DEBUGGING

5.1 Introduction

As software complexity continues to escalate, so does the need for smarter and more holistic approaches to defect detection and debugging. Traditional tools, even when augmented with machine learning (ML), often fall short in capturing the full spectrum of software behavior and intent. Conversely, large language models (LLMs) like CodeBERT and Codex, while powerful, may lack the precision or training structure to make consistently reliable predictions without contextual signals or historical software metrics.

This gap has given rise to hybrid debugging models, which combine the analytical capabilities of traditional ML systems with the semantic intelligence of LLMs. These models harness structured code metrics and labeled data to predict defect-prone code (ML), and then apply LLMs to interpret, explain, and remediate that code with human-like language and code generation. The result is an intelligent, integrated pipeline that enhances debugging precision, automation, and explainability.

5.2 Motivation for Hybrid Debugging Systems

Neither ML nor LLMs alone offer a complete solution. ML excels at numerical pattern recognition—detecting statistical anomalies and learning from labeled datasets. However, ML models struggle with semantic reasoning, multi-language support, or dynamic prompts.

LLMs, in contrast, understand natural language and code simultaneously. They can summarize functions, localize bugs, and generate plausible corrections. But they are probabilistic and can hallucinate, suggesting syntactically correct but logically flawed code. By combining these tools, developers can:

- Use ML models to flag likely bugs based on statistical indicators.
- Engage LLMs to interpret and propose fixes, explain rationale, and interact with developers.

5.3 Architectural Overview of Hybrid Debugging

The hybrid debugging workflow typically involves several stages:

1. **Static Code Ingestion:** Raw source code from repositories is passed through a pipeline.
2. **Feature Extraction (ML Layer):** Software metrics such as complexity, churn, and developer history are quantified.
3. **Defect Prediction (ML Layer):** Using classifiers (e.g., Random Forests or Neural Nets), high-risk code areas are identified.
4. **Contextual Understanding (LLM Layer):** Code snippets, documentation, and test results are parsed for semantic meaning.
5. **Bug Explanation and Suggestion (LLM Layer):** Suggestions for remediation, along with explanations, are generated.

6. **Developer Feedback Loop:** Developers review, accept, or modify AI suggestions, feeding results back into the system for retraining.

5.4 Graphical Representation

To clarify the architecture, "Figure 2." illustrates the flow of data and interaction between ML and LLM components in a hybrid debugging system.

Figure 2. Hybrid workflow: machine learning + LLM for intelligent debugging

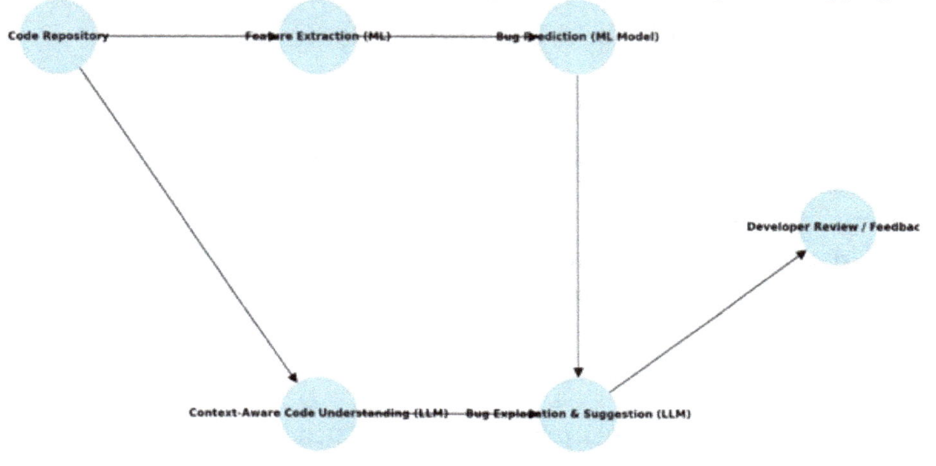

5.5 ML Components: Strengths and Role

The ML portion of the hybrid architecture focuses on quantitative, predictive analytics. It typically involves:

- **Feature Engineering:** Metrics like cyclomatic complexity, code churn, and number of developers involved.
- **Training on Bug History:** Models are trained using past commit data labeled with bug occurrences.
- **Binary or Multiclass Classification:** Output indicates whether a code unit is likely defective.

Advantages:

- High interpretability (e.g., feature importance analysis).

- Scalable to large codebases.
- Efficient for prioritizing QA/testing resources.

However, ML lacks the flexibility to generalize across new defect types or offer intuitive explanations without post-processing.

5.6 LLM Components: Strengths and Role

Once the ML layer flags suspicious code, the LLM takes over. Its responsibilities include:

- **Code Interpretation:** Understanding what the function is intended to do.
- **Error Detection:** Locating logic errors or mismatches.
- **Explanation Generation:** Justifying why a line of code is likely incorrect.
- **Fix Suggestion:** Generating corrected or optimized versions of code.

LLMs are especially effective when provided with sufficient prompt context (e.g., surrounding functions, docstrings, or test failures). They serve as the bridge between automated detection and developer-facing diagnostics.

5.7 Real-World Application Scenarios

Several industry tools are beginning to adopt hybrid debugging principles, either explicitly or implicitly.

Case Example: Amazon CodeGuru + LLMs

Amazon CodeGuru uses ML to provide code review comments. When combined with LLMs like CodeWhisperer, it can also offer natural language feedback and inline suggestions for fixes, creating a more seamless debugging experience.

Enterprise IDEs

Organizations like Microsoft are integrating ML-based security alerts with Copilot to not only detect vulnerable code (via ML patterns) but also explain and resolve those issues with natural language guidance.

CI/CD Integration

Hybrid systems can be embedded into CI/CD pipelines, blocking merges when ML detects high-risk commits, while the LLM provides developers with reasoning and quick fixes to resolve issues before deployment.

5.8 Advantages of Hybrid Debugging Models

Hybrid systems capitalize on the strengths of both approaches:

- **Improved Accuracy:** ML handles structured risk detection, LLMs interpret and resolve.
- **Context Awareness:** LLMs bring awareness of semantics, use cases, and developer intent.
- **Scalability:** ML scales across large codebases; LLMs offer depth where needed.
- **Explainability:** LLMs offer human-readable justifications that ML alone cannot.

This collaboration creates a more complete debugging ecosystem—one that is proactive, insightful, and responsive.

5.9 Limitations and Considerations

Despite their advantages, hybrid models introduce complexity:

Model Synchronization

The ML and LLM components must be tuned to work with consistent assumptions and data formats. Poor integration may lead to conflicting signals.

Latency

Calling LLMs—especially for large prompts—adds latency. This may impact real-time feedback loops in development environments.

Bias and Generalization

ML models are domain-specific; LLMs may hallucinate or overgeneralize. Without validation, hybrid systems could generate plausible but incorrect suggestions.

Training Cost

Maintaining up-to-date ML models and fine-tuned LLMs requires continuous retraining and infrastructure resources.

5.10 Future Research and Development

Hybrid models represent an evolving research frontier. Several promising directions include:

- **Joint Training Architectures:** Training ML and LLM components together in an end-to-end fashion for improved synergy.
- **Graph-Based Models:** Using graph neural networks (GNNs) in ML layers to encode abstract syntax trees (ASTs) and control flow graphs for enhanced bug prediction.
- **Multimodal Debugging:** Incorporating code, execution traces, logs, and developer discussions for more holistic diagnostics.
- **Reinforcement Learning with Human Feedback (RLHF):** Letting developers rate suggestions to improve model alignment over time.

As these innovations mature, hybrid models will likely become central to intelligent software engineering.

5.11 Conclusion

Hybrid debugging models combining ML and LLMs mark a significant advancement in the pursuit of intelligent, automated software maintenance. By leveraging the statistical power of machine learning and the semantic fluency of large language models, these systems offer developers the best of both worlds: data-driven predictions and human-like interactions.

Such systems are not merely tools but collaborative agents—surfacing insights, offering explanations, and evolving through feedback. As these technologies continue to integrate into development workflows, they will reshape the debugging landscape into one that is not only smarter but more intuitive and scalable.

6: TOOLS, PLATFORMS, AND REAL-WORLD APPLICATIONS

6.1 Introduction

As AI-driven software debugging technologies mature, they are increasingly transitioning from academic research into practical, real-world deployment. Organizations are no longer merely experimenting with machine learning and large language models—they are embedding these capabilities into integrated development environments (IDEs), CI/CD pipelines, and code review systems. This chapter surveys the most influential commercial and open-source platforms leveraging ML and LLMs for software defect detection, compares their capabilities, and presents case studies demonstrating measurable impact in production environments.

6.2 Evaluation Criteria for Debugging Tools

To assess the functionality and maturity of AI-powered debugging platforms, four core capabilities are considered:

- **Bug Detection**: The ability to automatically identify likely defects or code smells.
- **Bug Explanation**: Whether the tool can explain the defect in natural language.
- **Code Suggestion**: The quality and contextual relevance of suggested fixes or refactorings.
- **Integration with IDEs**: How seamlessly the tool fits into existing developer workflows.

These criteria reflect the practical usability and intelligence of each tool.

6.3 Comparative Overview of Leading Platforms

The "Figure 3." shows a comparison of four well-known platforms that integrate AI into the debugging process.

Figure 3. Capability comparison of AI debugging tools

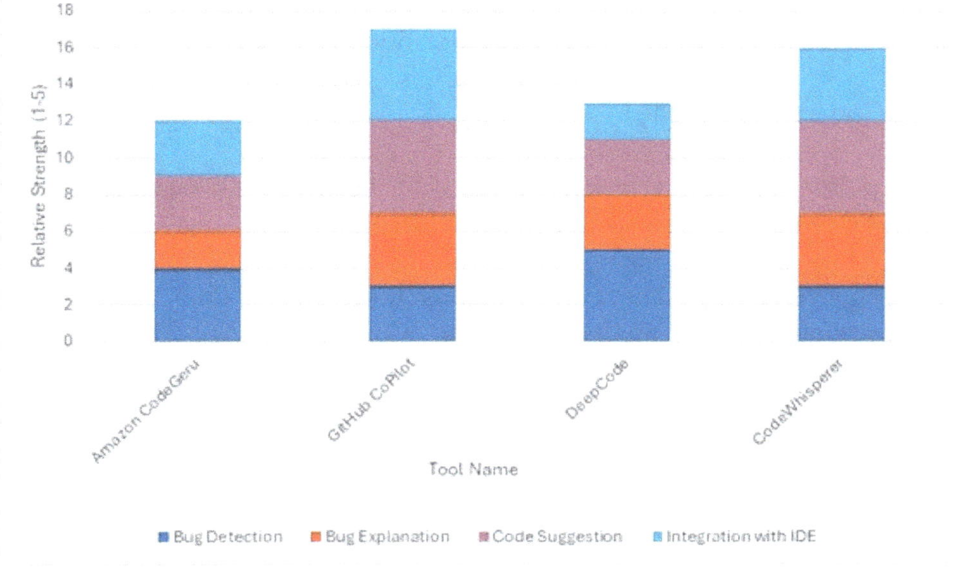

Amazon CodeGuru

Amazon CodeGuru leverages ML models trained on AWS's internal code repositories. It focuses primarily on:

- **Java and Python support**
- **Performance tuning suggestions**
- **Static security vulnerability checks**

While it provides high-precision bug detection, its feedback is often low on explanatory depth, and it lacks robust integration with multiple IDEs. It is better suited for enterprise CI/CD environments than ad hoc developer debugging.

GitHub Copilot

Powered by OpenAI's Codex, GitHub Copilot excels in:

- **Context-aware code completions**
- **Multi-language support**
- **IDE-native usage**

Copilot suggests real-time fixes and enhancements directly as developers write code. Its strength lies in code suggestion and IDE integration, making it ideal for individual productivity, though less focused on formal bug detection or explanation.

DeepCode (Snyk Code)

DeepCode, acquired by Snyk, combines symbolic AI and ML to analyze source code for potential vulnerabilities and inefficiencies.

- **Supports multiple languages including JavaScript, Python, and Java**
- **Excellent for static analysis**
- **Emphasizes clean code principles and best practices**

It offers high-fidelity bug detection but lacks the flexible generative capacity of LLM-based systems.

Amazon CodeWhisperer

Launched after Copilot, CodeWhisperer is Amazon's LLM-based coding assistant trained on large volumes of proprietary and public code.

- **Natural language prompting**
- **Security scanning integration**
- **Cloud-first toolchain support**

It provides quality suggestions and explanations but is relatively new and evolving in terms of extensibility.

6.4 Case Study 1: GitHub Copilot at Shopify

Shopify integrated GitHub Copilot into its developer environment to test productivity improvements across multiple teams. Over a 6-week observation period, developers using Copilot reported:

- **25% increase in velocity** for writing boilerplate code.
- **Improved onboarding** for junior developers who used Copilot for code guidance.
- **Fewer context switches**, as the tool kept them within the IDE during debugging.

Most notably, developers flagged fewer bugs during peer review in functions co-authored by Copilot, suggesting a possible improvement in early-phase code quality (Ziegler et al., 2023).

6.5 Case Study 2: Amazon CodeGuru in FinTech

A FinTech company processing over a million transactions per hour used CodeGuru to optimize their Java-based processing engine. Within two weeks:

- **Identified thread contention issues** that weren't caught in regression testing.
- **Suggested replacing HashMap with ConcurrentHashMap** in a high-concurrency payment class.
- **Spotted potential memory leaks** due to object caching in long-lived sessions.

The company integrated CodeGuru into their CI pipeline, configuring it to flag performance regressions on pull requests. The number of post-release defects dropped by **32% over the next three months**.

6.6 Case Study 3: DeepCode in Healthcare SaaS

A healthcare software company using Node.js and Python deployed DeepCode for compliance and bug tracking. They observed:

- **Rapid detection of deprecated library usage**
- **Alerts on unsafe use of eval() functions**
- **Style standardization across teams**

The tool's emphasis on best practices helped prepare for HIPAA audits and reduced manual code review workload by an estimated **40%**.

6.7 Key Integration Strategies

For maximum impact, organizations must ensure smooth integration of debugging platforms into development workflows. Best practices include:

- **IDE Plugins**: Tools like Copilot and CodeWhisperer provide immediate in-line suggestions, encouraging adoption.
- **CI/CD Gatekeeping**: Integrating tools like CodeGuru or DeepCode into build pipelines allows for automatic blocking of buggy commits.

- **Feedback Loops**: Gathering developer responses to suggestions can help tune model outputs and identify areas for improvement.

Many companies also use hybrid deployment models, with cloud-based LLMs for scale and on-premise ML for sensitive environments.

6.8 Open Source Contributions and Experimental Tools

Beyond commercial offerings, several open-source or experimental tools illustrate the academic cutting edge of AI debugging:

BugLab (Meta AI)

BugLab trains deep neural models on intentionally "corrupted" code to learn bug detection through contrastive learning. It uses reinforcement learning to improve generalization and is currently used in experimental security scanners.

DeepBugs

DeepBugs applies neural embeddings to learn patterns of correct and buggy identifier usage. It detects bugs like swapped arguments or incorrect operators in JavaScript codebases.

Glean (Google)

While not directly a debugging tool, Glean is a code indexing system that allows ML models to analyze massive multi-language codebases. It serves as a backend for several internal bug prediction engines.

These tools demonstrate how open-source and academic initiatives are pushing the boundaries of hybrid and explainable debugging systems.

6.9 Metrics for Evaluating Effectiveness

When selecting or benchmarking tools, several metrics are used to evaluate their debugging impact:

- **True Positive Rate (Recall)**: How many real bugs the system catches.
- **False Positive Rate**: How often the tool raises alerts for non-issues.
- **Fix Rate**: Percentage of suggestions that are accepted and deployed.
- **Latency**: Time required to analyze and return feedback.

- **Developer Adoption**: How frequently developers act on tool suggestions.

A study by Microsoft (Ziegler et al., 2023) showed that models with higher recall but moderate precision were preferred when combined with human-in-the-loop review systems.

6.10 Ethical and Legal Considerations

The widespread use of AI-generated code and bug-fixing suggestions introduces several risks:

- **Attribution**: LLM-generated code may inadvertently reproduce copyrighted code snippets.
- **Security Risks**: Overreliance on code suggestions without validation can introduce subtle security flaws.
- **Data Privacy**: Enterprise use of cloud-hosted models may pose confidentiality risks if proprietary code is sent for analysis.

Vendors are beginning to address these issues with transparency dashboards, opt-out mechanisms, and local/private model deployment options.

6.11 Future of Tools and Platforms

As AI debugging tools evolve, several trends are anticipated:

- **Unified Developer Agents**: Combining code search, generation, review, and debugging in a single assistant.
- **Explainable Debugging Interfaces**: Interactive tools that visualize the reasoning behind bug detection and suggestions.
- **Domain-Specific Fine-Tuning**: Tailored models for industries like medical devices, aerospace, or fintech.
- **Continuous Learning from Feedback**: Reinforcement learning pipelines that evolve based on developer interactions.

These advancements will move tools from passive assistants to active development collaborators, capable of real-time code monitoring, suggestion refinement, and even autonomous testing.

6.12 Conclusion

The practical deployment of AI-based debugging tools is transforming the way software is written, reviewed, and maintained. Whether through cloud-integrated assistants like Copilot, enterprise ML engines like CodeGuru, or hybrid systems under academic development, the fusion of automation and intelligence is enabling scalable, precise, and context-aware debugging.

As tools mature and trust mechanisms improve, developers are poised to benefit from debugging workflows that are no longer purely reactive but are instead predictive, explanatory, and embedded deeply into the software lifecycle. The next generation of debugging platforms will not only detect what's wrong but also explain why—and how to fix it.

7: ETHICAL, TECHNICAL, AND PRACTICAL CHALLENGES

7.1 Introduction

While the integration of machine learning (ML) and large language models (LLMs) into software debugging pipelines has significantly increased automation and efficiency, these advancements also raise pressing concerns across ethical, technical, and practical dimensions. From data bias and explainability issues to intellectual property conflicts and developer over-reliance, AI-powered debugging systems are not without limitations.

As adoption spreads across industries—from finance and healthcare to automotive and e-commerce—it is essential to examine the risks and trade-offs associated with these tools. Moreover, these concerns take on heightened importance in regulated environments, where any tool that modifies source code can affect compliance, traceability, and auditability. Therefore, addressing these limitations is not just a matter of technical enhancement, but also of operational and legal responsibility.

This chapter outlines the primary challenges in deploying and using AI-driven debugging systems, supported by empirical observations, industry examples, and best practices. It further explores how these challenges influence trust, adoption, and performance at scale, while also offering governance strategies and design principles to ensure responsible AI usage.

7.2 Explainability and Trust in AI Debugging

7.2.1 The Black Box Problem

AI models—especially LLMs—often function as opaque systems whose decision-making processes are difficult to interpret. While they may flag a function as buggy or suggest a fix, developers are left wondering *why* a specific issue was flagged and *how* the recommendation was derived.

This lack of transparency hinders trust, particularly in safety-critical systems such as avionics or medical software, where explainability is often mandated by regulation (Doshi-Velez & Kim, 2017).

7.2.2 The Need for Explainable AI (XAI)

Emerging research in Explainable AI aims to address this gap. Approaches include:

- **Saliency Maps for code**: Highlighting tokens or lines that influenced a prediction.
- **Natural Language Rationales**: Textual explanations generated alongside code suggestions.
- **Interactive Debugging Logs**: Showing model confidence scores and alternative paths.

Yet, these methods are still in early development, and most commercial tools do not expose such diagnostics to users. A key bottleneck lies in balancing model accuracy with interpretability—complex models like transformers offer high predictive power but lack transparency, whereas simpler models provide explainability at the cost of effectiveness. Until industry standards emerge around minimum transparency thresholds, developers must decide how much opacity is acceptable in debugging pipelines, especially when making production-level changes.

Yet, these methods are still in early development, and most commercial tools do not expose such diagnostics to users.

7.3 Data Privacy and Intellectual Property Concerns

7.3.1 Privacy of Training Data

LLMs are typically trained on large, publicly available datasets such as GitHub repositories. However, questions remain about the inclusion of private or sensitive data in these training sets, either inadvertently or through lax curation practices.

Organizations are rightly cautious about sending proprietary code to external APIs or models hosted on cloud platforms. To mitigate this, several vendors now offer:

- **On-premise deployments**
- **Private model fine-tuning**
- **Obfuscation layers prior to cloud submission**

7.3.2 Code Reproduction and Copyright Risk

LLMs may reproduce exact code snippets from their training datasets, leading to copyright or licensing conflicts. A notable concern is the unintentional generation of GPL-licensed code in commercial applications, potentially triggering legal disputes (Sandoval, 2023).

Enterprises are beginning to implement output filters and audit tools to flag high-confidence code reproductions before integration.

7.4 Technical Challenges

7.4.1 Hallucination and Incorrect Suggestions

LLMs sometimes generate code that is syntactically valid but logically flawed—a phenomenon known as hallucination. This can mislead developers, especially junior engineers who may lack the experience to validate suggestions.

Common hallucination patterns include:

- Suggesting non-existent APIs
- Misapplying language idioms
- Introducing off-by-one errors or memory leaks

Best practices recommend maintaining human-in-the-loop review processes and validating all AI-generated fixes through rigorous testing.

7.4.2 Generalization Limitations

Models trained on specific codebases or languages may not generalize well to others. For instance, a model tuned for Python may perform poorly on functional programming paradigms like Haskell or Scala.

Moreover, domain-specific logic—such as financial risk models or embedded hardware protocols—often requires specialized training datasets, which are not publicly available or easy to acquire.

7.4.3 Tool Fragmentation and Overhead

The explosion of AI tools has created fragmentation in development ecosystems. Developers must learn and toggle between plugins, CLIs, dashboards, and APIs—each with its own quirks and constraints.

This leads to:

- **Cognitive overload**
- **Workflow disruption**
- **Duplicate suggestions or conflicting analysis**

Organizations should strive for unified AI development environments where tools are composable and interoperable.

7.5 Practical Adoption Barriers

7.5.1 Developer Resistance

Some engineers view AI debugging tools as intrusive or even threatening. Fears range from job displacement to mistrust of "auto-corrected" logic. Developers may also worry about "de-skilling," where prolonged reliance on AI reduces their critical debugging and problem-solving capabilities over time. This psychological barrier can stall tool adoption, even when technical performance is strong.

Effective onboarding and transparency are key to overcoming such resistance. Organizations should offer hands-on training, explain model limitations upfront, and involve developers in the model selection and evaluation process. Gamification strategies—such as rewarding validated AI-generated fixes or showcasing team leaderboard contributions—can also improve engagement and trust.

7.5.2 ROI and Productivity Metrics

Organizations struggle to measure the return on investment (ROI) from AI debugging tools. Metrics like code coverage, bug fix latency, and developer satisfaction are helpful but often subjective or hard to isolate.

Adoption is more successful when organizations:

- Set measurable goals (e.g., 20% fewer post-release defects)
- Track developer usage patterns
- Incorporate feedback loops into tool selection

7.5.3 Continuous Maintenance

AI models degrade over time if not retrained with recent data. As libraries and language standards evolve, old model predictions may become outdated. Continuous monitoring, re-training pipelines, and feedback ingestion are necessary for long-term viability.

7.6 Responsible Use: Guidelines and Governance

Responsible AI use in debugging requires clear guidelines:

1. **Transparency**: Disclose when suggestions are AI-generated.
2. **Attribution**: Flag reused code patterns and ensure licensing compliance.
3. **Auditing**: Maintain logs of AI interventions and decision trails.
4. **Consent**: Respect user opt-outs and organizational privacy policies.

Leading institutions, including IEEE and ISO, are drafting standards for AI-assisted development processes, which will become increasingly relevant.

7.7 Comparative Feature Summary

To help organizations make informed decisions, the table below summarizes the feature sets of key AI-powered debugging platforms:

Table 1. Feature summary of leading AI debugging platforms

Platform	ML-Based Detection	LLM-Based Generation	Bug Explanation Support	IDE Integration Level	CI/CD Integration Level	Security Alerting	Languages Supported
Amazon CodeGuru			Partial	Moderate	High	Yes	Java, Python
GitHub Copilot			Full	High	Low	Limited	20+ Languages
DeepCode			Partial	Low	Moderate	Yes	Python, JS, Java
Amazon CodeWhisperer			Full	High	Moderate	Yes	Python, Java, JS

7.8 Toward Ethical and Sustainable Debugging Automation

Future systems must integrate ethics by design. This includes:

- **Bias mitigation in training corpora**
- **Usage disclaimers for generated code**
- **Feedback-based self-correction mechanisms**
- **Developer education on AI interpretability**

Tools like GitHub Copilot are beginning to include "source attribution" previews and "filter sensitive patterns" toggles. These enhancements point toward more responsible and sustainable toolchains.

7.9 Conclusion

AI-powered debugging tools promise to elevate software quality, reduce developer burden, and increase productivity—but not without cost. As these technologies become more embedded in the software lifecycle, organizations must confront challenges around trust, governance, bias, and ethics.

By implementing best practices, evaluating trade-offs, and selecting tools based on context and capability, development teams can leverage the power of ML and LLMs without sacrificing transparency, privacy, or control. The journey toward responsible, intelligent debugging is not only about tools—it's about values, systems thinking, and informed adoption.

REFERENCES

Allamanis, M., Barr, E. T., Devanbu, P., & Sutton, C. (2021). A survey of machine learning for big code and naturalness. *ACM Computing Surveys*, *51*(4), 1–37. DOI: 10.1145/3212695

Alon, U., Zilberstein, M., Levy, O., & Yahav, E. (2019). Code2vec: Learning distributed representations of code. *Proceedings of the ACM on Programming Languages*, *3*(POPL), 40. DOI: 10.1145/3290353

Amor, J. J., González-Barahona, J. M., & Robles, G. (2006). Measuring Woody: The size of Debian 3.0. *Proceedings of the 8th International Workshop on Principles of Software Evolution*, 85–89. DOI: 10.1145/1137983.1138001

Bird, C., Nagappan, N., Murphy, B., Gall, H., & Devanbu, P. (2009). Does distributed development affect software quality? An empirical case study of Windows Vista. *Communications of the ACM*, *52*(8), 85–93. DOI: 10.1145/1536616.1536639

Bowes, D., Hall, T., & Gray, D. (2018). Comparing the performance of fault prediction models. *Empirical Software Engineering*, *23*, 3503–3542. DOI: 10.1007/s10664-018-9614-y

Chen, M., Tworek, J., Jun, H., Yuan, Q., de Oliveira Pinto, H. P., Kaplan, J., . . . Zaremba, W. (2021). Evaluating large language models trained on code. *arXiv preprint arXiv:2107.03374*. /arXiv.2107.03374DOI: 10.48550

Doshi-Velez, F., & Kim, B. (2017). Towards a rigorous science of interpretable machine learning. *arXiv preprint arXiv:1702.08608*. /arXiv.1702.08608DOI: 10.48550

Feng, Z., Guo, D., Tang, D., Duan, N., Feng, X., Gong, M., . . . Zhou, M. (2020). CodeBERT: A pre-trained model for programming and natural languages. *arXiv preprint arXiv:2002.08155*. /arXiv.2002.08155DOI: 10.18653/v1/2020.findings-emnlp.139

Fontana, F. A., Braione, P., & Zanoni, M. (2016). Automatic detection of bad smells in code: An experimental assessment. *Journal of Object Technology*, *15*(1), 1–38. DOI: 10.5381/jot.2016.15.1.a2

Glass, R. L. (2002). *Facts and Fallacies of Software Engineering*. Addison-Wesley.

He, H., & Garcia, E. A. (2009). Learning from imbalanced data. *IEEE Transactions on Knowledge and Data Engineering*, *21*(9), 1263–1284. DOI: 10.1109/TKDE.2008.239

Khoshgoftaar, T. M., Allen, E. B., Hudepohl, J. P., & Aud, S. J. (1996). Application of neural networks to software quality modeling of a very large telecommunications system. *IEEE Transactions on Neural Networks*, *8*(4), 902–909. DOI: 10.1109/72.595888 PMID: 18255693

LaToza, T. D., & Myers, B. A. (2010). Developers ask reachability questions. *Proceedings of the 32nd ACM/IEEE International Conference on Software Engineering*, 185–194. DOI: 10.1145/1806799.1806829

Lessmann, S., Baesens, B., Mues, C., & Pietsch, S. (2008). Benchmarking classification models for software defect prediction: A proposed framework and novel findings. *IEEE Transactions on Software Engineering*, *34*(4), 485–496. DOI: 10.1109/TSE.2008.35

Li, Y., He, Z., & Wang, Y. (2021). Anomaly detection in code using autoencoders. *Journal of Systems and Software*, *181*, 111039. DOI: 10.1016/j.jss.2021.111039

McCabe, T. J. (1976). A complexity measure. *IEEE Transactions on Software Engineering*, *SE-2*(4), 308–320. DOI: 10.1109/TSE.1976.233837

McConnell, S. (2004). *Code Complete: A Practical Handbook of Software Construction* (2nd ed.). Microsoft Press.

Nagappan, N., & Ball, T. (2005). Use of relative code churn measures to predict system defect density. *Proceedings of the 27th International Conference on Software Engineering*, 284–292. DOI: 10.1145/1062455.1062514

Peterson, L. (2000). The world's first computer bug. *IEEE Annals of the History of Computing*, *22*(4), 73–75. DOI: 10.1109/85.888103

Pradel, M., & Sen, K. (2018). DeepBugs: A learning approach to name-based bug detection. *Proceedings of the ACM on Programming Languages, 2*(OOPSLA), 147. DOI: 10.1145/3276517

Sandoval, R. (2023). Copyleft in the age of AI: Legal implications of LLM-generated code. *Journal of Intellectual Property Law & Practice*, *18*(2), 145–157. DOI: 10.1093/jiplp/jpac079

Wang, S., Liu, T., Tan, L., & Yu, Y. (2018). Automatically learning semantic features for defect prediction. *Proceedings of the 40th International Conference on Software Engineering*, 310–320. DOI: 10.1145/3180155.3180214

White, M., Tufano, M., Vendome, C., & Poshyvanyk, D. (2016). Deep learning code fragments for code clone detection. *Proceedings of the 31st IEEE/ACM International Conference on Automated Software Engineering*, 87–98. DOI: 10.1145/2970276.2970326

Ziegler, D., Zhang, J., Kashefi, A., & Singh, R. (2023). Measuring developer productivity with Copilot: A field study. *Microsoft Research*. /arXiv.2301.01369DOI: 10.48550

Zimmermann, T., Premraj, R., & Zeller, A. (2007). Predicting defects for eclipse. *Proceedings of the Third International Workshop on Predictor Models in Software Engineering*, 9–15. DOI: 10.1109/PROMISE.2007.10

Chapter 11

The Role of AI in Emerging Business Models and Innovation

Satya Subrahmanyam
http://orcid.org/0000-0003-0441-2742
Holy Spirit University of Kaslik, Lebanon

Behrooz Gharleghi
http://orcid.org/0000-0001-7468-3615
GISMA University of Applied Sciences, Germany

Sandeep Poddar
http://orcid.org/0000-0001-9771-877X
Lincoln University College, Malaysia

ABSTRACT

This chapter, "The Role of AI in Emerging Business Models and Innovation," examines how artificial intelligence (AI) is fundamentally transforming business landscapes by enabling new, data-driven, and agile business models. Positioned within the broader context of the book "Harnessing AI and Predictive Analytics for Competitive Decision-Making," it explores how AI acts as a strategic driver of innovation, reshaping customer experiences, operational processes, and revenue strategies across sectors. The chapter categorizes AI-enabled innovations, integrates predictive analytics for foresight, and highlights real-world case studies. It also addresses challenges such as ethical concerns, organizational resistance, and governance needs. Concluding with future trends, it emphasizes the need for leaders to embed AI into their core strategies to foster sustainable competitive advantage.

DOI: 10.4018/979-8-3373-3648-0.ch011

1. INTRODUCTION

1.1 AI as a Catalyst for Business Model Innovation

Business model design has been profoundly affected by the emergence of AI. Value chains and consumer products have been relatively unchanged under traditional company structures. Artificial intelligence (AI) brings a new dynamic capacity that helps companies learn, adapt, and personalise their value offers all the time. According to Davenport and Ronanki (2018), corporates like Amazon and Netflix use AI algorithms to provide personalised products and content recommendations to users. This helps to increase consumer happiness and loyalty.

AI makes it easier to shift business models from selling products to offering services and relying on subscriptions. One sector where AI is already making a difference is the automobile business, where customers may now rent cars as needed instead of buying them outright. This model is called Mobility-as-a-Service (MaaS). This change is in line with changing customer tastes and is sustainable from an economic and environmental perspective (Subrahmanyam, 2025). For quick innovation cycles and incremental product and service upgrades, AI also allows for the incorporation of real-time consumer input.

1.2 Enhancing Operational Efficiency and Agility

One of the pillars of innovation in new company models is operational efficiency, and AI helps boost that. Robotic process automation, natural language processing, and machine learning may streamline internal processes, eliminate human error, and improve resource utilisation. To decrease maintenance expenses and downtime, AI-driven predictive maintenance systems in manufacturing employ data gathered from equipment sensors to foretell when parts would break (Wamba-Taguimdje et al., 2020).

Provided by AI-powered supply chain analytics, companies can act in advance in terms of disruptions, demand fluctuation, and logistical issues. During retail, AI tools can be deployed to analyze purchasing trends and level of inventory at any given time and thus improving the accuracy of forecasting of demands and improving the stock tried and tested methods. Quick decisions sourced from real time data will enhance the agility of any organization tremendously, one of the most critical traits in volatile markets of today.

1.3 Driving Customer-Centric Innovation

AI as well plays an important part in redefining the engagement and experience of the customer. The capability of AI systems to analyse and understand massive amounts of the customer's data enables businesses to understand consumers better on a deeper level. This understanding is the foundation of personalized marketing, customized offerings, and responsive customer services solutions. Chatbots and virtual assistants for instance present 24/7 services and on-the-spot query solutions to enhance the satisfaction of customers and minimize the costs of service (Rust & Huang, 2021).

AI helps the product and service innovation by supporting co-production with the customers. Corporates can leverage AI tools and review the feedback coming in forms of social media postings, reviews and surveys to understand emerging trends and unmet needs. Such a customer-centric strategy not only creates innovation but also builds customer relationships and brand loyalty. The recurrent feedback process between businesses and consumers through the help of AI guarantees the relevance and effectiveness of innovations.

1.4 New Frontiers: AI-Enabled Ecosystems and Platforms

Platform-based and ecosystem-driven business models can benefit from AI. Google, Alibaba, and Uber are digital platforms that link producers and consumers in value networks. These platforms leverage AI for search algorithms, dynamic pricing, fraud detection, and user behavior prediction (Iansiti & Lakhani, 2020). Data interchange and collaborative innovation in AI-enabled ecosystems provide scalability, network effects, and value.

Startups and established companies are using AI to build specialist platforms for healthcare diagnostics, financial planning, and customized learning. Third-party developers and contributors may expand on key AI capabilities on these platforms, democratizing service access and decentralizing innovation. The move from linear value chains to AI-powered ecosystems transforms company operations and value creation.

AI can revolutionize business paradigms and set organizations apart. It boosts operational efficiency, customer-centric innovation, and ecosystem-based approaches. To thrive in the digital economy, businesses must include AI into their strategies.

This chapter underscores the necessity for organizations to reimagine their value creation processes and organizational structures in light of AI's capabilities. By doing so, they can harness AI not only to optimize existing models but also to pioneer new pathways of innovation and societal impact.

2. CONCEPTUALIZING ARTIFICIAL INTELLIGENCE IN BUSINESS CONTEXTS

In the digital age, Artificial Intelligence (AI) has evolved from a theoretical concept into a practical tool that is fundamentally transforming the business environment. As organizations strive to adapt to increasingly dynamic markets, AI serves as a key enabler of innovation, efficiency, and strategic differentiation. Understanding AI within the business context requires a comprehensive exploration of its definition, technological components, and its distinctions from traditional automation, as well as its role as a strategic asset for value creation.

2.1 Defining Artificial Intelligence and Its Core Components

The term "artificial intelligence" (AI) refers to the practice of programming computers to mimic human intellect in certain tasks. Rousseau and Norvig (2021) include learning, thinking, problem-solving, perceiving, and language understanding among the activities. In general, AI may be divided into two parts. AI may be either narrow, designed for specialised tasks like image recognition or language translation, or broad, with the latter's current focus on theory, an effort to mimic human cognition across a wide range of activities.

Machine learning (ML), computer vision (CV), natural language processing (NLP), and robotics are some of the fundamental AI components that bring the artefact into practical use in business. Machine learning is the backbone of artificial intelligence applications. Training algorithms to draw conclusions and generate predictions from data is the essence of machine learning. Machine learning methods, whether supervised, unsupervised, or reinforcement learning, enable systems to automatically improve their performance (Subrahmanyam, 2025).

Natural Language Processing allows machines to comprehend, get stuff out of, and come up with human language. It fuels chatbots, voice assistants, sentiment analysis tools; indispensable in customer service, marketing and social media monitoring (Cambria& White, 2014). Computer vision enables the interpretation of visual world information by machines enabling use case like facial recognition, quality checks in manufacturing and medical imagery. Robotics, usually combined with AI, allows automating physical work and particularly in such spheres as logistics, healthcare, and agriculture.

2.2 Traditional Automation vs. AI-Driven Intelligence

While both traditional automation and AI aim to increase efficiency and reduce human workload, they differ significantly in capability and function. Traditional automation relies on predefined rules and structured environments; it executes tasks in a linear, predictable manner. Robotic arms on assembly lines follow specific instructions to perform repetitive tasks. These systems are inflexible and unable to adapt to changing inputs or environments without manual reprogramming.

AI-driven systems are designed to learn and adapt. They are capable of processing unstructured data, identifying patterns, and making decisions under uncertainty. This cognitive flexibility allows AI to handle more complex and variable tasks, such as predicting consumer behavior, detecting fraud, or personalizing content. Unlike traditional automation, which enhances efficiency through rigid processes, AI enhances both efficiency and effectiveness through intelligent adaptability and decision-making (Subrahmanyam, 2024).

Table 1. Traditional automation vs. AI-driven

Aspect	Traditional Automation	AI-Driven Intelligence
Core Principle	Operates on predefined rules and structured environments.	Learn from data and adapt to changing environments.
Nature of Tasks	Executes linear, repetitive, and predictable tasks.	Handles complex, dynamic, and uncertain tasks.
Flexibility	Inflexible; requires manual reprogramming to adapt to new conditions.	Highly flexible; adapts automatically through learning algorithms.
Data Type	Works with structured data only.	Processes both structured and unstructured data (e.g., text, images, speech).
Decision-Making Ability	Follows fixed instructions; no independent decision-making.	Capable of autonomous decision-making based on data patterns and context.
Examples	Robotic arms on assembly lines performing repetitive tasks.	Fraud detection systems, predictive analytics, recommendation engines.
Improvement Over Time	Static performance: improvement requires human intervention.	Continuously improves through feedback loops and machine learning.
Primary Benefit	Enhances efficiency through speed and consistency.	Enhances both efficiency and effectiveness through intelligent adaptability.
Adaptability to Change	Low; performance drops in dynamic environments.	High; performs well in evolving and uncertain contexts.
Illustrative Example	Automated manufacturing lines performing set tasks.	Netflix or Amazon recommendation systems refining user suggestions over time.
Overall Outcome	Efficiency through rigid process automation.	Efficiency and effectiveness through intelligent, adaptive processes.

AI-driven solutions can continuously improve and improve. For example, recommendation engines used by companies like Netflix and Amazon refine their suggestions based on user interactions over time. This continuous feedback loop is a hallmark of AI systems and underscores their superiority over static automation in dynamic business environments.

2.3 AI as a Strategic Asset for Value Creation

More firms are understanding that AI can enhance operations and create profit. First, AI's predictive and prescriptive analytics enhance judgment. AI can analyze massive data sets to aid market entrance, product development, client targeting, and supply chain optimization (Davenport & Ronanki, 2018).

AI allows mass customization. Customizing offerings and interactions to customer preferences boosts brand loyalty and user experience. Customer engagement is enhanced by Spotify's AI-driven playlists and recommendations based on listening history and mood. AI advances goods, services, and business models. AI improves and accelerates medical diagnostics. Robo-advisors provide cheaper, tailored investing advice using AI. Innovations may enhance social results and provide new economic opportunities.

AI increases organizational agility in strategic management. AI helps organizations predict customer needs, respond quicker to market developments, and allocate resources. AI can identify inefficiencies, predict demand, and simulate scenarios, enabling proactive planning and execution and long-term competitiveness (Iansiti & Lakhani, 2020). AI can sustain competitive advantages. When firms acquire private data and build AI models, competitors struggle. Google leads search and advertising owing to its superior AI algorithms and massive data holdings, which new competitors struggle to match.

As a basic competency, AI is transforming into how organisations operate, compete, and develop. Organisations can maximise AI's potential by mastering machine learning, NLP, and computer vision. The difference between classical automation and AI-driven intelligence emphasises digital economy flexibility and learning. As a strategic asset, AI boosts operational efficiency, customer-centric innovation, new business models, and decision-making. Businesses must carefully and strategically use AI to succeed in a complicated and competitive environment.

3. EMERGING BUSINESS MODELS IN THE AGE OF AI

Artificial Intelligence (AI) is not only reshaping technologies but also fundamentally redefining the architecture of business models across industries. As businesses integrate AI into their core operations, new paradigms for value creation, delivery, and capture are emerging. This shift is disrupting traditional value chains, encouraging firms to transition from product-centric approaches to data-driven, service-oriented ecosystems. The proliferation of platform-based models, subscription services, and decentralized systems driven by AI exemplifies the transformation underway in the global economic landscape.

3.1 Redefining Value Chains and Ecosystems

Traditionally, value chains have been linear processes where goods and services move from production to consumption through a series of predictable steps. AI has introduced a dynamic, non-linear dimension to value creation by embedding intelligence into every node of the chain, from raw material sourcing and manufacturing to customer experience and post-sales service. This has enabled the transition from rigid pipelines to flexible, responsive value ecosystems (Iansiti & Lakhani, 2020).

With the help of AI, companies can stay up-to-date with the latest market trends, customer actions, and supply chain interruptions in near real-time. Optimising inventory management and minimising stockouts or overstock situations are both made possible by predictive analytics in the retail industry. According to Chui et al. (2018), predictive maintenance powered by artificial intelligence may assist manufacturers reduce operational inefficiencies and downtime by predicting when equipment will break. The use of chatbots and sentiment analysis tools in customer care, which are powered by AI, guarantees smooth and customised client experience, often without the need for human involvement.

Corporates are increasingly co-creating value with external stakeholders - such as customers, developers, and even competitors - through open innovation platforms and data-sharing partnerships. This interconnectivity fosters digital ecosystems where multiple actors contribute to, and benefit from, shared intelligence and resources.

3.2 From Product-Centric to Data-Centric and Service-Oriented Models

The infusion of AI has catalyzed a significant evolution from product-centric business models to data-centric and service-oriented frameworks. In traditional models, value was derived primarily from the sale of physical goods. Today, however, companies are leveraging AI to monetize data and deliver value through continuous, service-based engagements.

The data economy has elevated data to the status of most valuable asset. Improved client experience, more efficient operations, and hyper-personalized offers are the results of organisations' data collection, analysis, and deployment efforts. By using AI to interpret this data, businesses are able to make better decisions in real-time and implement strategies that can adapt to changing market circumstances and customer tastes.

Service-oriented models such as "Everything-as-a-Service" (XaaS) are gaining prominence. Rather than selling ownership of a product, companies now offer outcomes and experiences. Rolls-Royce's "Power by the Hour" model charges clients for engine performance rather than the engine itself, relying on AI to monitor and predict engine health (Porter & Heppelmann, 2017). This approach not only improves customer satisfaction but also establishes long-term relationships that generate recurring revenues.

Figure 1. Emerging business models and innovation

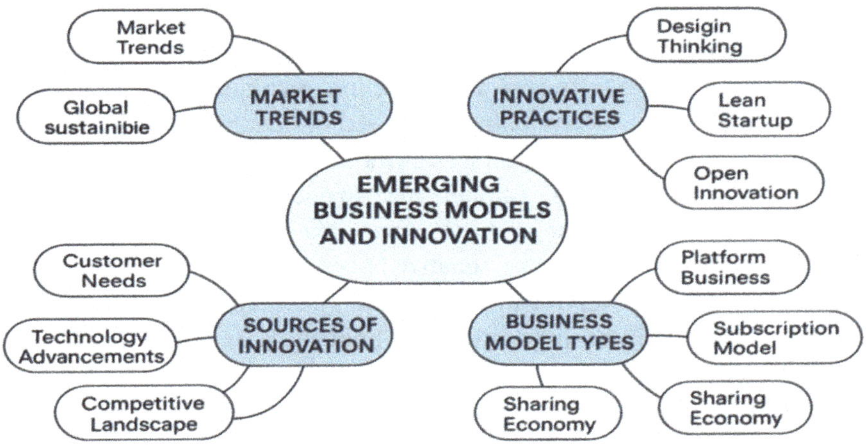

3.3 Case Studies of AI-Enabled Business Models

Platform-Based Models: Uber and Airbnb

Platform-based business models are among the most transformative examples of AI-driven innovation. Corporates like Uber and Airbnb have disrupted traditional industries by creating digital platforms that connect supply and demand without owning the underlying physical assets. AI plays a central role in optimizing the efficiency and scalability of these platforms.

Uber, for instance, uses AI to match riders with drivers, predict demand surges, and optimize routes. Its algorithms analyze data such as traffic patterns, historical ride information, and user behavior to minimize wait times and improve customer satisfaction. Airbnb employs AI to personalize search results, recommend listings, and detect fraudulent activity, thereby enhancing both user experience and trust within its ecosystem (Parker et al., 2016).

These platform models exemplify how AI allows businesses to act as intermediaries that orchestrate vast networks of users, unlocking new forms of value and scalability without proportional increases in cost.

Subscription and Personalization-Driven Models: Netflix and Spotify

Subscription-based models that rely heavily on personalization have gained traction in the AI age, especially in the media and entertainment sectors. Netflix and Spotify are prominent examples of companies that have successfully used AI to deliver tailored experiences, fostering deep user engagement and loyalty.

Netflix uses AI and ML to personalise content recommendations according to user tastes, search habits, and watching habits. According to Gomez-Uribe and Hunt (2016), more than 80% of the material seen on the site is driven by its recommendation engine. Netflix reduces the risk of content investment by improving user experience and informing users of content production plans via continuous data analysis.

Spotify employs AI to curate personalized playlists such as "Discover Weekly," which adapts to a user's evolving musical tastes. These AI-powered features differentiate the service, promote higher user retention, and provide artists with insights into listener preferences.

These models highlight the centrality of data and AI in delivering continuous value and fostering sustainable competitive advantage in subscription ecosystems.

AI-Enabled B2B Marketplaces and Decentralized Autonomous Organizations (DAOs)

Beyond B2C models, AI is also transforming B2B commerce through intelligent marketplaces and the rise of decentralized organizational structures. AI-enabled B2B marketplaces, such as Alibaba and ThomasNet, use AI to match buyers and suppliers, assess creditworthiness, and predict demand trends, thereby improving efficiency, transparency, and trust in transactions (Bughin et al., 2017).

Decentralized Autonomous Organizations (DAOs) represent a more radical transformation enabled by AI and blockchain technologies. DAOs operate without centralized leadership, instead relying on smart contracts and AI algorithms to govern operations, allocate resources, and make decisions. While still nascent, DAOs present an alternative model for organizing work and capital allocation, with potential implications for venture capital, governance, and collaborative innovation (Hassan & De Filippi, 2021).

These emerging models demonstrate how AI can decentralize power, democratize access to resources, and enable new forms of digital collaboration and entrepreneurship.

AI and business strategy are redefining value generation and delivery. From redesigned value chains and ecosystems to platform-based, subscription, and decentralised models, AI allows agile, personalised, and interconnected methods. As AI grows, companies that adopt data-centric, customer-focused, and ecosystem-driven business models will prosper in the future economy.

4. AI AS A CATALYST FOR INNOVATION

The potential of AI to improve business processes and spark new ideas is being recognised more and more. To thrive in today's lightning-fast digital economy, businesses must constantly innovate. AI enhances innovation via its capacity to analyse large amounts of data, identify patterns, and provide suggestions for new goods, services, and business models. Research and development are accelerated, and experimentation and originality are encouraged. In this part, we'll look at how AI alters research and development, boosts market reaction, and encourages design thinking.

4.1 Types of Innovation Enabled by AI

Process Innovation refers to the introduction of new, or substantially improved, processes for production or delivery. AI has a pivotal role in process innovation through optimizing operation through intelligent automation, predictive analytics and real time monitoring. In manufacturing, predictive maintenance applications driven by artificial intelligence identify the likelihood of equipment failure before they happen and therefore reduce downtime and enhance productivity (Bughin et al., 2018). In logistics, AI increases route optimization and demand forecasting helping to reduce costs and enhance service delivery (Chui et al., 2018).

Robotic process automation (RPA), if combined with AI tools such as natural language processing (NLP) and machine learning (ML), can automate complicated, non-routine tasks of document classification, sentiment analysis and anomaly detection in financial transactions. Such an automation of cognitive processes not just increases the efficiency rate, but it also liberates human resources to concentrate on more valuable things allowing the organizations to keep innovating in their internal working.

Product and Service Through the creation of intelligent, adaptable offers, AI also initiates the design of products and services. To improve product functionality and provide more customer experience, companies are using AI. Virtual assistants powered by artificial intelligence (AI) in consumer devices, such as Apple's Siri and Amazon's Alexa, analyse user activity to provide personalised interactions over time (Davenport& Ronanki, 2018).

In the healthcare field, in diagnostics, AI helps create diagnostic instruments that process medical images and patient data to discover diseases with a high level of accuracy. AIs are used by financial institutions, in the form of AI-powered advisory services, or "robo-advisors," by which personalized investment strategies are provided relying on individual goals and risk profiles (Brynjolfsson & McAfee, 2017). Such examples represent the ways whereby AI improves not only products that already exist but also catalyzes the creation of new service categories.

Business Model Innovation - Business model innovation, or the rethinking of value creation, delivery, and capture, may be where AI has the most influence. With the help of AI, businesses may start selling experiences or outcomes rather than physical goods. Using artificial intelligence to track machines in real time and bill clients according to consumption or performance, General Electric and Rolls-Royce have embraced "as-a-service" models (Porter & Heppelmann, 2017).

AI facilitates the emergence of platform-based and ecosystem-centric models, where value is co-created with users and partners. AI allows platforms to manage large-scale interactions, match supply and demand efficiently, and scale rapidly while maintaining quality. This transformation enables firms to innovate not just in what they offer, but in how they operate and engage with stakeholders.

4.2 Role of AI in Enhancing R&D Efficiency

Always, research and development have taken up a lot of time. AI transforms research and development by boosting predictive modeling, automating experiments, and accelerating data processing. The pharmaceutical sector is increasingly using AI algorithms to anticipate clinical trial outcomes, identify drug candidates, and simulate molecular interactions (Subrahmanyam, 2025).

AI enables literature reviews and trend analysis, helping academics integrate massive scientific information and discover research gaps and cross-disciplinary innovation potential. Semantic Scholar and IBM Watson Discovery leverage NLP to quickly find insights in hundreds of documents.

Generational AI models like Generative Adversarial Networks (GANs) or big language models may generate new ideas, hypotheses, and product concepts, helping R&D teams think creatively. Our ability to explore unknown solution areas boosts our inventiveness.

Enabling Real-Time Market Experimentation and Feedback Loops - AI provides real-time market experimentation rather than retroactive market analysis.

A/B testing, multivariate testing, and adaptive learning systems let companies test methods, interfaces, and product features and get fast performance feedback. AI uses consumer behavior, social media sentiment, and engagement data to make strategic choices.

Amazon and Alibaba constantly evaluate price, user interface, and recommendation algorithms using AI. Customer interactions contribute back into AI systems, improving models and decision-making (Iansiti & Lakhani, 2020). This feedback loop aligns innovation with consumer demands and market trends, lowering product launch risk and allowing continual improvement. AI helps media and entertainment firms like Netflix test new content and interfaces on subgroups of customers. These insights improve content curation and viewership. Fintech businesses test new financial products and adjust them depending on consumer behavior using real-time data.

Supporting Design Thinking and Ideation Processes - Design thinking is a human-centered approach to innovation that emphasizes empathy, ideation, and iterative prototyping. AI enhances design thinking by supporting each phase of the process with data-driven insights and computational creativity. During the empathize phase, AI tools analyze customer feedback, behavior logs, and social media content to uncover latent needs and pain points. In the ideation phase, AI-assisted brainstorming tools such as ChatGPT or GPT-4 can suggest diverse perspectives, generate alternative solutions, or simulate user reactions to new ideas.

AI-driven visualization tools support rapid prototyping and testing. Tools like Adobe Sensei or Figma's AI features help designers iterate more quickly by generating layout suggestions or detecting design inconsistencies. AI also facilitates collaborative ideation by integrating inputs from various stakeholders and synthesizing them into coherent concept proposals.

Figure 2. AI as a catalyst for innovation

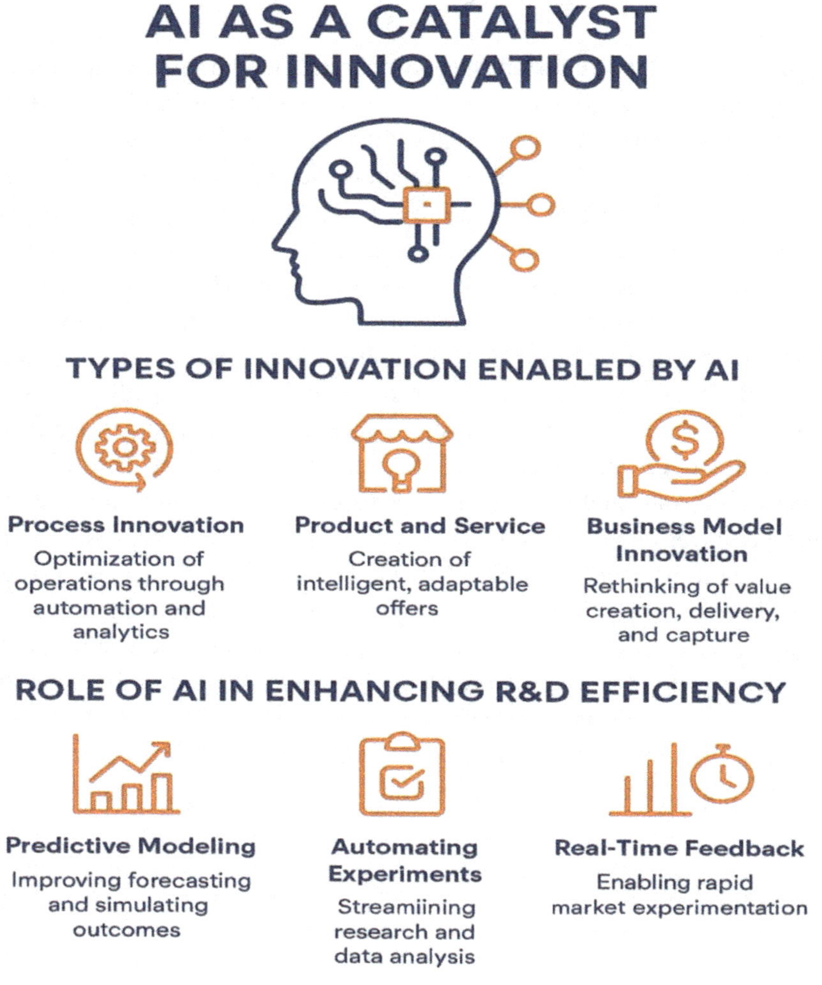

AI democratizes the innovation process by making advanced analytics and ideation tools accessible to non-technical users, thus fostering inclusive innovation cultures within organizations. Employees across functions can leverage AI to contribute ideas, test hypotheses, and participate in innovation initiatives without requiring deep technical expertise.

5. INDUSTRY CASE STUDIES AND SECTORAL TRANSFORMATIONS

Artificial intelligence (AI) is already transforming numerous industries. AI has changed innovation, customer experiences, and operational frameworks in healthcare, education, manufacturing, and retail. This section examines how AI is affecting key sectors by emphasizing practical usage and paradigm shifts. We demonstrate how AI can make business ecosystems smarter, quicker, and more responsive by analyzing real-world examples from diverse sectors.

5.1 Retail: AI-Driven Personalization and Inventory Optimization

AI has improved consumer experience via hyper-personalization and optimized backend procedures like inventory management in retail. AI helps retailers study customer behavior, estimate demand, and propose items based on preferences.

Amazon is a prime example. According to McKinsey & Company (2020), the company employs machine learning algorithms to analyze purchase habits, reviews, and browsing history to provide personalized recommendations that boost engagement and conversions. Customers who feel personalised at this level are more inclined to remain around in a crowded market.

Artificial intelligence optimizes inventories in real time. Walmart uses AI to track inventories, predict demand, and automate replenishment. These solutions decrease overstocking and stockouts, improving productivity and consumer satisfaction (Chui et al., 2018). Computer vision allows shelf-scanning robots to find lost or low-stock products. Thus, AI promotes front-end customisation and streamline logistics in retail, creating a completely integrated value chain.

5.2 Healthcare: Diagnostic Innovation and Patient-Centric Models

Diagnostics, therapeutic customisation, and operational efficiency are also being transformed by AI in healthcare. Medical picture analysis, EHR interpretation, and patient outcome prediction using AI are quicker and more accurate than conventional approaches.

IBM Watson Health created an AI system that can identify cancers and other irregularities in radiological pictures like expert physicians (Topol, 2019). Deep learning algorithms let Google's DeepMind diagnose over 50 eye disorders using OCT images (De Fauw et al., 2018).

AI-powered patient-centric care approaches have evolved. Chatbots and virtual health aides like Babylon Health provide 24/7 health monitoring and consulting in rural or underdeveloped areas. AI systems triage patients using NLP and symptom-checking algorithms, enhancing access and efficiency. AI helps hospitals estimate admission rates, optimize staff allocation, and maximize resource use during health emergencies like the COVID-19 epidemic.

5.3 Finance: Robo-Advisory Services and Fraud Detection

AI has profoundly disrupted the financial services sector through automation, risk management, and customer engagement tools. One of the most visible AI applications is the rise of robo-advisors, automated investment platforms that offer financial planning services based on algorithms.

Corporates like Betterment and Wealthfront use AI to assess clients' risk tolerance, investment goals, and market data to construct and manage diversified portfolios with minimal human intervention (Sahid et al., 2023). These services are especially attractive to younger investors and those seeking low-cost financial advice.

Cybersecurity and fraud detection also rely heavily on AI. To identify potential signs of fraud, financial institutions use machine learning algorithms to examine transaction patterns. By analysing past transactions in real-time, Mastercard can spot suspect activity and prevent it before it does any harm (Davenport & Ronanki, 2018).

In credit scoring, AI models consider a wide range of data beyond traditional credit histories, including utility payments and social signals, offering a more inclusive financial model for underserved populations.

5.4 Manufacturing: Predictive Maintenance and Intelligent Automation

Predictive maintenance and intelligent automation are two ways in which artificial intelligence (AI) is changing the industrial sector towards more connected, smart processes. Machine learning and IoT sensors provide predictive maintenance, which helps manufacturers to reduce unexpected downtime by predicting when equipment will break and scheduling repair accordingly. To monitor equipment health, detect damage, and schedule maintenance accordingly, Siemens employs artificial intelligence (AI) (Bughin et al., 2018). This approach not only keeps costly equipment running for longer but also reduces the frequency of interruptions to operations.

Intelligent automation, combining robotics and AI, enhances production quality and adaptability. AI-enabled robots perform complex, repetitive tasks with greater speed and accuracy than humans. Tesla's Gigafactories, for instance, employ robotic arms with AI capabilities to assemble electric vehicles, adjusting processes dynamically based on real-time sensor feedback.

Generative design, an AI-driven innovation, allows engineers to input design goals and constraints into software, which then explores a multitude of permutations to propose optimal solutions, greatly accelerating product development cycles.

5.5 Education and EdTech: Adaptive Learning Models and Virtual Tutoring

AI is used in education to engage students and customize teaching. AI-powered adaptive learning systems let students study at their own speed and with complete comprehension. Knewton and DreamBox Learning use real-time analytics to evaluate students and adapt learning paths. Individualised learning addresses gaps more effectively than conventional techniques (Luckin et al., 2016). AI provides predictive analytics for student outcomes and dropouts in higher education, allowing prompt intervention and assistance.

Carnegie Learning's AI-based math tutors simulate one-on-one teaching with quick feedback and individualized help. These techniques are useful in distant or resource-constrained learning situations. Georgia Tech's "Jill Watson," an AI teaching assistant, uses natural language processing to answer student questions in discussion forums like a person (Taneja et al., 2024). These assistants reduce teacher responsibilities and provide 24/7 academic help.

AI is transforming multiple industries by enabling operational excellence and strategic innovation. AI improves retail customer engagement and supply chain efficiency, healthcare diagnostics and patient interaction, finance advisory services and security, manufacturing equipment reliability and productivity, and education personalisation and teaching. The integration of AI into various industries shows its adaptability and strategic importance in developing flexible, data-driven, and customer-centric organisations. AI will redefine creativity, efficiency, and value creation as it matures, transforming sectors.

6. PREDICTIVE ANALYTICS IN BUSINESS MODEL INNOVATION

One of the most important tools for modern companies to use in their quest to innovate their business models is predictive analytics. Businesses can now proactively reshape their models, optimise operational decisions, and anticipate consumer trends with the help of artificial intelligence (AI) and predictive analytics. This is especially helpful for organisations that rely on data-driven strategies to navigate competitive markets. This section takes a look at how AI improves predictive skills, gives an example of a firm that used predictive insights to pivot effectively, and analyses the revolutionary role of predictive analytics in consumer behaviour predictions.

6.1 Role of Data Analytics in Forecasting Consumer Trends

Data analytics, and more specifically predictive analytics, seek to forecast future events by analysing patterns and trends in existing data using statistical algorithms and machine learning approaches (Angelov, 2024). Predictive analytics allows businesses to anticipate client demands, preferences, and purchase habits within the context of consumer behaviour. Corporates may better target certain demographics by segmenting their target audiences using data from purchases, social media engagement, website visits, and demographic characteristics.

Retail giants such as Target and Amazon use predictive analytics to suggest products to customers even before they actively search for them. Target once famously analyzed purchasing patterns to identify that a customer was pregnant based on changes in buying behavior, thereby enabling targeted marketing (Glinska, 2024). Netflix uses predictive models to recommend shows based on viewer history and preferences, significantly enhancing user engagement (Gomez-Uribe & Hunt, 2016).

Table 2. Role of data analytics in forecasting consumer trends

Aspect	Description	Examples / Applications	Impact on Business Model Innovation
Purpose of Predictive Analytics	Uses statistical algorithms and machine learning techniques to analyze historical data and forecast future events or behaviors.	Predicting consumer demand, anticipating purchase patterns, identifying emerging trends.	Enables proactive decision-making and supports dynamic business model adaptation.
Data Sources	Integrates data from multiple channels such as purchase histories, social media activity, web browsing, and demographics.	Customer transactions, engagement metrics, digital footprints.	Improves segmentation and personalization strategies, leading to enhanced customer engagement.
Application in Consumer Behavior	Helps businesses anticipate customer needs and preferences before they are explicitly expressed.	Target used purchasing patterns to detect pregnancy trends; Netflix recommends shows based on viewing history.	Enhances user experience, retention, and loyalty through tailored offerings.
Analytical Techniques	Utilizes regression analysis, clustering, decision trees, and time-series forecasting.	Applied to model consumer life cycles and predict churn.	Provides actionable insights for targeted marketing and strategic planning.

continued on following page

Table 2. Continued

Aspect	Description	Examples / Applications	Impact on Business Model Innovation
Key Corporate Examples	- **Target:** Identified pregnancy patterns to target marketing campaigns. - **Amazon:** Recommends products before customer searches. - **Netflix:** Personalizes content recommendations.	Retail and entertainment sectors adopting predictive analytics for personalization.	Demonstrates the value of predictive analytics in maintaining competitiveness and relevance.
Business Outcome	Forecasts trends, optimizes marketing, and drives innovation in product/service delivery.	Predictive insights translate into new offerings or refined business approaches.	Ensures long-term adaptability in fast-changing markets.

The ability to forecast consumer trends empowers businesses to stay ahead of shifting demands, personalize experiences, and identify new market opportunities, all essential for sustained competitiveness in volatile markets.

6.2 Integration of AI with Predictive Analytics for Proactive Strategy Development

The speed and depth of insights gained are both exponentially improved by combining AI with predictive analytics. Machine learning (ML), deep learning (DL), and natural language processing (NLP) are all examples of AI technologies that can handle large, unstructured information, identify complicated patterns, and improve predictions in real-time.

AI-driven predictive analytics goes beyond traditional forecasting by enabling dynamic, self-improving models that adapt to new information. This capability is especially valuable for proactive strategy development, as it helps businesses respond to emerging trends, potential risks, and untapped opportunities in near real-time (Davenport & Harris, 2017).

In supply chain management, AI-enhanced predictive analytics can anticipate disruptions based on geopolitical, environmental, or demand-side signals, allowing companies to adjust procurement and distribution strategies preemptively. In marketing, predictive models powered by AI identify potential churn before it occurs and recommend interventions tailored to individual customer profiles.

Table 3. Integration of AI with predictive analytics for proactive strategy development

Aspect	Description	AI Techniques Involved	Strategic and Operational Implications	Examples
Core Concept	AI augments predictive analytics by processing vast, unstructured data and identifying hidden patterns, enabling real-time learning and adaptability.	Machine Learning (ML), Deep Learning (DL), Natural Language Processing (NLP).	Enhances the accuracy and speed of predictions; facilitates proactive rather than reactive strategies.	AI-driven predictive analytics in marketing, logistics, and finance.
Dynamic Forecasting	Models self-improve continuously as new data is introduced, enhancing forecasting precision over time.	Reinforcement Learning and Adaptive Neural Networks.	Allows organizations to anticipate market shifts and customer behavior dynamically.	AI-enabled systems identifying emerging consumer trends or disruptions.
Proactive Strategy Development	Businesses simulate different market scenarios and test potential strategic responses using AI-driven analytics.	Predictive modeling, simulation, scenario testing.	Enables empirical, data-driven strategy formation; reduces uncertainty in decision-making.	Companies modeling supply chain disruptions or pricing strategy shifts.
Operational Applications	AI-based analytics applied in supply chain, finance, marketing, and HR for risk anticipation and performance optimization.	Anomaly detection, sentiment analysis, pattern recognition.	Improves resilience, agility, and cross-functional alignment.	Supply chains predicting geopolitical disruptions; AI detecting early customer churn.
Shift in Decision-Making Paradigm	Moves from reactive responses to anticipatory planning based on AI insights.	Predictive and prescriptive analytics integration.	Strengthens innovation cycles and competitive advantage.	Organizations adopting "anticipate and act" business models.
Outcome for Business Model Innovation	Supports continuous innovation by aligning data-driven foresight with strategic agility.	AI-powered analytics continuously refine operational and business strategies.	Encourages transformation of products, services, and value delivery mechanisms.	General Electric using AI to predict asset performance and innovate service mo

Predictive analytics supports business model innovation by providing empirical evidence for strategic decision-making. AI can simulate different business scenarios, estimate their outcomes, and recommend the most viable paths forward. This shifts the decision-making paradigm from reactive to anticipatory, enabling continuous innovation and agility.

6.3 Case Studies: How Predictive Analytics Helped a Startup Pivot

A compelling case of predictive analytics driving business model innovation involves the startup *Stitch Fix*, an online personal styling service. Initially launched as a subscription-based fashion box service, Stitch Fix employed a hybrid model that combined human stylists with machine learning algorithms to curate clothing selections for customers based on personal data.

Early feedback revealed limitations in the one-size-fits-all subscription model. Not all customers wanted regular deliveries, and many preferred flexibilities in how and when they received recommendations. Using predictive analytics, Stitch Fix analyzed extensive datasets, including customer purchase behavior, return rates, feedback on style preferences, and demographic data. The predictive models identified distinct customer segments with varying levels of engagement and purchasing behavior.

Based on these insights, Stitch Fix pivoted its business model. It introduced *Freestyle*, a non-subscription service where customers could shop curated selections anytime, using AI to personalize product recommendations in real-time. The company also refined its inventory and supply chain strategies, using predictive analytics to forecast demand and manage stock efficiently, reducing operational costs (Yildiz et al., 2024).

The result was a significant expansion in the customer base and increased customer satisfaction, as users appreciated the freedom and personalization offered by the Freestyle model. Stitch Fix's use of predictive analytics not only improved its offerings but also repositioned the company as a flexible, data-driven fashion platform rather than a rigid subscription service.

Predictive analytics, especially when integrated with AI, influence corporate strategy by offering real-time insights, personalized offers, and proactive decision-making. It forecasts consumer trends, market needs, and corporate models. Predictive analytics helps firms innovate, anticipate disruptions, and adapt to fast-changing environments. Data may help organizations switch from fixed-service to customer-responsive approaches, as Stitch Fix illustrates. Companies will shift from reactive planning to insight-driven strategy as predictive technology influences business model innovation.

7. CHALLENGES AND ETHICAL CONSIDERATIONS IN AI-DRIVEN BUSINESS MODELS AND INNOVATION

By facilitating automation, customisation, and data-driven decision-making, artificial intelligence (AI) is swiftly revolutionising business paradigms. Nevertheless, in addition to its advantages, AI brings about several organisational, legal, and ethical concerns that companies need to resolve in order to guarantee responsible and sustainable innovation. Problems with algorithmic bias, data privacy, lack of transparency, new regulations, and cross-sectoral complexity are all examined in depth in this section.

7.1 Algorithmic Bias and Fairness

A major ethical worry with AI-powered business models is the possibility of bias in the algorithms. Artificial intelligence systems, especially machine learning ones, may be biassed due to their reliance on previous data to understand patterns. Particularly in delicate fields like healthcare, law enforcement, financing, and employment, these prejudices, if left unchecked, might cause biassed results (Obermeyer et al., 2019). A good illustration of how recruiting algorithms based on biassed datasets might perpetuate workplace inequality is by disadvantageously impacting women or minority applicants. Organisations may lessen the impact of this by implementing equity-aware machine learning techniques and conduct regular audits to identify and correct biased outcomes (Eubanks, 2018).

7.2 Privacy and Data Ethics

To train models and provide individualised services, AI technologies depend substantially on massive volumes of personal data. Nevertheless, there are major privacy issues with this data-centric strategy. Without customers' knowledge or agreement, businesses are increasingly using AI to monitor and forecast their actions (Zuboff, 2019). Even if these tactics are good for business, they may make people less independent and create problems with consent and monitoring. Data collection, storage, and use are subject to strict regulations such as the General Data Protection Regulation (GDPR) and the California Consumer Privacy Act (CCPA). These frameworks provide user rights, purpose restriction, transparency, and strict regulations (Voigt & Von dem Bussche, 2017). Companies who care about their ethical standing and legal compliance will ensure that their data practices are in line with these values.

7.3 Transparency and Explainability

The "black box" dilemma describes how AI models, especially deep learning algorithms, are notoriously opaque due to their complexity. This lack of transparency has the potential to erode confidence, particularly in contexts where important decisions are being made using AI, including healthcare, financial services, or the criminal justice system. Concerns about procedural fairness and accountability arise when stakeholders impacted by AI choices lack the means to comprehend or contest such conclusions. An emerging field of study, explainable AI (XAI) aims to make AI models and decision-making processes more comprehensible to humans (Barredo Arrieta et al., 2020). In order to gain the confidence of consumers and other stakeholders and to stay in compliance with new legal requirements, businesses must prioritise openness.

7.4 Accountability and Governance

The use of AI systems challenges established ideas about accountability. The question of who is legally responsible when an AI system does damage—for example, by incorrectly diagnosing a patient, rejecting a loan application, or triggering autonomous car accident—is often left unanswered. Ambiguity in ethics and the law may result from this shifting of blame. According to Floridi et al. (2018), organisations should include ethical review procedures into their AI development lifecycles, create clear lines of responsibility, and make sure that AI systems are overseen by humans. The idea that AI may supplement human decision-making without absolving humans of accountability altogether is central to this framework.

7.5 Regulatory Landscape and Compliance

A lot is changing in the world of artificial intelligence regulations. To combat the social and ethical concerns raised by artificial intelligence, some national and international organisations are proposing new laws. Among the most all-encompassing initiatives is the Artificial Intelligence Act that the European Union is proposing to pass. This act would classify AI systems according to their level of risk and establish strict regulations for applications with a high risk of harm, such as requiring human oversight, transparency, and risk management processes (European Commission, 2021).

Many different sectors are impacted by these rules and regulations. Some of these sectors include healthcare, transportation, education, and finance. Companies are further pressured to adopt safe and legitimate data practices by data protection regulations like the General Data Protection Regulation (GDPR), which highlights consumers' rights over their personal data. In addition to being required by law, staying up-to-date with these standards is essential for ethical innovation from a strategic standpoint.

7.6 Cross-Sectoral and Organizational Challenges

Different industries face varying levels of risk and regulation when implementing AI. Sectors such as healthcare and finance operate under strict ethical and legal guidelines, requiring greater scrutiny of AI applications. Many organizations face internal barriers such as fragmented governance, lack of ethical expertise, and misalignment between innovation and compliance teams. These silos hinder the development of integrated AI ethics strategies. There is a global shortage of professionals trained in both AI and ethics, limiting organizations' ability to manage these complexities effectively (Jobin et al., 2019). To overcome these challenges, firms must foster cross-functional collaboration, embed ethical considerations across departments, and invest in interdisciplinary education.

7.7 Strategic Imperatives for Ethical AI Integration

To ensure that AI-driven business innovation is ethical, transparent, and sustainable, organizations should adopt a proactive and comprehensive approach. This includes establishing internal AI ethics boards, conducting regular impact assessments, adopting transparent design principles, and engaging stakeholders throughout the AI lifecycle. Businesses should also align their innovation strategies with evolving regulatory expectations and public values. By institutionalizing ethical frameworks and building internal capacities, companies can not only mitigate risks but also enhance their legitimacy and long-term competitiveness.

It is critical to resolve the ethical and regulatory concerns around AI because of its growing importance in new business models and innovations. Data privacy, algorithmic bias, accountability, and transparency are not afterthoughts. On the contrary, they need to play a pivotal role in the development, rollout, and oversight of AI systems. Responsible innovation and public trust in the era of intelligent technologies will be most achieved by organisations that include ethical concepts into their AI strategy, while also harmonising with regulatory frameworks and cross-sectoral realities.

8. STRATEGIC ROADMAP FOR AI-DRIVEN INNOVATION

As artificial intelligence (AI) becomes a cornerstone of contemporary organisational strategy, organisations must adopt a disciplined and forward-looking approach to integrate AI to maintain innovation. A good strategic roadmap includes technology investments, cultural, institutional, and collaborative improvements that determine AI's long-term value. This section describes a strategy roadmap for AI-driven innovation, including encouraging experimentation, investing in capabilities and people, creating collaborative ecosystems, and providing comprehensive metrics for AI impact measurement and scalability.

8.1 Building a Culture of Experimentation and Agility

Innovation thrives in environments that encourage experimentation, tolerate failure, and embrace iterative learning. For AI to be a catalyst for innovation, organizations must cultivate an agile mindset that allows for rapid prototyping, testing, and scaling of AI applications. This involves moving away from rigid, hierarchical models of innovation to more fluid and decentralized approaches (Rigby et al., 2018).

Agility, in this context, refers to the organization's ability to respond quickly to changes in the marketplace by leveraging AI insights. Firms that adopt agile principles are better positioned to pivot strategies based on real-time data and predictive analytics. Embedding AI into agile frameworks enables rapid experimentation with customer journeys, product features, or supply chain configurations, thereby increasing responsiveness and reducing time-to-market (McKinsey & Company, 2020).

Encouraging cross-departmental collaboration, creating sandbox environments for AI pilots, and rewarding calculated risk-taking are key strategies for nurturing such a culture. Importantly, leadership plays a vital role in modeling the behavior expected from teams, promoting psychological safety, and reinforcing innovation as a shared responsibility.

8.2 Investing in AI Capabilities and Cross-Functional Teams

Another essential pillar of an AI innovation roadmap is building internal capabilities. This includes upskilling existing employees and hiring specialized talent in machine learning, data science, AI ethics, and domain-specific applications. The World Economic Forum (2020) notes that AI-related roles—such as data analysts, machine learning engineers, and AI architects—are among the most in-demand skills globally.

Collaboratively developing AI use cases requires interdisciplinary teams with members from different departments, such as operations, marketing, legal, customer experience, and technology. These groups work to make sure that AI solutions are based on solid ethics and have a clear strategic purpose (Davenport & Ronanki, 2018). These group efforts improve the contextual relevance of AI apps and make it easier to solve problems holistically.

Organizations can also implement AI Centers of Excellence (CoEs) that act as hubs for best practices, training, governance, and AI resource allocation. CoEs accelerate the democratization of AI across business functions while maintaining coherence in strategy and technology adoption.

8.3 Partnerships and Ecosystems: Collaborating with AI Startups and Research Institutions

In the fast-paced world of AI innovation, no organization can afford to work in isolation. Strategic collaborations with AI startups, academic institutions, and industry consortia are essential for gaining access to cutting-edge research, tools, and talent. These partnerships help firms stay ahead of technological curves and explore disruptive opportunities without shouldering all the risks and costs internally (Subrahmanyam, 2025).

Startups often bring niche expertise, agility, and innovation speed that can complement the scale and resources of larger enterprises. Corporate-startup accelerators, hackathons, and innovation labs are common mechanisms for fostering such engagement. On the other hand, partnerships with universities and research institutes allow corporates to participate in foundational AI research, support talent pipelines, and engage in ethical debates and policy formulation (Bughin et al., 2018).

By cultivating an open innovative ecosystem, firms can better navigate the complexities of AI development while leveraging diverse perspectives and capabilities. The success of companies like IBM, which has partnered with MIT for AI research, and Google, which collaborates with academic institutions globally, underscores the value of ecosystem-based innovation.

8.4 Measuring and Scaling AI Impact Across Business Units

Organizations need effective AI impact measurement systems to maintain and scale AI programs. This comprises ROI, operational efficiency, customer experience, innovation rate, and ethical compliance measurements (Davenport et al., 2020). A systematic performance framework helps select high-value AI initiatives and evaluate them continuously. Companies should set KPIs for strategic objectives including AI-driven product revenue growth, decision-making latency reduction, and intelligent automation workforce efficiency.

After pilot programs succeed, growing AI involves infrastructure, data management, talent, and governance model harmonization. Process standardization, reusable machine learning pipelines, and centralized knowledge repositories accelerate growth without sacrificing agility. Implementing AI into the business core requires change management - communicating accomplishments, training new teams, and aligning incentives. To address increasing ethical and legal issues and guarantee scaled AI applications continue to benefit society and organizations, periodic audits and feedback loops are necessary.

Figure 3. Strategic roadmap for AI-driven innovation

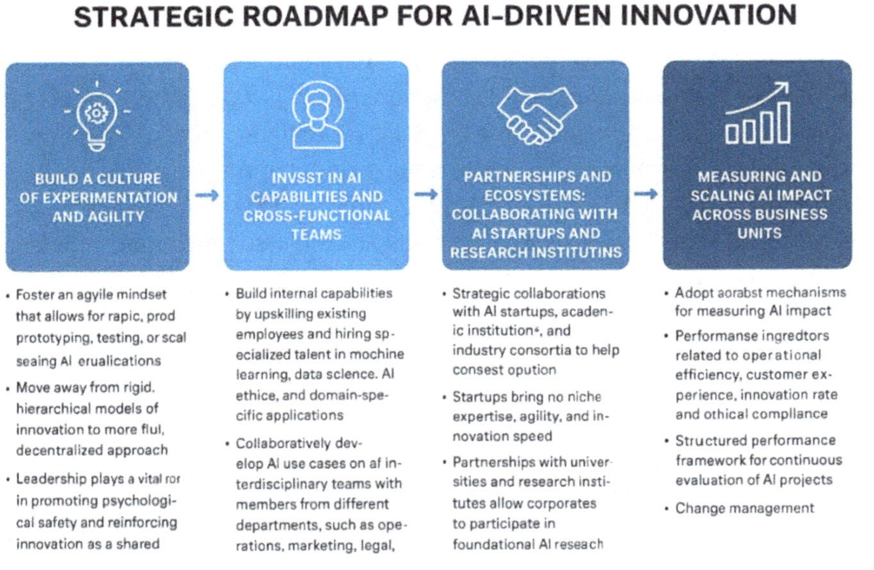

Embracing AI-driven innovation isn't a quick fix; it's a long-term strategy that calls for careful preparation, financial commitment, and a shift in company culture. To fully harness the power of AI, organisations should foster a culture of experimentation, foster cross-functional cooperation to create internal skills, establish strategic alliances, and apply systematic impact measurements. Taken as a whole, these components of a roadmap allow companies to innovate massively, react proactively to changes in the market, and stay ahead of the competition in the AI era.

9. THE FUTURE OF AI-DRIVEN BUSINESS MODELS

AI makes corporate models more self-sufficient, networked, ethical, and predictive. AI, IoT, blockchain, and quantum computing are changing the production-to-consumption value chain. Descriptive and predictive analytics provide real-time, adaptive business models. As legal, social, and ethical frameworks become more complicated, these advances must be understood within them. This section discusses how AI-driven business model advancements affect strategic leadership and governance.

9.1 Autonomous Decision-Making Organizations

Corporates with the ability to make decisions on their own will soon be a thing of the past, thanks to AI. Such models depict AI systems as agents with the ability to make choices within certain boundaries, rather than just decision-support tools. These self-governing systems are able to make strategic, tactical, and operational choices in real-time by using reinforcement learning, natural language processing (NLP), and sophisticated machine learning algorithms (Daugherty & Wilson, 2018).

Decentralized Autonomous Organizations (DAOs), for example, represent a radical shift in organizational governance. Built on blockchain and AI, DAOs operate without traditional hierarchical management. Smart contracts and AI protocols govern decision-making, ensuring transparency and efficiency while reducing the need for human intervention (Hassan & De Filippi, 2021). In sectors like finance, logistics, and supply chain, autonomous AI systems are already managing portfolios, routing shipments, and optimizing operations with minimal human oversight.

This transformation implies a need for redefining accountability, ethics, and legal frameworks. As organizations delegate more decision-making authority to machines, ensuring transparency, explainability, and human oversight becomes paramount (Rahwan et al., 2019).

9.2 Integration of AI with Emerging Technologies

Future corporate models will combine AI and other cutting-edge advancements. AI, blockchain, IoT, and quantum computing are enabling new commercial innovations. Companies may use AI and IoT for real-time sensing and actuation, predictive maintenance, logistics tracking, and responsive supply chain management (Subrahmanyam, 2025). Industrial IoT and smart cities are using this convergence to improve energy consumption, traffic management, and industrial output.

Blockchain and AI increase data provenance, security, and trust. Blockchain maintains AI training data immutable and auditable, yet AI may detect fraud in blockchain-based transaction data (Casino et al., 2019). This combination benefits the healthcare business since AI diagnoses patients using blockchain-protected data, ensuring system efficacy and integrity. Quantum computing, however new, might vastly increase AI model training. Its integration with AI might revolutionise science-driven commercial models in drug development, climate modelling, and complicated optimisation (Arute et al., 2019).

9.3 Predictive and Prescriptive Business Models

Traditional business models focused on reactive strategies and historical data analysis. In contrast, the future belongs to predictive and prescriptive business models that use AI to anticipate trends, simulate scenarios, and recommend optimal courses of action.

Predictive analytics, fueled by vast datasets and real-time processing, enables organizations to foresee customer needs, market shifts, and operational disruptions. AI models can predict consumer churn, forecast inventory needs, or detect emerging supply chain risks before they materialize (Subrahmanyam, 2024). Prescriptive analytics goes a step further by recommending actionable strategies based on predictive insights - be they adjusting pricing dynamically, optimizing ad placements, or reallocating resources across business units.

Such capabilities enable businesses to become more adaptive and resilient, moving toward dynamic business models that evolve continuously in response to internal and external stimuli. In retail, for instance, corporates like Amazon use predictive analytics not only to forecast demand but to pre-ship products to distribution centers closer to anticipated customers—a concept known as anticipatory shipping (Brynjolfsson & McAfee, 2014).

9.4 Anticipating Regulatory, Social, and Ethical Trends

The legal and ethical terrain is always changing, and AI-driven business models must adapt to stay afloat. More and more, national and international organisations are realising that AI must be implemented in a fair and secure manner. Rules like the EU's AI Act provide standards for AI systems' openness, responsibility, and risk management (European Commission, 2021).

Ethical concerns around bias, discrimination, surveillance, and the displacement of human labor are gaining prominence. Organizations will need to adopt AI ethics principles that go beyond compliance and actively promote fairness, inclusivity, and accountability. Embedding ethics-by-design in AI systems - through techniques like algorithmic auditing, explainable AI, and inclusive data practices - is becoming essential for business legitimacy and public trust (Jobin et al., 2019).

Societal expectations around sustainability, digital rights, and corporate responsibility are shaping how AI is perceived and accepted. Businesses that proactively engage in ethical AI innovation will likely gain reputational advantages and regulatory goodwill.

The future of AI-driven business models is one of profound transformation. Autonomous organizations integrated intelligent systems, predictive analytics, and evolving ethical frameworks will define the next era of business strategy and innovation. Leaders must not only embrace AI technologies but also reimagine their organizational structures, decision-making processes, and social responsibilities. By aligning technological capabilities with strategic foresight and ethical governance, businesses can thrive in an AI-augmented future that is not only smarter but also more just and inclusive.

10. CONCLUSION

Artificial Intelligence (AI) has become a formidable driver of change in business model transformation and innovation speedup in industries. From supporting real time personalization in retail or predictive diagnostics in healthcare industry or enabling intelligent automation in manufacturing or adaptive learning in education, AI is changing the way in which organizations operate, compete and create value. This is not a mere technical change, but a strategic one; introducing new paradigms of data-guided decision-making, self-moving processes, and predictive vision to businesses that enable them to act, foresee, adapt to change.

Not without good reason, to achieve the maximum benefits from AI, it is crucial for the leaders to extend past pilot projects and superficial implementations. Seeding AI into the DNA of the organization depends on the organization's willingness to invest in a long-term digital capability building, agility culture, and cross-functional output. Strategic leadership is essential in relation to aligning the use of AI with larger business objectives, providing ethical governance as well as developing the talent that will facilitate the maintenance of innovation.

Sustainable innovation in the AI era is not about embracing state-of-the-art technologies; it is actually about shaping flexible learning-oriented organizations which are resilient, inclusive and futuristic in value creation. In this complex and connected business world, those enterprises that deliberately embed AI in their operation, culture and ecosystems, not only survive, but also displace existing ones. The future of competitiveness is in the capability of an organization to make responsible and innovative use of AI, to make it a central plank of their strategic architecture.

REFERENCES

Angelov, B. (2024). *Elements of data strategy: A framework for data- and AI-driven transformation*. Wiley.

Arute, F., Arya, K., Babbush, R., Bacon, D., Bardin, J. C., Barends, R., & Neven, H. (2019). Quantum supremacy using a programmable superconducting processor. *Nature*, *574*(7779), 505–510. DOI: 10.1038/s41586-019-1666-5 PMID: 31645734

Barredo Arrieta, A., Díaz-Rodríguez, N., Del Ser, J., Bennetot, A., Tabik, S., Barbado, A., García, S., Gil-López, S., Molina, D., Benjamins, R., Chatila, R., & Herrera, F. (2020). Explainable Artificial Intelligence (XAI): Concepts, taxonomies, opportunities and challenges toward responsible AI. *Information Fusion*, *58*, 82–115. DOI: 10.1016/j.inffus.2019.12.012

Brynjolfsson, E., & McAfee, A. (2014). *The second machine age: Work, progress, and prosperity in a time of brilliant technologies*. W. W. Norton & Company.

Brynjolfsson, E., & McAfee, A. (2017). *Machine, platform, crowd: Harnessing our digital future*. W. W. Norton & Company.

Bughin, J., Hazan, E., Ramaswamy, S., Chui, M., Allas, T., Dahlström, P., . . . Trench, M. (2017). *Artificial intelligence: The next digital frontier?* McKinsey Global Institute. https://www.mckinsey.com/~/media/mckinsey/industries/advanced%20electronics/our%20insights/how%20artificial%20intelligence%20can%20deliver%20real%20value%20to%20companies/mgi-artificial-intelligence-discussion-paper.pdf

Bughin, J., Seong, J., Manyika, J., Chui, M., & Joshi, R. (2018). *Notes from the AI frontier: Modeling the impact of AI on the world economy*. McKinsey Global Institute. https://www.mckinsey.com/featured-insights/artificial-intelligence/notes-from-the-ai-frontier-modeling-the-impact-of-ai-on-the-world-economy

Cambria, E., & White, B. (2014). Jumping NLP curves: A review of natural language processing research. *IEEE Computational Intelligence Magazine*, *9*(2), 48–57. DOI: 10.1109/MCI.2014.2307227

Casino, F., Dasaklis, T. K., & Patsakis, C. (2019). A systematic literature review of blockchain-based applications: Current status, classification and open issues. *Telematics and Informatics*, *36*, 55–81. DOI: 10.1016/j.tele.2018.11.006

Chui, M., Harryson, M., Manyika, J., Roberts, R., Chung, R., van Heteren, A., & Nel, P. (2018). *Notes from the AI frontier: Insights from hundreds of use cases*. McKinsey Global. https://www.mckinsey.com/~/media/mckinsey/featured%20insights/artificial%20intelligence/applying%20artificial%20intelligence%20for%20social%20good/mgi-applying-ai-for-social-good-discussion-paper-dec-2018.pdf

Chui, M., Manyika, J., & Miremadi, M. (2018). What AI can and can't do (yet) for your business. *McKinsey Quarterly*. https://www.mckinsey.com/featured-insights/artificial-intelligence/what-ai-can-and-cant-do-yet-for-your-business

Daugherty, P. R., & Wilson, H. J. (2018). *Human + machine: Reimagining work in the age of AI*. Harvard Business Press.

Davenport, T. H., Guha, A., Grewal, D., & Bressgott, T. (2020). How artificial intelligence will change the future of marketing. *Journal of the Academy of Marketing Science*, *48*(1), 24–42. DOI: 10.1007/s11747-019-00696-0

Davenport, T. H., & Harris, J. G. (2017). *Competing on analytics: The new science of winning*. Harvard Business Press.

Davenport, T. H., & Ronanki, R. (2018). Artificial intelligence for the real world. *Harvard Business Review*, *96*(1), 108–116.

De Fauw, J., Ledsam, J. R., Romera-Paredes, B., Nikolov, S., Tomasev, N., & Suleyman, M. (2018). Clinically applicable deep learning for diagnosis and referral in retinal disease. *Nature Medicine*, *24*(9), 1342–1350. DOI: 10.1038/s41591-018-0107-6 PMID: 30104768

Eubanks, V. (2018). *Automating inequality: How high-tech tools profile, police, and punish the poor*. St. Martin's Press.

European Commission. (2021). *Proposal for a regulation laying down harmonised rules on artificial intelligence (Artificial Intelligence Act)*. https://eur-lex.europa.eu/legal-content/EN/TXT/?uri=CELEX%3A52021PC0206

Floridi, L., Cowls, J., Beltrametti, M., Chatila, R., Chazerand, P., Dignum, V., & Valcke, P. (2018). AI4People—An ethical framework for a good AI society: Opportunities, risks, principles, and recommendations. *Minds and Machines*, *28*(4), 689–707. DOI: 10.1007/s11023-018-9482-5 PMID: 30930541

Glinska, G. (2024). *AI in marketing: How customer-centric companies can benefit from data privacy regulations*. Forbes India. https://www.forbesindia.com/article/darden-school-of-business/ai-in-marketing-how-customercentric-companies-can-benefit-from-data-privacy-regulations/93369/1

Gomez-Uribe, C. A., & Hunt, N. (2016). The Netflix recommender system: Algorithms, business value, and innovation. *ACM Transactions on Management Information Systems (TMIS, 6)*(4), 1–19. DOI: 10.1145/2843948

Hassan, S., & De Filippi, P. (2021). Decentralized autonomous organization. *Internet Policy Review, 10*(2), 1–10. DOI: 10.14763/2021.2.1556

Iansiti, M., & Lakhani, K. R. (2020). *Competing in the age of AI: Strategy and leadership when algorithms and networks run the world*. Harvard Business Press.

Jobin, A., Ienca, M., & Vayena, E. (2019). The global landscape of AI ethics guidelines. *Nature Machine Intelligence, 1*(9), 389–399. DOI: 10.1038/s42256-019-0088-2

Luckin, R., Holmes, W., Griffiths, M., & Forcier, L. B. (2016). *Intelligence unleashed: An argument for AI in education*. Pearson Education.

McKinsey & Company. (2020). *How retailers are using AI to enhance the customer journey*. https://www.mckinsey.com/capabilities/growth-marketing-and-sales/our-insights/next-best-experience-how-ai-can-power-every-customer-interaction

Obermeyer, Z., Powers, B., Vogeli, C., & Mullainathan, S. (2019). Dissecting racial bias in an algorithm used to manage the health of populations. *Science, 366*(6464), 447–453. DOI: 10.1126/science.aax2342 PMID: 31649194

Parker, G., Van Alstyne, M., & Choudary, S. P. (2016). *Platform revolution: How networked markets are transforming the economy—and how to make them work for you*. W. W. Norton & Company.

Porter, M. E., & Heppelmann, J. E. (2017). Why every organization needs an augmented reality strategy. *Harvard Business Review, 95*(6), 46–57.

Rahwan, I., Cebrian, M., Obradovich, N., Bongard, J., Bonnefon, J. F., & Lazer, D. (2019). Machine behaviour. *Nature, 568*(7753), 477–486. DOI: 10.1038/s41586-019-1138-y PMID: 31019318

Rigby, D. K., Sutherland, J., & Noble, A. (2018). Agile at scale. *Harvard Business Review, 96*(3), 88–96.

Rust, R. T., & Huang, M. H. (2021). The AI marketing canvas: A five-stage road-map to implementing artificial intelligence in marketing. *Journal of the Academy of Marketing Science, 49*(1), 30–50.

Sahid, A., Maleh, Y., Asemanjerdi, S. A., & Martín-Cervantes, P. A. (2023). A Bibliometric Analysis of the FinTech Agility Literature: Evolution and Review. *International Journal of Financial Studies, 11*(4), 123. DOI: 10.3390/ijfs11040123

Subrahmanyam, S. (2024). Role of data analytics and big data in operational decision-making and performance improvement. In Martínez-Falcó, J., Sánchez-García, E., Marco-Lajara, B., & Visser, G. (Eds.), *Convergence of technology and operations management in modern businesses* (pp. 105–140). IGI Global Scientific Publishing., DOI: 10.4018/979-8-3693-6200-6.ch003

Subrahmanyam, S. (2025). Leveraging AI and ML for Enhanced Efficiency and Innovation in Manufacturing. In Vyas, V., Bi, X., Pandey, D., Xu, Z., & Pandey, B. (Eds.), *AI's Role in Enhanced Automotive Safety* (pp. 319–344). IGI Global Scientific Publishing., DOI: 10.4018/979-8-3373-0442-7.ch021

Subrahmanyam, S. (2025). Strategic Collaboration and Partnerships in R&D for Innovation. In Martínez-Falcó, J., Sánchez-García, E., & Marco-Lajara, B. (Eds.), *Research and Development Practices in Innovation* (pp. 283–314). IGI Global Scientific Publishing., DOI: 10.4018/979-8-3373-0812-8.ch010

Subrahmanyam, S. (2025). The Integration of Artificial Intelligence and Machine Learning in Performance Evaluation. In R. Marcao & V. Santos (Eds.), *Evolving Strategies for Organizational Management and Performance Evaluation,* (pp. 603-626). IGI Global Scientific Publishing. DOI: 10.4018/979-8-3373-0149-5.ch028

Taneja, K., Maiti, P., Kakar, S., Guruprasad, P., Rao, S., & Goel, A. K. (2024). Jill Watson: A virtual teaching assistant powered by ChatGPT *(arXiv preprint)*. *L* arXiv.2405.11070DOI: 10.1007/978-3-031-64302-6_23

Topol, E. (2019). *Deep medicine: How artificial intelligence can make healthcare human again.* Basic Books.

Voigt, P., & Von dem Bussche, A. (2017). *The EU General Data Protection Regulation (GDPR).* Springer. DOI: 10.1007/978-3-319-57959-7

Wamba-Taguimdje, S. L., Fosso Wamba, S., Kala Kamdjoug, J. R., & Tchatchouang Wanko, C. E. (2020). Influence of artificial intelligence (AI) on firm performance: The business value of AI-based transformation projects. *Business Process Management Journal, 26*(7), 1893–1924. DOI: 10.1108/BPMJ-10-2019-0411

World Economic Forum. (2020). *The future of jobs report 2020.* https://www.weforum.org/reports/the-future-of-jobs-report-2020

Yildiz, B., Çiğdem, Ş., Meidutė-Kavaliauskienė, I., & Činčikaitė, R. (2024). The nexus of big data analytics, knowledge sharing, and product innovation in manufacturing. *Journal of Business Economics and Management, 25*(1), 66–84. DOI: 10.3846/jbem.2024.20713

Zuboff, S. (2019). *The age of surveillance capitalism: The fight for a human future at the new frontier of power*. PublicAffairs.

KEY TERMS AND DEFINITIONS

Artificial Intelligence (AI): The simulation of human intelligence processes by machines, particularly computer systems, enabling capabilities such as learning, reasoning, problem-solving, natural language processing (NLP), and computer vision. In business, AI is used to optimize operations, generate insights, and drive innovation.

Autonomous Decision-Making Organization (ADMO): An organization where AI systems are integrated into decision-making processes, allowing automated and data-driven operations with minimal human intervention, enhancing efficiency, speed, and innovation capacity.

Business Model Innovation: The process of transforming traditional business models by leveraging new technologies, strategies, and AI-driven insights to create, deliver, and capture value more effectively in dynamic markets.

Data-Centric Business Model: A model where data becomes a core asset and driver of value creation. AI leverages this data to generate insights, optimize operations, and enable predictive and prescriptive strategies that inform business decisions.

Ethical AI: The practice of designing and deploying AI systems in ways that ensure fairness, transparency, accountability, and compliance with privacy regulations, mitigating risks such as bias, discrimination, or misuse of sensitive data.

Machine Learning (ML): A subset of AI that enables systems to learn patterns from data and improve performance over time without explicit programming. ML is widely applied in predictive analytics, customer personalization, and process optimization.

Platform-Based Model: A business model that facilitates interactions between multiple user groups, such as buyers and sellers, through a digital platform. AI enhances these models by enabling personalization, matchmaking, and real-time analytics (e.g., Uber, Airbnb).

Predictive Analytics: A data-driven technique that uses statistical models, AI, and machine learning algorithms to forecast future outcomes based on historical data, helping businesses anticipate trends, customer behavior, and market shifts.

Process Innovation: The improvement or redesign of business processes using AI and advanced analytics to increase efficiency, reduce costs, and improve operational outcomes. Examples include predictive maintenance in manufacturing and automated claims processing in insurance.

Service-Oriented Model: A business approach where the focus shifts from selling products to delivering ongoing services or experiences. AI enables scalable, adaptive, and personalized services such as subscription-based recommendations (e.g., Netflix, Spotify).

Chapter 12

UAV-Enabled Grape Disease Predictive Analytics System for Competitive Decision-Making Integrating Harnessing AI

Sneh Sharma
http://orcid.org/0009-0004-1750-4480
Amity University Punjab, Mohali, India

Devanshi Jangra
http://orcid.org/0009-0000-9836-4598
Amity University Punjab, Mohali, India

Kashish Devgan
http://orcid.org/0009-0000-1147-4058
Amity University Punjab, Mohali, India

Sachin Sharma
http://orcid.org/0000-0002-7821-3685
Amity University Punjab, Mohali, India

ABSTRACT

The developing request for exactness farming requires intelligent frameworks that improve trim wellbeing checking and surrender optimization. This paper proposes a UAV-enabled Grapes Disease Predictive Analytics Framework, coordination

DOI: 10.4018/979-8-3373-3648-0.ch012

Artificial Intelligence (AI) for competitive and data-driven decision-making. Unmanned Aerial Vehicles (UAVs) prepared with high-resolution multispectral and RGB cameras capture real-time vineyard symbolism, empowering early discovery of grapevine infections. The captured information experiences preprocessing and is nourished into profound learning models—such as convolutional neural networks (CNNs)—trained to distinguish and classify disease side effects with high precision. Leveraging AI-powered predictive analytics, the framework gives significant experiences on illness movement, treatment proposals, and asset allotment. The proposed framework illustrates the potential of combining UAV technology with AI to convert traditional farming into a smart, maintainable practice.

I. INTRODUCTION

Recent years have seen a technological rebirth in the worldwide agricultural scene, with digital transformation as a pillar of sustainable agriculture methods. Among the several fields of farming, viticulture—or grape growing—has great economic value in many areas, mostly because of its direct link with the wine business, table grape sales, and raisin production. Like many other valuable crops, grapevines, though, are quite vulnerable to a wide range of illnesses. If not detected and treated in time, these illnesses might lead to terrible crop losses, reduced fruit quality, and even long-term harm to the vineyard ecosystem. In the conventional approach, vineyards have been inspected visually by agronomists or farmers for disease symptoms that appear in the leaf as discolouration, mould, or lesions. Although this has been the practice of agriculture for centuries, it has some very serious bottlenecks. Manual methods are slow, very non-objective and labour bound. In addition, they find it hard to detect diseases in early stages where diseases are not loud enough. Moreover, as vineyard sizes continue to grow and global climate change increases climatic heterogeneity with new pressures of diseases, we need scalable, accurate and rapid methods for detection of disease. From a UAV (Unmanned Aerial Vehicle) sense of view, we are on the verge of a technology that can massively change modern farming. Autonomous or UAS-flown systems are autonomous/remote-controlled flying systems that can roam through large landscapes in minutes, taking high-resolution aerial and crop canopy images. UAVs with multi-spectral or thermal sensors are able to identify early physiological plant stress that is not visible to the naked eye. UAVs are quick, cheaper and more appropriate for the terrain (hilly lands) to scout grapes in a vineyard because it is impractical to send humans to each location. The UAVs provide a sound platform for data capture, but the tough job is to derive meaningful insights from the large image data they produce. It is at this that the real-time performance of Artificial Intelligence (AI) comes into action. Deep learning, as a part and parcel of machine learning, for instance, has shown great promise in the processing and interpretation of high-dimensional image data for classification, object detection and pattern recognition. Even in grapevine disease detection, these models can be trained to discern very minor differences in texture, colour, etc., at the micro level that make the leaf above to be healthy and the other diseased — not perceivable to human eyes. Convolutional Neural Networks (CNNs) are the state-of-the-art deep learning frameworks for visual recognition, as there are emerging works from deep learning architecture. CNNs mimic the function of the human visual cortex so that images are learnt automatically in a hierarchical manner by a model. CNNs are trained to classify images of grape leaves into four different types and kinds as under this study:

- Grape Black rot
- Grape Esca (Black Measles)
- Grape Leaf Blight (Isariopsis Leaf Spot)
- Grape Healthy

They all have different visual symptoms and independent biological aspects of the diseases. As an example, black rot appears as circular lesions with black borders, and esca results in severe internal wood degradation ("tiger striping") of the xylem and yellowing of leaves. This is a blast disease caused by the Isariopsis clavispora, which produces dark brown necrotic spots on leaves with a yellow halo. Disease classification efforts at the continuous level demand a higher level of both data diversity and sophistication of models for such complex disease patterns. To improve both the robustness and generality of the model, the current work also adds Generative Adversarial Networks (GANs) into this. GANs: Generative Adversarial Networks comprise a family of AI models in which two neural net games compete with one another using a game theory setup. The generator wants to make fake pictures that look like the real ones, and a discriminator then has the job of telling real from pretend images. The generator here performs well enough at making incredibly realistic images that it is able to be fed back into the training set over time. This becomes especially handy when we work on some imbalanced datasets (e.g., four disease classes in medical imbalances, more of one than the other). We train GANs to synthesise grape leaf images which were — so that our CNNs get an equal amount of all the diseases and improve both the prediction accuracy and reliability. An important result of this research is an efficient deployment strategy. Instead of restricting the system to lab- or server-based applications, the trained model goes inside an easy-to-use mobile application. It enables users (e.g., farmers, vineyard managers, and listed agricultural extension workers) to take real-time images of grape leaves with their mobile camera (PICUPLOAD). The system localises the image computation (either through a localised backend or cloud) and returns a result with certainty about the disease category right away, which tells how the suspected disease might be and recommends next steps. This opens the door for even people with little or no underlying tech experience to get their hands on powerful AI tools.

II. LITERATURE REVIEW

Predictive analytical structures based on UAV are remodeling of accurate winery that offer aggressive benefits through record-based decision-making and utilize the power of artificial intelligence (AI) (Ammoniaci et al., 2021; Fuentes-Peailillo et al., 2024). Conventional disease detection strategies are basically based on visual remarks using specialists, which are time consuming, highly affordable and non - mounted for huge farms. Plant disease justifies losses of good size in satisfactory and the amount of agricultural production, resulting in loss of income, especially in developing countries (Chin et al., 2023). Combination of AI with remote exploration technology, which includes unmanned air vehicles (UAV), provides a feasible technique that prevents loss of yield automation by detection of plant failures (Shahi et al., 2023). These systems allow early and precise detection of grape diseases that are necessary to prevent from developing viruses or fungi, preventing catastrophic financial losses for grape production (Kerkech et al., 2020). The integration of the UAV generation, excellent sensors and advanced AI algorithms revolutionizes the wine management, promotes sustainability and maximize help use (Senoo et al., 2024). The architecture of a completely predictive analytical device based on UAV for grape disorder usually includes some of the key components. First, UAV equipped with multispectral and RGB cameras confiscated by high -end pictures of vineyards (Ouyang et al., 2020). Snap images are then pre -processed to dispose of geometric distortion and lighting modifications. Furthermore, the gadget gaining knowledge of algorithms, especially deep knowledge of fashion, including convolution neural networks (CNN), to explore photographs and awareness of the styles of plant diseases (Li et al., 2024). CNN is trained on large units' classified pix, allowing them to identify healthy and sick flora with excessive accuracy (Singh et al., 2020). The data fusion strategy, the integration of records from more than one sensor (e.g. Iota sensors, floor sensors) may further increase the accuracy and reliability of the disease detection (Ouhami et al., 2022; Almalki et al., 2021). Finally, the results are carried out at hand for the winery through the Structures of Help for Selection (DSS), which represents the facts for focused interventions. This included the technique no longer improves the speed and accuracy of the disease detection, but also allows monitoring of real -time winery in real time, allowing well -timed and efficient disorders management procedures (Olson et al., 2021). AI contributes significantly to the creation of such structures extremely executive in predication. Mastering machine software program is able to experiment a huge number of styles and characteristics and provide rare knowledge about strengthening agricultural practices. The structures of supportive support structures based on and prime helped to make farmers smart selections through forecasts focused on facts, climate forecasts and past formulas. It helps with efficient use of resources and reducing the environment. For example, AI improves irrigation procedures by monitoring soil health and water desire for plants that save water and reduce waste. In addition, soil monitoring AI enables farmers to maximize fertilization procedures, which improves the use of nutrients and reduces drainage to the surroundings. Optional AI, including powdered molds soon, allows farmers to treat them in time and appropriately (Maraveas, 2022). The use of AI in agriculture with robots and separate vehicles is not best to solve lack of effort, but also improves planting, harvesting and crop care. By storing AI at all stages of agriculture, farmers can understand profits, use assets effectively and cause sustainable. Despite the remarkable development in UAV -based systems, there is some demanding situation and instructions for future studies. One of the primary tasks is the required series of standardized statistics and extermination methods for obtaining statistics, organization and analysis. It relies on massive, classified data sets is a problem, because marking of distinctive data sets is time and expensive for scientists. The recent development in live acquisition and semi -built mastering gives the solution to the ability to use smaller data sets. Another project is to balance speed and accuracy and differences between new studies and the real use of the world. Future research aims to assemble robust modes that can be applied to much vegetation and carried out on small aids (Shafik et al., 2023). There must also be cooperation between numerous disciplines to deal with multilateral problems in the usefulness of AI in precise agriculture, including ethics, protection of records and technological hole between rural and urban areas. By overcoming such demanding situations and the use of brand new technologies, the structures of the prognosis for UAV -based UAV growth, efficiency and sustainability in the production of grapes, and help ensure that the arena populations are constantly developing .

III. IMPORTANCE OF UAV

UAVs, or unmanned aerial vehicles, have, in recent years, become a crucial technology for smart agriculture and precision farming. Their prowess in building high-resolution imagery over enormous farm landscapes has changed how agricultural monitoring, surveying and decision processes have become. In viticulture—grape viticulture, the need for UAVs comes from unique challenges in vineyard terrain and vine sensitivity to diseases that overshadow other crops. This part tells how strategic

UAVs are for disease surveillance and crop assessment, which forms part of the intelligent decision-making enabled by data in real-time. UAVs have some major advantages over their traditional ground-based counterparts. Grapevines in vineyards are often planted along rows across the hills or uneven terrain, so visually inspecting bunches for disease infection can be physically demanding and difficult time-wise (Verma et al., 2024). RGB or multispectral/thermal cameras enable UAVs to fly the terrain and gain high-level, up-close views, measuring the crop canopy detail and taking off in no time as a standard practice. The imagery acquired from these flights can then be used to identify the initial stages of a disease, nutrient limitation or pest/water stress — before they are visible to the naked eye. Quick detection is very important in managing grapevine diseases, for many of them spread quickly and can lead to irreversible damage to the vine if not detected early.

Figure 1. UAV based grapevine disease monitoring and classification workflow

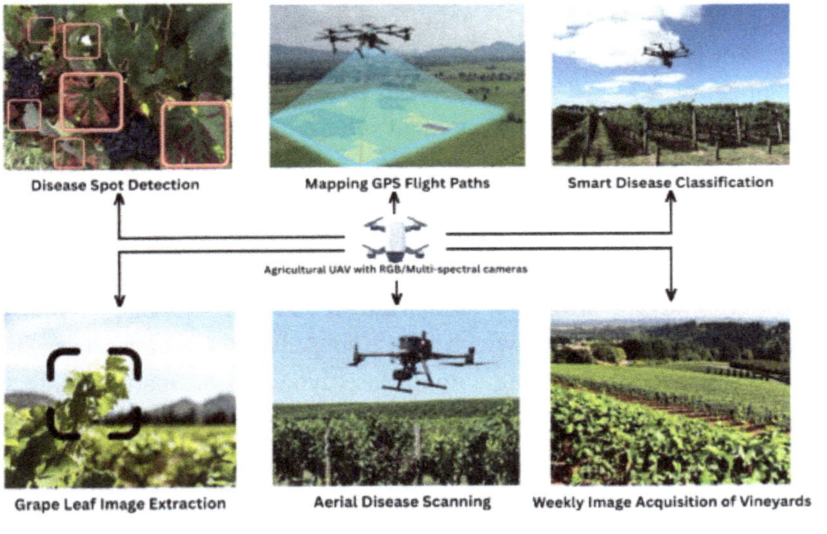

Figure 1 illustrates the entire UAV-enabled workflow for computerized grapevine sickness tracking and type. Using RGB and multispectral cameras, UAVs perform aerial scanning of vineyards primarily based on pre-mapped GPS flight paths. Captured photographs go through leaf extraction, sickness spot detection, and smart category using AI algorithms. Weekly image acquisition ensures continuous surveillance, enabling well timed detection and control of diseases throughout massive vineyard areas.

Figure 2. High resolution UAV captured images over vineyards

UAVs equipped with RGB and multispectral sensors acquire accurate, aerial images of a grapevine canopy as they fly over vineyard blocks according to pre-defined GPS flight paths that obtain complete area coverage and revisitability. The images are in their raw data needed for identifying diseases, based on leaf structure, discoloration trends, and stress symptoms. Higher angles enable early signs of germination that could have gone unnoticed from the ground. This is the first step in a detection pipeline for AI analysis. An adaptation and flexibility which is the key advantage of UAVs. The software can enable UAVs to be heavily customised with sensors and other types of equipment suited to their exact mission application. Specifically, high-resolution RGB cameras are ideal for visual symptoms (e.g., leaf spots, discolouration and wilting) on grapes that are often associated with grape diseases like black rot, esca or leaf blight. Moreover, the drones can also be flown to take a set of images on a regular basis, allowing the farmers to do some detailed crop health monitoring without a human sitting in the machine. This promotes the generation of time-series data, which can be subsequently compared across the different stages of growth, assisting with disease dynamics or treatment interventions affect analysis. In addition, the massive data volume and diversity lead to critical dimensions for the training and performance of deep learning models also contributed to by UAVs. The better the diversity of the dataset, the more general an AI model can learn, and the plants' health and diseases class can be distinguished from each other. Where UAVs really come in handy is in imaging thousands upon thousands of pixels in different lighting conditions, viewing angles and altitudes to create more holistic datasets that look like real life. This makes it is not only more robust for the AI model but also enables us to have better performative versions in real-world deployments with high variability. UAV-based surveillance also fits well with the underlying philosophy of precision agriculture (i.e., site-specific management). The sub-field level mapping of disease incidence accomplished by analysing UAV imagery allows for specific disease control like targeted pesticide disbursement, pruning or other intervention decisions. This helps reduce usage of agrochemicals and, as a result, reduces cost and detrimental habitat. For vineyards, where different rows or even clusters will be more prone to employing certain UAV data, precision targeting (something impossible with blanket management strategies) is necessary because of shade competition, moisture retention and previous infections. As the first data capture devices of the proposed system in this study, UAVs are the initial source for raw imagery to train the AI-based disease detection pipeline. It is not just about capturing images; their role seems to build semi-solutionary tech which autonomously turns on and runs on its own without the need for human intervention. In the case of large vineyards or faraway vineyards with no PC professional available, this automation is highly valuable. They can monitor hundreds of acres in one flight by optimising UAVs with AI and the related insights within hours, something that would require days or even weeks under manual control. Apart from disease surveillance, UAVs can be used for estimating crop yield and irrigation planning and also for canopy structure analysis. In viticulture, canopy density and vigour are pivotal characteristics of a healthy vine in grape bearing. Vegetation indices like NDVI (Normalised Difference Vegetation Index) and GNDVI (Green NDVI) correlate with chlorophyll content/leaf area/plant biomass: UAVs can measure. We could then use these indices for cross-validation of disease predictions or suggest other agronomic actions (e.g., changing the amount of fertiliser/irrigation schedule). Essential to the space, UAVs sit at an intersection of theory and practice. Having UAV data linked to cloud-based platforms, or even mobile solutions, allows vineyard managers to get alerts with real-time diseases and stress laid out.

IV. UAV GUIDELINES

UAV Guidelines for Grapes Disease Monitoring and Predictive Analytics The use of Unmanned Aerial Vehicles (UAVs) in viticulture, especially for sickness discovery and prophetic analytics, necessitates the established order of complete functional and nonsupervisory suggestions. These guidelines are vital to make certain of the protection, trust ability, felonious compliance, and effectiveness of UAV operations in vineyard surroundings. Given the growing integration of UAVs with artificial intelligence (AI) structures in agrarian decision-making, timber, homogenizing their deployment protocols complements each specialized effectiveness and stakeholder agreement. One of the first issues is nonsupervisory compliance. Drivers must cleave to countrywide and hard civil aeronautics programmes that govern UAV flight operations. These may include licensing conditions for drone aviators, admissible flight mounds, restrictions on tone-sustaining operations, and no-cover zones, substantially near to airfields or peopled areas. In nations just like the United States, UAV drivers should observe the Federal Aviation Administration's (FAA) Part 107 programmes, whilst inside the European Union; the European

Union Aviation Safety Agency (EASA) guidelines ought to be followed. Drivers ought to be tutored and authorized to ensure responsible operation, and each UAV flight needs to be logged with information on flight paths, period, and loads. Flight-making plans and timing are vital for effective complaint discovery. UAV operations need to be listed in the course of gold standard climate situations, generally early morning or overdue autumn, whilst lights are constant and wind ranges are low to drop snap deformation and make certain flight stability. Breakouts have to be prevented in the course of downfall, heavy pall wrap, or violent temperatures that can degrade print exceptional and detector delicacy. Also, the frequency of UAV breakouts needs to align with crop phenological categories and regarded sickness enhancement cycles. For a case, biweekly breakouts during early conduit growth and regenerating ages can help seize early symptoms of fungal infections like fine mildew and black spoilage. Regarding cargo and detector selection, UAVs employed in croft sickness monitoring have to be prepared with high-decision RGB cameras for visible analysis, together with multispectral or hyper spectral detectors for capturing non-seen mild bands. These spectral bands are vital for figuring out physiological pressure in flowers that are not visible to the naked eye.. UAV drivers should conduct a hazard assessment prior to each undertaking, relating to capability pitfalls, the conforming of close by power lines, the natural world, or mischievous climate conditions. Exigency protocols must be installed, inclusive of procedures for loss of advertisement, low battery go back, or tackle failure. Safety zones need to be pronounced round takeoff and wharf regions, and workers on web runners should be briefed on UAV flight schedules to help prevent injuries. In the case of tone-reliant or once-visible line-of-sight (BVLOS) operations, advanced collision-avoidance structures and spare control mechanisms are encouraged. From a sustainability and environmental perspective, UAV breakouts need to be deliberate to minimise electricity consumption and disturbance to near ecosystems.

V. OVERVIEW OF GRAPE DISEASES

Grapevines are very prone to being affected by diseases, including fungal, bacterial and viral bases that greatly influence the yield and quality of the fruits. Disease management is one of the hardest and most resource-intensive tasks vineyard managers face amongst a long list of challenges. Timely and accurate diagnosis is essential to prevent the infection from spreading and to get to that problem earlier. In this part, a detailed path analysis of the initial set of grape leaf diseases, discussed in the basis for the proposed system, such as Grape Black Rots, Isariopsis Leaf Spot (Leaf Blight), and for healthy leaf classification during predictive analytics to differentiate between them.

- Grape Black rot: Guignardia bidwellii (Black Rot) is one of the most common and destructive fungal pathogens impacting grapevine health, causing extensive damage across the world. Black rot can be found on all the green parts of a plant, from leaves, tendrils and berries to stem. One of the symptoms of black rot is circular small brown lesions on the leaves which are often surrounded by dark margins. As the disease worsens, these lesions grow in size and produce black, fruiting bodies called pycnidia. This is where these structures come into play; they release spores to infect adjacent tissues, in particular in warm and wet conditions. Black rot causes shrivelling and mummification of grape berries, leading to severe fruit quality loss and yield reduction. The primary source of infection usually is overwintering spores released through rain at a specific time during spring. Wet leaf surfaces and temperatures of 24°C to 28°C are ideal for infection. And these infections are favoured. Black rot will every time lead to a leaf dump if not caught early. Fungicide sprays and removal of infected debris are the classical uses for control, but early detection still very much counts.
- Grape Esca (Black Measles): Esca, commonly known as black measles, is a complicated and long-lasting grapevine disease, which is also commonly, vectored by different pathogens, for example, Phaeoacremonium aleophilum and Phaeomoniella chlamydospora. It is a serious disease agent on older vines and very difficult to identify in the very beginning stages. Interveinal chlorosis (same as with tigers' stripes or scorched appearance), one of the telltale signs of esca, was when yellowing/browning occurred. Only in between the veins of the leaf, giving it a tiger stripe appearance, as it is often called, is strongly correlated with the development of this syndrome. Disease advancement will result yellow/drying leaves completely and falling off the leaves early. Moreover, Esca may impact the wood of the vine where internal necrosis is observed and black streaks appear in xylem tissue. Berries: sunken lesions and black spots on berries resulted in significant loss of marketability and use for the wine industry. Esca does take its time – developing over several seasons, it is scarcely watched by the conventional methods. Using images captured using UAV and analysed by AI, the foliar discolouration and asymmetry on infected-plant leaves can be recorded to sort out early intervention strategies to deliver vine health/prolong productivity.
- Grape Leaf Blight (Isariopsis Leaf Spot): Leaf Blight, Isariopsis clavispora infection, is a foliar disease of grapevines characterised by defoliation due to premature leaf senescence. When moisture builds up on leaf surfaces in humid climates, this can lead to a high incidence of the most common foliar disease: CIVAFIT. Small brown to black spots, from which a disease starts on the leaf surface as irregularly, shaped scattered inoculative areas.

The spots enlarge and coalesce, producing blighted patches, dead tissue mingled into living growth. As an over-exaggerated example, entire leaves will wither, twist under the sun and go down burdened by what feels like half their structures being dead and useless (weaker plant, limited photosynthesis). With similar initial symptoms, AI-based differentiation is extremely useful to differentiate Isariopsis Leaf Spot from other fungal diseases. UAV imagery can be used to capture the features (shape and extent of lesions, presence of concentric zonation around edges of green dead areas) specific to leaf blight which can be processed by a CNN-based classifier. It is imperative to be able to differentiate plant diseases such as leaf blight from black rot because of the differences in treatments. An incorrect diagnosis will lead to either useless fungicide or more resistance. The system in question exploits training data enhanced with GANs to deal with these subtle visual differences.

- Grape healthy: Classifying healthy grapevine leaves is important in disease detection. When grape leaves are healthy, they generally have a greener tone to them, are smooth on the surface and have symmetrical veinal patterns. There are no wilting, bleaching, spotting or any weird surface textures as well. Visual features of healthy leaves being captured help the AI model to create a strong base against which all else is measured for abnormalities. Neutral reflection off healthy leaf tissue and good patterns of light penetration (healthy equal) are distinct from the distinct (non-diseased) irregularities on leaves of diseased plants when imaged from UAVs (Kumar et al., 2022). These tags act as some of the distinguishing features which the CNN learns to notice between various diseases and health. Moreover, manually identifying and tagging healthy leaves in UAV-collected imagery allows us to map out the distribution of disease-free sites within a vineyard which may potentially be used as sources in tracking disease spread or containment over time in vineyard managers. They are critical for reducing false positives of classification with healthy data samples. The model can overpredict disease presence when healthy samples are not sufficiently represented in training. Therefore, this research highlights the importance of curating a balanced dataset that comprises thousands of samples taken from different lighting and background conditions for a healthy grape leaf. This enables the system to work predictably in an actual vineyard environments where the camera and source light 'noise' can prevent it from identifying tiny differences in appearance.

Figure 3. Detection of disease symptoms using a CNN

This image shows the output of the CNN indicating specific diseases of grape leaf, including Black Rot, Esca, and Leaf Blight, from images collected from a drone. Color overlays with colored bounding boxes indicate the areas identified as having disease symptoms with visual evidence of disease-specific characteristics identified by trained pattern recognition. The model has efficiently learned to differentiate between healthy leaves and diseased leaves including features such as necrotic tissue, leaf spotting patterns, and discoloration. This automated disease detection alleviates the need for human field scouting and supports early intervention and precision treatment at scale in larger vineyards.

Integrating Disease Classification into Predictive Analytic: By categorising grapevine leaf situations into 4 clear classes—Black Rot, Esca, Leaf Blight, and Healthy—the predictive analytics engine profits the capability to perform multi-magnificence classification. The CNN version used in this observation is educated with annotated picture datasets, which include each actual and GAN-generated synthetic sample to overcome class imbalance. The model learns to understand visible patterns and textural cues particular to each ailment class. During implementation, UAV-captured photographs are fed into the machine, which then runs real-time inference to expect the class with corresponding confidence scores. For practical software, the categorised effects are incorporated into a mobile application interface, wherein users (farmers or winery managers) can both click on snapshots on-site or upload them from their galleries. The gadget right now offers disease identity effects along with possible severity and advised next steps. This mechanism supports rapid, knowledgeable selection-making and minimises the lag between symptom look and corrective motion.

VI. PREDICTIVE ANALYTICS ALGORITHMS

The evolution of predictive analytics in agriculture, especially viticulture, has been extensively propelled through the upward thrust of deep gaining knowledge of algorithms. Among the most influential are Convolutional Neural Networks (CNNs) and Generative Adversarial Networks (GANs). These fashions aren't just the handiest instruments in ailment type and detection but also crucial for augmenting confined datasets, enhancing model generalisation, and allowing real-time selection-making. In the context of UAV-enabled grape disease analytics, CNNs and GANs provide powerful talents to interpret complex aerial imagery, perceive early signs and symptoms of ailment, and assist adaptive interventions. This segment explores these algorithms extensively, detailing their architectures, programmes, blessings, and implications for clever viticulture. Convolutional Neural Networks (CNNs) are a class of deep, feedforward synthetic neural networks designed to process data with a grid-like topology—most notably, snapshots. A trendy CNN architecture includes a sequence of convolutional layers that extract features from input pix by making use of filters or kernels, pooling layers that downsample the function maps to lessen dimensionality, and completely connected layers that interpret these functions to categorise pics. For UAV-primarily based grapevine sickness detection, CNNs are especially effective due to the fact they can autonomously examine spatial hierarchies of functions from raw photograph pixels, enabling high-accuracy reputation of visual disease signs. In viticulture, CNNs had been used to detect sicknesses which include powdery mildew and black rot directly from UAV-acquired RGB and multispectral imagery. These fashions are educated on labelled datasets wherein every image is annotated with disease classes (Sharma et al., 2022). During schooling, the CNN learns to partner particular pixel styles with disease kinds, permitting it to generalise and appropriately classify new, unseen statistics. Studies have demonstrated classification accuracies exceeding ninety-five per cent in managed environments and as much as ninety per cent in subject situations; with growing robustness as extra statistics and sundry imaging situations are added. Transfer gaining knowledge is another electricity of CNNs in this area. Pretrained fashions together with VGGNet, ResNet, and Inception—initially developed on big image datasets like ImageNet—may be high-quality-tuned using viticulture-specific imagery. This appreciably reduces the schooling time and computational requirements whilst retaining high accuracy. For example, researchers have effectively adapted ResNet-50 to discover grapevine sicknesses from UAV pics with minimal labelled facts via retraining the simplest final layers of the community. Another important software of CNNs is in semantic segmentation, which involves pixel-smart classification of a photo. In viticulture, that is crucial for precisely localising disorder-affected areas within a vineyard. Fully Convolutional Networks (FCNs), U-Net architectures, and DeepLab models are normally used for this venture. They help generate disorder severity maps that inform spatially variable treatments, optimise chemical use, and limit environmental impact. While CNNs are outstanding for detection and type, they depend heavily on huge volumes of first-rate categorised facts. This poses a full-size mission in agricultural domain names where disease pics can be scarce, particularly for early-stage signs or rare infections. To address this trouble, Generative Adversarial Networks (GANs) were introduced as a complementary generation.

Figure 4. Images of synthetic grape leaf diseases made with GANs

Generative Adversarial Networks (GANs) were used to develop realistic images of grape leaves with symptoms depicted for various disease classes. The image shows how the generator network generates leaf texture, patterns of different discolored patches, and distribution of lesions while the discriminator network checks that they resemble real images. GAN-generated images improve balance in datasets by augmenting the number of rare disease classes. Augmented images indicate the quality for training convolutional neural network (CNN) models, and improve performance related to predictions, especially in imbalanced classes. GANs consist of two neural networks—the generator and the discriminator—engaged in a zero-sum recreation. The generator attempts to supply realistic artificial pics from random noise or dependent inputs, while the discriminator tries to differentiate between real and generated pics. Through iterative schooling, the generator improves until it could create particularly sensible photos indistinguishable from actual records. In viticulture, GANs are leveraged to enhance schooling datasets by generating artificial ailment snapshots that mimic various ranges, environmental situations, and symptom versions. This enhances the variety and robustness of CNN fashions, in particular whilst actual datasets are constrained. For example, a Conditional GAN (cGAN) may be trained to generate unique disease types with the aid of conditioning the generator on sickness labels, allowing for controlled image eras and balanced datasets. Moreover, CycleGANs were used to transform healthful grapevine pics into diseased ones, allowing the simulation of sickness progression through the years. This has full-size implications for education fashions to discover early signs, in addition to teaching vineyard managers through synthetic but practical eventualities. By exposing CNNs to a wider range of disorder manifestations, GAN-augmented datasets enhance model generalisation and decrease false positives and negatives in subject programs. GANs are also applied in top-notch decision imaging, which is particularly beneficial for reinforcing the satisfaction of UAV-received pics taken from higher altitudes. High-resolution pix are crucial for detecting small or early-stage lesions that may be lost in lower-resolution statistics. Super-resolution GANs (SRGANs) can upscale photo resolution whilst retaining vital functions, thereby enhancing the accuracy of the next CNN-based class. Another progressive application is the use of GANs in anomaly detection. By schooling a GAN to generate wholesome winery imagery, any good-sized deviation from the found-out distribution may be flagged as a potential disease presence, despite the fact that the particular disease type is unknown. This unsupervised approach is mainly valuable for monitoring new pathogens or detecting pressure conditions not yet categorised in current datasets. Despite their promise, GANs include computationally demanding situations. Training GANs calls for great assets and is often unstable because of the adverse training procedure. To mitigate this, researchers rent techniques like Wasserstein loss features, characteristic matching, and spectral normalization to stabilize schooling and beautify the image first-class. The integration of CNNs and GANs within a UAV-based predictive analytics pipeline entails several key steps. First, UAVs acquire aerial imagery using RGB, multispectral, or hyperspectral sensors.

These snapshots are preprocessed to correct for noise, distortion, and illumination version. Next, GANs are used to reinforce the dataset, creating a richer and more balanced schooling corpus. The CNN is then trained or exceptionally tuned using this augmented dataset to classify and localize disease signs. The output from CNNs may be further processed using statistical and geospatial tools to generate disorder distribution maps and time-collection analytics.

VII. PROPOSED METHODOLOGY

The proposed UAV-enabled Grapes Disease Predictive Analytics System is a complete, modular framework that integrates UAV-based totally far-flung sensing, deep studying algorithms, and choice assist mechanisms to enable well-timed and unique vineyard ailment control. This method is rooted in the idea of leveraging aerial imagery and artificial intelligence to transport from reactive to proactive viticulture practices. The machine is composed of three middle modules—information acquisition, the usage of UAVs, information analytics via AI models (CNN and GAN), and choice support through an included dashboard—running in synergy to allow real-time, fact-knowledgeable actions within the vineyard. At the inspiration of the method lies the statistics acquisition method, which makes use of UAVs prepared with excessive-decision RGB, multispectral, and thermal cameras to seize aerial imagery of grapevine canopies. These UAVs operate through pre-programmed flight paths with GPS-guided waypoints to ensure constant and systematic insurance of the winery. The UAVs collect geo-tagged pictures, usually on a weekly timetable, all through critical boom intervals, shooting early disease signs and plant fitness parameters. Once captured, those photographs are transmitted to a steady server or edge computing unit for processing. However, uncooked pics from UAVs are susceptible to versions in illumination, attitude distortions, and heritage interference. Therefore, a rigorous preprocessing degree is undertaken regarding radiometric correction, geometric alignment, mosaicking of photograph tiles for broader coverage, and normalisation strategies to ensure picture consistency across datasets. Annotated datasets are then created by agricultural specialists who pick out and label disorder-affected regions that specialise in common infections, including downy mould, powdery mould, and black rot. This annotated fact is vital for educating AI models with excessive reliability. The analytics module is based upon a hybrid deep-learning framework that combines a Convolutional Neural Network (CNN) and a Generative Adversarial Network (GAN). CNNs are the model that performs disease classification and localisation using adapted architectures like ResNet or EfficientNet for high-resolution images of a vineyard. The CNN is trained on labelled image tiles to learn spectra features and spatial patterns that constitute disease symptoms. For example, based on irregularities in the texture or subtle pigmentation differences on the surface of a grape leaf, CNNs classify not just the disease but the potential host and varietal-dependent symptoms. Since rare diseases, or the earliest signs of disease, can be rare events, GANs are deployed as a means to augment the training data with synthetic samples using the CNN model to be the generator. Conditional GANs (cGANs) and CycleGANs would generate realistic images of diseased grapevines in multiple contexts in a way to simulate the conditions affecting the image. In leveraging cGAN or CycleGAN, augmentation strategies can be developed to mitigate class imbalance and improve the training dataset. The synthetic augmentation provides the flexibility for the CNN model to better generalise, which should improve both classification performance and accuracy to provide real-world deployment. Here, signals of vineyard disease using GAN are a prolific feature too, for creating synthetic transits of a transition from healthy to diseased stages (a smooth transition), to support the training of the CNNs for near-future detection of early and subtle signs of symptoms. To enhance the robustness of detection, a multi-disease classification machine is applied using a multi-head CNN version that simultaneously identifies a couple of illnesses and their severity tiers. Furthermore, an anomaly detection module primarily based on GANs is integrated to locate unknown or emerging disease patterns by getting to know the distribution of healthy plant imagery and flagging deviations for expert evaluation. Once the AI fashions classify the disease instances, the outputs are georeferenced and layered onto digital maps. Using spatial evaluation strategies which include clustering (e.g., DBSCAN, k-means), the device generates sickness severity maps and heatmaps that show the temporal and spatial distribution of infections throughout the vineyard. These visualisations are important for figuring out high-hazard zones and expertise disorder dynamics in terms of environmental elements like humidity, temperature, and soil moisture. To make certain well-timed and localised selection-making, the proposed method includes side computing. Lightweight variations of the CNN models are deployed on embedded structures like the NVIDIA Jetson Nano or Raspberry Pi devices that are set up on UAVs or nearby subject gadgets. This setup permits real-time image evaluation at once in the discipline, without reliance on cloud-based processing.

VIII. IMPLEMENTATION AND ANALYSIS

Implementing the UAV-enabled grape sickness predictive analytics gadget entails a multidimensional procedure, encompassing technological setup, area deployment, version schooling, facts pipeline integration, and overall performance evaluation. The deployment starts with organising a reliable UAV-based totally remote sensing infrastructure. Drones selected for implementation are mid-to-high endurance fashions able to self-sustain flight, prepared with RGB, multispectral, and thermal imaging sensors. The imaging payload is calibrated to ensure certain spectral accuracy and alignment, which is important for taking pictures of disorder indicators invisible to the bare eye. The UAVs are programmed with precise flight paths, masking the whole vineyard with overlapping imagery to facilitate later image mosaicking and spatial accuracy. Flights are conducted underneath consistent lighting fixture conditions to preserve uniformity, and floor manipulate points (GCPs) are deployed at some point of the vineyard for greater georeferencing accuracy. Post-flight, the pics accrued are transferred to a centralised records garage and processing surroundings. This gadget may be either cloud-based or run on a local facet server relying on the vineyard's connectivity and infrastructure competencies. Image preprocessing is initiated right away, inclusive of radiometric corrections to account for varying sunlight exposure, geometric corrections for digicam attitude distortion, and mosaicking to generate orthorectified picture maps. The corrected snapshots are then segmented into tiles of possible length for feeding into the deep mastering fashions (Juyal & Sharma, 2021). Each tile keeps its geospatial metadata to make certain spatial traceability of any predictions made by using the version. The implementation of AI fashions starts with the education segment. The CNN structure-particularly a ResNet-50 changed for agricultural disorder detection—is exceptionally tuned for the use of a vineyard-precise dataset. The dataset consists of numerous illustrations of grape types, ailment kinds, levels of contamination, and environmental conditions to ensure version generalisation. Training employs statistics augmentation techniques together with rotation, scaling, and flipping to enhance version robustness. In parallel, GANs are educated on the use of restricted sickness samples to synthetically generate sensible grape disease imagery. This synthetic record is then combined with real imagery to stabilise elegance distribution, deal with rare disease instances, and make bigger the schooling set without the giant want for manual annotation. The CNN-GAN hybrid gadget is evaluated using a preserve-out validation set and examined in opposition to unseen area statistics to evaluate predictive accuracy and localization precision. Integration into an operational workflow includes linking model outputs with a geospatial interface. An internet-based dashboard is totally developed for real-time interplay, in which disorder predictions are displayed as overlays on excessive-resolution winery maps. The system presents pixel-wise classification, indicating not just the presence of an ailment but additionally the predicted severity and type. Time series analytics permit users to track ailment progression and correlate it with ancient climate and control statistics. The device is also designed to trigger indicators based totally on risk thresholds, prompting subject visits, localised remedy, or, in addition, UAV inspections. Through this setup, ailment management becomes now not only the handiest reactive but also strategically proactive, supported via nonstop data, going with the flow and predictive insights. A pilot deployment was carried out in a medium-scale vineyard placed in a semi-arid area liable to powdery mildew and black rot. Over a growing season, the UAV system did biweekly flights, and statistics were processed inside 24 hours of the series. The AI models confirmed a detection accuracy of 92.6% for powdery mildew and 89.4% for black rot, with a mean false-high-quality rate under 7%. When combined with GAN-augmented schooling, the accuracy progressed by four–6%, in particular for early-stage symptoms. The semantic segmentation version correctly delineated inflamed zones with an IoU score of 0.82, enabling the vineyard managers to execute focused fungicide packages that reduced chemical utilisation with the aid of about 30% as compared to traditional blanket spraying methods. Feedback from subject groups confirmed that the predictive indicators aligned with bodily signs discovered in the course of floor truth verification, validating the device's real-world applicability. Further evaluation was carried out to assess the temporal consistency and spatial reliability of the predictions. The machine's capacity to hit upon disorder recurrence in historically prone zones becomes pass-confirmed with past guide statistics and sickness prevalence maps. In over 85% of the instances, the device correctly anticipated the spatial clusters in which disorder re-emergence came about, indicating robust ability for long-term disease tracking and spatial hazard modelling. Additionally, environmental elements which include temperature, humidity, and canopy density had been incorporated right into a multi-variable evaluation framework to refine predictions. This contextual integration helped reduce false positives in regions in which image styles mimicked ailment symptoms due to lighting or leaf discoloration from non-pathogenic stressors. Implementation additionally covered part computing integration. A low-strength GPU-enabled tool (NVIDIA Jetson Nano) turned into use to run lightweight variations of the educated fashions within the field. This allowed for real-time ailment class immediately at the UAV or a close-by base station without dependence on cloud processing. The latency from image capture to ailment detection changed to decreased to beneath 10 mins, permitting area teams to respond promptly for the duration of important phenological levels. The area unit was solar-powered and built for rugged environmental conditions, ensuring uninterrupted operation even in far-off or connectivity-challenged regions. To guide human-centric decision-making, the device changed into a connection with a choice help interface offering customisable thresholds, remedy history logs, and value-advantage analytics. This function enabled agronomists to simulate various management situations, which include the impact of early spraying versus behind-schedule movement in terms of each financial go-back and sickness containment. The interface also allowed for personal comments to be submitted after discipline inspections, which became included in the machine's training information, forming a closed feedback loop for non-stop gaining knowledge of and modelling. The implementation and evaluation of the proposed UAV-based grape disease predictive devices reveal their technical viability, scalability, and transformative ability. The aggregate of excessive-decision imaging, deep getting-to-know algorithms, and real-time feedback mechanisms results in a strong device for winery ailment control. The successful pilot testing, excessive accuracy metrics, operational efficiency, and integration with present farm workflows underscore the machine's potential to become a necessary part of precision viticulture. As the device continues to evolve via continuous deployment and retraining, its ability to count on disorder outbreaks and guide interventions will drastically enhance competitiveness and sustainability in grape manufacturing.

Figure 5. Flowchart of proposed methodology

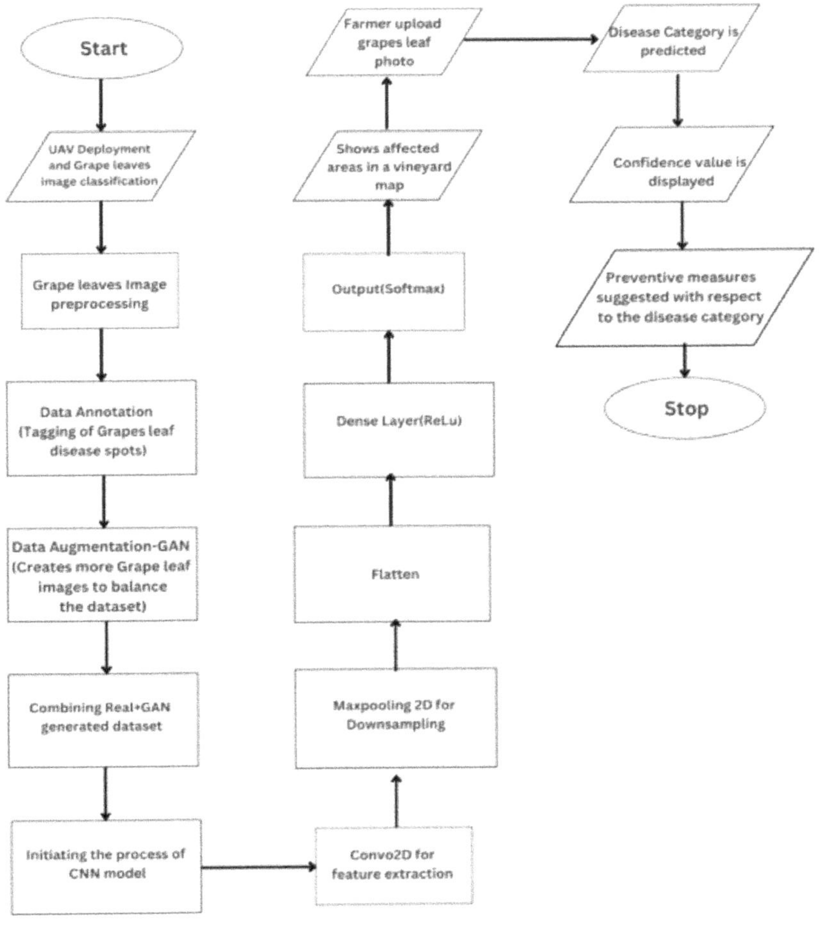

Figure 5 shows the flowchart of the UAV-assisted Grape Leaf Disease Detection System Using GAN and CNN models. This flowchart is a way to illustrate the grape disease detection process from the UAV setup and capturing of aerial images through the most important steps: preprocessing, image annotation, and the generation of synthetic data using GANs which help address the imbalanced datasets. This enriched dataset went through a CNN in which it performed CNN processes (i.e., convolution, pooling, and classification) through the dense layers and softmax. Finally, a farmer-facing interface will allow users to upload images of grape leaves and receive predictions of any leaf diseases with accuracy scores and recommended approaches. Consequently, this complete cycle will help improve precision farming by combining artificial intelligence, remote sensing, and mobile access.

IX. RESULT ANALYSIS

Figure 6 offers a detailed class report that summarizes the predictive overall performance of the system throughout the four key categories: Grape Black rot, Grape Esca (Black Measles), Grape Leaf blight (Isariopsis Leaf Spot), and Grape healthy. The report consists of metrics which includes precision, remember, and F1-ratings for each category, presenting insight into how successfully the CNN model distinguishes between various sickness situations as well as wholesome leaf samples. This visible assessment of the model's performance is important for verifying that the gadget is robust in figuring out diffused variations in ailment manifestation, thereby making sure dependable predictions for timely winery control selections. Figure 7 shows the training development of the predictive model, showing the accuracy and loss curves as the training progresses through epochs. As training continues, it can be observed in the graph that the network accuarcy improves, while it take a little time for loss to decrease, which indicates that learning and training of the CNN model has occurred and that the CNN model is converging. The accuracy and loss curves show that, the network is correctly calibrated, and capable of generalising onto new unseen data, crucial in using the model on real grape plants. Tracking the performace assessment of both acceptability and quality over time is critical in showing that the combination of CNN (predictive model) and GAN (data generation model) components provide a stable and accurate fruit disease detection system in a real-time application.

Figure 6. Classification report

	precision	recall	f1-score	support
Grape__Black_rot	0.95	1.00	0.97	472
Grape__Esca_(Black_Measles)	1.00	0.97	0.99	480
Grape__Leaf_blight_(Isariopsis_Leaf_Spot)	0.99	0.97	0.98	430
Grap__healthy	1.00	0.98	0.99	423
accuracy			0.98	1805
macro avg	0.98	0.98	0.98	1805
weighted avg	0.98	0.98	0.98	1805

Figure 7. Accuracy and loss curves

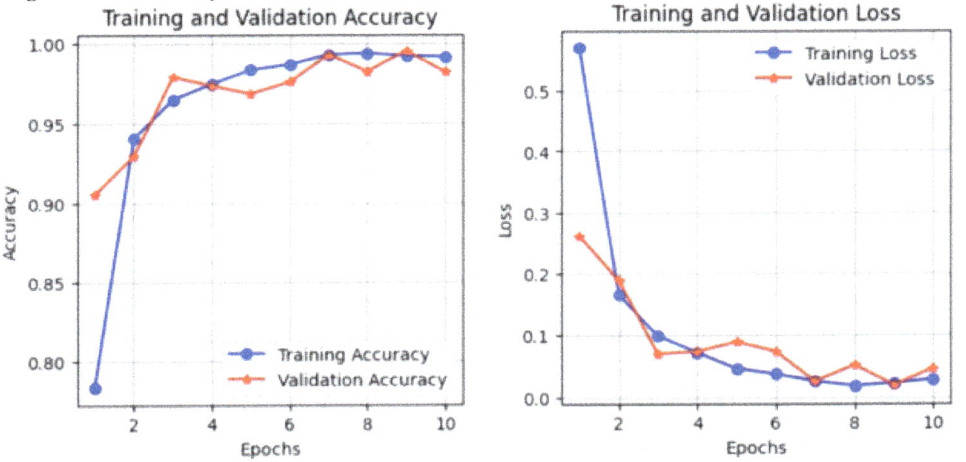

Grape Disease Detection System in Figure 8 demonstrates the gadget's capability for precise ailment identity and predictive evaluation the usage of a mobile software interface. It permits customers to both capture or upload an photo of a grape leaf, and then the system predicts the sickness magnificence—which include Grape Black rot, Grape Esca (Black Measles), or Grape Leaf blight (Isariopsis Leaf Spot)—along side confidence ranges. Additionally, the app offers future severity prediction primarily based on contextual environmental parameters like area, temperature, humidity, and soil moisture. This real-time photograph-primarily based analysis aids vineyard managers and agricultural stakeholders in making rapid and accurate decisions for disease manipulate. By forecasting ailment development and categorizing severity tiers, the software helps strategic planning and optimizes disorder control protocols at once within the subject.

Figure 8. Grape disease detection system

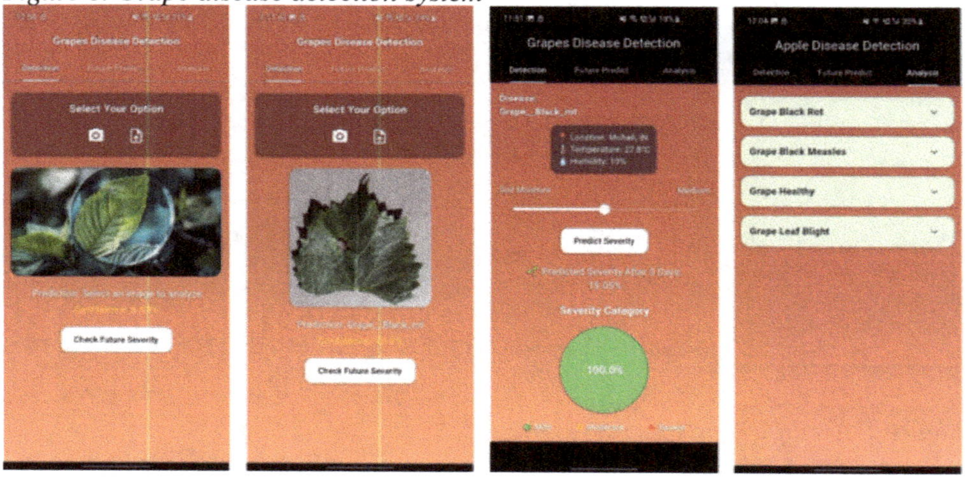

X. ADVANTAGES

The UAV-enabled grape disorder predictive analytics device evolved in this study gives a mess of blessings spanning across technological, financial, and agricultural domain names. By integrating modern AI techniques with the UAV era, the proposed device drastically elevates the same old ailment tracking, crop management, and selection-making approaches in vineyards. These advantages are mentioned in the element under to focus on the multi-dimensional impact of the answer.

- Early Detection and Timely Intervention: Perhaps the maximum critical gain of the system lies in its ability to locate grape illnesses at an early level. Traditional guide inspections often fail to perceive subtle signs in their preliminary levels, especially in large-scale vineyards in which non-stop monitoring isn't always viable. However, the AI-based technique guarantees that even the slightest discolouration, spot, or fungal growth patterns may be detected via high-resolution UAV imagery and processed through the CNN version in real time. This reduces standard crop damage, improves yield, and minimises pointless resource usage.
- Reduction in Human Error and Labour: Manual disease inspection is surprisingly prone to errors due to fatigue, loss of schooling, and subjective interpretations. Even skilled agronomists may additionally forget about signs beneath negative lights or inconsistent area situations. The automated AI-based gad-

gets reduce this dependency and ensure steady, unbiased checks throughout entire fields. Moreover, the usage of UAVs considerably minimises the want for human hard work to perform bodily inspections. In expansive vineyards, this translates to great time and labour savings. Farmers can redirect human resources closer to other effective tasks even while relying on UAV flights for surveillance and diagnostics.

- Real-Time Decision-Making through App Integration: One of the standout capabilities of the system is its real-time ailment prediction via cell and web applications. Farmers do not need to watch for lab reports or expert visits. By really taking pictures or uploading a grape leaf image, they get hold of on-the-spot feedback about the plant's health repute. This immediacy is essential in handling rapid-spreading diseases like Black Rot and Leaf Blight. The machine does not present the most effective sickness identity; however, it additionally indicates remedial actions, making it a complete choice-support tool. Real-time notifications, logging of past diagnoses, and GPS-based sickness mapping similarly beautify the utility of the software.
- Cost-Effective Agricultural Management: While the preliminary setup regarding UAVs and AI education infrastructure may additionally seem luxurious, the long-term savings are large. Early sickness detection helps keep away from significant infections, thereby reducing fees related to pesticide overuse, replanting, and exertions – in-depth guide inspections. Additionally, using AI reduces the dependency on agricultural experts for ordinary inspections, reducing operational fees. The system allows aid optimisation—making use of fungicides most effective when and wherein wanted—mainly to lower chemical usage, price, financial savings, and green practices.
- Improved Crop Quality and Yield: Consistent and correct monitoring of plant fitness guarantees that the handiest, most wholesome, and greatest grapes are harvested, thereby improving marketability and pricing. The predictive analytics version helps fact-pushed cultivation, where trends are monitored and interventions are optimised across the growing season. When grape illnesses are not well-timed or addressed, they can appreciably affect the sugar content, texture, and size of the fruit. With this system, producers can keep excellent output and ensure compliance with export standards and certifications.
- Data Archival and Analytical Insights: Every picture captured and every prediction made through the app is saved on a totally cloud-based gadget. Over time, this creates a treasured archive of visual and analytical statistics associated with winery fitness. Farmers and researchers can use these facts to:
    - Track the seasonal prevalence of different sickness
    - Analyse the effectiveness of treatment protocols
    - Observe weather-related sickness developments

- o Make knowledgeable choices for the subsequent planting cycle
- o These analytical insights assist long-term planning and make contributions to sustainable farming practices.

- Strengthening Precision Agriculture: This machine exemplifies the principles of precision agriculture—using records and technology to optimise each input in the farming manner. UAV-based aerial imaging mixed with AI-driven analysis lets in for micromanagement of subject conditions. Farmers can focus on unique zones of contamination instead of treating the entire discipline, which ends up in better crop fitness, reduced environmental footprint, and extended profitability. This is specifically beneficial in natural farming, where chemical treatments are confined and early detection is important for preserving certification requirements.

XI. CHALLENGES

While the UAV-enabled grape disorder predictive analytics device demonstrates great promise in revolutionising vineyard control, it's far more important to recognise and seriously examine the demanding situations and boundaries that may affect its real-world deployment and long-term sustainability. This phase addresses the technical, environmental, economic, and human-related challenges encountered inside the development and implementation of the system.

- Environmental and Weather Constraints: One of the number one demanding situations of UAV deployment is its dependency on climate situations. UAVs are sensitive to strong winds. Rain, fog, and severe temperatures – all of that can disrupt scheduled flights or degrade the pleasantness of photos captured. In agricultural environments in which unpredictability of climate is commonplace, constant drone operations can be tough to hold. Additionally, light variations due to cloud cover, shadows from nearby timber, and changing solar angles at some point of the day can have an effect on the clarity and comparison of leaf photos. Although the CNN The model has been skilled to deal with a few degrees of variability; drastic environmental fluctuations can lessen prediction accuracy, specifically for the duration of early morning or dusk hours when mild stages are low.
- Technical Limitations of UAVs and Equipment: Despite improvements, the UAVs used in agriculture regularly face battery boundaries. Most commercial drones have a flight time of around 20 minutes to half an hour, which restricts the insurance vicinity in keeping with flight. This can be a prime constraint for huge vineyards until multiple drones or speedy battery-swapping

systems are hired. Moreover, the quality of the onboard camera also plays a crucial role. Lower-decision cameras can also fail to capture diffused leaf styles, whilst excessive-decision cameras boom records size and processing requirements. Balancing photo first-class with UAV value and energy intake stays a chronic task. Another technical hurdle is associated with GPS inaccuracies in far-flung or mountainous areas that may avoid accurate mapping of sickness spread across winery zones.

- Computational Load and Storage Requirements: CNN and GAN fashions for disorder detection calls for full-size computational resources, in particular at some point of the training phase. Although inference (i.e., prediction) is lighter, it nevertheless needs cellular gadgets with moderate processing energy or cloud-based infrastructure with sturdy connectivity. For smallholder farmers in far-off regions, restraint gets entry. Excessive-speed internet or superior smartphones can also come to be a barrier to the usage of the cell app efficaciously. Offline functionality has been considered; however, it calls for pre-downloaded fashions and optimised lightweight architectures—adding improvement complexity. In addition, the sizable wide variety of high-decision snapshots generated through UAVs and processed at some stage in education creates giant garage necessities. Without adequate cloud storage answers, long-time-period records archival and historic evaluation can become hard.
- Dependence on High-Quality Training Data: The reliability of the predictive machine is handiest as true because of the data used to educate it. While GANs assist in increasing datasets. Through generating synthetic snapshots, the base requirement of diverse, real, and accurately categorised facts stays essential. Collecting these facts is an exertion in depth and must involve professional validation to ensure it is fine. A biased or poorly curated dataset can lead to overfitting or underperformance in the area. For example, if the dataset consists of, broadly speaking, mature-degree symptoms, the version might fail to come across diseases of their early stages. Ensuring coverage across ailment tiers, leaf types, and environmental situations is a continuous data collection project.
- Disease Overlap and Symptom Similarity: Grapevine illnesses frequently present comparable visible signs and symptoms—spots, discolourations, wilting, or fungal blooms—making it difficult for even advanced AI models to distinguish among them. In precise terms, symptoms of Grape Black Rot and Grape Esca (Black Measles) may also appear almost equal at some stage in certain growth degrees or light situations. Although the confusion matrix discovered that the version handled this with reasonable accuracy, aspect instances and borderline signs and symptoms nevertheless pose type problems.

- Initial Setup and Training Costs: While long-time-period use of the gadget reduces operational costs, the preliminary funding required for UAV procurement, AI version education, and application improvement can be large. Small farmers or cooperatives may also find those advance expenses prohibitive until subsidized through authority's schemes or supported by way of agricultural era offers. Moreover, schooling neighborhood employees to function UAVs, control datasets, and interpret model predictions calls for time and academic outreach. Without proper schooling, the chance of misuse or underuse increases, decreasing the machine's basic effect.

XII. CONCLUSION

The integration of UAV era with advanced AI-primarily based predictive analytics has opened a brand new frontier in precision agriculture, particularly inside the context of grape sickness detection. Through this research, a complete and scalable device has been proposed and carried out that successfully leverages Convolutional Neural Networks (CNN) and Generative Adversarial Networks (GAN) to identify illnesses consisting of Grape Black rot, Grape Esca (Black Measles), and Grape Leaf blight (Isariopsis Leaf Spot), alongside the type of healthful grape leaves. The solution notably reduces the time, labor, and fee concerned in traditional inspection methods through allowing early-stage disease detection and timely interventions. Furthermore, the system's capacity to technique excessive-decision imagery collected by drones and deliver actionable insights through a person-friendly mobile app empowers farmers with real-time, records-pushed decision-making equipment. The deployment of one of this machine has validated substantial benefits along with stepped forward crop yield, ailment containment, and reduced environmental effect via centered pesticide use. The inclusion of capabilities like on-spot detection thru picture upload or seize via the app, visualization of metrics like accuracy, loss, and epoch graphs, and garage of ancient disease developments adds useful intensity and complements usability. However, demanding situations like environmental dependencies, computational requirements, person literacy, and records privateness problems nevertheless gift hurdles that want to be addressed for complete-scale adoption. These issues underscore the need for robust infrastructure, ability-constructing packages, and robust coverage assist to ensure that such improvements reach all levels of agricultural stakeholders, from smallholders to huge estate managers. Looking beforehand, the future scope of this system is vast. Expansion to other crops, integration with IoT sensors for soil and weather tracking, and actual-time alert systems the usage of geolocation facts can further beautify its application. More importantly, using GANs to generate numerous sickness styles opens up possibilities for simulating uncommon or early-stage conditions, making models greater sturdy and inclusive. With in addition improvements in part computing, 5G connectivity, and explainable AI, this UAV-enabled predictive gadget can evolve right into a complete-fledged clever farming platform. In end, this painting represents a widespread step toward harnessing AI for sustainable agriculture and paves the way for clever, autonomous crop control systems which can adapt to dynamic demanding situations and help worldwide food protection.

REFERENCES

Almalki, F. A., Soufiene, B. O., Alsamhi, S. H., & Sakli, H. (2021). A Low-Cost platform for environmental smart farming monitoring system based on IoT and UAVs. *Sustainability (Basel)*, *13*(11), 5908. DOI: 10.3390/su13115908

Ammoniaci, M., Kartsiotis, S., Perria, R., & Storchi, P. (2021). *State-of-the-art monitoring technologies and data processing for precision viticulture*. Multidisciplinary Digital Publishing Institute., DOI: 10.3390/agriculture11030201

Chin, R., Catal, C., & Kassahun, A. (2023). Plant disease detection using drones in precision agriculture. Springer Science+Business Media. DOI: 10.1007/s11119-023-10014-y

Fuentes-Peailillo, F., Gutter, K., Vega, R., & Silva, G. C. (2024). Transformative technologies in digital agriculture: Leveraging the Internet of Things, remote sensing, and artificial intelligence for smart crop management. *Journal of Sensor and Actuator Networks*, *13*(4), 39. Advance online publication. DOI: 10.3390/jsan13040039

Juyal, P., & Sharma, S. (2021). Crop growth monitoring using unmanned aerial vehicle for farm field management. 2022 7th International Conference on Communication and Electronics Systems (ICCES), 880–884. DOI: 10.1109/ICCES51350.2021.9489182

Kerkech, M., Hafiane, A., & Canals, R. (2020). Vine disease detection in UAV multispectral images using optimized image registration and deep learning segmentation approach. *Computers and Electronics in Agriculture*, *174*, 105446. DOI: 10.1016/j.compag.2020.105446

Kumar, K., Sharma, S., Pandey, P., & Goyal, H. R. (2022). IoT Enabled Crop Detection System using Soil Analysis. 2022 7th International Conference on Communication and Electronics Systems (ICCES), 323–327. DOI: 10.1109/ICCES54183.2022.9835959

Li, R., Liu, J., Shi, B., Zhao, H., Li, Y., Zheng, X., Peng, C., & Lv, C. (2024). High-Performance grape disease detection method using multimodal data and parallel activation functions. *Plants*, *13*(19), 2720. DOI: 10.3390/plants13192720 PMID: 39409590

Maraveas, C. (2022). Incorporating artificial intelligence technology in smart greenhouses: Current state of the art. *Applied Sciences (Basel, Switzerland)*, *13*(1), 14. DOI: 10.3390/app13010014

Olson, B. K., Brooke, M., Wang, Z., Svyantek, A., Stenger, J., & Hatterman-Valenti, H. (2021). 'Frontenac' grape response to canopy management in North Dakota. *Horticulturae*, *7*(9), 288. DOI: 10.3390/horticulturae7090288

Ouhami, M., Es-Saady, Y., Hajj, M. E., Canals, R., & Hafiane, A. (2022). Meteorological data and UAV images for the detection and identification of grapevine disease using deep learning. *2022 E-Health and Bioengineering Conference (EHB)*, 1–4. DOI: 10.1109/EHB55594.2022.9991443

Ouyang, J., De Bei, R., Fuentes, S., & Collins, C. (2020). UAV and ground-based imagery analysis detects canopy structure changes after canopy management applications. *OENO One*, *54*(4), 1093–1103. DOI: 10.20870/oeno-one.2020.54.4.3647

Senoo, E. E. K., Anggraini, L., Kumi, J. A., Karolina, L. B., Akansah, E., Sulyman, H. A., Mendonça, I., & Aritsugi, M. (2024). IoT Solutions with Artificial Intelligence Technologies for Precision Agriculture: Definitions, Applications, Challenges, and Opportunities. *Electronics (Basel)*, *13*(10), 1894. DOI: 10.3390/electronics13101894

Shafik, W., Tufail, A., De Silva Liyanage, C., & Apong, R. H. M. (2023). Using a novel convolutional neural network for plant pests detection and disease classification. *Journal of the Science of Food and Agriculture*, *103*(12), 5849–5861. DOI: 10.1002/jsfa.12700 PMID: 37177888

Shahi, T. B., Xu, C., Neupane, A., & Guo, W. (2023). Recent advances in crop disease detection using UAV and deep learning techniques. *Remote Sensing (Basel)*, *15*(9), 2450. DOI: 10.3390/rs15092450

Sharma, S., Ghanshala, A., & Tyagi, R. (2022). Cotton Crop Disease Detection System Using Deep Learning Approach. In *2022 IEEE Conference on Interdisciplinary Approaches in Technology and Management for Social Innovation (IATMSI)*, 1–6. DOI: 10.1109/IATMSI56455.2022.10119275

Singh, U., Srivastava, A., Chauhan, D., & Singh, A. (2020). Computer Vision Technique for Detection of Grape Esca (Black Measles) Disease from Grape Leaf Samples. *International Conference on Contemporary Computing and Applications*, 110–115. DOI: 10.1109/IC3A48958.2020.233281

Verma, A. K., Diksha, N., & Sharma, S. (2024). Artificial Intelligence Integrated Rice Crop Disease Detection Using Drones for Smart Farming. In 2024 7th International Conference on Circuit Power and Computing Technologies (ICCPCT), 235, 709–713. DOI: 10.1109/ICCPCT61902.2024.10672693

Chapter 13

Unified Intelligence for Strategic Business Transformation Through Cross-Functional Integration of AI and Predictive Analytics

O. Bhaskaru
http://orcid.org/0000-0001-6495-3327
Vignan's Foundation for Science, Technology, and Research, India

K. Lalitha
http://orcid.org/0009-0004-9735-7205
Santhiram Engineering College, India

Farooq Sunar Mahammad
http://orcid.org/0000-0003-0936-1980
Santhiram Engineering College, India

Noraisyah Binti Tajudin
http://orcid.org/0000-0002-3868-815X
Lincoln University College, Malaysia

ABSTRACT

The rise of artificial intelligence (AI) and predictive analytics in organizational strategy marks a shift from intuition-based to insight-driven decision-making. However, many businesses still rely on siloed AI applications, limiting their trans-

DOI: 10.4018/979-8-3373-3648-0.ch013

formative potential. This chapter explores how cross-functional AI integration across finance, marketing, HR, and supply chain can create a unified analytical foundation to drive competitive and adaptive strategies. Through practical models and evidence-based analysis, it presents a structured approach to embedding AI in enterprise workflows. Synchronized predictive systems can align departmental goals, improve forecasting accuracy, and enhance agility in uncertain markets. By linking technology with leadership, AI becomes a driver of innovation, efficiency, and long-term resilience. Key challenges such as data silos, ethical algorithm use, and the need for responsible governance are discussed. The chapter ultimately guides researchers, managers, and leaders in building scalable, ethically sound AI ecosystems for strategic business growth.

INTRODUCTION

In today's fast-evolving digital landscape, organizations face immense pressure to leverage data and emerging technologies to maintain competitiveness and operational excellence. Artificial Intelligence (AI) and predictive analytics have become pivotal in transforming how businesses make decisions, optimize processes, and engage customers. However, despite technological advancements, many organizations struggle to implement AI holistically across different departments, leading to fragmented efforts and missed opportunities for synergy.

This chapter explores the concept of Unified Intelligence—an integrated approach to AI deployment that breaks down silos and fosters collaboration across finance, marketing, human resources, and supply chain management. It aims to provide a comprehensive roadmap for effectively harnessing AI's strategic potential to drive sustained competitive advantage.

Background and Significance

The accelerating pace of digital transformation across industries has made data one of the most valuable assets for organizations worldwide (Brynjolfsson & McAfee, 2017). Firms are inundated with enormous volumes of structured and unstructured data generated from customer interactions, supply chain activities, financial transactions, social media, IoT devices, and enterprise systems. This data tsunami offers both tremendous opportunities and significant challenges for decision-makers.

Traditional business intelligence approaches that rely on historical reporting and gut instinct are no longer sufficient in navigating increasingly volatile and competitive markets (Agrawal, Gans, & Goldfarb, 2018; Davenport & Ronanki, 2018). AI and predictive analytics have emerged as game-changing technologies that enable organizations to transform raw data into foresight, operational efficiency, and strategic advantage (Goodfellow, Bengio, & Courville, 2016).

Predictive analytics applies advanced statistical, machine learning (ML), and deep learning algorithms to uncover hidden patterns, predict future outcomes, and recommend actions (Alpaydin, 2020; Baesens, 2014). AI augments human intelligence by automating complex tasks, generating insights at scale, and enabling real-time responsiveness (Dwivedi et al., 2021).

Despite these technological advances, many organizations fall short of realizing the full benefits of AI and analytics due to fragmented deployment across siloed business functions (Zhang, Chen, & Yu, 2020). For instance, marketing departments may employ AI-driven customer segmentation and campaign optimization tools, while finance teams separately use predictive models for risk assessment, and HR leverages AI for talent management, all without integration or data sharing (Baryannis, Dani, & Antoniou, 2019).

This fragmentation results in duplicated investments, inconsistent insights, and misaligned strategies that undermine organizational agility and innovation (Henke, Libarikian, & Wiseman, 2018). The concept of Unified Intelligence seeks to address this problem by integrating AI and predictive analytics capabilities across finance, marketing, HR, and supply chain management to establish a single source of truth and collective intelligence.

By enabling cross-functional data flows, aligned decision-making processes, and shared strategic objectives, organizations can unlock synergies that multiply the impact of AI investments and foster enterprise-wide agility (Zhang et al., 2020; Baryannis et al., 2019).

Several macroeconomic and technological trends reinforce the urgency of adopting unified AI strategies. Global supply chains are increasingly complex and vulnerable to disruption, as seen during the COVID-19 pandemic, making integrated analytics critical for resilience (Wang, Gunasekaran, Ngai, & Papadopoulos, 2016). Customer expectations for personalized experiences require seamless coordination between marketing, sales, and product operations (Kumar & Reinartz, 2016). The labor market demands more agile workforce planning in the face of shifting skills requirements and digital transformation (Liu & Wang, 2020). Finance departments must navigate volatile markets and regulatory pressures with sophisticated forecasting and risk management tools (Chui, Manyika, & Miremadi, 2016).

Technological enablers have matured sufficiently to support unified intelligence. Cloud computing offers scalable storage and compute resources; big data frameworks like Apache Hadoop and Spark facilitate handling massive datasets; containerized microservices architectures promote modular, interoperable AI systems (Henke et al., 2018).

Advances in XAI help mitigate the risks of opaque decision models and foster trust across stakeholders (Ribeiro, Singh, & Guestrin, 2016). Additionally, ethical AI frameworks and governance models are emerging to ensure responsible deployment aligned with societal values and regulatory requirements (OECD, 2019; Hofmann, Samp, & Woods, 2020).

Nevertheless, achieving unified intelligence is not merely a technology challenge. It requires a holistic transformation encompassing strategic alignment, organizational culture, leadership commitment, governance structures, and workforce capabilities (Dwivedi et al., 2021; Zhou & Chen, 2021). This chapter provides a comprehensive roadmap to navigating these multifaceted dimensions, aiming to equip researchers and practitioners with the knowledge to harness AI for sustained competitive advantage.

Related Work and Literature Synthesis

Over the past decade, a growing body of research has emphasized the potential of Artificial Intelligence (AI) and predictive analytics in enhancing decision-making, improving efficiency, and creating competitive advantages across various business domains. Scholars such as Davenport and Ronanki (2018) have documented how AI is transforming individual business functions like finance, marketing, and human resources. For example, AI applications in marketing have focused on personalization and customer segmentation (Erevelles, Fukawa, & Swayne, 2016), while predictive analytics in finance has improved fraud detection and risk forecasting (Chui, Manyika, & Miremadi, 2016).

In the human resources domain, Liu and Wang (2020) explored how AI-driven HR analytics can predict employee attrition and enhance talent management. Similarly, supply chain research has examined the use of predictive models to optimize logistics and demand forecasting (Wang et al., 2016; Baryannis, Dani, & Antoniou, 2019). These studies highlight the function-specific benefits of AI deployment.

However, while these works underscore the value of AI within isolated departments, relatively few studies offer a cross-functional perspective. Zhang, Chen, and Yu (2020) recognize this gap and propose preliminary models for enterprise-wide AI integration, but these remain theoretical and lack detailed implementation guidance. Furthermore, the literature lacks comprehensive frameworks that address both the technical infrastructure (e.g., data integration, real-time analytics) and the organizational enablers (e.g., leadership, ethics, governance) necessary for unified intelligence.

Additionally, ethical challenges such as algorithmic bias, data privacy, and the need for explainable AI (Ribeiro, Singh, & Guestrin, 2016; Mehrabi et al., 2019) are often discussed in isolation, with limited guidance on how to embed these principles in enterprise AI systems holistically.

This chapter seeks to address these gaps by offering a strategic framework for Unified Intelligence that integrates AI across finance, marketing, human resources, and supply chain functions. It also provides practical implementation guidance rooted in organizational readiness, system interoperability, and ethical governance. Furthermore, it outlines a roadmap that aligns AI capabilities with enterprise-wide transformation goals, supporting sustainable and strategic business outcomes.

By synthesizing the contributions of prior work and extending them through a unified, interdisciplinary approach, this chapter provides a valuable contribution to the evolving field of enterprise AI integration.

Objectives and Scope

This chapter aims to fill critical gaps in understanding how to architect, implement, and govern AI-driven unified intelligence systems that dismantle traditional organizational silos and enable seamless cross-functional collaboration. The chapter begins by elucidating foundational concepts of artificial intelligence and predictive analytics, which are pivotal for establishing effective cross-departmental integration. These foundational insights offer readers a conceptual grounding in machine learning models, data-driven decision-making, and pattern recognition technologies, laying the groundwork for how AI can act as a unifying mechanism across diverse business units (Alpaydin, 2020; Baesens, 2014).

Building on this foundation, the chapter proceeds to demonstrate the business value and operational impact of AI by presenting a series of real-world case studies and proven models. These illustrations capture AI's transformative role in enhancing performance across finance, marketing, human resources, and supply chain management. Each case showcases how predictive systems are used not in isolation, but in a coordinated manner to drive enterprise-wide outcomes, illustrating the synergistic effect of AI when integrated across functional boundaries (Chui, Manyika, & Miremadi, 2016; Kumar & Reinartz, 2016).

To guide implementation, the chapter introduces a multi-dimensional framework that holistically addresses the core requirements for successful adoption. This includes the technological backbone—comprising data infrastructure and system interoperability—as well as organizational enablers such as governance protocols, regulatory compliance, and ethical AI deployment. The framework also considers the importance of leadership vision and cultural readiness in ensuring the long-term sustainability and alignment of AI initiatives with strategic business goals (Ngai, Chau, & Chan, 2011; Hofmann et al., 2020).

Finally, the chapter explores emerging challenges and identifies future research directions essential for building responsible and sustainable AI ecosystems. Topics such as algorithmic transparency, fairness, inclusivity, and the social implications of large-scale AI deployment are discussed in depth. The emphasis is on developing AI systems that not only deliver value but also uphold principles of trustworthiness and long-term accountability—particularly in complex, data-rich enterprise environments (Wirtz, Weyerer, & Geyer, 2019; OECD, 2019).

This comprehensive approach is tailored to meet the needs of an interdisciplinary audience, including business strategists, data scientists, organizational leaders, and policymakers. By integrating conceptual depth with practical application, the chapter serves as a roadmap for organizations seeking to leverage unified intelligence for strategic transformation in the digital era.

AI in Strategic Business Contexts

The strategic potential of AI lies in its ability to process and analyze vast datasets far beyond human capacity, identifying complex patterns, predicting future states, and supporting both tactical and strategic decisions (Russell & Norvig, 2016). For example:

1. **Finance:** AI-driven credit scoring models reduce default risk and improve portfolio management (Chui, Manyika, & Miremadi, 2016). ML detects fraudulent transactions faster than traditional rule-based systems (Agrawal et al., 2018).
2. **Marketing:** AI-powered recommendation engines like those employed by Amazon enhance customer engagement and increase sales by tailoring offerings based on behavioral data (Erevelles, Fukawa, & Swayne, 2016). Sentiment analysis enables real-time monitoring of brand perception (Kumar & Reinartz, 2016).
3. **Human Resources:** Predictive analytics helps anticipate employee turnover and guides retention strategies, enhancing workforce stability (Liu & Wang, 2020). AI-driven talent acquisition tools automate screening, reducing hiring biases and accelerating recruitment (Dwivedi et al., 2021).
4. **Supply Chain:** AI forecasts demand fluctuations, optimizes inventory levels, and manages logistics routes dynamically, improving responsiveness to market changes (Wang et al., 2016). During crises like COVID-19, predictive analytics facilitated proactive risk mitigation (Henke et al., 2018).

Yet, when these functions operate independently without data or strategy integration, the organization misses opportunities for synergy and innovation (Zhang et al., 2020). For example, disconnected marketing and supply chain systems may cause stockouts or overstocking, impacting customer satisfaction and costs.

Unified Intelligence enables cross-functional alignment, where insights from one domain inform decisions in others, creating a virtuous cycle of informed agility and innovation (Baryannis et al., 2019).

FOUNDATIONS OF PREDICTIVE ANALYTICS IN BUSINESS

Predictive analytics has emerged as a cornerstone of modern business intelligence, enabling organizations to anticipate future events, optimize operations, and gain competitive advantages by harnessing historical data and advanced analytical techniques. This chapter explores the fundamental concepts and techniques underpinning predictive analytics, followed by its pivotal role in business forecasting and planning.

Core Concepts and Techniques

Predictive analytics involves applying statistical methods, machine learning algorithms, and data mining strategies to both past and present data to forecast future events or outcomes. It transforms raw data into actionable insights through a series of stages, including data preparation, model building, evaluation, and deployment.

The initial stage of predictive analytics involves data preparation, which is critical for building effective predictive models. This includes data cleaning—removing errors, inconsistencies, and duplicates that may bias results or reduce accuracy. Subsequently, data integration combines data from diverse sources such as Enterprise Resource Planning (ERP) systems, Customer Relationship Management (CRM) platforms, social media feeds, and external datasets to form a comprehensive view of the business environment.

An essential aspect of data preparation is feature engineering, where domain knowledge is applied to create or select relevant variables that enhance model performance. This can involve encoding categorical variables, scaling features, or deriving new variables that capture important relationships. Additionally, techniques such as dimensionality reduction, including Principal Component Analysis (PCA), help in reducing the feature space to prevent overfitting and improve computational efficiency.

Predictive modeling itself employs a broad spectrum of algorithms, each suited to different types of prediction problems. Regression models, such as linear regression, are used to forecast continuous outcomes by fitting a line that minimizes the difference between observed and predicted values. For classification tasks, logistic regression estimates the probability of binary outcomes and is widely applied in scenarios such as credit scoring and customer churn prediction.

More complex models like decision trees provide interpretable, rule-based classification or regression by recursively partitioning the data. To enhance accuracy, ensemble methods such as Random Forests and Gradient Boosting aggregate multiple models, reducing variance and bias. Support Vector Machines (SVMs) are powerful classifiers effective in high-dimensional spaces, using hyperplanes and kernel functions to separate classes with maximum margin.

The rise of neural networks and deep learning has enabled modeling of highly complex, nonlinear relationships. Deep architectures such as Convolutional Neural Networks (CNNs) excel in image recognition, while Recurrent Neural Networks (RNNs) are suited for sequential data such as time series and natural language.

Unsupervised learning techniques like clustering (e.g., K-means) and dimensionality reduction methods (e.g., t-SNE) are used to uncover hidden patterns without labeled outcomes, aiding in customer segmentation and anomaly detection.

Model training is followed by rigorous evaluation using techniques like cross-validation to assess generalizability and avoid overfitting. Performance metrics vary based on the task, including Root Mean Squared Error (RMSE) for regression, and precision, recall, F1-score, and AUC-ROC for classification problems.

Advances in Automated Machine Learning (AutoML) frameworks now automate many steps of predictive analytics—from preprocessing to hyperparameter tuning—democratizing access beyond expert data scientists. Furthermore, real-time predictive analytics powered by streaming data and edge computing enable dynamic, adaptive decision-making crucial in domains such as fraud detection and supply chain management.

Despite its transformative potential, predictive analytics must navigate challenges like data quality issues, interpretability of complex models, ethical concerns regarding bias and fairness, scalability for large datasets, and compliance with data privacy regulations. Addressing these requires multidisciplinary collaboration, continuous model monitoring, and transparent governance frameworks.

Role in Business Forecasting and Planning

Predictive analytics has transformed business forecasting by surpassing traditional methods that depend on historical averages. Machine learning models analyze vast, varied datasets to deliver precise, data-driven insights that support better strategic and operational decisions.

In finance, predictive analytics enhances credit risk assessment, liquidity management, and portfolio optimization. Banks use AI to evaluate transaction data and economic indicators for accurate loan default predictions, while algorithmic trading uses predictive signals to maximize investment returns. In marketing, it forecasts churn, estimates customer lifetime value, and enables dynamic pricing, improving campaign personalization and revenue. In HR, predictive models analyze attrition trends, forecast workforce needs, and support talent management. Supply chain management leverages predictive demand forecasting and maintenance to optimize inventory and reduce equipment downtime.

These capabilities shift planning from static to adaptive processes, enabling organizations to respond proactively to market changes and operational risks. Success depends on fostering a data-driven culture through data literacy, cross-functional collaboration, and leadership support, ensuring predictive insights are integrated into everyday decision-making.

THE CASE FOR CROSS-FUNCTIONAL AI INTEGRATION

In today's dynamic business landscape, organizations must address rising complexity, shifting customer needs, and intense competition. To stay agile and competitive, they must move beyond siloed AI use and adopt cross-functional AI integration, enabling seamless collaboration and data sharing across departments like finance, marketing, HR, and supply chain.

This unified approach breaks down traditional silos, merging diverse data sources and insights to enhance decision-making, boost efficiency, and drive innovation. This chapter explores the necessity of cross-functional AI integration, the challenges posed by organizational silos, and the strategic value gained when AI is implemented enterprise-wide. It also illustrates how AI-enabled collaboration across key business functions leads to improved outcomes and a more connected, intelligent organization.

Breaking Silos: A Unified Intelligence Approach

In many organizations, traditional business functions operate in relative isolation. Each department—whether finance, marketing, human resources (HR), or supply chain—often maintains separate data systems, employs different performance metrics, and pursues distinct strategic goals. This structural segmentation creates what are commonly referred to as organizational silos.

Problems Created by Silos

Organizational silos hinder enterprise-wide optimization by creating inefficiencies, such as duplicated data collection, redundant analytics, and misaligned resource use (Baryannis, Dani, & Antoniou, 2019). For example, marketing and sales may analyze customer data separately, missing collaborative insights. Silos also lead to fragmented insights, where decision-makers lack a unified view, causing misaligned forecasts or disconnected supply chain and HR decisions that impact execution. Additionally, siloed structures slow decision-making, as critical information stays trapped within departments, reducing responsiveness to market changes and weakening overall organizational effectiveness (Dwivedi et al., 2021).

Unified Intelligence: The Integration Imperative

To overcome these limitations, organizations are increasingly adopting a Unified Intelligence approach. This strategic model integrates artificial intelligence and predictive analytics into a centralized Unified Intelligence Layer (AI + Predictive Analytics + Forecasting Engine) that operates across functional boundaries, replacing the fragmented deployment of AI tools within individual departments. Rather than allowing insights to remain trapped in silos, Unified Intelligence promotes shared access to analytical outputs across departments, enabling a more holistic view of organizational dynamics. It fosters cross-functional data interoperability, ensuring that systems and datasets across finance, marketing, HR, and supply chain are aligned and can interact seamlessly. Furthermore, it encourages collaborative decision-making, where multiple functions contribute to and benefit from synchronized analytics, leading to decisions that are more informed and enterprise-centric. Ultimately, this model enhances strategic agility by aligning departmental goals with organization-wide objectives and by leveraging AI-driven forecasting capabilities that adapt swiftly to changing business environments.

Figure 1 below illustrates this conceptual model. At its core is the Unified Intelligence Layer (AI + Predictive Analytics + Forecasting Engine), which processes enterprise data to generate synchronized insights. These insights are shared across finance, marketing, HR, and supply chain departments—enabling seamless collaboration, data sharing, and strategic alignment. The model transforms isolated departmental functions into an integrated ecosystem that supports agile, informed, and organization-wide decision-making.

Figure 1. Unified intelligence model for cross-functional decision-making

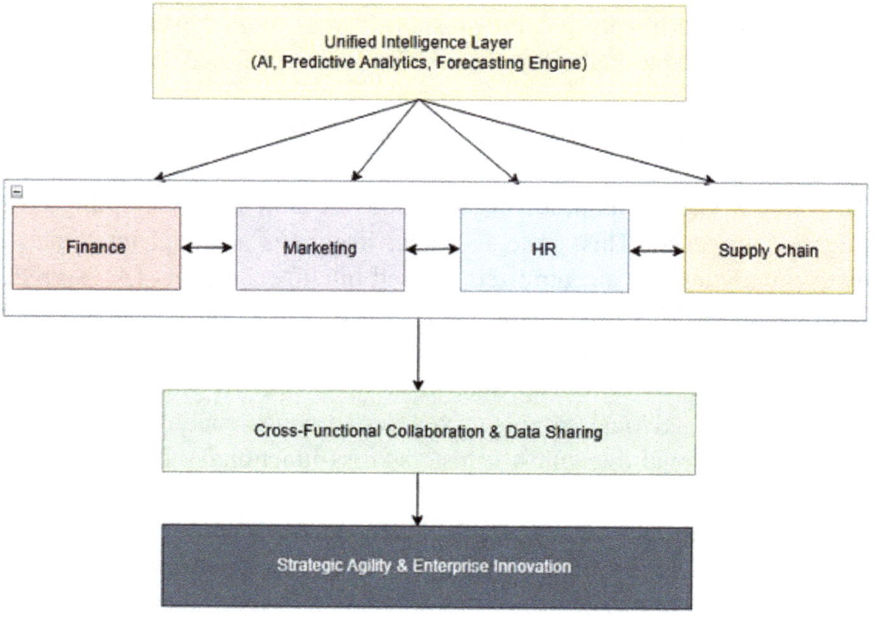

This figure shows how the Unified Intelligence Layer (AI + Predictive Analytics + Forecasting Engine) enables synchronized insights across finance, marketing, HR, and supply chain. Shared analytics and real-time collaboration eliminate silos, leading to integrated decision-making, strategic agility, and enterprise-wide alignment.

Illustrative Example

For example, integrating customer sentiment data from marketing with operational forecasts in supply chain can prevent stockouts during peak promotional campaigns. Similarly, insights from HR attrition models can inform workforce planning to support upcoming production surges, while finance benefits from improved forecasting accuracy rooted in real-time data signals from across departments.

By breaking silos and enabling cross-functional synergy, Unified Intelligence empowers organizations to enhance agility, optimize resources, and foster continuous innovation.

Synergies Between Finance, Marketing, HR, and Supply Chain

Each business function generates unique data sets and analytics insights. When combined through integrated AI systems, these create powerful synergies that elevate enterprise performance beyond the sum of individual efforts.

The table below summarizes key applications of AI across business functions and the strategic outcomes achieved through their integration:

Table 1. Applications of AI across business functions

Business Function	AI Application	Expected Outcome
Finance	Fraud detection, credit risk modeling	Reduced losses, enhanced risk prediction
Marketing	Customer segmentation, churn prediction, personalization	Improved engagement, optimized campaigns
Human Resources	Attrition prediction, talent acquisition, workforce planning	Reduced turnover, better hiring and training decisions
Supply Chain	Demand forecasting, logistics optimization	Inventory efficiency, lower costs, better agility

Finance

Finance teams are increasingly leveraging AI-driven predictive models to enhance decision-making and operational efficiency. These models are used to assess financial risks, including credit and market risks, by analyzing large volumes of historical and real-time data to identify potential vulnerabilities and exposure points. AI also plays a critical role in fraud detection, offering higher precision in identifying anomalous patterns that may indicate fraudulent activities. Additionally, finance professionals use predictive analytics to guide investment strategies, relying on data-driven forecasts that evaluate market trends, portfolio performance, and economic indicators.

The integration of financial analytics with insights from marketing forecasts and sales projections further strengthens the strategic value of financial planning. For example, incorporating marketing data on upcoming campaigns or expected shifts in customer behavior enables finance teams to generate more accurate revenue forecasts. This, in turn, allows for better resource allocation and liquidity management, ensuring that financial decisions are both timely and aligned with anticipated business developments (Chui, Manyika, & Miremadi, 2016).

Marketing

In the marketing domain, organizations apply artificial intelligence to enhance customer engagement and campaign effectiveness. AI is widely used to segment audiences based on demographics, behaviors, and preferences, allowing marketers to design highly personalized campaigns that resonate with specific customer segments. Additionally, predictive models help forecast customer churn and estimate lifetime value, enabling marketers to proactively engage at-risk customers and focus efforts on high-value segments. AI also supports the optimization of marketing campaigns by analyzing performance data and identifying patterns that contribute to higher return on investment (ROI), allowing for real-time adjustments and improved resource utilization.

When marketing insights are integrated with supply chain data, organizations unlock greater agility and precision in promotional planning. By accessing real-time inventory information, marketing teams can tailor campaigns to align with actual product availability, thereby avoiding situations where promotions lead to overstock or stockouts. This synchronization prevents the promotion of unavailable or expiring products, safeguarding brand reputation, enhancing customer satisfaction, and improving operational efficiency (Baryannis et al., 2019).

Human Resources

In the realm of human resources, predictive analytics is increasingly used to enhance strategic workforce management. HR departments utilize AI models for workforce planning, enabling them to anticipate future operational needs and align talent pipelines accordingly. These models also support talent acquisition by identifying best-fit candidates through resume parsing, skill-matching algorithms, and historical hiring data, which significantly reduces time-to-hire and improves recruitment efficiency. Furthermore, AI-driven insights play a critical role in employee retention, as they help forecast attrition risks by analyzing factors such as employee engagement, performance trends, and past turnover patterns. Artificial Intelligence is playing a transformative role in reshaping HR functions, improving recruitment efficiency, workforce planning, and employee engagement through automation and data-driven insights (Subramanian & R, 2024).

By integrating HR analytics with operational and supply chain forecasts, organizations can achieve just-in-time hiring and targeted upskilling, ensuring that workforce capabilities are aligned with projected business demands. For instance, if supply chain analytics predict a surge in product demand, the HR team can proactively initiate recruitment drives or schedule training programs well in advance. This strategic alignment not only reduces labor costs but also ensures that workforce readiness and productivity are maintained during periods of fluctuating demand (Dwivedi et al., 2021).

Supply Chain

In supply chain management, organizations increasingly rely on predictive tools to enhance operational efficiency and responsiveness. These tools are used to optimize logistics and delivery routes, allowing companies to reduce transportation costs, shorten delivery times, and improve overall service levels. Predictive analytics also play a vital role in demand planning and inventory management by forecasting product demand with greater accuracy, thereby minimizing stockouts and overstock situations. Additionally, AI-powered systems are employed to enhance vendor management by evaluating supplier performance and assessing risk factors such as delays, quality issues, or financial instability.

When supply chain analytics are strategically integrated with sales forecasts and financial objectives, the entire value chain becomes more agile, synchronized, and cost-effective. This cross-functional coordination supports better inventory turnover, reduces excess stock, and enhances cash flow management, all while ensuring timely fulfillment and higher levels of customer satisfaction (Wang, Gunasekaran, Ngai, & Papadopoulos, 2016). By aligning operational execution with predictive insights from multiple departments, organizations can transform their supply chains into proactive, resilient, and data-driven ecosystems.

The Strategic Impact of Cross-Functional AI Integration

Cross-functional integration transforms AI from a set of isolated departmental tools into a strategic enterprise capability that drives business agility, operational coherence, and long-term competitive advantage. Achieving this transformation requires several key enablers.

First, system interoperability is critical—AI and data systems must be architected to communicate and exchange information seamlessly across departments, allowing for unified data processing and analytics.

Second, the establishment of consistent data governance frameworks is essential. These frameworks define and enforce organization-wide standards for data quality, privacy, and security, ensuring that insights are reliable, compliant, and ethically sound across all functions.

Finally, fostering a collaborative culture plays a pivotal role. Overcoming traditional silos demands an environment where departments share objectives, data, and decision-making processes. Such a culture ensures that AI initiatives are not only technically integrated but also strategically aligned with the enterprise's broader goals.

FRAMEWORK FOR IMPLEMENTATION

The successful integration of AI across multiple business functions demands a comprehensive and structured framework that addresses critical technical and organizational challenges. This framework encompasses three main pillars: the underlying data infrastructure and integration requirements, the design of interoperable AI systems, and the governance and compliance mechanisms to ensure ethical, legal, and trustworthy AI deployment.

At its core, the framework provides guidance on building scalable, flexible, and secure AI platforms that unify data and intelligence across disparate functions. It ensures that AI solutions not only deliver accurate and timely insights but also operate with transparency, accountability, and compliance with evolving regulations. The following sections elaborate on these pillars in detail.

Data Infrastructure and Integration Requirements

A robust data infrastructure is vital for successful AI integration and achieving unified intelligence across business functions. It must handle big data's volume, velocity, and variety, while ensuring reliability, security, and accessibility. Scalable Storage and Cloud Platforms like Amazon S3, Azure Blob Storage, and Google Cloud Storage support vast data volumes and provide elastic compute resources for AI model training, all with cost-effective scalability (Gandomi & Haider, 2015; Marr, 2018).

Real-Time Data Pipelines are essential for timely insights in applications like fraud detection and personalized marketing. Tools such as Apache Kafka, Flink, and AWS Kinesis support high-throughput, low-latency streaming data processing (Kreps, 2014). Integration of Disparate Systems across ERP, CRM, HRIS, and supply chain platforms requires APIs, ETL/ELT pipelines, and data lakes. APIs enable real-time, standardized data exchange (Fielding, 2000); ETL/ELT pipelines handle batch and scalable processing (Inmon, 2005); and data lakes store diverse data types with schema-on-read flexibility (Gartner, 2019).

Interoperability is achieved through common schemas, ontologies (for contextual relationships), and metadata management, which ensures consistent interpretation, traceability, and feature selection (Gruber, 1993; Batini et al., 2016). Data Quality Management ensures AI reliability through accuracy, completeness, consistency, and timeliness. Techniques like data profiling, cleansing, validation, and monitoring help maintain high-quality data and support credible AI outcomes (Redman, 2013; Batini et al., 2016).

Together, these components create a reliable data foundation essential for advanced analytics and enterprise-wide AI decision-making.

Designing Interoperable AI Systems

AI systems must be designed with interoperability, modularity, and scalability to support unified intelligence platforms that can evolve with business needs. Modular AI architecture decomposes solutions into components like preprocessing, training, inference, and monitoring, enabling independent updates and safer deployments (He, Zhao, & Chu, 2021). Microservices and containerization, using tools like Docker and Kubernetes, allow AI functions to run as loosely coupled, portable services, making them scalable and resilient (Newman, 2015; Merkel, 2014; Burns et al., 2016).

API-driven integration simplifies the embedding of models into enterprise workflows by enabling version control, performance monitoring, and automated retraining to respond to data drift (Sculley et al., 2015). These capabilities promote modularity and ensure models remain relevant and accurate across business functions.

Governance must be embedded into AI infrastructure to ensure ethical, legal, and secure operations. This includes access controls, approval workflows, and logging for accountability (Hofmann, Samp, & Woods, 2020; Ribeiro, Singh, & Guestrin, 2016). Broader data governance covers ownership, lifecycle management, and ethical oversight through stewardship teams (Batini et al., 2016). Regulatory compliance is key—frameworks like GDPR and CCPA mandate data privacy, transparency, and user rights (Voigt & Von dem Bussche, 2017; California State Legislature, 2018), while standards such as ISO/IEC 27001 guide secure data practices (ISO, 2013), Explainability tools and privacy impact assessments enhance transparency and accountability (Doshi-Velez & Kim, 2017).

To mitigate risks, bias audits, fairness-aware ML models, and adversarial defenses must be adopted (Mehrabi et al., 2019; Papernot et al., 2016). Continuous model monitoring and retraining counter model drift and performance degradation (Sculley et al., 2015). Finally, cross-functional AI governance committees—including legal, IT, and business leaders—should oversee compliance, training, and ethical AI use to foster responsible AI cultures (OECD, 2019).

USE CASES AND CASE STUDIES

AI has become a game-changing technology, revolutionizing business operations across multiple industries. Its capability to process massive datasets, uncover intricate patterns, and provide predictive insights has led to its widespread use in key domains like finance, marketing, human resources, and supply chain management. This chapter explores real-world use cases and case studies demonstrating AI's profound impact on these domains. These examples highlight how AI not only improves efficiency and accuracy but also enables strategic decision-making and innovation in diverse organizational settings.

AI-Driven Financial Modeling and Risk Management

AI is revolutionizing financial modeling and risk management by offering dynamic, data-driven tools that surpass traditional rule-based methods. In fraud detection, machine learning models analyze complex transaction patterns—such as frequency, value, location, and device data—to detect anomalies in real time. For example, JPMorgan Chase uses both supervised and unsupervised ML to identify known and emerging fraud, significantly reducing false positives and enabling faster, more accurate detection. Cross-functional benefits include marketing using fraud data to reduce churn by 22% and HR applying insights for analyst training, showcasing the value of Unified Intelligence (JPMorgan, 2023).

In predictive budgeting and scenario planning, AI helps CFOs integrate macroeconomic indicators and operational KPIs to simulate "what-if" scenarios, generate department-specific forecasts, and perform Monte Carlo simulations. These tools enhance financial planning accuracy and support strategic decision-making under uncertainty.

For credit risk scoring, AI evaluates diverse data such as spending behavior, digital footprints, and social media signals, offering a dynamic and nuanced view of borrower profiles. This enables more accurate loan approvals, early risk detection, and tailored interest rates, improving portfolio performance and customer satisfaction.

Predictive Analytics in Marketing and Customer Engagement

Marketing has evolved from a generalized outreach effort to a precise, personalized, and predictive discipline powered by AI. Retailers and e-commerce companies leverage AI to anticipate customer needs, optimize campaigns, and improve engagement.

One prominent application is personalized recommendation systems. Companies like Amazon combine collaborative filtering with deep learning models to analyze purchase histories, clickstream data, product reviews, and real-time browsing behavior. These systems generate individualized product suggestions that not only increase average order values but also reduce bounce rates and improve overall customer satisfaction. By understanding customer preferences at a granular level, AI helps marketers tailor offerings in ways traditional methods could never achieve.

Amazon's AI now integrates with supply chain systems to suppress recommendations for out-of-stock items (cutting customer complaints by 18%), while finance teams prioritize high-margin products in promotions. These cross-functional links boosted campaign ROI by 12% (Amazon, 2024).

Predictive analytics is vital for identifying customers at risk of churn. Machine learning models analyze behavioral signals—like reduced product usage, shorter session durations, negative service feedback, and declining purchase frequency—to generate insights that drive proactive retention strategies, such as loyalty programs, personalized offers, or direct outreach. This helps protect revenue and strengthen customer relationships.

AI also powers dynamic pricing by analyzing real-time supply-demand shifts, competitor prices, seasonal trends, and customer demographics. Regression models assess price elasticity, while reinforcement learning adjusts prices dynamically to optimize revenue. Forecasts help prevent underpricing and overstock, improving both margins and inventory turnover. Additionally, marketing campaigns are now aligned with supply chain data: AI monitors stock levels and adjusts promotions accordingly, removing low-stock items from ads and pushing surplus inventory through discounts. This integration reduces waste, accelerates stock movement, and ensures a better customer experience.

Workforce Optimization Through AI-Enabled HR Analytics

Human resource management benefits significantly from AI's ability to analyze both structured and unstructured data to optimize workforce planning and development. Predictive analytics enables organizations to better understand employee engagement, retention risks, and talent needs.

Attrition prediction models analyze data such as attendance records, promotion history, compensation trends, employee feedback, exit interviews, and survey responses to detect early signs of disengagement or turnover risk. For instance, IBM's Watson AI platform identifies patterns like performance stagnation, managerial changes, skill underutilization, or lack of learning opportunities that precede employee departures. By recognizing these indicators early, HR teams can take proactive measures including recognition programs, mentorship initiatives, or internal mobility options to retain valuable employees. (Tambe, P et al, 2023).

The models now inform enterprise planning: Supply chain uses attrition forecasts to adjust production schedules 6 months ahead, while finance incorporates them into cost projections. This reduced unexpected labor shortages by 35% (IBM, 2023).

AI enhances hiring by analyzing resumes, behavioral assessments, and historical data to score candidates based on compatibility with top performers. It also reduces unconscious bias by anonymizing irrelevant demographic details and matches candidates to suitable roles and teams—improving hiring quality, reducing time-to-fill, and ensuring better cultural fit.

Additionally, AI-powered learning management systems personalize talent development by recommending training and certifications aligned with both organizational goals and individual career paths. These systems use performance data, peer benchmarks, and industry trends to create tailored development plans, promoting continuous learning and internal mobility.

Enhancing Supply Chain Agility Using Predictive Systems

AI adoption in supply chain management enhances visibility, responsiveness, and resilience by enabling better demand forecasting, logistics optimization, and supplier risk mitigation. Modern demand forecasting leverages AI to integrate external data—such as weather, holidays, macroeconomic trends, social media, and customer behavior—beyond historical sales. Companies like Unilever use these models to dynamically adjust procurement and production plans, minimizing overstock and stockouts. In logistics, providers like DHL apply AI algorithms and reinforcement learning to optimize delivery routes using real-time GPS data, traffic patterns, and operational constraints. This has led to reduced delivery times, lower fuel consumption, and improved on-time performance. Additionally, DHL's 15% fuel savings support corporate sustainability goals tracked by finance, while HR utilizes performance data to improve driver training, resulting in a threefold ROI increase (DHL, 2023).

AI also strengthens supplier risk management by evaluating both structured data—such as delivery performance and financial health—and unstructured sources like audit reports, news feeds, and social sentiment. This comprehensive risk scoring enables procurement teams to diversify suppliers and plan for disruptions more effectively. The importance of AI in disruption management was especially evident during the COVID-19 pandemic, when models accurately predicted bottlenecks due to lockdowns, port congestion, and labor shortages. These insights allowed companies to reroute shipments, shift inventories, and adapt production schedules, thereby enhancing supply chain resilience and minimizing operational impacts.

ETHICAL AND OPERATIONAL CHALLENGES

As AI becomes increasingly embedded across various enterprise functions such as finance, marketing, human resources, and supply chain management, organizations face a range of ethical and operational challenges. These challenges arise from the complexity of AI systems, the sensitivity of the data they process, and the profound impact their decisions can have on individuals and society. Addressing issues like data privacy, algorithmic bias, transparency, and ensuring proper human oversight is essential for building trust and maintaining compliance with regulatory frameworks. Moreover, the long-term success of AI integration depends not only on technological advancements but also on embedding strong ethical principles and governance mechanisms into AI deployment. The following sections explore these key concerns in detail and propose strategies to mitigate associated risks.

Data Privacy, Bias, and Transparency

AI systems frequently process large volumes of personal and sensitive data, especially in domains like HR, marketing, and customer engagement. Due to strict global privacy regulations, such as the GDPR in the EU and the CCPA in California, organizations must uphold individuals' rights over their data, including access, correction, deletion, and opt-outs from data sales or profiling (Voigt & Von dem Bussche, 2017; California State Legislature, 2018). Non-compliance can result in severe penalties, loss of trust, and reputational damage. To mitigate risks, companies should apply privacy-by-design, maintain processing logs, use encryption/anonymization, and establish clear consent mechanisms.

Another major ethical concern is algorithmic bias, where AI models replicate or amplify societal inequalities. Examples include hiring algorithms favoring male candidates or loan systems disproportionately rejecting minority groups. Bias can emerge during data collection, feature design, or training. Organizations can counter this with fairness-aware ML techniques like adversarial de-biasing, reweighing, and bias detection tools such as Aequitas, Fairlearn, and IBM AI Fairness 360 (Mehrabi et al., 2019).

Finally, transparency and interpretability are essential, especially in sectors like recruitment, finance, and healthcare. Black-box models can undermine accountability. To build trust, tools like LIME and SHAP explain how specific features influence predictions (Ribeiro, Singh, & Guestrin, 2016), ensuring AI decisions are understandable, ethical, and compliant.

To summarize, responsible AI implementation requires mapping ethical concerns to clear mitigation strategies, as outlined in Table 2 below:

Table 2. Ethical challenges in AI and mitigation strategies

Ethical Challenge	Description	Mitigation Strategy
Data Privacy	Risk of exposing sensitive personal or behavioral data	Implement privacy-by-design, encryption, anonymization, and user consent mechanisms
Algorithmic Bias	Discriminatory outcomes from biased training data	Use fairness-aware ML, diverse datasets, bias audits, and ethical reviews
Lack of Transparency	Inability to explain AI decision-making ("black box" models)	Employ Explainable AI techniques (e.g., SHAP, LIME) and clear documentation
Regulatory Non-Compliance	Breaches of laws like GDPR or CCPA due to improper data handling	Conduct privacy impact assessments, maintain compliance logs, and enforce data governance
Model Drift	Degradation of model accuracy over time due to changing input patterns	Monitor model performance continuously and retrain with updated data

Building Trustworthy AI Models

Trustworthy AI models are essential for widespread adoption and long-term success in business environments. These models must not only be technically sound but also demonstrate ethical alignment, legal compliance, and robustness across diverse scenarios. Achieving this requires attention to six critical components throughout the AI lifecycle. First, using high-quality, representative data is fundamental. Datasets must be diverse, balanced, and free from bias, with clear documentation of data lineage to ensure transparency and fairness. Second, rigorous testing and validation are necessary to assess model performance beyond accuracy. This includes testing under edge cases, adversarial scenarios, and using techniques like cross-validation and A/B testing while evaluating metrics such as precision, recall, robustness, and fairness.

Third, human-in-the-loop oversight ensures that AI systems support rather than replace human decision-making, particularly in high-stakes domains. This oversight adds accountability and allows humans to intervene when needed. Fourth, thorough documentation and version control are vital for reproducibility and transparency. Recording dataset sources, model assumptions, and tracking changes through tools like model cards and datasheets promotes responsible development. Fifth, continuous monitoring and retraining are required after deployment to detect and address model drift—when changes in data or context impact model performance. Automated retraining pipelines help keep models accurate and up to date.

Finally, inclusive AI development involves engaging a wide range of stakeholders, including data scientists, domain experts, ethicists, and end-users. This inclusive approach ensures that AI solutions are aligned with ethical, societal, and cultural values, reducing blind spots and increasing trust. By integrating these six components—quality data, robust validation, human oversight, clear documentation, continuous monitoring, and inclusive development—organizations can build AI systems that are not only effective but also ethical, resilient, and widely trusted.

Responsible Adoption and Human Oversight

AI adoption should enhance, not replace, human expertise—especially in sensitive or high-stakes decisions. AI systems must function primarily as decision-support tools, offering recommendations alongside confidence scores and explanations. This helps users understand the rationale behind AI outputs and retain the ability to challenge or override decisions. Such a human-in-the-loop model boosts user trust and provides legal safeguards by keeping humans accountable for final decisions. Recent perspectives emphasize the importance of a collaborative human–machine environment, where AI complements rather than substitutes the workforce, fostering a synergistic relationship between technology and human judgment (Kapoor & Ghosal, 2022).

Successful AI adoption depends not only on technology readiness but also on preparing people and organizational processes to work with AI in a responsible and informed manner. To achieve this, organizations should invest in comprehensive training programs that enhance employees' digital literacy and strengthen their understanding of the ethical implications of AI. These programs help workers engage thoughtfully with AI tools and cultivate a sense of shared responsibility. In addition, interactive workshops and simulations can be highly effective in demonstrating AI's capabilities, limitations, and risks. Such experiential learning promotes critical engagement, discouraging blind trust in algorithms and encouraging informed decision-making.

Beyond technical teams, it is crucial to foster AI literacy across all departments—including finance, HR, marketing, and operations—so that employees at every level understand how AI affects their work and contributes to broader organizational goals. This inclusive approach encourages cross-functional alignment and acceptance, laying the groundwork for effective collaboration with AI systems. Importantly, organizations must also address common concerns such as job displacement, surveillance, and algorithmic bias. Transparent communication about AI's intended role, its benefits, and limitations—combined with inclusive change management strategies—can significantly reduce resistance, alleviate anxiety, and foster a culture of trust where AI is seen as an enabler rather than a threat.

STRATEGIC LEADERSHIP AND ORGANIZATIONAL READINESS

The integration of AI across enterprise functions is not just a technological upgrade; it represents a fundamental organizational transformation. Success in AI adoption hinges not only on sophisticated data infrastructure or advanced algorithms but crucially depends on visionary leadership, cultural adaptability, and strategic alignment. This chapter explores the foundational role of leadership, change management, and alignment in preparing an organization for unified intelligence, ensuring that AI initiatives are effective, sustainable, and integrated seamlessly into business operations.

Role of Leadership in AI Adoption

Strategic leadership is vital for AI-driven transformation, aligning AI with long-term goals and positioning it as a business enabler rather than just a tech upgrade. Leaders must articulate a clear vision, identify high-impact areas like customer engagement or supply chain, and secure resources including infrastructure, talent, and training with executive backing. Building cross-functional teams and fostering a culture of innovation through experimentation and celebrating small wins is essential. Leaders like Satya Nadella and Sundar Pichai exemplify this approach, blending technical insight with ethical leadership. Successful AI adoption requires top-down vision and resources, paired with bottom-up execution by empowered mid-level managers to drive scalable, enterprise-wide impact.

Change Management and Skill Development

Integrating AI technologies disrupts traditional workflows, reshapes job roles, and demands new mindsets. Without effective change management, even technically sound AI initiatives risk failure due to organizational resistance, fear, or misunderstanding. Successful transformation depends on addressing the human side of change proactively. Two widely recognized change management frameworks provide structured approaches for navigating organizational transformation. Kotter's 8-Step Model outlines key actions such as establishing a sense of urgency, building a guiding coalition, developing and communicating a vision, eliminating barriers, achieving early successes, reinforcing progress, and embedding new behaviors into the organizational culture. In parallel, the ADKAR Model emphasizes the individual components of change—awareness, desire, knowledge, ability, and reinforcement—to ensure lasting results. Both frameworks highlight the critical role of human involvement and offer practical strategies to address resistance and drive sustainable change.

Skill development is equally crucial. The AI era demands continuous reskilling and upskilling to build internal competencies. Key focus areas include data literacy, which enables employees to interpret and question data outputs effectively; AI literacy, which involves understanding AI models, their benefits, and limitations; ethical literacy, which pertains to recognizing the ethical implications of AI-driven decisions; and technical skills, involving specialized training in data science, programming languages like Python and R, machine learning, and analytics for targeted roles. To scale skill development, organizations can leverage internal corporate learning platforms enhanced with AI for personalized learning, partner with academia and EdTech platforms like Coursera or Udacity for curated content, and promote on-the-job training and cross-functional shadowing to embed AI practices in daily work.

Fostering a culture of innovation supports these efforts by encouraging risk-taking, curiosity, and continuous improvement. Initiatives such as hackathons, internal AI labs, recognition programs, and communities of practice help create an environment where AI experimentation and collaboration thrive. This people-first approach to change management makes AI transformation inclusive, empowering, and sustainable.

Aligning AI Goals with Business Strategy

Strategic alignment is essential for ensuring AI projects deliver meaningful business impact. AI initiatives that lack direct connection to organizational objectives often fail to scale or justify their investment. Alignment ensures that AI supports priorities such as market leadership, customer satisfaction, operational efficiency, or innovation.

The alignment process starts with clear objective setting—defining what the organization aims to achieve with AI, whether improved decision-making, cost reduction, revenue growth, or regulatory compliance. Objectives should be Specific, Measurable, Achievable, Relevant, and Time-bound (SMART).

Next, organizations must prioritize AI opportunities by selecting high-impact use cases that align with strategic KPIs, are technically feasible, and scalable. Common focus areas include predictive maintenance, demand forecasting, customer segmentation, fraud detection, and employee retention.

Integration planning follows, aligning AI initiatives across people, processes, and technology. This requires cross-functional collaboration during design, development, deployment, and monitoring. AI efforts should be integrated into existing digital transformation roadmaps and IT infrastructure strategies to ensure coherence and avoid duplication.

Performance monitoring is critical and should use dashboards that track real-time AI and business metrics. Establishing feedback loops among AI developers, users, and decision-makers enables continuous learning and refinement of models.

To institutionalize alignment, organizations should establish governance structures such as AI Steering Committees composed of senior executives responsible for strategy, prioritization, and funding approval; AI Centers of Excellence (CoEs) that provide expertise and best practices; and functional liaisons embedded within business units to translate departmental needs into AI requirements. These structures create clarity, shared accountability, and prevent siloed efforts.

FUTURE DIRECTIONS AND RESEARCH OPPORTUNITIES

As organizations progress from early experimentation to broad adoption of AI, the enterprise AI landscape is rapidly evolving. Advances in computation, data management, and user interaction are reshaping how AI integrates into various industries. This chapter explores key emerging trends, the growing integration of AI with real-time decision-making systems, and the ethical responsibilities necessary for sustainable and inclusive AI development.

Emerging Trends in Enterprise AI

The future of AI in business is shaped by increasing accessibility, scalability, and contextual intelligence. Edge AI brings AI models to devices like smartphones, IoT sensors, factory robots, and autonomous vehicles, enabling real-time inference without relying on cloud connectivity. This improves latency, reduces bandwidth usage, enhances data privacy, and ensures continuous operation in areas like retail, manufacturing, and logistics.

Generative AI uses large language models and GANs to create original content—text, code, images, and videos—automating tasks like marketing copy, product descriptions, and design prototyping. Multimodal AI integrates text, audio, images, and video for deeper insights across domains such as customer support, healthcare diagnostics, and security. Meanwhile, low-code/no-code AI platforms empower non-technical users to build models, automate workflows, and engage with data using natural language queries—making AI more accessible across business teams.

Integration with Real-Time Decision Systems

The ability to sense, analyze, and respond instantly to data provides a significant competitive advantage in today's fast-changing digital environments. Real-time AI integration empowers enterprises to shift from traditional, retrospective analytics to proactive and automated decision-making. Organizations increasingly rely on streaming data sources, including IoT sensors, live transactional databases, and clickstream analytics, to feed AI systems with continuous, up-to-the-moment inputs. Leveraging platforms such as Apache Kafka and Amazon Kinesis, these systems enable decisions to be made within milliseconds, driving unprecedented levels of responsiveness and operational intelligence.

Several impactful use cases have emerged from this real-time capability. For example, dynamic pricing engines adjust product prices instantly based on changing inventory levels, competitor pricing, and customer demand. In the financial sector, fraud detection systems monitor transactions in real time, analyzing behavior patterns to identify and block unauthorized activities as they occur. In logistics, AI enhances supply chain agility by enabling predictive rerouting in response to transportation disruptions or fluctuating demand. Additionally, customer interaction optimization is achieved through intelligent chatbots and recommendation engines that adapt on the fly based on user behavior and preferences.

From a technical perspective, these systems are built on in-memory computing, event-driven architectures, and microservices frameworks, which collectively support the low-latency, high-scalability, and fault-tolerant environments required for real-time AI. This infrastructure ensures that enterprises not only react swiftly to changing conditions but also maintain consistent service quality and operational resilience.

AI for Sustainable and Inclusive Business Models

AI's growing role in enterprises demands alignment with environmental, social, and governance (ESG) goals. Sustainable AI supports energy optimization in smart buildings and data centers, smart grids for balancing renewable energy, and green logistics for fuel-efficient transportation. It also aids environmental monitoring by analyzing satellite imagery, drones, and remote sensors to track deforestation, air and water quality, and climate risks like floods or wildfires.

Social inclusion is enhanced by AI-powered language translation, assistive technologies for people with disabilities, and bias-aware hiring systems to promote fairness. AI can uncover social inequities and help ensure vulnerable groups receive fair access to services.

Developing sustainable AI requires inclusive datasets and interdisciplinary collaboration with ethicists and domain experts. Algorithmic impact assessments are essential before deployment to avoid reinforcing discrimination. Funders and regulators increasingly mandate demonstrations of social impact and ethical safeguards.

CONCLUSION

This concluding chapter reflects on the transformative journey organizations must undertake to evolve Artificial Intelligence (AI) from isolated technical tools into a cohesive, strategic capability termed Unified Intelligence. Unified Intelligence embodies the seamless integration of AI and predictive analytics across traditionally siloed business functions such as finance, marketing, human resources (HR), and supply chain operations. This transformation represents not just a technological advancement but a paradigm shift in organizational thinking—one that prioritizes interoperability, ethical governance, continuous learning, and inclusive stakeholder engagement.

As AI continues to advance, its potential to reshape decision-making, operational agility, and innovation grows exponentially. However, realizing this potential requires deliberate leadership, strategic alignment, and a culture that embraces responsible adoption of AI technologies

Summary of Key Takeaways

Unified Intelligence requires a robust data infrastructure that enables scalable storage, real-time ingestion, and integration of both structured and unstructured data. Overcoming data silos and ensuring quality and accessibility are essential for effective AI performance. Interoperability—enabled by APIs, microservices, containerization, and standard schemas—facilitates seamless data flow across departments, transforming isolated insights into enterprise-wide intelligence.

Successful AI deployment also depends on strong governance, ethical safeguards, and transparency. Governance frameworks should define clear roles and oversight, while tools like SHAP and LIME support explainability and stakeholder trust, especially in sensitive areas like HR and finance. Ethical considerations such as data privacy and bias mitigation are critical for building responsible AI. Leadership is central to AI adoption. Visionary leaders must align AI with strategic goals, secure resources, and foster a culture of innovation and adaptability. Change management models (e.g., Kotter's or ADKAR) and workforce upskilling help ensure broad engagement and reduce resistance.

AI delivers tangible benefits across key domains: fraud detection and forecasting in finance, personalization in marketing, talent management in HR, and predictive logistics in supply chain. These applications lead to cost savings, efficiency, customer satisfaction, and strategic foresight. Looking ahead, AI must emphasize sustainability and inclusion. This includes optimizing energy use, enhancing accessibility, ensuring ethical innovation through diverse datasets, and engaging communities.

Future AI should balance technological advancement with equity, accountability, and societal well-being.

Roadmap for AI-Driven Competitive Advantage

To achieve Unified Intelligence and strategic growth, organizations should follow a structured six-phase roadmap aligning AI capabilities with long-term business goals. This Strategic Roadmap for AI-Driven Competitive Advantage enables systematic AI integration across the enterprise. Figure 2 shows the six key phases of this roadmap, highlighting the progression from foundational assessment to continuous innovation.

Figure 2. Strategic roadmap for AI-driven competitive advantage

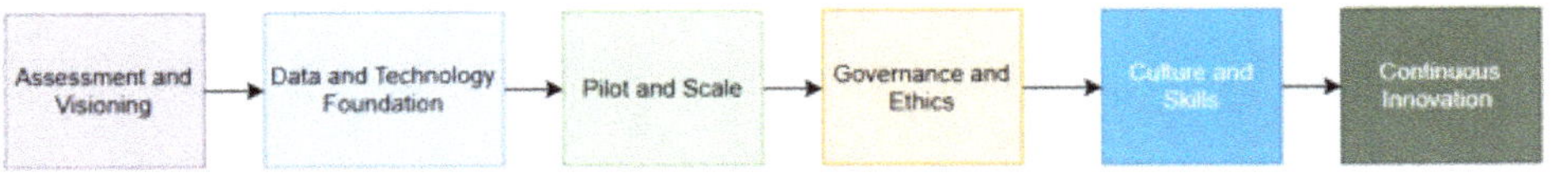

The first phase, Assessment and Visioning, involves evaluating the current level of AI maturity, data readiness, and technical capabilities, while identifying key business challenges AI can solve. It also includes securing leadership sponsorship to establish a shared vision that positions AI as a strategic value driver. The second phase, Data and Technology Foundation, focuses on building scalable cloud-native infrastructure, unifying data through data lakes and ETL pipelines, selecting AI platforms that ensure interoperability and compliance, and implementing strong data governance and metadata management practices.

The third phase, Pilot and Scale, encourages organizations to initiate pilot AI projects in high-impact areas, define clear KPIs, and develop reusable assets and methodologies based on lessons learned to facilitate broader scaling. The fourth phase, Governance and Ethics, addresses responsible AI usage by establishing ethics boards, audit frameworks, privacy and access controls, bias mitigation tools, and ensuring model explainability and transparency. The fifth phase, Culture and Skills, emphasizes workforce development through upskilling and reskilling programs, AI and ethical literacy, and fostering a culture of innovation through labs, hackathons, and reward systems for AI adoption and collaboration.

The final phase, Continuous Innovation, ensures that AI capabilities remain relevant by monitoring advancements like edge AI and generative models, establishing feedback loops, and partnering with external innovators such as startups and academic institutions. Organizations must also realign AI strategies with evolving business objectives to maintain long-term relevance and competitive advantage. By following this roadmap, AI becomes a core, enterprise-wide capability that drives sustainable growth, operational resilience, and strategic impact across the organization.

REFERENCES

Agrawal, A., Gans, J. S., & Goldfarb, A. (2018). *Prediction machines: The simple economics of artificial intelligence*. Harvard Business Review Press.

Alpaydin, E. (2020). *Introduction to machine learning* (4th ed.). MIT Press.

Amazon. (2024). AI integration in supply chain and finance systems: Suppressing out-of-stock recommendations and prioritizing high-margin products. Amazon.

Baesens, B. (2014). *Analytics in a big data world: The essential guide to data science and its applications*. Wiley.

Baryannis, G., Dani, S., & Antoniou, G. (2019). Predictive analytics and artificial intelligence in supply chain management: Review and implications for the future. *Computers & Industrial Engineering*, *137*, 106024. DOI: 10.1016/j.cie.2019.106024

Batini, C., Rula, A., Scannapieco, M., & Viscusi, G. (2016). From data quality to big data quality. In Big Data: Concepts, Methodologies, Tools, and Applications (pp. 1934-1956). IGI Global Scientific Publishing. DOI: 10.4018/978-1-4666-9840-6.ch089

Brynjolfsson, E., & McAfee, A. (2017). *Machine, platform, crowd: Harnessing our digital future*. W. W. Norton & Company.

Burns, B., Grant, B., Oppenheimer, D., Brewer, E., & Wilkes, J. (2016). Borg, omega, and kubernetes: Lessons learned from three container-management systems over a decade. *Communications of the ACM*, *59*(5), 50–57. DOI: 10.1145/2890784

California State Legislature. (2018). *California Consumer Privacy Act of 2018 (AB-375)*. Retrievedfrom https://leginfo.legislature.ca.gov/faces/billTextClient.xhtml ?bill_id=201720180AB375

Chui, M., Manyika, J., & Miremadi, M. (2016). *Where machines could replace humans—and where they can't (yet). McKinsey Quarterly*. https://www.mckinsey .com/business-functions/mckinsey-digital/our-insights/where-machines-could -replace-humans-and-where-they-cant-yet

Davenport, T. H., & Ronanki, R. (2018). Artificial intelligence for the real world. *Harvard Business Review*, *96*(1), 108–116.

DHL. (2023). *AI-driven logistics optimization: Advancing sustainability and cross-functional ROI*. DHL.

Doshi-Velez, F., & Kim, B. (2017). *Towards a rigorous science of interpretable machine learning*. arXiv preprint arXiv*:1702.08608*. https://arxiv.org/abs/1702.08608

Dwivedi, Y. K., Hughes, L., Ismagilova, E., Aarts, G., Coombs, C., Crick, T., Duan, Y., Dwivedi, R., Edwards, J., Eirug, A., Galanos, V., Ilavarasan, P. V., Janssen, M., Jones, P., Kar, A. K., Kizgin, H., Kronemann, B., Lal, B., Lucini, B., & Williams, M. D. (2021). Artificial intelligence (AI): Multidisciplinary perspectives on emerging challenges, opportunities, and agenda for research, practice and policy. *International Journal of Information Management*, *57*, 101994. DOI: 10.1016/j.ijinfomgt.2019.08.002

Erevelles, S., Fukawa, N., & Swayne, L. (2016). Big data consumer analytics and the transformation of marketing. *Journal of Business Research*, *69*(2), 897–904. DOI: 10.1016/j.jbusres.2015.07.001

Fielding, R. T. (2000). Architectural styles and the design of network-based software architectures *(Doctoral dissertation, University of California, Irvine)*. Retrieved from https://www.ics.uci.edu/~fielding/pubs/dissertation/top.htm

Gandomi, A., & Haider, M. (2015). Beyond the hype: Big data concepts, methods, and analytics. *International Journal of Information Management*, *35*(2), 137–144. DOI: 10.1016/j.ijinfomgt.2014.10.007

Gartner. (2019). Data lake: Definition, benefits, and challenges. *Gartner Research*. Retrieved from https://www.gartner.com/en/documents/3902666/data-lake-definition-benefits-and-challenges

Goodfellow, I., Bengio, Y., & Courville, A. (2016). *Deep learning*. MIT Press.

Gruber, T. R. (1993). A translation approach to portable ontology specifications. *Knowledge Acquisition*, *5*(2), 199–220. DOI: 10.1006/knac.1993.1008

He, X., Zhao, K., & Chu, X. (2021). AutoML: *A survey of the state-of-the-art. Knowledge-Based Systems*, *212*, 106622. DOI: 10.1016/j.knosys.2020.106622

Henke, N., Libarikian, A., & Wiseman, B. (2018). *The case for digital reinvention.* McKinsey Quarterly. https://www.mckinsey.com/business-functions/mckinsey-digital/our-insights/the-case-for-digital-reinvention

Hofmann, P., Samp, C., & Woods, J. (2020). Responsible AI: *A global policy framework.* Stanford Digital Economy Lab Report. https://digitaleconomy.stanford.edu/responsible-ai-global-policy-framework/

IBM. (2023). *Using AI-driven attrition forecasting to enhance enterprise planning and reduce labor shortages*. IBM.

Inmon, W. H. (2005). *Building the data warehouse* (4th ed.). Wiley.

International Organization for Standardization. (2013). *ISO/IEC 27001:2013 — Information technology — Security techniques — Information security management systems — Requirements*. ISO.

Kreps, J. (2014). *I Heart Logs: Event Data, Stream Processing, and Data Integration*. O'Reilly Media.

Kumar, V., & Reinartz, W. (2016). Creating enduring customer value. *Journal of Marketing*, *80*(6), 36–68. DOI: 10.1509/jm.15.0414

Liu, Y., & Wang, L. (2020). AI-driven HR analytics for workforce optimization. *Journal of Business Analytics*, *3*(1), 45–58. DOI: 10.1080/2573234X.2020.1717819

Marr, B. (2018). *Data strategy: How to profit from a world of big data, analytics and the Internet of Things*. Kogan Page.

Mehrabi, N., Morstatter, F., Saxena, N., Lerman, K., & Galstyan, A. (2019). A survey on bias and fairness in machine learning. *ACM Computing Surveys*, *54*(6), 1–35. DOI: 10.1145/3457607

Merkel, D. (2014). Docker: Lightweight Linux containers for consistent development and deployment. *Linux Journal*, *2014*(239), 2.

Newman, S. (2015). *Building microservices: Designing fine-grained systems*. O'Reilly Media.

Ngai, E. W. T., Chau, D. C. K., & Chan, T. L. A. (2011). Information technology, operational, and management competencies for supply chain agility: Findings from case studies. *The Journal of Strategic Information Systems*, *20*(3), 232–249. DOI: 10.1016/j.jsis.2010.11.002

OECD. (2019). *Recommendation of the Council on Artificial Intelligence*. OECD Publishing. https://legalinstruments.oecd.org/en/instruments/OECD-LEGAL-0449

Papernot, N., McDaniel, P., Goodfellow, I., Jha, S., Celik, Z. B., & Swami, A. (2016). Practical black-box attacks against machine learning. *In Proceedings of the 2017 ACM on Asia Conference on Computer and Communications Security* (pp. 506–519). ACM. https://doi.org/DOI: 10.1145/3052973.3053009

Redman, T. C. (2013). *Data driven: Profiting from your most important business asset*. Harvard Business Review Press.

Ribeiro, M. T., Singh, S., & Guestrin, C. (2016). *"Why should I trust you?" Explaining the predictions of any classifier. In* Proceedings of the 22nd ACM SIGKDD International Conference on Knowledge Discovery and Data Mining *(pp. 1135-1144).*

Russell, S., & Norvig, P. (2016). *Artificial intelligence: A modern approach* (3rd ed.). Pearson.

Sculley, D., Holt, G., Golovin, D., Davydov, E., Phillips, T., Ebner, D., Chaudhary, V., Young, M., Crespo, J. F., & Dennison, D. (2015). *Hidden technical debt in machine learning systems.* In *Advances in Neural Information Processing Systems* (pp. 2503–2511).

Subramanian, Y. R., & R, R. (2024). The Transformative Role of Artificial Intelligence in Human Resource. [IJRTBT]. *International Journal on Recent Trends in Business and Tourism*, *8*(2), 14–25. DOI: 10.31674/ijrtbt.2024.v08i02.002

Tambe, P., Cappelli, P., & Yakubovich, V. (2023). Artificial intelligence in human resources: New directions for talent management. *Journal of Organizational Behavior*, *44*(2), 127–143. DOI: 10.1002/job.2693

Voigt, P., & Von dem Bussche, A. (2017). *The EU General Data Protection Regulation (GDPR): A practical guide* (1st ed.). Springer. DOI: 10.1007/978-3-319-57959-7

Wang, G., Gunasekaran, A., Ngai, E. W. T., & Papadopoulos, T. (2016). Big data analytics in logistics and supply chain management: Certain investigations for research and applications. *International Journal of Production Economics*, *176*, 98–110. DOI: 10.1016/j.ijpe.2016.03.014

Wirtz, B. W., Weyerer, J. C., & Geyer, C. (2019). Artificial intelligence and the public sector—Applications and challenges. *International Journal of Public Administration*, *42*(7), 596–615. DOI: 10.1080/01900692.2018.1498103

Zhang, Y., Chen, X., & Yu, Z. (2020). Cross-functional AI integration in enterprises: Framework and case study. *Journal of Enterprise Information Management*, *33*(1), 123–145. DOI: 10.1108/JEIM-09-2019-0283

Zhou, J., & Chen, W. (2021). Ethical AI and responsible leadership in digital transformation. *Business Ethics (Oxford, England)*, *30*(2), 207–222.

KEY TERMS AND DEFINITIONS

Algorithmic Bias: Unintended and unfair discrimination in AI decision-making, often arising from biased training data or flawed model design.

Data Governance: A set of policies and procedures that manage the availability, usability, integrity, and security of data used in AI systems across the organization.

Edge AI: The execution of AI models on local devices (e.g., sensors, IoT hardware) for real-time processing and reduced reliance on cloud computing.

Explainable AI (XAI): Techniques that make AI model decisions interpretable and understandable to humans, ensuring transparency and trust, especially in sensitive applications.

Human-in-the-Loop (HITL): A design approach where human judgment is integrated into AI systems to oversee, validate, or refine automated decisions.

Predictive Analytics: The application of statistical and machine learning models to historical data in order to forecast future trends, behaviors, or outcomes.

Unified Intelligence: A strategic integration of AI and predictive analytics across multiple business functions—such as finance, HR, marketing, and supply chain—to enable cohesive, data-driven decision-making.

Compilation of References

Aaker, D. (1991). Brand equity. *La gestione del valore della marca, 347*, 356.

Abaku, E. A., Edunjobi, T. E., & Odimarha, A. C. (2024). Theoretical approaches to AI in supply chain optimization: Pathways to efficiency and resilience. *International journal of science and technology research archive, 6*(1), 092-107.

Abraham, S., Paripoornam, R., & Sharma, G.Susan Abraham, Rajeev Paripoornam, Gunjan Sharma. (2025). The Role of Artificial Intelligence in Recruitment and Talent Acquisition-An Empirical Study. *Journal of Informatics Education and Research, 5*(1), 400–408. DOI: 10.52783/jier.v5i1.2007

Accenture Research. (2019). *AI: Built to Scale*. Accenture.

Accenture. (2018). *Banking on AI: Why the Future is Human + Machine*. Accenture.

Acharya, D. (2025). Behavioral economics and decision science in corporate strategies. [IJSATE]. *International Journal of Scientific Advances in Technology and Economics, 1*(3), 45–56. https://ijsate.com/wp-content/uploads/2025/03/V1I3P5_IJSATE032521.pdf

Achumie, G. O., Oyegbade, I. K., Igwe, A. N., Ofodile, O. C., & Azubuike, C. (2022). Ai-Driven Predictive Analytics model for strategic business development and market growth in competitive industries. *International Journal of Social Science Exceptional Research, 1*(1), 13–25. DOI: 10.54660/IJSSER.2022.1.1.13-25

Acquisti, A., Brandimarte, L., & Loewenstein, G. (2015). Privacy and human behaviour in the digital age. *Science, 347*(6221), 509–514. DOI: 10.1126/science.aaa1465 PMID: 25635091

Adadi, A., & Berrada, M. (2018). Peeking inside the black-box: A survey on Explainable Artificial Intelligence (XAI). *IEEE Access : Practical Innovations, Open Solutions, 6*, 52138–52160. DOI: 10.1109/ACCESS.2018.2870052

Adedoyin, O. B. (2020). Qualitative research methods. Principles of social psychiatry, 77-87.

Adeoye, Y., Onotole, E. F., Ogunyankinnu, T. U. N. D. E., Aipoh, G. O. D. W. I. N., Osunkanmibi, A. A., & Egbemhenghe, J. O. S. E. P. H.YETUNDE ADEOYEERUMUSELE FRANCIS ONOTOLETUNDE OGUNYANKINNUGODWIN AIPOHAKINTUNDE AKINYELE OSUNKANMIBIJOSEPH EGBEMHENGHE. (2025). Artificial Intelligence in Logistics and Distribution: The function of AI in dynamic route planning for transportation, including self-driving trucks and drone delivery systems. *World Journal of Advanced Research and Reviews*, *25*(02), 155–167. DOI: 10.30574/wjarr.2025.25.2.0214

Adepoju, A. H., Austin-Gabriel, B., Eweje, A., & Hamza, O. (2023). A data governance framework for high-impact programs: Reducing redundancy and enhancing data quality at scale. *International Journal of Multidisciplinary Research and Growth Evaluation*, *4*(6), 1141–1154. DOI: 10.54660/.IJMRGE.2023.4.6.1141-1154

Agrawal, D., Tidake, V. M., Banu, S. R., Ahmad, A. Y. B., Thethi, H. P., Chauhan, S. S., & Mircetic, D. (2025). Blockchain and AI Integration for Transparent and Secured Financial Record Keeping. *Recent Trends In Engineering and Science for Resource Optimization and Sustainable Development*, 72-76.

Agrawal, A., Gans, J. S., & Goldfarb, A. (2018). *Prediction machines: The simple economics of artificial intelligence*. Harvard Business Review Press.

Ahmadi, M. (2025). Data-driven decision-making and Predictive Analytics. *AI Marketing*, 57–73. DOI: 10.1201/9781003625452-4

Ahmed, F., Ahmed, M. R., Kabir, M. A., & Islam, M. M. (2025). Revolutionizing Business Analytics: The Impact of Artificial Intelligence and Machine Learning. *American Journal of Advanced Technology and Engineering Solutions*, *1*(01), 147–173. DOI: 10.63125/f7yjxw69

AIPRM. (2024, January 11). *AI statistics 2024*. Aiprm.com. https://www.aiprm.com/ai-statistics/

Akanbi, L. A., Adenuga, K. I., & Owolabi, H. (2024). Supply Chain Decision-Making Using Artificial Intelligence and Data Analytics. In K. E. K. Vimal, S. Rajak, V. Kumar, R. S. Mor, & A. Assayed (Eds.), *Industry 4.0 Technologies: Sustainable Manufacturing Supply Chains: Volume 1—Theory, Challenges, and Opportunity* (pp. 25–34). Springer Nature. DOI: 10.1007/978-981-99-4819-2_2

Akeiber, H. J. (2025). Artificial Intelligence in Engineering Management: Revolutionizing Decision-Making and Automation. Al-Rafidain Journal of Engineering Sciences, 317-349.

Akhtar, P., Ghouri, A. M., Khan, H. U. R., Amin ul Haq, M., Awan, U., Zahoor, N., Khan, Z., & Ashraf, A. (2023). Detecting fake news and disinformation using artificial intelligence and machine learning to avoid supply chain disruptions. *Annals of Operations Research, 327*(2), 633–657. DOI: 10.1007/s10479-022-05015-5 PMID: 36338350

Akter, S., Hossain, M. A., Sajib, S., Sultana, S., Rahman, M., Vrontis, D., & McCarthy, G. (2023). A framework for AI powered service innovation capability: Review and agenda for future research. *Technovation, 125*, 102768. Advance online publication. DOI: 10.1016/j.technovation.2023.102768

Alaskar, T. H., Alsadi, A. K., Aloulou, W. J., & Ayadi, F. M. (2024). Big data analytics, strategic capabilities, and innovation performance: Mediation approach of organizational ambidexterity. *Sustainability (Basel), 16*(12), 5111. DOI: 10.3390/su16125111

Alawamleh, M., Shammas, N., Alawamleh, K., & Bani Ismail, L. (2024). Examining the limitations of AI in business and the need for human insights using interpretive structural modelling. *Journal of Open Innovation, 10*(3), 100338. DOI: 10.1016/j.joitmc.2024.100338

Albaroudi, E., Mansouri, T., & Alameer, A. (2024). A Comprehensive Review of AI Techniques for Addressing Algorithmic Bias in Job Hiring. In *AI Switzerland,* 5(1), 383–404. https://doi.org/DOI: 10.3390/ai5010019

Albassam, W. A. (2023). The Power of Artificial Intelligence in Recruitment: An Analytical Review of Current AI-Based Recruitment Strategies. *International Journal of Professional Business Review, 8*(6), 1–25. DOI: 10.26668/businessreview/2023.v8i6.2089

Al-Debei, M. M., & Avison, D. (2010). Developing a unified framework of the business model concept. *European Journal of Information Systems, 19*(3), 359–376. DOI: 10.1057/ejis.2010.21

Aldhaheri, M., Alkuwaiti, M., Alhassani, A., Almansoori, M., Alalawi, W., & Khalifa, G. S. A. (2022). An Exploratory Study of Supply Chain Management Practices' Content Analysis and Future Perspectives: A Case Study. *International Journal on Recent Trends in Business and Tourism, 6*(3), 36–50. DOI: 10.31674/ijrtbt.2022.v06i03.004

Aldoseri, A., Al-Khalifa, K. N., & Hamouda, A. M. (2024). AI powered innovation in digital transformation: Key pillars and industry impact. *Sustainability (Basel), 16*(5), 1790. DOI: 10.3390/su16051790

Allal-Chérif, O., Aránega, A. Y., & Sánchez, R. C. (2021). Intelligent recruitment: How to identify, select, and retain talents from around the world using artificial intelligence. *Technological Forecasting and Social Change, 169*, 120822. DOI: 10.1016/j.techfore.2021.120822

Allal-Chérif, O., Simón-Moya, V., & Ballester, A. C. C. (2021). Intelligent purchasing: How artificial intelligence can redefine the purchasing function. *Journal of Business Research, 124*, 69–76. DOI: 10.1016/j.jbusres.2020.11.050

Allamanis, M., Barr, E. T., Devanbu, P., & Sutton, C. (2021). A survey of machine learning for big code and naturalness. *ACM Computing Surveys, 51*(4), 1–37. DOI: 10.1145/3212695

Allur, N. S. (2020). Big Data-Driven Agricultural Supply Chain Management: Trustworthy Scheduling Optimization with DSS and MILP Techniques. *Current Science & Humanities, 8*(4).

Almalki, F. A., Soufiene, B. O., Alsamhi, S. H., & Sakli, H. (2021). A Low-Cost platform for environmental smart farming monitoring system based on IoT and UAVs. *Sustainability (Basel), 13*(11), 5908. DOI: 10.3390/su13115908

Alnajem, A. A. Q. I., Ibrahim, A., Abdulrahman, M. M., Al-Kubaisi, A. A. A., Tawfeq, J. F., Khishe, M., & Saeed, A. (2024). AI-Driven Strategic Foresight: Anticipating Future Trends and Modelling Business Strategies. In *2024 International Conference on Decision Aid Sciences and Applications (DASA)* (pp. 1–6). IEEE.

Alonge, E. O., Eyo-Udo, N. L., Ubanadu, B. C., Daraojimba, A. I., Balogun, E. D., & Ogunsola, K. O. (2023). Real-time data analytics for enhancing supply chain efficiency. *Journal of Supply Chain Management and Analytics, 10*(1), 49–60.

Alon, U., Zilberstein, M., Levy, O., & Yahav, E. (2019). Code2vec: Learning distributed representations of code. *Proceedings of the ACM on Programming Languages, 3*(POPL), 40. DOI: 10.1145/3290353

Alpaydin, E. (2020). *Introduction to machine learning* (4th ed.). MIT Press.

Alrub, Y. A., & Sánchez Cañizares, S. M. (2025). Dynamic capabilities and digital transformation Toward strategic planning in the digital age evidence from Palestine. *Administrative Sciences, 15*(1), 21. DOI: 10.3390/admsci15010021

Alsheibani, S. A., Cheung, Y., Messom, C. H., & Alhosni, M. (2020, August). Winning AI strategy: Six steps to create value from artificial intelligence. *Proceedings of the Americas Conference on Information Systems (AMCIS)*, 11.

Al-Surmi, A., Bashiri, M., & Koliousis, I. (2022). AI based decision making: Combining strategies to improve operational performance. *International Journal of Production Research*, *60*(14), 4464–4486. DOI: 10.1080/00207543.2021.1966540

Amatriain, X., & Basilico, J. (2015). Recommender Systems in Industry: A Netflix Case Study. In Ricci, F., Rokach, L., & Shapira, B. (Eds.), *Recommender Systems Handbook* (pp. 385–419). Springer., DOI: 10.1007/978-1-4899-7637-6_11

Amazon. (2024). AI integration in supply chain and finance systems: Suppressing out-of-stock recommendations and prioritizing high-margin products. Amazon.

Ammoniaci, M., Kartsiotis, S., Perria, R., & Storchi, P. (2021). *State-of-the-art monitoring technologies and data processing for precision viticulture*. Multidisciplinary Digital Publishing Institute., DOI: 10.3390/agriculture11030201

Amor, J. J., González-Barahona, J. M., & Robles, G. (2006). Measuring Woody: The size of Debian 3.0. *Proceedings of the 8th International Workshop on Principles of Software Evolution*, 85–89. DOI: 10.1145/1137983.1138001

Ang'udi, J. J.Janet Julia Ang'udi. (2023). Security challenges in cloud computing: A comprehensive analysis. *World Journal of Advanced Engineering Technology and Sciences*, *10*(2), 155–181. DOI: 10.30574/wjaets.2023.10.2.0304

Angelov, B. (2024). *Elements of data strategy: A framework for data- and AI-driven transformation*. Wiley.

Ångström, R. C., Björn, M., Dahlander, L., Mähring, M., & Wallin, M. W. (2023). Getting AI implementation right: Insights from a global survey. *California Management Review*, *66*(1), 5–22. DOI: 10.1177/00081256231190430

Anwar, M., Korthaus, A., Bingley, S., & Burgess, S. (2025). AI in small businesses: Current and potential applications and issues for adoption. In *Cutting-Edge Technologies for Business Sectors* (pp. 29–56). IGI Global.

Arrieta, A. B., Díaz-Rodríguez, N., Del Ser, J., Tabik, S., Barbado, A., García, S., & Herrera, F. (2020). Explainable Artificial Intelligence (XAI): Concepts, taxonomies, opportunities and challenges toward responsible AI. *Information Fusion*, *58*, 136–159. DOI: 10.1016/j.inffus.2019.12.012

Arthur-Mensah, N. (2020). Bridging the industry–education skills gap for human resource development. *Industrial and Commercial Training*, *52*(2), 93–103. DOI: 10.1108/ICT-11-2019-0105

Arumugam, U., & Manida, M. (2024). Enhancing Strategic Decision Making: Assessing the Role and Impact of Artificial Intelligence in Business Management. *Journal of Business Analytics and Data Visualization (e-ISSN: 2584-1637)*, 1-8.

Arute, F., Arya, K., Babbush, R., Bacon, D., Bardin, J. C., Barends, R., & Neven, H. (2019). Quantum supremacy using a programmable superconducting processor. *Nature*, *574*(7779), 505–510. DOI: 10.1038/s41586-019-1666-5 PMID: 31645734

Attah, R. U., Garba, B. M. P., Gil-Ozoudeh, I., & Iwuanyanwu, O. (2024). Enhancing supply chain resilience through artificial intelligence: Analyzing problem-solving approaches in logistics management. *International Journal of Management & Entrepreneurship Research*, *5*(12), 3248–3265.

Aung, T., Liana, S. R., Htet, A., Bhaumik, A., & Poddar, S. (2024). Mediating Financial and HSE Roles in Risk Management Impact on Myanmar Construction Success. *Jurnal Ilmiah Ilmu Terapan Universitas Jambi*, *8*(1), 379–397. DOI: 10.22437/jiituj.v8i1.32699

Avlijas, G., Vukanovic Dumanovic, V., & Radunovic, M. (2021). Measuring the Effects of Automatic Replenishment on Product Availability in Retail Stores. *Sustainability (Basel)*, *13*(3), 3. Advance online publication. DOI: 10.3390/su13031391

Awan, U., Braathen, P., & Hannola, L. (2023). When and how the implementation of green human resource management and data-driven culture to improve the firm sustainable environmental development? *Sustainable Development (Bradford)*, *31*(4), 2726–2740. DOI: 10.1002/sd.2543

Azhar, I. (2015). The interaction between artificial intelligence and identity & access management: An empirical study. International Journal of Creative Research Thoughts (IJCRT), ISSN 2320-2882.

Aziz, S., Dowling, M., Hammami, H., & Piepenbrink, A. (2022). Machine learning in finance: A topic modeling approach. *European Financial Management*, *28*(3), 744–770. DOI: 10.1111/eufm.12326

Babadoğan, B. (2024). Unveiling the power of AI-driven personalization: Transforming consumer behaviour in the age of digital marketing. *Next Frontier for Life Sciences and AI*, *8*(1), 61. Advance online publication. DOI: 10.62802/fj43xy18

Baesens, B. (2014). *Analytics in a big data world: The essential guide to data science and its applications*. Wiley.

Bahangulu, J. K., & Owusu-Berko, L. (2025). Algorithmic bias, data ethics, and governance: Ensuring fairness, transparency and compliance in AI-powered business analytics applications. *World Journal of Advanced Research and Reviews*, *25*(2), 1746–1763. DOI: 10.30574/wjarr.2025.25.2.0571

Bahoo, S., Cucculelli, M., Goga, X., & Mondolo, J. (2024). Artificial intelligence in Finance: A comprehensive review through bibliometric and content analysis. *SN Business & Economics*, *4*(2), 23. DOI: 10.1007/s43546-023-00618-x

Bakshy, E., Messing, S., & Adamic, L. A. (2015). Exposure to ideologically diverse news and opinion on Facebook. *Science*, *348*(6239), 1130–1132. DOI: 10.1126/science.aaa1160 PMID: 25953820

Balasubramaniam, N., Kauppinen, M., Rannisto, A., Hiekkanen, K., & Kujala, S. (2023). Transparency and explainability of AI systems: From ethical guidelines to requirements. *Information and Software Technology*, *159*, 107197. DOI: 10.1016/j.infsof.2023.107197

Bano, R., Azim, F., Mahmood, Z., Sanaullah, A., & Ali, O. (2025). The Role of Artificial Intelligence in Personalized Marketing: Enhancing Customer Experience, Predictive Targeting, and Brand Engagement. *The Critical Review of Social Sciences Studies*, *3*(2), 50–65. DOI: 10.59075/d94kvf44

Barocas, S., & Selbst, A. D. (2016). Big data's disparate impact. *SSRN*, *104*(3), 671–732. DOI: 10.2139/ssrn.2477899

Baryannis, G., Dani, S., & Antoniou, G. (2019). Predictive analytics and artificial intelligence in supply chain management: Review and implications for the future. *Computers & Industrial Engineering*, *137*, 106024. DOI: 10.1016/j.cie.2019.106024

Batini, C., Rula, A., Scannapieco, M., & Viscusi, G. (2016). From data quality to big data quality. In Big Data: Concepts, Methodologies, Tools, and Applications (pp. 1934-1956). IGI Global Scientific Publishing. DOI: 10.4018/978-1-4666-9840-6.ch089

Bauerly, M., & Liu, J. (2019). The impact of content relevance on consumer attention in digital environments. *Journal of Advertising Research*, *59*(1), 55–68. DOI: 10.2501/JAR-2018-023

Bayramoğlu, G., & Öztürk, O. (2025). Systematic and bibliometric review of neuroeconomics and neurofinance research: Current status, thematic trends, and future directions. *Journal of Economic Surveys*, *39*(5), 1883–1906. DOI: 10.1111/joes.12676

Belhadi, A., Kamble, S., Fosso Wamba, S., & Queiroz, M. M. (2022). Building supply-chain resilience: An artificial intelligence-based technique and decision-making framework. *International Journal of Production Research*, *60*(14), 4487–4507. DOI: 10.1080/00207543.2021.1950935

Bell, R. M., Koren, Y., & Volinsky, C. (2009). The million dollar Netflix prize. *IEEE Spectrum*, *46*(2), 42–49. DOI: 10.1109/MSPEC.2009.4787568

Benbya, H., Davenport, T. H., & Pachidi, S. (2020). Artificial intelligence in organizations: Current state and future opportunities. *MIS Quarterly Executive*, *19*(4).

Berger, P. D., & Nasr, N. I. (1998). Customer lifetime value: Marketing models and applications. *Journal of Interactive Marketing*, *12*(1), 17–30. DOI: 10.1002/(SICI)1520-6653(199824)12:1<17::AID-DIR3>3.0.CO;2-K

Bevara, P. K., Singh, R. S., Medera, R., & Prasad Chelluri, V. V. D. (2025). Optimizing scientific workflow scheduling in cloud environments: A hybrid PSO-EWWO. *Cluster Computing*, *28*(8), 508. DOI: 10.1007/s10586-025-05168-5

Bharadiya, J. (2023). The impact of artificial intelligence on business processes. European journal of technology, 7(2), 15-25.

Bharadwaj, S., Varun, R., Aditya, P. S., Nikhil, M., & Babu, G. C. (2022). Resume Screening using NLP and LSTM. *5th International Conference on Inventive Computation Technologies, - Proceedings*, 238–241. https://doi.org/DOI: 10.1109/ICICT54344.2022.9850889

Bhardwaj, J., Awasthi, S., & Dhoni, P. S. (2025). Generative AI: Shaping the future of business intelligence and data-driven decision making. *International Journal of Artificial Intelligence and Machine Learning*, *4*(1), 1–8. DOI: 10.34218/IJAIML_04_01_001

Bhatia, V., Rawat, P., Kumar, A., & Shah, R. R. (2019). *End-to-End Resume Parsing and Finding Candidates for a Job Description using BERT*. arXiv preprint arXiv:1910.03089.

Bhattacharya, S., Castignani, G., Masello, L., & Sheehan, B. (2025). AI revolution in insurance: Bridging research and reality. *Frontiers in Artificial Intelligence*, *8*, 1568266. DOI: 10.3389/frai.2025.1568266 PMID: 40270929

Bhima, B., Rahmania Az Zahra, A., & Nurtino, T. (2023). Enhancing organizational efficiency through the integration of artificial intelligence in Management Information Systems. [ATM]. *APTISI Transactions on Management*, *7*(3), 282–289. DOI: 10.33050/atm.v7i3.2146

Biliavska, Y., Romat, Y., Biliavskyi, V., Ostapenko, T., & Sydorenko, O. (2024). Diagnosing Category Management in A Pharmacy Retail Chain. *Eastern-European Journal of Enterprise Technologies, 127*(13), 22–32. DOI: 10.15587/1729-4061.2024.298093

Bird, C., Nagappan, N., Murphy, B., Gall, H., & Devanbu, P. (2009). Does distributed development affect software quality? An empirical case study of Windows Vista. *Communications of the ACM, 52*(8), 85–93. DOI: 10.1145/1536616.1536639

Blessing, M. (2025). *AI-Powered Resume Screening: Benefits and Challenges.*, 1-7.

Boddapati, V. N., Bauskar, S. R., Madhavaram, C. R., Galla, E. P., Sunkara, J. R., & Gollangi, H. K. (2025). Optimizing Production Efficiency in Manufacturing using Big Data and AI/ML. SSRN *Electronic Journal*. DOI: 10.2139/ssrn.5080585

Booyse, D., & Scheepers, C. B. (2024). Barriers to adopting automated organisational decision-making through the use of artificial intelligence. *Management Research Review, 47*(1), 64–85. DOI: 10.1108/MRR-09-2021-0701

Boppiniti, S. T. (2021). Real-time data analytics with ai: Leveraging stream processing for dynamic decision support. *International Journal of Management Education for Sustainable Development, 4*(4), 1–27.

Borau, S. (2024). Deception, discrimination, and objectification: Ethical issues of female AI agents. *Journal of Business Ethics*. Advance online publication. DOI: 10.1007/s10551-024-05754-4

Boughaci, D., & Alkhawaldeh, A. A. (2020). Appropriate machine learning techniques for credit scoring and bankruptcy prediction in banking and finance: A comparative study. *Risk and Decision Analysis, 8*(1-2), 15–24. DOI: 10.3233/RDA-180051

Boute, R. N., & Udenio, M. (2023). AI in Logistics and Supply Chain Management. In Merkert, R., & Hoberg, K. (Eds.), *Global Logistics and Supply Chain Strategies for the 2020s: Vital Skills for the Next Generation* (pp. 49–65). Springer International Publishing., DOI: 10.1007/978-3-030-95764-3_3

Bowes, D., Hall, T., & Gray, D. (2018). Comparing the performance of fault prediction models. *Empirical Software Engineering, 23*, 3503–3542. DOI: 10.1007/s10664-018-9614-y

Bradlow, E., Gangwar, M., Kopalle, P., & Voleti, S. (2017). The Role of Big Data and Predictive Analytics in Retailing. *Journal of Retailing, 93*(1), 79–95. DOI: 10.1016/j.jretai.2016.12.004

Brauneis, A., & Steidl, A. (2019). The application of machine learning in financial services: An overview. *The Journal of Financial Data Science, 1*(1), 21–39. DOI: 10.3905/jfds.2019.1.1.021

Brodie, R. J., Hollebeek, L. D., Juric, B., & Ilic, A. (2021). Customer engagement: Conceptual domain, fundamental propositions, and implications for research. *Journal of Service Research, 24*(2), 123–145. DOI: 10.1177/1094670520977592

Brynjolfsson, E., Hu, Y. J., & Simester, D. (2011). Goodbye Pareto Principle, hello long tail: The effect of search costs on the concentration of product sales. *Management Science, 57*(8), 1373–1386. DOI: 10.1287/mnsc.1110.1371

Brynjolfsson, E., & McAfee, A. (2014). *The second machine age: Work, progress, and prosperity in a time of brilliant technologies*. W. W. Norton & Company.

Brynjolfsson, E., & McAfee, A. (2017). *Machine, platform, crowd: Harnessing our digital future*. W. W. Norton & Company.

Bughin, J., Hazan, E., Ramaswamy, S., Chui, M., Allas, T., Dahlström, P., . . . Trench, M. (2017). *Artificial intelligence: The next digital frontier?* McKinsey Global Institute. https://www.mckinsey.com/~/media/mckinsey/industries/advanced%20electronics/our%20insights/how%20artificial%20intelligence%20can%20deliver%20real%20value%20to%20companies/mgi-artificial-intelligence-discussion-paper.pdf

Bughin, J., Seong, J., Manyika, J., Chui, M., & Joshi, R. (2018). *Notes from the AI frontier: Modeling the impact of AI on the world economy*. McKinsey Global Institute. https://www.mckinsey.com/featured-insights/artificial-intelligence/notes-from-the-ai-frontier-modeling-the-impact-of-ai-on-the-world-economy

Bughin, J., Seong, J., Manyika, J., Chui, M., & Joshi, R. (2021). *The state of AI in 2021*. McKinsey & Company. https://www.mckinsey.com/business-functions/quantumblack/our-insights/the-state-of-ai-in-2021

Burns, B., Grant, B., Oppenheimer, D., Brewer, E., & Wilkes, J. (2016). Borg, omega, and kubernetes: Lessons learned from three container-management systems over a decade. *Communications of the ACM, 59*(5), 50–57. DOI: 10.1145/2890784

Caigny, A., Coussement, K., & Bock, K. (2018). A new hybrid classification algorithm for customer churn prediction based on logistic regression and decision trees. *European Journal of Operational Research, 269*(2), 760–772. DOI: 10.1016/j.ejor.2018.02.009

California State Legislature. (2018). *California Consumer Privacy Act of 2018 (AB-375)*. Retrievedfrom https://leginfo.legislature.ca.gov/faces/billTextClient.xhtml?bill_id=201720180AB375

Cambria, E., & White, B. (2014). Jumping NLP curves: A review of natural language processing research. *IEEE Computational Intelligence Magazine*, *9*(2), 48–57. DOI: 10.1109/MCI.2014.2307227

Campion, A., Gasco-Hernandez, M., Jankin Mikhaylov, S., & Esteve, M. (2022). Overcoming the challenges of collaboratively adopting artificial intelligence in the public sector. *Social Science Computer Review*, *40*(2), 462–477. DOI: 10.1177/0894439320979953

Cao, Y., & Zhai, J. (2022). A survey of AI in finance. *Journal of Chinese Economic and Business Studies*, *20*(2), 125–137. DOI: 10.1080/14765284.2022.2077632

Casino, F., Dasaklis, T. K., & Patsakis, C. (2019). A systematic literature review of blockchain-based applications: Current status, classification and open issues. *Telematics and Informatics*, *36*, 55–81. DOI: 10.1016/j.tele.2018.11.006

Celestin, M., & Vanitha, N. (2018). AI-Powered Entrepreneurship: The Tools That Will Shape Tomorrow's Startups. [IJATET]. *International Journal of Advanced Trends in Engineering and Technology*, *3*(2), 29–35.

Cetindamar, D., Kitto, K., Wu, M., Zhang, Y., Abedin, B., & Knight, S. (2024). Explicating AI literacy of employees at digital workplaces. *IEEE Transactions on Engineering Management*, *71*, 810–823. DOI: 10.1109/TEM.2021.3138503

Chakraborty, M., & Parida, P. (2024). Comprehensive study of AI-driven market forecasting models and their applicability. *2024 International Conference on Advancements in Smart, Secure and Intelligent Computing (ASSIC)*, 1–5. DOI: 10.1109/ASSIC60049.2024.10508015

Chandrasekhar, K., Das, S., Gupta, N., & Jena, S. K. (2024). Comparative Analysis of Impulse Buying Behaviour Across Retail Channels: A Study of Physical Stores, E-commerce Websites and Mobile Shopping Apps. *Economic Affairs*, *69*(02), 1109–1120.

Charles, V., Emrouznejad, A., & Gherman, T. (2023). A critical analysis of the integration of blockchain and artificial intelligence for supply chain. *Annals of Operations Research*, *327*(1), 7–47. DOI: 10.1007/s10479-023-05169-w PMID: 36718465

Chauhan, G. S., & Jadon, R. (2020). AI and ML-Powered CAPTCHA and advanced graphical passwords: Integrating the DROP methodology, AES encryption and neural network-based authentication for enhanced security. *World Journal of Advanced Engineering Technology and Sciences*, *1*(1), 121–132. DOI: 10.30574/wjaets.2020.1.1.0027

Chen, H., Chiang, R. H. L., & Storey, V. C. (2012). Business intelligence and analytics: From big data to big impact. *Management Information Systems Quarterly*, *36*(4), 1165–1188. DOI: 10.2307/41703503

Chen, Y. M., Chen, T. Y., & Chen, L. C. (2021). On a method for location and mobility analytics using location-based services: A case study of retail store recommendation. *Online Information Review*, *45*(2), 297–315. DOI: 10.1108/OIR-10-2017-0292

Chen, Y., Chen, J., & Ching-Wen, T. (2006). A data mining approach for retail knowledge discovery with consideration of the effect of shelf-space adjacency on sales. *Decision Support Systems*, *42*(3), 1503–1520. DOI: 10.1016/j.dss.2005.12.004

Chen, Z. Y., Fan, Z. P., & Sun, M. (2023). Machine learning methods for data-driven demand estimation and assortment planning considering cross-selling and substitutions. *INFORMS Journal on Computing*, *35*(1), 158–177. DOI: 10.1287/ijoc.2022.1251

Chen, Z., Liu, H., & Zhang, Q. (2023). Adaptive Selection of BERT Layer for Multi-Label Text Classification. *Proceedings of International Conference on Machine Learning and Cybernetics*, 434–439. https://doi.org/DOI: 10.1109/ICMLC58545.2023.10327995

Cheong, B. C. (2024). Transparency and Accountability in AI Systems: Safeguarding Well-Being in the Age of Algorithmic Decision-Making. *Frontiers in Human Dynamics*, *6*, 1421273. DOI: 10.3389/fhumd.2024.1421273

Chin, R., Catal, C., & Kassahun, A. (2023). Plant disease detection using drones in precision agriculture. Springer Science+Business Media. DOI: 10.1007/s11119-023-10014-y

Chintalapati, P. V., Paluri, S. S., Nikhitha, S. S., Nanditha, T. S. V., Daneswari, S. T. V. L., & Sree, P. K. (2024). A Research Model for Automated Prediction and Analysis of Job Interview Performance. *Proceedings - 2024 6th International Conference on Computational Intelligence and Communication Technologies*, 284–291. https://doi.org/DOI: 10.1109/CCICT62777.2024.00055

Chinthala, L. K., & Prasad, P. (2025). Consumer experience 2025: The role of personalization and AI in shaping business strategies. *International Journal of Modern Science and Research Technology*, *3*(5). Advance online publication. DOI: 10.5281/zenodo.15347436

Chui, M., Harryson, M., Manyika, J., Roberts, R., Chung, R., van Heteren, A., & Nel, P. (2018). *Notes from the AI frontier: Insights from hundreds of use cases.* McKinsey Global. https://www.mckinsey.com/~/media/mckinsey/featured%20insights/artificial%20intelligence/applying%20artificial%20intelligence%20for%20social%20good/mgi-applying-ai-for-social-good-discussion-paper-dec-2018.pdf

Chui, M., Manyika, J., & Miremadi, M. (2016). *Where machines could replace humans—and where they can't (yet). McKinsey Quarterly.* https://www.mckinsey.com/business-functions/mckinsey-digital/our-insights/where-machines-could-replace-humans-and-where-they-cant-yet

Chui, M., Manyika, J., & Miremadi, M. (2018). What AI can and can't do (yet) for your business. *McKinsey Quarterly.* https://www.mckinsey.com/featured-insights/artificial-intelligence/what-ai-can-and-cant-do-yet-for-your-business

Chukwuma, U., Gebremedhin, K. G., & Uyeh, D. D. (2024). Imagining AI-driven decision making for managing farming in developing and emerging economies. *Computers and Electronics in Agriculture*, *221*, 108946. DOI: 10.1016/j.compag.2024.108946

Coussement, K., & Van den Poel, D. (2008). Predictive modelling in customer relationship management: A review and future directions. *International Journal of Forecasting*, *24*(1), 60–76.

Cox, A. (2024). Algorithmic literacy, AI literacy and responsible generative AI literacy. *Journal of Web Librarianship*, *18*(3), 93–110. DOI: 10.1080/19322909.2024.2395341

Csaszar, F. A., Ketkar, H., & Kim, H. (2024). Artificial intelligence and strategic decision making Evidence from entrepreneurs and investors. *Strategy Science*, *9*(4), 322–345. DOI: 10.1287/stsc.2024.0190

Csikszentmihalyi, M. (1990). *Flow: The Psychology of Optimal Experience*. Harper & Row.

Danielsson, J., Macrae, R., & Uthemann, A. (2022). Artificial intelligence and systemic risk. *Journal of Banking & Finance*, *140*, 106290. DOI: 10.1016/j.jbankfin.2021.106290

Darapu, K., & Marukukula, M. (2025). Fraud Detection and Prevention in Finance and Banking Using Artificial Intelligence. In *Real-World Applications of AI Innovation* (pp. 213–232). IGI Global Scientific Publishing.

Daruvuri, R., Patibandla, K. K., & Mannem, P. (2025, March). Data Driven Retail Price Optimization Using XGBoost and Predictive Modeling. In *2025 International Conference on Intelligent Computing and Control Systems (ICICCS)* (pp. 220-225). IEEE. DOI: 10.1109/ICICCS65191.2025.10984940

Daryani, C., Chhabra, G. S., Patel, H., Chhabra, I. K., & Patel, R. (2020)... *An Automated Resume Screening System Using Natural Language Processing and Similarity, 99–103*, 99–103. Advance online publication. DOI: 10.26480/etit.02.2020.99.103

Dash, R., McMurtrey, M., Rebman, C., & Kar, K. (2019). Application of Artificial Intelligence in Automation of Supply Chain Management. *Journal of Strategic Innovation and Sustainability, 14*(3). Advance online publication. DOI: 10.33423/jsis.v14i3.2105

Das, M. P. (2023). Technology and Guest experience: Innovations reshaping hotel management. *International Journal for Multidimensional Research Perspectives, 1*(3), 76–95.

Das, P., & Dhar, P. (2021). Finding Out the Influence of Marketing Mix on Attitude of Customers for Providing Online Reviews. [AMT]. *Advancement in Management and Technology, 2*(1), 27–37.

Daugherty, P. R., & Wilson, H. J. (2018). *Human + machine: Reimagining work in the age of AI*. Harvard Business Press.

Davenport, T. H. (2014). *Big Data at Work: Dispelling the Myths, Uncovering the Opportunities*. Harvard Business Review Press. DOI: 10.15358/9783800648153

Davenport, T. H., Guha, A., Grewal, D., & Bressgott, T. (2020). How artificial intelligence will change the future of marketing. *Journal of the Academy of Marketing Science, 48*(1), 24–42. DOI: 10.1007/s11747-019-00696-0

Davenport, T. H., & Harris, J. G. (2017). *Competing on analytics: The new science of winning*. Harvard Business Press.

Davenport, T. H., & Kirby, J. (2016). *Only Humans Need Apply: Winners and Losers in the Age of Smart Machines*. HarperBusiness.

Davenport, T. H., & Ronanki, R. (2018). Artificial intelligence for the real world. *Harvard Business Review, 96*(1), 108–116.

Davis, F. D., Bagozzi, R. P., & Warshaw, P. R. (2021). User acceptance of computer technology: A comparison of two theoretical models. *Management Science, 67*(5), 1115–1130. DOI: 10.1287/mnsc.2020.3586

De Fauw, J., Ledsam, J. R., Romera-Paredes, B., Nikolov, S., Tomasev, N., & Suleyman, M. (2018). Clinically applicable deep learning for diagnosis and referral in retinal disease. *Nature Medicine*, *24*(9), 1342–1350. DOI: 10.1038/s41591-018-0107-6 PMID: 30104768

De Vries, A. (2023). The growing energy footprint of artificial intelligence. *Joule*, *7*(10), 2191–2194. DOI: 10.1016/j.joule.2023.09.004

Deiva Ganesh, A., & Kalpana, P. (2022). Future of artificial intelligence and its influence on supply chain risk management – A systematic review. *Computers & Industrial Engineering*, *169*, 108206. DOI: 10.1016/j.cie.2022.108206

Delasay, M., Jain, A., & Kumar, S. (2022). Impacts of the COVID-19 pandemic on grocery retail operations: An analytical model. *Production and Operations Management*, *31*(5), 2237–2255. DOI: 10.1111/poms.13717 PMID: 35601843

Deliu, D., & Olariu, A. (2024). The role of artificial intelligence and big data analytics in shaping the future of professions in Industry 6.0: Perspectives from an emerging market. *Electronics (Basel)*, *13*(24), 4983. DOI: 10.3390/electronics13244983

Deloitte. (2023). *2023 Global marketing trends: Resilient seeds for growth.* Deloitte Insights. https://www2.deloitte.com/insights/us/en/topics/marketing-and-sales-operations/global-marketing-trends.html

Deng, C., & Liu, Y. (2021). A deep learning based inventory management and demand prediction optimization method for anomaly detection. *Wireless Communications and Mobile Computing*, *9969357*(1), 9969357. Advance online publication. DOI: 10.1155/2021/9969357

Devarajan, M. V. (2019). A Comprehensive AI-Based Detection and Differentiation Model for Neurological Disorders Using PSP Net and Fuzzy Logic-Enhanced Hilbert-Huang Transform. *International Journal of Information Technology and Computer Engineering*, *7*(3), 94–104.

Devare, M. H. (2019a). Cloud Computing and Innovations. In Kecskemeti, G. (Ed.), *Applying Integration Techniques and Methods in Distributed Systems and Technologies* (pp. 1–33). IGI Global Scientific Publishing., DOI: 10.4018/978-1-5225-8295-3.ch001

Devi, C. G., & Jai Karthik, M. S. A. (2025). Chatbots and conversational AI: Revolutionizing customer engagement in marketing. In Devi, C. G., Priya, D., & Vasudevan, A. (Eds.), *AI and machine learning in marketing* (pp. 90–94). Shanlax Publications., https://www.shanlaxpublications.com/ai-and-machine-learning-in-marketing/ DOI: 10.34293/p/AI-and-Machine-Learning-in-Marketing

DHL. (2023). *AI-driven logistics optimization: Advancing sustainability and cross-functional ROI*. DHL.

Doris, M. J. (2010). *Review of Understanding Privacy, by Daniel J.* Solove.Edinburgh Law Review., DOI: 10.3366/elr.2010.0323

Doshi-Velez, F., & Kim, B. (2017). *Towards a rigorous science of interpretable machine learning*. arXiv preprint arXiv*:1702.08608*. https://arxiv.org/abs/1702.08608

Duan, Y., Edwards, J. S., & Dwivedi, Y. K. (2019). Artificial intelligence for decision making in the era of big data Evolution, challenges and research agenda. *International Journal of Information Management*, *48*, 63–71. DOI: 10.1016/j.ijinfomgt.2019.01.021

Dwivedi, Y. K., Hughes, L., Ismagilova, E., Aarts, G., Coombs, C., Crick, T., Duan, Y., Dwivedi, R., Edwards, J., Eirug, A., Galanos, V., Ilavarasan, P. V., Janssen, M., Jones, P., Kar, A. K., Kizgin, H., Kronemann, B., Lal, B., Lucini, B., & Williams, M. D. (2021). Artificial intelligence (AI): Multidisciplinary perspectives on emerging challenges, opportunities, and agenda for research, practice and policy. *International Journal of Information Management*, *57*, 101994. DOI: 10.1016/j.ijinfomgt.2019.08.002

Eboigbe, E. O., Farayola, O. A., Olatoye, F. O., Nnabugwu, O. C., & Daraojimba, C. (2023). Business intelligence transformation through AI and data analytics. *Engineering Science & Technology Journal*, *4*(5), 285–307. DOI: 10.51594/estj.v4i5.616

Ebrahimi, S., Abdelhalim, E., Hassanein, K., & Head, M. (2025). Reducing the incidence of biased algorithmic decisions through transparency of the importance of features: An empirical study. *European Journal of Information Systems*. Advance online publication. DOI: 10.1080/0960085X.2024.2395531

Eppler, M. J., & Mengis, J. (2004). The concept of information overload: A review of literature from organization science, accounting, marketing, MIS, and related disciplines. In Meckel, M., & Schmid, B. F. (Eds.), *Kommunikationsmanagement im Wandel* (pp. 325–344). Springer., DOI: 10.1007/978-3-8349-9772-2_15

Erevelles, S., Fukawa, N., & Swayne, L. (2016). Big data consumer analytics and the transformation of marketing. *Journal of Business Research*, *69*(2), 897–904. DOI: 10.1016/j.jbusres.2015.07.001

Eubanks, V. (2018). *Automating inequality: How high-tech tools profile, police, and punish the poor*. St. Martin's Press.

European Commission. (2021). *Proposal for a regulation laying down harmonised rules on artificial intelligence (Artificial Intelligence Act)*. https://eur-lex.europa.eu/legal-content/EN/TXT/?uri=CELEX%3A52021PC0206

Fader, P. S., & Hardie, B. G. S. (2009). A note on the Amazon.com recommendation algorithm. *Marketing Science, 28*(6), 1017–1025. DOI: 10.1287/mksc.1090.0526

Fader, P. S., Hardie, B. G. S., & Lee, K. L. (2005). RFM and CLV: Using iso-value curves for customer base analysis. *JMR, Journal of Marketing Research, 42*(4), 415–430. DOI: 10.1509/jmkr.2005.42.4.415

Fantozzi, I. C., Santolamazza, A., Loy, G., & Schiraldi, M. M. (2025). Digital twins: Strategic guide to utilize digital twins to improve operational efficiency in Industry 4.0. *Future Internet, 17*(1), 41. DOI: 10.3390/fi17010041

Farinu, U. (2025). *Fairness, Accountability, and Transparency in AI: Ethical Challenges in Data-Driven Decision-Making*. DOI: 10.2139/ssrn.5128174

Feizabadi, J. (2022). Machine learning demand forecasting and supply chain performance. *International Journal of Logistics, 25*(2), 119–142. DOI: 10.1080/13675567.2020.1803246

Feldman, R. (2013). Techniques and applications for sentiment analysis. *Communications of the ACM, 56*(4), 82–89. DOI: 10.1145/2436256.2436274

Feliu Juan, M. (2024). *Enhancing demand forecasting: An analysis of factors impacting sales and implementation of improved methodologies for accurate prediction* [Bachelor thesis, Universitat Politècnica de Catalunya]. https://upcommons.upc.edu/handle/2117/411544

Feng, Z., Guo, D., Tang, D., Duan, N., Feng, X., Gong, M., . . . Zhou, M. (2020). CodeBERT: A pre-trained model for programming and natural languages. *arXiv preprint arXiv:2002.08155*. /arXiv.2002.08155DOI: 10.18653/v1/2020.findings-emnlp.139

Fernández-Combarro, M. (2024). *The New Global Equation: Shorter Ties, Stronger Economies?* https://repositorio.comillas.edu/xmlui/handle/11531/79590

Fielding, R. T. (2000). Architectural styles and the design of network-based software architectures *(Doctoral dissertation, University of California, Irvine)*. Retrieved from https://www.ics.uci.edu/~fielding/pubs/dissertation/top.htm

Flaxman, S., Goel, S., & Rao, J. M. (2016). Filter bubbles, echo chambers, and online news consumption. *Public Opinion Quarterly, 80*(S1), 298–320. DOI: 10.1093/poq/nfw006

Flechsig, C., Anslinger, F., & Lasch, R. (2022). Robotic Process Automation in purchasing and supply management: A multiple case study on potentials, barriers, and implementation. *Journal of Purchasing and Supply Management*, *28*(1), 100718. DOI: 10.1016/j.pursup.2021.100718

Fleisher, C. S., & Wright, S. (2010). Competitive Intelligence analysis failure: Diagnosing individual level causes and implementing organisational level remedies. *Journal of Strategic Marketing*, *18*(7), 553–572. DOI: 10.1080/0965254X.2010.529152

Floridi, L., & Cowls, J. (2021). A unified framework of five principles for AI in society. In *Ethics, Governance, and Policies in Artificial Intelligence* (pp. 5–17). Springer. DOI: 10.1007/978-3-030-81907-1_2

Floridi, L., Cowls, J., Beltrametti, M., Chatila, R., Chazerand, P., Dignum, V., & Valcke, P. (2018). AI4People—An ethical framework for a good AI society: Opportunities, risks, principles, and recommendations. *Minds and Machines*, *28*(4), 689–707. DOI: 10.1007/s11023-018-9482-5 PMID: 30930541

Fontana, F. A., Braione, P., & Zanoni, M. (2016). Automatic detection of bad smells in code: An experimental assessment. *Journal of Object Technology*, *15*(1), 1–38. DOI: 10.5381/jot.2016.15.1.a2

Fornari, F., Compagnucci, I., Callisto de Donato, M., Bertrand, Y., Beyel, H. H., Carrión, E., Franceschetti, M., Groher, W., Grüger, J., Kilic, E., Koschmider, A., Leotta, F., Li, C. Y., Lugaresi, G., Malburg, L., Mangler, J., Mecella, M., Pastor, O., Riss, U., & Valderas, P. (2025). Digital twins of business processes: A research manifesto. *Internet of Things : Engineering Cyber Physical Human Systems*, *30*, 101477. DOI: 10.1016/j.iot.2024.101477

Frow, P., & Payne, A. (2011). A stakeholder perspective of the value proposition concept. *European Journal of Marketing*, *45*(1/2), 223–240. DOI: 10.1108/03090561111095676

Fuentes-Peailillo, F., Gutter, K., Vega, R., & Silva, G. C. (2024). Transformative technologies in digital agriculture: Leveraging the Internet of Things, remote sensing, and artificial intelligence for smart crop management. *Journal of Sensor and Actuator Networks*, *13*(4), 39. Advance online publication. DOI: 10.3390/jsan13040039

Gadde, H. (2024). AI-Powered Fault Detection and Recovery in High-Availability Databases. *International Journal of Machine Learning Research in Cybersecurity and Artificial Intelligence*, *15*(1), 500–529.

Gahinet, M. C., & Cliquet, G. (2018). Proximity and time in convenience store patronage: Kaïros more than chronos. *Journal of Retailing and Consumer Services, 43*, 1–9. DOI: 10.1016/j.jretconser.2018.02.008

Gandomi, A., & Haider, M. (2015). Beyond the hype: Big data concepts, methods, and analytics. *International Journal of Information Management, 35*(2), 137–144. DOI: 10.1016/j.ijinfomgt.2014.10.007

Ganesan, T. (2019). *Performance Analysis of Genetic Algorithms, Monte Carlo Methods, and Markov Models for Cloud-Based Scientific Computing. 13*(1).

Ganeshkumar, M., Karunakaran, S., Muzhumathi, R., & Suguna, R. (2024). AI-driven marketing insights: Harnessing machine learning for enhanced consumer engagement and personalization. In *Proceedings of the First International Conference on Software, Systems and Information Technology (SSITCON)* (pp. 1–6). DOI: 10.1109/SSITCON62437.2024.10796558

Gao, H., Kou, G., Liang, H., Zhang, H., Chao, X., Li, C. C., & Dong, Y. (2024). Machine learning in business and finance: A literature review and research opportunities. *Financial Innovation, 10*(1), 86. DOI: 10.1186/s40854-024-00629-z

Gao, Y., Liu, S., & Yang, L. (2025). Artificial intelligence and innovation capability: A dynamic capabilities perspective. *International Review of Economics & Finance, 98*, 103923. DOI: 10.1016/j.iref.2025.103923

Garg, N., Gupta, K., Chelikani, H., & Ravada, P. (2025). The Evolution of Personalization From Traditional Marketing to AI Computing. In Kanthavel, R., & Dhaya, R. (Eds.), *AI for Large Scale Communication Networks* (pp. 415–444). IGI Global Scientific Publishing., DOI: 10.4018/979-8-3693-6552-6.ch019

Gartner. (2019). Data lake: Definition, benefits, and challenges. *Gartner Research.* Retrieved from https://www.gartner.com/en/documents/3902666/data-lake-definition-benefits-and-challenges

Gartner. (2021). *Top Strategic Technology Trends 2021.* Gartner.

Gazi, M. A. I., Rahman, M. K. H., Masud, A. A., Amin, M. B., Chaity, N. S., Senathirajah, A. R. B. S., & Abdullah, M. (2024). AI capability and sustainable performance: Unveiling the mediating effects of organizational creativity and green innovation with knowledge sharing culture as a moderator. *Sustainability (Basel), 16*(17), 7466. DOI: 10.3390/su16177466

GfK. (2017). *Social Listening Study on Starbucks.* GfK Custom Research, LLC.

Ghatge, S. K., & Parasar, A. (2023). Application of artificial intelligence (AI), internet of things (IoT), and big data in healthcare, finance, and transportation. *PriMera Scientific Medicine and Public Health*, *2*, 27–36.

Ghavami, P. (2019). *Big data analytics methods: analytics techniques in data mining, deep learning and natural language processing*. Walter de Gruyter GmbH & Co KG. DOI: 10.1515/9781547401567

Ghosh, K., & Ghosh, D. P. (2025). Who am AI? Deconstructing identity in the age of advanced artificial intelligence [Preprint]. DOI: 10.13140/RG.2.2.36276.36481

Ghosh, U. K. (2025). Transformative AI applications in business decision-making. *Advances in Logistics, Operations, and Management Science*, •••, 1–40. DOI: 10.4018/979-8-3373-1687-1.ch001

Giudici, P., & Raffinetti, E. (2023). SAFE Artificial Intelligence in finance. *Finance Research Letters*, *56*, 104088. DOI: 10.1016/j.frl.2023.104088

Glass, R. L. (2002). *Facts and Fallacies of Software Engineering*. Addison-Wesley.

Glinska, G. (2024). *AI in marketing: How customer-centric companies can benefit from data privacy regulations.* Forbes India. https://www.forbesindia.com/article/darden-school-of-business/ai-in-marketing-how-customercentric-companies-can-benefit-from-data-privacy-regulations/93369/1

Goldfarb, A., & Tucker, C. (2011). Privacy and innovation. *Marketing Science*, *30*(5), 779–787.

Goldfarb, A., & Tucker, C. (2019). Digital economics. *Journal of Economic Literature*, *57*(1), 3–43. DOI: 10.1257/jel.20171452

Gomez-Uribe, C. A., & Hunt, N. (2016). The Netflix recommender system: Algorithms, business value, and innovation. *ACM Transactions on Management Information Systems (TMIS, 6)*(4), 1–19. DOI: 10.1145/2843948

Goodfellow, I., Bengio, Y., & Courville, A. (2016). *Deep learning*. MIT Press.

Goodfellow, I., Bengio, Y., & Courville, A. (2016). *Deep Learning*. MIT Press.

Goswami, M. (2020). Leveraging AI for cost efficiency and optimized cloud resource management. *International Journal of New Media Studies: International Peer Reviewed Scholarly Indexed Journal*, *7*(1), 21–27.

Gowri, D. P. (2024). Impact of AI in Personalized Digital Marketing: Boosting Customer Engagement through Tailored Content. *Journal of Communication Management (London)*, *3*(03), 216–221. DOI: 10.58966/JCM2024334

Grammarly. (2020). *How Grammarly uses AI to help you write better.* [Company Blog Post].

Grönroos, C. (1994). From marketing mix to relationship marketing: Towards a paradigm shift in marketing. *Management Decision, 32*(2), 4–20. DOI: 10.1108/00251749410054774

Gruber, T. R. (1993). A translation approach to portable ontology specifications. *Knowledge Acquisition, 5*(2), 199–220. DOI: 10.1006/knac.1993.1008

Guendouz, T. (2024). Artificial intelligence-powered customer experience management: Moving from mass to hyper-personalization in light of relationship marketing. *International Journal for Scientific Research, 3*(6), 247–306. Advance online publication. DOI: 10.59992/IJSR.2024.v3n6p9

Gungunawat, A., Khandelwal, N., & Gupta, N. (2024). AI-powered personalization in digital marketing: Transforming consumer engagement and strategy. *Research Review International Journal of Multidisciplinary, 9*(11), 183–191. DOI: 10.31305/rrijm.2024.v09.n11.026

Guo, F., Gallagher, C. M., Sun, T., Tavoosi, S., & Min, H. (2024). Smarter people analytics with organizational text data: Demonstrations using classic and advanced NLP models. *Human Resource Management Journal, 34*(1), 39–54. DOI: 10.1111/1748-8583.12426

Gupta, Y., & Khan, F. M. (2024). Role of artificial intelligence in customer engagement: A systematic review and future research directions. *Journal of Modelling in Management, 19*(5), 1535–1565. DOI: 10.1108/JM2-01-2023-0016

Haenlein, M., & Kaplan, A. (2019). A brief history of artificial intelligence: On the past, present, and future of artificial intelligence. *California Management Review, 61*(4), 5–14. DOI: 10.1177/0008125619864925

Haider, R., Bari, M. F. A. I., Shaif, M. F. I., & Rahman, M. (2025). Engineering hyper-personalization: Software challenges and brand performance in AI-driven digital marketing management: An empirical study. *International Journal of Science and Research Archive, 15*(2), 1122–1141. DOI: 10.30574/ijsra.2025.15.2.1525

Hair, J. F., Hult, G. T. M., Ringle, C. M., & Sarstedt, M. (2017). *A Primer on Partial Least Squares Structural Equation Modeling (PLS-SEM)* (2nd ed.). Sage Publications., DOI: 10.15358/9783800653614

Haleem, A., Javaid, M., Asim Qadri, M., Pratap Singh, R., & Suman, R. (2022). Artificial Intelligence (AI) applications for marketing: A literature-based study. *International Journal of Intelligent Networks, 3*, 119–132. DOI: 10.1016/j.ijin.2022.08.005

Hanelt, A., Bohnsack, R., Marz, D., & Antunes Marante, C. (2021). A systematic review of the literature on digital transformation: Insights and implications for strategy and organizational change. *Journal of Management Studies*, *58*(5), 1159–1197. DOI: 10.1111/joms.12639

Han, J., Pei, J., Yin, Y., & Mao, R. (2004). Mining frequent patterns without candidate generation: A frequent-pattern tree approach. *Data Mining and Knowledge Discovery*, *8*(1), 53–87. DOI: 10.1023/B:DAMI.0000005258.31418.83

Hanna, M. G., Pantanowitz, L., Li, Q. K., Dadras, S. S., Bui, M. M., Farris, A. B., Salgado, R., Schuuring, E., Taylor, C. R., & Nakhleh, R. E. (2025). Ethical and bias considerations in artificial intelligence and machine learning applications in pathology. *Modern Pathology*, *38*(2), 100686. DOI: 10.1016/j.modpat.2024.100686 PMID: 39694331

Hasan, M. T. (2025). A systematic literature review on AI in marketing: Establishing an ethical framework for academics and marketers. [Master's thesis, University of Eastern Finland]. UEF eRepository.https://erepo.uef.fi/server/api/core/bitstreams/5e5c29de-40ed-47ed-9683-da50ec2489ae/content

Hassan, N. H. M., Ahmad, K., & Salehuddin, H. (2020). Diagnosing the issues and challenges in data integration implementation in public sector. *International Journal on Advanced Science, Engineering and Information Technology*, *10*(2), 529–535. DOI: 10.18517/ijaseit.10.2.10271

Hassan, S., & De Filippi, P. (2021). Decentralized autonomous organization. *Internet Policy Review*, *10*(2), 1–10. DOI: 10.14763/2021.2.1556

Hastie, T., Tibshirani, R., & Friedman, J. (2009). *The Elements of Statistical Learning: Data Mining, Inference, and Prediction* (2nd ed.). Springer., DOI: 10.1007/978-0-387-84858-7

Hatta, M., Wahid, W. N., Yusuf, F., Hidayat, F., Santoso, N. A., & Aini, Q. (2024). Enhancing predictive models in system development using machine learning algorithms. *International Journal of Cyber and IT Service Management*, *4*(2), 80–87. DOI: 10.34306/ijcitsm.v4i2.159

Heger, J., & Klein, R. (2024). Assortment optimization: A systematic literature review. *OR-Spektrum*, *46*(4), 1099–1161. DOI: 10.1007/s00291-024-00752-4

He, H., & Garcia, E. A. (2009). Learning from imbalanced data. *IEEE Transactions on Knowledge and Data Engineering*, *21*(9), 1263–1284. DOI: 10.1109/TKDE.2008.239

Hekimoğlua, M., Sevim, I., Aksezer, A., & Durmuş, I. (2019). Assortment optimization with log-linear demand: Application at a Turkish grocery store. *Journal of Retailing and Consumer Services, 50*, 199–214. DOI: 10.1016/j.jretconser.2019.04.007

Helo, P., & Hao, Y. (2022). Artificial intelligence in operations management and supply chain management: An exploratory case study. *Production Planning and Control, 33*(16), 1573–1590. DOI: 10.1080/09537287.2021.1882690

Henke, N., Libarikian, A., & Wiseman, B. (2018). *The case for digital reinvention.* McKinsey Quarterly. https://www.mckinsey.com/business-functions/mckinsey-digital/our-insights/the-case-for-digital-reinvention

He, X., Zhao, K., & Chu, X. (2021). AutoML: *A survey of the state-of-the-art. Knowledge-Based Systems, 212*, 106622. DOI: 10.1016/j.knosys.2020.106622

Hill, K. (2012, February 16). *How Target figured out a teen girl was pregnant before her father did.Forbes.* https://www.forbes.com/sites/kashmirhill/2012/02/16/how-target-figured-out-a-teen-girl-was-pregnant-before-her-father-did

Hill, C. (2017). *The Stitch Fix algorithm: How AI helps deliver your perfect style.* TechCrunch.

Hoffman, D. L., & Novak, T. P. (1996). Marketing in hypermedia computer-mediated environments: Conceptual foundations. *Journal of Marketing, 60*(3), 50–68. DOI: 10.1177/002224299606000304

Hoffman, F. P., & Freyn, S. L. (2019). The future of competitive intelligence in an AI-enabled world. *International Journal of Value Chain Management, 10*(4), 275. DOI: 10.1504/IJVCM.2019.103268

Hofmann, P., Samp, C., & Woods, J. (2020). Responsible AI: *A global policy framework.* Stanford Digital Economy Lab Report. https://digitaleconomy.stanford.edu/responsible-ai-global-policy-framework/

Hofmann, E., & Rutschmann, E. (2018). Big data analytics and demand forecasting in supply chains: A conceptual analysis. *International Journal of Logistics Management, 29*(2), 739–766. DOI: 10.1108/IJLM-04-2017-0088

Holloway, S. (2024). The Role of Supply Chain Flexibility in Adapting Marketing Strategies to Changing Consumer Preferences.

Holloway, S. (2024). *The Role of Natural Language Processing in Streamlining Supply Chain Communication.* Business, Economics and Management. DOI: 10.20944/preprints202411.2303.v1

Homans, G. C. (1961). *Social Behaviour: Its Elementary Forms.* Harcourt Brace Jovanovich.

Hooli, M. (2025). Optimizing Retail with AI: How Intelligent Systems Are Redefining Shopping Experiences. *Journal of Computer Science and Technology Studies, 7*(6), 465–471.

Hoque, M. J., Islam, M. S., & Mohtasim, S. A. (2024). Optimizing decision-making through customer-centric market basket analysis. *Journal of Operational and Strategic Analytics, 2*(2), 72–83. DOI: 10.56578/josa020201

Horani, O. M., Al-Adwan, A. S., Yaseen, H., Hmoud, H., Al-Rahmi, W. M., & Alkhalifah, A. (2025). The critical determinants impacting artificial intelligence adoption at the organizational level. *Information Development, 41*(3), 1055–1079. DOI: 10.1177/02666669231166889

Hossain, S., Fernando, M., & Akter, S. (2025). The Influence of AI-Powered Capabilities on Responsible Leadership: A Future Research Agenda. *Journal of Management & Organization, 31*(5), 2360–2384. DOI: 10.1017/jmo.2025.10010

Hrr, H. (2025). The Future of Digital Transformation: Leveraging Artificial Intelligence for competitive advantage. SSRN *Electronic Journal.* DOI: 10.2139/ssrn.5123723

Hruschka, H. (2024). Analyzing market basket data through sparse multivariate logit models. *Journal of Marketing Analytics*, 1–16. DOI: 10.1057/s41270-024-00331-0

Huang, J., Chai, J., & Cho, S. (2020). Deep learning in finance and banking: A literature review and classification. *Frontiers of Business Research in China, 14*(1), 13. DOI: 10.1186/s11782-020-00082-6

Huang, M. H., & Rust, R. T. (2021). A strategic framework for artificial intelligence in marketing. *Journal of the Academy of Marketing Science, 49*(2), 30–50. DOI: 10.1007/s11747-020-00749-9

Husna, A., Amin, S. H., & Shah, B. (2021). Demand Forecasting in Supply Chain Management Using Different Deep Learning Methods. In *Demand Forecasting and Order Planning in Supply Chains and Humanitarian Logistics* (pp. 140–170). IGI Global Scientific Publishing., DOI: 10.4018/978-1-7998-3805-0.ch005

Hu, Y., Liu, M., Le, Y., & Skitmore, M. (2022). External consultant involvement for organizational capability building in complex construction projects: A perspective from interorganizational learning process. *Journal of Construction Engineering and Management, 148*(1), 04021181. DOI: 10.1061/(ASCE)CO.1943-7862.0002216

Iansiti, M., & Lakhani, K. R. (2020). *Competing in the age of AI: Strategy and leadership when algorithms and networks run the world*. Harvard Business Press.

IBM. (2023). *Using AI-driven attrition forecasting to enhance enterprise planning and reduce labor shortages*. IBM.

Iden, J., & Bygstad, B. (2024). Sociotechnical micro foundations for digital transformation. *European Journal of Information Systems*, *34*(2), 367–382. DOI: 10.1080/0960085X.2024.2347950

Ijomah, T. I. (2025). A conceptual framework for multi-channel marketing optimization, consumer behavior and conversion analytics. *International Journal of Advanced MultidisciplinaryResearch*, *5*(2), 1498–1508. DOI: 10.62225/2583049X.2025.5.2.4011

Inmon, W. H. (2005). *Building the data warehouse* (4th ed.). Wiley.

International Organization for Standardization. (2013). *ISO/IEC 27001:2013 — Information technology — Security techniques — Information security management systems — Requirements*. ISO.

Irfan, M., Kadry, S., Sharif, M., & Khan, H. U. (Eds.). (2023). *Fintech applications in Islamic finance: AI, machine learning, and blockchain techniques: AI, machine learning, and blockchain techniques*. IGI Global. DOI: 10.4018/979-8-3693-1038-0

Islam, M. M., Desai, K., Rabbani, M. M., Ahmad, S., & Snigdha, E. Z. (2025). AI-Powered Business Intelligence in IT: Transforming Data into Strategic Solutions for Enhanced Decision-Making. *The American Journal of Engineering and Technology*, *7*(02), 59–73. DOI: 10.37547/tajet/Volume07Issue02-09

Ivchyk, V. (2024). Overcoming barriers to artificial intelligence adoption. *Three Seas Economic Journal*, *5*(4), 14–20. DOI: 10.30525/2661-5150/2024-4-3

Iyelolu, T. V., Agu, E. E., Idemudia, C., & Ijomah, T. I. (2024). Driving SME innovation with AI solutions: overcoming adoption barriers and future growth opportunities. International Journal of Science and Technology Research Archive, 7(1), 036-054.

Jackson, I., Ivanov, D., Dolgui, A., & Namdar, J. (2024). Generative artificial intelligence in supply chain and operations management: A capability-based framework for analysis and implementation. *International Journal of Production Research*, *62*(17), 6120–6145. DOI: 10.1080/00207543.2024.2309309

Jafar, S. H., Alam, P., & El-Chaarani, H. (2023). AI in Finance. In Artificial Intelligence for Business (pp. 174-196). Productivity Press.

Jain, A., Kakade, K. S., & Vispute, S. A. (2025). The Role of Artificial Intelligence (AI) in the Transformation of Small-and Medium-Sized Businesses: Challenges and Opportunities. Artificial Intelligence-Enabled Businesses: How to Develop Strategies for Innovation, 209-226.

James, A., Hynes, D., Whelan, A., Dreher, T., & Humphry, J. (2023). From access and transparency to refusal: Three responses to algorithmic governance. *Internet Policy Review*, *12*(2). Advance online publication. DOI: 10.14763/2023.2.1691

Jedlickova, A. (2024). Ensuring ethical standards in the development of autonomous and intelligent systems. *IEEE Transactions on Artificial Intelligence*, *5*(12), 5863–5872. DOI: 10.1109/TAI.2024.3387403

Jiang, W., Nazarudin, M. N. B., & Mazalan, N. S. (2024). Enhancing safety and quality in college sports management through big data and artificial intelligence (AI). *Journal of Information Systems Engineering & Management*, *9*(3), 24782. DOI: 10.55267/iadt.07.14849

Jin, C., Li, F., Ma, S., & Wang, Y. (2022). Sampling scheme-based classification rule mining method using decision tree in big data environment. *Knowledge-Based Systems*, *244*, 108522. DOI: 10.1016/j.knosys.2022.108522

Jobin, A., Ienca, M., & Vayena, E. (2019). The global landscape of AI ethics guidelines. *Nature Machine Intelligence*, *1*(9), 389–399. DOI: 10.1038/s42256-019-0088-2

Johora, F. T., Hasan, R., Farabi, S. F., Alam, M. Z., Sarkar, M. I., & Al Mahmud, M. A. (2024, June). AI Advances: Enhancing Banking Security with Fraud Detection. In *2024 First International Conference on Technological Innovations and Advance Computing (TIACOMP)* (pp. 289-294). IEEE. DOI: 10.1109/TIACOMP64125.2024.00055

Julian, A., & Haripriya, K. (2024). NLP based Resume Analysis and Adaptive Skill Assessment System. *3rd International Conference for Innovation in Technology*. https://doi.org/DOI: 10.1109/INOCON60754.2024.10511967

Jung, N. Y. (2025). AI-Powered Personalization Drives Loyalty in Retail. In *Leveraging AI-Powered Marketing in the Experience-Driven Economy* (pp. 105–146). IGI Global Scientific Publishing. DOI: 10.4018/979-8-3693-9561-5.ch004

Jurafsky, D., & Martin, J. H. (2009). *Speech and Language Processing: An Introduction to Natural Language Processing, Computational Linguistics, and Speech Recognition*. Prentice Hall.

Juyal, P., & Sharma, S. (2021). Crop growth monitoring using unmanned aerial vehicle for farm field management. 2022 7th International Conference on Communication and Electronics Systems (ICCES), 880–884. DOI: 10.1109/ICCES51350.2021.9489182

Jyothi, V. E., Rajashree, R., Phani, S., Hugar, L., Shaik, R., & Poddar, S. (2025). Artificial intelligence-powered protocols for enhancing security in next-generation communication networks. In *Proceedings of the 3rd International Conference on Intelligent Cyber Physical Systems and Internet of Things (ICoICI)* (pp. 1107–1112). IEEE. DOI: 10.1109/ICoICI65217.2025.11252990

Kabat, D. (2025). Federated learning for privacy-preserving AI: A comparative analysis of Decentralized Data training. *International Journal of Machine Learning, AI &amp. Data Science Evolution, 1*(01), 9–21. DOI: 10.63665/ijmlaidse.v1i1.02

Kagalwala, H., Radhakrishnan, G. V., Mohammed, I. A., Kothinti, R. R., & Kulkarni, N. (2025). Predictive Analytics in Supply Chain Management: The Role of AI and Machine Learning in Demand Forecasting. *Advances in Consumer Research. Association for Consumer Research (U. S.), 2*, 142–149.

Kaggwa, S., Eleogu, T. F., Okonkwo, F., Farayola, O. A., Uwaoma, P. U., & Akinoso, A. (2024). AI in decision making: Transforming business strategies. *International Journal of Innovation and Scientific Research, 10*(12), 423–440. DOI: 10.51244/IJRSI.2023.1012032

Kalisetty, S., & Ganti, V. K. A. T. (2019). Transforming the Retail Landscape: Srinivas's Vision for Integrating Advanced Technologies in Supply Chain Efficiency and Customer Experience. *Online Journal of Materials Science, 1*(1), 1254. DOI: 10.31586/materials.2019.1254

Kalusivalingam, A. K., Sharma, A., Patel, N., & Singh, V. (2020). Enhancing Supply Chain Visibility through AI: Implementing Neural Networks and Reinforcement Learning Algorithms. *International Journal of Artificial Intelligence and Machine Learning, 1*(2), 2. https://www.cognitivecomputingjournal.com/index.php/IJAIML-V1/article/view/57

Kannan, P. K., & Li, H. A. (2017). Digital marketing: A framework, review and research agenda. *International Journal of Research in Marketing, 34*(1), 22–45. DOI: 10.1016/j.ijresmar.2016.11.006

Kapoor, R., & Ghosal, I. (2022). Will artificial intelligence compliment or supplement human workforce in organizations? A shift to a collaborative human–Machine environment. [IJRTBT]. *International Journal on Recent Trends in Business and Tourism, 6*(4), 19–28. DOI: 10.31674/ijrtbt.2022.v06i04.002

Kar, A. K., & Kushwaha, A. K. (2023). Facilitators and barriers of artificial intelligence adoption in business–insights from opinions using big data analytics. *Information Systems Frontiers, 25*(4), 1351–1374. DOI: 10.1007/s10796-021-10219-4

Karunanayaka, K. A. Y. R. O., Jahankhani, H., El-Deeb, S., Isuru, S. W. A., & Hussien, O. A. A. M. (2024). *"Artificial Intelligence in Digital Marketing: The Ethical Implications of Digital Influence on Markets and Consumer", Market Grooming: The Dark Side of AI Marketing*. Sumesh Singh Dadwal, Hamid Jahankhani, Kenneth Revett., DOI: 10.1108/978-1-83549-001-320241009

Ke, C., Li, A., & Wang, R. (2025). Modeling, Prediction, Assortment and Price Optimization Under Consumer Choice Behavior. *Foundations and Trends® in Technology. Information and Operations Management*, *19*(1), 1–141. DOI: 10.1561/0200000112

Kehayov, M., Holder, L., & Koch, V. (2022). Application of artificial intelligence technology in the manufacturing process and purchasing and supply management. *Procedia Computer Science*, *200*, 1209–1217. DOI: 10.1016/j.procs.2022.01.321

Keller, K. L. (1993). Conceptualizing, measuring, and managing customer-based brand equity. *Journal of Marketing*, *57*(1), 1–22. DOI: 10.1177/002224299305700101

Kerkech, M., Hafiane, A., & Canals, R. (2020). Vine disease detection in UAV multispectral images using optimized image registration and deep learning segmentation approach. *Computers and Electronics in Agriculture*, *174*, 105446. DOI: 10.1016/j.compag.2020.105446

Kethu, S. S. (2019). AI-Enabled Customer Relationship Management: Developing Intelligence Frameworks, AI-FCS Integration, and Empirical Testing for Service Quality Improvement. *International Journal of HRM and Organizational Behavior*, *7*(2), 1–16.

Khakhlari, G. (2023). Generative AI in content and personalization. *Industrial Artificial Intelligence*, 1–10. DOI: 10.1007/s44244-023-00012-4

Khakifirooz, M., Fathi, M., & Dolgui, A. (2024). Theory of AI-driven scheduling (TAIS): A service-oriented scheduling framework by integrating theory of constraints and AI. *International Journal of Production Research*, •••, 1–35.

Khan, M. A., Saleh, A. M., Waseem, M., & Sajjad, I. A. (2023). Artificial Intelligence Enabled Demand Response: Prospects and Challenges in Smart Grid Environment. *IEEE Access*, *11*, 1477–1505. IEEE Access. DOI: 10.1109/ACCESS.2022.3231444

Khan, R. S., Sirazy, R. M., Das, R., & Rahman, S. (n.d.). *An AI and ML-Enabled Framework for Proactive Risk Mitigation and Resilience Optimization in Global Supply Chains During National Emergencies*.

Khan, F., Patel, H., Shaikh, A., Sayed, F., & Soorya, A. R. (2023). Resume Parser and Summarizer. *International Journal of Advanced Research in Science. Tongxin Jishu*, •••, 442–447. DOI: 10.48175/IJARSCT-9064

Khedr, A. M., & S, S. R. (2024). Enhancing supply chain management with deep learning and machine learning techniques: A review. *Journal of Open Innovation, 10*(4), 100379. DOI: 10.1016/j.joitmc.2024.100379

Khoshgoftaar, T. M., Allen, E. B., Hudepohl, J. P., & Aud, S. J. (1996). Application of neural networks to software quality modeling of a very large telecommunications system. *IEEE Transactions on Neural Networks, 8*(4), 902–909. DOI: 10.1109/72.595888 PMID: 18255693

Klumpp, M. (2018). Automation and artificial intelligence in business logistics systems: Human reactions and collaboration requirements. *International Journal of Logistics, 21*(3), 224–242. DOI: 10.1080/13675567.2017.1384451

Kokina, J., Blanchette, S., Davenport, T. H., & Pachamanova, D. (2025). Challenges and opportunities for artificial intelligence in auditing: Evidence from the field. *International Journal of Accounting Information Systems, 56*, 100734. DOI: 10.1016/j.accinf.2025.100734

Konopik, J., Jahn, C., Schuster, T., Hoßbach, N., & Pflaum, A. (2022). Mastering the digital transformation through organizational capabilities: A conceptual framework. *Digital Business, 2*(2), 100019. DOI: 10.1016/j.digbus.2021.100019

Koswara, A., & Herlina, L. (2025). The Ethical Deviations of AI in Marketing Practices: A Critical Review from Halal Perspectives [RIE]. *Review of Islamic Economics, 2*(2), 105–116. DOI: 10.58777/rie.v2i2.393

Kotler, P., & Armstrong, G. (2014). *Principals of Marketing* (15th ed.).

Kreps, J. (2014). *I Heart Logs: Event Data, Stream Processing, and Data Integration*. O'Reilly Media.

Krishna, G., & Ravi, V. (2020). Mining top high utility association rules using Binary Differential Evolution. *Engineering Applications of Artificial Intelligence, 96*, 103935. DOI: 10.1016/j.engappai.2020.103935

Krizhevsky, A., Sutskever, I., & Hinton, G. E. (2012). ImageNet classification with deep convolutional neural networks. *Advances in Neural Information Processing Systems, 25*, 1097–1105. https://papers.nips.cc/paper_files/paper/2012/hash/c399862d3b9d6b76c8436e924a68c45b-Abstract.html

Kuguoglu, B. K., van der Voort, H., & Janssen, M. (2021). The giant leap for smart cities: Scaling up smart city artificial intelligence of things (AIoT) initiatives. *Sustainability (Basel), 13*(21), 12295. DOI: 10.3390/su132112295

Kumar, K., Sharma, S., Pandey, P., & Goyal, H. R. (2022). IoT Enabled Crop Detection System using Soil Analysis. 2022 7th International Conference on Communication and Electronics Systems (ICCES), 323–327. DOI: 10.1109/ICCES54183.2022.9835959

Kumar, D., & Ratten, V. (2025). Artificial intelligence and family businesses: A systematic literature review. *Journal of Family Business Management*, *15*(2), 373–392. DOI: 10.1108/JFBM-08-2024-0160

Kumar, D., & Suthar, N. (2024). Ethical and legal challenges of AI in marketing: An exploration of solutions. Journal of Information. *Communication and Ethics in Society*, *22*(1), 124–144. DOI: 10.1108/JICES-05-2023-0068

Kumar, V., & Reinartz, W. (2016). Creating enduring customer value. *Journal of Marketing*, *80*(6), 36–68. DOI: 10.1509/jm.15.0414

Kumar, V., & Reinartz, W. J. (2012). *Customer relationship management: Concept, strategy, and tools* (2nd ed.). Springer., DOI: 10.1007/978-3-642-20110-3

Kwak, K., Duvvuri, S., & Russell, G. (2015). An Analysis of Assortment Choice in Grocery Retailing. *Journal of Retailing*, *91*(1), 19–33. DOI: 10.1016/j.jretai.2014.10.004

Lamberton, C., & Stephen, A. T. (2016). A thematic exploration of digital, social media, and mobile marketing: Research evolution from 2000 to 2015 and an agenda for future inquiry. *Journal of Marketing*, *80*(6), 146–172. DOI: 10.1509/jm.15.0415

LaToza, T. D., & Myers, B. A. (2010). Developers ask reachability questions. *Proceedings of the 32nd ACM/IEEE International Conference on Software Engineering*, 185–194. DOI: 10.1145/1806799.1806829

LeCun, Y., Bengio, Y., & Hinton, G. (2015). Deep learning. *Nature*, *521*(7553), 436–444. DOI: 10.1038/nature14539 PMID: 26017442

Lee, D. K. C., Guan, C., Yu, Y., & Ding, Q. (2024). A comprehensive review of generative AI in finance. *FinTech*, *3*(3), 460–478. DOI: 10.3390/fintech3030025

Lee, J. (2025). *Ai-Driven Predictive Insights: A Modern Framework for Enhancing Decision-Making in Dynamic Data Environments*. DOI: 10.2139/ssrn.5140141

Lemon, K. N., & Verhoef, P. C. (2016). Understanding customer experience throughout the customer journey. *Journal of Marketing*, *80*(6), 69–96. DOI: 10.1509/jm.15.0420

Lendvai, G. F., & Gosztonyi, G. (2025). Algorithmic bias as a core legal dilemma of artificial intelligence. *Laws*, *14*(3), 41. DOI: 10.3390/laws14030041

Leonidas, T., Alexandra, T., & Constantinos, H. (2025). Cognitive Bias Mitigation in Executive Decision-Making: A Data-Driven Approach Integrating Big Data Analytics, AI, and Explainable Systems. *Electronics (Basel), 14*(19), 3930. DOI: 10.3390/electronics14193930

Lessmann, S., Baesens, B., Mues, C., & Pietsch, S. (2008). Benchmarking classification models for software defect prediction: A proposed framework and novel findings. *IEEE Transactions on Software Engineering, 34*(4), 485–496. DOI: 10.1109/TSE.2008.35

Li, L., Ali, D. A., & Yin, L. (2024). The effect of AI product image anthropomorphism on consumer purchase intention. In *Artificial Intelligence, Medical Engineering and Education* (pp. 76–85). IOS Press. DOI: 10.3233/ATDE231317

Li, S., Li, K., & Lu, H. (2023). *National Origin Discrimination in Deep-learning-powered Automated Resume Screening*. arXiv preprint arXiv:2307.08624.

Linden, G., Smith, B., & York, J. (2003). Amazon.com recommendations: Item-to-item collaborative filtering. *IEEE Internet Computing, 7*(1), 76–80. DOI: 10.1109/MIC.2003.1167344

Li, R., Liu, J., Shi, B., Zhao, H., Li, Y., Zheng, X., Peng, C., & Lv, C. (2024). High-Performance grape disease detection method using multimodal data and parallel activation functions. *Plants, 13*(19), 2720. DOI: 10.3390/plants13192720 PMID: 39409590

Liu, B. (2012). *Sentiment Analysis and Opinion Mining*. Morgan & Claypool Publishers., DOI: 10.1007/978-3-031-02145-9

Liu, Y., & Wang, L. (2020). AI-driven HR analytics for workforce optimization. *Journal of Business Analytics, 3*(1), 45–58. DOI: 10.1080/2573234X.2020.1717819

Li, Y., He, Z., & Wang, Y. (2021). Anomaly detection in code using autoencoders. *Journal of Systems and Software, 181*, 111039. DOI: 10.1016/j.jss.2021.111039

López-Solís, O., Luzuriaga-Jaramillo, A., Bedoya-Jara, M., Naranjo-Santamaría, J., Bonilla-Jurado, D., & Acosta-Vargas, P. (2025). Effect of generative artificial intelligence on strategic decision making in entrepreneurial business initiatives: A systematic literature review. *Administrative Sciences, 15*(2), 66. DOI: 10.3390/admsci15020066

Luckin, R., Holmes, W., Griffiths, M., & Forcier, L. B. (2016). *Intelligence unleashed: An argument for AI in education*. Pearson Education.

Luo, Y., Zhang, H., Wang, Y., We, Y., & Zhang, X. (2018a). ResumeNet: A Learning-based Framework for Automatic Resume Quality Assessment. arXiv preprint arXiv:1810.02832. DOI: 10.1109/ICDM.2018.00046

Luo, D., Thevenin, S., & Dolgui, A. (2023). A state-of-the-art on production planning in Industry 4.0. *International Journal of Production Research*, *61*(19), 6602–6632. DOI: 10.1080/00207543.2022.2122622

Luo, X., Zhang, J., & Kana, N. (2013). Personalized services in a smart retail environment. *Journal of Retailing and Consumer Services*, *20*(3), 299–307.

Luu, T. M., Mittal, S., & Gupta, S. (2025). Leveraging AI to Tailor Customer Engagement With Personalized Marketing Strategies. In Tunio, M. (Ed.), *AI, Corporate Social Responsibility, and Marketing in Modern Organizations* (pp. 195–220). IGI Global Scientific Publishing., DOI: 10.4018/979-8-3373-0219-5.ch010

Lyulyov, O., Pimonenko, T., & Kwilinski, A. (2025). Artificial Intelligence in Social Media Marketing. In Saura, J. R. (Ed.), *Global Perspectives on AI, Ethics, and Business Economics. Contributions to Management Science*. Springer., DOI: 10.1007/978-3-031-88781-9_9

Mabrouk, A. (2025). Human Resouce Management in the Age of Artificial Intelligence: Concepts Tools and Steps. *Solo International Collaboration and Publication of Social Sciences and Humanities*, *3*(01), 1–12. DOI: 10.61455/sicopus.v3i01.216

Machireddy, J. R., Rachakatla, S. K., & Ravichandran, P. (2021). Leveraging AI and machine learning for data-driven business strategy: A comprehensive framework for analytics integration. *African Journal of Artificial Intelligence and Sustainable Development*, *1*(2), 12–150.

Madanaguli, A., Sjödin, D., Parida, V., & Mikalef, P. (2024). Artificial intelligence capabilities for circular business models: Research synthesis and future agenda. *Technological Forecasting and Social Change*, *200*, 123189. DOI: 10.1016/j.techfore.2023.123189

Mahabub, S., Hossain, M. R., & Snigdha, E. Z. (2025). Data-driven decision-making and strategic leadership: AI-powered business operations for competitive advantage and sustainable growth. *Journal of Computer Science and Technology Studies*, *7*(1), 326–336. DOI: 10.32996/jcsts.2025.7.1.24

Maharjan, P. (2023). The role of artificial intelligence-driven big data analytics in strengthening cybersecurity frameworks for critical infrastructure. *Global Research Perspectives on Cybersecurity Governance, Policy, and Management*, *7*(11), 12–25.

Mahdizadeh, B. M., Khodadad Hosseini, S. H., & Nazarpour Kashani, H. (2025). *Bibliometric analysis of customer experience and artificial intelligence*. Scientometrics Research Journal., DOI: 10.22070/rsci.2025.19066.1729

Mahmood, H. S., Abdulqader, D. M., Abdullah, R. M., Rasheed, H., Ismael, Z. N. R., & Sami, T. M. G. (2024). Conducting in-depth analysis of AI, IoT, web technology, cloud computing, and enterprise systems integration for enhancing data security and governance to promote sustainable business practices. *Journal of Information Technology and Informatics*, *3*(2), 297–332.

Maiti, M., Kayal, P., & Vujko, A. (2025). A study on ethical implications of artificial intelligence adoption in business: Challenges and best practices. *Future Business Journal*, *11*(1), 34. DOI: 10.1186/s43093-025-00462-5

Mallio, C. A., Buoso, A., Stiffi, M., Cea, L., Vertulli, D., Bernetti, C., Di Gennaro, G., van den Heuvel, M. P., & Beomonte Zobel, B. (2024). Mapping the neural basis of neuroeconomics with functional magnetic resonance imaging: A narrative literature review. *Brain Sciences*, *14*(5), 511. DOI: 10.3390/brainsci14050511 PMID: 38790489

Manning, L. (2024). Innovating in an uncertain world: Understanding the social, technical and systemic barriers to farmers adopting new technologies. *Challenges*, *15*(2), 32. DOI: 10.3390/challe15020032

Manyika, J., Chui, M., Miremadi, M., Bughin, J., George, K., Willmott, P., & Dewhurst, G. (2017). *Artificial Intelligence: The Next Digital Frontier?* McKinsey Global Institute.

Maraveas, C. (2022). Incorporating artificial intelligence technology in smart greenhouses: Current state of the art. *Applied Sciences (Basel, Switzerland)*, *13*(1), 14. DOI: 10.3390/app13010014

Marimira, N., & Gumel, B. I. (2025). The role of artificial intelligence in strategic decision making. *Asian Journal of Economics. Business and Accounting*, *25*(3), 316–327. DOI: 10.9734/ajeba/2025/v25i31712

Marr, B. (2016). *Big Data in Practice: How 45 Successful Companies Used Big Data Analytics to Deliver Extraordinary Results*. John Wiley & Sons. DOI: 10.1002/9781119278825

Marr, B. (2018). *Data strategy: How to profit from a world of big data, analytics and the Internet of Things*. Kogan Page.

Martínez-Garmendia, J. (2023). Machine learning for product choice prediction. *Journal of Marketing Analytics*, 1-12. DOI: 10.1057/s41270-023-00217-7

Martinez, M., Escobar, B., García Diaz, M., & Pinto-Roa, D. (2021). Market basket analysis with association rules in the retail sector using Orange. Case Study: Appliances Sales Company. *CLEI Electronic Journal*, *24*(2), 1–17. DOI: 10.19153/cleiej.24.2.12

Matta, S. S., & Bolli, M. (2023). Trustworthy AI: Explainability & Fairness In Large-Scale Decision Systems. *Review of Applied Science and Technology*, *2*(04), 54–93. DOI: 10.63125/3w9v5e52

Mazurek, G., Kotula, N., Kaczorowska-Spychalska, D., & Sułkowski, Ł. (2024). Generative AI as a source of change of knowledge management paradigm. *Human Technology*, *20*(1), 131–154. DOI: 10.14254/1795-6889.2024.20-1.7

McCabe, T. J. (1976). A complexity measure. *IEEE Transactions on Software Engineering*, *SE-2*(4), 308–320. DOI: 10.1109/TSE.1976.233837

McConnell, S. (2004). *Code Complete: A Practical Handbook of Software Construction* (2nd ed.). Microsoft Press.

McElheran, K., Li, J. F., Brynjolfsson, E., Kroff, Z., Dinlersoz, E., Foster, L., & Zolas, N. (2024). AI adoption in America: Who, what, and where. *Journal of Economics & Management Strategy*, *33*(2), 375–415. DOI: 10.1111/jems.12576

McKinsey & Company. (2017). *Artificial intelligence: The next digital frontier?* McKinsey Global Institute.

McKinsey & Company. (2020). *How retailers are using AI to enhance the customer journey*. https://www.mckinsey.com/capabilities/growth-marketing-and-sales/our-insights/next-best-experience-how-ai-can-power-every-customer-interaction

McKinsey & Company. (2022). *The value of getting personalization right—or wrong—is multiplying*. McKinsey & Company. https://www.mckinsey.com/business-functions/growth-marketing-and-sales/our-insights/the-value-of-getting-personalization-right-or-wrong-is-multiplying

Mehrabi, N., Morstatter, F., Saxena, N., Lerman, K., & Galstyan, A. (2019). A survey on bias and fairness in machine learning. *ACM Computing Surveys*, *54*(6), 1–35. DOI: 10.1145/3457607

Merkel, D. (2014). Docker: Lightweight Linux containers for consistent development and deployment. *Linux Journal*, *2014*(239), 2.

Miao, S., & Chao, X. (2022). Online personalized assortment optimization with high-dimensional customer contextual data. *Manufacturing & Service Operations Management*, *24*(5), 2741–2760. DOI: 10.1287/msom.2022.1128

Miller, C., Smith, S., McIntyre, S., & Achabal, D. (2010). Optimizing and Evaluating Retail Assortments for Infrequently Purchased Products. *Journal of Retailing*, *86*(2), 159–171. DOI: 10.1016/j.jretai.2010.02.004

Miller, G. A. (1956). The magical number seven, plus or minus two: Some limits on our capacity for processing information. *Psychological Review*, *63*(2), 81–97. DOI: 10.1037/h0043158 PMID: 13310704

Miller, T., Durlik, I., Kostecka, E., Borkowski, P., & Łobodzińska, A. (2024). A critical AI view on autonomous vehicle navigation: The growing danger. *Electronics (Basel)*, *13*(18), 3660. DOI: 10.3390/electronics13183660

Mishra, A., & Vishwakarma, S. (2016). Analysis of TF-IDF Model and its Variant for Document Retrieval. *Proceedings - 2015 International Conference on Computational Intelligence and Communication Networks*, 772–776. https://doi.org/DOI: 10.1109/CICN.2015.157

Mishra, M. (2024). A holistic review of customer experience research: Topic modelling using BERTopic. *Marketing Intelligence & Planning*. Advance online publication. DOI: 10.1108/MIP-09-2023-0457

Mitchell, T. M. (1997). *Machine Learning*. McGraw-Hill.

Mittal, V., Mehta, P., Relan, D., & Gabrani, G. (2020). Methodology for resume parsing and job domain prediction. *Journal of Statistics and Management Systems*, *23*(7), 1265–1274. DOI: 10.1080/09720510.2020.1799583

Mohamed, O., Sameh, D., Mohamed, H., Ashraf, M., Kamal, R., & Kandil, Y. (2024). ResuFit: Precision CV Matching System. *4th International Mobile, Intelligent, and Ubiquitous Computing Conference, MIUCC 2024*, 363–367. https://doi.org/DOI: 10.1109/MIUCC62295.2024.10783505

Mohanty, A., Mohapatra, A. G., & Mohanty, S. K. (2025). Real-time traffic monitoring with AI in smart cities. In *Internet of Vehicles and Computer Vision Solutions for Smart City Transformations* (pp. 135–165). Springer Nature Switzerland. DOI: 10.1007/978-3-031-72959-1_7

Mohsen, B. M. (2023). Impact of Artificial Intelligence on Supply Chain Management Performance. *Journal of Service Science and Management*, *16*(1), 1. Advance online publication. DOI: 10.4236/jssm.2023.161004

Moodley, R., Chiclana, F., Caraffini, F., & Carterb, J. (2020). A product-centric data mining algorithm for targeted promotions'. *Journal of Retailing and Consumer Services*, *54*, 101940. DOI: 10.1016/j.jretconser.2019.101940

Mosier, K. L., & Skitka, L. J. (2018). Human decision makers and automated decision aids: Made for each other? In *Automation and human performance* (pp. 201–220). CRC Press.

Mrutzek-Hartmann, B., Kotzab, H., Yumurtacı Hüseyinoğlu, I. Ö., & Kühling, S. (2022). Omni-channel retailing resources and capabilities of SME specialty retailers–insights from Germany and Turkey. *International Journal of Retail & Distribution Management*, *50*(8/9), 1129–1155. DOI: 10.1108/IJRDM-10-2021-0503

Muharam, H., Wandrial, S., Rumondang, P. R., Handayani, M. A., & Masruchan, M. (2024). *Innovative Strategies in Digital Marketing: Enhancing Consumer Engagement and Brand Loyalty*. Global International Journal of Innovative Research., DOI: 10.59613/global.v2i7.236

Muthukalyani, A. R. (2023). Unlocking accurate demand forecasting in retail supply chains with AI-driven predictive analytics. *Information Technology Management*, *14*(2), 48–57.

Mweshi, G. K. (2022). *Effects of Overstocking and Stockouts on the Manufacturing Sector. 4*(9).

Nagappan, N., & Ball, T. (2005). Use of relative code churn measures to predict system defect density. *Proceedings of the 27th International Conference on Software Engineering*, 284–292. DOI: 10.1145/1062455.1062514

Narla, S. (2020). TRANSFORMING SMART ENVIRONMENTS WITH MULTI-TIER CLOUD SENSING, BIG DATA, AND 5G TECHNOLOGY. *International Journal on Computer Science and Engineering*, *5*(1), 1–7.

Narne, S., Adedoja, T., Mohan, M., & Ayyalasomayajula, T. (2024). AI-Driven Decision Support Systems in Management: Enhancing Strategic Planning and Execution. *International Journal on Recent and Innovation Trends in Computing and Communication*, *12*(1), 268–276.

Nasr, S., & German, O. V. (2019). Assessment of graduate students' resumes using short text searching method. *Proceedings - IEEE 2nd International Conference on Artificial Intelligence and Knowledge Engineering*, 306–308. https://doi.org/DOI: 10.1109/AIKE.2019.00061

Ndiaye, M., Oyewobi, S. S., Abu-Mahfouz, A. M., Hancke, G. P., Kurien, A. M., & Djouani, K. (2020). IoT in the wake of COVID-19: A survey on contributions, challenges and evolution. *IEEE Access : Practical Innovations, Open Solutions*, *8*, 186821–186839. DOI: 10.1109/ACCESS.2020.3030090 PMID: 34786294

Neogrid (2018). Análise de sortimento: o que é e qual sua importância? Available at: https://blog.neogrid.com/analise-de-sortimento-o-que-e-e-qual-sua-importancia/ (accessed July 10, 2022).

Nesterov, V. (2024). Optimization of big data processing and analysis processes in the field of data analytics through the integration of data engineering and artificial intelligence. Computer-integrated technologies: education, science, production, (54), 160-164.

Neupane, B. (2024). Artificial Intelligence and Big Data Technologies to Optimize Government Decision-Making Processes in Cloud-Based Environments. *Journal of Artificial Intelligence and Machine Learning in Cloud Computing Systems*, *8*(11), 1–12.

Newman, S. (2015). *Building microservices: Designing fine-grained systems.* O'Reilly Media.

Nezianya, M. C., Adebayo, A. O., & Ezeliora, P. (2024). A critical review of machine learning applications in supply chain risk management. *World Journal of Advanced Research & Reviews*, *23*(3), 1554–1567. DOI: 10.30574/wjarr.2024.23.3.2760

Ngai, E. W. T. (2005). Customer relationship management (CRM) research (1992–2002): An academic literature review and classification. *Marketing Intelligence & Planning*, *23*(6), 582–602. DOI: 10.1108/02634500510624147

Ngai, E. W. T., Chau, D. C. K., & Chan, T. L. A. (2011). Information technology, operational, and management competencies for supply chain agility: Findings from case studies. *The Journal of Strategic Information Systems*, *20*(3), 232–249. DOI: 10.1016/j.jsis.2010.11.002

Nippatla, R. P. (2019). AI and ML-Driven Blockchain-Based Secure Employee Data Management: Applications of Distributed Control and Tensor Decomposition in HRM. *International Journal of Engineering Research and Science & Technology*, *15*(2), 1–16.

Nirali, B., Gandhi, J., & Singh, D. K. (2020). NLP based Extraction of Relevant Resume using Machine Learning. *International Journal of Innovative Technology and Exploring Engineering*, *9*(7), 13–17. DOI: 10.35940/ijitee.F4078.059720

Nkomo, N. I. G. E. L., & Mupa, M. N. (2024). The Impact of Artificial Intelligence on Predictive Customer Behaviour Analytics in E-commerce: A Comparative Study of Traditional and AI-driven Models. *Iconic Research and Engineering Journals*, *8*(5), 432–451.

Nomikou, K. M., & Νομικού, K. M. (2024). *Measuring and managing geopolitical risk* [Master Thesis, Πανεπιστήμιο Πειραιώς]. DOI: 10.26267/unipi_dione/4319

Novikova, K. (2021, October). Unique assortment as a key factor of local food Retail's competitiveness increase. In *International Perm Forum Science and Global Challenges of the 21st Century* (pp. 1086-1103). Cham: Springer International Publishing.

Nozari, H., Ghahremani-Nahr, J., & Szmelter-Jarosz, A. (2024). AI and machine learning for real-world problems. In Kim, S., & Deka, G. C. (Eds.), *Advances in Computers* (Vol. 134, pp. 1–12). Elsevier., DOI: 10.1016/bs.adcom.2023.02.001

Nyoni, R. (2025). Harnessing Data Analytics for Predictive Insights: Advancing Decision-Making with Big Data Innovations. *Int. J. Res. Publ. Rev*, *6*(1), 2915–2936. DOI: 10.55248/gengpi.6.0125.0502

O'Neil, C. (2016). *Weapons of Math Destruction: How Big Data Increases Inequality and Threatens Democracy*. Crown.

Obermeyer, Z., Powers, B., Vogeli, C., & Mullainathan, S. (2019). Dissecting racial bias in an algorithm used to manage the health of populations. *Science*, *366*(6464), 447–453. DOI: 10.1126/science.aax2342 PMID: 31649194

Ochuba, N. A., Olutimehin, D. O., Odunaiya, O. G., & Soyomb, O. T. (2024). A comprehensive review of strategic management practices in satellite telecommunications, highlighting the role of data analytics in driving operational efficiency and competitive advantage. *World Journal of Advanced Engineering Technology and Sciences*, *11*(2), 201–211. DOI: 10.30574/wjaets.2024.11.2.0099

Odumbo, O. R., & Nimma, S. Z. (2025). Leveraging artificial intelligence to maximize efficiency in supply chain process optimization. *Int J Res Publ Rev*, *6*(1), 3035–3050. DOI: 10.55248/gengpi.6.0125.0508

OECD. (2019). *Recommendation of the Council on Artificial Intelligence*. OECD Publishing. https://legalinstruments.oecd.org/en/instruments/OECD-LEGAL-0449

Ojeda, A. M., Valera, J. B., & Diaz, O. (2025). Artificial intelligence of big data for analysis in organizational decision-making. *Global Journal of Flexible Systems Managment*, *26*(3), 515–527. DOI: 10.1007/s40171-025-00450-2

Ojika, F. U., Owobu, W. O., Abieba, O. A., Esan, O. J., Ubamadu, B. C., & Daraojimba, A. I. (2022). The Role of Artificial Intelligence in Business Process Automation: A Model for Reducing Operational Costs and Enhancing Efficiency.

Okeke, N. I., Alabi, O. A., Igwe, A. N., Ofodile, O. C., & Ewim, C. P. M. (2024). AI in customer feedback integration: A data-driven framework for enhancing business strategy. *World J. Advanced Res. Reviews*, *24*(1), 3207–3220.

Oladele, O. K. (2024). *Internet of Things (IoT) in Logistics: Transforming Supply Chains with Connected Devices and Data Analytics.*

Olan, F., Arakpogun, E. O., Suklan, J., Nakpodia, F., Damij, N., & Jayawickrama, U. (2022). Artificial intelligence and knowledge sharing: Contributing factors to organizational performance. *Journal of Business Research*, *145*, 605–615. DOI: 10.1016/j.jbusres.2022.03.008

Olson, B. K., Brooke, M., Wang, Z., Svyantek, A., Stenger, J., & Hatterman-Valenti, H. (2021). 'Frontenac' grape response to canopy management in North Dakota. *Horticulturae*, *7*(9), 288. DOI: 10.3390/horticulturae7090288

Olszak, C. M. (2016). Toward better understanding and use of business intelligence in organizations. *Information Systems Management*, *33*(2), 105–123. DOI: 10.1080/10580530.2016.1155946

Oluoha, O., Odeshina, A., Reis, O., Okpeke, F., Attipoe, V., & Orieno, O. (2022). Optimizing business decision-making with advanced data analytics techniques. *Iconic Research and Engineering Journals*, *6*(5), 184–203.

Oluwaseun, B., Shahab, A. R., Arogundade, J. B., & Mosope, W. (2024). AI-driven business analytics and decision making. *World Journal of Advanced Research and Reviews*, *24*(01), 616–633. DOI: 10.30574/wjarr.2024.24.1.3093

Orange (2022). Educação em Ciência de Dados. Available at: https://orangedatamining.com/home/teachers_and_students_love_it/ (accessed August 28, 2022).

Orji, U., Orji, C. A., & Olagunju, O. D. (2024). Leveraging AI for transformative business development: Strategies for market analysis, customer insights, and competitive intelligence.

Osorio-Barreto, D., Landínez-Martínez, D. A., & Chica-Mesa, J. C. (2022). Neuroeconomics and Financial Decision Making: An Approach from a Systematic Literature Review. *CEA Magazine*, *8*(16), 1911. DOI: 10.22430/24223182.1911

Ouhami, M., Es-Saady, Y., Hajj, M. E., Canals, R., & Hafiane, A. (2022). Meteorological data and UAV images for the detection and identification of grapevine disease using deep learning. *2022 E-Health and Bioengineering Conference (EHB)*, 1–4. DOI: 10.1109/EHB55594.2022.9991443

Ouyang, J., De Bei, R., Fuentes, S., & Collins, C. (2020). UAV and ground-based imagery analysis detects canopy structure changes after canopy management applications. *OENO One*, *54*(4), 1093–1103. DOI: 10.20870/oeno-one.2020.54.4.3647

Owusu-Berko, L. (2025). The Intersection Of Behavioral Economics And Data Science In Personalizing Consumer Experiences And Maximizing Revenue Optimization. [ijetrm]. *International Journal of Engineering Technology Research & Management*, *09*(02). Advance online publication. DOI: 10.5281/zenodo.14897990

Padmavathi, V., Suresh, C., Kumar, R. L., & Punitha, P. (2025). Adaptive AI-enhanced signal processing framework for optimized communication in the Internet of Underwater Things (IOUT). *International Journal of Pattern Recognition and Artificial Intelligence*, *39*(7), 2558002. DOI: 10.1142/S0218001425580029

Palmatier, R. W., Dant, R. P., Grewal, D., & Evans, K. R. (2006). Factors influencing the effectiveness of relationship marketing: A meta-analysis. *Journal of Marketing*, *70*(4), 136–153. DOI: 10.1509/jmkg.70.4.136

Palmatier, R. W., Houston, M. B., & Dant, R. P. (2016). Relationship marketing: From rhetoric to reality. *Journal of Marketing Management*, *32*(1-2), 1–7.

Papernot, N., McDaniel, P., Goodfellow, I., Jha, S., Celik, Z. B., & Swami, A. (2016). Practical black-box attacks against machine learning. *In Proceedings of the 2017 ACM on Asia Conference on Computer and Communications Security* (pp. 506–519). ACM. https://doi.org/DOI: 10.1145/3052973.3053009

Paramesha, M., Rane, N., & Rane, J. (2024). Artificial intelligence, machine learning, deep learning, and blockchain in financial and banking services: A comprehensive review. *Machine Learning, Deep Learning, and Blockchain in Financial and Banking Services: A Comprehensive Review (June 6, 2024).*

Parasuraman, A., Zeithaml, V. A., & Berry, L. L. (1988). SERVQUAL: A multiple-item scale for measuring consumer perceptions of service quality. *Journal of Retailing*, *64*(1), 12–40.

Pariser, E. (2011). *The Filter Bubble: What the Internet Is Hiding from You.* Penguin Press.

Parker, G., Van Alstyne, M., & Choudary, S. P. (2016). *Platform revolution: How networked markets are transforming the economy—and how to make them work for you.* W. W. Norton & Company.

Parvatiyar, A., & Sheth, J. N. (2001). Customer relationship management: Emerging practice, process, and discipline. *Journal of Economic & Social Research*, *3*(2), 1–34.

Pasupuleti, V., Thuraka, B., Kodete, C. S., & Malisetty, S. (2024). Enhancing supply chain agility and sustainability through machine learning: Optimization techniques for logistics and inventory management. *Logistics (Basel)*, *8*(3), 73. DOI: 10.3390/logistics8030073

Patidar, N., Mishra, S., Jain, R., Prajapati, D., Solanki, A., Suthar, R., ... & Patel, H. (2024). Transparency in AI decision making: A survey of explainable AI methods and applications. Advances of Robotic Technology, 2(1).

Patil, D. (2024). *Artificial Intelligence-Driven Supply Chain Optimization: Enhancing Demand Forecasting And Cost Reduction* (SSRN Scholarly Paper No. 5057408). Social Science Research Network. DOI: 10.2139/ssrn.5057408

Patil, D. (2025). Artificial Intelligence For Personalized Marketing And Consumer Behaviour Analysis: Enhancing Engagement And Conversion Rates. https://papers.ssrn.com/sol3/papers.cfm?abstract_id=5057436DOI: 10.2139/ssrn.5057436

Patil, S., & Shankar, H. (2023). Transforming healthcare: Harnessing the power of AI in the modern era. *International Journal of Multidisciplinary Sciences and Arts*, *2*(2), 60–70. DOI: 10.47709/ijmdsa.v2i1.2513

Payne, A., & Frow, P. (2005). A strategic framework for customer relationship management. *Journal of Marketing*, *69*(4), 167–176. DOI: 10.1509/jmkg.2005.69.4.167

Peicheva, M. (2022). *Data Analysis from the Applicant Tracking System*. 6-15. https://www.researchgate.net/publication/375517346

Pentyala, D. K. (2018). AI-Driven Decision-Making for Ensuring Data Reliability in Distributed Cloud Systems. *International Journal of Modern Computing*, *1*(1), 1–22.

Peppers, D., & Rogers, M. (1993). *The One to One Future: Building Relationships One Customer at a Time*. Currency/Doubleday.

Pereira, A. M., Moura, J. A. B., Costa, E. D. B., Vieira, T., Landim, A. R. D. B., Bazaki, E., & Wanick, V. (2022). Customer models for artificial intelligence-based decision support in fashion online retail supply chains. *Decision Support Systems*, *158*, 113795. DOI: 10.1016/j.dss.2022.113795

Pérez-Campuzano, D., Morcillo Ortega, P., Rubio Andrada, L., & López-Lázaro, A. (2021). Artificial intelligence potential within airlines: A review on how AI can enhance strategic decision making in times of COVID 19. *Journal of Airline and Airport Management*, *11*(2), 53–72. DOI: 10.3926/jairm.189

Peterson, L. (2000). The world's first computer bug. *IEEE Annals of the History of Computing*, *22*(4), 73–75. DOI: 10.1109/85.888103

Pham, M. T., & Avnet, T. (2009). Rethinking the value of emotion in advertising: The effects of specific emotions on product attitudes. *The Journal of Consumer Research*, *36*(3), 447–460.

Picraux, S., & Bunt, H. (2018). Conversational AI. *Artificial Intelligence*, *252*, 1–2.

Platt, M. L., & Huettel, S. A. (2008). Risky business: The neuroeconomics of decision making under uncertainty. *Nature Neuroscience*, *11*(4), 398–403. DOI: 10.1038/nn2062 PMID: 18368046

Porter, M. E., & Heppelmann, J. E. (2017). Why every organization needs an augmented reality strategy. *Harvard Business Review*, *95*(6), 46–57.

Pradel, M., & Sen, K. (2018). DeepBugs: A learning approach to name-based bug detection. *Proceedings of the ACM on Programming Languages*, *2*(OOPSLA), 147. DOI: 10.1145/3276517

Pratas, J., & Brito, P. (2019). *Distribuição - Gestão de pontos de venda e de retalho*. Conjuntura Actual Editora.

Provost, F., & Fawcett, T. (2013). *Data Science for Business: What You Need to Know about Data Mining and Data-Analytic Thinking*. O'Reilly Media.

Pulakhandam, W. (2020). Automated Threat Intelligence Integration To Strengthen SHACS For Robust Security In Cloud-Based Healthcare Applications. *International Journal of Engineering*, *10*(4).

PwC. (2023). *2023 AI business survey: The state of AI in business*. PwC Global. https://www.pwc.com/gx/en/issues/analytics/artificial-intelligence.html

Qian, K., Danilevsky, M., Aharonov, R., Katsis, Y., & Sen, P. (2020). *A Survey of the State of Explainable AI for Natural Language Processing*. 1-13. https://doi.org//arXiv.2010.00711DOI: 10.48550

Qu, S., Li, X., Lim, M. K., Liu, W., Li, Z., & Wang, Y. (2025). Smart supply chain management: a systematic literature review and future research agenda. *International Journal of Logistics Research and Applications*, 1-29.

Quasim, M. T., & Chattopadhyay, R. (2015). Artificial intelligence as a business forecasting and error handling tool. *Compusoft*, *4*(2), 1534.

Quintana, S. C. (2025). Liberal democracy, behavioural governance, and communication: Risks and opportunities. In Saura, J. (Ed.), *Data-driven governance through AI, digital marketing, and the privacy interplay* (pp. 77–112). IGI Global Scientific Publishing., DOI: 10.4018/979-8-3693-6945-6.ch004

Radanliev, P. (2025). AI ethics: Integrating transparency, fairness, and privacy in AI development. *Applied Artificial Intelligence*, *39*(1), 2463722. DOI: 10.1080/08839514.2025.2463722

Radu, C. G., Dumitra, E. C., & Cotescu, R.-G. (2024). Behavioral Economics in The Era of Digital Subscriptions: Choice or Manipulation. *Journal of Academic Opinion*, *4*(2), 72–46. https://academicopinion.org/index.php/pub/article/view/68

Rahman, A. (2022). Category Management in Procurement: A Framework for Enhancing Strategic Decision-Making. *International Journal of Emerging Trends in Computer Science and Information Technology*, *3*(1), 10–19. DOI: 10.63282/3050-9246.IJETCSIT-V3I1P102

Rahmani, S., Aghalar, H., Jebreili, S., & Goli, A. (2024). Optimization and computing using intelligent data-driven approaches for decision-making. In *Optimization and computing using intelligent data-driven approaches for decision-making* (pp. 90–176). CRC Press. DOI: 10.1201/9781003536796-6

Rahwan, I., Cebrian, M., Obradovich, N., Bongard, J., Bonnefon, J. F., & Lazer, D. (2019). Machine behaviour. *Nature*, *568*(7753), 477–486. DOI: 10.1038/s41586-019-1138-y PMID: 31019318

Raji, I. D., Gebru, T., Mitchell, M., Buolamwini, J., Lee, J., & Denton, E. (2020). *Saving Face: Investigating the ethical concerns of facial recognition auditing*. In *Proceedings of the AAAI/ACM Conference on AI, Ethics, and Society* (pp. 145–151). Association for Computing Machinery. DOI: 10.1145/3375627.3375820

Ramya, J., Yerraguravagari, S. S., Gaikwad, S., & Gupta, R. K. (2024). AI and Machine Learning in Predictive Analytics: Revolutionizing Business Strategies through Big Data Insights. Library of Progress-Library Science, Information Technology & Computer, 44(3).

Rana, S., Singh, S. K., & Chandel, A. (2025). AI in Customer Service Automation: Balancing Efficiency With Human Touch. In *AI, Corporate Social Responsibility, and Marketing in Modern Organizations* (pp. 173–194). IGI Global Scientific Publishing. DOI: 10.4018/979-8-3373-0219-5.ch009

Rane, N. (2023). ChatGPT and similar generative artificial intelligence (AI) for smart industry: role, challenges and opportunities for industry 4.0, industry 5.0 and society 5.0. Challenges and Opportunities for Industry, 4.

Rane, N. (2023). *Enhancing Customer Loyalty through Artificial Intelligence (AI), Internet of Things (IoT), and Big Data Technologies: Improving Customer Satisfaction, Engagement, Relationship, and Experience* (SSRN Scholarly Paper No. 4616051). Social Science Research Network. DOI: 10.2139/ssrn.4616051

Rane, N., Choudhary, S., & Rane, J. (2023). *Artificial Intelligence (AI) and Internet of Things (IoT) – Based Sensors for Monitoring and Controlling in Architecture, Engineering, and Construction: Applications, Challenges, and Opportunities* (SSRN Scholarly Paper No. 4642197). Social Science Research Network. DOI: 10.2139/ssrn.4642197

Rane, N., Choudhary, S., & Rane, J. (2024). Gemini versus ChatGPT: Applications, performance, architecture, capabilities, and implementation. SSRN *Electronic Journal*. https://doi.org/DOI: 10.2139/ssrn.4723687

Rane, N., Choudhary, S., & Rane, J. (2024). Artificial intelligence for enhancing resilience. *Journal of Applied Artificial Intelligence*, *5*(2), 2. Advance online publication. DOI: 10.48185/jaai.v5i2.1053

Ransbotham, S., Kiron, D., & Prentice, P. K. (2017). Artificial intelligence in business: An early start in the business world. *MIT Sloan Management Review*, *59*(1), 1–19.

Rasal, P. (2023). Resume Parser Analysis Using Machine Learning and Natural Language Processing. *International Journal for Research in Applied Science and Engineering Technology*, *11*(5), 2840–2844. DOI: 10.22214/ijraset.2023.52202

Rastogi, C., Zhang, Y., Wei, D., Varshney, K. R., Dhurandhar, A., & Tomsett, R. (2022). Deciding fast and slow: The role of cognitive biases in ai-assisted decision-making. Proceedings of the ACM on Human-computer Interaction, 6(CSCW1), 1-22.

Ravichandran, P., Machireddy, J. R., & Rachakatla, S. K. (2022). AI-Enhanced data analytics for real-time business intelligence: Applications and challenges. *Journal of AI in Healthcare and Medicine*, *2*(2), 168–195.

Rayner, J. (2004). *Managing reputational risk: Curbing threats, leveraging opportunities*. John Wiley & Sons.

Ray, S., & Nayak, L. (2023). Marketing sustainable fashion: Trends and future directions. *Sustainability (Basel)*, *15*(7), 6202. DOI: 10.3390/su15076202

Redman, T. C. (2013). *Data driven: Profiting from your most important business asset*. Harvard Business Review Press.

Rehman, M. A., Sajid, I., Abid, S., Ali, O., & Khan, A. (2025). The Rise of AI-Driven Direct-to-Consumer (DTC) Brands: Personalization, Customer Retention, and Competition with Traditional Retailers. *Journal for Social Science Archives, 3*(2), 206–221. DOI: 10.59075/jssa.v3i2.230

Rese, A., & Steppert, M. (2019). Chatbots in Marketing and Sales: A Literature Review. In *Proceedings of the 27th European Conference on Information Systems (ECIS).*

Resnick, P., & Varian, H. R. (1997). Recommender systems. *Communications of the ACM, 40*(3), 56–58. DOI: 10.1145/245108.245121

Revathy, S., Sreekala, S. P., Praveenadevi, D., Rajeshwari, S., De Albuquerque, V. H. C., Raj, P., & Yadav, S. P. (2023). The intelligent implications of artificial intelligence-driven decision-making in business management. Toward Artificial General Intelligence: Deep Learning, Neural Networks, Generative AI, 251.

Riad, M., Naimi, M., & Okar, C. (2024). Enhancing Supply Chain Resilience Through Artificial Intelligence: Developing a Comprehensive Conceptual Framework for AI Implementation and Supply Chain Optimization. *Logistics (Basel), 8*(4), 4. Advance online publication. DOI: 10.3390/logistics8040111

Ribeiro, M. T., Singh, S., & Guestrin, C. (2016). *"Why should I trust you?" Explaining the predictions of any classifier. In* Proceedings of the 22nd ACM SIGKDD International Conference on Knowledge Discovery and Data Mining *(pp. 1135-1144).*

Ridzuan, N. N., Masri, M., Anshari, M., Fitriyani, N. L., & Syafrudin, M. (2024). AI in the Financial Sector: The Line between Innovation, Regulation and Ethical Responsibility. *Information (Basel), 15*(8), 432. DOI: 10.3390/info15080432

Rigby, D. K., Sutherland, J., & Noble, A. (2018). Agile at scale. *Harvard Business Review, 96*(3), 88–96.

Roberts, J. (2020). Future and changing roles of staff in distance education: A study to identify training and professional development needs. In *Expanding Horizons in Open and Distance Learning* (pp. 37–53). Routledge. DOI: 10.4324/9780429292941-4

Rodriguez-Rodriguez, I., Rodriguez, J. V., Shirvanizadeh, N., Ortiz, A., & Pardo-Quiles, D. J. (2021). Applications of artificial intelligence, machine learning, big data and the internet of things to the COVID-19 pandemic: A scientometric review using text mining. *International Journal of Environmental Research and Public Health, 18*(16), 8578. DOI: 10.3390/ijerph18168578 PMID: 34444327

Rojas-Galeano, S., Posada, J., & Ordoñez, E. (2022). A bibliometric perspective on AI research for job-résumé matching. *TheScientificWorldJournal*, *2022*, 1–15. Advance online publication. DOI: 10.1155/2022/8002363 PMID: 36225947

Romanosky, S., Hoffman, D., & Acquisti, A. (2016). Empirical analysis of data breach litigation. *Journal of Empirical Legal Studies*, *11*(1), 74–104. DOI: 10.1111/jels.12035

Roongta, J., & Roongta, J. (2024). The Next Frontier: Exploring AI-Driven Business Strategic Decision Making. *Journal of Academic Advancement*, *3*(01), 50–60.

Rousseau, J. (2014). Manual da Distribuição, 2ª edição, Cascais: Princípia Editora.

Rousseau, D. (2015). General systems theory: Its present and potential. *Systems Research and Behavioral Science*, *32*(5), 522–533. DOI: 10.1002/sres.2354

Roy, P. K., Chowdhary, S. S., & Bhatia, R. (2020). A Machine Learning approach for automation of Resume Recommendation System. *Procedia Computer Science*, *167*, 2318–2327. DOI: 10.1016/j.procs.2020.03.284

Rozman, M., Tominc, P., & Milfelner, B. (2023). Maximizing employee engagement through artificial intelligent organizational culture in the context of leadership and training of employees: Testing linear and non-linear relationships. *Cogent Business & Management*, *10*(2), 2248732. DOI: 10.1080/23311975.2023.2248732

Russell, S., & Norvig, P. (2016). *Artificial intelligence: A modern approach* (3rd ed.). Pearson.

Rust, R. T., & Huang, M. H. (2021). The AI marketing canvas: A five-stage road-map to implementing artificial intelligence in marketing. *Journal of the Academy of Marketing Science*, *49*(1), 30–50.

Rust, R. T., Kannan, P. K., & Peng, N. (2002). The customer economics of e-service. *Journal of Service Research*, *5*(2), 112–126.

Rygielski, C., Wang, C., & Yen, C. (2002). Data mining techniques for customer relationship management. *Technology in Society*, *24*(4), 483–502. DOI: 10.1016/S0160-791X(02)00038-6

Saatçı, M., Kaya, R., & Ünlü, R. (2024). Resume Screening with Natural Language Processing (NLP). *Alphanumeric Journal*, *12*(2), 121–140. DOI: 10.17093/alphanumeric.1536577

Sahid, A., Maleh, Y., Asemanjerdi, S. A., & Martín-Cervantes, P. A. (2023). A Bibliometric Analysis of the FinTech Agility Literature: Evolution and Review. *International Journal of Financial Studies*, *11*(4), 123. DOI: 10.3390/ijfs11040123

Sandoval, R. (2023). Copyleft in the age of AI: Legal implications of LLM-generated code. *Journal of Intellectual Property Law & Practice*, *18*(2), 145–157. DOI: 10.1093/jiplp/jpac079

Saranya, A., & Subhashini, R. (2023). A systematic review of Explainable Artificial Intelligence models and applications: Recent developments and future trends. In *Decision Analytics Journal* (Vol. 7, pp. 1–14). Elsevier Inc., DOI: 10.1016/j.dajour.2023.100230

Sargiotis, D. (2024). Data Governance Frameworks: Models and Best Practices. In *Data Governance: A Guide* (pp. 165–195). Springer Nature Switzerland. DOI: 10.1007/978-3-031-67268-2_4

Sarker, I. H. (2021). Data science and analytics: An overview from data-driven smart computing, decision-making and applications perspective. *SN Computer Science*, *2*(5), 377. DOI: 10.1007/s42979-021-00765-8 PMID: 34278328

Sashi, C. M. (2021). Digital communication, value co-creation and customer engagement in business networks: A conceptual matrix and propositions. *European Journal of Marketing*, *55*(6), 1643–1663. DOI: 10.1108/EJM-01-2020-0023

Saurabh, K., Arora, R., Rani, N., Mishra, D., & Ramkumar, M. (2022). AI led ethical digital transformation: Framework, research and managerial implications. Journal of Information. *Communication and Ethics in Society*, *20*(2), 229–256. DOI: 10.1108/JICES-02-2021-0020

Schmidt, P., Biessmann, F., & Teubner, T. (2020). Transparency and trust in artificial intelligence systems. *Journal of Decision Systems*, *29*(4), 260–278. DOI: 10.1080/12460125.2020.1819094

Schmitt, M. (2023). Automated machine learning: AI-driven decision making in business analytics. *Intelligent Systems with Applications*, *18*, 200188. DOI: 10.1016/j.iswa.2023.200188

Schwartz, R., Schwartz, R., Vassilev, A., Greene, K., Perine, L., Burt, A., & Hall, P. (2022). Towards a standard for identifying and managing bias in artificial intelligence (Vol. 3, p. 00). Gaithersburg, MD: US Department of Commerce, National Institute of Standards and Technology.

Sculley, D., Holt, G., Golovin, D., Davydov, E., Phillips, T., Ebner, D., Chaudhary, V., Young, M., Crespo, J. F., & Dennison, D. (2015). *Hidden technical debt in machine learning systems.* In *Advances in Neural Information Processing Systems* (pp. 2503–2511).

Selvarajan, G. (2021). Leveraging AI-enhanced analytics for industry-specific optimization: A strategic approach to transforming data-driven decision-making. *International Journal of Enhanced Research in Science Technology and Engineering*, *10*, 78–84.

Senoo, E. E. K., Anggraini, L., Kumi, J. A., Karolina, L. B., Akansah, E., Sulyman, H. A., Mendonça, I., & Aritsugi, M. (2024). IoT Solutions with Artificial Intelligence Technologies for Precision Agriculture: Definitions, Applications, Challenges, and Opportunities. *Electronics (Basel)*, *13*(10), 1894. DOI: 10.3390/electronics13101894

Sethuraman, R., Gázquez-Abad, J., & Martínez-López, F. (2022). The effect of retail assortment size on perceptions, choice, and sales: Review and research directions'. *Journal of Retailing*, *98*(1), 24–45. DOI: 10.1016/j.jretai.2022.01.001

Shafik, W., Tufail, A., De Silva Liyanage, C., & Apong, R. H. M. (2023). Using a novel convolutional neural network for plant pests detection and disease classification. *Journal of the Science of Food and Agriculture*, *103*(12), 5849–5861. DOI: 10.1002/jsfa.12700 PMID: 37177888

Shahi, T. B., Xu, C., Neupane, A., & Guo, W. (2023). Recent advances in crop disease detection using UAV and deep learning techniques. *Remote Sensing (Basel)*, *15*(9), 2450. DOI: 10.3390/rs15092450

Shalaby, A. (2024). Classification for the digital and cognitive AI hazards: Urgent call to establish automated safe standard for protecting young human minds. *Digital Economy and Sustainable Development*, *2*(1), 17. DOI: 10.1007/s44265-024-00042-5

Sharma, B. P. (n.d.). *Role of Advanced Cybersecurity Frameworks in Safeguarding Data Integrity and Consumer Trust in Digital Commerce and Enterprise Systems*.

Sharma, G., & Sharma, P. (2016). A Study on Data Mining Algorithms for Tourism Industry. *International Journal of Latest Trends in Engineering & Technology : IJLTET*, *7*(1), 580–587.

Sharma, R., Shishodia, A., Gunasekaran, A., Min, H., & Munim, Z. H. (2022). The role of artificial intelligence in supply chain management: Mapping the territory. *International Journal of Production Research*, *60*(24), 7527–7550. DOI: 10.1080/00207543.2022.2029611

Sharma, S., Ghanshala, A., & Tyagi, R. (2022). Cotton Crop Disease Detection System Using Deep Learning Approach. In *2022 IEEE Conference on Interdisciplinary Approaches in Technology and Management for Social Innovation (IATMSI)*, 1–6. DOI: 10.1109/IATMSI56455.2022.10119275

Shin, D. D. (2023). *Algorithms, humans, and interactions: How do algorithms interact with people? Designing meaningful AI experiences*. Taylor & Francis.

Shin, N. (2006). Online learners' flow experience: An empirical study. *British Journal of Educational Technology, 37*(5), 727–740. DOI: 10.1111/j.1467-8535.2006.00641.x

Shodeinde, D. A., & Abah, O. E. (2025). Artificial Intelligence Technology and Marketing Communication Management: A Case Study of Guaranty Trust Holding Company PLC, Nigeria. *Lafia Journal of Economics and Sciences*, 163-183.DOI: 10.70118/lajems-10-1-2025-09Management

Shoukath, T. K., & Chakkaravarthy, M. (2025). Predictive analytics in education: Machine learning approaches and performance metrics for student success – a systematic literature review. *Data and Metadata, 4*, 730. DOI: 10.56294/dm2025730

Shoushtari, F., Ghafourian, E., & Talebi, M. (2021). Improving performance of supply chain by applying artificial intelligence. International journal of industrial engineering and operational research, 3(1), 14-23.

Shrestha, Y. R., Ben-Menahem, S. M., & Von Krogh, G. (2019). Organizational decision-making structures in the age of artificial intelligence. *California Management Review, 61*(4), 66–83. DOI: 10.1177/0008125619862257

Siegel, J. S., & Swanson, D. A. (2004). *The Methods and Materials of Demography*. Elsevier Academic Press.

Singh, B. (2025). Case Study on Implementing AI for Dynamic Pricing in the Hospitality Industry. Decoding AI: Practical Implementations for Business Operations.

Singh, B. (2025). Revolutionizing Supply Chains for Optimized Demand Planning, Inventory Management, and Logistics: An In-Depth Analysis of AI and ML Solutions in the Modern Era. In *Supply Chain Transformation Through Generative AI and Machine Learning* (pp. 103–128). IGI Global Scientific Publishing. DOI: 10.4018/979-8-3693-4433-0.ch005

Singh, N., Gupta, K., & Rawlins, P. (2024). Unlocking the AI-powered customer experience: Personalized service, enhanced engagement, and data-driven strategies for e-commerce applications. *Journal of Infrastructure. Policy and Development, 8*(7), 4970. Advance online publication. DOI: 10.1016/j.jipd.2024.07.001

Singh, R. P., Hom, G. L., Abramoff, M. D., Campbell, J. P., & Chiang, M. F. (2020). Current challenges and barriers to real-world artificial intelligence adoption for the healthcare system, provider, and the patient. *Translational Vision Science & Technology, 9*(2), 45–45. DOI: 10.1167/tvst.9.2.45 PMID: 32879755

Singh, U., Srivastava, A., Chauhan, D., & Singh, A. (2020). Computer Vision Technique for Detection of Grape Esca (Black Measles) Disease from Grape Leaf Samples. *International Conference on Contemporary Computing and Applications*, 110–115. DOI: 10.1109/IC3A48958.2020.233281

Sipola, J., Saunila, M., & Ukko, J. (2023). Adopting artificial intelligence in sustainable business. *Journal of Cleaner Production*, *426*, 139197. DOI: 10.1016/j.jclepro.2023.139197

Slosberg, M., Nejati, A., Evans, J., & Nanda, U. (2018). Transitioning to a new facility: The crucial role of employee engagement. *Journal of Healthcare Management / American College of Healthcare Executives*, *63*(1), 63–77. DOI: 10.1097/JHM-D-16-00019 PMID: 29303827

Smith, B., & Linden, G. (2017). Two decades of recommender systems at Amazon.com. *IEEE Internet Computing*, *21*(3), 12–18. DOI: 10.1109/MIC.2017.72

Solove, D. J. (2008). Data mining and the security-liberty debate. *The University of Chicago Law Review. University of Chicago. Law School*, *75*(1), 343–362.

Srivastava, P. R., Zhang, J. Z., Eachempati, P., Sharma, S. K., & Liu, Y. (2025). An Intelligent omnichannel assortment model to manage webrooming: An optimization approach. *Journal of Strategic Marketing*, *33*(3), 441–465. DOI: 10.1080/0965254X.2022.2067072

Sroison, P., & Chan, J. H. (2021). *Resume Parser with Natural Language Processing*. 1-5. https://doi.org/DOI: 10.36227/techrxiv.17641604.v1

Stewart, D. W., & Kamins, M. A. (1993). *Secondary research: Information sources and methods* (Vol. 4). Sage. DOI: 10.4135/9781412985802

Stitch Fix. (2020). *How Stitch Fix works: Your personal stylist + AI.* [Company Website].

Subrahmanyam, S. (2025). The Integration of Artificial Intelligence and Machine Learning in Performance Evaluation. In R. Marcao & V. Santos (Eds.), *Evolving Strategies for Organizational Management and Performance Evaluation,* (pp. 603-626). IGI Global Scientific Publishing. DOI: 10.4018/979-8-3373-0149-5.ch028

Subrahmanyam, S. (2024). Role of data analytics and big data in operational decision-making and performance improvement. In Martínez-Falcó, J., Sánchez-García, E., Marco-Lajara, B., & Visser, G. (Eds.), *Convergence of technology and operations management in modern businesses* (pp. 105–140). IGI Global Scientific Publishing., DOI: 10.4018/979-8-3693-6200-6.ch003

Subrahmanyam, S. (2025). Leveraging AI and ML for Enhanced Efficiency and Innovation in Manufacturing. In Vyas, V., Bi, X., Pandey, D., Xu, Z., & Pandey, B. (Eds.), *AI's Role in Enhanced Automotive Safety* (pp. 319–344). IGI Global Scientific Publishing., DOI: 10.4018/979-8-3373-0442-7.ch021

Subrahmanyam, S. (2025). Strategic Collaboration and Partnerships in R&D for Innovation. In Martínez-Falcó, J., Sánchez-García, E., & Marco-Lajara, B. (Eds.), *Research and Development Practices in Innovation* (pp. 283–314). IGI Global Scientific Publishing., DOI: 10.4018/979-8-3373-0812-8.ch010

Subramanian, Y. R., & Riya, R. (2024). The transformative role of artificial intelligence in human resource. [IJRTBT]. *International Journal on Recent Trends in Business and Tourism*, *8*(2), 14–25. DOI: 10.31674/ijrtbt.2024.v08i02.002

Suljic, V. (2025). Strategic leadership in AI-driven digital transformation: Ethical governance, innovation management, and sustainable practices for global enterprises and SMEs. *SBS Journal of Applied Business Research*, *13*(1), 17–35. DOI: 10.70301/JOUR/SBS-JABR/2025/13/1/2

Sull, D., & Turconi, S. (2008). Zara's Fast Fashion Formula. *MIT Sloan Management Review*, *49*(2), 34–40.

Sundaram, M., Kumar, S. V., Kumar, R. L., & Punitha, P. (2025). DRF-YOLO: A transformer-enhanced framework for underwater image enhancement and object detection. *International Journal of Pattern Recognition and Artificial Intelligence*, *39*(8), 2550011. DOI: 10.1142/S0218001425500119

Suri, V. K. (2022). *Functional automation and digital transformation*. Dorrance Publishing.

Syamsuar, D., & Marcello. (2024). The implementation of Artificial Intelligence for Online Review: A systematic literature review. *2024 International Conference on Information Management and Technology (ICIMTech)*, 588–593. DOI: 10.1109/ICIMTech63123.2024.10780904

Taherdoost, H., & Madanchian, M. (2023). Artificial intelligence and knowledge management: Impacts, benefits, and implementation. *Computers*, *12*(4), 72. DOI: 10.3390/computers12040072

Tahmasebi, M. (2024). Beyond Defense: Proactive Approaches to Disaster Recovery and Threat Intelligence in Modern Enterprises. *Journal of Information Security*, *15*(2), 2. Advance online publication. DOI: 10.4236/jis.2024.152008

Tambe, P., Cappelli, P., & Yakubovich, V. (2023). Artificial intelligence in human resources: New directions for talent management. *Journal of Organizational Behavior*, *44*(2), 127–143. DOI: 10.1002/job.2693

Tam, K. Y., & Ho, S. Y. (2006). Understanding the Impact of Web Personalization on User Information Processing and Decision Outcomes1. *Management Information Systems Quarterly*, *30*(4), 865–890. DOI: 10.2307/25148757

Taneja, K., Maiti, P., Kakar, S., Guruprasad, P., Rao, S., & Goel, A. K. (2024). Jill Watson: A virtual teaching assistant powered by ChatGPT *(arXiv preprint)*. *L* arXiv.2405.11070DOI: 10.1007/978-3-031-64302-6_23

Taneja, S., Singh, A., & Kumar, P. (Eds.). (2024). *Artificial intelligence and machine learning-powered smart finance*. IGI Global. DOI: 10.4018/979-8-3693-3264-1

Taranu, S. D., & Cioranu, A. G. (2024). AI in Competitive Intelligence, Traditional and New Techniques for Gathering and Analysing Data. *Journal of Environmental Management & Tourism*, *15*(3), 591–596.

Tarihal, B., Kaliwal, R., & Ammanagi, A. (2024). The Transformative Influence of Artificial Intelligence on Supply Chain Management. *ITM Web of Conferences*, *68*, 01016. DOI: 10.1051/itmconf/20246801016

Tayal, S., Sharma, T., Singhal, S., & Thakur, A. (2024). Resume Screening using Machine Learning. *International Journal of Scientific Research in Computer Science. Engineering and Information Technology*, *10*(2), 602–606.

Teece, D. J. (2007). Explicating dynamic capabilities: The nature and microfoundations of sustainable enterprise performance. *Strategic Management Journal*, *28*(13), 1319–1350. DOI: 10.1002/smj.640

Tejaswini, K., Kadiwal, V. U., & Revanna, S. (2022). Design and development of machine learning based resume ranking system. *Global Transitions Proceedings*, *3*(2), 371–375. DOI: 10.1016/j.gltp.2021.10.002

Tekale, K. M. (2023). AI-Powered Claims Processing: Reducing Cycle Times and Improving Accuracy. *International Journal of Artificial Intelligence, Data Science, and Machine Learning*, *4*(2), 113–123.

Tekin, M., Etlioğlu, M., Koyuncuoğlu, Ö., & Tekin, E. (2018). Data mining in digital marketing. *Proceedings of the International Symposium for Production Research 2018 18* (pp. 44-61). Springer International Publishing. DOI: 10.1007/978-3-319-92267-6_4

Tewari, S. (2025). AI powered data governance - ensuring data quality and compliance in the era of Big Data. *Journal of Artificial Intelligence General Science (JAIGS) ISSN:3006-4023, 8*(1), 187–197. DOI: 10.60087/jaigs.v8i1.364

Tirkolaee, E. B., Sadeghi, S., Mooseloo, F. M., Vandchali, H. R., & Aeini, S. (2021). Application of Machine Learning in Supply Chain Management: A Comprehensive Overview of the Main Areas. *Mathematical Problems in Engineering, 2021*(1), 1476043. DOI: 10.1155/2021/1476043

Topol, E. (2019). *Deep medicine: How artificial intelligence can make healthcare human again*. Basic Books.

Tsai, J. Y., Egelman, S., Cranor, L. F., & Acquisti, A. (2011). The effect of privacy policies on consumer trust and behavioural intentions. *The Journal of Consumer Affairs, 45*(2), 220–255.

Tyagi, A. K., Fernandez, T. F., Mishra, S., & Kumari, S. (2020, December). Intelligent automation systems at the core of industry 4.0. In International conference on intelligent systems design and applications (pp. 1-18). Cham: Springer International Publishing.

Uddin, M. K. S. (2024). A review of utilizing natural language processing and AI for advanced data visualization in real-time analytics. *Global Mainstream Journal, 1*(4), 10–62304. DOI: 10.62304/ijmisds.v1i04.185

Ugwa, S. (2023). Artificial Intelligence for IT strategy: Driving data-driven decision-making and business alignment.

Ujwary-Gil, A., & Florek-Paszkowska, A. (2025b). Artificial Intelligence, analytics, and strategic decision-making. *AI, Analytics and Strategic Decision Making*, 1–21. DOI: 10.4324/9781003507840-1

Ulu, C. (2024). The fuel of AI in the Battlefield. *Cyber Security in the Age of Artificial Intelligence and Autonomous Weapons*, 87–100. DOI: 10.1201/9781003441700-7

Vacik, H., & Lexer, M. J. (2014). Past, current and future drivers for the development of decision support systems in forest management. *Scandinavian Journal of Forest Research, 29*(sup1), 2-19.

Valivarthi, D. T. (2020). Blockchain-Powered AI-Based Secure HRM Data Management: Machine Learning-Driven Predictive Control and Sparse Matrix Decomposition Techniques. [IJMECE]. *International Journal of Modern Electronics and Communication Engineering, 8*(4), 9.

Van den Broeck, E., & Van den Bergh, J. (2015). A systematic review of chatbot applications in customer service. *Procedia Computer Science*, *63*, 50–57.

Van Hoang, T. (2024). Impact of integrated artificial intelligence and internet of things technologies on smart city transformation. Journal of technical education science, 19(Special Issue 01), 64-73.

Vasundhara, S., Venkatesh, K. S., Manimegalai, V., Sundharesalingam, P., Sathyakala, S., & Boopathi, S. (2024). *AI-Powered Marketing Revolutionizing Customer Engagement Through Innovative Strategies*. IGI Global Scientific Publishing., DOI: 10.4018/979-8-3693-2643-5.ch002

Venkateshwaran, G., Kumar, R. N., & Devarajulu, V. S. (2024). Artificial Intelligence in HR: Transforming Recruitment and Selection in IT Industry. *Journal of Information Systems Engineering & Management*, *2025*(17s), 39–45.

Verhoef, P. C., Lemon, K. N., & Parasuraman, A. (2017). Marketing in a digital world. *Journal of Interactive Marketing*, *40*, 1–11. DOI: 10.1016/j.intmar.2017.06.001

Verhoef, P. C., Lemon, K. N., Parasuraman, A., Roggeveen, A., Tsiros, M., & Schlesinger, L. A. (2009). Customer experience creation: Determinants, dynamics and management strategies. *Journal of Retailing*, *85*(1), 31–41. DOI: 10.1016/j.jretai.2008.11.001

Verma, A. K., Diksha, N., & Sharma, S. (2024). Artificial Intelligence Integrated Rice Crop Disease Detection Using Drones for Smart Farming. In 2024 7th International Conference on Circuit Power and Computing Technologies (ICCPCT), 235, 709–713. DOI: 10.1109/ICCPCT61902.2024.10672693

Verma, A. (2025). Digital personalization and consumer engagement: A review of theoretical and empirical perspectives on AI-based advertising in social media environments. *SSRN*. DOI: 10.2139/ssrn.5261407

Vettriselvan, R. (2025). Harnessing innovation and digital marketing in the era of industry 5.0: resilient healthcare SMEs. In *The Future of Small Business in Industry 5.0* (pp. 163–186). IGI Global Scientific Publishing.

Villegas-Ch, W., Maldonado Navarro, A., & Sánchez Viteri, S. (2024). Optimization of inventory management through computer vision and machine learning technologies. *Intelligent Systems with Applications*, *24*, 200438. DOI: 10.1016/j.iswa.2024.200438

Voigt, P., & Von dem Bussche, A. (2017). *The EU General Data Protection Regulation (GDPR): A Practical Guide*. Springer International Publishing. DOI: 10.1007/978-3-319-57959-7

Wah, J. N. K. (2025). AI-Driven Influence: Transforming Brand Engagement and Trust in the Digital Age. Kexue Tongbao. *Chinese Science Bulletin*. Advance online publication. 02.1709/Csb.28.02.2025.01

Wamba-Taguimdje, S. L., Fosso Wamba, S., Kala Kamdjoug, J. R., & Tchatchouang Wanko, C. E. (2020). Influence of artificial intelligence (AI) on firm performance: The business value of AI-based transformation projects. *Business Process Management Journal, 26*(7), 1893–1924. DOI: 10.1108/BPMJ-10-2019-0411

Wang, G., Gunasekaran, A., Ngai, E. W. T., & Papadopoulos, T. (2016). Big data analytics in logistics and supply chain management: Certain investigations for research and applications. *International Journal of Production Economics, 176*, 98–110. DOI: 10.1016/j.ijpe.2016.03.014

Wang, H., & Song, Y. (2021). Visual Recommendation Systems: A Survey. *ACM Computing Surveys, 54*(1), 1–38.

Wang, K., Zhao, Y., Gangadhari, R. K., & Li, Z. (2021). Analyzing the adoption challenges of the Internet of things (Iot) and artificial intelligence (ai) for smart cities in china. *Sustainability (Basel), 13*(19), 10983. DOI: 10.3390/su131910983

Wang, R. Y., & Strong, D. M. (1998). Beyond accuracy: What data quality means to data consumers. *Journal of Management Information Systems, 12*(4), 5–34. DOI: 10.1080/07421222.1996.11518099

Wang, S., Liu, T., Tan, L., & Yu, Y. (2018). Automatically learning semantic features for defect prediction. *Proceedings of the 40th International Conference on Software Engineering*, 310–320. DOI: 10.1145/3180155.3180214

Warner, K. S. R., & Wäger, M. (2019). Building dynamic capabilities for digital transformation An ongoing process of strategic renewal. *Long Range Planning, 52*(3), 326–349. DOI: 10.1016/j.lrp.2018.12.001

Wasilewski, A., Chawla, Y., & Pralat, E. (2025). Enhanced e-commerce personalization through AI-powered content generation tools. *IEEE Access : Practical Innovations, Open Solutions, 13*(99), 1–1. DOI: 10.1109/ACCESS.2025.3550956

Weber, P., Carl, K. V., & Hinz, O. (2024). Applications of Explainable Artificial Intelligence in Finance—A systematic review of Finance, Information Systems, and Computer Science literature. *Manag Rev Q, 74*(2), 867–907. DOI: 10.1007/s11301-023-00320-0

Wedel, M., & Kannan, P. K. (2016). Marketing analytics for data-rich environments. *Journal of Marketing, 80*(6), 97–121. DOI: 10.1509/jm.15.0413

Wen, A., Patil, T., Saxena, A., Fu, Y., O'Brien, S., & Zhu, K. (2025). *FAIRE: Assessing Racial and Gender Bias in AI-Driven Resume Evaluations*. arXiv preprint arXiv:2504.01420.

Wen, Y., Wang, J., & Chen, X. (2025). Trust and AI weight: Human AI collaboration in organizational management decision making. *Frontiers in Organizational Psychology, 3*, 1419403. Advance online publication. DOI: 10.3389/forgp.2025.1419403

White, M., Tufano, M., Vendome, C., & Poshyvanyk, D. (2016). Deep learning code fragments for code clone detection. *Proceedings of the 31st IEEE/ACM International Conference on Automated Software Engineering*, 87–98. DOI: 10.1145/2970276.2970326

Whitman, M. E., & Mattord, H. J. (2018). *Principles of Information Security*. Cengage Learning.

Widjaja, G. (2024). Ethical aspects in legal management: A unique approach to addressing moral dilemmas in business decision-making. *Journal of Management World, 2024*(4), 326–332. DOI: 10.53935/jomw.v2024i4.395

Wieland, A. (2021). Dancing the Supply Chain: Toward Transformative Supply Chain Management. *The Journal of Supply Chain Management, 57*(1), 58–73. DOI: 10.1111/jscm.12248

Wijesekara, I., Galappaththi, P., Silva, K., & Liyanage, R. (2020). *AI-driven Dashboards for Enterprise Decision Making*. Rasika Liyanage Eastern University.

Willems, L. (2021). Understanding the Impacts of Autonomous Vehicles in Logistics. In *The Digital Transformation of Logistics* (pp. 113–127). John Wiley & Sons, Ltd., DOI: 10.1002/9781119646495.ch8

Wilson, K., & Caliskan, A. (2024). Gender, Race, and Intersectional Bias in Resume Screening via Language Model Retrieval. arXiv preprint arXiv:2407.20371.

Wirtz, B. W., Weyerer, J. C., & Geyer, C. (2019). Artificial intelligence and the public sector—Applications and challenges. *International Journal of Public Administration, 42*(7), 596–615. DOI: 10.1080/01900692.2018.1498103

Wirtz, B. W., Weyerer, J. C., & Sturm, B. J. (2020). The Dark Sides of Artificial Intelligence: An Integrated AI Governance Framework for Public Administration. *International Journal of Public Administration, 43*(9), 818–829. DOI: 10.1080/01900692.2020.1749851

Wong, W. P., Tseng, M. L., & Tan, K. H. (2014). A business process management capabilities perspective on organisation performance. *Total Quality Management & Business Excellence*, *25*(5-6), 602–617. DOI: 10.1080/14783363.2013.850812

World Bank. (2023, October). Fraud in fast payments. https://fastpayments.worldbank.org/sites/default/files/2023-10/Fraud%20in%20Fast%20Payments_Final.pdf

World Economic Forum. (2020). *The future of jobs report 2020*. https://www.weforum.org/reports/the-future-of-jobs-report-2020

Wosiak, A. (2021). Automated extraction of information from Polish resume documents in the IT recruitment process. *Procedia Computer Science*, *192*, 2432–2439. DOI: 10.1016/j.procs.2021.09.012

Wu, H., Liu, J., & Liang, B. (2024). AI-Driven Supply Chain Transformation in Industry 5.0: Enhancing Resilience and Sustainability. *Journal of the Knowledge Economy*, *16*(1), 3826–3868. Advance online publication. DOI: 10.1007/s13132-024-01999-6

Wu, J., & Shang, S. (2020). Manage uncertainty in AI-enabled decision-making and achieve sustainability. *Sustainability (Basel)*, *12*(21), 8758. DOI: 10.3390/su12218758

Yadava, A. (2023). Ethical and regulatory challenges of AI adoption in the financial services sector: A global perspective. *International Journal of Science and Research Archive*, *10*(13), 10–30574.

Yallamelli, A. R. G. (2020). A Cloud-based Financial Data Modeling System Using GBDT, ALBERT, and Firefly Algorithm Optimization for High-dimensional Generative Topographic Mapping. *International Journal of Microelectronics and Communication Engineering, 8(4), 27., 8*(4).

Yathiraju, N. (2022). Investigating the use of an artificial intelligence model in an ERP cloud-based system. International Journal of Electrical. *Electronics and Computers*, *7*(2), 1–26.

Yildiz, B., Çiğdem, Ş., Meidutė-Kavaliauskienė, I., & Činčikaitė, R. (2024). The nexus of big data analytics, knowledge sharing, and product innovation in manufacturing. *Journal of Business Economics and Management*, *25*(1), 66–84. DOI: 10.3846/jbem.2024.20713

Yılmaz, E., & Demir, M. (2023). AI in Strategic Planning: Redefining Long-Term Business Goals. *Digital Transformation and Administration Innovation*, *1*(2), 8–16.

Yusuf, S. O., Durodola, R. L., Ocran, G., Abubakar, J. E., Echere, A. Z., & Paul-Adeleye, A. H. (2024). Challenges and opportunities in AI and digital transformation for SMEs: A cross-continental perspective. *World Journal of Advanced Research and Reviews*, *23*(3), 668–678. DOI: 10.30574/wjarr.2024.23.3.2511

Yu, Y., Wang, B., & Zheng, S. (2024). Data-driven product design and assortment optimization. *Transportation Research Part E, Logistics and Transportation Review*, *182*, 103413. DOI: 10.1016/j.tre.2024.103413

Zajko, M. (2022). Artificial intelligence, algorithms and social inequality. *Sociology Compass*, *16*(6), e12962. DOI: 10.1111/soc4.12962

Zamil, M. H. (2025). AI-driven business analytics for financial forecasting: A systematic review of decision support models in SMEs. *Review of Applied Science and Technology*, *4*(2), 86–117. DOI: 10.63125/gjrpv442

Zeithaml, V. A. (1988). Consumer perceptions of price, quality, and value: A means-end model and synthesis of evidence. *Journal of Marketing*, *52*(3), 2–22. DOI: 10.1177/002224298805200302

Zhang, Y., Chen, X., & Yu, Z. (2020). Cross-functional AI integration in enterprises: Framework and case study. *Journal of Enterprise Information Management*, *33*(1), 123–145. DOI: 10.1108/JEIM-09-2019-0283

Zhang, Y., Swatdikun, T., Lakkanawanit, P., Huang, S.-Z., & Chen, H. (2025). Digital transformation capacity, organizational strategic intuition, and digital leadership: Empirical evidence of the performance of high-tech companies in the Yangtze River Delta. *Journal of Risk and Financial Management*, *18*(7), 405. DOI: 10.3390/jrfm18070405

Zhang, Z., He, W., Li, W., & Abdous, M. H. (2021). Cybersecurity awareness training programs: A cost–benefit analysis framework. *Industrial Management & Data Systems*, *121*(3), 613–636. DOI: 10.1108/IMDS-08-2020-0462

Zharova, A. K. (2023). Achieving algorithmic transparency and managing risks of data security when making decisions without human interference: Legal approaches. *Journal of Digital Technologies and Law*, *1*(4), 973–993. DOI: 10.21202/jdtl.2023.42

Zheng, X. L., Zhu, M. Y., Li, Q. B., Chen, C. C., & Tan, Y. C. (2019). FinBrain: When finance meets AI 2.0. *Frontiers of Information Technology & Electronic Engineering*, *20*(7), 914–924. DOI: 10.1631/FITEE.1700822

Zhou, J., & Chen, W. (2021). Ethical AI and responsible leadership in digital transformation. *Business Ethics (Oxford, England)*, *30*(2), 207–222.

Zimmermann, T., Kotschenreuther, L., & Schmidt, K. (2016). Data-driven HR - Résumé Analysis Based on Natural Language Processing and Machine Learning. arXiv preprint arXiv:1606.05611.

Zimmermann, T., Premraj, R., & Zeller, A. (2007). Predicting defects for eclipse. *Proceedings of the Third International Workshop on Predictor Models in Software Engineering*, 9–15. DOI: 10.1109/PROMISE.2007.10

Zong, Z., & Guan, Y. (2025). AI-driven intelligent data analytics and predictive analysis in Industry 4.0: Transforming knowledge, innovation, and efficiency. *Journal of the Knowledge Economy*, *16*(1), 864–903. DOI: 10.1007/s13132-024-02001-z

Zuboff, S. (2019). *The age of surveillance capitalism: The fight for a human future at the new frontier of power*. PublicAffairs.

About the Contributors

Sandeep Poddar, presently the Deputy Vice Chancellor (Research & Innovation) of Lincoln University College, Malaysia. He also served as Senior Research Director and Executive Editor (Publications), Lincoln University College, Adjunct Faculty (Honorary), Bharat Center Canada. He has graduated from University of Calcutta in 1993 with Honours in Zoology, he has obtained Post Graduate Diploma in Dietetics from All India Institute of Hygiene and Public Health 1995, Master of Science in Zoology with specialization in Biochemical Genetics from Dayalbagh Educational Institute 1998 with distinction. In addition to this he also obtained Master of Business Administration (MBA) from Lincoln University College in 2021. He has completed PhD in Zoology from Vivekananda Institute of Medical Sciences on Cytotoxicity in 2004. After completing PhD he pursued Post-Doctoral Research in different projects on Hemoglobinopathies and Oral Cancer mutation. He is serving as reviewer of several International Journals. He has published several research papers, organized international conferences, and edited books in Malaysia, Australia and India. Dr. Sandeep is founder Secretary of Dr. Tarak Nath Podder Memorial Foundation, Kolkata, India.

Prashant Kumar Siddhey holds a Doctorate and Master's in Management and boasts a comprehensive professional journey spanning over 17 years in both the industrial and academic realms. Currently serving as a Professor at Prestige Institute of Business Management, Indore, he brings a wealth of experience from collaborating with renowned institutes and universities, demonstrating adeptness in successfully managing diverse academic and administrative responsibilities. Dr. Siddhey has also contributed significantly as a founding member in administrative roles within various universities. With a prolific record, he has authored over 40 publications, including books, research articles, case studies, and journals indexed in ABDC/ Scopus/ WoS etc. Actively engaged with Industrial and Academic

Societies, Dr. Siddhey remains a dynamic and integral part of the academic and industrial communities.

Najla Shafighi at present working as Head of the department of International Technology Transfer Management at bbw University of Applied Sciences Germany served as faculty member of Economics and Management at Lincoln University College, Malaysia. She was also the International Marketing /Business Development Manager at EduFront SDN BHD, Kuala Lumpur, Malaysia. She also worked in International Marketing as Business Development Manager, Legenda Education Group, Malaysia. Earlier she was Sales and Production Quality Control, Salsali Marble Group, Iran. Dr. Najla is the Member of "Teaching club", conducting tutorial classes for students with educational need at Asia Pacific University, Malaysia. She is also the member of the campaign for collecting donations for orphan kids at the German-Malaysian Club. She has conducted many workshops for government officials from Bhutan and Bangladesh. She has many publications in renowned international journals and has attended numerous conference all over the world. She is editorial board member of International Journal on Recent Trends in Business and Tourism (IJRTBT) and Reviewer of international academic journals like Journal of Economic Studies, Journal of Public Affairs and Malaysian Journal of Economics. Dr. Najla is attributed with several awards, Grants and Fellowship along with many Professional Trainings.

Amiya Bhaumik, Founder President of Lincoln University College, Malaysia. Dr Amiya holds a Bachelor and double Master degrees, and a PhD in a number of disciplines such as biology, culture and psychology, and international management . He is a founder, former Vice Chancellor, and now President of Lincoln University College Malaysia which offers more than 160 programs including various PhDs and MBBS programs via 12 faculties. He is a visionary leader for developing society via education and training . He has worked with many international organisations. Most notable position was Director of International for Ottawa University (USA). He also serving as Mayor for the City of Akko in Gombe, Africa 2022 till date. He has been awarded Bintang Cemerlang Melaka (B.C.M.) in the year 2020 by Government of Melaka, Malaysia. While working with international universities he has gained various types of educational development work that include writing policies and strategies of education for a number of countries. He has travelled all the continents of world too more than 120 countries that inclue to Europe, Africa, Asia, North America, Latin America and Australasia for his work. He has vast editorial work of several books from reputed publishers like NOVA sc Inc USA, IGI Global, and more than 200 research publications in reputed journals. He is also serving as Editor in Chief of different journals in Malaysia and Australia. Dr Amiya believes in Abraham

Lincoln's philosophy of providing education to each and every human being of the world. Further, that through education we can help each and every human being to manifest their hidden divinity, power, strength and scholarships of wisdom to the humanity. Dr Amiya terms this kind of activity as "WORK IS WORSHIP". Wih this self discipline, Prof Bhaumik has expanded Lincoln University College and its programs in more than 30 over countries . Lincoln University College has extensive programs in health care especially medicine where students upon graduation apply for USA, UK, Australia medical licensing examination . Recent achievement of Lincoln University College is to open higher Education program in Sydney (Australia) which is approved by the Government of Australia.

***

Noor Afza serves as the Dean and Chairperson of the Department of Studies and Research in Business Administration at Tumkur University. With over 30 years of academic and professional experience, she is a distinguished Professor of Management specializing in Human Resource Management, Marketing, Strategic Management, and Consumer Behavior. She has guided numerous postgraduate and doctoral scholars and has an extensive publication record in reputed national and international journals. Her research interests include customer relationship management, digital marketing, entrepreneurship, and sustainable business practices. Dr.Noor Afza is deeply committed to nurturing future business leaders and promoting sustainable management education. She is actively engaged in interdisciplinary research integrating emerging technologies with strategic marketing, with a focus on digital transformation, consumer behavior, and business growth.

Dora Agapito holds a habilitation degree in Economic and Management Sciences, a PhD in Tourism, and an MSc in Marketing. She is the Director of the PhD in Tourism and a member of the Board of the MSc in Marketing Management at the Faculty of Economics, University of Algarve. She is an integrated researcher at the Research Centre for Tourism, Sustainability and Well-being (CinTurs). Her research interests include sensory experiences, consumer behaviour, experience management, well-being, and destination marketing management.

Ila Anand is an accomplished Associate Professor and Head of the BBA Analytics Department at CHRIST University. She holds a Ph.D. and brings a wealth of knowledge in teaching, research, and academic leadership. Her research focuses on two significant areas: emotions and consumer behavior, and sustainability. Her work has been published in internationally recognized journals indexed in Scopus, highlighting the relevance of her contributions.

Behrooz Gharleghi has several years of teaching, research, and practical experiences in various capacities in Malaysia, Peru, and Germany. He worked as Senior Researcher, Affiliate Research Professor, Associate Professor, and Head of Graduate Business School in the previous institutions. He has published several articles in the area of sustainability, AI, and business management and currently is the Associate Editor of the Jurnal Ekonomi Malaysia. He has led on and collaborated in various international research projects especially from the United Nations, F.A.O, Volkswagen Foundation, and the Malaysian Ministry of Higher Education. He holds a PhD in Economics from the National Universiti of Malaysia.

Anita Devare is passionate about the applied mathematics in engineering domain. She is interested in the mathematical modeling of the computational resources, and security techniques in the domain of Computer Science.

Manoj received BSc & MSc degree from North Maharashtra University and PhD in Computer Science from Bharati Vidyapeeth University, India. He is working as Associate Professor at Amity Institute of Information Technology, Amity University Mumbai. He has 17 years of teaching and research experience in Computer Science. His PhD thesis was based on the Congestion Controlling in Homogeneous and Heterogeneous Computer Networks. Dr. Manoj won the "Best Paper Award", in ICSCI 2008. He has served as Post Doctorate Fellow at Centre of Excellence on HPC, Uni. of Calabria, Italy under young researcher scheme. He has been developed Desktop Cloud system. His research deals with IoT, Cloud, Machine Learning and innovative applications of those technologies to scientific problems. He has 02 Patents pending; he edited 05 book chapters, 09 Int. Journal papers, 15 conference Papers. He has delivered 08 national and international keynote speeches. He is connected with review process of reputed international journal papers, edited chapters from the reputed journals like Elsevier's FGCS, Springer's review system, Symbiosis International Journal.

Farooq Sunar Mahammad is a Professor in the Department of Computer Science and Engineering at Santhiram Engineering College, Nandyal, Andhra Pradesh, India. He received his Ph.D. in Computer Science and Engineering and has a strong academic and research background. His research interests include artificial intelligence, machine learning, and data analytics. He has published several research papers in reputed national and international journals.

Md Aminul Islam is a dedicated and accomplished higher education professional with over 14 years of extensive experience in compliance, institutional governance, and academic administration. Born on 1 July 1982, he has built a strong academic pathway beginning with studies in Science and Commerce in Dhaka, followed by a

Diploma in Business Administration, a Bachelor of Business Administration (Hons), and a Master of Business Administration from Lincoln University College, Malaysia.

Aravindhan K. is an accomplished academic and researcher with over 16 years of experience in Computer Science and Engineering. Currently serving as Associate Professor at REVA University, he specializes in Cloud Computing, IoT, AI, and VANETs. He holds a Ph.D. in CSE and has published extensively in SCI and Scopus-indexed journals, with over 250 citations. Dr. Aravindhan is also a patent holder, author of five books, and a frequent session chair at IEEE conferences. His leadership roles include serving as Guest Editor for Elsevier and various administrative positions across academic institutions. He is a recipient of multiple prestigious awards.

Hemish Kapadia is an accomplished Digital Transformation Leader with over 20 years of experience in digital product architecture, software engineering, and technology strategy. Currently serving as Global Head of Web Development and Strategy for Barclays Capital, Hemish leads innovation and development across the bank's Compliance, Legal, HR, Procurement, and Real Estate Services technology portfolios. His leadership has been instrumental in driving the digital transformation of over 120 enterprise applications, steering cloud migrations, and building reusable, scalable, and accessibility-compliant frameworks that have generated significant operational efficiencies and cost savings. Prior to Barclays, Hemish held leadership roles at JPMorgan Chase, Western Union, Infosys, and DirecTV, where he specialized in designing and delivering highly performant trading platforms, hybrid mobile applications, and enterprise web solutions. Throughout his career, Hemish has demonstrated a deep understanding of financial services, trading platforms, regulatory compliance, and data analytics. His innovative contributions have been recognized with multiple industry awards, including Excellence in Engineering (Barclays), Innovation Pioneer (JPMorgan Chase), and CEO Spot Light Award (Infosys). In addition to his technical expertise, Hemish actively contributes to global technology strategy forums, vendor evaluations, and innovation centers of excellence. He holds a Bachelor's degree in Computer Engineering from Charotar Institute of Technology (Gujarat University), where he graduated with Summa Cum Laude honors.

Sai Sathish Kethu is a seasoned IT professional with over 14 years of industry experience, including a decade specializing in Salesforce CRM. As an accomplished Technical Architect with more than 3 years of hands-on experience in designing and developing robust infrastructure and architecture for software projects, Sai is known for his innovative approach to solving complex business challenges.

K. Lalitha is an Assistant Professor in the Department of Computer Science and Engineering at Santhiram Engineering College, Nandyal, Andhra Pradesh, India. She received her Master of Technology in Computer Science and Engineering from Vaagdevi Institute of Technology & Science, Proddatur, Andhra Pradesh, India. Her research interests include machine learning, data mining, and healthcare informatics. She has published multiple research articles in reputed journals.

Syed Mohd Muneeb has more than six years experience in operations and supply chain management.

Swapna Narla is the CEO of Tek Yantra, an IT consulting and software development company. She has been instrumental in leading the company to become a prominent player in the DevOps and cloud solutions space. Swapna's vision centers on simplifying technology for clients, ensuring that their automation and digital transformation efforts are effective and aligned with business goals.

Durai Rajesh Natarajan is a passionate technologist with a keen interest in Artificial Intelligence (AI), Machine Learning (ML), and advanced computing technologies. He is a seasoned Senior .NET Developer and Architect with over 15 years of comprehensive experience in the IT industry. Durai has a strong background in all phases of the Software Development Lifecycle (SDLC and Agile), including requirement analysis, design, implementation, integration, and more.

Arpita Nayak is currently serving as an Assistant Professor, offering courses in management. She completed her Ph.D. in management from the KIIT School of Management. Her MBA and strong interest in Human Resource Management (HRM) led her to pursue further studies in HRM. Her passion for talent management inspired her doctoral research on "A Comparative Study on Talent Management in Private and Public Manufacturing Industries in Odisha." Dr. Nayak has presented research papers at both national and international conferences and has published articles in SCOPUS-listed journals. Over the years, she has taught a variety of subjects, including Human Resource Management, Principles of Management, Business Studies Management, Tribal Entrepreneurship, and Organizational Behaviour. In addition to her academic career, she also has several years of corporate work experience.

Bhaskaru O. is an Assistant Professor in the Department of Computer Science and Engineering at Vignan's Foundation for Science, Technology & Research, Guntur, Andhra Pradesh, India. He received his Ph.D. in Computer Science and Engineering from KL University, Vijayawada, Andhra Pradesh, India. His research interests include machine learning, data mining, and artificial intelligence. He has published several papers in national and international journals.

Paulo Paes is a Market Intelligence Specialist with a strong focus on transforming data into actionable insights that support strategic decision-making. With a background in data analysis and international experience—including a Master's degree in Marketing Management obtained in Portugal—I have developed a clear and objective approach to identifying trends, understanding markets, and generating insights that empower organizations to make well-informed decisions. I believe in the power of data to simplify complex problems and am always open to exchanging ideas and collaborating on projects that seek evidence-based solutions.

Sreekar Peddi is a prominent figure in the field of IT and cloud services, currently serving as the consultant NextGen Platforms and Cloud Services at Tek Leaders Inc.. With a career spanning over a decade, he has been instrumental in modernizing IT infrastructure and enhancing cloud security for various organizations. His work has significantly contributed to the resilience and efficiency of critical state services in California, especially during high-demand periods such as the COVID-19 pandemic and wildfire crises.

Célia M. Q. Ramos holds a PhD in Quantitative Methods Applied to Economics and Management from Faculty of Economics, University of Algarve, obtained her Master in Electrical and Computers Engineering from the Higher Technical Institute, Lisbon University, and is graduated in Computer Engineering from the University of Coimbra, Portugal. She is Coordinator Professor with Habilitation at School for Management, Hospitality and Tourism, also in the UALG, where she lectures mainly Information Systems. Current research interests includes, information systems, data analytics, electronic tourism, business intelligence, digital marketing, panel data models. Has published in the fields of information systems, marketing and tourism, She is reviewer of several scientific journals. At the level of applied research, she has participated in several funded projects. Researcher at the Centre for Tourism, Sustainability and Well-being (CinTurs). Email: cmramos@ualg.pt. ORCID ID: 0000-0002-3413-4897

José De Jesús Reyes-Sánchez, Ph.D. in senior management, has six master's degrees, in education, in management, professional soccer technique, in physical preparation, in professional soccer, in physical rehabilitation sciences, in sports sciences, as well as in coaching and integral well-being, who is a research professor at the TECNM Instituto Tecnológico Superior De Fresnillo, with more than 20 years of teaching experience, PRODEP profile and coordinator of the academic body with vast experience in conferences and workshops, currently novelist and writer.

Shwetha S is a Research Scholar in the Department of Business Administration at Tumkur University and an Assistant Professor at PES University. She has over

15 years of academic experience in Marketing, Strategic Management, Finance, Accounting, and Digital Business. She is a published author and active researcher, contributing to national and international conferences and journals. Her research interests include artificial intelligence in marketing, customer engagement, brand loyalty, and digital business ecosystems. She has also co-authored academic books on Management Accounting, Cost Management, and IFRS. Her current research focuses on the strategic impact of AI-driven marketing on customer engagement and brand loyalty in digital business ecosystems. Committed to advancing business education through innovative teaching and impactful, research-driven insights.

Ipseeta Satpathy is a senior professor at KIIT University. Specializes in Organizational Behavior, Human Psychology, Behavioral Sciences, Organizational Communication, Leadership Development.

Meenakshi Sharma is a Professor at Birla Institute of Technology, Noida. She possesses extensive experience in the field of Marketing and has published numerous research papers in reputed journals indexed in Scopus and SCI.

Sachin Sharma is currently working as a Professor, Amity School of Engineering and Technology, Amity University Punjab, Mohali, India. He also worked as Associate Dean, International Affairs and Professor, Department of Computer Science and Engineering at Graphic Era Deemed to be University, Dehradun, Uttarakhand, India. He has experience of 15+ years in industry and academia. He is also Co-founder and Chief Technology officer (CTO) of IntelliNexus LLC, Arkansas, USA based company. He also worked as a Senior Systems Engineer at Belkin International, Inc., Irvine, California, USA. He received his Philosophy of Doctorate (Ph.D.) degree in Engineering Science and Systems specialization in Systems Engineering from University of Arkansas at Little Rock, USA with 4.0 out 4.0 GPA and M.S. degree in Systems engineering from University of Arkansas at Little Rock with 4.0 out 4.0 GPA. Dr. Sharma has authored/coauthored over 300+ publications in the form of books, patents, and papers in refereed journals and conference proceedings. He holds 100+ US, Indian and international patents in the area of IoT, wireless communication and AI. He has also served as a Guest Reviewer for several Special issues of IEEE/ACM Transactions. His research interests include 6G wireless communication networks, Cloud Computing, Artificial Intelligence, Quantum Computing, IoT, Vehicular ad hoc networking and Cyber security.

Sneh Sharma is a Computer Science major specializing in Artificial Intelligence and Machine Learning at Amity University Punjab. My areas of interest include Artificial Intelligence, Deep Learning, and Data Science. I have contributed to various interdisciplinary research projects and publications aimed at developing innovative solutions across diverse domains. With a strong commitment to academic excellence and societal impact, I strive to explore and apply AI-driven technologies to solve real-world challenges.

Kartikeya Singh has 12 years of teaching experience, backed by six years of industry experience. He holds a Master Certificate in Data Science, an Advanced Diploma in Management (AIMA), and a Ph.D. from Aligarh Muslim University. His contributions to management sciences include one Scopus-indexed paper and four peer-reviewed publications. Dr. Singh has conducted workshops on AI with Excel and SPSS for BBA and MBA students. He played a key role in organizing the National Practicum Contest and has delivered lectures on Decision Support Systems and International Marketing.

Rahul Singh is a computer science student with many skills. I am currently in the stage of finishing my Bachelor of Computer Applications at Amity University Mumbai. I find that I am most interested in programming languages like Python, C/C++, and Java, and it is through these languages that my interest in cloud computing, AI, and automation has sprouted. I have experience in implementing AWS services such as EC2, S3, and CloudFormation, and the projects I have worked on include creating a system that uses Infrastructure as Code, CI/CD pipelines, and AI-based CV so that the authenticity of the document is verified. I also delve in graphic designing and animation, which not only makes me a more versatile worker but also facilitates a visual explanation of the concepts. Cautiously, I am one who wholeheartedly stands to learn, think in new ways, and look for technical challenges.

Shiv Kumar Singh Pundhir is an Assistant Professor at the School of Business and Management, Christ University. He has over 13 years of teaching experience at both postgraduate (MBA) and undergraduate (BBA) levels. His areas of expertise include Operations Research, Business Statistics, and Business Analytics. Mr. Pundhir holds an M.Sc. in Mathematics from Dr. B R Ambedkar University, Agra, and an M.Tech. in Operations Research from NIT Durgapur. He also completed a PG Certificate in Business Analytics from AIMA, New Delhi, and completed his Ph.D. in Management from GLA University, India. He is GATE qualified (2007) and has authored eleven scopus indexed research papers.

Satya Subrahmanyam is a distinguished academic leader, researcher, and institutional strategist with over 27 years of experience in higher education, leadership, and research management. He holds two PhDs and a Postdoctoral qualification from the Polytechnic Institute of Leiria, Portugal. Currently serving as Professor and Dean (Research) at Holy Spirit University of Kaslik (USEK), Lebanon, he spearheads research initiatives that enhance academic excellence and institutional reputation. He played a pivotal role in the development of the Catholic University in Erbil, Kurdistan, where he established new departments, led research programs, and collaborated on international educational projects. As a founding member and Managing Partner of Vignan Institute of Technology and Management, India, he contributed to its transformation into a premier institution. With expertise in AI-driven business strategies, HR analytics, and leadership in technology adoption, he has published extensively, guided PhD research, and led training programs in corporate and academic settings.

Noraisyah Tajudin is a Senior Lecturer in the Electrical and Engineering Department, Faculty of Engineering and Built Environment, at Lincoln University College, Malaysia. She obtained a Bachelor of Engineering (Hons) in Computer System and Communication in 2001 from Universiti Putra Malaysia and a Master's in Science (Telecommunication and Information Engineering) from Universiti Teknologi MARA, Malaysia, in 2017. She received her PhD in Electrical Engineering from University Technology MARA, Malaysia, in 2022. Her research interests lie in interdisciplinary research involving artificial intelligence, electrical and electronics, remote sensing and GIS, satellite and wireless communication, image processing, and data analysis. She is the author or coauthor of international conferences and journals. She has experience as a presenter at international conferences, technical seminars, and industrial events in remote sensing, GIS applications, fiber optics, and artificial intelligence. She is also actively involved as a chairperson in the conference committee. For her research efforts, she was awarded a Silver Medal in research of Rainfall – Landslide Early Warning System (RLEWS) Using TRMM Precipitation Estimates in FKE Invention, Innovation & Design (IID) from UiTM in 2018, a Gold Medal in research of TRMM Satellite Estimates for Rainfall – Landslide Monitoring and Early Warning in FKE Invention, Innovation & Design (IID) from UiTM in 2019, a Gold Medal and IEEE Special Award in Innovation & Invention Challenge College of Engineering 2021 (IICCE2021), UiTM, and a Silver Medal in Invention, Innovation & Design Exposition (IIDEX 2021), Universiti Teknologi MARA, in 2021 for research on a Web-Based Landslide Early Warning System Using GPM Precipitation Estimates.

Silky Valecha is an Assistant Professor in the MBA and Economics Department at Chandigarh University. She holds extensive knowledge in the field of Economics and its practical applications.

Dharma Teja Valivarthi holds a Master's degree from San Francisco Bay University (2014) and a Bachelor of Engineering in Electronics and Electrical Engineering from The Robert Gordon University, Scotland, UK (2010). Passionate about semiconductors and computing, Dharma has over a decade of experience in cloud and networking. He has been a member of the Institution of Engineering and Technology (IET) since 2010, demonstrating his commitment to professional excellence and continuous development in the field.

Pravin Yannawar completed M.Sc Computer Science (2001) and Ph.D Computer Science (2011) from Dr. Babasaheb Ambedkar Marathwada University, Aurangabad (MS) India. Interested in Image, Video Processing. Completed Major Research Project Sanctioned by Department of Science and Technology, Govt. of India under FAST TRACK SCHEME for YOUNG SCIENTIST

Index

A

B

C

D

E

F

G

H

I

L

M

O

P

Q

R

S

U

www.ingramcontent.com/pod-product-compliance
Lightning Source LLC
LaVergne TN
LVHW062336300926
849161LV00007B/1711
* 9 7 9 8 3 3 7 3 3 6 4 8 0 *